THE OXFORD ILLUSTRATED HISTORY OF THE BIBLE

THE OXFORD ILLUSTRATED HISTORY OF THE BIBLE

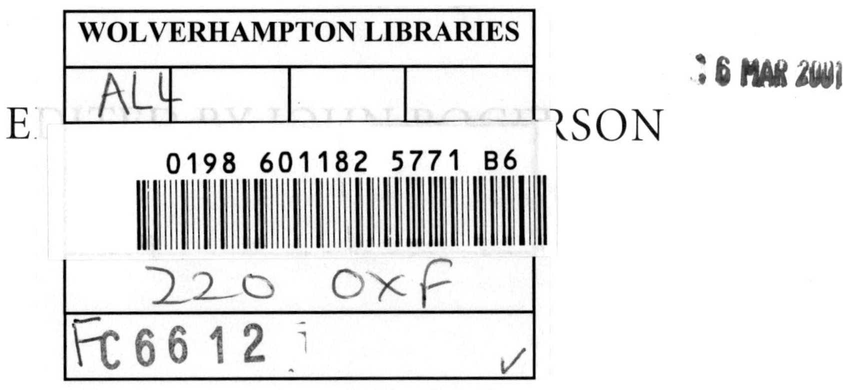

E[illegible]RSON

OXFORD
UNIVERSITY PRESS

OXFORD
UNIVERSITY PRESS

Great Clarendon Street, Oxford OX2 6DP

Oxford University Press is a department of the University of Oxford.
It furthers the University's objective of excellence in research, scholarship,
and education by publishing worldwide in

Oxford New York
Athens Auckland Bangkok Bogotá Buenos Aires Calcutta
Cape Town Chennai Dar es Salaam Delhi Florence Hong Kong Istanbul
Karachi Kuala Lumpur Madrid Melbourne Mexico City Mumbai
Nairobi Paris São Paulo Shanghai Singapore Taipei Tokyo Toronto Warsaw

with associated companies in Berlin Ibadan

Oxford is a registered trade mark of Oxford University Press
in the UK and in certain other countries

Published in the United States
by Oxford University Press Inc., New York

First published 2001

British Library Cataloguing in Publication Data
Data available

Library of Congress Cataloging in Publication Data
Data available

ISBN 0-19-860118-2

10 9 8 7 6 5 4 3 2 1

Printed by Giunti Industrie Grafiche
Prato, Italy

Contents

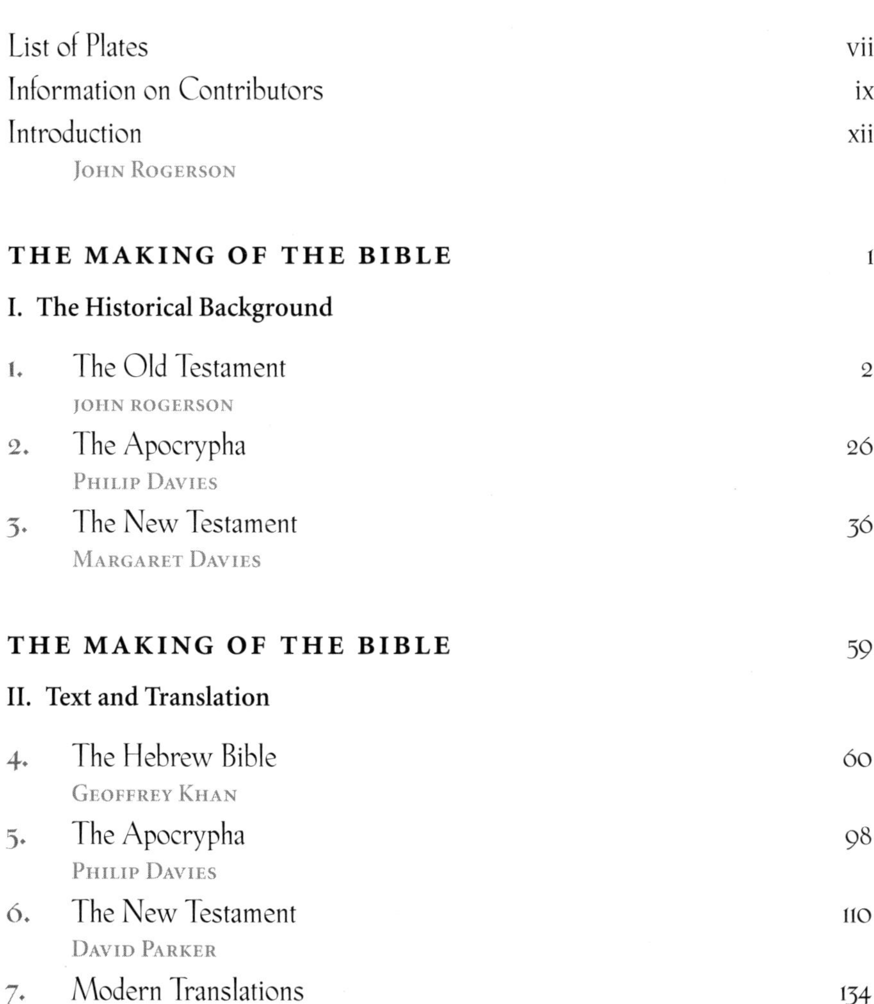

List of Plates

Information on Contributors

Philip Alexander is Professor of Post-Biblical Jewish Studies, University of Manchester, and Co-Director of the University of Manchester Centre for Jewish Studies. His recent publications include 'The King Messiah in Rabbinic Judaism' in J. Day (ed.), *King and Messiah in Israel and the Ancient Near East* (1998) and 'From Son of Adam to Second God: Transformations of the Biblical Enoch' in M. E. Stone and H. Bergren (eds.), *Biblical Figures outside the Bible* (1998). His current research interests include the history of Judaism in the Second Temple and Talmudic periods, early Jewish Bible interpretation, and the Jewish background to Christian origins.

George Habib Bebawi is Director of Studies at the Institute for Orthodox Christian Studies, University of Cambridge. He is a graduate of the Coptic Orthodox Seminary, Cairo, in 1961, completing his PhD at Cambridge in 1970 on 'Some Aspects of the Sacramental Theology of the Coptic Church'. He is now preparing a work on 'Islamic Objections to the Doctrine of the Trinity from the 9th to the 14th century' for the Selly Oak Islamic Centre.

M. Daniel Carroll R. (Rodas) is Professor of Old Testament at Denver Seminary. He has written *Contexts for Amos: Prophetic Poetics in Latin American Perspective* (1992) and has just edited *Rethinking Contexts, Rereading Texts: Contributions from the Social Sciences to Biblical Interpretation* (2000). His current major project is a commentary on the book of Amos for the New International Commentary Series.

Ronald E. Clements is Professor Emeritus of Old Testament Studies, King's College, University of London. His major publications include *A Century of Old Testament Study* (1978), and *Old Testament Prophecy. From Oracles to Canon* (1995). He has written several commentaries on Old Testament books and is currently engaged on research into the origin and composition of the book of Isaiah.

Margaret Davies recently retired from the Department of Biblical Studies at Sheffield University. Her publications include *Matthew* (1993), and the Epworth Commentary on *The Pastoral Epistles* (1996). Her main interest is in ethics.

Philip R. Davies is Professor of Biblical Studies at the University of Sheffield. His major publications include *In Search of Ancient Israel* (1992), *Whose Bible Is It Anyway?* (1995) and *Scribes and Schools. The Canonization of the Hebrew Scriptures* (1998). He is also the author of numerous books and articles on the Dead Sea Scrolls.

G. R. Evans lectures in history and theology in Cambridge, and is a former British Academy Research Reader in Theology. She is author of books on medieval theology including *Augustine on Evil* (1983), *The Language and Logic of the Bible* (2 vols. 1984–5), *Bernard of Clairvaux* (2000), and on modern ecumenical theology and theological method, and on the governance of universities.

David Jasper is Professor of Literature and Theology and Dean of Divinity at the University of Glasgow. His recent publications include *The Sacred and Secular Canon in Romanticism* (1999) and *Religion and Literature: A Reader* (with Robert Detweiler, 2000). He is at present working on a study of trends in postmodern theology.

Geoffrey Khan is Reader in Semitic Philology at the University of Cambridge. His major publications include *Studies in Semitic Syntax* (Oxford 1988), *Karaite Bible Manuscripts from Cairo Genizah* (Cambridge 1990), *Arabic Legal and Administrative Documents from the Cambridge Genizah Collections* (Cambridge 1993), *A Grammar of Neo-Aramaic* (Leiden 1999). He is currently working on medieval Hebrew grammatical texts.

David Parker is Reader in New Testament Textual Criticism and Palaeography in the University of Birmingham. His major publications include *Codex Bezae. An Early Christian Manuscript and Its Text* (1992), *The Living Text of the Gospels* (1997), and *John Calvin, Commentarius in Epistolam Pauli ad Romanos* (1999). He is editor of the International Greek New Testament Project.

Stanley E. Porter is Research Professor in New Testament at the University of Surrey Roehampton. His major publications include *Verbal Aspect in the Greek of the New Testament* (1989), *Idioms of the Greek New Testament* (1992), *Katallasso in Ancient Greek Literature* (1994), *The Paul of Acts* (1999), and *The Criteria for Authenticity in Historical-Jesus Research* (2000). He is currently researching in the area of early Christian hymns and creeds.

Henning Graf Reventlow is retired Professor of Exegesis and Theology of the Old Testament at the University of the Ruhr, Bochum, Germany. His major publications include *The Authority of the Bible and the Rise of the Modern World* (1984), and *Epochen der Bibelauslegung* (1990–); he is currently preparing the concluding vol. 4.

John Rogerson is Emeritus Professor of Biblical Studies at the University of Sheffield and was Head of Department from 1979 to 1994. His many publications include *Old Testament Criticism in the Nineteenth Century: England and Germany* (1984), *Atlas of the Bible* (1985), *The Old Testament World* (with Philip Davies, 1989), *W. M. L. de Wette. An Intellectual Biography* (1992), *The Bible and Criticism in Victorian Britain* (1995), *An Introduction to the Bible* (1999), and *Chronicle of the Old Testament Kings* (1999). He is hoping to complete a Theology of the Old Testament.

Luise Schottroff was Professor of New Testament at the universities of Mainz and Kassel. She retired in 1999. Her major publications in the last years include *Lydia's Impatient Sisters. A Feminist Social History of Early Christianity* (1995, German 1994) and *Kompendium Feministischer Bibelauslegung* (editor, together with Marie-Theres Wacker;1999). She is currently completing a work on Paul.

Yvonne Sherwood is Lecturer in Biblical Studies and Jewish Studies at the University of Glasgow. She writes on the Bible in dialogue with gender theory, literary theory, popular culture, and Jewish interpretation. She is the author of *The Prostitute and the Prophet: Hosea's Marriage in Literary-Theoretical Perspective* (1996) and *A Biblical Text and Its Afterlives: The Survival of Jonah in Western Culture* (2000).

Gerald West is Professor of Hebrew Bible in the School of Theology, University of Natal, South Africa, and Director of the Institute for the Study of the Bible, a project of the School of Theology which links academic biblical studies with poor and marginalized readers of the Bible. His publications include *Biblical Hermeneutics of Liberation: Modes of Reading the Bible in the South Africa Context* (1995) and *The Academy of the Poor: Towards a Dialogical Reading of the Bible* (1999). He is currently editing (with Musa Dube) a collection of essays to be published as *The Bible in Africa: Transactions, Trajectories and Trends.*

David F. Wright is Professor of Reformed and Patristic Christianity at The University of Edinburgh. He edited *The Bible in Scottish Life and Literature* (1988), and has written extensively on Martin Bucer and John Calvin. He was chief editor of *The Dictionary of Scottish Church History and Theology* (1993).

Introduction

JOHN ROGERSON

That the Bible should have a history may cause some surprise. Surely the Bible *is* history. It begins with the creation of the universe and the story of the first humans, Adam and Eve. It is still popularly supposed that if something is mentioned in the Bible, that thing must go back to earliest recorded human history. Books or television programmes which seek to confirm the history contained in the Bible often arouse great interest. So what is meant by the history of the Bible?

It is a curious fact that, although the Bible can be purchased in a bookshop like any other book, it is in fact unlike any other book. This is not simply a matter of the different translations that can be found in a bookshop. Other books, for example Dante's *Divine Comedy*, may be found in two or more translations. The unusual thing about the Bible is that a bookshop that has more than one version for sale will probably have on its shelves Bibles with differing contents. Some may include a section entitled 'The Apocrypha' between the Old and New Testaments while others may have no such section. The number of books in the Old Testament section may vary, while of Bibles that do include a separate Apocrypha some will have a bigger Apocrypha than others. These facts are striking because we do not normally expect books that bear the same title to vary in their contents. But the difference between the Bible and other books needs to be pressed further. It has been noted that some Bibles contain more books than others, yet it is wrong, strictly speaking, to use the word 'books' of the items that are collected together in Bibles. The Old Testament is, in fact, a collection of scrolls, scrolls that originally existed separately, and which were not put into a form in which they could be bound together in one volume until several centuries into the Common Era, and that means, in some cases, many centuries after their composition. This point is well made by the observation that the apostle Paul never saw a Bible. But even the process of converting originally separate scrolls or, in the case of the New Testament epistles, odd sheets of papyrus, into a form in which they could be bound into one volume was affected by the fact that it took several centuries for the churches to agree about which writings should be included and which left out. In fact, the various branches of the church have never agreed about the exact contents of the Bible, which is one reason why it is possible to buy Bibles with varying contents in bookshops today.

On the face of it this is very alarming. A sceptic might argue that the lack of agreement over the contents of the Bible is an indication of its worthlessness, or that claims made about its importance and authority have been exaggerated. How can a book be authoritative if there is no agreement about its contents?

Yet the fact that disparate writings composed over a period of at least 800 years came to be included together in one volume, even if there was not complete agreement about its exact contents, is an indication of enormous trouble taken over writings precisely because they were regarded as being of the utmost significance. The surprising thing about the Bible is that it should exist at all, given the time-span of the composition of its separate items and the complicated processes of their transmission. By the time that the earliest extant Hebrew manuscripts of the Old Testament were written in the first century BCE (they were found among the Dead Sea Scrolls at or near Qumran) these writings had come to be regarded as scripture; that is, writings inspired by God which communicated his will for his people Israel, and the whole of humankind. Even if we did not have these manuscripts, we would know from the New Testament of the existence of these Jewish scriptures, in terms of which the life, death, and resurrection of Jesus of Nazareth had been understood by himself and his earliest followers. Somehow, writings as disparate as laws, popular stories, dynastic annals, proverbs, laments, love stories, and psalms, to mention only those in the Old Testament, came to be regarded as scripture. Two communities of faith, in which there could be a diversity of opinions, came to regard certain writings as foundation documents, as writings which described their identity, told their past story, and offered fresh and contemporary insights and challenges through the medium of interpretation.

A history of the Bible charts what we know of the processes that led from the writing, editing, and copying of the items collected together in the Bible to their appearance in the forms familiar to us, and available in bookshops today. In the course of reading this history there will inevitably be surprises. Those who are used to reading *four* gospels will be surprised to discover that, as early as the second century, attempts were made to combine them into *one* narrative, and that these harmonies were so popular for several centuries in certain parts of the church that they all but displaced the four gospels. Again, because we are used to reading printed texts which reproduce exactly what an author has written, it comes as a surprise to learn that this is not the case with the Bible. This problem is particularly acute with regard to the New Testament, because the rapid spread of the church throughout the Roman empire and beyond led to the development of divergent local texts, which remained untouched by later attempts to introduce some form of standardization. As one contributor to this volume observes, the text of the New Testament has not yet been decided, by which he means that new discoveries and the refinements of the methods of textual criticism may necessitate revisions to the standard editions of the Greek New Testament upon which translations into English and other languages are based.

A completely different situation exists with regard to the texts of the Old Testament and the Apocrypha. Geoffrey Khan's essay describes the work of the Jewish scholars who, in the early centuries of the Common Era, were able to produce a standard text for the Hebrew Bible. This standard text is the basis for contemporary scholarly Hebrew Bibles and for translations of the Hebrew Bible/Old Testament. However, biblical manuscripts found among the Dead Sea Scrolls differ in some respects from the standard Hebrew Bible, and it will be interesting to see whether anyone tries to produce a text of the Hebrew Bible that is chosen from all the manuscripts now available, and which attempts to reconstruct the 'best' readings. The situation for the Apocrypha is different again. There is no standard text, and some books of this section exist in differing versions, some of which can be found in English translations available today.

The history of the Bible does not end with an account of how the original writings ended up in volumes that can be purchased in bookshops. Once the writings of the Old and New Testaments were regarded as scripture they became the object of interpretation—a process already begun in the use of the Old Testament in the New. The way that the Old Testament was interpreted differed fundamentally in the Jewish and Christian communities, both of which regarded its texts as scripture. Judaism accorded the utmost authority to the laws in the books of Exodus to Deuteronomy, believing them to have been revealed by God to Moses. Supplemented by an oral law, also believed to have been revealed to Moses, these laws indicated to observant Jews how God wished them to obey him in every detail and particular of daily life. At the same time, the interpretation of the non-legal parts of the Hebrew Bible became the opportunity for a deeper exploration of the meaning of scripture. Passages from many parts of the Hebrew Bible could be related to any other part, multiple interpretations could be proposed, and anecdotes, stories, and examples drawn from everyday life enriched a way of reading the Bible that has been described as pure poetry.

By contrast, Christian use of the Old Testament was more prosaic, even where it preferred allegorical and spiritual senses to the literal sense. It was not denied that God had revealed his law to Moses, but simply asserted that much of this law was not binding upon Christians. Where the Old Testament was interpreted literally, its stories were used as object-lessons, indicating examples to be avoided or followed. Where it was interpreted allegorically or spiritually, it referred primarily to Christ. A striking instance of this, not discussed in the present volume, is the use of the psalms. The early church took over from the synagogue the extensive use of psalms in worship, but in the process the psalms ceased to be Jewish texts and became Christian ones.

Two striking examples of this are Psalms 22 and 68, the former having been quoted by Christ on the cross (Matt. 27: 46, Mark 15: 34), the latter being quoted in Ephesians 4: 8. Psalm 22 was seen to contain so much that echoed Christ's passion—for example, phrases such as 'they pierced my hands and my feet' (Psalm 22: 17 Septuagint—the Hebrew has 'my hands and my feet were like a lion') and 'they divided my garments among them, and for my vesture they cast lots' (Psalm 22:

19, cf. John 19: 24), not to mention its sudden switch to praise at verse 23 as though prefiguring the resurrection—that the psalm was used as a prophecy, if not an account of Christ's passion. The opening words of Psalm 68, 'Let God arise ...' were taken to refer to the resurrection, while verse 12, 'God gave the word', was clearly a reference to Christ's incarnation in this type of interpretation.

A history of the Bible that outlines the different ways in which it has been used during the past two thousand years gives the lie to the idea that the Bible has always been understood in one particular way, and that in order to be true to 'biblical principles' it is necessary to adhere to what is mistakenly believed to be this one way in which it has always been understood. More often than not, what are held to be timeless 'biblical principles' turn out to be comparatively recent interpretations that have been embraced by powerfully self-confident churches that claim a monopoly of the truth. The fact that an interpretation may be recent does not, of course, prove it to be mistaken or misleading. However, when it is set in the context of the whole history of interpretation it can be seen for what it is—the way in which the Bible has answered the needs of a particular church at a particular time, without necessarily establishing an interpretation that will never be superseded or which excludes all other possible approaches to the Bible.

In an ideal world, a work such as the present volume would have a much wider scope than the practicalities and economics of present-day publishing allow, if one affordable volume is to be produced. The *Cambridge History of the Bible* ran to three volumes and about 1,800 pages, and Henning Graf Reventlow, author of the chapter on the early church, is producing a series of massive volumes on the different epochs of biblical interpretation. However, the present, more modest book not only covers the basic ground; its final section, on contemporary interpretation, brings the subject up to date in a way not attempted by other works.

Ideally, it would have been good to be able to treat at least two topics that do not appear in this book, the use of the Bible in art, and its use in music. The illustrations in this volume taken from the work of artists, whether they were scribes, illuminators of manuscripts, sculptors, carpenters, or painters, provide a small glimpse into the vast world of the way in which biblical themes have inspired artistic endeavours. In fact, the use of the Bible in art is a new, and burgeoning, feature of contemporary biblical studies as it interacts with other branches of the humanities, especially cultural studies. The use of the Bible in music is yet to emerge in the way that its use in art has recently taken off, yet there is abundant material here for study. Anyone who has heard Handel's oratorio *Jephtha* and who has been surprised at the way in which the tragic ending of the biblical story (Jephthah's sacrifice of his only daughter) has been transformed into a much happier ending will have chanced upon a deep vein of interpretation. For medieval Jewish interpretation there was sufficient ambiguity in the text of Judges 11: 39 for it to be suggested that Jephthah's daughter became a virgin for life instead of being sacrificed by her father. Sixteenth- and seventeenth-century dramas exploited the same idea, linking Jephthah's daughter's story with Euripides' Greek play *Iphigenia*, and provided names for characters such as

Jephthah's daughter who are otherwise anonymous in the biblical account. Handel's librettist thus stood in an established tradition when he gave the oratorio a happier ending. Another area of research would be the use of the Bible in the 200 extant church cantatas composed by J. S. Bach in the first half of the eighteenth century. Bach's librettists took considerable liberties with the interpretation of the biblical texts upon which the cantatas were based and which, together with the sermon, provided extensive meditation on the New Testament readings prescribed for each Sunday. The aim of the librettists was to enable individual worshippers to enter into an intimate and mystical relationship with Christ, often in defiance of what would be regarded today as responsible interpretation of the biblical material. A modern instance of the interaction between the Bible and music would be Arnold Schoenberg's *Moses and Aaron.*

In the nineteenth century there was much discussion in Britain about whether the Bible should be studied 'like any other book'. There were those who argued against doing this, fearful of what the outcome would be. They lost the argument and the Bible showed that it could more than stand up to the most searching and detailed scrutiny that any text, let alone a religious text, has ever been subjected to. Something of that scrutiny, extending for nearly two thousand years, is described in the present volume while the final section shows that, far from being exhausted, the Bible has found a new lease of life in the past thirty years as it has inspired groups working for a better world and a better humanity.

THE MAKING OF THE BIBLE

I. The Historical Background

1 The Old Testament

JOHN ROGERSON

How, when, and why was the Old Testament written? The obvious place to look for an answer to these questions is in the texts themselves; if this is done, some answers are forthcoming. Exodus 24: 7 refers to 'the book of the covenant' which Moses read to the people at Mt Sinai, while Exodus 34: 27 reports that Moses wrote 'the words of the covenant, the ten commandments' on the stone tablets according to God's instructions. Many of the regulations concerning priesthood and sacrifice in Leviticus and Numbers begin with the formulas 'the Lord said/spoke to Moses/Aaron', implying their divine origin mediated through Moses and Aaron. Deuteronomy is an address by Moses to the Israelites gathered in the plains of Moab. In 1 Samuel 10: 25 Samuel writes in a book 'the rights and duties of the kingship', while 1 Kings 4: 32 attributes 3,000 proverbs and 1,005 songs to Solomon. The prophet Isaiah is told to seal the testimony and the teaching (i.e. to write them down) among his disciples, while Jeremiah dictates two sets of prophecies to Baruch, the first of which is destroyed by King Jehoiakim (Jeremiah 36).

Out of the hints found in the Old Testament a view of its authorship emerged as early probably as the second century CE, and is recorded in the Babylonian Talmud *Baba Bathra* 14b–15a. This attributed 'his book' (almost all of Genesis to Deuteronomy) and Job to Moses; the book of Joshua and eight verses of the Torah (presumably Deut. 34: 5–12 recording the death of Moses) to Joshua; the books of Judges, Ruth, and 1 and 2 Samuel to Samuel; and the Psalms to David assisted by ten elders, including the first Adam, Melchisedek, and Abraham. Jeremiah was credited with 1 and 2 Kings, Jeremiah, and Lamentations, and Hezekiah and his helpers (cf. Prov. 25: 1) with Isaiah, Proverbs, Song of Songs, and Ecclesiastes. The remainder were attributed to the 'Men of the Great Synagogue' and Ezra.

Views similar to, but not identical with, these were to establish themselves in Christian scholarship and to last into the nineteenth century. They can still be found in the young churches of the developing world which are innocent of biblical criticism, and in a modified form in Western conservative churches. The conservative Study Bible based on the New International Version, first published in 1985, ascribes the 'bulk of the Pentateuch' to Moses, assigns a prominent role to Solomon in composing the book of Proverbs, and defends the unity of Isaiah (i.e. Isaiah wrote all 66 chapters) and the authorship of the book of Daniel by Daniel in the sixth century BCE.

The traditional views of authorship had two strengths. First, they provided a clear account of the origin of the faith of Israel. It was divine revelation communicated directly to individuals such as Moses. Secondly, if the authors of Old Testament books were known, it became possible to regard them as writers inspired by God. The seemingly neutral question 'who wrote a particular book?' became closely tied up with theories about the authority and inspiration of the Old Testament such that to question traditional views of the authorship of a book could be regarded as an attack on that book's status as inspired scripture. This is a difficulty still felt by Christians who are not necessarily 'fundamentalists'.

This is not the place to describe how and why the traditional views of authorship were abandoned from the late eighteenth century onwards in academic scholarship. This abandonment did, however, have serious consequences for the study of the Old Testament. The traditional views accounted for the origin of the faith of Israel. Where, however, did this faith come from if it was no longer possible to accept at face value statements such as 'the Lord spoke to Moses, saying ...'? If, as is often maintained, much of the priestly and sacrificial legislation in Leviticus and Numbers is a development dating from the sixth century BCE rather than something revealed to Israel at the outset, how is the history of Israel's faith to be reconstructed?

W. M. L. de Wette (1780–1849) in his study in Basel. De Wette's reconstruction of the history of the ancient Israelite cult (1804–7) was a formative point in modern biblical criticism.

This question must now be addressed, because it is fundamental to any attempt to sketch the origin and formation of the traditions and books that make up the Old Testament; and it has to be said at the outset that only some broad indications can be given. As a first step, several attempts to account for the origin of the faith of Israel and the traditions witnessing to it will be considered. Some or all of them may be familiar to readers, and their strengths and weaknesses are informative.

A consensus that emerged in academic scholarship in the latter part of the nineteenth century was that the prophets of Israel, especially those of the eighth century (Isaiah of Jerusalem, Hosea, Amos, and Micah) were the main force behind the formation of Israel's faith. Reacting against Canaanite fertility cults and despotic rulers, the prophets proclaimed ethical monotheism and social justice, and challenged Israel to look beyond its national interests to God's universal rule. Failure to respond to these challenges would bring divine punishment upon the people, who had been chosen by God for responsibilities and not for complacency. The sixth-century prophets (Jeremiah, Ezekiel, and the author of Isaiah 40–55 usually known as Deutero-Isaiah) enabled Judah to survive the Babylonian exile by proclaiming that it was divine punishment for Israel's unfaithfulness. As a result, new and deeper lessons about sin, punishment, and vicarious suffering were learnt. Some of these insights were consolidated into the developing sacrificial ritual of the post-exilic Jerusalem temple with its emphasis on atonement. At the same time, personal piety found expression in the composition and use of the psalms, while contact with Hellenism from the late fourth century resulted in the Old Testament 'wisdom' traditions (Proverbs, Job, Ecclesiastes).

This consensus was set in the context of various developmental and evolutionary schemes. One approach, influential in Britain, traced in the Old Testament a progressive development of religious belief, from animism, polytheism, and henotheism (belief that the God of Israel was supreme among gods) to monotheism (belief that the God of Israel was the only God). It was also held that Israel had experienced a progressive moral and ethical development. The Old Testament thus became the record of a progressive revelation or education. Other approaches focused upon Israel's social development: from a 'nomadic' people to one surrounded by fertility cults in a settled land; from a loose association of 'tribes' to a dynastic state ruling other small states. A popular source for Israel's faith was the supposed clarity and purity of the desert in which there were no shades of grey, and where God's moral being and ethical demands could be more readily apprehended than elsewhere.

Gerhard von Rad (1901–71) a leading Old Testament scholar of the 20th century.

A major factor highlighted by this consensus was that if appeal was no longer made to a divine revelation communicated to known authors of biblical writings as the origin of the faith of Israel, substitute theories had to be found; and these were likely to be taken from secular views that were popular at the time. Belief in progress and in the history of the human race as a process directed by divine providence had a profound influence upon Old Testament scholars. It enabled them to ascribe to a 'primitive' stage of Israel's moral and religious development narratives such as those describing Joshua's slaughter of whole populations at God's command.

In the twentieth century two notable attempts were made to correct or modify the nineteenth-century consensus and to offer alternative explanations of the origins of Israel's faith. The first, associated with the American scholar W. F. Albright and his students J. Bright and G. E. Wright, believed that archaeology supported a mildly critical, traditional reading of the Old Testament. The

Ancestors (Abraham, Isaac, and Jacob) were located in second millennium Mesopotamia and Syria/Palestine and the Exodus from Egypt was dated in the thirteenth century. The faith of Israel originated in acts of God in history such as the Exodus, events which could be dated and reconstructed with the aid of historical and archaeological research. What made them 'acts of God' was the testimony to this fact in the biblical traditions. Wright's books *Biblical Archaeology* and *God who Acts: Biblical Theology as Recital* were classic statements of this position.

The second approach, that of the German scholar Gerhard von Rad, was more sceptical about what could be known about figures such as Moses and the Ancestors and events associated with them in the biblical record such as the Exodus. It did not so much search for the origins of Israel's faith as concern itself with proclamations of that faith that von Rad connected with two great festivals in particular, one which celebrated the occupation of the land, and one which celebrated the law-giving at Mt Sinai. The datum, in other words, was the faith that was confessed, rather than the revelations or events that gave rise to the faith. Those parts of the confession that referred to revelatory events, such as the Exodus, referred to happenings beyond the scope of historical research, either because the necessary evidence was not available, or because theological reflection upon the events and the celebratory retelling of them had altered them beyond recognition in the tradition. According to von Rad the core of the Pentateuch was to be found in the 'creed' recited at the festival of first-fruits, according to Deuteronomy 26: 5–9:

> A wandering Aramean was my ancestor; he went down into Egypt and lived there as an alien, few in number, and there he became a great nation, mighty and populous. When the Egyptians treated us harshly and afflicted us, by imposing hard labour on us, we cried to the Lord, the God of our ancestors; the Lord heard our voice and saw our afflictions, our toil and our oppression. The Lord brought us out of Egypt with a mighty hand and an outstretched arm, with a terrifying display of power, and with signs and wonders; and he brought us into this place.

Two other features of von Rad's position were important: belief in the 'Solomonic Enlightenment', a period in the tenth century in which the traditions relating to Israel's faith began to be written down; and acceptance of Albrecht Alt's attempt to identify the 'God of the fathers' (i.e. the Ancestors) by means of comparative studies. According to Alt the 'God of the fathers' (a common phrase in the tradition) identified a manifestation of the divine to a particular person, whose descendants then worshipped that manifestation as, for example, the God of Abraham or the God of Nahor (Gen. 31: 53), Abraham and Nahor being the names of Ancestors to whom, it was believed, the deity had been manifested. This accounted for the traditions about Abraham and the other Ancestors.

Since the work of Wright and von Rad (both of whom died in the early 1970s) Old Testament studies have undergone a transformation in radical directions which have completely changed the landscape of the discipline. New literary-critical study of the Pentateuch and the 'historical' books (Joshua to 2 Kings) has suggested later dates for their composition. The nineteenth-century consensus dated the sources for these books from the tenth/ninth to the seventh/sixth centuries BCE. There is now a tendency to regard all of them as post-exilic. Von Rad's 'Solomonic Enlightenment' has been abandoned. At the same time, archaeological research has produced an account of the history of Syria/Palestine that suggests that Israel, Judah, Moab, Ammon, and Edom did not begin to emerge as 'states' until the ninth/eighth centuries BCE. The biblical accounts of the empire of David and Solomon hardly fit in with this picture, although it is going too far to deny the existence of David and Solomon. Events such as the Exodus or the time of the Ancestors are now so remote compared with the proposed dates for the traditions about them that they have become invisible as far as any historical attempt to recover them is concerned. At the same time, much more has become known about the popular religion of Israel thanks to the researches of Othmar Keel and his associates on cylinder seals, amulets, and suchlike.

The task, not only of writing a history of Israel, but of accounting for the faith of Israel and therefore the origin and growth of the Old Testament traditions has become more formidable than ever. Unlike New Testament scholars whose task is to trace the growth of specifically Christian scripture from Jesus of Nazareth, Old Testament specialists are faced with a faith that developed within a nation, in circles that often came into conflict with the rulers and ordinary people of that

The sun god emerging from a complex of lotus leaves, from an engraved Tridacna shell from Arad, southern Judah, 7th century BCE. Compare the description of the vision of God in Ezekiel ch. 1.

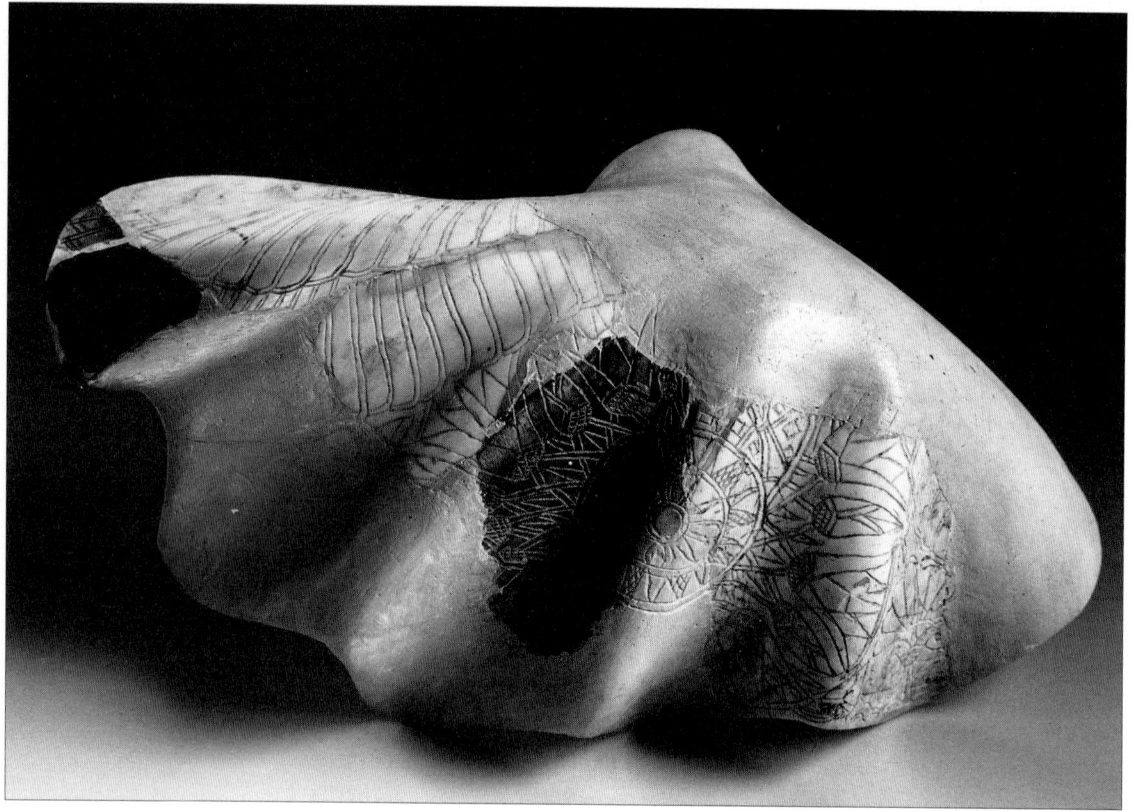

The God of thier Ancestors.

Core of Pentateuch?;
Deuteronomy 26:5-9.
A wandering Aramean was my ancestor
(who is the God of the "wandering Aramean?")
The wandering Aramean entered Egypt,
performed a work, then left Egypt.

"the faith of Israel, and therefore the origin and
growth of the Old Testament traditions."

Highlighted part of a stele naming Israel, and erected by the Egyptian pharaoh Merneptah *c.*1207 BCE, recording victories in a campaign in Canaan. How far this reference relates to later historical entities called Israel is hotly disputed.

nation. Furthermore, the 'history' of the nation that these circles produced was not a history in the modern sense. Although the writers used historical sources such as royal chronicles, their aim was not to present a chronological account of the nation's fortunes but to write what has been called a 'decision history'—a story containing incidents with outcomes that would challenge readers/hearers to faith in God. Also, the religious beliefs and practices of the post-exilic community were explained in terms of an overall story that was projected back to the creation of the world. In what follows, an attempt will be made to sketch the origins of Israel's faith and the growth of its scripture in the light of present Old Testament studies, and taking into account the dynamics indicated in the preceding sentences.

ISRAEL'S ORIGINS

'Israel is laid waste, its seed is no more.' These words from the 27th line of an inscription from the reign of the Egyptian pharaoh Merneptah (variously dated 1224–1214 or 1212–1202) is the earliest known reference to Israel. It indicates through its determinative (a sign that precedes a name and indicates whether the name is that of a god, or a person, or a country,) that a group organized along tribal lines is meant. Thus, towards the end of the thirteenth century BCE there existed, probably in ancient Palestine, a people that was sufficiently distinct for it to be recognized and named by a foreign invader. It is interesting that, however the first part of the name Israel is to be understood (it has been connected with *sara*, 'to fight', 'to rule', or 'to heal', or with *yashar*, 'upright'), the second part is 'El', the common Semitic word for 'God'. The group is thus named according to the general Semitic term for 'God' rather than the distinctive name for the God of Israel, YHWH, thought to have been pronounced Yahweh. The earliest non-biblical reference to Yahweh in connection with Israel is in the Inscription of Mesha, king

Jebel Musa, reaching 2273 m (7455 ft) and traditionally identified as Mt Sinai (the Arabic name means 'the mountain of Moses'), is part of a cluster of mountains in the southern part of the Sinai peninsula.

of Moab in the first half of the ninth century BCE. Lines 17 and 18 read: 'I took from there [i.e. Nebo] the [vessels of] Yhwh'. The inscription also indicates that the kingdom of Israel ruled by Omri (*c*.885–874), who is named in the inscription in lines 4–5, had outposts in Transjordan, with holy places at which Yahweh was worshipped.

To the question 'how and when did Yahweh become the God of Israel?' no definite answer can be given if appeal is made to non-biblical sources only. However, attention has been drawn to the occurrence of what is probably a shortened form of the name, Yhw, in Egyptian sources from the time of Amenophis III (1391–1353), one reference being to 'Yhw in *shasu*-land'. This may be a reference to a sacred mountain or mountain-god, which has been tentatively located in Seir or ancient Edom. The mention of *shasu* draws attention to a nomadic people living in this and other regions. This information can be compared with the Old Testament claims that the name Yahweh was revealed to Moses at the mountain of God in the Sinai wilderness (Exodus 3: 1–12), as well as with references in poetic parts of the Old Testament to a 'coming' of Yahweh from Seir. Thus the 'Song of Deborah' states 'Lord [i.e. Yahweh], when you went out from Seir, when you marched from the region of Edom, the earth trembled' (Judg. 5: 4, cf. Ps. 68: 7–8).

Comparisons of biblical texts with extra-biblical evidence must be handled carefully. They do not prove that the biblical texts are 'true' in a strictly historical sense. Exodus 3: 1–12 is no doubt a post-exilic and sophisticated theoretical reflection in its present form. The comparisons do, however, provide a plausible, and necessarily provisional, larger context into which biblical texts can be placed. On the basis of the above and similar comparisons as well as recent archaeological research a tentative picture of Israel's origins can be sketched as follows.

In the second half of the thirteenth century BCE there was a migration of peoples from northern Transjordan to the central hill country of Palestine, the area of the later northern kingdom, Israel. The reasons for the migration are unknown; they may have had political or environmental causes, or both. This could well have included the entity, or part of it, that is mentioned as Israel in the Merneptah stele of 1219 or 1207. This group may have then been joined by a group of *shasu* who brought with them faith in a God Yahweh who had helped them to escape from Egyptian overlordship. Faith in Yahweh as the God of Israel then became one of the distinguishing features of Israel as it struggled for survival with the Canaanites and then with the Philistines in Palestine itself, as well as with neighbouring peoples in Transjordan.

An important moment of crisis in the formation of the people came with the arrival of the Philistines, who established themselves in the coastal plain in southern Palestine, probably in the last third of the twelfth century BCE. They were part of the larger movement of 'sea peoples' who migrated by sea and land from somewhere in the north-eastern Mediterranean region, and who are mentioned in Egyptian sources from Ramesses III. Towards the end of the eleventh century they began to expand into the central hill country of Palestine, at the expense of the tribes there who constituted Israel.

At this point another puzzle presents itself. No mention has been made so far of Judah. According to the biblical sources, Judah's first king was David, whose capital, Jerusalem, became the capital of the united kingdom of Israel and Judah under David and Solomon. After the destruction of the northern kingdom, Israel, by the Assyrians in 722–721 BCE Judah took over the role and traditions of Israel. The origin, exact form, and meaning of the name Judah are unknown. Biblical and extra-biblical texts vary the form between *Yehud* and *Yehudah* among others. Whether the name is a personal name or a place name is disputed; suggested meanings range from 'praise' (Gen. 29: 35, 49: 8) to 'may Yahweh be victorious'. According to the present state of archaeological research it seems that the area of Judah, that is, the southern hill country, was settled later and less densely than the northern hill country and Galilee, where Israel was established. There are good environmental reasons for this. Rainfall increases in Palestine as one goes northwards, and Judah lacks the fertile valleys that become increasingly evident the further north one goes towards the Jezreel valley. It is true that the Shephelah, or lowlands, a transitional set of hills between the coastal plain and the Judaean hills, is a much more fertile region; but the Philistines bordered, and no doubt controlled, this area. A major puzzle is how, if the biblical account is correct, this small, less-favoured region came, under David and Solomon, to dominate the much larger and potentially more powerful kingdom of Israel. It may be possible to give an answer if the biblical material is handled carefully.

In 1 Samuel the Philistine attempt to expand into the central hill country is given as the reason for the institution of kingship in Israel, with Saul as the first king. Although this connection is no doubt too simple (Saul may have been more of a paramount chief than a king and the Philistine threat only the sufficient

Saul appears in 1 Samuel in the roles of judge, ecstatic prophet, and king. Here, Julius Schnorr von Carolsfeld (1794–1874) depicts Saul's anointing as king by Samuel.

cause), it will serve here. The Philistine expansion destabilized the area of Judah and Israel and united their inhabitants against the invader. The emergence of a national leader from the territory most immediately threatened (Benjamin) was a natural consequence. However, an interesting feature of the narrative in 1 Samuel is the insistence that Saul had the backing of, or was even a member of, ecstatic prophetic groups that were zealous in their devotion to Yahweh. Twice comes the proverb 'Is Saul also among the prophets?' (1 Sam. 10: 11–12; 19: 24), and Samuel, the apparent leader of the prophets, is instrumental in promoting and deposing Saul as king. In the final form of the tradition, Samuel has become a composite figure combining the features of priest and judge with that of ecstatic prophet. It is arguable, however, that the role of ecstatic prophet brings us closest to the historical figure of Samuel. If the association of ecstatic prophetic activity with the appointment of Saul is correct, the rise of the kingship must be seen as more than a political response to the threat of an invader. There was a strong religious element also; and the tradition in 1 and 2 Samuel, which is not exactly sympathetic to Saul in its final form, retains evidence that Saul had tried to carry out religious reforms during his reign (1 Sam. 28: 3b; 2 Sam. 21: 1–2).

David, who succeeded where Saul failed, is an enigmatic figure. If the genealogy of 2 Samuel 17: 24 and other pieces of information (2 Sam. 10: 1–2) are authentic, David's mother would seem to have been at one time the wife of the Ammonite king Nahash, who was Saul's adversary according to 1 Samuel 11. Certainly, David seems to have taken advantage of the Philistine crisis to establish himself as a kind of freebooter heading a group of adventurers who were fiercely loyal to a man who was evidently a charismatic leader. Initially temporarily allied with Saul, David aroused the latter's suspicions and was forced eventually to desert to the Philistines. Confined to the area of southern Judah, David adopted the dual strategy of forging diplomatic links with the villagers of Judah while raiding the Amalekites in the Negev. After Saul had been defeated by the Philistines, David became king of Judah and then of Israel, before defeating the Philistines and setting up his capital in Jerusalem (2 Sam. 5).

These processes can best be understood if we set them in the context of a world where borders between states were not lines drawn on maps, and where rulers had little centralized control over the areas that they claimed to rule. Philistine 'control' of Israel would have amounted to the occupation of frontier and strategic cities from which demands for food and labour could be imposed upon the immediately surrounding villages (cf. 1 Sam. 13: 17). None the less, this was an affront to the Israelites and especially to the ecstatic prophetic groups. Since warfare was essentially battle for control of border or strategic towns, a charismatic leader with a small brave and accomplished group of fighters could dislodge an enemy from these sites within his own country and could even seek to expand beyond it by capturing key cities of neighbouring peoples. If David indeed created a small 'empire', it was in the sense of capturing border and strategic towns that enabled him to claim authority over a whole territory. The actual control of such territory would be limited to immediate areas around towns in which garrisons were installed.

ISRAEL'S RELIGION

A historical sketch has been a necessary diversion from the religious and literary questions that this chapter is seeking to address. It has drawn attention to the ecstatic prophetic groups; it has now to be asked what can be guessed about the religion of David. The tradition in 2 Samuel 6 credits David with bringing to Jerusalem the ark of the covenant, a cult object that had apparently at one point been captured by the Philistines. In 1 Samuel 4: 4 the ark is called the 'ark of the covenant of the Lord of hosts' and in Numbers 10: 35–6 it is associated with the earthly and heavenly armies of Yahweh by way of words that also occur in Psalm 68 and which, as mentioned earlier, speak of Yahweh coming in a warlike manner from the south. The words are 'Arise O Lord, let your enemies be scattered, and your foes flee before you' (Num. 10: 35–6, cf. Ps. 68: 1). The ark was possibly a visible symbol of the warlike presence of Yahweh among his people, which had been brought to Palestine by *shasu* groups who settled in Israel. Indeed, the adoption of Yahweh by Israel may have resulted from the belief that the ark had assisted them in their struggles with their neighbours to establish their independence. That David should have adopted this cult object is perhaps an indication that his own faith was a soldier's belief in a God who was his helper in war. At any rate, the stories of Saul and the ecstatic prophets, and of David and the ark, point to two features that were to be formative in the development of Israel's faith and thus the production of the Old Testament: a northern prophetic element, and the establishment of the worship of Yahweh in Jerusalem.

It has long been supposed in critical scholarship that when David captured Jerusalem he found there both an established priesthood presided over by a priest-king, Zadok, and a cult that contained 'Canaanite' elements. Hints of this pre-existing religion have been found in psalms such as 110, where the king is made a priest 'after the order of Melchizedek' and Psalm 91 where God is named as 'the Most High' and 'the Almighty' as well as Yahweh. Psalm 46, which speaks of the river that flows beneath the city of God, contains another possible allusion to 'Canaanite' beliefs. Without meaning to reject these suggestions, it should be noted that current scholarship is divided about how much of the city of Jerusalem existed at the time of David, while it has also been argued that the 'Canaanite' fea-

Excavations at the city of David, Jerusalem, carried out in the 1970s and 1980s reveal remains from the 10th to the 6th centuries BCE. Some scholars date the 'stepped stone structure' (*centre*) to the time of David.

tures of the Jerusalem cult are later developments rather than beliefs and practices that Israelite faith incorporated from a pre-Davidic Jerusalem cult. Only time will tell which of these views is the more likely to be correct.

The delineation of the ecstatic prophets in the north and the Jerusalem cult in the south is only a preliminary step in tracing the faith of Israel. The prophetic groups lived on the margins of society, while the Jerusalem cult was that of a royal rather than a national temple. To discover the religious situation of the people in general it is necessary to consider the evidence from personal names, extra-biblical inscriptions, and artistic representations on seals and amulets. The evidence from personal names is not easy to handle because of textual variations between parallel passages (King Abijam in 1 Kgs. 14: 31, 15: 1, etc. is Abijah in the parallel account in 2 Chr. 12: 16, 13: 1, etc.) and differences between the Hebrew and the ancient Greek translation known as the Septuagint. The list of names of the 30 heroes of David in 2 Samuel 23: 24–39 bristles with such difficulties. Bearing all these problems in mind, it is nevertheless striking that the recorded names of the kings of Israel and Judah begin by having no element of the name Yahweh, and that this element only gradually becomes more common. The first northern king whose name has an element of Yahweh is Ahaziah (853–852), the first southern king (assuming that Abijam rather than Abijah is correct) is Jehoshaphat (871–848). Of the nineteen kings of the northern kingdom, Israel, only seven contain an element of Yahweh while of the twenty kings of Judah (not counting David and Solomon) fourteen contain this element. The greater presence of Yahweh elements in Judah is probably due to the close connection between the king and the cult of Yahweh in Jerusalem, while of the seven names with Yahweh elements in the northern kingdom five follow one after the other from 853 to 782, the period of major political activity of the prophetic groups led by Elijah and Elisha, who were fiercely loyal to Yahweh and who encouraged their sympathizer Jehu to execute a *coup d'état* in 841 (2 Kgs. 9).

Hebrew inscriptions, bearing in mind that their survival and discovery is haphazard, indicate the presence of personal names combined with Yahweh from the eighth century onwards (practically no Hebrew inscriptions are known from before this time). From the information in Graham Davies's *Ancient Hebrew Inscriptions* (1991), there are roughly thirteen such names from sites in Judah in the eighth century, eight from the seventh century, and twenty from the late seventh to early sixth centuries. These figures do not include names ending in -yah or -iyah. On the other hand, the Samaria ostraca, dated from the second half of the eighth century, contain seven personal names with the element *ba'al*, the name of the 'Canaanite' god of the storm. This supports the view presented in the books of Kings that the northern kingdom, Israel, or at any rate its capital Samaria (the Samaria ostraca derive from places close to, and linked to, Samaria) was open to 'Canaanite' influences.

Much interest has been aroused by the discovery in 1975–6 of two inscribed jars at Kuntillet-Ajrud, a kind of caravanserai 50 km. south of Kadesh-barnea, in the Negev. Dated *c.*800 BCE, they were evidently written and painted on by travellers, and among the inscriptions are references to 'Yahweh of Samaria', 'Yahweh of Teman', and 'Yahweh and his Asherah'. The references seem to indicate that for the travellers, at any rate, Yahweh was worshipped as a localized deity in Samaria and in the south of Edom (i.e. Teman; and see above for the connection between Yahweh and this region). The reference to Yahweh's Asherah is probably to the sacred pole or tree that represented Asherah, because it is not possible (as far as is known) to add a suffix with the meaning 'his' to a proper name in Hebrew in the way that 'his' is added to 'Asherah' in the inscription. What this indicates is that popular religion associated a fertility symbol, the Asherah pole or tree, with the worship of Yahweh, a practice strongly condemned in the Old Testament (1 Kgs. 15: 13). The iconography of Israel and Judah shows the influence of Egyptian and Assyrian religious symbols upon Israelite popular religion; but it also shows that, at the end of the seventh century, a strenuous effort was made by officials in Judah to avoid 'pagan' symbols. The seals from around this time have no symbols, and contain simply the names of the officials concerned. Their presence confirms the account of the cultic reform carried out by Josiah from 622 BCE onwards (2 Kgs. 22–3).

The consideration of such things as personal names, inscriptions, and iconography generally confirms the picture given in the books of Kings, according to which the religion of Israel in the period 950–587 was syncretistic. The worship of Yahweh was carried on at many sites called, derogatively, 'high places' in the Old Testament; but other deities were worshipped, including Baal, and fertility practices were associated with Yahweh in the form of the Asherah pole or tree. The situation in Israel and Judah can be described in terms of three competing types of religion: those of official Yahwism (the religion of the court), popular Yahwism (the religion of the ordinary people), and prophetic Yahwism (the religion of prophetic groups probably on the margins of society). However, there were probably important differences between Israel and Judah.

The Lachish ostraca were discovered in 1935 and date from *c.*587 BCE. Evidently written from an outpost and sent to Lachish, they cast vivid light on the last days of Judah before its capitulation to Nebuchadnezzar.

Israel was more open to syncretism at the level of official religion, with the result that the prophetic groups frequently clashed with the kings of Israel, and encouraged soldiers and administrators with prophetic sympathies either to subvert official policies or to attempt *coups d'état*. An instance of the former is the high official Obadiah's concealment of prophets during the reign of Ahab (873–853) when the king's foreign-born wife promoted her own religion and tried to eliminate the Yahweh prophets (1 Kgs. 18: 3–4). An instance of the latter is the *coup d'état* of Jehu (841–813) instigated by Elisha (2 Kgs. 9).

In Judah, which was much smaller territorially and where Jerusalem's influence became increasingly dominant, prophets such as Hosea and

Amos directed their attention to Israel. However, Micah was bitterly critical of Jerusalem towards the end of the eighth century, as were Jeremiah and Ezekiel just over a century later. The two slightly different manifestations of Yahwism, in Israel and Judah at royal and prophetic level, were brought together following the destruction of the northern kingdom, Israel, by the Assyrians in 722/721 BCE. Royal chronicles and other written or oral traditions were brought from the north to Judah by groups, including prophetic groups, seeking refuge in the one remaining country where Yahweh was officially worshipped.

It was most likely at this time, during the reign of Hezekiah (727–698), that the first steps were taken towards the production of the Old Testament as we know it. Hezekiah had the necessary scribal resources, and in the presence of the northern prophetic groups plus a desire to resist Assyria and extend his jurisdiction over as much of the former northern kingdom as possible, the motivation to put in train the production of the initial account of the history of the people from the time of Abraham onwards. His scribes made use of royal chronicles, stories emanating from prophetic groups, and stories of local and popular heroes and heroines. Abraham and Isaac were most likely Judahite heroes, their stories being set in southern Judah (Hebron) and the Negev, while Jacob was a northern hero, his story centring on Bethel, Shechem, Transjordan, and Haran. The fact that the Judahite Abraham precedes the Israelite Jacob, whose name is changed to Israel and who becomes the ancestor of the twelve tribes of Israel (Gen. 29; 32: 22–32) is best explained by the supposition that the stories were put together in Judah when Israel no longer existed as a political force.

How the overall story was continued down to Hezekiah's time can only be guessed at. We are on firmest ground with the royal chronicles, described in the books of Kings as the 'Book of the Chronicles of the Kings of Judah/Israel' (see 1 Kgs. 14: 19, 29). Their general accuracy can be checked against Egyptian and Assyrian records from time to time, from the invasion by Sheshonq I of Egypt in 925 BCE (1 Kgs. 14: 25–8) through the mention of Omri in the Inscription of Mesha (see above), to Ahab, Jehu, Azariah (Uzziah), and Hezekiah himself being mentioned in Assyrian sources. This does not

The inscription of Mesha, king of Moab *c.*850 BCE, was discovered in 1868 in Dhiban (ancient Dibon), Jordan. It mentions the Israelite king Omri as well as the God of Israel, YHWH.

mean, of course, that every detail is correct from a modern historical point of view. The stories of Elijah and Elisha, that dominate the books of Kings from 1 Kings 17 to 2 Kings 10, contain legendary elements and narratives that sometimes cannot be fitted in to the historical scheme; but the general framework can be trusted. What cannot be known is how much of the story from Jacob to the time of David existed in this initial draft. Because tradition abhors a vacuum it is likely that the narrative included the Exodus (Hosea 11: 1), stories about Moses, Joshua, and some or most of the 'judges' ending with Samuel and Saul. The difficulty is that it is almost impossible to work back from the final forms of these accounts to the form that they might have had in the initial version.

This initial version was the product of official Yahwism as represented in Jerusalem under the patronage of a king (Hezekiah) who allowed himself to be advised by a prophet, Isaiah. Its aim was to legitimize Jerusalem and its Davidic dynasty as chosen by Yahweh, as well as to assert that the whole land of Israel, north and south, had been promised to the descendants of the Judahite Ancestor, Abraham. However, the account also no doubt stressed the importance of loyalty to Yahweh over against other deities, and used stories as object-lessons to point out the consequences of disloyalty. It is also likely that the reign of Hezekiah was the time in which the laws found in Exodus 21–3 were officially promulgated. These restricted any period of slavery for males to six years and were generally supportive of the poor and disadvantaged (e.g. Exodus 22: 21–7).

The promise of Hezekiah's reign was cruelly disappointed. Invaded by the Assyrian king Sennacherib in 701, Judah was devastated and Hezekiah was forced to pay tribute (2 Kgs. 18: 13–16). For the next sixty years Judah was a vassal state of Assyria and 'pagan' religion flourished at the official and popular levels. In 640, by which time Assyrian power had declined to the

Part of an Assyrian relief of the siege and capture of the city of Lachish in Judah by Sennacherib in 701 BCE. The relief was discovered in the palace of Sennacherib in Nineveh.

point of no return (the Assyrian empire would last for not more than a further thirty years), parties favourable to prophetic Yahwism were able to intervene in the politics of Judah and place on the throne the 8-year old Josiah (2 Kgs. 21: 19–22: 2). His reign (640–609) produced a religious reorganization in Judah that turned Jerusalem from a royal to a national sanctuary. All other sanctuaries were closed down and all traces of 'paganism' were purged from the Jerusalem cult. In terms of the threefold distinction between official, popular, and prophetic religion, it can be said that official religion, inspired by the prophetic, sought to control popular religion as never before in Judah or Israel, a move made possible by the increasing administrative control of Jerusalem over Judah. This controlling of popular religion is instanced in making the passover a national festival to be observed only in Jerusalem. The origins of the passover are obscure and its exact form of observance prior to Josiah unknown; but it was probably a local or family observance of some kind, originating in the northern kingdom.

Josiah's reform had a major impact on the formation of the Old Testament. It was inspired by or gave rise to the deuteronomistic movement, which was a combination of high official and prophetic circles. These produced a first draft of Deuteronomy, and edited the existing story of Israel from the time of Abraham, bringing it down to the time of Josiah (2 Kgs. 23: 24–5) and adding deuteronomistic frameworks to books such as Judges. The framework in Judges sets the stories of

Statue of the Egyptian pharaoh Necho II (ruled 610–595 BCE) who intervened in Old Testament history by killing king Josiah at Megiddo in 609.

various heroes and heroines in a recurring cycle of the Israelites turning to other gods, oppression by a foreign power as God's punishment for the apostasy, the raising up by God of a deliverer in response to the request of the people, and a period of 'rest' following the deliverance, before the cycle is repeated. Deuteronomy was probably modelled on the types of vassal treaty that were current in the Near East at the time. These contained a historical prologue setting the context for the treaty (Deut. 4: 44–11: 31), stipulations required to be observed by the vassal (Deut. 12–26), and details of penalties that would be exacted if the vassal was disloyal. Interesting parallels have been pointed out between Deuteronomy 28 and the vassal treaties of the Assyrian king Esarhaddon (681–669 BCE). One of the features of deuteronomistic theology, deriving from the vassal treaty scheme, was a recasting of past history to show that disasters that had befallen Israel were divine punishments resulting from disloyalty to Yahweh. In particular, disloyalty to Yahweh was understood in terms of worshipping other gods.

Another feature of the deuteronomic reform was the introduction of new social measures to counteract poverty and to support the officials whose shrines had been closed down. For example, a three-year tithe was commanded whose produce was to be distributed locally to Levites (dispossessed local cultic officials) and to the disadvantaged (Deut. 14: 28–9). Further, a seven-yearly system of release was commanded in which loans to fellow Israelites were written off (Deut. 15: 1–6). Women slaves were given the same right of release as men slaves (Deut. 15: 12–18; cf. Exod. 21: 7–11 where women slaves do not have this right).

The deuteronomic reform was brought to an end by Josiah's death in 609 BCE at the hands of the Egyptian pharaoh Necho II and for the remainder of the existence of Judah (to 587) the kingdom was in effect a vassal state to Egypt and then Babylonia. These reverses allowed popular religion to be freed from official control, and the books of Jeremiah and Ezekiel contain abundant evidence that ordinary people turned to 'pagan' deities and away from the austere official and prophetic Yahwism that had apparently failed, given Judah's loss of independence.

From the destruction of the temple in 587 to the end of the Persian period (333) Israelite history enters a phase about which little information has survived, and yet in which the Old Testament and its faith came near to reaching the forms in which we know them. It can be surmised that in this period priestly, scribal, and prophetic interests combined in the context of a small temple-based community in Jerusalem to consolidate trends that had been apparent for some considerable time. However, the loss of the Jerusalem temple and the Babylonian exile made a lasting impression upon this closing stage of the formulation of the faith and its writings.

In the first place, in the absence of political rule (the last Davidic king was Jehoiachin, who died some time after 560 BCE), religious rule by priests took on new importance, while prophetic activity became primarily concerned with the editing and expanding of teaching deriving from the prophets of earlier generations. Secondly, there was much less scope for popular religion in a temple-based community centred in a Judah that was now smaller than it had been before 587. The southern part of Judah, for example, had been occupied by Edomites.

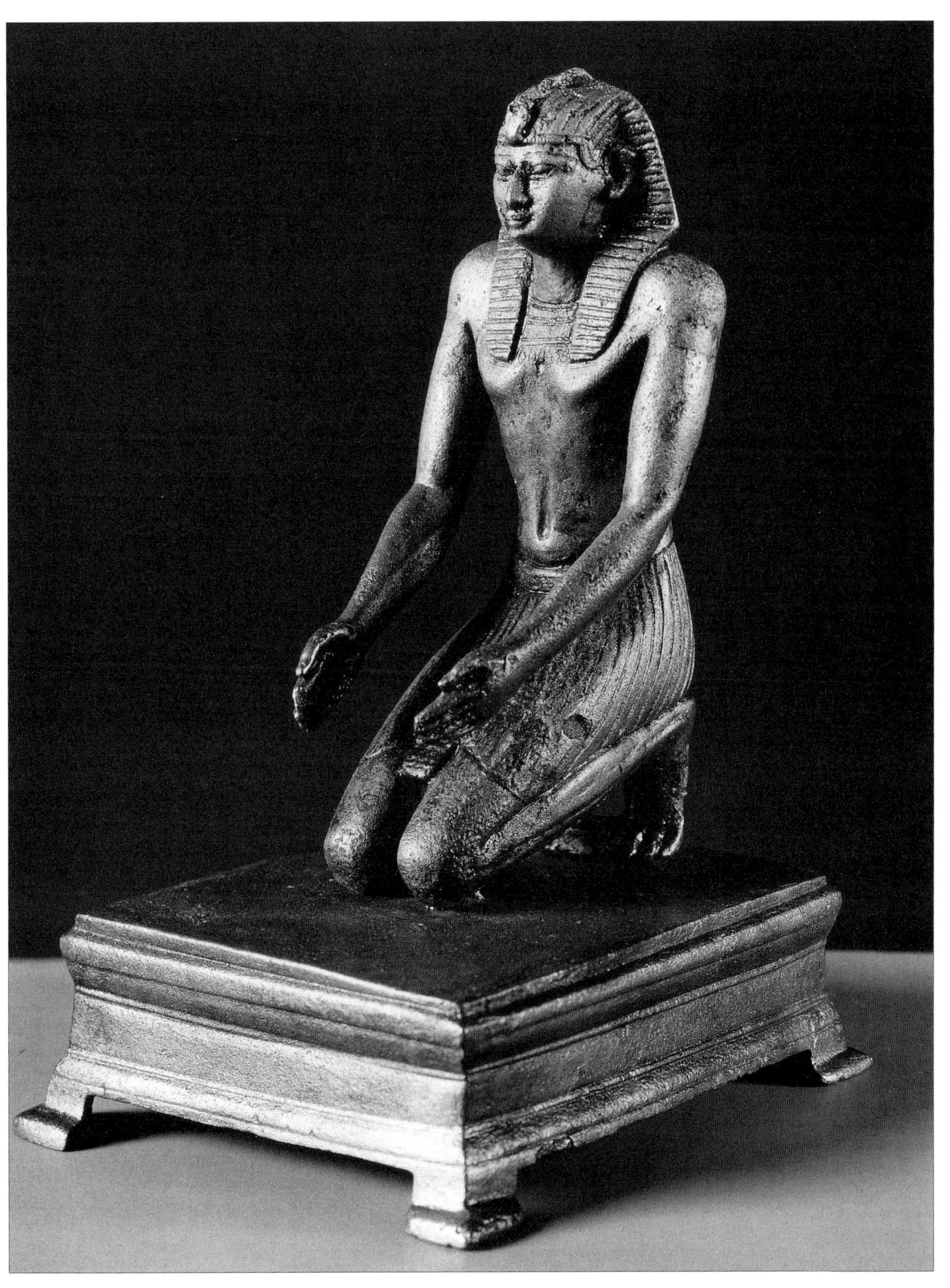

Thirdly, official religion in the sense of the religion of the court no longer existed, and neither did prophetic religion in the sense of the religion of marginal groups fiercely loyal to Yahweh, who intervened in politics from time to time. In fact, religion in Judah was now well on the way to becoming a faith based upon writings that were regarded as scripture.

To the Persian period (539–333 BCE) can be assigned the editing of the Pentateuch into its final form and the substantial completion of the prophets, which included the books of Joshua, Judges, Samuel, and Kings as well as Isaiah, Jeremiah, Ezekiel, and the twelve Minor Prophets. The story beginning with Abraham was prefaced by the primeval history (Gen. 1–11) and supplemented by the ritual and priestly material now found in Exodus, Leviticus, and Numbers. In the Former Prophets (Joshua to Kings) the story was brought down to the destruction of the temple and the release from prison of the last king, Jehoiachin, in 560 (2 Kgs. 25: 27–30). Also, sections were edited or expanded to meet situations arising from the destruction of the temple in 587 and the Babylonian exile. For example, Solomon's prayer of dedication of the temple in 1 Kings contains sections which imply that there are Jews in the diaspora (i.e. not living in Palestine) for whom the temple will be a place towards which they pray (1 Kgs. 8: 46–53). It says nothing about the temple as a place of sacrifice. A good example of the work on the Latter Prophets is Isaiah, where sayings deriving from at least three prophets, Isaiah of Jerusalem (eighth century), Deutero-Isaiah (mid-sixth century), and Trito Isaiah (late sixth century) were brought together, along with attempts to give the work some unity by thematically linking the closing chapters with the opening ones.

Bust of Alexander the Great whose defeat of the Persian empire in 333 BCE and subsequent conquest of Syria, Palestine, and Egypt ushered in the Hellenistic era of Jewish history.

The third section of the Hebrew Bible, the Writings, was less complete by the end of the Persian period. The Psalms, some of which dated from the First Temple period, were probably in their present form as far as Psalm 106. The Proverbs, many of which dated from the time of Hezekiah or earlier, were prefaced by chapters 1–9 which set them in an explicitly Yahwistic theological framework, albeit one which was closer to official Yahwism than to prophetic Yahwism. Also complete by the middle of the fourth century BCE were the so-called Chronicler's history (Chronicles, Ezra, and Nehemiah) and books such as Lamentations (most likely occasioned by the destruction of Jerusalem) and Ruth. It is difficult to determine whether works such as Job, Ecclesiastes, Song of Songs, and Esther were complete by 333 BCE.

This uncertainty stems mostly from lack of knowledge about social conditions in Judah in the first half of the fourth century BCE and whether changes were beginning to occur before Alexander the Great defeated the Persians and incorporated Syria/Palestine into the Hellenistic environment that would profoundly affect it up to and well beyond the coming of Roman rule in 63 BCE. Certainly, the advent

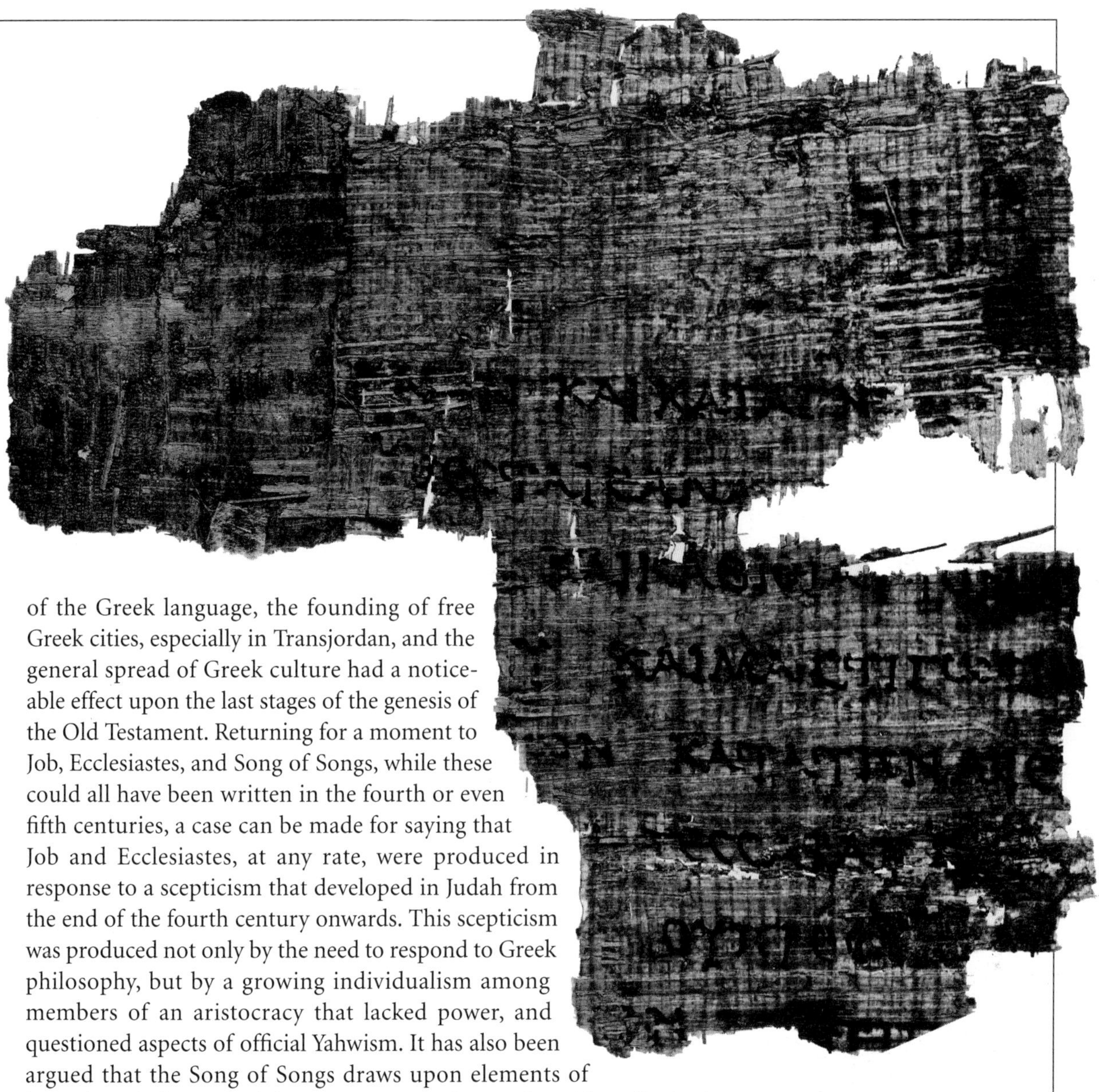

of the Greek language, the founding of free Greek cities, especially in Transjordan, and the general spread of Greek culture had a noticeable effect upon the last stages of the genesis of the Old Testament. Returning for a moment to Job, Ecclesiastes, and Song of Songs, while these could all have been written in the fourth or even fifth centuries, a case can be made for saying that Job and Ecclesiastes, at any rate, were produced in response to a scepticism that developed in Judah from the end of the fourth century onwards. This scepticism was produced not only by the need to respond to Greek philosophy, but by a growing individualism among members of an aristocracy that lacked power, and questioned aspects of official Yahwism. It has also been argued that the Song of Songs draws upon elements of 'pagan' mythology, which became increasingly popular with Hellenization.

The 2nd century CE Rylands fragment of Deuteronomy 25: 1–3 is one of the earliest remains of the Old Testament in Greek. Greek translations of the Bible were one of the long-term outcomes of Alexander's conquests.

Whatever the truth of these arguments, Hellenization was responsible for the need for the Old Testament to be translated into Greek from the mid-third century BCE, for the benefit of Jews living in Egypt. There was also the clash with Hellenism which resulted in the Maccabean revolt against the Seleucid ruler of Judah, Antiochus IV, from 168 or 167 to 164. This resulted in the writing of the book of Daniel (in Hebrew and Aramaic) and the production of the books 1 and 2 Maccabees in the Apocrypha, the former in Hebrew, the latter in Greek.

The existence of the Apocrypha indicates that what was said above about Old Testament books being completed in the Persian period needs to be qualified. The Apocrypha contains 1 Esdras, a work based upon part of 2 Chronicles 35–6,

Ezra 1: 1–10: 44, and Nehemiah 7: 72–8: 13, but evidently using a Hebrew text differing from that which has become traditional for those books; 1 Esdras also contains two sections (1: 23–4 and 3: 1–5: 6) which have no parallel in the Old Testament. Overall, it provides a more integrated and interesting version of material, most of which is in the Old Testament.

CONCLUSION

It is now time to review the point which has been reached in comparison with the opening pages. There, it was pointed out that the Old Testament's view of how Israel's faith originated is that it was revealed by God supremely to Moses, but also to other people such as Abraham and the prophets. Authors drawn from this privileged group were then responsible for writing the Old Testament. The outline given above has indicated something much more complicated—a series of interactions between official, popular, and prophetic Yahwism in the context of the historical ups and downs of a small people surrounded by, and often victim to, the ambitions of powerful empires. Also, brief consideration of the Apocrypha has indicated that the processes of formation and development of Israel's faith and the production of its scriptures was something ongoing. The discovery of the Dead Sea Scrolls, for example, has shown how, in the first century BCE, there were diverse and competing strands within the broad stream of the Judaism of the time. In a way, the Qumran group might be compared with the prophetic religion of earlier times, seeing that it lived on the margins of society and was fiercely critical of the official Judaism of the time.

The Qumran group is also instructive with regard to attitudes to scripture. On the assumption that the Temple Scroll and the biblical commentaries were the work of the same group, the Qumran sectarians regarded certain works as sacred and therefore susceptible of interpretation. This is seen in the commentaries on books such as Habakkuk and Nahum, the prophecies of which are interpreted in terms of the group's history and leaders. On the other hand, the Temple Scroll is an attempt to fill a gap in the Bible. There is no record in the Old Testament of explicit instructions from God about the form and dimensions of the Jerusalem temple. Exodus 35–40 contains an account of the construction of the portable

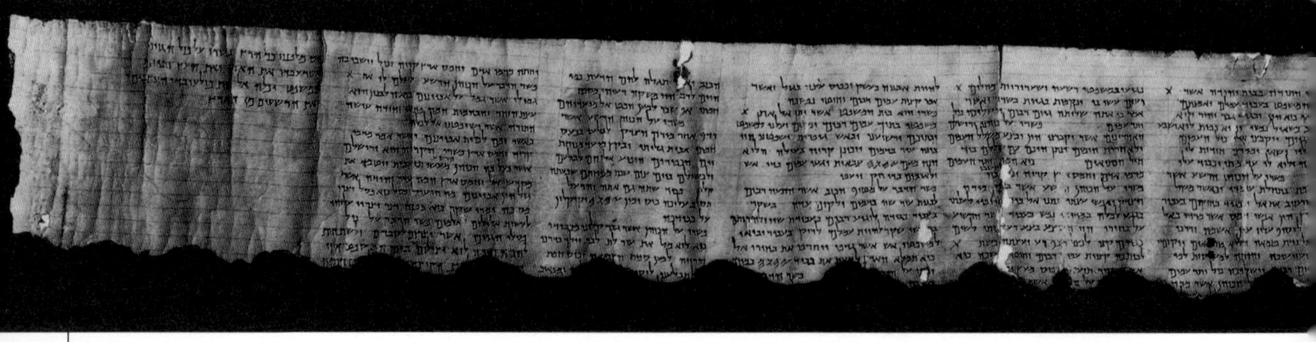

The commentary, or pesher, on the book of Habakkuk from Cave 1 at Qumran interprets the biblical text in terms of recent events in the life of the Qumran sect.

tabernacle according to God's instructions which served the Israelites in the wilderness; 1 Kings 6–7 describes how Hiram built the Jerusalem temple for Solomon. No doubt the description of the tabernacle in Exodus is dependent upon the later Second Temple. The point is that the Old Testament contains no specific instructions from God about the construction of the Jerusalem temple; and it is this lack which the Temple Scroll remedies, in the form of a direct address of God to Moses about the building of a temple. Thus, as late as the first century BCE, there was a group within Judaism that claimed and attributed revelations of God to Moses regarding vital matters of religion.

If modern scholarship proposes a gradual development of the faith of Israel as opposed to an initial revelation to a founder such as Moses, this does not mean that we are left with vagaries. However the faith of Israel may have developed (and subsequent research and discoveries may modify or alter the sketch proposed in this chapter) the end result was that the texts that were produced and the faith that they implied had what has been called a family likeness. The main features of this 'family likeness' were:

- belief in Yahweh as the God of Israel and as the only God, the creator of the universe;
- belief in Israel as the people chosen and called by Yahweh to service and obedience, that would lead to Yahweh being acknowledged by the other nations;
- belief in Jerusalem as the place chosen by Yahweh for a temple to honour his name, and belief in Yahweh's choice of the house of David to rule over Israel;
- belief in Yahweh's laws as revealed to Moses;
- belief in a re-creation of the heavens and the earth when Yahweh would establish a peace and justice longed for by the nations.

Not all of these features are to be found in every book of the Old Testament, but they are implied. Ecclesiastes, for example, always uses the general Hebrew word for God rather than the name Yahweh, and makes no mention of Israel or of its being specially chosen and commissioned by Yahweh. But its view, that humans live in a world created by God, who is also the creator of individual humans and

ויתלו את המן

to whom their spirits return at death, would be impossible without the general background of belief outlined above. Indeed, the scepticism in Ecclesiastes and Job comes precisely from problems arising from the need to relate Israelite monotheism to the sufferings of innocent people and the many injustices that go unpunished, when Israelite monotheism had not yet developed a belief in the afterlife. Again, a book such as Esther which, in its Hebrew version, notoriously fails to mention God none the less depicts the Jews as a distinct entity singled out for hatred and destruction by Haman, and thus implying a unique Jewish national self-consciousness and praxis which could arouse hostile feelings against the Jewish people.

Readers of the list of features making up the 'family likeness' may be surprised by the omission of belief in the coming of the Messiah. Of course, by the beginning of the Common Era various types of 'Messianic' belief had developed, including the coming of a 'prophet like unto Moses' (Deut. 18: 15), a return of Elijah (Mal. 4: 5), and a royal (Davidic) or priestly anointed one (which is what 'Messiah' means). However, in the Old Testament only the elements of these later expectations are present, and are subordinate to the view that God himself will redeem his people and renew the created order.

The hanging of Haman and his sons, an incident in the book of Esther, from the Leipzig Mahzor, Upper Rhine, Germany, 1st quarter of the 14th century. The text is the *piyyut* (liturgical hymn) for the festival of Purim.

2 The Apocrypha

PHILIP DAVIES

DEFINITION AND HISTORY

Apocrypha means '[books] hidden away' and is the name given to those books found in the Old Testament of ancient Greek (Christian) Bibles but not in the Hebrew scriptures of Judaism. (There is one exception: 2 Esdras/4 Ezra.) Only two such books (the Wisdom of Solomon and 2 Maccabees) were for certain composed in Greek; the rest were either certainly or probably written originally in Aramaic or Hebrew. Also included in the Apocrypha is material included in the Greek version of Old Testament books but absent from the Hebrew editions: the Greek versions of the book of Daniel contain a 'Prayer of Azariah' and 'Song of the Young Men' in chapter 3, and the stories of Susanna and Bel and the Serpent (or Dragon) as chapters 13 and 14. The Greek edition of the book of Esther also incorporates some additional material. The existence of an Apocrypha arises from the recognition within Christian churches of different Hebrew and Greek canons, and, where the Hebrew canon has been preferred, how the additional material should be presented and evaluated.

Why the 'additional' books and parts of books came to be called 'apocryphal' is not clear. There is a Jewish tradition, narrated in 4 Ezra 14: 44–8 (written at the end of the first century CE), that Ezra the scribe was ordered by God to dictate 94 holy books that had been lost in the Babylonian exile. Ezra was then instructed to 'make public the 24 books that you wrote first, and let the worthy and unworthy read them, but keep the seventy that were written last, in order to give them to the wise among your people'. Thus, it is possible that the 'apocryphal' books were understood by some Jews, and Christians, to have belonged to these 70 books that were 'hidden' from public access (and thus not in the official list of scriptural writings).

The starting-point, then, for the emergence of a class of 'apocryphal' writings is the establishment of a scriptural list of books in Hebrew, probably during the first century BCE under the Hasmonaeans. While 4 Ezra (see above) numbered these books as 24, Josephus, writing at about the same time (*Against Apion* 1: 37–43) counted 22. (It is, however, possible to reconcile these figures in a number of ways.) But although this list of sacred writings was accepted in Palestine, and endorsed by the rabbis, there is no reason to think that an official, fixed list of Jewish scriptures was immediately and universally accepted. The Qumran scrolls, for example, dating mostly from the first century BCE to early first century CE, do not give clear evidence of a completely fixed list, though certain books, including those of the Law and Prophets, were undoubtedly regarded as scriptural. But the inclusion among the scrolls of manuscripts of 1 Enoch, Jubilees, Tobit, and ben Sira (the last two later included in the Apocrypha), shows that among some circles in Palestine the list of holy books may have been greater and perhaps less rigid.

Outside Palestine, it also seems unlikely that Jewish communities everywhere followed the list of holy books accepted in Palestine and endorsed by the rabbis. There was in any case a much richer Jewish literature in Greek than in Hebrew or Aramaic, at least to judge by what has survived. The Law and Prophets (but with the Prophets including Daniel, unlike the Hebrew scriptures) corresponded to the Hebrew canon (with the minor difference on Daniel), but we have no direct evidence regarding other books. The increased authority of the rabbis as definers of Judaism led to new Greek translations of the Hebrew scriptures, and thus the rejection of any additional material. The contents of what Christians were calling the 'Old Testament' were not, however, affected by rabbinic policy.

There are in the New Testament few allusions to, and no quotations from, any of the apocryphal books. Most early church writers quoted from these as from scripture. It is impossible to say that the apostolic church accorded any distinct status to holy books of the Jews that circulated only in Greek. This is not to say that they were unaware of discrepancies between Hebrew and Greek scriptural canons. The *Dialogue with Trypho* of Justin Martyr (100–165) already reflects an awareness on the part of learned Christians that the scriptures of the Jews that they possessed in Greek did not exactly correspond to those in Hebrew. Some patristic writers (who knew Hebrew and the Jewish scriptures (Origen, Melito, Jerome) indeed regarded only their contents as belonging to the 'Old Testament'.

This does not mean that the Christian church itself inherited a completely fixed Old Testament canon. For this reason there is no single definitive list of apocryphal books. Christians were, however, the first to collect scriptures into a single book (a 'codex'), and thus create 'Bibles'. This habit itself prompted the question of what should or should not be included in a Bible. But no 'original' list of apocryphal books can be drawn up because none of the earliest Christian biblical codices (Alexandrinus, Sinaiticus, and Vaticanus, from the fourth and fifth centuries CE) has exactly the same contents or sequence. For example, the Epistle of Jeremiah and Baruch are not preserved in Codex Sinaiticus (it is not known whether they were originally present), and none of the books of Maccabees was contained in Codex Vaticanus. The Prayer of Manasses is included only in Alexandrinus, though only as part of an appendix to the Psalter not found in the other two codices.

The isolation of 'apocryphal' books as a group (and thus the collective name 'Apocrypha') came about from a new translation of the Bible into Latin (known as the Vulgate) in the fourth century CE by Jerome, in which he used the original Hebrew for the Old Testament (the earlier Old Latin translation had been from

Greek and, of course, included 'apocryphal' books). Jerome was then confronted with the problem that certain Old Testament books were not found in the Hebrew scriptures of the Jews (which Jerome regarded as the authentic Old Testament). Once the Roman church chose to translate its Old Testament from Hebrew, of course, the status of these books would be problematic. Jerome deemed the additional books 'apocryphal', and was unwilling to supply a translation from the Greek. (He also separated the additional material in Esther and Daniel.) The remaining books were in fact added to the Vulgate, but their status continued to be uncertain, partly because many Vulgate manuscripts contained Jerome's preface and notes, in which he distinguished between 'canonical' and 'edifying' books. In the sixteenth century Luther also regarded the latter as being non-scriptural, and combined them in a separate section at the end of his German translation of the Bible (1545), under the title 'Apocrypha' (his reason seems to have been that the Roman Catholic doctrines of purgatory, prayers for the dead, and salvation by good works, which Luther rejected, were found only in the apocryphal books). The Reformation brought to a head the issue of canon, and in reaction to Luther, the Roman Catholic Council of Trent (1545–63) at last definitively affirmed that certain apocryphal books were canonical. These were: Tobit, Judith, the Wisdom of Solomon, Ecclesiastes, Baruch, 1–2 Maccabees, and additions to Esther and Daniel. These writings were thus placed among the other Old Testament books, though they were acknowledged as 'deuterocanonical' ('subsequently canonized'). However, this declaration left certain other books, previously included in the Vulgate, not canonized and these were included at the end of the Old Testament. They are regarded as 'apocryphal' but they do not form a definitive Apocrypha. Strictly speaking, 'Apocrypha', as now used in biblical scholarship, is a Protestant category.

The rather confusing position can be summed up as follows: there are books in the ancient Greek Bibles but not the Hebrew Bible; there are books included as 'Apocrypha' in Protestant Bibles, and there are books accepted by the Council of Trent as 'secondarily canonized'. All three collections could be, and sometimes are, treated as 'the Apocrypha'. Thus, for example, 3–4 Maccabees was not canonized by the Catholic Church but is included in all the early Greek Bibles. Psalm 151 is included in the Psalter of ancient Greek Bibles, but not in the Vulgate. The Prayer of Manasses, on the other hand, has somehow crept into the Apocrypha, even though it is not in two of the three earliest Greek Bibles and was not canonized at the Council of Trent. The book 4 Ezra/2 Esdras is in no ancient Greek Bible, but finds a place in the Apocrypha, though also not canonized by the Council of Trent!

Quite apart from the problem of exact contents, the canonical status of the Apocrypha has also continued to vary between Christian denominations. These books (defined according to Luther) were accepted by the Church of England as suitable for instruction but not for doctrine. The Westminster Confession, however, ruled these books out of scripture altogether. Protestant Bibles, although at first containing this material as a separate section (as in the Thomas Matthew

Bible, the Geneva Bible, and, originally, the King James Version), subsequently tended to drop the Apocrypha altogether, while in the Roman Catholic Church, despite the decision of Trent, there has remained a view in some quarters that these books have a secondary status.

The slightly different Old Testament canons of the Orthodox churches, based on the Greek, not the Latin Bible, are not considered here, but it is worth noting that differences exist over the status of 'deuterocanonical' books as well. The Greek-speaking church had also been aware of discrepancies between Hebrew and Greek canons, but not until the seventeenth century did the question of which books were truly canonical formally arise. In 1672 at the Synod of Jerusalem, the books of Wisdom, Judith, Tobit, Bel and the Dragon (not Susanna!), 1–4 Maccabees, and Ecclesiasticus (Sirach) were declared canonical. The Russian Orthodox Church, by contrast, agrees with Protestant Christianity in regarding as non-canonical all Old Testament books not existing in Hebrew.

Recent English Bibles, aiming to be inclusive and perhaps less doctrinaire, are tending to include the Apocrypha again, either among the other Old Testament books (as in the earliest Christian Bibles) or as a separate collection. However, as in the New Revised Standard Version, the result is a Bible that no Christian church has ever recognized or recognizes! But this may be a salutary reminder that there is indeed no single Christian 'Bible' or 'canon', a fact that may lead to a less doctrinaire use of scripture, especially among Protestants.

THE BOOKS OF THE APOCRYPHA: A SURVEY

The contents of the Apocrypha are, as observed earlier, not definitive, and because they did not originate as a group, their own origins are quite diverse.

1 Esdras, entitled Esdras A in the Greek manuscripts and 3 Ezra/Esdras in the Vulgate (where it appears as an appendix to the New Testament), consists of a version of 2 Chronicles 35–6, Ezra 1–10, and Nehemiah 8: 1–13. It also includes a major addition (3: 1–5: 6), a story of three courtiers, one of them Zerubbabel, who wins a contest of wits set by King Darius. The origin of this book is obscure; most scholars think it later than the corresponding biblical books, but it is clearly not a translation of the existing Hebrew text and may well represent an alternative recension of material shared by the canonized Ezra-Nehemiah. It can thus be dated anywhere between the fourth century BCE and first century CE.

2 Esdras is now generally better known as 4 Ezra (its Vulgate designation), since the name 2 Esdras in the old Greek Bibles and the Vulgate denotes the book of Nehemiah. 4 Ezra is not represented in any of the ancient Greek manuscripts, and was written towards the end of the first century CE. It is a composite work, of apocalyptic character, and the original Jewish composition, comprising chapters 3–14, has been expanded by a Christian introduction and epilogue, in which God turns away from Israel and towards the Gentiles. The original Jewish composition is composed of a series of seven visions given to Salathiel (identified with Ezra), reflecting the recent destruction of Jerusalem and the

theological problems posed by this catastrophe for the nature of God and the redemption of the people of Israel. There are also some (varied) speculations about the messianic future.

Wisdom, or the Wisdom of Solomon, is one of the two originally Greek compositions in the Apocrypha, and is generally agreed to have been composed by an Alexandrian Jew, probably in the first century BCE. It claims Solomonic authorship (ch. 7), personifies Wisdom as an agent of divine activity in Israel's history as well as the creation of the world, extols the Jewish people, condemns idolatry, and reviles Egyptians, dwelling at length on their defeat at the time of the Exodus. It also accepts a doctrine of resurrection. In all, while displaying some influence of Greek philosophy and rhetoric, it expresses the classic tenets of late Second Temple Judaism (and the aspirations of Alexandrian Jews to full citizen status within the city).

Sirach is also known as ben Sira (but never ben Sirach!), and is a Greek translation by his grandson of a work by a Jerusalem scribe early in the second century BCE. In the early twentieth century a Hebrew text was recovered from the Cairo Genizah and more recently still some fragments in Hebrew, dating to about the first century BCE, were found at Masada. The Vulgate title of the books is Ecclesiasticus ('church book'), and is not to be confused with Ecclesiastes (which is in the Hebrew Bible).

The book is largely a collection of proverbial sayings and passages of moral instruction, mixing some contemporary wisdom of the Hellenistic age with the traditional ethics of Palestinian Judaism. Its most famous section is the historical review 'in praise of our ancestors' (chs. 44–9). Ben Sira was a book known and respected also among the rabbis, and given by some of them perhaps an almost, but not quite, scriptural status.

The Additions to Esther are the product of differences between the Hebrew and Greek texts of the book, such that Jerome's Latin translation omitted a good deal of what was previously familiar to Christian readers. Jerome gathered the additional material and placed it at the end. This material was not intended to be read as if it were the proper ending of the book; yet this is often the effect of such a rearrangement. The additions alone make no sense without the rest of the book.

There are six additions in the Greek, which occur right at the beginning (numbered in the Vulgate as chs. 11–12); after 3: 13 (numbered in the Vulgate 13: 1–7); after 4: 17 (in the Vulgate 13: 8–14: 19 and 15); after 8: 12 (in the Vulgate ch. 16), and at the end, after 10: 3 (in the Vulgate 10: 4–11: 1). These additions respectively narrate Mordecai's dream and his service to the king (only alluded to in the Hebrew version); provide the text of the king's decree to exterminate the Jews; contain Mordecai's prayer; expand Esther's confrontation with the king; give the text of the second royal decree; and narrate the fulfilment of Mordecai's dream. Overall, the Greek version enhances divine participation in the story (entirely absent in the Hebrew) and glorifies further the figures of Esther and Mordecai. The content of the Additions to Esther (or some) was known to Josephus in the first century CE and so represents an early version of the book known to many Jews.

Judith is explicitly set in the Assyrian period, though many details belong to the Persian era, and Nebuchadnezzar is depicted as the Assyrian king! The story tells how this king wished to rule the world, but the inhabitants of Syria and Palestine would not accept his rule, and were thus invaded by the general Holofernes. Although warned by a non-Jew, Achior, not to besiege the Israelite city of Bethulia, Holofernes does so. Judith, a pious widow resident in the city, appears only halfway through the book. She rescues the situation by taking herself into the enemy camp, engineering a romantic meeting with the general, and beheading him before escaping to her city. Thus the siege is abandoned, Achior converts to the God of Israel, and Judith reverts to her role, releasing her slave into freedom before her death. In its celebration of a female warrior, the story is reminiscent of Judges 4 and 5, and it may well have been written in, or just after, the period of Seleucid persecution in the mid-second century BCE.

Tobit, like Judith, is set in the Assyrian period. The hero, an exceptionally pious Jew, had been punished by the king for burying a corpse in contravention of a royal decree, but was later reinstated. However, after burying yet another corpse, Tobit is blinded by bird-droppings. With the prompting of Raphael, an angel disguised as a human being, Tobit's son Tobias goes to Media to seek money left by Tobit there, and on the way hooks a fish that will later heal his father's blindness. On arrival in Ecbatana, Raphael suggests that Tobias marries Sarah, a relative of Tobias who has already lost seven bridegrooms on her wedding night to Asmodeus, a demon. On their wedding night, Tobias burns the fish's entrails and repels the demon as far as Egypt, where Raphael binds him. After much celebration, the married couple return to Nineveh and Tobias heals his father's blindness with the fish gall. Raphael discloses his identity, explains his mission, and bids Tobias and Tobit to write down the story for the instruction of others. Tobit composes a hymn of thanksgiving in which the return to Jerusalem and rebuilding of the Temple are anticipated. Later, on his deathbed, Tobit remembers the prophecies against Nineveh and tells his son to take his family elsewhere.

The story is a mixture of romance, didactic instruction, and court-tale, intertwining folk-themes and the vicissitudes of a pious hero with the exile of Israel and its future liberation. It was certainly inspired by an older and very popular tale of Ahiqar, a courtier of Sennacherib, who is mentioned in the book as Tobit's nephew. Tobit exists in a shorter and a longer version; the shorter is preserved in Vaticanus and the longer in Sinaiticus; the King James version reproduces the former and the New English Bible the latter. Jerome translated it into Latin from an Aramaic manuscript that he said he had before him, and fragments of several manuscripts of Tobit (in Hebrew and Aramaic) have been found among the Dead Sea Scrolls, suggesting a time of composition in the third or early second century BCE.

Together with the canonical Lamentations and the apocryphal Epistle of Jeremiah, Baruch comprises an addition, or supplement, to the book of Jeremiah. Baruch contains three psalms or poems, probably originally independent of each other, prefaced by an introduction that claims as their author Baruch, the scribe of Jeremiah. These are dated to five years after the capture of Jerusalem by the

Babylonians, and are said to have been read out to the king and the people in Babylonia (perhaps an idea inspired by Jer. 36). In response, the people fast and send the Temple vessels back to Jerusalem, with money for offerings on the altar.

The first of the three pieces is a psalm of repentance in two parts. It begins by remembering the continual sins of the people and acknowledges their righteous punishment. Its second part asks for forgiveness and restoration. The second psalm is a hymn in praise of divine wisdom and the third is a song of exhortation, calling on the Israelites to endure their exile and be comforted. This last psalm, apparently addressed by Baruch to Jerusalem, is full of scriptural allusions, notably to Isaiah 40–55.

The angel Raphael accompanying Tobias on his various quests as described in the book of Tobit in a painting, *Tobias and the Angel*, attributed to Andrea del Verrocchio.

The dating of this work is extremely difficult; the exilic theme may point to a period of distress, such as the second century BCE or even the first century CE; but such a conclusion is not at all certain.

The Epistle of Jeremiah, often incorporated within Baruch as its last chapter, already recognized by Jerome (in his Commentary on Jeremiah) as a 'pseudepigraph', is probably inspired by the letter in Jeremiah 29 to the exiled Judaeans in Babylonia. This later apocryphon represents itself as an earlier letter, written before their departure, and its entire theme is a warning against idolatry. Like Daniel 9, it also multiplies Jeremiah's prediction of 70 years of exile by anticipating an exile of 'up to seven generations', though this is probably no hint for a calculation of when the work was written. The invective against idolatry is such a common theme that it cannot help establish date or provenance, either.

The Additions to Daniel represent additional material in the Greek edition of the book—of which more than one ancient version has been preserved. But both translations contain (*a*) a prayer and a song performed while the three youths are in the furnace (inserted in ch. 3); (*b*) the story of Susanna, and (*c*) the story of Bel and the Dragon (or Snake).

Susanna was placed at the beginning of Daniel in the Greek and the Old Latin Old Testament, but Jerome moved it to the end; Bel and the Dragon has always been the very last part. The 'Prayer of Azariah' and 'Song of the Three Youths' are generally thought to have been translated from Hebrew or Aramaic originals, but were hardly composed for this setting, and must have been taken from elsewhere. The original language of Susanna has always been disputed, even in Jerome's day (as he notes in his Commentary on Daniel). Whether it was originally connected with Daniel is also uncertain. The same is true of the story (or stories) of Bel and the Dragon, which probably featured another hero who has later been identified as Daniel.

The first of these additions comprises two liturgical pieces as well as a narrative framework. A brief opening narrative link, in which the heroes walk about in the fire, precedes the Prayer of Azariah (= Abed-nego), one of the youths. Like Daniel 9, this is a prayer of confession for the sins of Israel, expressing loyalty and asking for deliverance. It is followed by an account of how the furnace flames are stoked, and consume those nearby, after which an angel comes to join the youths. Then comes a hymn of praise of the three youths, each line beginning with the word 'bless' or 'blessed', celebrating for the most part the divine acts of creation, though it ends with thanks for the deliverance of the three men from persecution. The motive for the insertion of the prayer and hymn into the story may have been to stress the value of prayer and thanksgiving in times of persecution, possibly to counteract the impression in the book of Daniel that the events of history are determined by God without human intervention.

Both Susanna and Bel and the Dragon have the flavour of detective fiction: Susanna, who lives in Babylon, is a pious young married woman falsely accused of adultery by lewd elders. By revealing discrepancies in each elder's testimony, the young Daniel exposes their falsehood and they are executed.

Scenes illustrating events in 1 Maccabees, from the Winchester Bible: (*Upper register*) Antiochus IV decrees the worship of an idol, while the priest Mattathias strikes off the head of a Jew who is complying, having first killed Antiochus' officer. (*Middle register*) Judas Maccabeus defeats Antiochus' general Nicanor (1 Maccabees 7:26–50). (*Lower register*) Judas Maccabeus is killed, and his burial is attended by mourners (1 Maccabees 9:1–22).

Bel and the Dragon comprises two stories, both about the stupidity of idolatry. In the first, King Cyrus is induced to worship the god Bel (= Baal) because the god appears to consume food and wine left for him every day. By having ashes strewn over the floor of the temple, Daniel proves to the king that the priests and their families return and eat the food themselves. In the second story, a huge dragon or snake is worshipped as a god, which Daniel kills by stuffing cakes of tar, fat, and hair into its mouth. In the aftermath, Daniel is put into a lions' den. There he is visited by the prophet Habakkuk (transported to him by an angel) and eventually Daniel is released unharmed.

Of the four books of Maccabees, the first two are clearly in the Apocrypha, and in the Roman Catholic Old Testament. The status of the third and fourth is ambiguous. All four are included in Alexandrinus and 1 Maccabees in Sinaiticus (none in Vaticanus), but only the first two were canonized at Trent and 3 and 4 Maccabees are not included in the Protestant Apocrypha. Generally agreed to have been composed in Hebrew, 1 Maccabees is an account of the origins of the proscription of the Jewish religion by Antiochus and an account of the deliverance brought about through a divinely chosen family/dynasty (the work is strongly pro-Hasmonaean). It was clearly an authoritative source in antiquity, and used by Josephus (*War* and *Antiquities*). However, 2 Maccabees is clearly a Greek composition, written in Alexandria, assuming the form of a letter written to establish the celebration of Hanukkah, and dwelling on the persecutions of Jewish martyrs, especially an old man called Eleazar and seven brothers, urged on by their mother. The moral of the story is less the salvation of the Jews historically than the resurrection and glorification of the martyr. Probably also written in Alexandria, 3 Maccabees is not about the Maccabees at all, but takes place in Egypt, under King Ptolemy IV, though it borrows themes from 1 and 2 Maccabees: a foiled attempt to enter the Temple, a righteous Jew called Eleazar, elephants, persecution of Jews, and angelic intervention. It ends (as do most chapters of Daniel) with a change of mind by the king. Clearly a development of 2 Maccabees, 4 Maccabees deals at even greater length with the exemplary behaviour of martyrs, though its purpose is also to demonstrate the great virtue that obedience to the Jewish law brings.

The Prayer of Manasses is represented in ancient Greek Bibles only by Alexandrinus, and then as part of an addendum to the psalms. The Council of Trent did not canonize it, and some Protestant Bibles omit it. But in the Vulgate manuscripts it became attached to the end of 2 Chronicles. It is inspired by the account in 2 Chronicles 33 that this wicked king was taken to Babylon and 'sought the favour of the Lord his God and humbled himself greatly before the God of his fathers'. A prayer of Manasseh is also mentioned in the pseudepigraphical work 2 Baruch (64–5) and a manuscript fragment from Qumran Cave 4 contains a 'Prayer of Manasseh, king of Judah, when the king of Assyria imprisoned him'. But it is a different text from the Greek prayer. Following the traditional form of such a prayer, it confesses sin, exalts God's power and mercy, asks forgiveness, and praises God in anticipation of a favourable response.

3 The New Testament

MARGARET DAVIES

THE NEW TESTAMENT IN ITS FAMILIAR FORM

How did our New Testament come into being? This apparently simple historical question soon unravels into many other questions. Our New Testament is the second and much shorter part of contemporary printed editions of the Christian Bible in vernacular translations. These we find in the libraries, bookshops, churches, and homes of people who live in countries where the various denominations and sects of Christianity are tolerated, approved, or supported. The English word 'Bible' derives from the ancient Greek word *biblia* which is plural and diminutive, used for little papyrus books or scrolls, or the place where they are kept. In other words, 'Bible' suggests that this is a collection of writings. How and why were just these writings collected together, and when, where, why, by whom, and for whom were they originally written? Moreover, how did it come about that the Jewish scriptures, the first and much longer part, came to be designated 'the Old Testament', and the second, shorter part 'the New Testament'? 'Testament' is also derived from an ancient word, but this time a Latin word referring to the expression of a person's wishes. Apart from its use as titles for the two parts of Christian Bibles, it is most common in contemporary English for written documents which express people's wishes about the inheritance of their property after their deaths. Do these titles therefore suggest that these writings are expressions of someone's wishes, and is that someone to be identified with the Christian God? And, if so, why are there two different testaments, two different expressions of this God's wishes, and why is one designated 'old' and the other 'new'?

We have now noticed that two key English terms in regard to our topic are actually borrowings. This gives us a sense that the Bible is understood as a collection of writings brought together and given titles at times when Greek or Latin was used by Christian communities, or rather by the literate élite of those communities. Why are two ancient languages involved? In the fourth century BCE, the Macedonian Greek-speaking warrior Alexander conquered Greece, Asia Minor, and the Middle East, including Syria, Palestine, the Persian empire, and Egypt. After his death, his Greek-speaking successors ruled these areas, and founded

Greek cities. Hence, Hellenistic Greek, a later development of classical Greek, became the common language of diplomacy, commerce, and élite literature in these eastern Mediterranean regions. Of course, peoples in these areas continued to speak or write in their own languages—Aramaic and Hebrew in Palestine, for example—but educated people and merchants would also learn to speak and write in Greek. Most New Testament manuscripts from the third and fourth centuries CE which have survived are written in Hellenistic Greek. Most of the New Testament books, however, contain some expressions which seem to be Greek translations of idioms more at home in Semitic languages, the indigenous languages of the Middle East; for example, 'the son of the human being' or 'a son of a human being' which occurs in New Testament gospels (e.g. Matt. 8: 20; Mark 8: 31; Luke 21: 27; John 5: 27). This Greek expression is found in no Greek writings uninfluenced by either Greek versions of the Jewish scriptures, where the phrase occurs without the definite article (e.g. Ps. 8: 4; Ezekiel 2: 1; Daniel 7: 13), or Greek translations of other Semitic languages like Aramaic or Syriac. How far particular Semitisms in the New Testament are to be explained as conscious or unconscious imitations of the style of Greek versions of the Jewish scriptures, or as translations into Greek of earlier Aramaic or Syriac oral or literary traditions, is matter for debate. What is remarkable is that those books which now comprise the New Testament were originally written in Greek, not in Aramaic, probably the language in which Jesus taught. That they were in Greek suggests that they were written by and for people who lived in the small urban centres of the eastern Mediterranean world, rather than for peasants who lived in the countryside, where they would speak indigenous languages.

During the first century BCE Latin-speaking Roman generals began, from their base in Italy, to conquer and bring under Roman control countries bordering the Mediterranean to the east, west, and south. For example, Jerusalem was captured by Pompey in 63 BCE. In the eastern Mediterranean, however, Greek continued to function as the language of diplomacy, trade, and élite literature, while in the west Latin came to serve the same purposes. Codex Bezae, a fifth-century codex of the New Testament Gospels and Acts, contains both Greek and Latin versions.

We should also notice that we have inherited another word for titles of the two parts of the Bible: 'the Old Covenant' and 'the New Covenant'. The word 'covenant', however, is not a direct borrowing but a translation into English of the Greek word *diatheke*. 'Covenant' refers to an agreement, bargain, or compact between different parties. It is used, for example, in the 'National Covenant' of 1638 which sought to defend Presbyterianism in Scotland. Today, 'covenant' refers most commonly to a legal agreement either to do some specified action or to provide some benefit for a named person or institution. Do the Old and New Covenants therefore signify a compact between God and a community or communities of people, or between the creator and creation? The ancient Greek word *diatheke*, however, like the ancient Latin word 'testament', can refer to expressions of a person's wishes, as, for example, in some manuscripts of Galatians 3: 15; but it is also used in New Testament contexts, like those relating Jesus' last supper with his associates (Matt. 26: 28; Mark 14: 24; some manuscripts of Luke 22: 20; 1 Cor. 11: 25; and in Luke 22: 20 and 1 Cor. 11: 25 the adjective 'new' occurs), where 'covenant' seems a more appropriate translation. Similarly, some New Testament quotations from the Jewish scriptures in Greek (e.g. Rom. 11: 27; Heb. 8: 10) also use the word in this sense, perhaps suggesting that New Testament references imitate and interpret those already known from Greek versions of the Jewish scriptures. In the fourth century CE the *Church History* of Eusebius (265–340 CE) uses the term *endiathekos* to refer to a collection of writings considered of prime importance to Christians (III. 3.1; XXV. 6; VI. 14.1).

Our contemporary vernacular versions of the New Testament are printed on paper in the form of a book. Printing dates from the fifteenth century in Europe and electronic printing from the twentieth century. Before that, and even into the nineteenth century, official and important documents were written manually by professional scriveners who could write in a neat, legible script, either copying or working from dictation. Paper, made from compactly interlaced fibres of rags, straw, or wood into thin sheets, was increasingly used as Western printing developed and expanded. The manuscripts of our New Testament books, however, were not written on paper but on carefully prepared animal hides or on papyrus manufactured from the papyrus plant which grew abundantly in Egypt and less plentifully in other parts of the Middle East. Since it took much human effort to prepare papyrus and parchment, these materials were far more expensive than paper is today.

A statuette of an Egyptian scribe of the 5th dynasty (2498–2345 BCE). The scribe adopts the traditional posture of a scribe with the papyrus spread out on his knees.

Moreover, the form of modern books which we take for granted, with their thin pages, printed on both sides, sewn or glued together, and bound between protective covers in easily portable sizes and weights, is also a modern convenience, developed with the spread of literacy. Papyrus and parchment were thicker, so literary artefacts were bulkier and heavier. The forms of ancient texts, the time and expense needed to produce them, and the relatively small number of people who could read or write (most people would come to know texts from hearing them read) meant that collections of manuscripts were made under the patronage of rich rulers in cities like Athens, Alexandria, and Pergamum, or in cultic centres where priests could read and write, as in the temple at Jerusalem. Other religious communities could acquire and preserve texts with the help of patrons, but only very rich individuals would own texts and keep them at home.

Two forms of texts were used in the early Christian era: the scroll, written in columns along its longer extent on one side only and rolled up when not in use (see Rev. 5: 1), and the codex, a larger and heavier version of our book. We should notice the different effects of these two forms. Manageable individual scrolls could not have included the whole New Testament; each would have contained no more than a single narrative or a collection of short epistles. These individual scrolls were probably kept together but it is unclear whether users could distinguish those which now comprise our New Testament from those which now comprise the Christian Old Testament and from other writings valued by Christians. Codices, on the other hand, could contain a number of narratives or epistles. For example, the two codices of the third-century Chester Beatty papyri contain the four gospels and Acts in one volume and Pauline epistles addressed to communities in the other, and the fourth-century CE Codex Sinaiticus contains an Old Testament and all the books now comprising our New Testament, as well as two other early Christian works, the Epistle of Barnabas and the Shepherd of Hermas. The form of the codex determines what is included and what is excluded, as well as the order in which individual books are presented. Whether for this purpose the codex was deliberately promoted by Christian leaders until it became the universal form of Christian scriptures is yet another debated question. Some scholars have suggested, for example, that a collection of Paul's letters to seven communities could be preserved most effectively in a codex. Jewish communities continued to favour the scroll form for their scriptures.

Our form of the New Testament, bound in a book, therefore, indicates the contents of the New Testament and the order in which its individual components appear. We have become accustomed to these features, but they are puzzling in a number of ways. There are four separate gospels, each presenting a theological appreciation of aspects of Jesus' life, public ministry, crucifixion, and

Codex Sinaiticus, discovered by Constantin Tischendorf in the monastery of St Catherine on Mt Sinai in 1844, indicates what an ancient codex of the Bible in Greek looked like.

resurrection, but they differ in detail and are sometimes contradictory. For example, the gospels according to Matthew, Mark, and Luke describe Jesus' last meal with his disciples as a Passover meal, eaten during the evening after the Passover lambs had been sacrificed in the Jerusalem temple, and go on to relate Jesus' crucifixion on the following day; but the Gospel according to John presents Jesus' crucifixion as coinciding with the sacrifice of the Passover lambs. Again, the Gospel according to Matthew locates the resurrected Jesus' appearances to his disciples in Galilee, the Gospel according to Luke in Jerusalem, and the Gospel according to John in Jerusalem (ch. 20) and in Galilee (ch. 21). Why were four gospels included instead of one, or why were they not combined into a single version, as was attempted in the second-century CE Diatessaron of Tatian? By the second half of the second century, Christian apologists like Irenaeus, bishop of Lyons, found it necessary to justify the collection of four gospels, no more and no less, by appealing to cultural constructs like the four corners of the world to suggest their universal significance (*Against Heresies*, III. ii. 8). The Acts of the Apostles, probably the second volume to the Gospel according to Luke, may owe its inclusion to recognition of common authorship. Much of that work relates the missionary activities of Saul or Paul, and if we read the New Testament in the order in which it is now presented, the portrait of Paul in Acts may influence our readings of the epistles attributed to him which immediately follow, in spite of tensions which scholars discern between Acts and the Pauline letters in terms of their theologies, christologies, church organization, and Paul's companions and itinerary.

The collection of epistles attributed to Paul now forms the second longest series of texts after the four gospels. Again their preservation may seem surprising, since they address particular topical concerns which, at first sight, preclude them from more general interest. Why were they preserved and how were they collected? In our present New Testament there are thirteen separate epistles which explicitly name Paul as the sender, nine addressed to seven communities, and four addressed to three individuals. But there is also the Epistle to the Hebrews, which some used to attribute to Paul; the text itself does not claim Pauline authorship, although the reference to Timothy (13: 23), mentioned as a companion of Paul in other epistles, can be read to suggest Pauline authorship. If we consider this corpus as a whole (including Hebrews), however, fourteen is two multiplied by seven, and seven can be taken as the perfect, complete, and indivisible number, doubled to suggest the importance of Paul, the apostle to the Gentiles, that is, to all the non-Jewish peoples of the world (compare the seven letters in Rev. 2–3). Some contemporary scholars have argued, for example, that 2 Corinthians is a combination of two original epistles (chs. 1–9 and chs. 10–13), or have given reasons for supposing that some New Testament epistles attributed to Paul were not originally written by him. Whether or not these arguments are convincing in their own terms, the present arrangement of fourteen epistles into a corpus suggests a deliberate attempt at intimating their significance through numbers.

There then follows in our New Testament another collection of epistles, attributed to individuals, one to James, two to Peter, three to John, and one to Jude. In other words this collection consists of four writers' seven epistles, the significance of which has already been suggested. The New Testament now ends with John's visionary narrative of God's final judgement and the new Jerusalem's descent from heaven, a text which is structured through the number seven. It is appropriately placed because it looks forward to the end of human wickedness and suffering, and a new beginning.

This New Testament also seems to mirror the Old Testament in many respects, especially if the book of the twelve Minor Prophets, from Hosea to Malachi, is placed before those of Isaiah, Jeremiah, Lamentations, Ezekiel, and Daniel, as it was in some versions of the Christian Old Testament, so that it ends with the eschatological visions of Ezekiel and Daniel. Then the New Testament Apocalypse of John, which develops imagery from Ezekiel and Daniel, would mirror the ending of the Old Testament, and the other eschatological language and visions of the gospels and epistles would make better sense as a continuation of an Old Testament arranged in that way. The four gospels could also be understood as reflecting the Torah in their presentations of Jesus as a second Moses and as a faithful Israelite; and the Torah looks forward to Israel's entry into the promised land as the gospels look forward to believers' entry into the eschatological kingdom. The Acts of the Apostles, which relates a theological history of the early churches, including depictions of their leading prophetic figures' preaching and miracles, could be seen as mirroring the Old Testament theological histories' depictions of prophetic preaching and miracles, especially in 1 Samuel to 2 Kings. The New Testament epistles attributed to named individuals also seem to correspond to the prophetic books attributed to named prophets, and some of the New Testament authors refer to themselves as 'slaves of God' in the manner of Old Testament prophets (e.g. Rom. 1: 1; Phil. 1: 1; Jas. 1: 1; 2 Peter 1: 1; Jude 1: 1, cf. 1 Kgs. Septuagint 21: 28; Ps. 105.26; Zech. 1.6). There are no entire New Testament books in the form of the poetic Old Testament books of Job, Psalms, Proverbs, Ecclesiastes, and the Song of Solomon, although there are short expressions of poetry and proverbs within New Testament books. Once we begin to notice these features, we realize that the present form of our New Testament is neither arbitrary nor entirely accidental.

Moreover, the whole Bible has been read as a grand all-encompassing narrative, a divine comedy, according to which human beings are created by the generous God to live in a beneficent world, but human 'hardness of heart', expressed in neglect of this creator, violence towards others, and greed, led to their alienation from God, each other, and the rest of creation, until God's messiah and God's holy spirit inspired and transformed human hearts to live in hope of a renewed physical, political, and social world, from which all forms of evil would be excluded. It is this kind of reading which assumes a division between the Jewish scriptures and the following writings through the use of the terms the 'Old Testament' and the 'New Testament'.

Head of Constantine I (307–37 CE) whose conversion to Christianity in 313 was a turning point in the history both of the Roman empire and the Christian church.

CHRISTIAN CHURCHES AND THEIR SCRIPTURES IN THE FOURTH CENTURY CE

Within the texts of our New Testament there are references to 'the writings or scriptures' or to 'the law and the prophets' and quotations from them which treat them as authoritative and interpret them, but these are references to the Jewish scriptures. In other words, New Testament writers knew at least some of the Jewish scriptures and ways of interpreting them, and assumed that readers would share their recognition of scriptural authority, whether they were Jews or not. Jude 14–15's quotation from Enoch, which finally formed no part of the Christian Bible, suggests that the contents of the Jewish scriptures were not yet fixed. Neither Jewish nor New Testament writings, however, call these Jewish scriptures 'the Old Testament'. Only after the books which now comprise our New Testament were gathered together and formally recognized were the Jewish scriptures described with this title by Christians, and placed before the New Testament writings. Let us begin, then, by considering the writings of fourth-century Christian bishops and other church leaders which use these and other terms.

After a century which included the most extensive persecutions of Christians by Roman officials within the empire, the new Roman warrior ruler of the western empire, Constantine, in 313 CE, issued an edict from Milan which accepted that Christians posed no threat to Roman hegemony, and Constantine became the patron of Christianity. In 324 he defeated his rival in the east and became emperor of the whole empire, moving his capital to Byzantium on the Bosphorus, rebuilding and renaming the city Constantinople. It is easier for us to discern his political than his religious motives for promoting Christianity, and he may even have recognized a tension between his activities as emperor and Christian practice by putting off his own baptism till just before his death. Widespread adherence to Christianity, in the countryside as well as the cities, administered hierarchically by well-educated male bishops, open to universal admissions and favourably inclined towards Roman power, meant that the Christian churches could become a unifying institution which bolstered Constantine's authority. Whether the emperor ruled the church, or the bishops, as representatives of the churches, were supreme in religious and social matters were disputed issues during the following centuries. New Testament writings' emphasis on renewal at God's eschatological judgement, which does not exclude renewal in present anticipation of this future, nevertheless allowed some church leaders to accept Roman rule as a necessary interim organization of political life.

By the fourth century most Christian communities existed within the Roman world, and earlier Roman victorious wars against Jewish freedom fighters in Judaea and Galilee, during 66–74 CE, including Roman destruction of the Jerusalem temple, and 132–35 CE, led to the development of Christian centres away from Jerusalem, in Alexandria, Caesarea, Antioch, Rome, Carthage, and, with Constantine's patronage, Constantinople. Constantine himself promoted the building of Christian basilicas, the name itself indicating his royal patronage, at sites in Palestine traditionally associated with Jesus' birth, ministry, crucifixion, and resurrection, and these too developed as places of Christian pilgrimage, organization, and learning. Hence, the vast majority of Christians were united in their experience as communities of believers under Roman rule, their leaders in correspondence and meeting with one another.

As patron of Christianity, Constantine promoted the resolution of religious issues through ecumenical, that is empire-wide, and local councils of bishops to ensure unity. The ecumenical council at Nicaea in 325, for example, sought to settle disputes between so-called Arian and orthodox church leaders. Since these leaders appealed to Christian writings as well as to the Jewish scriptures in support of their views, bishops considered which Christian writings should be accorded most authority. Moreover, as patron, Constantine ordered fifty copies of the Christian scriptures to be prepared for churches in Constantinople, according to Eusebius' *Life of Constantine* (IV. 36–7). In other words, royal patrons helped to promote and preserve Christian scriptures. But which Christian writings should be accorded greatest authority? We have already noticed that codices like Sinaiticus from the fourth century contain writings which no longer form part of our New Testament. How many other Christian writings might have been valued by some Christians we cannot be sure, because those which were rejected by church councils were less likely to be reproduced than those which were promoted. Nevertheless, some seem to have been sufficiently popular for copies of them to be circulated in following centuries, some of which have survived. For example, the pseudonymous epistle of Paul to the Laodiceans (see Col. 4: 16), which seems to include quotations from Philippians and Galatians, remained popular for many centuries, as did the pseudonymous correspondence between Paul and Seneca, the leading Roman Stoic philosopher contemporary with Paul; the Acts of Paul and Thecla, a remarkable woman preacher and ascetic; and 3 Corinthians (see 1 Cor. 5: 9). Equally popular were the Protevangelium of James, which is an account of Mary's miraculous birth, her upbringing, and her unconsummated marriage to the widower Joseph, and the Infancy Story of Thomas, which depicts Jesus as an infant prodigy, both these texts serving to enhance reputations through stories of miracles. In the middle of the twentieth century, a whole Christian library of ancient texts was discovered at Nag Hammadi in Egypt. The Coptic manuscripts date from about 400 CE, but seem to be Coptic translations of earlier Greek texts which may go back to the third century CE. Many of these texts express a Gnostic form of Christianity, previously known from refutations by Christian opponents. The Gospel of Thomas is closest to our New Testament gospels' sayings of Jesus. Other texts include the Gospel of Philip and the Gospel of Truth. These and other ancient Christian writings which form no part of our New Testament can be read in English translations in Hennecke's *The New Testament Apocrypha.*

Some texts of Christian council decisions in the fourth century about which Christian writings were to be treated in what ways have survived. These decisions, however, contain lists of titles and do not provide us with the actual contents of each book. For the contents themselves, we have to rely on the manuscripts that have survived. The council of Laodicea in Phrygia (363 CE), for example, forbade the reading of private psalms and 'uncanonical books' in church, and encouraged the public reading of only 'canonical books' of the New Testament and Old Testament (canon 59). This is one of the first uses of the word 'canon' in the sense of books accepted for public readings, books considered as sufficiently authoritative to be included in the New Testament, along with the Jewish scriptures. In later manuscripts of this council's decisions, a list of the books comprising the New Testament is appended, which corresponds to those included in our New Testament except that Revelation is not mentioned, in this agreeing with the lectures of Cyril (*c.*315–386 CE), bishop of Alexandria, to catechumens (*Catecheses*, iv. 33–6), and with the decision of the later synod of Trullan (692 CE). The earliest listing of all 27 books of our New Testament occurs in Athanasius' *Festal Epistle* 39 (*c.*367 CE). This list of what is called 'canonical scriptures' was approved by the synod of Carthage (397 CE), the surviving written account of which refers back to its earlier acceptance at a synod in Hippo Regius (393 CE).

The Latin Muratorian Canon, which forms part of a damaged collection of Christian writings, is difficult to date, and I include it here for convenience, but it is just possible that it is a translation of a Greek synopsis about Christian texts, going back as far as the second century CE. There are no references to the Gospel according to Matthew or Mark, but they seem to be presupposed by its reference to that of Luke as the third gospel and that of John as the fourth. Next is mentioned the Acts of the Apostles, thirteen epistles of Paul, one epistle of Jude and two of John, the Wisdom of Solomon, and the Apocalypses of John and Peter, although it is noted that 'some' are not willing to read the Apocalypse of Peter in church. The Shepherd of Hermas is said to be valuable private reading but not to be read at public services. Other Christian writings by named individuals like Valentinus and Basilides, known from other writings as Christian Gnostic teachers in the second half of the second century, are described as unacceptable for either private or public reading. Scholars disagree, not only about the possible dating of any original of this list, but also about its significance. Why, for example, is 1 Peter not mentioned, and why is the Wisdom of Solomon included? The style suggests that this Latin manuscript was written by a careless scribe, so its list can hardly be taken as evidence for anything more than the honour accorded to the books named in a manner known from other early Christian writings.

A sense of some of the difficulties facing fourth-century church leaders in their attempts to control what Christians would read or hear read can be gained from Eusebius' *Church History*, III. 25.1–7. This refers to the New Testament as consisting of 'the holy quaternion of the Gospels', the Acts of the Apostles, the epistles of Paul (the number not given, but in III. 3.4 and III. 38.2 the Epistle to the Hebrews is said to be 'disputed'), 'the extant former Epistle of John', and 'the Epistle of Peter'. The Apocalypse of John is recognized as a possible but uncertain candidate for inclusion. A second group of books is called 'disputed' but 'familiar to the majority': 'the Epistle of James as it is called', the Epistle of Jude, the second Epistle of Peter, and 'those that are called second and third John, whether they belong to the evangelist or to another of the same name'. A third group, called 'spurious', apparently in the sense that they are not generally accepted for public reading in churches, is said to comprise the Acts of Paul, the Shepherd of Hermas, the Apocalypse of Peter, the Epistle of Barnabas, and the teachings of the apostles. Again the Apocalypse of John is mentioned. Also in this group 'some' are said to have 'counted the Gospel of the Hebrews, with which those of the Hebrews who have accepted Christ take special pleasure'. This work is apparently mentioned and quoted in other Christian literature, for example, by Clement in Alexandria at the end of the second century, and by Origen (185–253 CE), but no copy has survived. A final group of writings is described as 'those which the heretics put forward under the name of apostles', mentioning the gospels of Peter, Thomas, and Matthias, and 'the Acts of Andrew and John and the other apostles'.

Is it possible for us to discern the *criteria* used in this discussion to decide whether a particular Christian writing should be included in or excluded from the New Testament? Since three centuries of Christian writing preceded the fourth century, one criterion for acceptance is general and long use of a work in public assemblies among Christian communities throughout large parts of the Roman empire. In the case of the Epistle to the Hebrews, for example, although its authorship by Paul was disputed, its time-honoured public reading in churches of the eastern empire ensured it a place in the New Testament, just as the long practised public reading of the Apocalypse of John in churches of the western empire eventually led to its inclusion. A second criterion seems to have been the widely and long accepted belief that a book was written by one of the twelve apostles of Jesus or by the apostle Paul. Nevertheless, whether such attribution was accepted or not depended on other criteria, since many books existed that were attributed to apostles.

Moreover, in the case of the four gospels that were accepted into the New Testament, during the first half of the second century references in Christian literature which appear to come from one or other of these gospels were not distinguished by the names of Matthew, Mark, Luke, or John. Only in the second half of the second century does this happen. Should we suppose that each of them originally served as the only gospel for a particular area? If this were so, since the gospels according to Matthew, Mark, and Luke exhibit literary interdependence, one or more of them must have been known more widely; but whether the newer version was intended to replace or to supplement the older version is not known. We should notice especially that the Gospel according to Mark survived as a separate book, in spite of 90 per cent of Mark appearing in Matthew and 50 per cent in Luke. Also, whether the Gospel according to John is to be understood as dependent on one or more of the others is disputed among contemporary scholars. Moreover, many critical scholars now doubt that the gospels according to Matthew and John could have been written by those apostles. Most remarkable, however, is that the gospels according to Mark and Luke are not attributed to apostles. Does this mean that they became known by those authors' names and were widely read in Christian churches before apostolic attribution became important as a criterion of acceptability and authority? When such attribution did become important, the Gospel according to Mark was said to take up the preaching of Peter. For example, that Mark was the interpreter of Peter is attributed by Eusebius' *Church History*, III. 39.15 to Papias, bishop of Hieropolis in Phrygia, who may have lived between 70 and 140 CE, and whose *Expositions of the Sayings of the Lord* is mentioned by Eusebius, but no copies have survived. In the case of the Gospel according to Luke, *Against Marcion*, iv. 2 by Tertullian (*c.*160–220 CE) identifies this Luke as the companion of the apostle Paul (see Col. 4: 14; 2 Tim. 4: 11; Philemon 24; and Lucius of Cyrene is mentioned in Acts 13: 1, cf. Rom. 16: 21).

Another criterion for deciding which Christian books should be included in the New Testament is implied by Eusebius' discussion. Of those books which should be repudiated, we read: 'The thought and purpose of their contents are completely out of harmony with true orthodoxy and clearly show themselves that they are forgeries of heretics' (*Church History*, III. 25.7). In other words, those who were deciding what constitutes the New Testament were also discussing what expressions of Christian belief were acceptable or not. In matters of doctrinal disagreement, appeal was made to Christian texts that were considered ancient, so questions about which text was ancient and authoritative, how it was to be interpreted, and which expressions of belief were 'in harmony' with particular apostolic writings were intimately bound together, and, inevitably, were entangled with power politics among Christian bishops and their royal patrons.

Eusebius' *Church History*, III. 25.7 also suggests another criterion for discovering which texts are 'forgeries': 'The character of the style also is far removed from apostolic usage.' This criterion is widely used by critical scholars today in distinguishing, for example, which of the New Testament epistles attributed to Paul are authentic and which are pseudonymous, and it was the early recognition that the style of the Epistle to the Hebrews is different from that of other Pauline epistles that made its inclusion in the New Testament a matter for debate. The epistles 1 and 2 Timothy and Titus, attributed to Paul, are now considered pseudonymous by many scholars, as they were in some early Christian writings. For example, in the second half of the second century, Tatian rejected 1 and 2 Timothy as pseudonymous and accepted only Titus as Pauline. But all three were considered 'orthodox' and Pauline by those bishops whose decisions about the contents of the New Testament prevailed. The teachings of 1 Timothy and Titus, with their references to an exclusively male church leadership of elders, bishops, and, probably, deacons, their acceptance of Roman rule and Roman social organization, their attempts to exclude false teachers, and their insistence on women's subordination to men would have been congenial to male bishops from the second century onwards.

Another criterion which modern readers might have expected to be used in decisions about which texts should comprise the New Testament, however, was not used: the criterion of 'inspiration'. The reason for this is that both verbal and written expressions of belief by many Christians were understood to be 'inspired' (see Eusebius, *Orations of Constantine*, 2; Augustine, *Epistle*, 82.2; Gregory of Nyssa *Hexaemeron*, proem.). Moreover, the criteria discussed above are *discerned* from Eusebius' discussion and other fourth-century writings which have come down to us. Nowhere are such criteria formally listed and the relative importance of one against another weighed.

These fourth-century discussions and decisions about the contents of the New Testament were made by literate élite male leaders of the churches under the auspices of the emperor Constantine and his successors. Actual manuscripts of the New Testament were also commissioned and preserved by these leaders, who themselves read, and in some cases also wrote, other Christian books that they considered useful for the developing life of the churches: epistles, homilies, refutations, apologies, histories, commentaries, and theologies. These men's interests, especially in excluding 'unorthodox' theologians, affected the ways in which they read the ancient Christian texts which came to form the New Testament just as our interests affect our ways of reading the New Testament. Our interest in history as we understand it, for example, means that most of us now find early Christian 'orthodox' readings as alien as we find Arian readings, especially in their practice of allegorical interpretations. Most of the non-canonical Christian texts that were preserved and have survived from the second century CE onwards can be read to express 'orthodoxy' as that was defined in the centuries that followed, but some texts which were considered 'unorthodox' have survived by accident, as in the case of some writings in the library at Nag Hammadi. We have to assume, however, that most texts that proved uncongenial to later church leaders have been lost. For example, some Greek writings by Origen (*c*.185–253 CE), who was condemned for 'heresy' during his lifetime and after his death, have come down to us only in damaged copies or in Latin translation, or not at all.

I have referred to Christian bishops and other church leaders as members of a male literate élite minority within the churches and within society at large. The majority of Christians in the fourth century would have come to know Christian texts by hearing extracts from them read in church assemblies, and what was read to them would have depended on availability and on the particular preferences of the literate leaders of their own communities. The effects on future developments in Christianity of the emperors' patronage and of decisions by bishops should therefore be recognized. The spread to local churches of codices containing and defining Christian scriptures, the development and use of lectionaries listing which parts of scripture were to be read over cycles of years, and the integration of these readings into developing liturgies, including expositions of scripture, potentially gave power to the literate over the illiterate. This is to assume, however, that all illiterate Christians were schooled as catechumens, that they often attended church assemblies, and that they understood Greek in the eastern empire and Latin in the western empire, or that they heard the New Testament read in translations into languages (Coptic or Syriac, for example) which they could understand. Even so, those who heard what was read to them could interpret what they heard in their own ways; and 'inspiration' could be claimed and recognized by people who were not bishops, and not even members of the clergy. Occasionally, we gain glimpses of this happening in the writings of their opponents. For example, the movement named after one of its leaders, Montanus, which originated in Phrygia during the second half of the second century but spread among Christians in both the east and the west of the Roman empire, claimed that not only Montanus but also two women, Prisca and Maximilla, were inspired by God's spirit prophetically to announce the imminent arrival of the heavenly Jerusalem on earth (see, for example, Epiphanius, bishop of Salamis in Cyprus, who died in 403 CE, *Heresies*, 48.2–11). The movement was opposed by synods of bishops but attracted not only large numbers of ordinary Christians but also the support of the Christian theologian Tertullian from about 212 CE onwards.

Before leaving the fourth century, we need briefly to consider two other features of the New Testament to which we are accustomed: the titles of our New Testament books and the order in which they now appear. Other features, like divisions of books into chapters and verses, and footnotes which indicate some important variant readings or cross-references, have been added since the fourth century for convenience in personal reading and study. Authors of ancient narratives often refer to their own work with different rather than a single, formal descriptive title (e.g. the first-century CE Jewish historian Josephus refers to his early work about the Jewish war against the Romans in a variety of ways: *Jewish Antiquities*, I.xi.4; XIII.iii.3; v. 9; *Life*, 74). Moreover, when texts were written on scrolls, a description of the contents would appear on a strip attached at the end that could be seen for purposes of identification when the scroll was rolled up. Within the scroll, the author and description of the contents would appear at the end. That each of our New Testament 'gospels' is called by the singular 'gospel' or good news, which suggests how they should be read, and then distinguished from the others by the expression 'according to Matthew, Mark, Luke, or John', intimates that they provide four different versions of a single good news. This shows that the titles were added only after all four were formally recognized as authoritative. The titles of the epistles and of Revelation which appear in our New Testament take up the information of their introductions. In other words, the titles familiar to us were given to New Testament books by later collectors.

There is also some variety in the order in which New Testament books appear in ancient manuscripts and lists. We have already noted the ways in which our New Testament contents are grouped: four gospels, Acts, the epistles of Paul, the general epistles, and Revelation. Some of these groups were sometimes ordered differently. For example, in Codex Sinaiticus, the Pauline epistles follow the gospels, and Acts follows the Paulines. Most other ancient Greek manuscripts which have survived, however, place the general epistles immediately after Acts and before the Paulines. There is also some variety of order within the groups. Our order of the gospels: Matthew, Mark, Luke, John, was popularized by Eusebius and by Jerome (*c.*346–420 CE), whose Latin translation became the official version of western churches. But the fifth-century Codex Bezae gives the order: Matthew, John, Luke, Mark, placing the two narratives attributed to apostles first. Other sequences, however, are occasionally found in manuscripts that have survived.

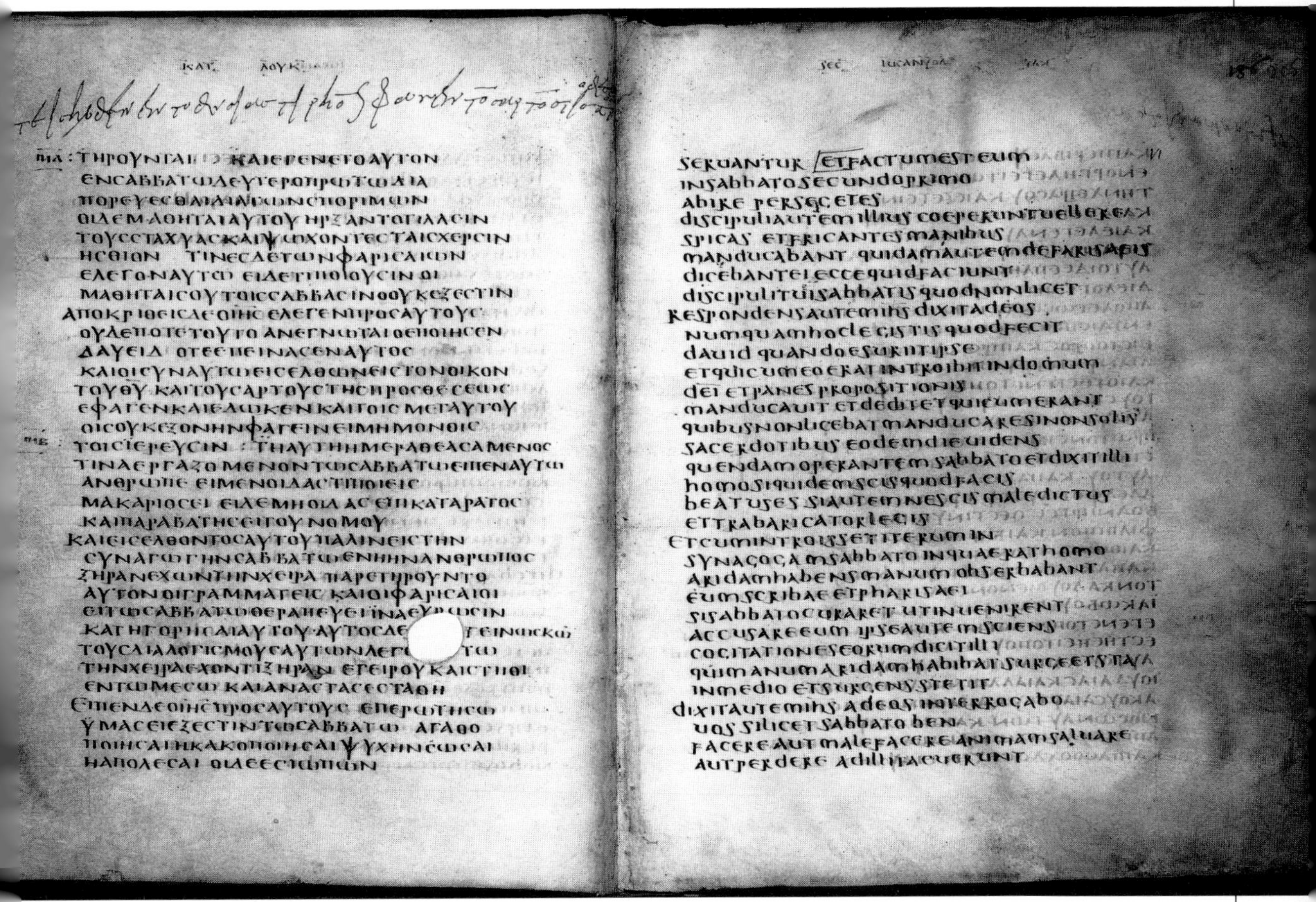

The bilingual Greek and Latin 5th-century Codex Bezae, presented to Cambridge University in 1581 by the reformer Theodore Beza. It shows Luke 6: 1ff. and contains the additional passage about the man working on the sabbath.

Our present arrangement of the Paulines places those to communities first and those to individuals second, and within those sections, the epistles are arranged in order of decreasing length, except that Galatians precedes the slightly longer Ephesians, and Hebrews is placed last. This position of Hebrews is found in most surviving Greek manuscripts, suggesting that it was recognized as non-Pauline, but in a Chester Beatty papyrus it follows Romans, and in the fourth-century Codex Vaticanus and Codex Sinaiticus it follows 2 Thessalonians, these two arrangements grouping it with Pauline letters to communities. In a minority of later manuscripts other arrangements are found. The sequence of the general epistles in our New Testament is: James, 1 and 2 Peter, 1, 2, and 3 John, Jude; and this is the order most common in the oldest surviving Greek codices, Vaticanus, Sinaiticus, and the fifth-century Alexandrinus. Again it seems to be based on decreasing length, except that epistles attributed to the same author appear together. But the list of the council of Carthage (397 CE) gives the order: 1 and 2 Peter, 1, 2 and 3 John, James, Jude, an order of decreasing length in which length is calculated by combining all the epistles attributed to a single author.

CAN THE TEXTS OF THE NEW TESTAMENT BE ACCURATELY DATED?

We have noticed that time-honoured acceptance of a text by most churches was one of the implied criteria for its inclusion in the New Testament. How far back can we now trace the existence and use of its individual books? In the fourth-century codices Vaticanus and Sinaiticus, we have actual Greek copies of all the books which now appear in our New Testament, as well as some which do not now form part of it, and from the third century CE we have actual Greek copies of the four gospels and Acts, and the Pauline epistles to communities in the Chester Beatty papyri. Fragments of New Testament texts in other papyri from Egypt have also survived. Dating these fragments is difficult but the following seem to date from the third century: P53 (Matthew and Acts), P92 (Ephesians and 2 Thessalonians), P20 (1 and 2 Thessalonians), P72 (1 and 2 Peter and Jude), P9 (1 John), P12 and P13 (Hebrews), and P18 (Revelation). Some other fragments seem to go back to the second century: P52, which may even go back to the first half of the second century, contains fragments of the Gospel according to John, as do the slightly later P66 and P90; P4, P64, and P67 seem to have formed parts of a single codex containing the gospels according to Matthew and Luke; P77 is part of another text of Matthew; and P32 is part of a text of the Paulines. That these papyri fragments have survived is due to the dry climate of Egypt, but they indicate that three of our four gospels and some of our Pauline epistles existed there during the second century, and this suggests that texts originally written and received among churches in one part of the Roman empire were circulated and accepted by churches in other parts of the empire by the second century CE. One of the most intriguing papyrus fragments to have survived from the first half of the second century, the Egerton papyrus, contains narratives reminiscent of some in our four gospels, perhaps written from memory either of those texts or of their sources.

References to texts now comprising our New Testament and some quotations from them also occur in the writings of Christian apologists and theologians from the second half of the second century. I have already mentioned Irenaeus' defence of our four gospels, and the Muratorian canon, an original version of which may go back to this period. Scholarly studies of the development of the Christian canon emphasize that, during this period, the activities of Marcion, a Christian teacher at Rome *c.*144 CE, were opposed by 'orthodox' bishops like Irenaeus, and that, since Marcion's activities included his promotion of his own versions of the Gospel according to Luke and the Pauline epistles, and his rejection of the Jewish scriptures, 'orthodox' bishops defended not only the Jewish scriptures and their versions of Luke and the Paulines, but also other Christian writings. Moreover, these 'orthodox' bishops also sought to refute the teachings of Gnostics like Valentinus and Basilides, whose followers preserved their or their disciples' writings.

When we move back to the beginning of the second century and the end of the first century, we have to rely on apparent quotations, allusions, or references to our New Testament books in other Christian literature as evidence of their existence, since, apart from P52's fragmentary text of John, no actual manuscripts have survived. Except for the Shepherd of Hermas, the Didache, and Eusebius' much later claims to be quoting Papias' *Expositions*, all these Christian writings are epistles. In such literature, it is often impossible to decide whether reference to a saying of Jesus is an inexact quotation from one of our gospels or not. For example, Clement of Rome's epistle to the Corinthians 13: 2 (*c.*96 CE) cites 'words of the Lord' which could echo Matthew 5: 7; 6: 14–15; 7: 1–2,12; Luke 6:31, 36–8; and 46: 7–8 could echo Mark 9: 42; Matthew 18: 6–7; Luke 17: 1–2. In 24.5, a homily on 1 Corinthians 15: 36ff. seems to take up the imagery of the parable of the sower (Matt. 13: 3; parallels in Mark 4: 3, Luke 8: 5). With regard to 1 Corinthians, however, in ch. 47 Clement encourages his recipients to read the epistle which 'the blessed apostle Paul' had sent them, assuming that they still had a copy and that Clement in Rome knew that epistle too. The epistles of Ignatius, bishop of Antioch in Syria, written on his journey to Rome where he was martyred in 110 CE, seem to echo phrases from the Pauline epistles, especially 1 Corinthians 15: 8–10. There could also be allusions to the gospels according to Matthew and John, but none of these is a formal or exact quotation of our versions. In the Didache, the date of which is itself uncertain but it may come from this period, there are two quotations from Matthew, in 8.2 (Matt. 6: 5ff.) and 9.5 (Matt. 6: 6), together with other echoes of that book. Unfortunately, we have to rely on Eusebius' fourth-century versions of Papias' work, and I have already mentioned the connection made between Mark and the apostle Peter attributed to him. Eusebius also attributes the following statement about Matthew to Papias: 'Matthew composed the sayings in the Hebrew dialect, and each one interpreted them as best he could' (*Church History*, III. 39.16). This cannot be a description of our Matthaean Gospel which is written in Greek and is not a translation of a Hebrew or Aramaic original. Eusebius also mentions that Papias knew Revelation, 1 John, and 1 Peter (*Church History*, III. 39.6, 17). Given the paucity of evidence from this period, scholars have attempted to date each of the New Testament books on the basis of features in the texts themselves.

Let us begin with the Pauline epistles, arguably the earliest writings of our New Testament. We have noticed that Clement knew 1 Corinthians in Rome. Moreover, one of the Pauline epistles is not addressed to a single city but to 'the churches of Galatia' (Gal. 1: 2), and there may have been more than one assembly of Christians in a single city addressed in other epistles. Also Colossians 4: 16, an epistle which many scholars consider pseudonymous, requires recipients to ensure that it is read also by the church of the Laodiceans, and requires the Colossian church to read the Laodicean letter. Even if Colossians is pseudonymous, it is unlikely that it would invent an unheard-of practice. Was a single copy of an epistle received and then circulated? Would each church assembly make a copy before passing it on to another? We find each of the Pauline epistles difficult to understand when we have the text in front of us to read and re-read, whereas original recipients would have heard it read (cf. 2 Peter 3: 16). It is therefore likely that copies would have been retained by individual churches. But what would have encouraged wider circulation? In spite of their attention to specific concerns of churches in particular places, these epistles also explore issues of more general interest. I shall mention the most obvious. They seek to justify the admission of non-Jews into the church without their practising commands in the Jewish scriptures concerning circumcision and food regulations, and this practice prevailed in the centuries that followed; yet they also quote and interpret the Jewish scriptures as authoritative. They express eschatological expectations, including references to Jesus' resurrection and the hope of believers' future resurrection, even discussing the nature of eschatological existence. They provide a variety of interpretations of the significance of Jesus' crucifixion. They encourage believers to live from God's inspiration, and to welcome endowments which are understood as special charismatic gifts to individuals for the community's benefit; they explore believers' political relations with Roman power, and social relations within communities and with outsiders; they encourage recipients to follow Paul's example in suffering persecution without retaliation; and they repeatedly argue and state that Paul's work is the expression of God's call and that God sent him as a missionary apostle. All these matters remained important for subsequent generations of Christians. It would be surprising, therefore, had Pauline epistles not been circulated and collected. Nevertheless, Acts does not mention Paul's practice of writing letters and shows no knowledge of those that have survived.

The Pauline epistles suggest by their references to other followers of Jesus like Simon Peter, to problems like those concerned with Gentile admission into churches, and to events, that they originate from the 50s and 60s of the first century. Of course forgeries written later can adopt such features in order to mask their later origin, but the existence of forgeries themselves suggests both that Paul himself did write letters and that these were circulated. Most scholars agree that the following epistles are authentically Pauline: Romans, 1 and 2 Corinthians, Galatians, Philippians, 1 Thessalonians, and Philemon. It is interesting that these amount to seven epistles. Apparently, not all of Paul's epistles have survived (e.g. 1 Cor. 5: 9), and, unfortunately, correspondence from communities to Paul (e.g. 1 Cor. 7: 1) and reactions to his preaching and writings can only be inferred from his own epistles. Once his epistles were more generally known, however, it was possible for others who wanted their own views to be taken seriously to write in his name. Scholars now agree, for example, that the epistle to the Laodiceans, 3 Corinthians, and the correspondence between Paul and Seneca are pseudonymous, but they disagree about the possible authenticity of the other epistles attributed to Paul in the New Testament. Colossians and Ephesians, which are related, are considered inauthentic by some, while others accept Colossians as authentic but regard Ephesians as pseudonymous, and still others accept the authenticity of both. Similarly, 2 Thessalonians is accepted as genuine by some but not by others. The majority of scholars now regard 1 and 2 Timothy and Titus as pseudonymous, and all scholars today regard Hebrews as non-Pauline. Accepting all of these brings the number of Paulines to fourteen.

Dating the New Testament gospels is more difficult since very general considerations are involved. When would it have been either necessary or expedient for accounts of Jesus' life, teachings, miracles, crucifixion, and resurrection to be written instead of, or as well as, preached orally, and why are they so short? If we possessed only the Pauline epistles, we would gather that Jesus was to be accepted as the Jewish messiah, who was crucified and resurrected, and who was expected to return at the eschaton, but we would learn very little of his teachings and nothing at all of his miracles. Even the preaching attributed to first-generation missionaries in Acts adds little but general references to his miracles. Scholars suggest, however, that the deaths of Jesus' original followers and the continuation of the churches into a second generation would have encouraged or necessitated the writing of accounts in order to preserve what was known of him. As mentioned earlier, the gospels according to Matthew, Mark, and Luke exhibit literary interrelations in Greek, but whether those literary relations suggest that Mark was used as a source by Matthew and Luke, or that Mark used both Matthew and Luke as sources; whether Matthew and Luke used another source (Q), now lost, or Luke used both Matthew and Mark; and whether only more complicated interrelations adequately account for the versions we have, are matters of continuing debate. The verbatim agreements among these three gospels, however, suggest that they seek to conserve what was available, and both their shortness and their use of the Greek language (rather than Aramaic) mark them as second-generation compositions.

The only other possible argument for a more definite dating concerns the question whether these narratives presuppose knowledge of the Jewish war against Rome which led to the destruction of the Jerusalem temple in 70 CE. Jesus is presented prophesying the temple's destruction (Matt. 24: 2; parallel Mark 13: 2, and see Matt. 23.38; parallel Luke 21: 5) but the saying contains nothing about its destruction by fire as Josephus' eyewitness account does. The parable in Matthew 22: 7, however, refers to the destruction and burning of 'their city', presumably Jerusalem. Moreover the apocalyptic discourse of Mark 13 and Matthew 24 predicts not only wars, but takes up the language of Daniel to refer to a desolating sacrilege, which the reader is to understand. This, however, could refer either to the temple's destruction or to the earlier threat posed by the emperor Caligula's sending his statue to be erected in the Jerusalem temple, instructions which were not carried out. The Lucan parallel section in chapter 21 does not include a reference to a desolating sacrifice but, in 21: 20–4, provides a more graphic description of a foreign army's destroying Jerusalem which suggests it was written after that event. Whether these apocalyptic discourses are all to be understood as separating the destruction of Jerusalem from the eschaton is disputed. Those who argue that each of these gospels shows knowledge of the Jerusalem temple's destruction date all of them after 70 CE. Which of them is considered earlier and which later depends on whichever hypothesis about their literary relations is accepted. The conservative nature of these narratives may itself suggest that they could be preserving other Greek sources which are now lost, and the relative though not complete accuracy of their references to geographical and social features of Palestinian life during the most likely time of Jesus' public ministry, in the 20s and 30s of the first century, suggest that they draw on earlier written or oral sources. But we also notice that each differs from the others in details, and each creates its own distinct impression of Jesus for their churches, serving purposes that we can only tentatively infer from the narratives themselves and their interrelations.

Most scholars, but not all, regard the Gospel according to John as the latest of those included in the New Testament, and therefore date it at the end of the first century. Features of that gospel which make the hypothesis plausible are as follows. The speeches attributed to Jesus read like Christian meditations on his significance after his life, death, and resurrection, rather than the preaching of a prophet of the eschaton in parables, similes, and wisdom sayings like those in the other gospels. There are fewer distinctions among Jewish groups than in the other gospels, and often Jewish groups are called simply 'the Jews'. The long farewell discourses attributed to Jesus at his last meal with his disciples in John 13–17 are distinctive and seem to be concerned with reassuring his followers that God's spirit, uniquely called the Paraclete or helper, would inspire them to remain faithful in the face of persecution during an unspecified period before the eschaton. Whether the gospel also expresses what is called a 'high Christology' which sets it later than the others depends, of course, on how the text itself is interpreted and what possible history of Christological perceptions is reconstructed. Those scholars who argue that the fourth gospel shows literary dependence on the other three consider it to be last for that reason.

The Acts of the Apostles is almost universally regarded as the second volume of the Gospel according to Luke, as the dedication which introduces each suggests. That this narrative relates a history of the early church which looks forward to its continuing into another generation (see the speech attributed to Paul in Acts 20) has led to its being dated at the end of the first century, in spite of its failure specifically to depict the death of Paul, though it can be read as hinting that he would die at Rome (Acts 20: 36–7; 21: 10–14). What source material was available to the author is unknown. Some scholars still attribute the work to a companion of Paul, interpeting the use of the first person plural 'we' and 'us' in some sections as a reflection of the author's experience, but others doubt that a companion of Paul could have remained completely ignorant both of his practice in writing to churches and of the contents of his letters.

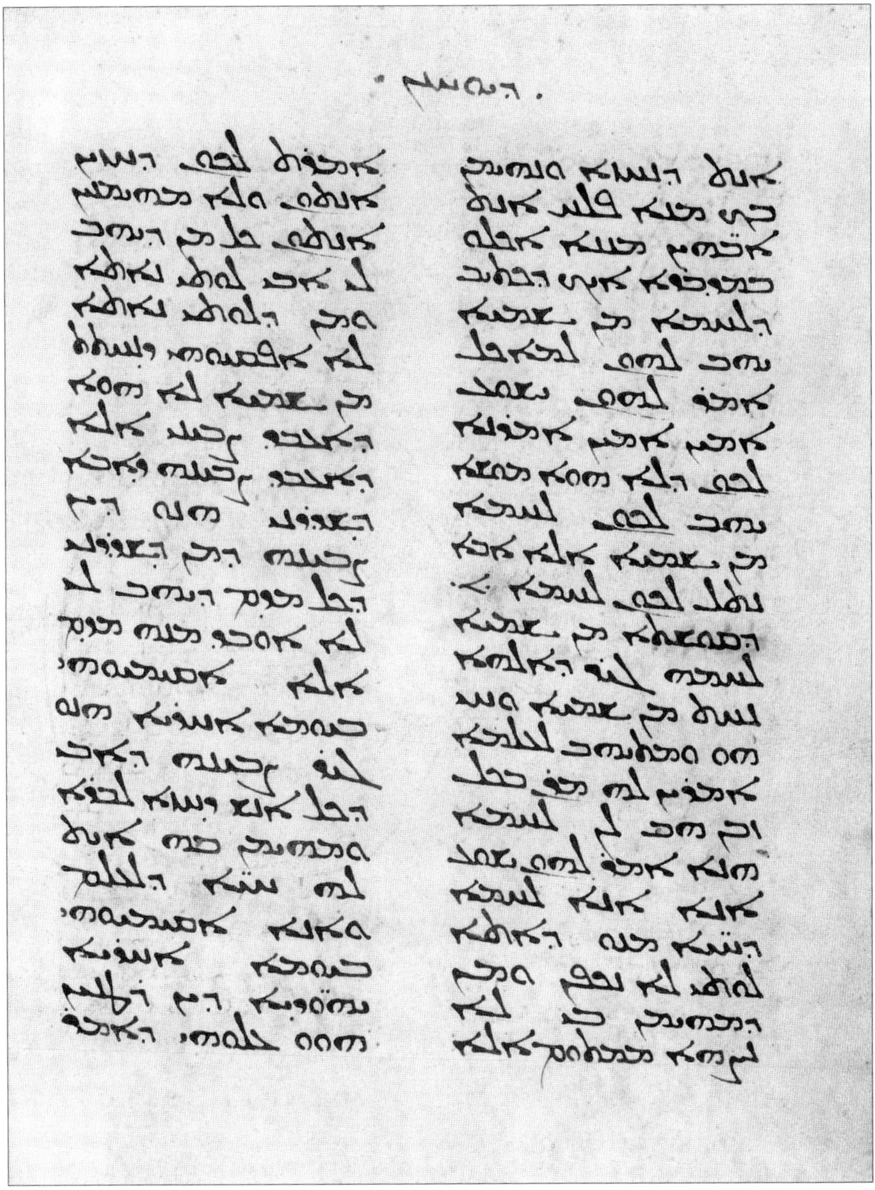

John 6: 30–41 in the 5th-century Curetonian Syriac manuscript. This was acquired in 1842 from the monastery of St Mary Deipara in the Nitrian desert (Egypt) and is named after W. Cureton of the British Museum who first identified it.

Hebrews and the general epistles are the most difficult New Testament texts to date. Do their form and general address suggest that they presuppose knowledge of a collection of Pauline epistles, already valued outside the churches to which they were originally sent? The distinctively Pauline expression 'in Christ' seems to be imitated in 1 Peter (1 Peter 3: 16; 5: 11); James seems to counter an interpretation of the Pauline distinction between faith and works, even using the Pauline appeal to Abraham for different ends (James 2: 14–24); 2 Peter 3: 15–16 specifically refers to Paul's 'difficult' writings. Moreover, although these epistles and the Johannine epistles are attributed to Aramaic-speaking Jewish Christians, they are written in competent Greek styles and use imagery and vocabulary which suggest that their authors benefited from a Hellenistic Greek education. Moreover, the style of 1 Peter is different from that of 2 Peter, and 2 Peter is closely related to Jude. Scholars dispute whether 1 John is written in a style sufficiently distinct from that of the fourth gospel to warrant attribution to a different author. We have noticed too that in later centuries the general epistles of James, 2 Peter, 2 and 3 John, and Jude were not universally accepted and that their attributions were doubted: 2 Peter and Jude seem to oppose Christian teachers in the manner that 1 and 2 Timothy and Titus do, but all these epistles refer to opponents in derogatory terms conventionally used in non-Christian Hellenistic philosophical writings' references to their opponents, so that these opponents' teaching cannot be reconstructed in detail and dated; 1 Peter refers to persecution, not only of Christian missionaries and leaders, but of whole communities (4: 12–19), but whether this persecution is to be identified with that which the Roman governor of Bithynia, Pliny, describes in his letter to the emperor Trajan (Epistle 96) in 112 CE, or to a purported earlier persecution of Christians in that area (see 1 Peter 1: 1) under the emperor Domitian in 96 CE is disputed. It is for these reasons that the general epistles are usually dated at the end of the first century or the beginning of the second century and are regarded as pseudonymous.

The Revelation of John also pictures widespread violent persecution of Christians, but mainly, though not exclusively (see 2: 13), as an expectation for the future. The seven letters it contains are addressed to believers in Asia Minor. This work claims to be written by John (1: 1,4) from the island of Patmos (1: 9), situated off the west coast of Asia Minor, but does not specifically say that this John was one of Jesus' disciples. John was a common name in the first centuries CE. The style is distinctive, not least because of its frequent use of Semitisms, and sufficiently so to make it impossible to attribute Revelation to the author(s) of the Johannine Gospel and epistles, in spite of some common imagery, especially the picture of Jesus as a slain lamb.

At the beginning of this chapter, I asked the questions: when, where, why, by whom, and for whom were the individual books of the New Testament written? Except in the case of the authentic Pauline epistles, these questions cannot be answered with confidence, and even trying to reconstruct Pauline addressees is a risky task, since inferring answers from the texts themselves, without reliable and detailed external evidence, is a procedure that can lead to no more than plausible hypotheses. That one of the implied criteria for including a book in the New Testament was apostolic authorship, and that scholars doubt the apostolic authorship of many New Testament texts, should not disturb us greatly. This was only one criterion among many. Another was that these books had been found useful to Christian life in the first centuries. Looking back and reading these texts after 2,000 years, we may regret certain of their features: their anti-Judaism, the insistence of some of them on the subordination of women to men, and the acceptance of the institution of slavery by some of them. Moreover, the process of defining the New Testament seems to have expressed desires to exclude what some literate male leaders disliked. Of even greater regret are the terrible cruelties perpetrated down the centuries by Christians who have appealed to these features for justification of their deeds. Christian cruelty can be opposed, however, not only by appeal to other parts of the Christian scriptures, but by the recognition that all written texts are open to interpretations and that interpreters are themselves responsible for their readings. Finally, Christianity, although honouring its scripture, is not strictly a religion of the book. Christians express belief in the creator God and the resurrected Jesus from whom they expect inspiration in the present.

THE MAKING OF THE BIBLE

II. Text and Translation

4 The Hebrew Bible

GEOFFREY KHAN

The printed editions of the Hebrew Bible that are in use today are based on medieval manuscripts deriving from the school of the Masoretes of Tiberias. The Masoretes were scholars who devoted themselves to preserving the traditions of writing and reading the Bible. Their name derives from the Hebrew term *masora* or *masoret*, the meaning of which is generally thought to be 'transmission of traditions'. The Tiberian Masoretes were active over a period of several centuries in the second half of the first millennium CE. The medieval sources refer to several generations of Masoretes, some of them belonging to the same family. The most famous of these families is that of Aharon ben Asher (tenth century). The Masoretes continued the work of the *soferim* ('scribes') of the Talmudic and Second Temple periods, who were also occupied with the correct transmission of the biblical text.

The Tiberian Masoretic tradition gradually took shape over two or three centuries and continued to grow until it was finally fixed and the activities of the Masoretes ceased at the beginning of the second millennium. During the same period, circles of Masoretes are known to have existed also in Iraq, but the Tiberian Masoretic tradition had become virtually exclusive in Judaism by the late Middle Ages and has been followed by all printed editions of the Hebrew Bible.

The Tiberian Masoretic tradition is recorded in numerous medieval manuscripts. The majority of these were written after 1100 CE and are copies of older manuscripts made in various Jewish communities. The earlier printed editions are based on these late medieval manuscripts. The most authoritative of these early editions was the so-called second Rabbinic Bible (i.e. the Bible text combined with commentaries and translations, known as *Miqra' ot Gedolot*) edited by Jacob ben Hayyim ben Adoniyahu and printed at the press of Daniel Bomberg in Venice between 1524 and 1525. This came to be regarded as a *textus receptus* and was used as the basis for many subsequent editions of the Hebrew Bible.

A small number of surviving manuscripts are first-hand records of the Tiberian Masoretic tradition. The fixed tradition was transmitted by generations of scribes. Some of the modern editions of the Bible are based on these early manuscripts, for example, the *Biblia Hebraica* from the third edition (1929–37) onwards, *The Hebrew University Bible*, ed. M. Goshen-Gottstein (1975, 1981), the editions by A. Dotan (1976) and M. Breuer (1977–82), and the modern edition of the Rabbinic Bible by M. Cohen (1992–).

The Tiberian Masoretic tradition can be divided into the following components:

1. The consonantal text of the Hebrew Bible.
2. The indications of divisions of paragraphs.
3. The accent signs, which indicated the musical cantillation of the text and also the position of the main stress in a word.
4. The vocalization, which indicated the pronunciation of the vowels and some details of the pronunciation of the consonants in the reading of the text.
5. Notes on the text, written in the margins of the manuscript.
6. Masoretic treatises. Some manuscripts have appendices at the end of the biblical text containing various treatises on aspects of the teachings of the Masoretes.

These six items are all in written form. In addition the Masoretic tradition also contained an orally transmitted component in the form of a reading tradition. The reading tradition was partially represented in graphic form by the vocalization and accent signs, but these did not record all of its details. The orally transmitted Tiberian reading tradition, therefore, should be treated as an additional component of the Tiberian Masoretic tradition. The reading tradition complemented the consonantal text, but it was independent of it to a certain degree, and sometimes contained a different reading from what was represented by the consonantal text. In such cases the traditional Masoretic terminology distinguishes the *qere* ('what is read') from the *ketiv* ('what is written').

It is this complex of components, written and oral, that formed the Tiberian Masoretic tradition. A careful distinction must be made between the components of the tradition that the Masoretes had a direct role in creating and the components that were inherited from an earlier period. The core components that were inherited from earlier tradition include the consonantal text, the paragraph divisions, the oral reading tradition, and some of the contents of the textual notes. The other components, i.e., the accent and vocalization signs (but not the reading tradition that the signs represented, and the majority of the textual notes and treatises, were developed by the Masoretes in the Masoretic period. At the end of the Masoretic period the written components of the Tiberian Masoretic tradition had become fixed and were transmitted in this fixed form by later scribes. By contrast, the oral component, that is, the Tiberian reading tradition, was soon forgotten and appears not to have been transmitted much beyond the twelfth century.

Within the Tiberian school there were various streams of tradition that differed from one another in small details and were associated with the names of individual Masoretes. The differences that we know the most about were between

Aharon ben Asher and Moshe ben Naphtali, who belonged to the last generation of Masoretes in the tenth century. The points of disagreement between these two Masoretes are recorded in lists at the end of many of the early Tiberian Bible manuscripts. A source from the eleventh century refers to the possibility of following either the school of Ben Asher or that of Ben Naphtali, without any evaluation.

The Ben Asher school finally became supreme only when it was espoused by the influential Jewish scholar Moses Maimonides (1135–1204). When he was resident in Egypt, Maimonides examined a manuscript with vocalization and accents written by Aharon ben Asher and pronounced it to be the model that should be followed. It is likely that the book of differences between Ben Asher and Ben Naphtali (*Kitab al-Khulaf*) was composed by Misha'el ben 'Uzzi'el shortly after this pronouncement of Maimonides.

The Tiberian Masoretic manuscripts are codices, that is, books consisting of collections of double-leaves that were stitched together. The Hebrew Bible began to be written in codex form during the Masoretic period. Previously, before about 700 CE, it was always written in a scroll. After the introduction of the codex, scrolls continued to be used for writing the Hebrew Bible. Each type of manuscript, however, had a different function. The scrolls were used for public liturgical reading in the synagogues whereas the codices were used for study purposes and non-liturgical reading. The scroll was the ancient form of manuscript that was hallowed by liturgical tradition and it was regarded as unacceptable by the Masoretes to change the custom of writing the scroll by adding the various written components of the Masoretic tradition that they developed, such as vocalization, accents and marginal notes. The codex had no such tradition behind it and so the Masoretes felt free to introduce into these types of manuscript the newly developed written Masoretic components. We may say that the liturgical scroll remained the core of the biblical tradition whereas the Masoretic codex was conceived as auxiliary to this. This distinction of function between liturgical scrolls and Masoretic codices has continued in Jewish communities down to the present day. Occasionally in the Middle Ages Masoretic additions were made to scrolls if they had, for some reason, become unfit for liturgical use. The scrolls also differed from Masoretic codices in the addition of ornamental strokes called *taggim* to the Hebrew letters.

The task of writing codices was generally divided between two specialist scribes. The copying of the consonantal text was entrusted to a scribe known as a *sofer*, who also wrote scrolls. The vocalization, accents, and Masoretic notes, on the other hand, were generally added by a scribe known as a *naqdan* ('pointer', i.e. vocalizer) or by a Masorete. In the early period, coinciding with or close to the time when the Masoretes were active, we can distinguish between various types of Hebrew Bible codices. The type of codex that has been referred to in the preceding discussion is what can be termed a 'model' codex, which was carefully written and accurately preserved the written components of the Tiberian Masoretic tradition. Such manuscripts were generally in the possession of a community, as is shown by their colophons, and were kept in a public place of study and worship for consultation and copying. References to various model codices and their readings are found in the Masoretic notes, for example, Codex Mugah, Codex Hilleli, Codex Zambuqi, and Codex Yerushalmi. Sometimes accurately written manuscripts also contain the text of an Aramaic Targum (interpretative translation).

In addition to these model Masoretic codices, there existed numerous so-called popular Bible codices, which were generally in the possession of private individuals. These were not always written with such precision and usually did not include all the written components of the Tiberian Masoretic tradition. Often they contain no accents or Masoretic notes but only vocalization, and this may deviate from the standard Tiberian system of vocalization in a number of details. A conspicuous feature of some popular codices is that they adapt the written consonantal text to make it correspond to the reading tradition more closely. An extreme case of this is represented by a corpus of Hebrew Bible manuscripts that contain an Arabic transcription of the reading tradition. These were used by some Karaite Jews. Some popular Bible manuscripts are no more than *aides-mémoire* to the reading tradition, in that they were written in a shorthand form known as *serugin*. In these texts the first word of a verse is written in full, followed by a single letter from each of the other important words in the verse. Some popular Bible manuscripts were accompanied by an Aramaic Targum or an Arabic translation and commentary. There were, therefore, three classes of Hebrew Bible manuscript in the early Middle Ages: (1) scrolls used for public reading in the liturgy; (2) model Masoretic codices, the purpose of which was to preserve the full biblical tradition, both the written tradition and the reading tradition; (3) popular manuscripts that aided individuals in the reading of the text.

We describe here briefly two of the surviving model Tiberian Masoretic codices that have come to be regarded as among the most important and have been used in modern critical editions. They all reflect a basically uniform Masoretic tradition, though no two manuscripts are completely identical. The differences are sometimes the result of scribal errors and other times due to a slightly different system of marking vocalization or accents that is followed by the *naqdan*.

The Aleppo Codex

In the colophon of this manuscript it is stated that the Masorete Aharon ben Asher added the vocalization, accents, and Masoretic notes. It is thought to be the manuscript that Maimonides examined when he pronounced that Ben Asher's tradition was superior to that of other Masoretes. It should be regarded, therefore, as the authorized edition in Jewish tradition. When Malmonides saw the manuscript, it was kept in Egypt, possibly in the Ben-Ezra synagogue in al-Fustat, which later became famous for its 'Genizah'. From the later Middle Ages, however, it was kept in Aleppo. In 1948 the synagogue in which it was kept in Aleppo was set on fire and only about three-quarters of the original manuscript were preserved.

The surviving portions are now kept in Jerusalem in the library of the Ben-Zvi Institute. This manuscript forms the basis of a number of Israeli editions of the Hebrew Bible, including the *Hebrew University Bible*, the edition of M. Breuer, and the modern Rabbinic Bible (*Ha-Keter*) edited by M. Cohen.

A page showing Exodus 14: 28 to 15: 14 from the St Petersburg Manuscript (Firkovitch I, B 19a). Written in 1009, it contains the complete text of the Hebrew Bible and was the basis for the third edition of the *Biblia Hebraica* (Stuttgart 1919–37).

St Petersburg, National Library of Russia, Firkovitch 1 B 19a

The colophon of this manuscript states that it was written in 1009 and subsequently corrected 'according to the most exact texts of Ben Asher'. It differs slightly from the Aleppo Codex in a few minor details. The manuscript has been preserved in its entirety and it contains the complete text of the Bible. Paul Kahle made this the basis of the third edition of *Biblia Hebraica* (Stuttgart 1929–37) and it has been used for all subsequent editions. It is also the basis of the edition of the Hebrew Bible by A. Dotan.

In the Middle Ages Hebrew Bible manuscripts were also written with systems of vocalization and accents that differed from those of the Tiberian Masoretic tradition. Some of these systems are adaptations of the Tiberian system, such as the so-called 'expanded' Tiberian system, which extends some of the principles found in the standard Tiberian vocalization.

Other systems use different sets of signs. These include the Palestinian and Babylonian systems of vocalization, which are found in numerous manuscripts from the Middle Ages. There is no uniformity within the two systems and it is possible to identify a range of sub-systems. By the late Middle Ages these systems had been almost completely supplanted in manuscripts by the standard Tiberian Masoretic tradition. As far as can be established, the earliest forms of the Palestinian and Babylonian vocalization systems have many features that are independent of the Tiberian system, but gradually the Tiberian tradition exerted its influence and, indeed, some manuscripts are little more than transcriptions of the Tiberian tradition into Babylonian or Palestinian vowel signs.

A reconstruction of the Entrance to the Genizah (store room) in the Karaite synagogue in Old Cairo.

The model Tiberian codices such as the Aleppo Codex and manuscript Firkovitch 1 B 19a were kept in the libraries of synagogues until modern times. The majority of the popular manuscripts from the Middle Ages and the manuscripts with Palestinian and Babylonian vocalization have been preserved mainly in fragmentary form in the Cairo Genizah. This was a repository for worn-out sacred writings that was discovered by scholars in the Ben-Ezra synagogue of al-Fustat (Old Cairo) in the nineteenth century.

We shall now examine the background of each of the components of the Tiberian Masoretic tradition.

THE CONSONANTAL TEXT

The term consonantal text refers to the Hebrew letters of the biblical text without the vocalization, accents, and Masoretic notes. Although this term is widely used in biblical scholarship, it is not completely appropriate as far as the Tiberian Masoretic text is concerned since this consists not only of letters representing consonants but also many letters that represent vowels, whose use is not consistent. In the ensuing discussion the Masoretic consonantal text is referred to as MCT.

Among the early model Masoretic codices there are only sporadic differences in the consonantal text. They are all in virtually complete agreement with regard to the distribution of the vowel letters. The differences that do occur can usually be explained as an error in copying. Similarly the numerous biblical Masoretic manuscripts written after 1100 only exhibit minute variants in the consonantal text. The collation of hundreds of late medieval manuscripts by Kennicott and De Rossi in the late eighteenth century showed that the Tiberian text was accurately copied down to the period of the first printed editions. The small deviations in the consonantal text that are found in some of the later manuscripts are likely to be mistakes or intentional changes of late scribes and do not preserve an earlier text that differed from what is found in the earlier model Tiberian codices. It is, nevertheless, possible to distinguish between scribal practices in Sephardi (Spanish, Portuguese, and eastern) manuscripts and those in Ashkenazi (European) manuscripts. The Sephardi manuscripts have, in general, preserved the Tiberian Masoretic text in its minute details of orthography more accurately than the Ashkenazi ones. The accurate transmission of the standard Tiberian consonantal text is found also in the unvocalized scrolls that have been preserved from the Middle Ages.

By contrast to the late medieval manuscripts, many of the popular biblical manuscripts of the early Middle Ages which have been found in the Cairo Genizah deviate from contemporary model Tiberian codices. In general they use vowel letters far more frequently. Where the *qere* differs from the *ketiv*, popular manuscripts sometimes have the text of the *qere* in the consonantal text.

Early medieval manuscripts with different systems of vocalization generally exhibit the orthography of the standard Tiberian text. Some manuscripts with Palestinian vocalization have a slightly fuller orthography, with more vowel letters than the standard text. This suggests that they were popular manuscripts intended for private use. Manuscripts with Babylonian vocalization, most of which can be assumed to have been written in Iraq, correspond to the Tiberian consonantal text very closely and differ only in a few details. These differences are generally related to orthography, the division of words, or the harmonization of the *ketiv* with the *qere*. Small divergences such as these between the 'Easterners' and the 'Westerners' are mentioned in the Tiberian Masoretic notes and also in lists appended to Tiberian manuscripts.

With regard to the ordering of the biblical books, those of the Pentateuch and the Former Prophets were arranged in all manuscripts in a fixed order, but there was a certain amount of variation in the order of books in the Latter Prophets

Solomon Schechter examining Genizah fragments in the Cambridge University Library.

and Writings. The order that is customary today is the one that is used in the first printed editions. The differences from the early printed editions in the Latter Prophets are found mainly in late medieval Ashkenazi manuscripts. The order of the Writings differs from the present custom in the early Masoretic manuscripts such as the Aleppo Codex and the Firkovitch 1 B 19a. The division of the biblical books into chapters and the numbering of verses that are found in modern printed editions do not derive from Jewish tradition but were transferred from a tradition followed in manuscripts of the Latin Vulgate version that was established in the thirteenth century by Archbishop Stephen Langton in England.

Between the end of the Second Temple period (70 CE) and the time of the earliest surviving medieval Masoretic codices (ninth century) very few Bible manuscripts are extant. The codex was not used to write Bibles before the Masoretic period, which began around 700 CE. As remarked above, it was adopted by the Masoretes as an alternative to the traditional scroll to give them freedom to add vocalization, accents, and marginal notes. All extant Bible manuscripts that were written before the earliest attested Masoretic codices are, therefore, scrolls that contain only the consonantal text.

Some biblical scrolls that have been preserved in synagogue libraries and the Cairo Genizah have been dated to the eighth century or earlier. Fragments of biblical scrolls have been discovered in the Judaean desert (Nahal Hever and Wadi Murabba'at) which were written around the beginning of the second century CE. There are no biblical manuscripts that can be dated to the intervening centuries in the middle of the first millennium CE.

Despite the passage of hundreds of years the manuscripts from Nahal Hever and Wadi Murabba'at contain a consonantal text that is virtually identical with that of the medieval Masoretic manuscripts, including in details of orthography. It is clear that the consonantal text was copied by scribes with great accuracy from one generation to the next. This concern for precise transmission is reflected in the many rules for writing biblical scrolls that are prescribed in the Babylonian and Palestinian Talmuds. These were collected together shortly after the Talmudic period in the treatise *Massekhet Sefer Torah* and, slightly later, in the more detailed work *Massekhet Soferim*. Talmudic literature mentions a number

Remains of a scroll of Leviticus from Cave 11 at Qumran, written in paleo-Hebrew script.

of rabbis who took a close interest in the biblical text, such as R. Meir, R. Hananel, and R. Shmuel ben Shilat. There was an awareness among the Babylonian rabbis that the most accurate transmission of the text was to be found in Palestine. The careful transmission of the text at the beginning of the millennium is also reflected by the introduction of rules of biblical hermeneutics by Hillel the Elder in the first century CE and their use by the Tannaim, since these presuppose the existence of an inviolable, authoritative text. The exegetical importance attached by Rabbi Aqiva (d. 135 CE) to grammatical particles such as *'et* and *gam* also reflected the stability of the text.

The many biblical scrolls that were discovered at Qumran provide abundant evidence for transmission of the consonantal text in the Second Temple period. These are the earliest surviving biblical manuscripts. The scrolls are datable to a period ranging from the third century BCE to the first half of the first century CE. From the first or second century BCE we also have the so-called Nash papyrus, a single sheet of papyrus discovered in Egypt in 1902 and now in the possession of the Cambridge University Library, which contains the text of the Decalogue. This, however, appears to be a liturgical rather than biblical text.

Some of the Qumran manuscripts, though not necessarily the oldest, are written in an early type of Hebrew script, close to the Phoenician form of script that is found in earlier Hebrew epigraphic texts. Most are written in the 'Assyrian' square script that resembles the medieval scripts in the basic forms of letters. The Qumran scrolls show us that during this period a multiplicity of consonantal texts were transmitted in manuscripts.

The majority of the scrolls, however, exhibit a text that is very close to the Masoretic consonantal text, and have been termed 'proto-Masoretic' manuscripts. These differ from the medieval manuscripts only in a few orthographic details and in isolated words. The tradition of the Masoretic consonantal text, therefore, can be traced back to the earliest surviving Bible manuscripts in the Second Temple period.

A number of passages in rabbinic literature refer to the concern of the Jewish authorities in the Second Temple period for the precise copying of biblical manuscripts. The temple employed professional 'correctors' or 'revisers' (*magihim*) to ensure that the text was copied correctly. In the temple court there were model manuscripts, which

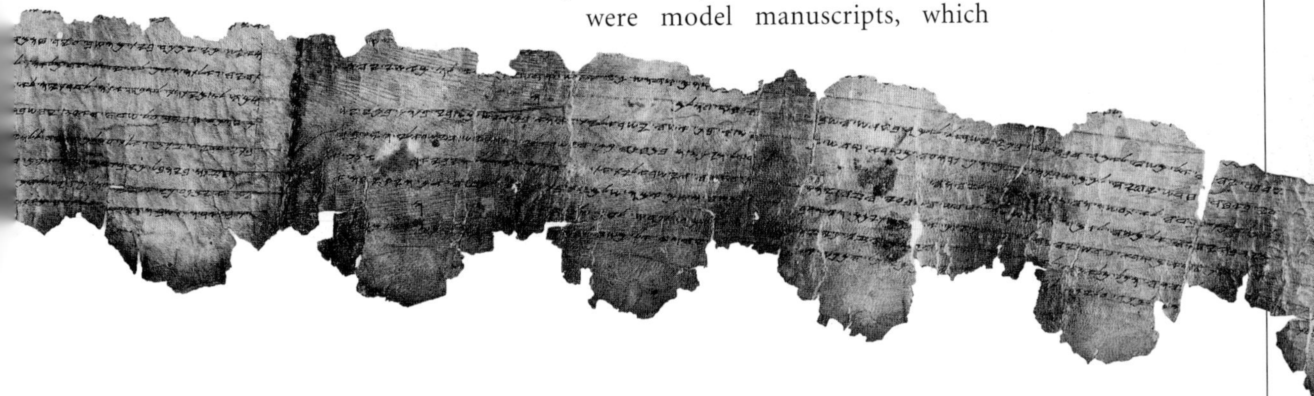

appear to have contained the standard text that was sanctioned by the Jewish authorities. It is said that once a year all the scrolls of the Pentateuch had to be taken to the temple for revision.

In Talmudic literature there are reports of three scrolls of the Pentateuch that were found in the Temple court. These differed from one another in small details. They were carefully collated and differences were corrected towards the majority reading. The purpose of this activity is not completely clear. It may have been a means of sanctioning the authorized text against other rival texts. Alternatively, the reports may reflect efforts that were made in the Second Temple period to level variants in texts belonging to the proto-Masoretic tradition. Judging by the extant proto-Masoretic manuscripts from Qumran, there was indeed a slightly higher degree of variation in the Second Temple period than is found in manuscripts from later periods. Whatever the precise interpretation may be of the Talmudic account of the three scrolls, it is clear that the Jewish authorities recognized an authorized text in the Second Temple period. It is generally thought that this authorized text is to be identified with the type of text found in the proto-Masoretic manuscripts from Qumran, which was subsequently transmitted with great precision after the destruction of the temple. Some signs of textual collation include dots written above, and in one case (Ps. 27:13) also below, certain letters, and inverted *nuns* (the Hebrew letter 'n'), which are written before and after Numbers 10: 35–6 and Psalm 107: 23–8. It has been argued that the insistence on scribal exactitude in handing down written records in general at this period was partly inspired by the Greek tradition of textual criticism.

Before the discovery of the Qumran scrolls, scholars were aware of the existence of texts of the Hebrew Bible that differed in places substantially from the Tiberian consonantal text. These divergent texts were identified in the Samaritan Pentateuch and the reconstructed Hebrew Vorlage of the Septuagint Greek version. It used to be thought that these texts and the Tiberian Masoretic text constituted three separate recensions.

The Samaritan Pentateuch was first made available to scholars when Morinus printed it in 1632 in the Paris Polyglot. The earliest manuscripts are datable to the Middle Ages. They are written in an early type of Hebrew script that resembles the form of script that was in use in the Hasmonean period (second–first century BCE). There is no consensus among scholars as to when the Samaritans seceded from Judaism, though a date some time in the Second Temple period is generally favoured rather than a pre-exilic date which is claimed by the Samaritans themselves. It may have been as late as the second century BCE, which would conform with the aforementioned palaeographical evidence.

The Samaritan Pentateuch differs from the Tiberian Masoretic consonantal text in a number of respects. In the majority of cases these differences are due to deliberate changes introduced by scribes, reflecting the fact that a freer attitude was taken to the transmission of the text than was the case with the proto-Masoretic and Masoretic text. These scribal interventions include various types of harmonizing alterations that remove internal inconsistencies in content, orthography, and grammar. The orthography generally exhibits a more liberal use of vowel letters than is found in the Tiberian consonantal text and the guttural letters are often interchanged, owing to their weakening in the reading tradition. Finally various ideological changes have been made, the most conspicuous of which is the substitution of 'Mount Gerizim', which was the centre of the Samaritan cult, for 'Jerusalem' in verses referring to Jerusalem as the central place of worship.

Among the Qumran scrolls scholars have now identified biblical texts that resemble that of the Samaritan Pentateuch. These have been termed 'pre-Samaritan' texts. Broadly, they exhibit the same type of harmonizations in

Samaritan high priest in Nablus, Palestine, with a Scroll of the Pentateuch. The Samaritans believe that the scroll was written by Abisha, a great grandson of Aaron, but it is a medieval text whose earliest parts date from 1149 CE.

content, spelling, and grammar but not the changes motivated by Samaritan ideology. In the Second Temple period, therefore, the pre-Samaritan texts were not specifically associated with the Samaritan religious group. The Samaritans adopted this text for no particular reason, other than, perhaps, on account of it differing from the proto-Masoretic text, which was associated with the central Jewish authorities.

The Septuagint Greek translation of the Bible is an indirect witness to the Hebrew biblical text, yet since its Vorlage (i.e. the Hebrew text which it used) differs significantly from the Tiberian Masoretic text in some places, it is of great significance. The name of this translation derives from the tradition (recorded in the apocryphal composition known as the Epistle of Aristeas) that the translation of the Hebrew Pentateuch into Greek was assigned by King Ptolemy II Philadelphus (285–246 BCE) to 72 elders in Egypt. The reliability of this tradition is a matter of debate. Some scholars have held that the Septuagint was not the first attempt at translation but a standardization of previous Greek versions. It is now generally agreed, however, that the Septuagint version of the Pentateuch was a single original translation that was made in the third century BCE, as is stated in the Epistle of Aristeas. The translation of the rest of the Hebrew Bible was made in the following two centuries. A few papyrus fragments of the Septuagint have been discovered, though the main sources of the text are a number of manuscripts written in Greek uncials (capital letters) dating from the fourth to the tenth century CE.

There are major difficulties in reconstructing the Hebrew Vorlage of the Septuagint. The majority of apparent divergences between the translation and MCT are likely not to be the result of a different Hebrew Vorlage but rather due to the exegesis of the translator, a concept of etymology different from our own, or corruptions in the transmission of the Greek text. The style of the translation varies in degrees of literalness. This reflects the approaches of different translators. Some sections are very free and even paraphrases, which makes any certain reconstruction of the Hebrew Vorlage impossible. Retroversions of the Greek into Hebrew are far safer in the literal sections of the Septuagint. Some of the more certain cases of a reconstructed Vorlage that differs from the Masoretic text include translations that diverge radically from the Masoretic text but can be explained by assuming an interchange of a consonant in the word concerned. The degree of certainty is greater in the transcription of proper names that point to a form in the Hebrew Vorlage that differs from the MCT in one of its letters, for example, Genesis 10: 4, MCT *ddnym*; Greek *rhodioi*; reconstruction *rdnym*. Another case where the Vorlage can safely be assumed to differ from MCT is where the translation contains a lengthy addition or omission in comparison with MCT or a different arrangement of material, none of which can reasonably be explained to have arisen by exegesis. This applies, for example, to the book of Jeremiah, the Septuagint version of which is shorter than MCT by one-sixth, and also to the books of Joshua and Ezekiel, which contain both omissions and additions relative to MCT.

At Qumran a number of biblical scrolls have been found that contain a Hebrew text that is closer to the Septuagint than the MCT. The value of these Qumran manuscripts is that they often support reconstructions of the Vorlage of the Septuagint with a text that diverges from MCT.

The Qumran scrolls that have been discussed so far include the proto-Masoretic texts, the pre-Samaritan texts, and the texts that are close to the Septuagint. In addition to these there is a group of biblical scrolls that are not closely related to any of these three types of text, but exhibit inconsistent patterns of agreement with all of them as well as significant divergences. These demonstrate that the textual transmission in the Second Temple period took place in a multiplicity of forms and had not been completely reduced to three clearly separate recensions, as used to be thought. The proto-Masoretic type of text, nevertheless, was recognized as authoritative in mainstream Judaism and appears to have been the most common one that was in use.

A final category of biblical scroll that is found at Qumran is represented by manuscripts that are written according to what E. Tov terms 'Qumran scribal practice'. These are thought to have been produced by a school of scribes that was active at Qumran. Many of the biblical scrolls belonging to the other categories may have been brought to Qumran from elsewhere.

The Isaiah Scroll from Cave 1 at Qumran (IQIsa[a]) is a thousand years older than the medieval manuscripts which preserve the massoretic text of the Hebrew Bible.

The biblical scrolls written according Qumran practice do not reflect a tradition of precise and conservative copying but rather exhibit numerous interventions of the scribe. They can be categorized as popular texts that were not bound to the preservation of a textual tradition but adapted to facilitate the reading of the text. The orthography is expanded with the abundant use of vowel letters, which often reflect a different form of morphology from what one finds in the Tiberian Masoretic tradition. The orthography reflects a weakening in the pronunciation of the guttural consonants, which no doubt was caused by the influence of the vernacular language. The scribes also adapted the text when there was a grammatical irregularity (as is found in pre-Samaritan texts).

The Qumran scrolls, therefore, attest to a multiplicity of texts that coexisted with an authoritative text that had been espoused by the central Jewish authorities. This variety of texts that is found in Qumran may well reflect the situation that was found throughout the Jewish communities of Palestine, though at present we have no way of verifying this. The sectarian community in Qumran did not pay allegiance to the mainstream Jewish authorities and so may have felt less bound by the authoritative text. It may be significant in this regard that the fragments of biblical scrolls that have been found at Masada and in the Judaean desert, which were in use by Jews who were loyal to mainstream Judaism, all contain the authoritative, proto-Masoretic text.

After the destruction of the temple in 70 CE the proto-Masoretic text was the only text tradition that continued to be transmitted in Jewish communities. This was not necessarily due to a concerted effort to eliminate all other traditions, or, as Kahle claimed, to unify the variant traditions by a process of official levelling. The description of the collation of the three manuscripts in the temple, nevertheless, suggests that some process of textual unification may have been carried out within the proto-Masoretic tradition itself during the Second Temple period. The role of a Jewish council meeting at Jamnia shortly after the destruction of the temple does not seem to have been as decisive in this matter, as Kahle had held. The exclusive transmission of the proto-Masoretic tradition in Judaism is more likely to be the consequence of historical events. The text of the Septuagint Greek translation was adopted by Christianity, the pre-Samaritan text by the Samaritans. The Qumran sectarian community was destroyed. The Pharisaic authorities who had espoused the proto-Masoretic text as authoritative constituted the only organized Jewish group that survived.

The custom of writing popular texts, however, such as the scrolls written according to Qumran practice, in which the scribes felt a degree of freedom from a precise textual tradition, no doubt continued throughout the first millennium CE. In rabbinic literature there are references to readings deviating from MCT that were found in what is known as the Severus scroll. This appears to have been a popular text. It was written in the Second Temple period, but continued to be used in the rabbinic period, having been donated to the Jews by the Roman emperor Alexander Severus (222–35). The readings cited from this manuscript reflect an imprecise copying with adaptation of orthography to pronunciation.

Several biblical citations in rabbinic literature reflect slight deviations from the MCT, which may also have originated in similar popular manuscripts or have been quoted imprecisely from memory. In a few cases, the variant readings of these citations coincide with other known texts from the Second Temple period. These variant readings, however, were not officially tolerated.

As we have seen, popular biblical manuscripts are found among the early medieval manuscripts. Many of the Masoretic notes that were incorporated into the Tiberian Masoretic tradition also have the purpose of guarding against the tendencies that are reflected in popular manuscripts, implying that these tendencies must have existed among some scribes. Apart from a punctilious attention to orthography, the notes also warn against the harmonization of constructions that are irregular grammatically. The latter type of notes are introduced by the phrase 'one may suppose' (*sevirin*) or 'one may suppose mistakenly'.

In the first millennium CE revisions were made of the Septuagint Greek translation to adapt it to the Hebrew textual tradition that had become exclusive in Judaism. Three of these Greek revisions were collated by Origen in the middle of the third century CE in his Hexapla. This contained six columns containing the following texts: the consonantal text of the Hebrew Bible, the transliteration of the Hebrew into Greek, the revisions of Aquila, Symmachus, and the Septuagint, and in the final column a revision attributed to Theodotion. The Septuagint text in the fifth column was annotated, indicating where it differs from the Hebrew. A later

A palimpsest (a manuscript whose original writing has been erased and replaced by a later writing) of part of Origen's Hexapla, the latter being the underscript.

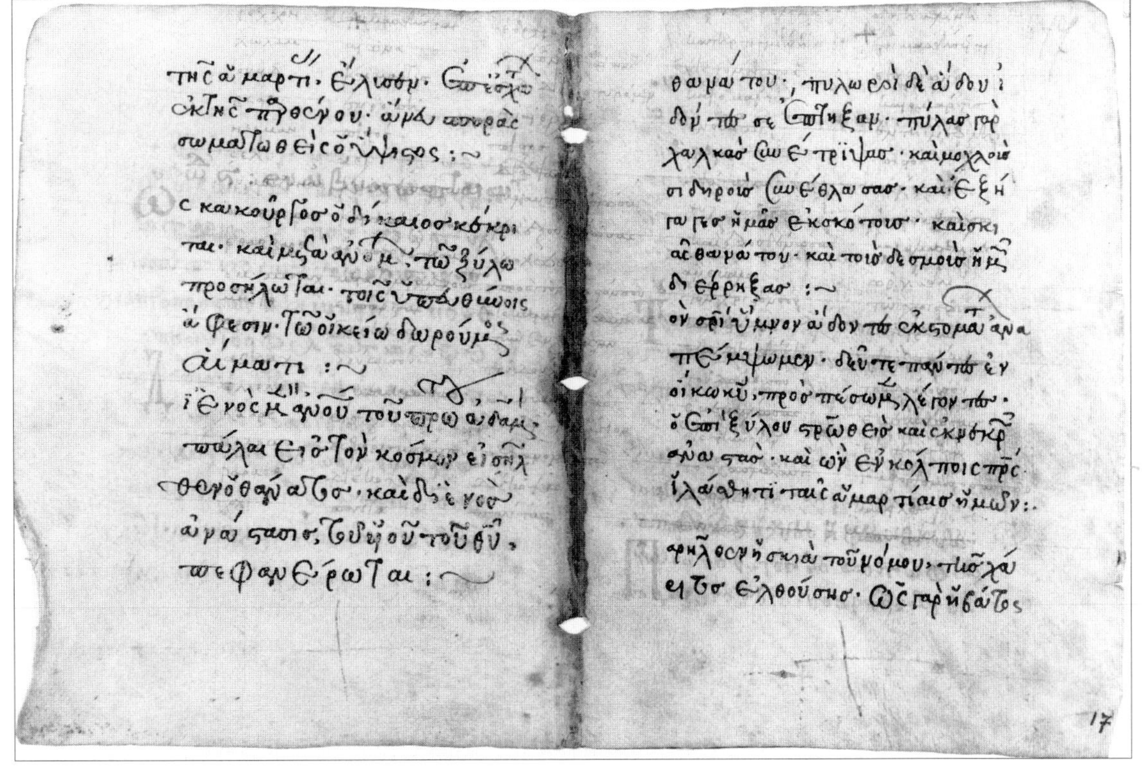

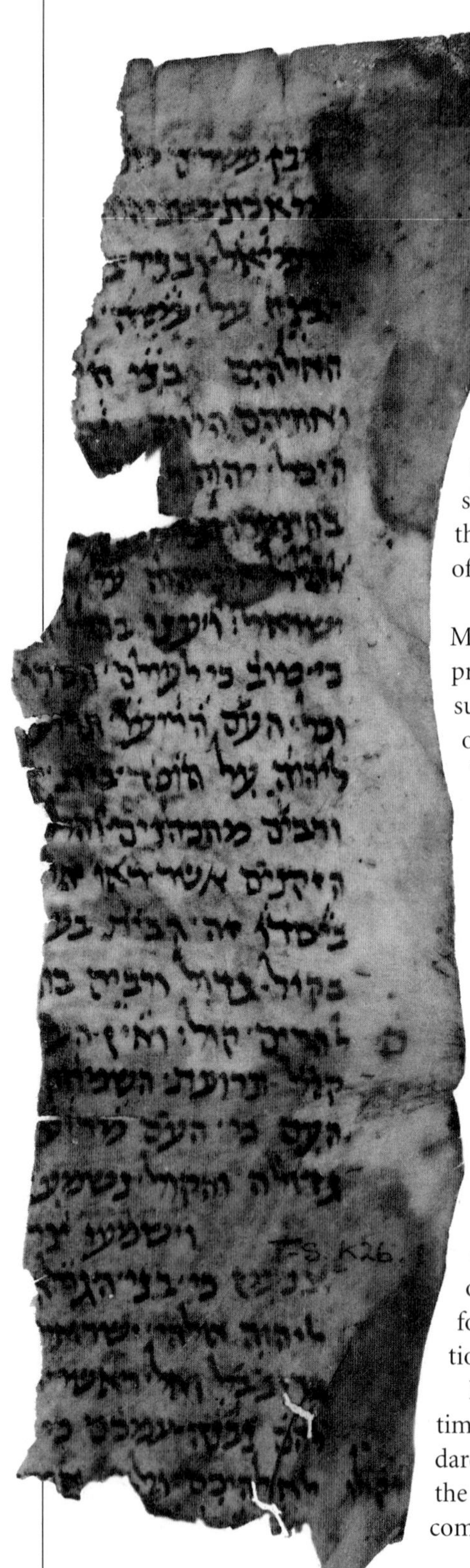

revision of the Septuagint was made by Lucian, who died in 312 CE. Since the Greek translation of the Bible served as the official text for Christianity at the beginning of the first millennium CE, many Christian translations of the Bible were made directly from the Greek rather than the Hebrew. The most important of these is the Old Latin translation (the Vetus Latina), which preserves many readings of the original Greek translation that have been lost in the subsequent revisions. All translations that were made directly from the Hebrew in the first millennium are based on the Masoretic text tradition. These include the Jewish Aramaic Targumim (first half of the millennium), the Latin Vulgate of Jerome (346–420 CE), the Jewish Arabic translations (tenth–eleventh centuries), and also most of the Syriac Peshitta version (first half of the millennium). As was remarked with regard to the Septuagint, however, the Hebrew Vorlage of these translations is often disguised by exegetical renderings.

The consonantal text that was incorporated into the Tiberian Masoretic tradition is a textual tradition that was transmitted with precision since at least the third century BCE, the time of the earliest surviving manuscripts from the Second Temple period. The history of the consonantal text before the earliest manuscripts is theoretical. The recent discovery of two minute silver amulets from Ketef Hinnom datable to the seventh or sixth century BCE that contain fragments of the priestly blessing in Numbers 6: 24–6 do not cast any significantly new light on this issue. Several general points concerning the earlier history of the text, however, can be made here.

The extant proto-Masoretic manuscripts show that the text had been fixed not only in content but also in orthography by the third century CE. This orthography is broadly uniform across all biblical books, though there is a slightly greater tendency for using vowel letters in the later books. It cannot, however, have been the original orthography of all the books that was used when they were first committed to writing. The composition of the majority of the books is dated several centuries earlier in the pre-exilic period when, judging by extant inscriptions, the orthography was much more defective, with vowel letters used only rarely. It is generally believed that these were written in some form at this earlier period, though the first stages of their composition may have been oral.

Hebrew orthography gradually employed more vowel letters as time progressed. At some stage an attempt was made to impose a standard orthography on the entire text. The slight discrepancies between the early and late books reflect the fact that this editorial work did not completely eliminate the original chronological differences in orthography. By comparison with independently attested epigraphic material, scholars have dated the broad profile of the orthographic practices fixed in the proto-Masoretic text to approximately the period 500–300 BCE. Some of the later biblical books were actually composed in this period, so it is possible that the MCT orthography in these texts is close to the original.

Fragment of Ezra 3 with Palestinian vocalization from the Cairo Genizah.

This was a key period in the formation of the Hebrew Bible as we know it today. It coincided broadly with the canonization of the Pentateuch and the Prophets. The emergence of this concept of a clearly circumscribed canon of sacred literature no doubt was the main factor that motivated concern for the exact preservation of its text. Some time during this period a change was made in biblical manuscripts from the early Hebrew script to the square script, which was first developed for the writing of Aramaic in the Persian empire. According to rabbinic tradition it was Ezra who instigated this change of script after the return from the Babylonian exile. Some scholars attribute the fixing of the orthography of the proto-Masoretic text also to the activities of Ezra, who lived some time between the fifth and fourth centuries BCE. Some of the later biblical books may have been originally written in square script. As remarked above, however, the Qumran discoveries show that biblical manuscripts were still being copied in the old Hebrew script several centuries after this reform. Even in some manuscripts that are written in the square script the tetragrammaton (the divine name *yhwh*) continued to be copied in the early script, apparently reflecting a greater scribal conservatism on account of its sanctity. There are reasons to assume that the biblical text that was fixed for the proto-Masoretic tradition in the second half of the first millennium BCE did not contain the original form of the text.

The MCT contains many difficulties that appear to have arisen from scribal errors in the transmission of the text predating the time in which it was fixed. These errors, which are usually visual, include the incorrect copying of individual letters and words, the false division of words, the conflation of variants, and the omission or addition of material. The scribal corruptions must have been present in the manuscripts that were used for establishing the authoritative text. Superior readings are sometimes found in Qumran manuscripts that lie outside this authoritative tradition or in the reconstructed Vorlage of the Septuagint. In some cases, moreover, where two parallel texts from the same source are found in the MCT, one of the texts preserves a superior reading to the other (e.g. 2 Sam. 22=Ps. 18; 2 Kings 18: 13–20: 19=Isa. 36: 1–38: 22=2 Chron. 32: 1–20).

The MCT also exhibits various intentional scribal changes to bring the text into line with contemporary linguistic usage, theology, and exegesis. It is often difficult, however, to distinguish between changes introduced during the literary recension of the text and those that were made during its transmission after the literary growth was complete. The extensive linguistic adaptation of the biblical sources in Chronicles is no doubt attributable to the stage of literary composition, yet the Chronicler may be regarded as both a scribe and an author since he copied earlier texts as well as rewriting sections and composing new ones.

A possible case of linguistic adaptation introduced by scribes in the transmission is the interpretation of the archaic enclitic *mem* as a plural ending. An example of a scribal change for theological reasons is the replacement of the name *ba'al* in theophoric names to *boshet*, 'shame'. The original text with *ba'al* was clearly felt at a later period to be theologically undesirable. In parallel passages between Samuel and Chronicles the original form of name with the element *ba'al* is often retained in the Chronicles passage whereas it has been changed to *boshet* in the Samuel parallel (e.g. Saul's fourth son is *'eshba'al* in 1 Chron. 8: 33 and 9: 39 but *'ish boshet* in 2 Sam. 2: 8ff., 3: 8ff., 4: 5ff.). This indicates that, possibly purely by chance, the manuscripts of Chronicles used to establish the proto-Masoretic text preserved an older scribal tradition than the manuscripts of Samuel. The manuscripts used for the text of Samuel, moreover, also contained a relatively large number of unintentional scribal corruptions compared to those used for other books. A scribal change for the sake of euphemism in connection with God may be identified in 2 Samuel 12: 9: 'Why did you despise *the word of* the Lord?', whereas the Lucianic Greek version appears to preserve the original text: 'Why did you despise the Lord?'

There are some possible signs of intentional scribal changes that were introduced late in the Second Temple period. The text 'city of destruction' in Isaiah 19: 18, for example, appears to have been changed from an original 'city of the sun', which referred to Heliopolis. This reading is found in a Qumran manuscript (1QIsa) and is reflected by some of the ancient versions. Heliopolis was the site of the rival temple built by Onias in the first half of the second century BCE and the change of the text to the ominous name 'city of destruction' was apparently instigated by the disapproving Jewish authorities of Jerusalem. By the Talmudic period a scribal change had been introduced into the text of Judges. 18: 30 by correcting the earlier text 'Moses' to 'Manasseh'. The purpose of this was to avoid the ascription of the erection of an idol to one of the descendants of Moses. This was achieved by inserting a superscribed *nun* after the *mem*. Although the reading 'Manasseh' is referred to in Talmudic literature, some of the early versions such as the Vulgate and the Vetus Latina, read 'Moses'. It is no doubt on account of the lateness of the change that the original text was graphically modified rather than replaced.

We should mention here the rabbinic tradition of the 'corrections of the scribes' (*tiqqune soferim*). These are places in the Bible in which, according to rabbinic tradition, the original text was changed by scribes to avoid undesirable expressions in relation to God. One such case is Genesis 18: 22: 'And Abraham was still standing before God.' Here, according to tradition, the text originally read 'And God was still standing.' The number of *tiqqune soferim* differs according to the various sources. Some scholars believe that they originate in rabbinic exegesis of the passages concerned as euphemisms rather than in traditions of actual changes to the text. The earlier traditions refer to scripture using a substitute rather than scribes changing the text. Another rabbinic tradition is that of the *'iṭṭur soferim* according to which the scribes removed a letter, usually a conjunctive *waw*. Thus Genesis 18: 5, 'afterwards you may pass on', is said to have originally been 'and afterwards you may pass on'. The background of this tradition is unclear.

After the fixing of an authoritative text in Judaism, however, the need for theological adaptations and the solution of philological difficulties was increasingly supplied by exegesis of various forms. Before the time of the fixing of the MCT the various biblical books underwent a long period of literary growth, during which several recensions were often made. The fact that some of the other textual traditions contain texts of biblical books that have a considerably different form from what is found in the MCT has been explained by the theory that these represent texts that stem from different periods of literary growth of the books. The various parallel passages in the MCT, which appear to have originated in the same source, in many cases exhibit differences from one to another. In some cases, as we have seen, this is due to scribal changes, intentional or unintentional, in the transmission of the text. In other cases it reflects the free approach to textual sources that existed during the process of composition and literary growth.

MARKING OF PARAGRAPHS

The second component of the Tiberian Masoretic tradition is the division of the text into paragraphs according to content. The paragraphs (known as *pisqa'ot* or *parashiyyot*) are of two types: the *parasha petuḥa* ('open paragraph'), which marked major divisions in content, and the *parasha setuma* ('closed paragraph'), which was a sub-division of the *petuḥa*. These differ in the way in they are marked. At the beginning of a *petuḥa* paragraph, the first word was written at the beginning of a new line. If the preceding line ended near the left margin, a whole line was left blank. A *setuma* was marked by leaving a space of nine letters after the preceding text on the same line. If there was not enough room left on the same line the following line was indented. In late medieval manuscripts and in many printed editions the letter *pe* is added in the space to mark a *petuḥa*, or the letter *samekh* to mark a *setuma*.

The places where each of these two types of paragraph were marked was a fixed component of the Tiberian Masoretic tradition. Some medieval Bible manuscripts contain lists of the *petuḥa* and *setuma* paragraphs. Similar lists were sometimes written in separate manuscripts. Some variation in paragraph division is found among the medieval manuscripts, though there is general uniformity. Maimonides includes in his *Mishneh Torah* a list of the paragraph divisions in the Pentateuch according to a manuscript of Aharon ben Asher, and by this means sanctioned the Ben Asher stream of Masoretic tradition not only in the marking of paragraphs but in its entirety. As remarked earlier, this led to the adoption of the Ben Asher tradition in Judaism.

The Tiberian Masoretes incorporated the practice of paragraph division from an earlier tradition. It is mentioned in rabbinic texts from about the third century CE. The same system of marking divisions starting new lines and leaving

Fragment from *Hidāyat al-Qāri* (The guide for the reader), a work in Arabic on the Tiberian pronunciation tradition and accent system.

spaces is found in the manuscripts from Qumran, both biblical and non-biblical. There is a large degree of agreement between the paragraphing of the Qumran biblical scrolls and that of the medieval manuscripts, which indicates that the tradition can be traced back to the Second Temple period. This division into units and sub-units of content is an expression of the exegesis of the text that was applied to it at a certain stage in its transmission.

ACCENTS

The accent signs are marked above and below the words in the Tiberian Masoretic text. They represent the musical motifs to which the biblical text was chanted in public reading. This chant gave solemnity to the reading and expressed the sanctity of the text. It also had an exegetical function in two respects. The chant marked the semantic and syntactic connections between words and phrases. It also marked the position of the stress in a word, which can be crucial for understanding the correct meaning, for example, *shavú*, 'they captured', but *shávu*, 'they returned'.

One uniform system of accent signs is used throughout the Bible except for the poetic books Job, Proverbs, and Psalms, which have a different system. Accent signs are found also in manuscripts with Babylonian and Palestinian vocalization.

The precise musical contour denoted by the various Tiberian accent signs is unknown, yet from a number of sources we can reconstruct their basic pitch and syntactic function. The most important early treatises in this respect are the *Diqduqe ha-te'amim* ('The fine rules of the accents') written in Hebrew by Aharon ben Asher (tenth century CE) and the *Hidāyat al-Qāri* ('The guide for the reader') written in Arabic by 'Abu al-Faraj Harun (eleventh century CE). It is not clear what relation the surviving cantillation traditions of the various Jewish communities have with the Tiberian system.

The accents are divided into 'disjunctives' and 'conjunctives'. The disjunctive accents mark some kind of break in the sense and require the reader to pause slightly. The conjunctive accents are marked on words between the disjunctives, showing that they form part of a phrase ending at the following disjunctive. In the standard Tiberian Masoretic tradition all words that bear a stress are marked with an accent sign. In some manuscripts with Babylonian and Palestinian vocalization, on the other hand, only disjunctive accents are marked.

All the conjunctive accents express the same degree of syntactic connection whereas the disjunctives express different degrees of pause. For this reason, in the less developed accent systems found in Babylonian and Palestinian manuscripts it was considered more important to mark disjunctives than conjunctives. The two major pausal accents, *silluq* and *atnaḥ*, mark the end and dichotomy of the verse respectively. The division of the biblical text into verses is, in fact, defined by the accent system. The two halves of a verse can be split into a hierarchy of smaller units with other disjunctive accents, the pausal value of which can be categorized according to the level of the hierarchy of division that they mark.

מתלא אלסכון פי אלאלף ומא אשבה   על
אלתאלת אלהים בראשית   נקיא
שוא מתחרך לא [illegible]וד שוא מתחרך
לא פי אול כלאם ולא פי וסטה ולא פי
אכרה לאן אלכלאם אנמא יכון מתחרך
ומא אלחק אלמתחרך פהו אקל חרכה
מן אלמתחרך אדא אבתדא באלשוא
ואלסאכן קד יתבעה מא פלדלך לם
יקתרנא אלמתחרכין כמא יקתרנא
אלסאכנין   פמתי שואיין סאכנין
לא יקתרנא אלא פי אכר כלמה מתל
וַיֵּשְׁבְּ וַיִּ[illegible]ְת וְסָבַת ואמא אן למא
סכן אלשוא אלדי תחת מן וישב ואלדי [illegible]

The Tiberian Masoretes developed the written accent signs to represent the chant but they did not create the chant itself. The tradition of reading the Bible with musical cantillation can be traced back several centuries before the Masoretic period. There are references to the teaching of biblical cantillation in Talmudic literature. One passage mentions the use of the right hand by the teacher or leader of the congregation to indicate the accents of the reading. The term 'stops of the accents', which is found in Talmudic literature, reflects the function of the accents to mark syntactic division. The association of the chant with the interpretation of the meaning of the text was recognized, as is shown by the Talmudic interpretation of Nehemiah 8: 8: 'And they read from the book, from the law of God, clearly: *they gave the sense and [the people] understood the reading*', which is said to refer to the reading with accents. Evidence for the division of the biblical text by accents in the Second Temple period is found in a Septuagint manuscript from the second century BCE that has spaces corresponding to the major pausal accents of the Tiberian tradition. There is no evidence of the use of written accent signs before the time of the Masoretes. It was the achievement of the Masoretes to create a written notation to record a tradition of cantillation that they received from an earlier period.

As remarked above, the disjunctive accents mark syntactic divisions. Since the syntax could in many cases be interpreted in more than one way, the accents reflect one particular exegesis of the text. In Deuteronomy 26: 5, for instance, the disjunctive accent on the first word of the clause *'arami* (Aramean) indicates that it is syntactically separated from the following word and so the two should be interpreted as subject and predicate rather than noun and attributive adjective. The sense is, therefore, 'An Aramaean [i.e. Laban] was seeking to destroy my father' and not 'my father was an Aramaean about to perish'. In Isaiah 40: 3 the accents mark a major syntactic break after the word *qore* (cries). This indicates that 'in the wilderness' belongs to what follows and the phrase was interpreted as having the sense 'The voice of the one that cries "Prepare in the wilderness the way of the Lord"'. The interpretation reflected by the accents generally corresponds to what is found in rabbinic literature and the Aramaic Targumim, which contain elements of early rabbinic exegesis. The aforementioned interpretation of Deuteronomy 26: 5, for instance, is found in Targum Onqelos and also Midrashic literature, from where it was incorporated into the Passover liturgy (Haggadah). The traditional Jewish interpretation of the verse is also found in the Latin Vulgate.

There is evidence that in the Second Temple period the exegesis of the syntax of the biblical text did not always correspond to that of the Tiberian accents. This is seen in the Septuagint translation, which often reflects a different syntactic division of the verse. From the Pesher commentaries found in Qumran, moreover, it appears that the delimitation of biblical verses did not always correspond to the placement of the final pausal accent (*silluq*) in the Tiberian tradition. It should be taken into account, however, that, just as there were a large range of consonantal textual traditions at this period, it is likely that there were a variety of exegetical traditions regarding the syntax of the text. This is seen in the case of Isaiah 40: 3. In the New Testament 'the voice of one crying in the wilderness' of Matthew 3: 3 reflects an interpretation that is different from the one reflected by the Tiberian accents. In the *Manual of Discipline* from Qumran (IQS 8: 13–14), however, the introit 'a voice calls' is omitted and the teacher uses the verse to exhort the sectarians 'to prepare a way in the wilderness', that is, to establish a community there. This shows that the Masoretic interpretation of the syntax was also current at that period. The version found in Matthew 3: 3 is apparently an exegetical reworking to support the call of John the Baptist from the wilderness. Another case is Deuteronomy 26: 5. The interpretation in conformity with the accents, 'An Aramaean was seeking to destroy my father', can be traced to the Second Temple period. Midrashic literature, however, indicates that there was also an ancient tradition of interpreting it: 'My father is an Aramaean about to perish'. It is likely that the exegetical tradition of the Masoretic accents has its origin in the teachings of mainstream Pharisaic Judaism.

As was remarked above, the division of the text into paragraphs (*parashiyyot*) in the Tiberian Masoretic text, which has roots in an ancient tradition, also reflects a division of the text according to the interpretation of its contents. In a number of places, however, the paragraph divisions do not coincide with the end of a verse according to the accents. This is known as *pisqa be-emtsa 'pasuq* 'a paragraph division within a verse' (e.g. Gen. 35: 22, 1 Sam. 16: 2). The reason for this appears to be that the paragraph division of the written text and the division expressed by the cantillation are two different layers of exegetical tradition which occasionally do not correspond with one another.

Within the accent system itself one can sometimes identify different layers of tradition. One possible example of this is the decalogue in Exodus 20: 13–16. The accentuation of this passage is unusual in that most words have two different accents. The explanation of this double accentuation is apparently that it reflects two layers of tradition. According to one layer of tradition the four commandments are presented in four separate verses, whereas in another they form together one accentual unit.

THE VOCALIZATION AND THE READING TRADITION

The next component of the Tiberian Masoretic tradition that we shall consider is the vocalization. This consists of a set of signs that were written below, above and sometimes within the letters of the consonantal text. The vocalization system includes signs to represent vowels and also signs to represent syllable division (*shewa*), consonant gemination (*dagesh*), the distinction between the two types of pronunciation of the so-called *bgadkfat* consonants (*dagesh*) and the consonantal pronunciation of a letter (*mappiq*). The vocalization notation, in fact, marks more than phonology. It reflects syntactic divisions in the same way as the accents, in that it marks differences between the pronunciation of words that occur at syntactic pauses and those that occur within syntactic units. The *dagesh* sign is sometimes used, moreover, in an exegetical function to distinguish meaning. A few isolated cases of this are found in the Tiberian tradition, such as the *dagesh* in the *mem* of 'Abimelech' in Genesis 26: 1 to indicate that this is a different Abimelech from the one mentioned in chapters 20–1, and in the *lamed* of the word *lo* (meaning 'not') when collocated with the homophonous word *lo* (meaning 'to him'), for example Proverbs 26: 17. This usage of *dagesh* is more widespread in the Babylonian vocalization.

As is the case with the accent signs, the vocalization signs are a written notation that was developed by the Masoretes to record a reading tradition. It is not possible to establish exactly when the vocalization and accent signs were created. Neither the vocalization signs nor, as we have seen, the accent signs are mentioned in Talmudic literature or in other sources from the first half of the first millennium CE. Jerome (346–420 CE) expressly states that the Jews do not use signs to denote the vowels. In the earliest Masoretic codices datable to the ninth century, however, the notation of the vocalization and accents is fully developed, so the first stages of its development are likely to have taken place at least a century earlier.

In the time of the Tiberian Masoretes and also for a certain period after their activities ceased both the Tiberian sign system and the Tiberian reading tradition were regarded as authoritative. The form of sign system that became standardized represents a fixed stage in the development of the notation. Some extant manuscripts with non- standard Tiberian vocalization preserve more primitive stages of its development and others exhibit more developed stages. In the standard Tiberian system a vestige of a more primitive stage of development can be identified in the vocalization of the *qere* (what is read) of the tetragrammaton (*yhwh*) with *shewa* on the *aleph* of *'adonai.* One can compare this to the continuing use of the early Hebrew script to write the tetragrammaton in Qumran manuscripts that are otherwise written in square script (see above).

The other vocalization systems (Babylonian and Palestinian) exhibit various degrees of assimilation to the Tiberian system in the extant manuscripts. The Hebrew grammarians in the tenth and eleventh centuries, and also other learned scholars, all followed the Tiberian vocalization and the Tiberian reading tradition, which it reflected, whether they were resident in Palestine, Iraq, North Africa, or Spain. The Tiberian vocalization system soon became the standard one and replaced all other systems in the transmission of the Bible. The transmission of the Tiberian reading tradition, on the other hand, soon came to an end. It is not completely clear why this happened. For one or two generations after the last Masoretes teachers of the Tiberian reading tradition could still be found in Palestine, but not, it seems, in all Jewish communities. The Spanish grammarian Ibn Janaḥ (eleventh century) expressed regret that in Spain there were no traditional readers and teachers (*ruwat wa-'asḥab al-talqin*) with a first hand knowledge of the Tiberian reading. The reading tradition may have become extinct through lack of trained teachers. Whereas the signs of the vocalization system could be copied by any scribe in any community, the oral transmission of the reading which depended on a small circle of teachers could not keep abreast of the large expansion of the transmission of the written Tiberian tradition in manuscripts throughout the Jewish world. As a result, the Tiberian vocalization signs came to be read according to the various local traditions of Hebrew pronunciation, most of them heavily influenced by the vernacular languages of the communities concerned. It is only recently, by studying previously neglected medieval sources, that we have been able to reconstruct the original Tiberian reading tradition. This does not correspond to the descriptions that are found in modern textbooks of biblical Hebrew, all of which present a form of pronunciation that was not that of the Tiberian Masoretes.

In a large number of places the reading tradition that is reflected by the vocalization does not correspond to the consonantal text. In the majority of cases the divergence relates to the pronunciation of single vowels in a single word. Sometimes there is a difference in the whole word, as in 2 Kings 20: 4 where 'the city' is written and 'court' is read, or the division of words. In a few isolated cases the discrepancy amounts to omissions or additions of words or phrases, as in Jeremiah 31: 38 where 'behold days' is written and 'behold days are coming' is read. The Masoretes indicated in their marginal notes the places where these discrepancies occurred. There are approximately 1,500 of these notes. Some elements of the consonantal text are regularly read in a way that does not correspond to what is written. These are not marked in the Masoretic notes. The most common word where this occurs is the tetragrammaton (*yhwh*), which is read either as *'adonai* (my Lord) or as *'elohim* (God). It also applies to the reading of some elements of morphology. The regular discrepancy between the written form of 'Jerusalem' (*yrwshlm*) and the reading tradition with final *-ayim* is likewise a morphological difference.

There is no uniform trend in the deviations of the reading tradition from the consonantal text. In a few isolated cases the reading tradition replaces possibly offensive words with a euphemism; for example, 1 Samuel 5: 9 *ketiv*: 'haemorrhoids' (the meaning is not completely certain), *qere*: 'tumours'. The avoidance of pronouncing the tetragrammaton, moreover, is presumably theologically motivated. In the vast majority of cases, however, the *qere* does not appear to be an intentional change of the written text.

The most satisfactory explanation for this phenomenon is that the reading was a separate layer of tradition that was closely related to, but nevertheless independent from, the tradition of the consonantal text. Contrary to a view that is still widely held today, the reading tradition was not a medieval creation of the Masoretes but was an ancient tradition that the Masoretes recorded by their notation system. This tradition had been faithfully passed on orally from teacher to pupil over many generations. There is no evidence that the Masoretes reformed the reading tradition and felt free to introduce exegetical or linguistic innovations of their own.

In the discussion of the history of the reading tradition we should distinguish its textual form from its linguistic form. There is evidence that both of these aspects have ancient roots. The textual differences between the reading and the written text are referred to in Talmudic literature. Some of the Qumran scrolls from the Second Temple period have in a number of places the text of the Tiberian *qere*. One may trace back the text of *qere* forms even further, into the period of literary growth of the biblical books. This is shown by the fact that the *ketiv* of the text of Chronicles often corresponds to the *qere* of its earlier biblical source. An example of this is the word *migrasheha*, 'its surrounding pasture-lands', which is used in association with the lists of Levitical cities in Joshua 21 and 1 Chronicles 6. The Chronicler is clearly using the text of Joshua 21 as his literary source. In the original text in Joshua the word is always written as a singular form but it is read in the reading tradition as a plural. This reflects a later interpretation of an originally singular form as a plural. This 'later' interpretation, however, is no later than the consonantal text of Chronicles, where it is written as a plural. Even if we do not attribute this interpretation to the author of the Chronicles passage, there are good grounds for arguing that the text of the reading tradition of Joshua 21 is as old as the consonantal text of 1 Chronicles 6. Linguistic features of the Tiberian reading tradition that differ from what is represented in the consonantal text are reflected by some Qumran manuscripts. This is seen, for example, in the form of some of the pronominal suffixes.

As we have seen, in the Middle Ages various ways of pronouncing biblical Hebrew are reflected in different systems of vocalization. The Tiberian, Babylonian, and Palestinian systems of vocalization not only use different sets of signs but also reflect clearly distinct forms of pronunciation. Indeed in manuscripts within the Babylonian and Palestinian systems one can identify several varieties of pronunciation. In addition to these three traditions of pronunciation, there is the Samaritan tradition, which was not recorded in written notation but has been passed down orally. Although the Tiberian, Babylonian, and Palestinian systems differ from one another, it is clear that they are closely related in comparison with the Samaritan pronunciation of Hebrew, which is significantly different from all three. We can identify two broad streams of pronunciation tradition, the Samaritan and the non-Samaritan. The close relationship of the Babylonian reading tradition with the Tiberian and Palestinian could be explained as a result of its being transferred from Palestine to Babylonia by Jewish scholars after the Bar-Kochba revolt. These Palestinian scholars also established the first rabbinic academies in Babylonia at this time. Similarly the official Targumim of Onqelos and Jonathan appear to have been transferred from Palestine to Babylonia in the same period.

A number of the differences within the non-Samaritan group appear to have arisen through the influence of the vernacular languages. This applies especially to the Palestinian pronunciation, which exhibits many features that are characteristic of Aramaic, the vernacular of the Jews for most of the first millennium CE. A number of Aramaic features can also be identified in the Babylonian pronunciation of Hebrew, though it appears that it differed from contemporary vernacular Aramaic in a number of ways and was a conservative tradition. The Tiberian system appears to have been very conservative and was relatively unaf-

Fragment of Numbers 11 with Babylonian vocalization, from the Cairo Genizah (10th–11th centuries CE).

fected by vernacular influence. The greater concern for conservatism in the Tiberian and Babylonian traditions is reflected by the fact that a corpus of detailed Masoretic annotations was developed by the Masoretes of Tiberias and Babylonia, but manuscripts with Palestinian vocalization exhibit only sporadic marginal notes, mainly concerning *qere* and *ketiv*. We may compare this to the varying degrees of conservativeness in the transmission of the Aramaic Targumim. Targum Onqelos of the Pentateuch preserves a form of literary Aramaic that was used in Palestine at the beginning of the first millennium CE. The text of this Targum was stable in the Middle Ages and Masoretic notes were developed to ensure its accurate transmission. The so-called Palestinian Targumim, on the other hand, reworked earlier Targumic traditions in the vernacular Aramaic of Palestine. Their text was by no means fixed and so no Masoretic notes were developed in association with their transmission. Another feature that reflects the concern for accurate transmission is the fact that the Tiberian Masoretic tradition developed a full system of vocalization, in which every word and virtually every letter had its vocalization sign, even if this denoted zero (*shewa*). Manuscripts with Babylonian and Palestinian vowel signs do not exhibit such a consistently full system. This especially applies to Palestinian vocalization, which is generally marked only sporadically on isolated words.

It was no doubt for this reason that in the Middle Ages the Tiberian reading tradition was the preserve of a small number of scholars who had received special training. The Palestinian pronunciation, which was close to the Aramaic vernacular, was far more widespread. The Sephardi pronunciation traditions of Hebrew, which are still followed today in many of the eastern Jewish communities, are derived historically from Palestinian pronunciation. The Babylonian pronunciation, which was also more widespread in the medieval Jewish communities than Tiberian pronunciation, has survived down to the present day in the reading traditions of the Yemenite Jews.

We have already discussed the evidence for the existence in the Second Temple period of certain textual and linguistic elements of the Tiberian reading tradition that differ from the consonantal text. The linguistic features in the Qumran manuscripts that correspond to the Tiberian reading tradition indicate that these features were not introduced into the reading tradition in the Middle Ages. There is also evidence that the Tiberian reading tradition resisted the influence of the Aramaic vernacular during its transmission in the first millennium CE. This is seen clearly in the reading tradition of the Aramaic portions of the Bible. In numerous places the reading tradition of biblical Aramaic reflects a different morphology from that of the consonantal text. This reflects the independence of the two traditions. The Aramaic morphology of the reading tradition, however, is not the same as the morphology of Jewish Palestinian Aramaic, the dialect that was spoken by Jews in Palestine throughout the Byzantine and early Arab period, but has earlier roots. Jewish Palestinian Aramaic was spoken by the Masoretes during most of the Masoretic period so this is evidence that the Tiberian reading tradition was not influenced by the vernacular speech of its transmitters. Indeed there are features of non-Semitic pronunciation in loanwords from non-Semitic languages that were preserved from the original period of composition right down to the period of the Masoretes, centuries after contact of the transmitters of the tradition with the source language had ceased. This demonstrates the incredible conservatism of the Tiberian reading tradition.

We have seen that some linguistic features of the Tiberian reading tradition are attested in the Qumran manuscripts. However, Qumran sources also reflect various features of phonology and morphology that are alien to the Tiberian tradition. This applies also to the reading tradition of Hebrew reflected in transcriptions of Hebrew words (mainly proper nouns) that are found in the Septuagint. Some of the distinctive linguistic features of the Samaritan tradition can be traced back to the Second Temple period.

During the Second Temple period, therefore, there were a variety of reading traditions of the Hebrew Bible which differed from one another both linguistically and also textually. The lack of correspondence of some forms of pronunciation with the Tiberian reading tradition should not lead us to conclude that the Tiberian tradition is a later development. There is evidence of the extreme conservatism of the Tiberian tradition and it is likely that a form of pronunciation that is very close to the Tiberian tradition existed in Second Temple times side by side with other traditions of pronunciation. The fact that transcriptions in the Septuagint, for example, often have an *a* vowel in an unstressed closed syllable (e.g. *Mariam*) where in Tiberian Hebrew it has developed into an *i* (*Miryam*) should not be interpreted as demonstrating the *chronological* antecedence of the Septuagint reading tradition, although it may reflect *typologically* an earlier stage of development. It is relevant to take into account that in the development of the dialects of a language some dialects may be more conservative of earlier linguistic features than other dialects spoken at the same period. Some features in the transcriptions of the Septuagint and other early sources that differ from Tiberian phonology can, in fact, be explained as the result of influence from the Aramaic vernacular, which was resisted by the standard Tiberian tradition. Likewise, where the Qumran biblical scrolls reflect a different pronunciation from the Tiberian one, it should not be assumed that the Tiberian is a later development. Some Qumran scrolls that are written according to the Qumran scribal practice, for instance, exhibit a weakening of the guttural consonants, whereas these are stable in the Tiberian tradition. It is clear that the Qumran scribes were influenced by vernacular pronunciation whereas the Tiberian tradition is conservative and has preserved the original distinction between the guttural letters.

Similarly, where the reading tradition of the consonantal text reflected by the Septuagint differs textually from the Tiberian, it does not necessarily follow that the Septuagint tradition is the original one and the Tiberian is a later development. There is, in fact, considerable textual agreement between the vocalization reflected by the Septuagint and the Tiberian one. This shows that there must have been a large degree of continuity in the reading tradition. The places where the vocalization adopted by the Septuagint translator differs from the Tiberian tradition can in some cases be shown to be the result of uncertainty and conjecture and so the Tiberian vocalization, although later, would preserve the older, more accurate tradition.

The precise relationship of the Tiberian tradition with the Babylonian and Palestinian traditions is not completely clear. There was a complicated web of relations between the traditions of reading the Hebrew Bible in the Second Temple period, just as there was between the various forms of the consonantal text of the Bible. As remarked above, the Babylonian and Palestinian reading traditions are more closely related linguistically to the Tiberian than to the Samaritan, yet some linguistic features of the reading tradition reflected by the Septuagint transcriptions are found in the Babylonian traditions but not in the Tiberian.

As remarked above, the Tiberian vocalization marks syntactic divisions by distinctive pausal forms of words. In the majority of cases the occurrence of these pausal forms correspond to the divisions expressed by the accents. In a few cases, however, they conflict with the accents, for example, in Deuteronomy 6: 7 ('when you sit in your house and when you go on the road'). Here a pausal form occurs on 'in your house' but according to the accents the major pause should occur on

An Arabic transcription of Exodus 1: 22 to 2: 5 from the Hebrew Bible, written in the 11th century by a Karaite scribe. The Karaites were a group within Judaism.

'on the road' not on 'in your house'. Note also Deuteronomy 5: 14 'you, your son, your daughter, and your maidservant', where a pausal form occurs even with a conjunctive accent ('and your daughter'). Cases such as these suggest that the tradition of vocalization and the tradition of accents were independent from each other to some extent. We see, therefore, that the vocalization tradition is a layer of tradition that is not only separate from the consonantal text but also from the accents. So the reading tradition, which includes both vocalization and accents, comprises two separate layers.

The separateness of the reading tradition from the tradition of the consonantal text is reflected in the fact that in the Talmudic period different exegesis was applied to each layer. Some of the rabbis followed the principle that both the consonantal text and the reading tradition were authoritative sources. Rabbinic literature contains numerous examples of a different interpretation being made of the two levels of the text. This is also reflected in the rabbinic form of exegesis that is expressed by the formula *'al tiqre ... 'ella* 'do not read ... but ...'. The purpose is probably to express an interpretation of the consonantal text that differs from the reading tradition rather than to record a variant reading tradition. It is not clear how far back this exegetical practice can be traced.

Another sign of the independence of the reading tradition from the written transmission is the existence of transcriptions of the reading tradition into other alphabets. We have seen that in the Middle Ages the Karaite Jews transcribed the reading of the Hebrew Bible into Arabic script. They also occasionally transcribed the Hebrew of the Mishnah and other rabbinic literature, which themselves had an orally transmitted reading tradition, but never medieval Hebrew texts such as legal texts or Bible commentaries that had no reading tradition and circulated only in written form. At an earlier period the reading tradition of the Hebrew Bible was represented in Greek transcription. The clearest evidence for this is the second column of Origen's Hexapla, which contained a full Greek transcription of the reading of the Hebrew text. From internal evidence it appears that this transcription was taken from an earlier source datable to no later than the first century CE. Similar transcriptions of the reading tradition may have been used by Greek-speaking Jews in the Second Temple period, although there is no direct evidence to substantiate this hypothesis.

The recitation of the Hebrew Bible in Jewish worship is presented as an established custom in the New Testament (Luke 4: 16ff., Acts 15: 21). It is mentioned by Philo (*c.*20 BCE–50 CE) and Josephus (first century CE) and is likely to go back several centuries earlier. Public reading of the Pentateuch (or parts of it) is referred to in the Bible (Deut. 31: 9–11, Neh. 8: 1–8). It can be argued that the very existence of Bible manuscripts implies the contemporary practice of public recitation, since in the Second Temple period a large proportion of the Jewish population must have been illiterate. We have seen that the consonantal text of the Tiberian Masoretic tradition can be traced back to the earliest attested manuscripts from the Second Temple period (third century BCE) and, on the basis of orthography, can be carried back further, possibly to the time of Ezra. Rabbinic

A page from the Aleppo Codex showing Proverbs 5: 18 to 6: 31. The Masoretic notes can be clearly seen in the margins.

traditions concerning the recitation with accents are linked to Ezra. In the introduction to the medieval treatise *Hidāyat al-Qāri* ('The guide for the reader'), the transmission of the Tiberian reading tradition is traced back to Ezra. These statements should, of course, be approached with caution and they cannot be verified. It is clear, however, that the Tiberian reading tradition has ancient roots. When the proto-Masoretic consonantal text was fixed it was already corrupted by scribal errors. It reflected, moreover, literary recensions of some of the biblical books that were different from what is found in other transmissions. In most cases the Tiberian reading tradition has been adapted to the words in the consonantal text that have been corrupted by earlier scribes. The reading tradition, furthermore, although deviating from the consonantal text in some places, does not reflect a radically different literary recension. On these grounds the reading tradition is unlikely to be older than the period in which the proto-Masoretic consonantal text was fixed. A number of linguistic features suggest that the vocalization should not be dated to an earlier period. Some archaic forms of Hebrew morphology that are preserved in the consonantal text, for instance, are harmonized in the vocalization to the standard form, which is reflected by the majority of the consonantal text. Furthermore, judging by north-west Semitic epigraphy from the beginning of the first millennium BCE, final case vowels were still in use in Canaanite languages in the period when the earliest biblical passages were composed, but these do not appear in the vocalization. It should be taken into account, however, that some of the later biblical books were probably composed after the process of fixing the proto-Masoretic text had started. Linguistic differences between these compositions and the earlier books are clearly reflected by the consonantal text. There is also some evidence that the historical layering is reflected by differences in the vocalization, and that in the main the linguistic roots of the vocalization of the Bible are in the Second Temple period.

Exegetical alterations can be found in the reading tradition, just as they can in the proto-Masoretic consonantal text. Examples of this practice are cases where an original expression of 'seeing the face of God' is changed into the theologically more acceptable 'appearing before God' by reading the verb as a *niph'al* (passive) rather than as a *qal* (active), for example Deuteronomy 16: 'Three times a year all your males shall appear before the Lord, your God.' This change is clear where the verb is an infinitive and it lacks the expected initial *he* of the *niph'al* form in the consonantal text, for example, 'When you go up to appear before the Lord, your God.' This change in the reading tradition is reflected already in the translation of the Septuagint and the Targumim, which demonstrates that it has ancient roots.

The proto-Masoretic manuscripts from Qumran exhibit a basically homogeneous text, but are by no means identical in all details. The text of the reading tradition that became accepted as the standard can be regarded as an oral form of a proto-Masoretic text which differed in some details from the written form that became standardized. The linguistic form (phonology and morphology) of the reading tradition is likely to represent one of various types that existed in the Second Temple period.

יהי מקורך ברוך ושמח מאשת נעורך
אילת אהבים ויעלת חן דדיה ירוך בכל
עת באהבתה תשגה תמיד ולמה
תשגה בני בזרה ותחבק חק נכריה
כי נכח עיני יהוה דרכי איש וכל
מעגלתיו מפלס עוונתיו ילכדנו
את הרשע ובחבלי חטאתו יתמך
הוא ימות באין מוסר וברב אולתו ישגה

בני אם ערבת לרעך תקעת לזר כפיך
נוקשת באמרי פיך נלכדת באמרי פיך
עשה זאת אפוא בני והנצל כי באת
בכף רעך לך התרפס ורהב רעיך
אל תתן שנה לעיניך ותנומה לעפעפיך
הנצל כצבי מיד וכצפור מיד יקוש

לך אל נמלה עצל ראה דרכיה וחכם
אשר אין לה קצין שטר ומשל
תכין בקיץ לחמה אגרה בקציר מאכלה
עד מתי עצל תשכב מתי תקום
משנתך מעט שנות מעט תנומות
מעט חבק ידים לשכב ובא
כמהלך ראשך ומחסרך כאיש מגן

אדם בליעל איש און הולך עקשות פה
קרץ בעינו מלל ברגלו מרה באצבעתיו
תהפכות בלבו חרש רע בכל עת
מדנים ישלח על כן פתאם יבוא אידו

פתע ישבר ואין מרפא

שש הנה שנא יהוה ושבע תועבת
נפשו עינים רמות לשון שקר
וידים שפכות דם נקי לב חרש
מחשבות און רגלים ממהרות לרוץ
לרעה יפיח כזבים עד שקר
ומשלח מדנים בין אחים

נצר בני מצות אביך ואל תטש
תורת אמך קשרם על לבך תמיד
ענדם על גרגרתך בהתהלכך
תנחה אתך בשכבך תשמר עליך
והקיצות היא תשיחך כי נר מצוה
ותורה אור ודרך חיים תוכחות מוסר
לשמרך מאשת רע מחלקת לשון
נכריה אל תחמד יפיה בלבבך
ואל תקחך בעפעפיה כי בעד
אשה זונה עד ככר לחם ואשת
איש נפש יקרה תצוד

היחתה איש אש בחיקו ובגדיו
לא תשרפנה אם יהלך איש
על הגחלים ורגליו לא תכוינה
כן הבא אל אשת רעהו לא ינקה
כל הנגע בה לא יבוזו לגנב כי
יגנוב למלא נפשו כי ירעב
ונמצא ישלם שבעתים את כל הון

MASORETIC NOTES AND TREATISES

The Tiberian Masoretic tradition included the writing of notes in the margins of the Bible codices. The purpose of these was to ensure the accurate transmission of the text. The notes belong to various categories. Some of these have been mentioned already in the preceding discussion. The majority relate to the orthography of the consonantal text, with special attention to the use of vowel letters. The orthographical notes are statistical in form; thus Amos 9: 9 *yippol* (shall fall); Masoretic note: '[this word occurs] seven times spelled *plene*' (i.e. fully). One of the most common notes states simply that the form, at least in the orthography in which it occurs, is unique in the Bible ('there is no [other form]'). Sometimes the note includes information on closely related forms to avoid confusion; thus 1 Chronicles 8: 6 *'eḥud*; Masoretic note: 'Unique, elsewhere in the Bible *'ehud* (with *he* not *ḥet*) is used'. The notes also give statistical information about the combinations of words, vocalization, accents, and forms that are unusual from the point of view of syntax or spelling. These types of notes are all written in the side margins of the text in abbreviated form (known as the Masorah Parva). At the top and bottom of the page further notes are given (known as the Masorah Magna) that elaborate on the abbreviated notes by giving the references by key words to the verses that are included in the statistics.

In medieval Palestine the reading of the Pentateuch in the liturgy was completed in a three-year cycle. For this purpose the Pentateuch was divided into 154 (according to some traditions 167) weekly portions known as *sedarim*. The beginning of these *sedarim* are marked in the early Tiberian manuscripts from Palestine. In Babylonia the reading of the Pentateuch was completed in a year by dividing it into 54 portions. There is evidence that the custom of the one-year cycle of reading also had Palestinian roots. This would support the view expressed above that the Babylonian reading tradition is closely related to the Tiberian and Palestinian ones. In the later Middle Ages the Babylonian practice of a one-year cycle of reading became the standard one in Judaism.

The Masoretic notes contain general statistical information concerning the number of verses, words, and letters in the whole Bible and also the middle word and the middle letter of books, the Pentateuch, and the Bible as a whole. These were added at the end of the texts concerned, together with other lists, in what is known as the Masorah Finalis. The purpose of this was to prevent the additions or omissions of words or even letters in the standard text.

Other items that were incorporated into the Masoretic notes include indications where the *qere* differs from the *ketiv*, the so-called *sevirin* (cases where a different text might be erroneously supposed—see above), differences between 'the Easterners' (Babylonians) and the 'Westerners' (Tiberians), and differences between various streams in the Tiberian Masoretic tradition. There are also references to 'corrections of the scribes' (*tiqqune soferim*) and 'omissions of the scribes' (*'iṭṭur soferim*), which were incorporated into the Masorah from earlier Talmudic traditions. The references to differences between *qere* and *ketiv* and the gathering of statistical information concerning the biblical text are also mentioned in Talmudic literature. According to the Babylonian Talmud (Kiddushin 30a) the *soferim*, the forebears of the Masoretes, acquired their name from the fact that they counted (Hebrew *spr*) all the letters of the Pentateuch. Indeed, as is shown by the translation of the word in Ezek. 20: 37 by the Greek Septuagint as 'number', the term *masoret* was probably originally understood in the sense of 'counting'. This connection with the Talmudic interpretation of the term *soferim* may be more than coincidental, in that *masoret* may have been intended originally to refer to the activity of the *soferim*. Most of the elements of the Masoretic notes, in fact, can be traced back to traditions that predate the Masoretic period. The language of the Masoretic notes is also indicative of their date. The majority are in Jewish Palestinian Aramaic, which was the vernacular of Jews in the Byzantine and early Arab period. A few isolated terms in the notes are in Hebrew. Some of these may be of Mishnaic origin; others appear to belong to a late layer of tradition datable to the ninth or early tenth century. At this later period the Masoretes used Hebrew also in independent treatises.

The Masoretic notes complemented the other components of the Tiberian Masoretic tradition yet they had a certain independence of transmission, in that the notes in a manuscript did not always correspond to the text, vocalization, and

Fragment from the Masoretic treatise *Sefer Okhlah we-Okhlah.*

accents that were copied in the same manuscript. The notes were incorporated into a printed edition in full for the first time in the sixteenth-century Second Rabbinic Bible edited by Jacob ben Hayyim.

In the late Masoretic period (ninth–tenth centuries CE) independent Masoretic treatises were written. These systematized the information dispersed in the marginal notes and also expanded on them. One of these, *Diqduqe ha-ṭeʿamim* 'The fine rules of the accents', is attributed to Aharon ben Asher. Most, however, are anonymous. Sometimes they are attached to the end of Bible manuscripts and other times are written separately. One of the longest is *Okhlah we-Okhlah*, which is a series of lists of various contents, including pairs of words differing from each other in one detail. By the beginning of the eleventh century, Masoretic treatises were written in Arabic, for example *Kitab al-Khulaf*, 'The book of differences [between Ben Asher and Ben Naphtali]' by Misha'el ben 'Uzzi'el and a treatise on the *shewa*. Some of these later treatises were not written by Masoretes themselves, for example *Hidāyat al-Qāri* 'The guide for the reader', which was a work by the eleventh-century Karaite 'Abu al-Faraj Harun.

One of the ways in which the Masoretic activity was expanded in this period was in the development of grammatical analysis, the rudiments of which are found in some Masoretic texts that are appended to Bible manuscripts and in works containing grammatical notes on the biblical text. After the end of the Masoretic period Hebrew grammatical thought was developed further as a separate discipline.

CONCLUDING REMARKS

In the foregoing discussion, we have examined the components of the Tiberian Masoretic tradition. These consist of the Tiberian reading tradition and six written components. The written components were transmitted by scribes but the Tiberian reading tradition was soon forgotten and the Tiberian Masoretic text was read in Jewish communities with other reading traditions.

The written components, apart from the Masoretic treatises and the Masoretic notes, represent ancient traditions that can be traced back hundreds of years before the Masoretes into the Second Temple period. Some elements of the Masoretic notes can be traced to the Talmudic period. The various components constituted closely related but to some extent independent layers of tradition which were not completely harmonized with each other.

5 The Apocrypha

PHILIP DAVIES

THE APOCRYPHA AS A WHOLE

Fragments of the Old Latin translation of Ezekiel as discovered in the binding of another codex. The translation originates from North Italy in the 5th century.

The existence of an 'Apocrypha' arises mainly from the presence in one or more of the earliest Greek biblical codices (Alexandrinus, Sinaiticus, Vaticanus) of a number of books whose absence from the Jewish scriptural canon led Jerome to omit them at first from his translation into Latin (the Vulgate) as undeserving of canonical status. Subsequently he, or others, supplied translations from the Greek. The one complete exception is 2 Esdras/4 Ezra, which is in none of the ancient Greek Bibles, and the Prayer of Manasses constitutes a semi-exception, since it is not included in them as an independent book.

However, the contents of Latin Bibles have fluctuated over the centuries, and their contents did not necessarily correspond over time exactly to those of the Greek Bibles (which, in any case, did not preserve exactly the same list of books). Thus, it is not the case that the 'Apocrypha', effectively created as a category by Protestants, simply embraces those books in a Greek Bible but not a Hebrew one. However, that is effectively how the contents of the Apocrypha originated.

The books of the Apocrypha derive immediately from Greek texts. However, while in some cases Greek is the original language, in some a translation from another language is either known or suspected to have occurred. Even where Greek is the original language, we do not necessarily have only one Greek text form, let alone identical Greek texts, thanks to the process of continual copying and sometimes deliberate revision. Hence most of the books of the Apocrypha have an interesting textual history of their own, and it is therefore necessary to examine them individually.

1 ESDRAS

This book is confusingly known as 1 Esdras or Esdras A in the Greek Bibles (Esdras is the Greek spelling of Ezra), as well as in the Old Latin and the Syriac. But in the Vulgate it is named 3 Esdras. Of the early Greek texts, that which is preserved in Codex Alexandrinus is generally agreed to be the best of those preserved.

1 Esdras is unique in being only *partly* a translation of a Hebrew book. 1: 1–2: 15 is clearly a translation of 2 Chronicles 35: 1–36: 23, 1 Esdras 2: 16–30 a translation of Ezra 4: 7–24, and Esdras 5: 7–9: 55 a translation of Ezra 2: 1–10: 44 (with the omission of Ezra 4: 6–23), plus Nehemiah 7: 73–8: 12. But there it ends in the middle of a sentence! The material in 1 Esdras 3: 1–5: 6, containing the story of Darius' bodyguards, is, on the other hand, entirely new.

What, then, is the relationship of the book to its biblical counterparts? It cannot simply be assumed that the biblical texts are the more original and that 1 Esdras has inserted a new tale from somewhere into the middle of a Greek translation. In any case, there is a (rather inelegant) Greek translation of Ezra itself (Esdras B) in the Greek Old Testament, which is different and follows the contents of the Hebrew/Aramaic. And in any case, 1 Esdras is not based exactly, as is the Greek translation of Ezra, on the received Hebrew/Aramaic Masoretic text.

Perhaps 1 Esdras reflects a quite early form of the material. It has been argued that the order of the material in 1 Esdras is more logical, providing a continuous account of Ezra's mission by leaving out Nehemiah 1–7. This might point to harmonizing revisions, but equally to an early version of an Ezra story. The fact that the historian Josephus at the end of the first century CE used 1 Esdras rather than the biblical Ezra-Nehemiah may suggest that the biblical form of these books was not necessarily the standard edition in his own day. Challenges to the once widely held view that Chronicles-Ezra-Nehemiah was composed as a single work have complicated the picture further: the suggestion that 1 Esdras is a truncated version of the entire 'Chronicler's work' is now less plausible.

Thus, it remains possible that the author of 1 Esdras wished to create an 'Ezra story' from the biblical material. Yet most scholars agree that Nehemiah 8 once belonged to Ezra, and it has been argued recently that Ezra and Nehemiah were once quite separate books before being artificially and clumsily united—so that 1 Esdras might well preserve a more original state of affairs than the biblical versions.

The view of most modern scholars is that 1 Esdras and the biblical Ezra-Nehemiah both go back to a common prototype. But that prototype may well have been an early form of a book of Ezra, independent of Nehemiah, which diverged into a form that was combined with a Nehemiah story to form the biblical Ezra-Nehemiah, and into another form later translated as 1 Esdras.

2 ESDRAS

2 Esdras is also, and less confusingly, known as 4 Ezra (its Vulgate designation), since the name 2 Esdras in the old Greek Bibles and in the Vulgate denotes the book of Nehemiah. Originally composed in either Hebrew or Aramaic by a Jew, it was translated into Greek, but neither the original nor the Greek has survived. Instead, it was translated, from the Greek, into a number of languages including Latin, from which it was taken into the Vulgate, as well as being translated further into other languages. But even the translations from Greek fall into two textual traditions: Latin and Syriac represent one and Ethiopic, Georgian, and Coptic another.

TITLES GIVEN TO BOOKS ASSOCIATED WITH EZRA (AND NEHEMIAH) IN SELECTED VERSIONS

Document	Old Testament book of Ezra	Old Testament book of Nehemiah	Paraphrase of 2 Chronicles chs. 35–6, the whole book of Ezra; Nehemiah 7: 38–8: 12; Plus a tale about Darius' bodyguards	A Latin Apocalypse
Septuagint	2 Esdras		1 Esdras	
Latin Vulgate	1 Esdras	2 Esdras	3 Esdras	4 Esdras
Many later Latin manuscripts	1 Esdras		3 Esdras	2 Esdras = chs. 1–2 4 Esdras = chs. 3–14 5 Esdras = chs. 15–16
Great Bible (1539) Douai Bible (1609–1610)	1 Esdras	2 Esdras	3 Esdras	4 Esdras
Russian Bible, Moscow Patriarchate (1956)	1 Esdras	Nehemiah	2 Esdras	3 Esdras
Geneva Bible (1560) Bishops' Bible (1568) King James Version (1611) Revised Standard Version (1957)	The book of Ezra	The book of Nehemiah	1 Esdras	2 Esdras

Source: B. M. Metzger, 'The Fourth Book of Ezra', in J. H. Charlesworth, *Old Testament Pseudepigrapha* (New York: Doubleday, 1983), i. 516.

A further complication is that the original Jewish form of the book, dated to the end of the first century CE, consists only of chapters 3–14, since in its Greek form it was also expanded by one or more Christians adding an introduction (chs. 1–2) and an appendix (chs. 15 and 16). These extra sections have persisted into the Latin translation, though they were recognized as additions, and in some manuscripts named separately as 2 and 5 Esdras respectively, while some scholars refer to them as 5 Ezra and 6 Ezra!

The most recent phase in the book's history is the discovery in 1874 of a Latin text of the book containing an additional passage of 70 verses between 7: 35 and 7: 36, omitted from the King James version. This passage, present in many of the ancient translations and even in eighteenth-century English and American Bibles, was included in the Revised Version and all subsequent English Bibles; its verses are numbered 7: 36–105. Since this passage denies the value of prayers for the dead, it may have been deliberately removed from early Latin manuscripts.

WISDOM

One of the textually least problematic books in the Apocrypha, this work was originally composed in Greek, despite the occasional suggestion that it, or its first half, had been composed in Hebrew or Aramaic. The few traces of Semitisms indicate no more than a Jewish author echoing the phraseology of the scriptures.

SIRACH

The Wisdom of Jesus ben Sira ('Sirach' is the Greek name; 'ben Sirach' is incorrect), is a translation, as the prologue tells us, by his grandson of a work in Hebrew by Joshua ben Sira. Named simply 'Sirach' in the Greek Bibles, it was designated as 'Ecclesiasticus' (the church [book]) in the Vulgate, perhaps because of its use in Christian liturgy. The work was certainly known and respected by Jews, and is mentioned in the Mishnah and Talmud. But until the end of the nineteenth century no Hebrew text was known. In 1896 fragments of four (later identified as six) medieval Hebrew manuscripts of the work were found in a synagogue Genizah in Cairo. More recently, bits of Hebrew manuscripts of Ben Sira have been found at Qumran Cave 2 (2Q18) and at Masada. (Even more interestingly, Ben Sira 51: 13–20 is contained within the Qumran Psalms manuscript 11QPs[a].) These ancient fragments confirm that the medieval manuscripts are reliable copies of the earlier text. They also confirm that Ben Sira's grandson did not always translate correctly!

However, it seems likely from the evidence of the Greek versions that two basic forms of the Hebrew text may have once existed. The original was rendered by Ben Sira's grandson; an expanded form was later consulted by a Greek translator in revising the existing Greek translation. But, as is frequently the case of a much-copied work, the Greek manuscripts now available show a mixture of the two Greek forms.

Since a Latin translation of the work already existed (and probably he had no access to a Hebrew text), Jerome did not make a new translation of the book for the Vulgate. One curiosity of this Old Latin translation (made from the Greek) is that it preserves what we know to have been the original order, in which 33: 13b–36: 16a took the place of 30: 25–33: 1a and vice versa. All other extant Greek manuscripts (and thus all modern versions) have the altered sequence. The later Syriac translation was, as is often the case, made from the Hebrew but with reference to the Greek.

The result of this complicated history is that the Greek and Latin texts of Ben Sira are very corrupt, and the rediscovery of Hebrew manuscripts has made the task of textual criticism easier though still very far from simple.

ADDITIONS TO ESTHER

The 'Additions to Esther' are six passages included by the Jewish translator (second or first century BCE) of the text included in the Septuagint (preserved in Codex Vaticanus), and known as Greek B. The translator, incidentally, gives his name as Lysimachus in 11: 1 (this colophon is not reproduced in modern Bible translations). These additions, probably made to compensate for what were seen as theological defects in the story, are found in no extant Hebrew manuscript, and none of the later Jewish translations from the (by then) standardized (Masoretic) Hebrew text (those attributed to Aquila, Symmachus, and Theodotion) has them.

From this expanded Greek version of the book the Old Latin version was made. For the Vulgate, however, Jerome translated from the Hebrew, and gathered into an appendix the extra material he found in his Latin version, noting where in the story they belonged. Unfortunately, later scribes did not always notice Jerome's notes and simply copied the additional material as a (nonsensical) continuation of the story. Modern Bibles that include the Apocrypha as a supplementary section print these additions separately, but of course they make no sense apart from the rest of the book of Esther.

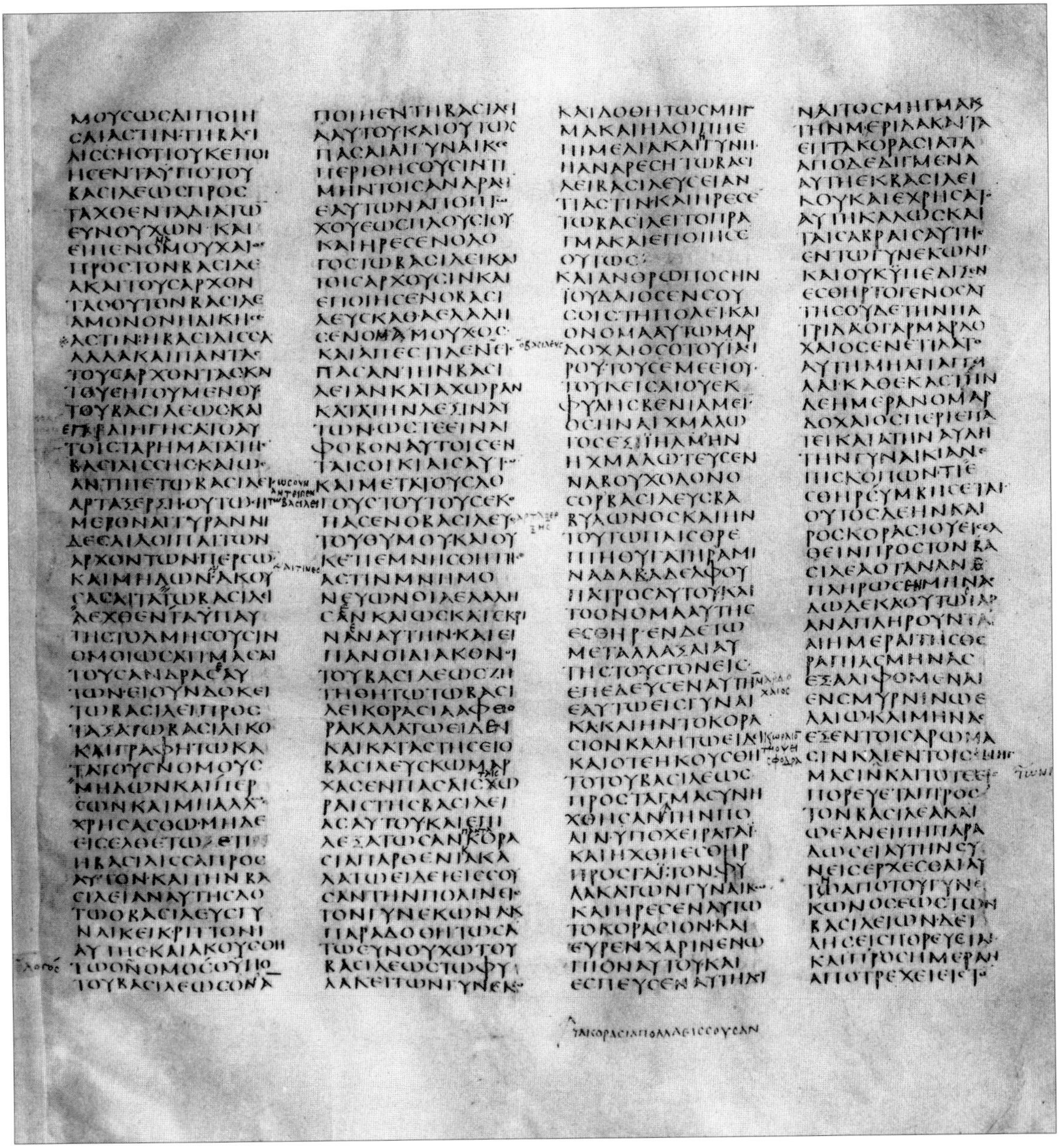

A page from Codex Sinaiticus of the Greek version of Esther, 1: 15 to 2: 14.

But although only the additions belong to the Apocrypha, their textual history cannot be fully explained without considering the history of Greek Esther as a whole. To begin with, additions B and E, comprising the edicts of Haman and Mordecai, and probably F, were created in Greek, but A and D are quite possibly translated from Hebrew or Aramaic, and may therefore have been in the translator's Hebrew text of Esther. The translation, then, cannot be simply regarded as Greek additions to the Hebrew text that we know. Furthermore, the Greek B translation attests numerous small differences, mostly omissions, in comparison with the received, Masoretic text of Esther. These are probably, though not certainly, due to stylistic considerations.

There also exists a second Greek version, known as the A text. It too contains the additions that the B text has. But scholars do not agree over whether this A text is a recension of the earlier B text or a new translation from Hebrew. It seems on the whole to be different, though the differences are much less in the additions. This leads one to suspect that the additions were taken into the A text from the B text, and not from a Hebrew text (and, as noted earlier, additions B and E never existed in Hebrew).

Clines has made the interesting suggestion that Esther A was made from a proto-Masoretic Hebrew, i.e. an ancestor of the received Hebrew text. He bases this conclusion largely on the ending of the A text, which is briefer than the Hebrew. It covers the events narrated in the 34 verses of the Hebrew (7: 9–9: 15) in only ten verses. Put simply, Clines believes that the ending of the Masoretic text has been expanded from an earlier Hebrew text from which Greek A was translated, and that Greek A, shorn of the additions, points us to the original form of the story. Clines's view opposes that of Tov, who regards Greek A as a recension of Greek B, which on balance is perhaps more convincing, though certainty is not possible.

These considerations do not affect the basic observation that the additions to Esther are all secondary to any *extant* Hebrew version. However, unlike the Greek additions to Daniel, the case of Greek Esther shows that the development of Greek and Hebrew texts of this admittedly late (second or first century BCE) narrative overlap chronologically to some extent, something that remains in principle a possibility for any biblical book, given what we now know from the Qumran scrolls about the flexibility of the Hebrew scriptural text.

JUDITH

The only textual issue in the book of Judith is the question of its original language: Aramaic or Hebrew? That the Greek displays a highly biblical style does not of itself indicate a Semitic original, but there are large number of constructions native to the Hebrew (not Aramaic) language and, more significantly, Moore has suggested a number of places where the Greek has misread a Hebrew word.

However, while the Old Latin and the other ancient versions are rendered from the Greek, Jerome's Vulgate translation is not from a Hebrew, but from an Aramaic text (with or without some reference to the Old Latin). Compared to the

Greek, it appears rather paraphrastic, but whether this is accounted for in Jerome's Aramaic source or in his own translation we cannot know; the former would seem more likely.

There are Hebrew versions of the story of Judith, but these are medieval translations from the Latin.

TOBIT

Before the discoveries at Qumran, opinion was divided on the original language of Tobit. The problem remains partly unresolved, since while the scrolls fairly clearly indicate a Semitic rather than a Greek original, their one Hebrew and four Aramaic manuscripts do not determine the issue any more precisely.

But there remain problems over the Greek version, of which there are two forms: a shorter, as preserved in Codex Vaticanus and Codex Alexandrinus, and a longer version, with some 1,700 words more, as in Codex Sinaiticus. (There is, in fact, a third form, known as Recension C, only partial but preserving a text that mixes the other two.) Modern English Bibles remain divided in their choice between the texts of Sinaiticus and the other two ancient Greek codices.

In general, textual criticism tends to favour a shorter rather than a longer text, since expansion is more common in transmission than compression. But this is only a general principle, and, while it was once applied to Tobit, recent opinion has moved in favour of the longer text as the more original. That judgement is apparently supported by the Qumran manuscripts, and certainly the longer recension underlies the Old Latin translation. Jerome, however, as he did in the case of Judith, adapted the Old Latin with reference to an Aramaic version which is no longer extant.

BARUCH

Baruch (also known as 1 Baruch) is contained in Codex Vaticanus and Codex Alexandrinus, as an appendix to the book of Jeremiah, immediately before Lamentations; Codex Sinaiticus omits it. It is also not included in the earliest manuscripts of the Vulgate, and Jerome commented that it was not read by Jews, and so would not make a fresh translation, leaving the Old Latin (translated from the Greek) to be included in later Vulgate Bibles.

The book is commonly divided by scholars into two (sometimes more) parts, possibly by different authors, and possibly in different original languages. Generally, the first part (1: 1–3: 8) is believed to have been composed in Hebrew, while on 3: 9–5: 9 there is no consensus. Thackeray argued that the Greek translator of Baruch 1: 1–3: 8 was the same as the second Greek translator of Jeremiah, who rendered chapters 29–51. More recently, Tov has suggested that Jeremiah 29–51 and Jeremiah 52 represent a revision of an older Greek translation, still preserved in Jeremiah 1–28. But in either case, whether Baruch 3: 9–5: 9 was ever a translation, rather than a Greek composition, remains disputed.

The story of how Daniel rescues Susanna from false accusations by two elders occurs in the Greek additions to the book of Daniel, and is here depicted by Albrecht Altdorfer in the painting entitled *Susanna in the Bath* (1526).

THE EPISTLE OF JEREMIAH

In codices Alexandrinus and Vaticanus, this follows Baruch as a kind of appendix to Jeremiah; like Baruch, it not was not originally included by Jerome, but the Old Latin translation was later incorporated into the Latin Bible. Again like Baruch, there is no Hebrew version extant, though a fragment of the Greek text has been found at Qumran Cave 7 (7Q2), a cave which contained only Greek manuscripts.

Scholars are divided on whether this work was translated from Hebrew or composed in Greek. Moore argues that because it alludes to a verse in the Hebrew book of Jeremiah but not the Greek (10: 5) its author knew a Hebrew rather than a Greek text of the book. He also points to several instances of alleged mistranslation. (Torrey had earlier argued for an Aramaic original.) All important ancient versions derive from the Greek, and the Semitic original, if there was one, remains elusive.

THE ADDITIONS TO DANIEL

As with Jeremiah and Esther, the ancient Greek translations reflect both a different Hebrew original from that preserved in the Masoretic text, and also additions originally composed in Greek, with only the major additions being later removed and assigned to an Apocrypha. Of these three additions, one, the 'Prayer of Azariah and the Three Young Men', belongs in the body of the book of Daniel (ch. 3), while the other two, Susanna and Bel and the Dragon (or Snake) are free-standing narratives.

As with Esther, there exist two ancient Greek translations of the biblical book: the Old Greek text, usually that found in the ancient codices (and previously referred to as the Septuagint version), and one assigned to Theodotion, which in this case has replaced it in these codices, and is used by most ancient versions.

As far as the Additions are concerned, both Greek translations have almost identical texts in the Prayer of Azariah, but they are different in Susanna and slightly different in Bel and the Dragon. How this is to be explained remains unclear. The Theodotion text of Susanna differs from the Old Greek first of all in its placement of the story within Daniel as a whole. In the Old Greek version it comes as chapter 13, after the end of the material in the Masoretic Daniel, while in Theodotion it comprises chapter 1. There are also a number of additions in Theodotion (e.g. vv. 11, 15–18, 20–1, 24–7, 46–7, 49–50) which perhaps enhance the tale. It is not clear how to explain these differences. Moore suggests that there was a different Semitic text available to each Greek translator, and because Theodotion exhibits more Hebraic Semitisms, perhaps an Aramaic for the Old Greek and a Hebrew for Theodotion (recall that there were manuscripts of Tobit in both Hebrew and Aramaic at Qumran). Milik has argued for Aramaic as the original language of the story. But the Theodotion translator must have had access to the Old Greek version, because there is so much verbal agreement

between the two and may even be regarded to some extent as a revision of the Old Greek (so Di Lella). The evidence for a Semitic original is thus substantial but not conclusive.

Bel and the Dragon (ch. 13 in the Old Greek and ch. 14 in Theodotion) actually comprises two stories, and in both parts the two Greek translations again differ. Again, as with Susanna, the explanation may be that each worked from a different Semitic text, perhaps a different Semitic language. Verbal agreement between the two Greek translations is evident only in vv. 23–4 and 33–9, raising the question of whether, or how, the later translation consulted the earlier.

As with Esther, the evidence of the Greek versions of Daniel may suggest that a Semitic version of the Daniel collection continued to expand beyond the stage represented by its canonized Masoretic form, before being rendered into Greek.

1 MACCABEES

Both Origen and Jerome knew that 1 Maccabees had been composed in Hebrew (Jerome saw a copy), but no Hebrew text has survived. The only preserved Greek translation is literal and contains several translation errors, and it is widely agreed that the Old Latin version was made from a different Greek rendering (Goldstein even suggests, perhaps too ambitiously, that the translators were able to consult the Hebrew).

2 MACCABEES

Unlike 1 Maccabees, this book was evidently composed in Greek. Both its language and style are thoroughly Greek in nature. Among the early Greek Bible codices, only Alexandrinus has preserved this book, while of the ancient versions, all made from a Greek text, the most important is the Old Latin. The Vulgate includes a Latin text older than Jerome, who obviously did not bother to translate it.

THE PRAYER OF MANASSES

The Prayer of Manasses (or 'Manasseh', the Hebrew form of the name) is represented in ancient Greek codices only by Alexandrinus, and then as part of an addendum to the psalms. Only in later Vulgate Bibles did it become attached to the end of 2 Chronicles (which mentions a prayer spoken by Manasseh, 33: 18–19). There are also several Syriac manuscripts of the prayer, but the brevity of the piece makes it difficult to decide what the relationship of the Syriac to the Greek text may be.

No Hebrew or Aramaic version of this prayer has been found; a fragment of a 'Prayer of Manasseh, king of Judah, when the king of Assyria imprisoned him' from Qumran Cave 4 is an entirely different composition. (So is the prayer of Manasseh mentioned in the pseudepigraphical work 2 Baruch 64–5.)

Nevertheless, a number of scholars maintain that it was originally composed in Hebrew rather than in Greek. In either event, it follows closely the traditional form of the Jewish penitential prayer and was obviously one of a number of ancient attempts to fill a perceived gap in the biblical record.

6 The New Testament

DAVID PARKER

Fifty generations separate the earliest Christian writers from the first printed Greek New Testaments of the sixteenth century; another seventeen stand between that epoch and our own. That first period consisted of a huge process of copyings, increasingly distant from the original texts. The second period has proved to be a reversal of that process. It is therefore possible to tell the two stories together, to describe the Greek manuscripts and the translations of the New Testament through the history of European scholarship.

SIXTEENTH-CENTURY SCHOLARSHIP AND ITS INFLUENCE

When the humanists of the Renaissance looked around them, they became critical of the dependence of western Christendom on the Latin Bible, the Vulgate. More and more, they studied Greek manuscripts and noted its differences from them. They concluded that, since the New Testament writings were first composed in Greek, these differences must necessarily be due to corruptions in the Latin. And so, in accordance with their general desire to rebuild on the Graeco-Roman foundations of our civilization, they wished to restore the Greek New Testament to its rightful place as the source and originator of the Latin text, and therefore its superior. The printing press was the means to this end. Although such ambitions were expressed in the fifteenth century, it was only in the second decade of the sixteenth that they were realized. Two editions claim the right of priority. The Complutensian Polyglot, produced at Alcalá in Spain, was the first text to be printed. Its New Testament volume, with the text in Greek, with a Graeco-Latin glossary, is dated 10 January 1514. But the Pope was slow to grant permission for its release, and the Dutchman Desiderius Erasmus decided to forestall it. With the Greek, his own text, and the Vulgate in parallel

Erasmus of Rotterdam (1466/9–1536), one of the pioneers of New Testament textual criticism, from the painting by Holbein.

A page from Erasmus's Greek New Testament of 1516, showing Luke 10: 16–30 alongside his Latin version of the same passage.

150 ΕΥΑΓΓΕΛΙΟΝ

ἀθετῶν ὑμᾶς, ἐμὲ ἀθετεῖ, ὁ δὲ ἐμὲ ἀθετῶν ἀθετεῖ τὸν ἀποστείλαντά με. ὑπέστρεψαν δὲ οἱ ἑβδομήκοντα μετὰ χαρᾶς λέγοντες, κύριε, καὶ τὰ δαιμόνια ὑποτάσσεται ἡμῖν ἐν τῷ ὀνόματί σου, εἶπεν δὲ αὐτοῖς. ἐθεώρουν τὸν σατανᾶν ὡς ἀστραπὴν ἐκ τοῦ οὐρανοῦ πεσόντα. ἰδοὺ δίδωμι ὑμῖν τὴν ἐξουσίαν τοῦ πατεῖν ἐπάνω ὄφεων καὶ σκορπίων καὶ ἐπὶ πᾶσαν τὴν δύναμιν τοῦ ἐχθροῦ, καὶ οὐδὲν ὑμᾶς οὐ μὴ ἀδικήσει. πλὴν ἐν τούτῳ μὴ χαίρετε, ὅτι τὰ πνεύματα ὑμῖν ὑποτάσσεται. χαίρετε δέ, ὅτι τὰ ὀνόματα ὑμῶν ἐγράφη ἐν τοῖς οὐρανοῖς. ἐν αὐτῇ τῇ ὥρᾳ ἠγαλλιάσατο τῷ πνεύματι ὁ ΙΗΣΟΥΣ, καὶ εἶπεν, ἐξομολογοῦμαί σοι πάτερ, κύριε τοῦ οὐρανοῦ καὶ τῆς γῆς, ὅτι ἀπέκρυψας ταῦτα ἀπὸ σοφῶν καὶ συνετῶν καὶ ἀπεκάλυψας αὐτὰ νηπίοις. ναὶ ὁ πατήρ, ὅτι οὕτως ἐγένετο εὐδοκία ἔμπροσθέν σου. πάντα παρεδόθη μοι ὑπὸ τοῦ πατρός μου, καὶ οὐδεὶς γινώσκει, τίς ἐστιν ὁ υἱός, εἰ μὴ ὁ πατήρ. καὶ τίς ἐστιν ὁ πατὴρ εἰ μὴ ὁ υἱός, καὶ ᾧ ἐὰν βούληται ὁ υἱὸς ἀποκαλύψαι. καὶ στραφεὶς πρὸς τοὺς μαθητὰς, κατ' ἰδίαν εἶπεν. μακάριοι οἱ ὀφθαλμοὶ οἱ βλέποντες ἃ ὑμεῖς βλέπετε. λέγω γὰρ ὑμῖν, ὅτι πολλοὶ προφῆται καὶ βασιλεῖς ἠθέλησαν ἰδεῖν ἃ ὑμεῖς βλέπετε καὶ οὐκ εἶδον, καὶ ἀκοῦσαι ἃ ἀκούετε, καὶ οὐκ ἤκουσαν. καὶ ἰδοὺ νομικός τις ἀνέστη ἐκπειράζων αὐτὸν καὶ λέγων. διδάσκαλε τί ποιήσας, ζωὴν αἰώνιον κληρονομήσω; ὁ δὲ εἶπεν πρὸς αὐτόν, ἐν τῷ νόμῳ τί γέγραπται; πῶς ἀναγινώσκεις; ὁ δὲ ἀποκριθείς, εἶπεν. ἀγαπήσεις κύριον τὸν θεόν σου ἐξ ὅλης τῆς καρδίας σου. καὶ ἐξ ὅλης τῆς ψυχῆς σου, καὶ ἐξ ὅλης τῆς ἰσχύος σου, καὶ ἐξ ὅλης τῆς διανοίας σου, καὶ τὸν πλησίον σου ὡς σεαυτόν. εἶπεν δὲ αὐτῷ. ὀρθῶς ἀπεκρίθης, τοῦτο ποίει καὶ ζήσῃ. ὁ δὲ θέλων δικαιοῦν ἑαυτὸν εἶπεν πρὸς τὸν ΙΗΣΟΥΝ. καὶ τίς ἐστί μου πλησίον; ὑπολαβὼν δὲ ὁ ΙΗΣΟΥΣ εἶπεν. ἄνθρωπός τις κατέβαινεν ἀπὸ ἱερουσαλὴμ εἰς ἱεριχὼ, καὶ λῃ-

σταῖς

^Καὶ στραφεὶς πρὸς τὰς μαθητὰς εἶπε,

EVANGELIVM

uos ſpernit me ſpernit. Qui autem me ſpernit, ſpernit eũ qui miſit me. Reuerſi ſunt autem ſeptuaginta cum gaudio dicentes. Domine, etiam dæmonia ſubijciuntur nobis in nomine tuo. Ait aũt illis. Videbam ſatanam ſicut fulgur de cœlo cadentem. Ecce do uobis poteſtatem calcandi ſuper ſerpẽtes & ſcorpiones, & ſuper omnem uirtutem inimici & nihil uobis nocebit. Veruntamen in hoc nolite gaudere, quod ſpiritꝰ uobis ſubijciuntur. Gaudete autem, ꝙ nomina ueſtra ſcripta ſunt ĩ cœlis. In ipſa hora exultauit ĩ ſpiritu ſancto & dixit. Cõfiteor tibi pater domine cœli & terræ, ꝙ abſcondiſti hæc a ſapientibus & prudentibus, & reuelaſti ea paruulis. Etiã pater, qm̃ ſic placuit ante te. ^Omnia mihi tradita ſũt a patre meo, & nemo ſcit quis ſit filius niſi pater, & quis ſit pater niſi filius, & cui uoluerit filius reuelare. Et cõuerſus ad diſcipulos ſuos ſeorſim dixit. Beati oculi q uidẽt q̃ uos uidetis. Dico em̃ uobis, ꝙ multi ꝓphetæ & reges uoluerunt uidere quæ uos uidetis, & nõ uiderũt, & audire q̃ auditis, & nõ audierũt. Et ecce quidã legiſꝑitus ſurrexit tentans illũ & dicens. Magiſter, qd faciẽdo uitã æternã poſſidebo? At ille dixit ad eũ. In lege qd ſcriptũ eſt? Quõ legis? Ille r̃ndẽs dixit. Diliges dñm deũ tuũ ex toto corde tuo, & ex tota anima tua & ex totis uiribus tuis, & ex tota mẽte tua, & ꝓximũ tuũ ſicut teipſũ. Dixitq; illi. Recte r̃ndiſti. Hoc fac & uiues Ille aũt uolens iuſtificare ſeipſum dixit ad Ieſum. Et quis eſt meus ꝓximꝰ? Suſcipiẽs aũt Ieſus dixit. Homo quidã deſcẽdebat ab Hieruſalẽ in hierico & inci-

dit in

^Et conuersus ad discipulos dixit,

columns, it became the first *published* Greek New Testament on its appearance in 1516. Erasmus worked fast—too fast, it has been said. Certainly, the number of printing errors has earned it the description of the most inaccurate book ever printed. But such blemishes were easily corrected in subsequent editions. From today's vantage point we may see one more serious factor which determined many of the problems of the subsequent three and a half centuries. Erasmus was in Basel in 1516, and he used the manuscripts which he happened to find there. There were only six which he used and, as chance would have it, they were all fairly recent: the oldest, which he trusted least, was a tenth-century copy bearing a much older form of text. The rest date from various points between then and the fifteenth century. None of them contained more than a part of the New Testament, so that he rarely relied on more than two copies. Moreover, Erasmus could find no manuscript containing the final verses of Revelation. He made this lack good by translating back from Latin to Greek, thereby creating a number of completely new readings.

The printed text thus began its history on a base as far from the manuscripts of the early centuries as it is possible to be. The consequences of this were enormous, for the manuscripts on which Erasmus most heavily relied represented a late form of the text, one that is different in many places from those of earlier centuries. It is known as the 'Byzantine Text', for it is a kind of text which was produced in the Byzantine empire. It began to be formed from the sixth century, and was increasingly the only kind of text of the New Testament to be copied, down to the end of the Byzantine empire in the fifteenth century. Although its text is principally different in the cumulative effect of small changes, it should first be observed that this later text contained some large passages absent in early copies. Some of these have regularly been the focus of controversy. One is Mark 16: 9–20, the 'Longer Ending' of Mark's Gospel. Mark ended his gospel abruptly and shockingly at 16: 8. This was surprising to early Christianity, which by the end of the second century had produced several alternative endings. One short coda is found only in one Latin manuscript. The other, 16: 9–20, is found in virtually every Greek manuscript. None of those few which omitted it was known to Erasmus. The other long passage is John 7: 53–8: 11 (the story of the woman taken in adultery). Again, this was firmly established in the Byzantine Text. Only a few early copies survive, attestation to the fact that this tradition was introduced into the gospel later, perhaps a century or more after its compilation. Another telling passage is Luke 22: 44f., the story of Christ's bloody sweat. This is another legendary addition to the text. Finally we note 1 John 5: 7f. (the 'Johannine comma'), which will be discussed below. But it is often the small details which are the more telling: details which bring the New Testament into closer accord with orthodox doctrine, such as the addition 'son of God' at Mark 1: 1, which will be discussed later; harmonizations, which remove differences between the gospels, particularly the first three; changes of wording or grammar which improve the Greek; clarifications of obscurities, such as the change from 'the only begotten God' to 'the only begotten *Son*' at John 1: 18; and removals of

(*facing*) The psalms, which were attributed to David, were believed by the church to contain prophecies of Christ and his passion. David is thus portrayed as both king and prophet by the Master of Riofrio (c.14th cent).

AVID
REI PROFETA

The sacrifice of Isaac (Genesis 22), portrayed by Domenichino (1581–1641), is an important text for Jews, Christians, and Muslims. Isaac was not, in fact, killed but was saved when God provided a ram as a substitute.

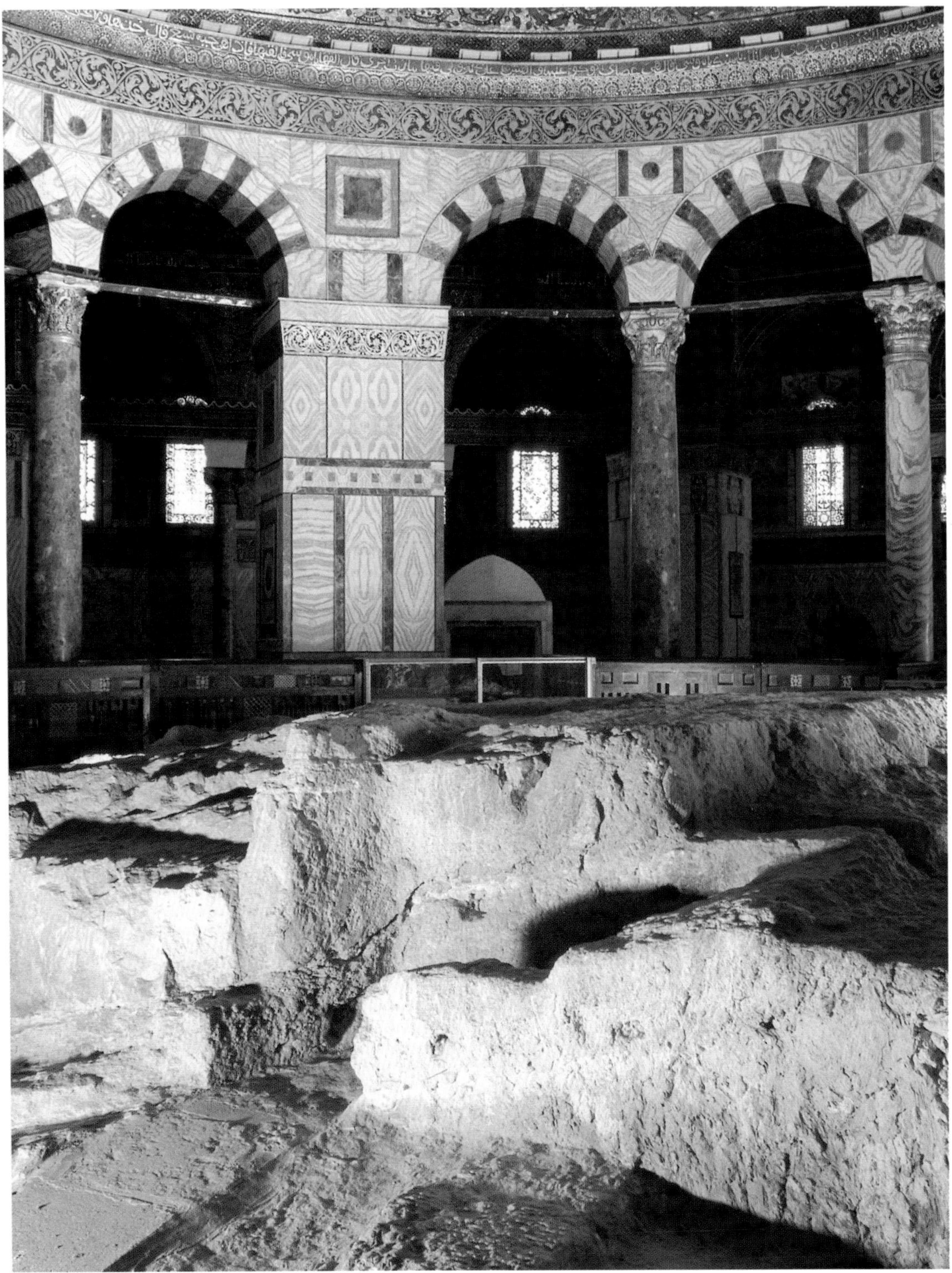

The Dome of the Rock in Jerusalem was completed in 691/2 CE, and is connected in Islamic tradition with Sura 17:2 of the Qur'an, which was understood to describe Mohammed's ascension to heaven (and back) from the sacred rock.

Scenes of martyrdom illustrating stories taken from 2 and 4 Maccabees and relating to the prohibition of Judaism by Antiochus IV in 169/8–164 BCE. The manuscript comes possibly from the middle Rhine region, *c.*1428.

The book of Judith recounts how Judith delivered her people from the Assyrian commander Holofernes by getting him drunk in his tent and decapitating him. The painting here of *Judith with the Head of Holofernes* is by Cristofano Allori (1577–1621).

The Church of the Nativity in Bethlehem was built by the emperor Constantine in 326 CE. Its floor can be seen beneath the present 6th-century structure, which replaced Constantine's church when the latter was destroyed by fire.

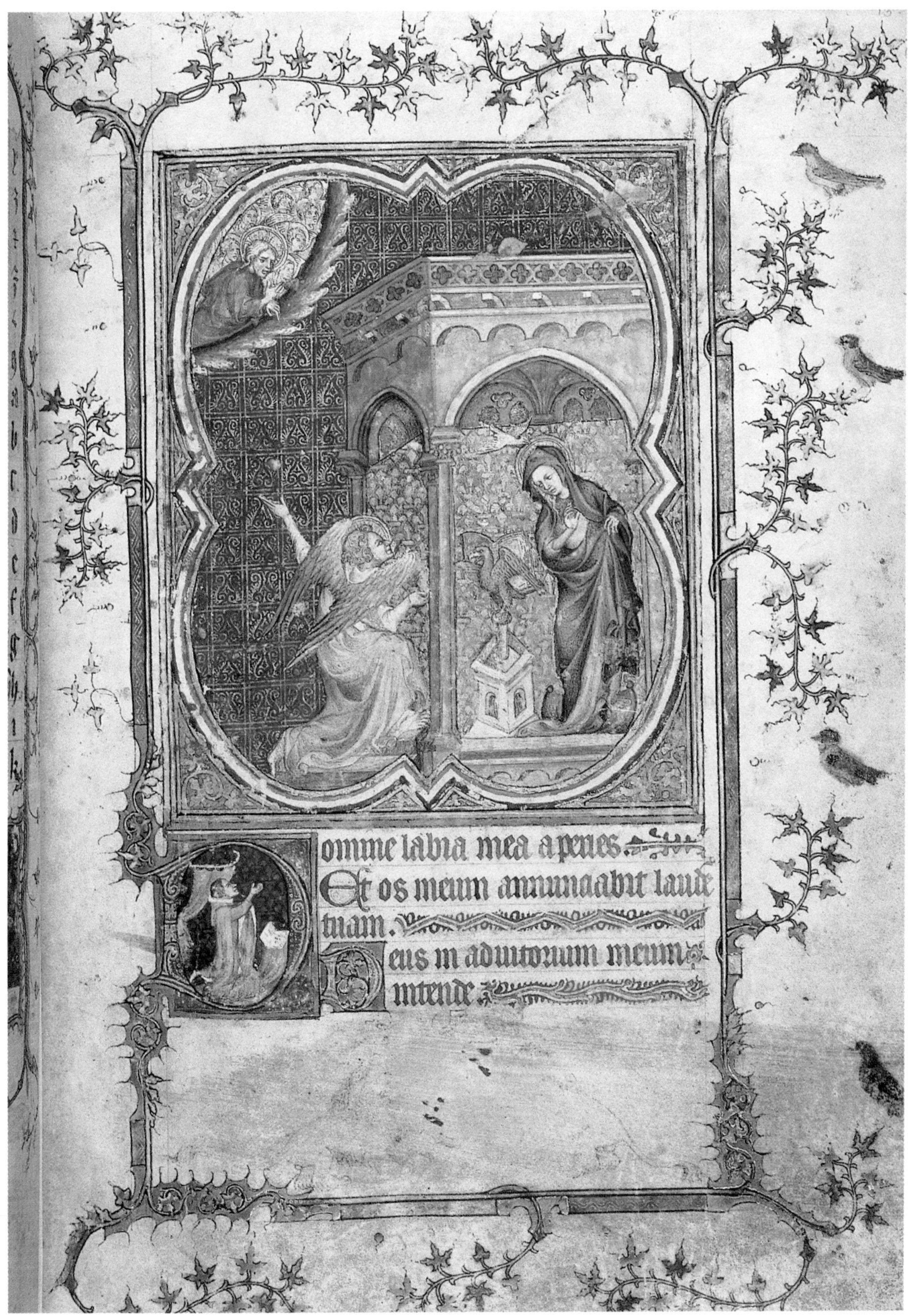

The Annunciation records the incident in Luke 1:26 when the angel Gabriel announced to Mary that she would bear a son. It is portrayed here in an illuminated manuscript prepared in France for the Duke of Burgundy (1342–1404).

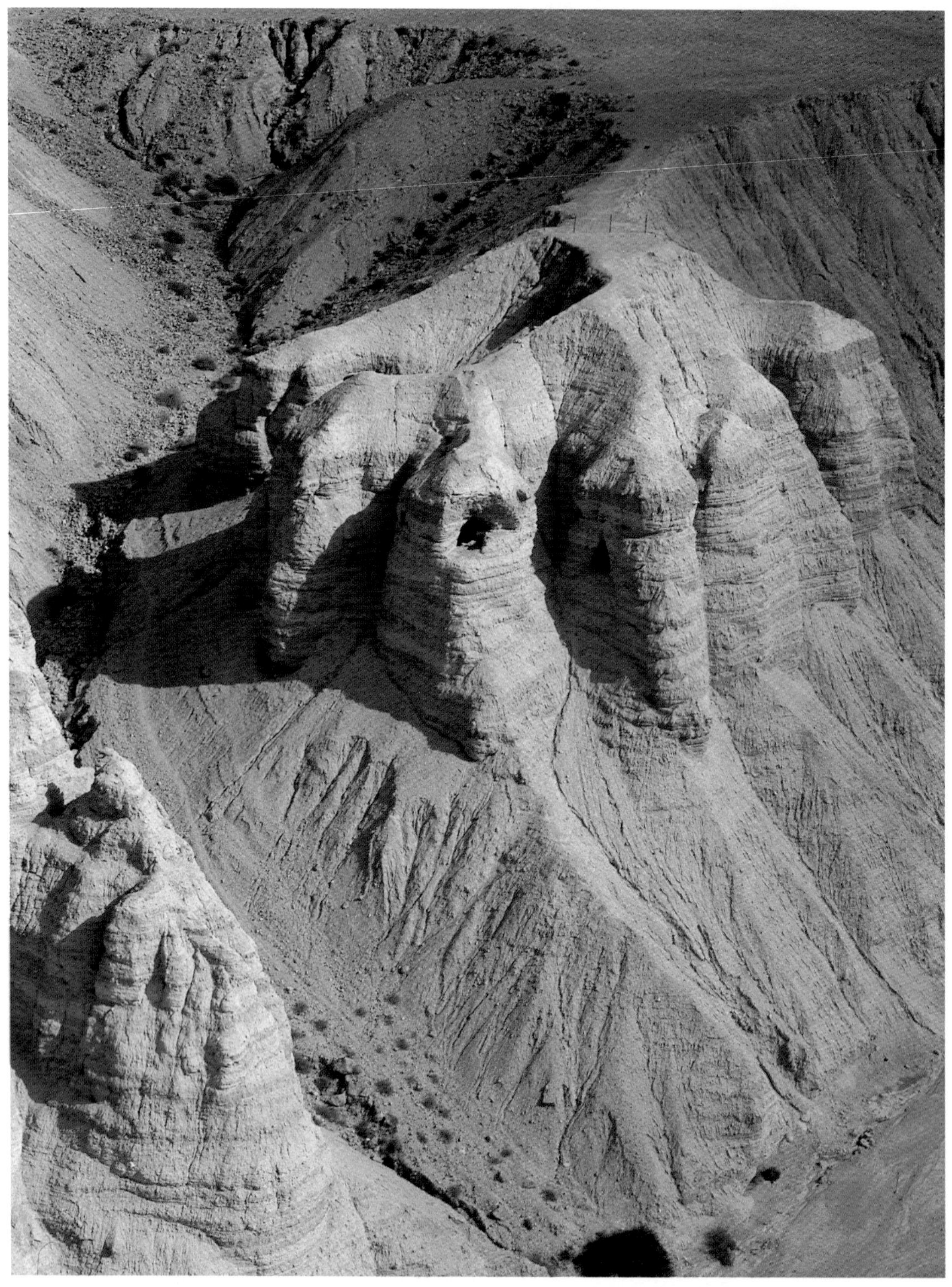

Cave IV at Qumran, at the far edge of the promontory on which the community buildings stood, contained some of the most important biblical and non-biblical fragments found among the Dead Sea Scrolls.

confusions. Such influences were at work from the very beginning of the process of the transmission of the New Testament writings, and they had made a strong impact by the time that the manuscripts of the Byzantine period came to be copied. The characteristics of the Byzantine text are that it attempted to keep everything it possibly could: any verse or story which had been brought into the New Testament; in detail, we find additions to names of Jesus, expansions (note how a congregation tends to add 'Amen' spontaneously in the middle of a reading if a doxology or phrase such as 'This is the very word of the Lord' is used).

It was on manuscripts of this late period that Erasmus relied. That Erasmus's Greek text was thus 'corrupt' is clear to us. But to his contemporaries that it was Greek was enough to commend it. Its influence was immediate, and felt far beyond the studies of the humanists. For it was from Erasmus's text, in this or one of his four subsequent editions, that Luther made his German version in 1522, that Tyndale produced his English New Testament of 1526, and translations into other tongues, such as Tuscan (1530) and Spanish (1543), were made. Other versions were based either on Erasmus's Latin translation (such as the Dutch version of Doen Pietersz, the 1533 Czech New Testament, Olivétan's French translation of 1535, a revision of an earlier Vulgate-based text) or on Luther's German (such as the 1526 Dutch Bible, and the 1524 Danish version). Thus the new vernacular Bibles, in this period generally associated with the spread of the Reformation, owed much of their innovative character to Erasmus.

It would be a gross over-simplification to claim that all traditionalists favoured the Latin Vulgate, and all progressives and reformers the Greek text. But this issue did become a touchstone of sixteenth-century debate. Thus, for example, as the equal struggle of Henrician reform in England swayed to and fro, successive translations were made from Greek or from Latin texts, as Henry accorded the precedence to one group or the other.

The progressive party claimed that the differences between the Greek text and the Vulgate demonstrated the latter to be corrupt, since the original must necessarily be prior to the version. The traditionalists invoked the authority of the church and the weight of tradition. Thus it was that the Council of Trent in 1546 declared the Vulgate to be sacred and canonical, and that in many places preference for the Greek text was more a theological than a scholarly matter. But, whatever your persuasion, it became increasingly difficult to undertake biblical study without any reference at all to the printed Greek text. This simple and evident fact is the foundation of modern study of the New Testament.

In spite of the Complutensian Polyglot, and in spite of a remarkably independent-minded edition of 1534 by the Frenchman Simon de Colines, it was Erasmus's editions that were to be the parents of the text of the subsequent centuries. He produced five in all (1516, 1519, 1522, 1527, and 1535), of which the third, with the Greek, his own Latin translation, and the Vulgate in parallel columns, was the most influential. Next in line to him are the editions of Robert Estienne (Stephanus) (1503–59), one in a famous line of scholar-printers, first of Paris and then, from 1551, of Geneva. To Stephanus we owe several considerable

Stephanus's 1550 edition of the Greek New Testament, the first to contain variant readings, showing Matthew 1: 1 to 1: 15. Note the absence of chapter and verse divisions and the cursive nature of the printed Greek.

ΤῸ ΚΑΤᾺ ΜΑΤΘΑΙ͂ΟΝ ἍΓΙΟΝ

ΕΥ̓ΑΓΓΈΛΙΟΝ.

α
γ
Βίβλος γενέσεως Ἰησοῦ Χρι- A Λουκ.γ.Ε
στοῦ, υἱοῦ Δαβίδ, υἱοῦ Ἀβραάμ. Ἀ- Γεν.κβ.Δ.
βραὰμ ἐγέννησε τὸν Ἰσαάκ. Ἰσαὰκ & κε.Δ
δὲ ἐγέννησε τὸν Ἰακώβ. Ἰακὼβ δὲ ἐγέν- Γεν.κθ.Δ.
νησε τὸν Ἰούδαν καὶ τοὺς ἀδελφοὺς αὐτοῦ. & λη.Η
Ἰούδας δὲ ἐγέννησε τὸν Φαρὲς καὶ τὸν
Ζαρὰ ἐκ τῆς Θάμαρ. Φαρὲς δὲ ἐγέννησε α.Παρ.β.Α
τὸν Ἐσρώμ. Ἐσρὼμ δὲ ἐγέννησε τὸν Ἀράμ. Ἀρὰμ δὲ ἐγέννησε Ῥουθ δ.Δ
τὸν Ἀμιναδάβ. Ἀμιναδὰβ δὲ ἐγέννησε τὸν Ναασσών. Ναασσὼν
δὲ ἐγέννησε τὸν Σαλμών. Σαλμὼν δὲ ἐγέννησε τὸν Βοὸζ ἐκ τῆς
Ῥαχάβ. Βοὸζ δὲ ἐγέννησε τὸν Ὠβὴδ ἐκ τῆς Ῥούθ. Ὠβὴδ δὲ ἐγέν- Ῥουθ δ.Δ
νησε τὸν Ἰεσσαί. Ἰεσσαὶ δὲ ἐγέννησε τὸν Δαβὶδ τὸν βασιλέα. Δα- α.Βασ.ις.Α
βὶδ δὲ ὁ βασιλεὺς ἐγέννησε τὸν Σολομῶντα ἐκ τῆς τοῦ Οὐρίου. Σο- & ιζ.Β β.Βασ.ιβ.Ζ
λομὼν δὲ ἐγέννησε τὸν Ῥοβοάμ. Ῥοβοὰμ δὲ ἐγέννησε τὸν Ἀ- α.Παρ.γ.Β
βιά. Ἀβιὰ δὲ ἐγέννησε τὸν Ἀσά. Ἀσὰ δὲ ἐγέννησε τὸν Ἰωσαφάτ. B
Ἰωσαφὰτ δὲ ἐγέννησε τὸν Ἰωράμ. Ἰωρὰμ δὲ ἐγέννησε τὸν Ὀζίαν.
Ὀζίας δὲ ἐγέννησε τὸν Ἰωάθαμ. Ἰωάθαμ δὲ ἐγέννησε τὸν Ἄ-
χαζ. Ἄχαζ δὲ ἐγέννησε τὸν Ἐζεκίαν. Ἐζεκίας δὲ ἐγέννησε τὸν Μα-
νασσῆ. Μανασσῆς δὲ ἐγέννησε τὸν Ἀμών. Ἀμὼν δὲ ἐγέννησε τὸν β.Παρ.λγ.Α δ.Βασ.κα.Δ
* τὸν Ἰακείμ. Ἰακεὶμ δὲ ἐγέννησε τὸν. Ἰωσίαν. Ἰωσίας δὲ ἐγέννησε *τὸν Ἰεχονίαν καὶ τοὺς ἀδελφοὺς αὐ- α.παρ.γ.Γ δ.Βασ.κγ.Η
τοῦ, ἐπὶ τῆς μετοικεσίας Βαβυλῶνος. Μετὰ δὲ τὴν μετοικεσίαν Βα- & κδ.Α β.παρ.λς.Β
βυλῶνος Ἰεχονίας ἐγέννησε τὸν Σαλαθιήλ. Σαλαθιὴλ δὲ α.Παρ.γ.Γ
ἐγέννησε τὸν Ζοροβάβελ. Ζοροβάβελ δὲ ἐγέννησε τὸν Ἀβιούδ.
Ἀβιοὺδ δὲ ἐγέννησε τὸν Ἐλιακείμ. Ἐλιακεὶμ δὲ ἐγέννησε τὸν Ἀ-
ζώρ. Ἀζὼρ δὲ ἐγέννησε τὸν Σαδώκ. Σαδὼκ δὲ ἐγέννησε τὸν Ἀ-
χείμ. Ἀχεὶμ δὲ ἐγέννησε τὸν Ἐλιούδ. Ἐλιοὺδ δὲ ἐγέννησε τὸν Ἐ-

a.i.

inventions. The first is the system of verse numberings, introduced in his edition of 1551. The division of the text into chapters is considerably older. Our system is attributed to Stephen Langton, archbishop of Canterbury (d. 1228). But there were still earlier systems: several are known to us from the fourth century or even earlier. In these the chapter or section lengths are considerably less. In one of them, for example, the Gospel of Matthew is divided into 170 portions (this is Codex Vaticanus, which will be described in more detail below). Stephanus's second innovation is less obvious, but more significant. In order to understand it, we must retrace our steps.

From the beginning, Erasmus's text excited criticism. It was naturally the places where he printed a Greek text evidently different from the Vulgate that were treated with the most scepticism. Opponents of Erasmus realized very quickly that the best way to fight him was to find Greek manuscripts with readings which supported the Vulgate. Almost inevitably, certain passages became storm centres. One almost blushes to repeat this well-worn tale, but it illustrates most neatly the point at issue. One important passage of debate was 1 John 5: 7f., translated in the Authorized Version as 'For there are three that bear record in heaven, the Father, the Word, and the Holy Ghost: and these three are one'. It is in the Vulgate, but Erasmus did not find it in his Greek manuscripts, and therefore omitted it. But, when pressed, he rashly stated that he would print the passage in his next edition, if there could be found one Greek manuscript containing it. Such a manuscript was produced (I use the word in the senses both of 'written' and of 'made available'), and Erasmus kept his promise. This was evidently unscientific. Admittedly, there are one or two other Greek manuscripts containing the verse, the oldest of the fourteenth century. Today we can see both the appeal of such an orthodox declaration, and how it reflects a degree of theological formulation which lay far in the future when 1 John was written. The textual evidence now available shows it to have been formulated in Latin Christianity, in response to doctrinal controversy. This story illustrates the difficulties of editing the New Testament. The production of editions of the classics was often difficult enough. But in editing the Greek New Testament, there were two huge problems. The first was the sensitivity of the subject matter. Every generation has argued about the text of the Bible, both in the original and in translation. Jerome's Vulgate, itself sanctified by the sixteenth century, had caused a riot in one church eleven hundred years previously when the faithful heard it, because the learned saint had decided that Jonah's gourd was really an ivy. Small wonder, then, that passages touching on the person of Christ and on the holy Trinity should cause controversy. The second problem was scientific.

The humanists were concerned to recover authentic texts. Thus, they demonstrated various spuria to be forgeries. These included the correspondence of Paul and Seneca (a set of fourteen letters allegedly exchanged between Paul and the Roman philosopher Seneca, in fact written in Latin in the fourth century), 3 Corinthians (a second-century letter that is found with one from the Corinthians to Paul, both separately and in the Acts of Paul) and Paul's Epistle to the Laodiceans (produced at some point between the second and fourth centuries, purporting to be the letter mentioned in Col. 4: 16). They sought also to recover authentic and reliable copies of texts. But how to establish the age of an undated manuscript and to gauge the accuracy of its text were disciplines hardly even born. With a manuscript tradition as vast and as complicated as the New Testament, the difficulties were enormous. The first stage was to gather evidence. We can see how the need was recognized, from the argument over 1 John 5. It was Stephanus who found a convenient way, in his edition of 1550, of setting out the information. He provided the variant readings (or at any rate some of them) of fifteen manuscripts. These readings were printed in the margin, and each manuscript was designated by a Greek numeral, as α', β', down to $\iota\epsilon'$. This compendious way of providing valuable information is essentially still in use today.

Stephanus's text was, as has been said, based on that of Erasmus. That is to say, he printed Erasmus's text except in those places where he deliberately chose to change the wording. His text in turn was the base used by Theodore Beza (1519–1605), the successor of Calvin in the Genevan church, in his ten editions. These were produced between 1565 and 1611. It is with Beza that two noteworthy manuscripts come fully into notice. Stephanus's text was as Byzantine as Erasmus's. Into Beza's hands, however, came two far older manuscripts. Both, coincidentally, were bilingual, consisting of a Greek text with a Latin translation. One, containing the gospels and Acts, we now know to date from about the year 400. To Beza it was simply *vetustissimus*, 'very old', the Greek being written in a majuscule hand. This manuscript was markedly different from any other used by either Erasmus or Stephanus (although Stephanus had examined it, it being one of the fifteen codices cited by him in 1550, he did not adopt its readings). While Beza doubted its accuracy, he was initially convinced of the authenticity of a story which it contained at the end of Luke 6: 4: 'On the same day, seeing somebody working on the sabbath, he [Jesus] said to him, "Man, if you know what you are doing, then you are blessed; but if you do not, then you are accursed and a transgressor of the law"'. He included this otherwise unattested story in his edition of 1563, but then dropped it. In the end, he gave the manuscript away to Cambridge University, expressing the hope that it would be buried in obscurity. That was not to be. It is to these events that the manuscript owes its name of Codex Bezae Cantabrigiensis. The second manuscript, of the Pauline epistles, was less ancient by a good century, and less distinctive. But the fifth century is still early enough for it be recognized as 'very old', and its distinctive character again gave occasion for thought. It is the leader of a group of bilingual manuscripts of Paul, which give us a fourth-century text current in the west. South Italy and Sardinia are both possible places where it was copied. Coming to Beza from the town of Clermont in northern France, it is known as the Codex Claromontanus. This habit of naming manuscripts from the place of discovery, or the name of their discoverer, or the library where they now live, continues, particularly where the manuscript is ancient, distinctive, or important. It was fortunate that these two manuscripts were found when they were. For they demonstrated a problem which Erasmus could not have anticipated: the degree and number of differences between different copies of the Greek New Testament. It seemed that these early texts sometimes supported the Vulgate against the printed text. But the supporter of the Vulgate must also feel perplexed, for the Latin text of both these manuscripts was not at all of the Vulgate type: they represent two of the many Old Latin, pre-Jerome versions.

The sixteenth century saw also the printing of editions of some of the important early versions of the New Testament. The most significant of these was the Peshitta Syriac, published in 1555. The Peshitta is the form of Syriac text which by the fifth century was emerging as the most widely used and ecclesiastically approved text of Syrian Christianity. It developed, by a gradual process of revision, out of far more ancient Syriac versions. It thus, with the Vulgate, stood as one of the great versions of the early church. The value of the versions became apparent fairly soon: they are a witness to the manuscript or manuscripts used by the translator. If the translation is ancient, then we have evidence for the text of a long lost ancient manuscript. This same period saw also the publication of the writings of many early Christian writers. Where these writers quote the New Testament, they again provide a testimony to a now lost text. These enterprises were fraught with the same problems as those of editing the Greek New Testament: the number of manuscripts was huge (in the case of a writer like Chrysostom, even greater than the New Testament, while his works are many times more voluminous), and nobody could yet find the best of these manuscripts. But these editions at any rate laid the foundations and provided the material for later generations to build on and to improve.

A number of English versions were produced in this period. They seem to have no connection with the Wyclif Bible, perhaps because of linguistic and theological developments, perhaps because the reformers wished to follow the Greek text, and not the Latin Vulgate on which Wyclif was based. It begins with William Tyndale. There was then a period of cautious reform and conservative reaction, which lasted until the end of Henry VIII's reign. The version of this period which was destined to have the longest use was Miles Coverdale's Bible of 1535, for his version of the Psalter (revised for the Great Bible, made in 1540) is that found in the Book of Common Prayer. The next major advance came about during Mary's reign, when a group of exiles who had gone to Geneva set about a new translation. Known as the Geneva Bible, it enjoyed great popularity among English Protestants for the rest of the century and to the end of the next. It showed sound scholarship. However, it was to be superseded by the famous revision inaugurated in the reign of James I. It was from the Greek text of the kind produced by Beza that the translators of the Authorized Version worked, their edition appearing in 1611. In this it was little different from the Geneva Bible, except that the text had changed somewhat in the intervening years. The revisers consulted other sources, including earlier translations. But it is the text descended from Erasmus that is their base.

English Catholics also produced a translation. Made from the Vulgate, though not without consultation of other sources, it was published at Rheims in 1582.

From Beza is descended a text printed in Leiden in 1633. It claims in its preface to be the 'text received by all', the *textus receptus.* And indeed it did, in its many many printings, actually attain the distinction of being for some two centuries the only generally and readily available Greek text. It is sometimes said that a publisher's blurb achieved this. But it is nearer the mark to say that theologians get the text which they deserve. The spectacle of a procession of textual phantoms arising from early Christianity was not particularly welcome to seventeenth-century Europe, either Protestant or Roman Catholic. The former quickly came to accord in practice to the Greek text the same privileged position of authority that the Vulgate occupied among the latter. Thus the two camps each possessed an authoritative text. The one had the virtue of being in the language in which the writings were originally produced, but the defect that it was based on extremely late copies. The latter had the defect that it could only claim to be a version, and it was in fact known also in a late and corrupt form. But if the theologians were thus entrenched, some scholars were more adventurous. For the next stage, we must follow Codex Bezae across the waters from the Continent to England.

THE IMPACT OF NEW MATERIALS

The growth of mercantile dealings between England and the Levant was accompanied by political and cultural interests, and these had their effect on New Testament manuscript studies. To the seventeenth century we owe the expansion of those manuscript collections which were in time to flow into the holdings of the British Library and of Bodley. One of the most dramatic first fruits of this was the gift by the patriarch of Alexandria to King Charles I of the Codex Alexandrinus, a copy of the entire Bible that had been produced in the fifth century. While in the gospels this manuscript represents an early form of the Byzantine Text, elsewhere it contains a purer text. But even in the gospels there was much that was new to excite the scholar. Along with the exploration of the east went linguistic opportunities, and thus further study of the versions. The most splendid achievement in this respect was Brian Walton's Polyglot, published in London between 1654 and 1657. It contains the New Testament in Greek, Latin (the Vulgate and a modern version), Syriac, Ethiopic, Arabic, and Persian (only in the gospels).

The study of one of the most important of the early versions soon received an important boost. The Latin text of the New Testament had undergone as many changes in the manuscript copying as had the Greek. It became clear that there were early materials quite different from the Vulgate. The latter is associated with the name of Jerome, who undertook a translation in 382. In fact, what he did was to revise one of the many existing versions of the gospels. He does not seem to have translated, or rather, revised, any other part of the New Testament. What is known as the Vulgate was a collection of various other Old Latin versions of the rest of the

New Testament into association with Jerome's gospels. The study and collection of the pre-Jerome versions is associated with the name of Pierre Sabatier (1682–1742), a French scholar who was one of the Benedictine scholars known as the Maurists. He edited all the material then known, in three volumes published posthumously. Only in recent years has his work been superseded.

To the generation after Walton belongs one of the most important figures in this account. John Mill (1645–1707), Fellow of Queen's College, Oxford, devoted 30 years of his life to collating manuscripts and versions. 'To collate' in this connection means to compare a witness with a base text, and to record all divergencies from it. In 1707, two weeks before his death, his great edition appeared. It brought together, for the first time, the materials then available for reconstructing a text older than the received text. Mill did not in fact print a new text. What he did was to print the received text, recording beneath it all the variants which he had collected. It has been stated that he collected 30,000 variant readings. In addition, he wrote a long introduction in which the principle witnesses were discussed, and the problems described.

A portrait of John Mill (1645–1707) in Queen's College, Oxford. Mill was an important figure in the development of the textual criticism of the New Testament and produced an edition with an extensive critical apparatus.

The reaction was violent. Even though Mill had printed the received text, the very fact that he listed variations from it was regarded by many as playing into the hands of Latitudinarians, Deists, and Atheists, as threatening the historical truth of Christianity, and as providing the materials for proving the New Testament not to be the dictated Word of God. Textual criticism was suspect. Certainly, people had got used to the idea that the familiar printed text was *the* original text. To be told that this text might be a corruption of what the evangelists and apostles had written, and to hear that the church had not preserved this text incorruptible from the very beginning, were ideas that many preferred to fight than to consider. Such was the weight of opposition, with the accusation of heresy and the threat of ejection, that it was to be a century before scholars dared to do more than to print the received text and to express their own preferences in the margin.

This was precisely the course of action followed by J. A. Bengel (1687–1752), who published an edition in 1734. Disturbed by Mill's huge collection of variations between the witnesses, Bengel carefully studied them all. He reached the conclusion that no article of doctrine was affected by them. But even this orthodox and conservative conclusion did not protect him from severe criticism. He was marked as a dangerous man. It was not simply the conclusions, it was even the practice of textual criticism of which at least some churchmen disapproved. The concept of a verbally inspired and infallible text had become too dear to Protestantism for the harsh light of textual reality to be tolerable. However, times were to change.

But it was not only to the theologian that Mill's *apparatus criticus* (the name given to the collection of variants at the bottom of each page) presented a challenge. There were also many problems for the textual critic. Nevertheless, the weakness of the received text became quite clear. Particularly, the significance of the frequent agreement of early manuscripts and versions against was appreciated. On the whole, the agreement of early witnesses against the received text was noted more frequently than their disagreement with one another. In the case of the bilingual manuscripts Bezae and Claromontanus, Mill argued that the idiosyncrasies of their Greek columns were the consequence of the influence of the Latin, thus finding an argument which would explain the degree of difference, enabling one to posit a purer base text essentially in common with other early witnesses.

The principles of Richard Bentley (1662–1742), probably the greatest English critic of any age, also emphasize the agreement of the oldest manuscripts. For the gospels there were now four regarded as pre-eminent. Two of them have been described—codices Alexandrinus and Bezae. A third, Codex Ephraemi Rescriptus (so called because the manuscript was re-used to copy some works of Ephraem), contains the entire Bible. Copied in the fifth century, it is one of the leading witnesses to the New Testament text. The fourth, Codex Vaticanus, was still imperfectly known, although its value was recognized. It will be described at a later point. Bentley also used a manuscript in Cambridge of the ninth century, Codex Augiensis, which contains the epistles of Paul in Greek with a Latin translation. He recognized its value, although the full story of its text has only been unravelled in recent years. It is a later representative of the text first known from Codex Claromontanus. Bentley believed that the oldest and best Greek and Latin manuscripts agreed with each other, and that this was the original text. He was not the first scholar to explore this possibility, but he was probably the most influential. He was right, to the extent that the Vulgate, particularly in the gospels, is modelled on a Greek text similar to some of the old Greek manuscripts known to Bentley.

THE ADVENT OF PALAEOGRAPHY

The rapid growth of the number of known manuscripts, brought about principally by explorations and cataloguings in European libraries, led towards the end of the seventeenth century to the formation of a discipline that is indispensable to the analysis of texts: palaeography, the study of the development and character of handwriting. Two French scholars were responsible for this development. The first was Bernard de Montfaucon (1655–1741), the second Jean Mabillon (1632–1707). They provided the essential prerequisites: the classification of hands into different types, an explanation of the relationship between these types, and an account of the development of each. The oldest New Testament manuscript to contain a colophon explicitly stating its date was finished on 7 May 835. Without such information, although there is sometimes some sort of indirect evidence, it is almost invariably necessary to use the handwriting as a means of dating. In this science, Montfaucon and Mabillon led the way. Although there were errors—generally, out of proper caution, dating tended to be rather late than early—subsequent advances have confirmed that the first framework was sound. The classification of hands into different types, principally for Greek writing the two types of majuscule (the precursors of upper-case letters) and minuscule (from which modern lower case is ultimately derived) is basic. The former was the principal book hand down to the eighth/ninth centuries, when the latter took over.

Today European and indeed world-wide travel is an easy matter. In the eighteenth century it was not. The great scholar J. J. Wettstein (1693–1754) did his travelling in his youth, and spent the rest of his life examining the materials which he had gathered, and discussing it with correspondents, on whom he relied for further information. In spite of the obstacles—how often one had not noted information which twenty years later appeared vital, how easy it was to be misled by second-hand information—Wettstein's edition (1751–2) provided a wealth of information. Besides the variant readings, the linguistic and intellectual parallels which he noted have made his work a treasure house for generations.

The work of Bentley, Bengel, and Wettstein show two important developments in the way in which manuscripts and their texts were studied. The first was the first coherent steps towards giving a history of how the texts had changed. Bentley noted the ways in which fourth- and fifth-century manuscripts were different from those copied later. Bengel was able to compare enough manuscripts to place them in two groups, the Asiatic and the African. The details of his scheme have long proved unsatisfactory, but the concept has become basic. In particular, the recognition that different texts circulated in different parts of the early Christian world (perhaps the genetic comparison of a particular subspecies of plant or animal developing in a particular area will explain the idea) has been of great importance.

The second area was the development of rules, 'canons', for determining how to choose between two or more variant readings. For example, Bengel articulated the rule that 'the difficult reading should be preferred to the easy one'. The point is that a scribe or a reader would be more likely to replace what was written with what they thought should have been written, in places where the author was in some way obscure. To Wettstein we owe the rule that 'manuscripts must be evaluated by their significance, not their number'. That is, one does not prefer the reading supported by the greater number of witnesses. For the greater number of manuscripts may all be descended from a single copy that was wrong at this point, while the few manuscripts which oppose it may be derived from one which was here correct.

The century that followed was significant above all in the printing of editions to replace the Received Text. First came Bowyer's text of 1763. William Bowyer (1699–1777), a London scholar-printer, put Wettstein's preferences (which he had only indicated in the margin) into the text, and provided more changes of his own where he found better readings in the manuscripts. In addition, he placed a number of suspected interpolations in square brackets, such as John 7: 53–8: 11, the doxology of the Lord's Prayer in Matthew, and those verses in 1 John 5 which Erasmus had reinserted. Edward Harwood (1729–94) followed in 1776 with an even bolder text. He printed the text of three manuscripts: Codex Bezae for the gospels and Acts, Codex Claromontanus for Paul, and Codex Alexandrinus for the rest.

Bengel's theory of groups was further developed by J. S. Semler (1725–91), who identified three in his contribution to the discipline, an expanded edition of Wettstein's introduction (1764). It was now clearly recognized that what had been named the western recension by Semler was very distinctive, against the Alexandrian and eastern texts. The claim that this Western Text is consistently better than the other two has been upheld by some people ever since. But the majority of scholars were becoming aware of the virtues of the Alexandrian witnesses. This trend was encouraged by the researches of J. J. Griesbach (1745–1812), who gave these three text-types their common names Alexandrian, Western, and Byzantine. Griesbach was also the first scholar to show how three types of evidence might be used in recovering each of these three text-types: Greek manuscripts, early versions, and Fathers. Thus, his materials for reconstructing the Alexandrian text included various majuscule and minuscule manuscripts, translations into Coptic, Armenian, Ethiopic, and Syriac, and quotations from the New Testament in the writings of Origen, Clement of Alexandria, Eusebius, Cyril of Alexandria, and Isidore of Pelusium. It was the evident Alexandrian location of some of these writers, together with the Coptic, that most strongly justified the name of the text-type. The place of Alexandria in the ancient world as a centre for the preservation, study, and copying of classical texts added weight to the claim.

NINETEENTH-CENTURY SCHOLARSHIP

Griesbach provided the most thorough history of the text. He also developed further the canons of criticism, listing fifteen in all. The task of the student of the New Testament text was emerging as containing two stages. The first was the reconstruction of the history of the text and the recovery of the early forms in which it existed. The second was the comparison of these forms, and the applications of the canons, in order to ascertain, where they differed, which was the more recent. The greatest advances in these directions was found in two nineteenth-century editions. Karl Lachmann (1793–1851) provided the first. He did not set out to reconstruct the original text, but to recover that which was prevalent in the late fourth century. To do this he used a tiny number of witnesses—four Latin manuscripts, and four Greek. What was revolutionary was that he did not work by revising an existing printed text. He started from his selected manuscripts, and followed through the principles that had first been enunciated by Bentley a century earlier. The result was something radically different from the received text. Not surprisingly, it was received negatively by many theologians and church leaders. But to the textual critic it offered new horizons. These possibilities were fully explored in England, first by S. P. Tregelles. Tregelles (1813–75) was a Cornishman of humble origins, who had independently worked towards the principles followed by Lachmann. In two respects his work was superior to the German's: he studied manuscripts (having travelled widely), and he used more in the creation of his text. His edition, published in 1857–72, laid the foundations for the edition which was to cap all other alternatives to the received text hitherto produced. But before examining that, it is necessary to catch up on the search for manuscripts.

Lobegott Friedrich Constantin von Tischendorf (1815–74) was born near Leipzig. In 1844 and 1859 he discovered the Codex Sinaiticus at St Catherine's monastery on Mt Sinai, on which the 8th edition of his Greek New Testament (1869–72) was largely based.

The scholar who had done most to make materials available, and indeed who continues to hold the palm, not only for this but in the incredible accuracy of his work, is Constantin Tischendorf (1815–74). This man spent his entire life, one might suppose, either in a library or on his way to the next. When he had exhausted Europe, he moved on to Asia. In his youth he transcribed the difficult fifth-century palimpsest in Paris, Codex Ephraemi Rescriptus, thus making more of its text certain and available. This work remains the primary source for its citation. In his *Monumenta Sacra Inedita*, and in many other productions, Tischendorf edited many of the principal early sources for the New Testament. He also produced critical editions of both the Old and the New Testament in Greek, of the latter in Latin, and of other texts. But his name is above all associated (to his honour and his discredit) with one manuscript. It was in the monastery of St Catherine on Mt Sinai that, in 1844, he was shown leaves of a magnificent codex which, as it transpired, contained the entire Bible and had been produced in the mid-fourth century. Thus of a stature and age comparable to Codex Vaticanus, though of a poorer textual quality, it was close enough to it to add great weight to the belief that this text was much better than any other available. Tischendorf's role in subsequent events, including the removal of part of this manuscript to Leipzig, and part to St Petersburg (whence it came to London in 1933) does not place him in the best possible light. But the use which he made of it testifies to his unparalleled abilities as a collector of evidence. In his eighth and last edition of the Greek New Testament (1869–72) Tischendorf provided the fullest *apparatus criticus* of the New Testament until then available. The text is too partial to his beloved Codex Sinaiticus to be of value, but the *apparatus* is still to be consulted frequently and carefully by anyone conducting a serious investigation into textual evidence.

B. F. Westcott (1825–1901) and F. J. A. Hort (1828–92) in their epoch-making *The New Testament in the Original Greek* followed as far as was possible the recognition of the superiority of one manuscript. Just as it had been found that

Portrait of F. J. A. Hort (1828–92). His collaborative work with B. F. Westcott profoundly affected late-19th- and 20th-century New Testament textual criticism.

the Alexandrian text-type was superior in quality to the others, so it had emerged that one manuscript of this type was of matchless quality. Codex Vaticanus, fully available in a bad transcription (Cardinal Mai's) since 1857, in a better one (Tischendorf's) since 1867, and in a third competent one of 1868, formed the foundation of Westcott and Hort's text, and Codex Sinaiticus was its main supporter.

Curiously enough, although its recognition came so late, Codex Vaticanus had always been known. It first appears in modern times in a late fifteenth-century catalogue of the Vatican Library. Its omission of the passage in 1 John which had proved so vexatious to Erasmus was reported to him as early as 1521. An edition of the Septuagint based upon it was published in 1587. It was collated a number of times in the seventeenth and eighteenth centuries. After the transcriptions mentioned above, a photographic edition of the whole Bible was produced in 1889–90, and ones of the New Testament in 1904, 1965 (the latter on the occasion of the Second Vatican Council), and 2000. Copied towards the middle of the fourth century, this magnificent copy of the entire Bible (though it lacks the books of the Maccabees, and the end is missing, so that we do not know whether it ever contained Revelation) shows both consistency of spelling and accuracy of copying, and a quality in the text thus carefully reproduced. It is thus possible to conclude that this text is the product of a tradition of scholarly copying. Tending towards brevity rather than expansion both in details and in larger blocks of text, its virtues struck Westcott and Hort so forcibly that they allocated it and one other manuscript to their 'Neutral' text-type, a phrase indicating that, unlike the other types, it had not been subject to revision.

The period in which Westcott and Hort worked coincided with a revision of the Authorized Version. While some of the purpose was to bring the Bible into more modern English, there were also those who wanted a translation derived from a better Greek text. The two editors were themselves also revisers, and their up-to-date opinions were available to the committee. But some of their opponents, defenders of the traditional Received Text, were also present, and did not always lose the day. But in many ways the Revised Version, though a failure as a piece of English literature, popularized the revolution in textual criticism which Westcott and Hort embodied.

Their edition consisted of a volume of text, and a volume of introduction. There was no *apparatus criticus*. This economy of presentation might mask the degree of hard work that had led to it: two centuries of struggle against the received text, of travel from library to library, of learning ancient tongues in order to study the versions, of reading church Fathers in search of biblical quotations. The lists of manuscripts known at particular periods provide a pointer to the vast expansion of information available to the scholar. We saw that fifteen were cited by Stephanus. Mill's edition refers to nearly 100, and Wettstein's to about 220. About a thousand manuscripts were known at the beginning of Tischendorf's career, and three times that number fifty years later. C. R. Gregory's list of 1908, which set out the numbering system in use today, contained 4,000. That has been extended today past the five and a half thousand mark.

To a certain extent the work was cumulative. The discovery of a new manuscript led to an assessment of its readings, the comparison of this new evidence with existing knowledge, and a tentative conclusion. But in fact much of the

Codex Vaticanus, one of the most important witnesses to the text of the New Testament, open at Luke 10: 6–29.

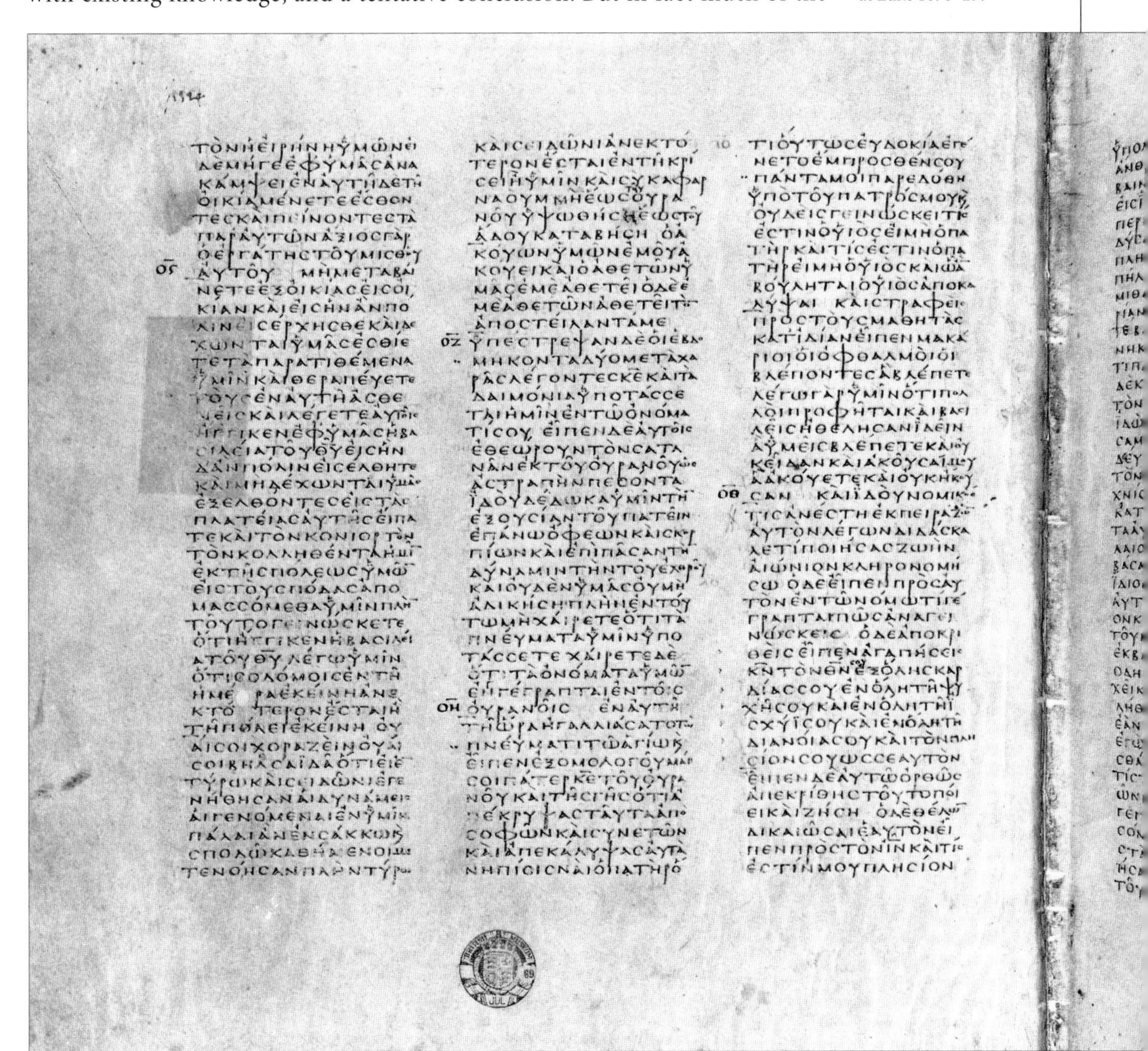

work has had to be done again and again. Many early editions of the church Fathers were as corrupt as the received text was for the New Testament. The tendency was always for copyists of patristic texts to substitute their familiar scriptural texts for those older forms known to the Fathers, so these citations were particularly liable to corruption. Each new and better edition required a fresh examination of the biblical quotations. Moreover, standards of accuracy improved, and collations became more complete. Earlier editions cited only selected readings from a manuscript. Increasing scientific accuracy required the inclusion of all a manuscript's readings. Several ways were developed of providing the necessary information.

The most prodigal of space was to print a complete transcription of a manuscript. Properly effected, this would preserve the line endings of the manuscript, show any corrections as exactly as possible as they appeared, include any marginalia, and describe all secondary hands and indicate by which hand each correction or marginal note was made. This method requires particularly high accuracy, since the whole manuscript has to be copied out by hand, and then typeset. By the middle of the nineteenth century most of the major witnesses had been made available to research in this way. Some of the finest editions are those in specially cut founts imitating the scribe's hand. Since then, photographic reproduction has to some extent supplanted the transcription. But while it can generally reproduce better, it cannot interpret, and for a number of manuscripts one continues to consult the views of those who spent months or even years in the scribe's company. Palimpsests (manuscripts which have been reused by erasing the original text and writing over it) are also sometimes as hard or harder to read in facsimile than they are in the flesh, particularly since the nineteenth-century habit of treating the parchment with chemical to bring up the original ink has generally left a veneer impenetrable to every colour of light in the spectrum. More economical than the transcription and the reproduction is the collation. Many witnesses have been made available in this way, and the results subsequently incorporated into editions. The provision of the evidence of a version is harder. Few editors of the Greek New Testament are going to be perfectly fluent in every necessary language, so the original may not help. But putting it into Greek will require great caution. In many places, it will be uncertain which of several Greek readings the version favours, and in others its idiosyncrasy may be due to the translator or even to the language, and so silence is best. The same silence is necessary where a patristic text is concerned. The Father may have quoted wrongly from memory, or if he is preaching may have paraphrased the text in order to emphasize a point.

Thus the situation stood in the beginning of the last quarter of the nineteenth century. The materials had apparently been gathered, and the evidence analysed, and *The New Testament in the Original Greek* represented the pinnacle of achievement. Of course, not everyone thought so, and the Received Text continued to have its defenders. Indeed, it still does (the support is universally amongst conservative scholars, many of whom adhere to it on doctrinal grounds, principally that Providence could not have left the church so long without the pure Word). But the twentieth century has proved as exciting a period as the nineteenth. Tischendorf would have been delighted to have lived in it.

TWENTIETH-CENTURY DEVELOPMENTS

Hitherto, all new manuscripts had been found in libraries, either as uncatalogued volumes, or as palimpsests, or as materials used to stiffen binding. And all had been written either on parchment or on paper (first used in the thirteenth century). None in Greek was older than the second quarter of the fourth century. The decade that saw the publication of Westcott and Hort saw also a number of

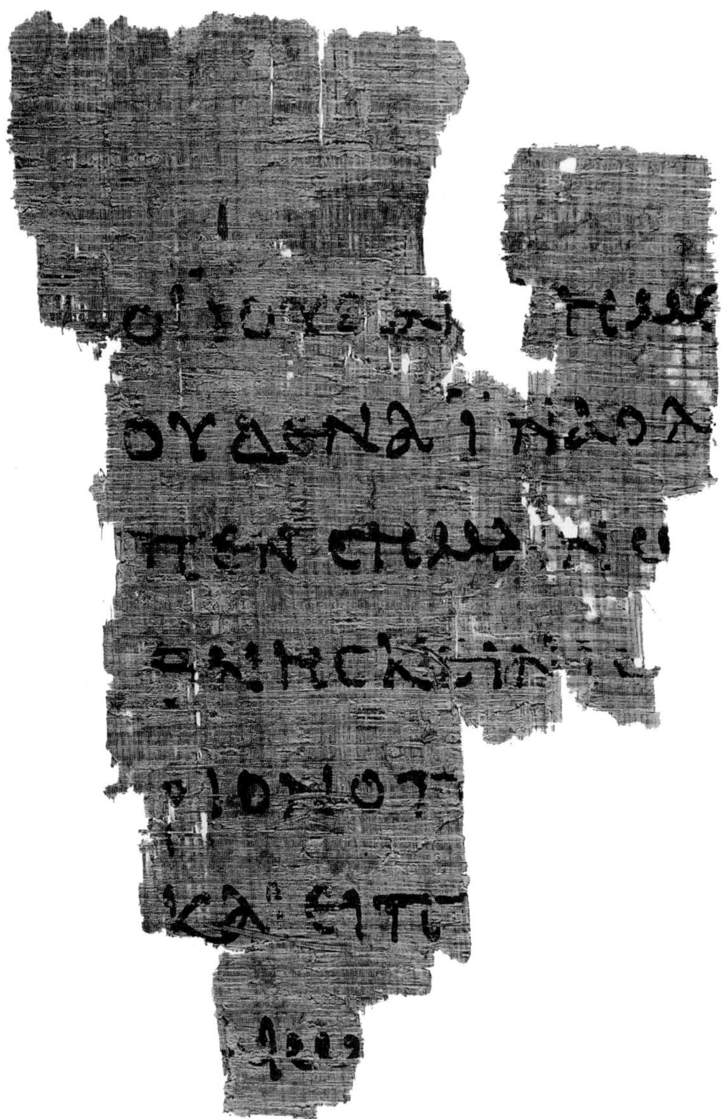

The Rylands fragment of John's Gospel, containing John 18: 31–3, 37ff. and known as P52 is the earliest extant fragment of the New Testament. It is dated to the period 125–150 CE.

large-scale archaeological excavations in Egypt. Some of these began to turn up discarded papyrus copies of all manner of texts. Most were legal papers, letters, accounts, bills, surveys, school exercises, censuses. But many were literary texts: Greek and Latin authors, early Christian writings, and copies of the Greek scriptures. Most finds have been scraps of manuscripts, perhaps half a page, or even just a few lines. Others contain parts of a number of leaves. A few are more substantial, and a tiny number contain most of a New Testament writing. At the end of the nineteenth century, two scholars named Grenfell and Hunt chose a site which had every prospect of being a rich source of early Christian material—the town of Oxyrhynchus. Their success was spectacular: they reported that the craftsman making metal boxes to store the finds could not keep up with the excavators. Today, a century on, the Oxyrhynchus papyri are still being published. So far, 65 volumes, containing the text of 4,441 papyri, have been published. Of these, 33 contain a New Testament text. But it was not until the 1930s that the first substantial texts were found. The Chester Beatty papyri (so called after the collector who purchased them) contain three of particular interest, all of the third century. The first manuscript, which contains the four gospels and Acts (remnants of all five books survive), was produced in the third century. There is another of a similar date which contains Paul's letters, which is a particularly important witness to the text. The third contains the book of Revelation, and remains the oldest extensive copy. At a similar time there was found a scrap of half a dozen verses of John's Gospel which, dated to the period 125–50, is still the oldest surviving copy of any part of the New Testament. This find at once knocked on the head the theory that the fourth gospel might have been composed as late as 150, for here was a copy written before that date turning up in Egypt.

But the real significance of these finds was that they predated the fourth-century manuscripts which nineteenth-century scholarship, culminating in Westcott and Hort, had believed to contain a text closest to that of the authors of the New Testament text. Would the evidence of these older witnesses confirm this, and with it the theory of groupings of manuscripts which had been proposed? The evidence at first was inconclusive. It had been claimed in 1924 that some manuscripts contain a 'Caesarean text', that is, one which came from and was in use in Caesarea. The Chester Beatty gospel manuscript cast some doubt on this, for it appeared to have some of the features of the Caesarean text, but not all. Other papyri likewise showed some characteristics of the later texts, but not all, or showed characteristics of more than one later text. The theory began to emerge that there was a 'Constantinian watershed'. The persecution by the Emperor Diocletian, lasting between the years 303 and 312, had seen the destruction of many Christian books. It seemed possible that, with the Peace of Constantine in 312, the church had used its comparatively small stock of surviving books to produce a number of 'standards'. Churches whose books had been destroyed needed replacements, and in an era of growth many new copies were needed for new churches. As a result, much of the variety of earlier generations was lost. This theory also explained the peculiarities of the 'Western Text', and especially of

Codex Bezae. Although this manuscript seemed, by comparison with the Codex Vaticanus, to preserve the text of the gospels rather imperfectly, it was noted that it had many readings in common with the two oldest versions, the Old Syriac and the Old Latin. These agreements had to come from a similar second-century base text. The degree of its difference from other post-Constantinian manuscripts was due to the fact that it is a reminder of an earlier age when texts differed much more from each other, and when there was less interest in control. It is true of many writings that the manuscript tradition was free in the earliest period of its copying, and that it stabilized thereafter. This, it was becoming clear, was the case with the New Testament. The study of other pre-Constantinian materials substantiated the case. Even before the impact of the discovery of extensive papyri, some scholars in the generation after Westcott and Hort were examining this problem. The name of F. C. Burkitt (1864–1935) stands pre-eminent among them. His studies encouraged him to examine the early Syriac and Latin versions, and to appreciate the significance of their agreements.

The quotations from the New Testament in the mid-second-century apologist and teacher Justin Martyr, who worked in Rome, and of other second- and third-century writers, added to the oldest Syriac and Latin evidence, suggested that the later text forms were developed after the Peace of Constantine. The Byzantine text was latest, emerging in the course of the fourth and fifth centuries. The Western Text, as we have seen, was formed from older materials. That left the Alexandrian text, to which the two codices Sinaiticus and Vaticanus belonged. The problem was that there was clear evidence that the Western Text dated from the second century. But the Alexandrian Text seemed to be better. On the canons of criticism developed by earlier generations, it was generally agreed where the two texts differed, that the Alexandrian was the better. For example, scribes tended to harmonize the gospels; that is, to change the text of one to make it more like the others. This tendency is found far more strongly in Codex Bezae than in the Alexandrian Text.

Light was shed on this problem with the publication in 1956 and 1961 of the most extensive papyri of all. P75 (all the papyri are listed in a numerical sequence, each prefaced with P for papyrus) contains Luke and over half of John, and is dated to about 200. In a thorough investigation of its text of Luke, C. M. Martini showed that it contained substantially an earlier form of the text found in Codex Vaticanus: the same careful spelling, the same tendency to restraint, many of the same readings. Each is written in a quality hand of its time. Thus, it is now clear, what was to develop into the Alexandrian Text was already in existence by the year 200. The pressing question whether it is older still has yet to be answered. Was it a careful product of a late second-century scholar, tidying up a hopelessly confused text as well as he could, or was it derived from copies which avoided at least some of the second-century freedom? A degree of editing is indisputable: there are a number of places where the Hellenistic Greek of the evangelists has been 'Atticized', that is, improved to the literary taste of a later age, where classical Greek was the writer's model.

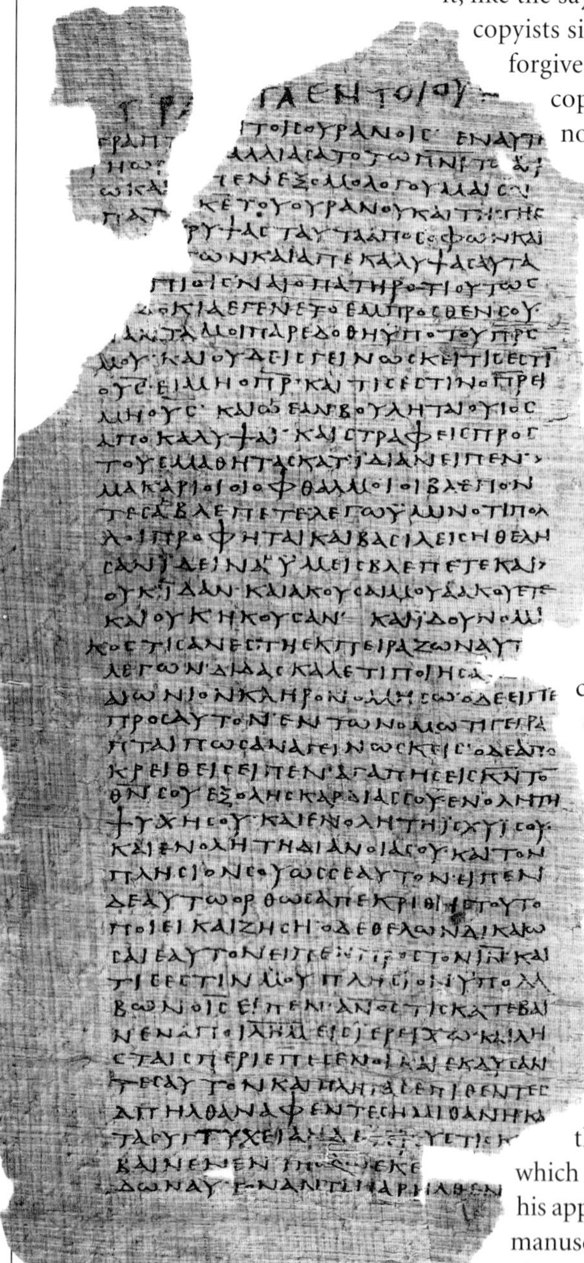

Bodmer papyrus P75 written in the period 175–225, and showing Luke 10: 20–32.

The origins of the Alexandrian Text is one of the biggest questions in New Testament studies. All that can be said at present is that there were no tight controls by anyone on the second-century text. Phrases and sayings were altered, brought into the text (like the story of the woman taken in adultery in John 7: 53–8: 11, or the Long Ending of Mark, 16: 9–20) or—less often—dropped out of it, like the saying at Luke 23: 34. It seems probable that Christian copyists simply left out Jesus' saying at his crucifixion, 'Father, forgive them, for they know not what they do.' The text was copied to make sense to the communities who used it, not to preserve the precise words of the author.

P66, found at the same time as P75, is a manuscript of John which contains some of the materials from which later recensions emerged. There are frequent corrections by the scribe, mostly of mistakes which he had made, but a few changing the text, so that it shows two readings found later in different manuscripts.

The list of papyri is now past the hundred mark. Not all are ancient or significant—some are comparatively insignificant copies written as late as the seventh century. But many have dramatically changed the course of modern research. Unfortunately, few are extensive. Often, we have just a tantalizing glimpse of a text last read 1,700 years or more ago. It is partly for this reason that the changes to printed texts in their wake has been less dramatic than the abandonment of the Received Text. P75, which could have had a huge influence, has on the whole encouraged editors and translators to stay with Westcott and Hort, whose Codex Vaticanus the papyrus so closely anticipates. However, the fact that they have cast some doubt on the age of the later texts has caused one school of criticism to abandon the significance of manuscripts entirely.

No editor of the New Testament follows a single manuscript. In any place where manuscripts vary, he will adopt the reading here of one manuscript, there of another, selecting in each place the reading which he considers to be that written by the author. In fact, his approach is eclectic. But most editors come to rely on one manuscript rather than another, and where there is nothing to choose between readings, will follow a trusted guide. Against this, one approach is altogether to reject the value of manuscripts as trusted bearers of good readings, and instead to evaluate the variant readings solely on the basis of the question 'What is this author most likely to have written?' This approach, known as 'thoroughgoing eclecticism', has proved particularly valuable in matters of style. The names C. H. Turner, G. D. Kilpatrick, and J. K. Elliott are associated with the recovery of many shades of meaning, by studying an author's usage where the manuscripts agree, and extrapolating the evidence to find the reading consonant with his style where they differ.

It is but a short step to find out the author's theological ideas, and to reject those readings which bear the mark of later debate or more advanced Christian thought. This has not been such a primary concern of the thoroughgoing eclecticists, nor indeed until recently of any textual critics. In previous centuries, their battles were with defenders of the *textus receptus*, who regarded even the critical apparatus as an evil to be resisted. It is thus no surprise to find the textual critics taking the line that no readings in the manuscripts affect any point of doctrine, and rarely touch on matters of substance. A little reflection on the degree of theological debate, usually text-centred, in most periods of Christian history, may lead one to question this. And indeed the degree to which variations between manuscripts came into being as a result of theological controversy has come to be more fully appreciated. A good example appears in the very first verse of Mark's Gospel, with the later addition of the words 'Son of God' to 'The beginning of the Gospel of Jesus Christ'. If the beginning of Mark is read without these words, one comes to verse 12 and the proclamation 'This my beloved son' rather differently. It might appear that Jesus only became son of God at his baptism. This adoptionist position was fiercely argued at a later date. One can see how Mark, who was innocent of the later question, wrote a rather heretical-seeming beginning, which a later copyist corrected, since he did not believe that the evangelist could have meant to imply such a dreadful thing.

HARMONIES

One especially fascinating aspect of modern study has been the gradual recovery of the material referring to a lost document from early Christianity, indeed the slow realization that this document had once existed. Harmonies of the canonical gospels into a single continuous narrative were popular down to the early modern period. Late nineteenth- and early twentieth-century research has revealed that the medieval versions were to a greater or lesser extent descended, with many variations and developments, from two second-century harmonies, which had had an immense influence in their time, both on the minds of those who knew them and on the text of the separate gospels. The first of these to be fully appreciated was Tatian's Diatessaron. Tatian, a native of Syria who at one time taught in Rome, produced his Diatessaron in either Greek or Syriac (there are supporters of each theory). This remarkable achievement, a working together not merely of stories but of phrases and words, predominated as *the* gospel book of Syrian Christianity down to the fifth century and beyond. From it are derived important versions in

Arabic, Persian, Latin, several dialects of Middle Italian, Dutch, and early English (a manuscript owned by Samuel Pepys). One other vital witness is a commentary on the Diatessaron by the Syriac writer Ephraem. Until recently, this was known only in an Armenian translation. But portions of a copy in Syriac have been found. Not a scrap of Tatian's Diatessaron survives, and it is only possible to reconstruct his text and sequence of material by painstaking analysis of the various witnesses. A tiny fragment of parchment, found in the early 1930s in the course of excavations at Dura Europos on the Euphrates, was initially thought to contain the Diatessaron. Certainly, it was a harmony (the end of the crucifixion story, with the beginning of the pericope about Joseph of Arimathea). It is in Greek, and this suggested that Tatian might have written in that language. On the other hand, some possible Syriacisms were found in the text, suggesting that it might be a translation. Thus, the fragment cast only uncertain light on the basic issue of the language in which Tatian wrote. Subsequent study, however, has demonstrated that the text is unlikely to be the Diatessaron, and is an otherwise unknown harmony.

It is rarely possible to be sure of Tatian's exact wording. However, it has become increasingly clear that he had a considerable influence on the text of the separate gospels, especially in Syriac and Latin. But it also became clear that not all harmonies could have stemmed directly from Tatian, and there must have been an even older lost Harmony. There was an earlier Harmony produced by Justin Martyr, which is completely lost. It is striking that Justin never cites from the canonical gospels in a form found also in later manuscripts of the gospels, and that he refers to these texts not as gospels but as the Memoirs of Jesus.

THE CURRENT POSITION

In many other areas of study the situation has developed comparatively rapidly in the past century. Sabatier's edition of the Old Latin remained a standard reference work for two centuries. Increasingly, however, it needed to be supplemented by reference to many editions of manuscripts subsequently discovered. These include several ancient fourth-century copies, of great interest. The foundation by the monks of Beuron, Baden-Württemberg, of the Vetus Latina Institüt made it possible to set about replacing Sabatier. Their edition of the materials not only provides the readings of the manuscripts, but also the text of thousands of citations from early Latin Christian writers. For good measure, the editors analysed the material, reconstructing the base texts represented by the manuscripts and citations. The most remarkable centre of all is the Institut für Neutestamentliche Textforschung, Münster, Germany. Founded by Kurt Aland in 1959, and now under the directorship of Professor Barbara Aland, it has produced an extraordinary number of works that have become indispensable tools of the trade: catalogues of manuscripts, lexica, concordances, editions of Greek and versional manuscripts, lists of variant readings, editions of the Greek New Testament, textual studies. In addition, its collection of microfilms and photographs of Greek and versional manuscripts makes the Institute the world's centre for New Testament manuscript studies.

Collaborative work in the English-speaking world has been largely focused in the International Greek New Testament Project, a British and American venture founded in 1948. A detailed collection of variant readings from Luke's Gospel was published in 1984–7, and since then work on the Gospel of John has progressed steadily.

It thus becomes clear, not only that the earliest forms of the text of the gospels was very different to that known to later generations, but that in large parts of early Christianity, the gospels were less influential than the single harmonized version. The contrast with P75, the precursor of the Alexandrian Text produced only a generation after Tatian, is marked. And it is here that we are at a standstill, for we lack the materials to recover earlier forms of the text, and are still searching for a methodology to undertake the quest. The time has not yet come to despair. But the present barrier of the second century is as great as the Constantinian watershed proved a hundred years ago.

Meanwhile, the making of translations continues, and a number of materials have been prepared especially for this purpose. The United Bible Societies' *Greek New Testament*, first published in 1966, is now in its fourth revised edition (1993). As well as full information about the variations in the text adjudged by its editors to be the most significant, it contains information about the punctuation adopted by various editors and translators. A companion volume produced by B. M. Metzger discusses the variants in the *apparatus* and gives the reasons why the editors selected the reading which they have printed in their text. This text is now identical with the most widely used edition, the *Novum Testamentum Graece* of the Institut für Neutestamentliche Textforschung. This, known as Nestle–Aland from the names of past (Eberhard Nestle and then his son Edwin, followed by Kurt Aland) and present (Barbara Aland) editors, is now in its 27th edition. With the most comprehensive small *apparatus criticus*, in an up-to-date format, it undoubtedly provides the best working text for anyone studying the New Testament.

It is sometimes said that the comparatively few differences between Nestle–Aland and Westcott and Hort indicate that the papyri have had surprisingly little impact on the process of editing the text. However, this is partly because the process of evaluating the new materials is still under way. We do not know what changes the editors of the future will make, once the evidence of the papyri has been fully assimilated. It is also true to say that a single text (that of Nestle–Aland and the United Bible Societies) has become dominant. If one were to take into account other twentieth-century editions which are less widely used, the real complexity of the situation would become more apparent. For example, G. D. Kilpatrick produced most of an edition (*A Greek English Diglot for the Use of Translators*) which follows quite different principles. But it was abandoned by the British and Foreign Bible Society when they joined in the United Bible Societies venture. There is thus less uniformity than at first appears. The text of the New Testament has changed greatly since the time of Erasmus and his fellow pioneers. A late medieval text became a fourth-century one, and that in turn has at least in part become an even older one. What is to come is still unsure.

7 Modern Translations

STANLEY E. PORTER

INTRODUCTION

Translation of the Bible into English has taken two major turns. The first was the rise of vernacular translations that in some ways anticipated but also encouraged and supported events surrounding the Reformation. Not only did this result in such monumental linguistic accomplishments as Luther's German translation, which in effect 'invented' modern German (1522), but there were a number of important English translations as well. English translations of this time include those of Tyndale (1526), Coverdale (1535), Rogers (who used the name Matthew) and who completed Tyndale's Bible (1537), the Great Bible (1539), Geneva Bible (1560), and Bishops' Bible (1568). These English versions were drawn on in various ways, especially Tyndale's, in publication of the Authorized Version (or King James Bible) of 1611. The enduring effect of this monument of English translation is far from past, as the survey below indicates. The second major turn in translation of the Bible into English occurred in the last few years leading up to the turn of the nineteenth century, with publication of the English Revised Version and the American Standard Version (see below). Since that time, there has been a veritable avalanche of translations of the Bible into English (both British and American) versions, with well over 115 different versions of the Old and New Testaments produced, according to one reckoning. The history of this Bible translating, and resultant publishing industry (with millions of copies sold), is a story in itself that merits brief recounting. However, perhaps equally if not more important are the issues regarding translation of the Bible that such industry has raised.

HISTORICAL SURVEY OF TRANSLATIONS

Owing to the huge number of translations produced over the last 100 years, it is impossible here to comment upon each of them, or even to mention them all. Nevertheless, an intriguing narrative can be recounted of the history and development of English Bible translation over the last century, beginning with the English Revised Version and American Standard Version, and ending with the

THE

HOLY BIBLE

CONTAINING THE

OLD AND NEW TESTAMENTS

AND THE APOCRYPHA

TRANSLATED OUT OF THE ORIGINAL TONGUES: BEING THE VERSION SET FORTH A.D. 1611 COMPARED WITH THE MOST ANCIENT AUTHORITIES AND REVISED

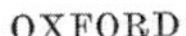

OXFORD

PRINTED AT THE UNIVERSITY PRESS

LONDON: OXFORD UNIVERSITY PRESS

AMEN HOUSE, E.C. 4

Bourgeois 8vo Refs.

(*Above left*) Title page of the Revised Version with Apocrypha, which was first published as a complete translation (with Apocrypha) in 1895.

(*Above right*) Samuel Rolles Driver (1846–1914) was an outstanding Hebrew scholar, and a member of the translation committee of the Revised Version of the Old Testament from 1875 to 1884. He played a decisive role in enabling biblical criticism to be accepted in Britain.

Contemporary English Version. The story is one filled with agreements and some serious disagreements, even disputes, the influence of powerful personalities and strongly held convictions, the commendatory work of numerous translation committees and the perhaps not always so commendable compromise that such work requires, and the diligent and often thankless work of numerous individuals, some of whom remain virtually unknown and others of whom put their names at the head of their translations.

Because of its many virtues, as well as the theological and political climate of the times, the Authorized Version eventually achieved supremacy among English translations, attaining this in the second part of the seventeenth century. Despite this, in the eighteenth and nineteenth centuries there had been several efforts either to improve or to replace it (one scholar estimates that there were as many as 70 private versions of the Bible published in English between 1611 and 1881). Among the more reputable versions, efforts by such notables as John Wesley (1775), Noah Webster (1833), and Henry Alford (1869), combined with discoveries of earlier manuscripts and the development of textual criticism (see pp. 147–152 below), set the stage for the formation in 1870 of a committee to oversee revision of the Authorized Version. Members of the committee belonged to a number of Christian denominations, and there was an equivalent American committee formed, which made suggestions regarding American usage. The revision worked within the guidelines that changes were to bring the version into line with recent discoveries regarding manuscripts, correct errors, and clarify ambiguities or inconsistencies, but without making unnecessary changes to the Authorized Version. At the time of its first appearance (1881 for the New Testament, then 1885 for the Old Testament, and 1895 for the Apocrypha), the Revised Version caused a significant stir, selling over 2 million copies in the first few days of its publication. Nevertheless, the perhaps inevitable conservatism of the revision committee, which saw itself as maintaining the language of the Authorized Version, resulted in a less than acceptable product. Of course, some readers were bothered that certain cherished passages, especially in the New Testament, were now confined to the margins or deleted altogether due to reconsideration of the text (e.g. John 5: 3–4; Acts 8: 37; 1 John 5: 7), which for the New Testament generally followed that of B. F. Westcott and F. J. A. Hort, who were working on an edition of the Greek text at the same time. The reconstructed Greek text of the Authorized Version, with the Revised Version's variants noted, was issued in 1881 by F. H. A. Scrivener. More importantly, however, it is generally thought that there was less consideration of English style, again especially in the New Testament, than there should have been, and than there was in the original Authorized Version. In particular, the effort to render each Hebrew and Greek word with the same English word, a more conservative practice than the Authorized Version itself displayed, led to tedium and flatness in reading. Thus, despite the more up-to-date text, and fidelity to the original languages, the Revised Version was probably best used as a study Bible, but not as a pew Bible. The American version of the Revised Version, known as the American Standard Version, was published in 1901 (without the Apocrypha), being completed by essentially the same American committee as had worked in a consultative capacity with the British committee that had produced the English Revised Version. However, the American committee was less conservative than its English counterpart and incorporated more changes into the text in an effort to eliminate archaisms, as well as take American usage into consideration. This version was more popular in the United States than its counterpart was in Britain. Despite—or perhaps because of—the ultimate failure to become replacements of the Authorized Version, these translations suitably paved the way for a spate of modern versions in the twentieth century.

The committee approach to translation of the Revised Version, however, had not been successful. Instead, once the need for modern English versions had been illustrated by the shortcomings of the Revised Version and its American counterpart, a number of individuals in the first half of the twentieth century undertook to produce personal versions, motivated by differing circumstances and resulting in a number of credible and well-received translations. To a large extent, the personal translations gave renewed impetus for the possibility of committee translations, which have subsequently dominated translation in the second half of the century. This is not to say that there have not been personal translations throughout the century, but their acceptance in the first half of the century was generally much greater.

There are a number of personal translations worth mentioning, virtually all of them attempting to be modern English renderings. Richard Weymouth's translation was the outgrowth of his having worked with other translation projects, as well as his own interest in Greek language as a classical scholar, and his work in textual criticism (he earlicr published his own Greek text, *The Resultant Greek Testament* (1886), collating a large number of Greek editions). He produced a translation (1903) of the New Testament into contemporary English as a supplement to other versions, not as a substitute for Bible versions to be read in church. Weymouth's translation went through several revisions, and was eventually published in the United States. Its strengths were that it reflected translation of the Greek text by someone who was familiar with it for other than strictly theological reasons, and that it differentiated the purposes for which translations might be made.

A better-known personal translation is that of James Moffatt, the Scottish pastor and scholar. Moffatt actually published two separate translations. The first was *The Historical New Testament*, published in 1901, but the one for which he is known today is his New Translation, with the New Testament appearing in 1913 and the Old Testament in 1924, and the combined version in 1926. It was this Bible that later became the basis of the Moffatt Bible Commentary on the New Testament (1928–49), which had a number of distinguished contributors besides Moffatt himself. Moffatt was a very innovative translator, concerned to overcome the archaisms of the Authorized Version and reflect what he considered the most important advances in understanding of the Hebrew and Greek texts of the Testaments. As a result, many of his renderings have a noteworthy freshness and vividness, but that is also what has been considered the problem with the translation. Despite its becoming probably the most popular modern language version of the first half of the century, with the New Testament more highly regarded than the Old, it has been accused of being too free and easy with the text, both in terms of changes that Moffatt made to the ordering of the text of the Old Testament and in his renderings themselves. For example, Moffatt placed Job 40: 15–34 in square brackets at the end of Job and Jeremiah 45: 1–5 between verses 7 and 8 of chapter 36. He also used different typefaces to distinguish pentateuchal sources. For the New Testament, Moffatt used von Soden's Greek text (1913), which he considered a major step forward, although later textual critics do not share that opinion. Nevertheless, Moffatt's contribution

James Moffatt (1880–1944) produced innovative translations of the Bible (New Testament 1913, Old Testament 1924). A native of Glasgow, he held posts in Oxford and Glasgow, and New York where he died.

to modern English translation of the Bible should be recognized as the important effort that it was, resulting not only in his two translations, but also in his involvement with the Revised Standard Version, though he died before it was completed.

Whereas the first two personal translations of substance were done by British scholars, the first American English personal translation of lasting value was made by Edgar J. Goodspeed with J. M. P. Smith. A New Testament scholar who had a keen interest in the recently discovered and published papyri (he edited a number himself), Goodspeed, as the name of the version—An American Translation—reflects, was concerned to produce one that was actually in American English and suitable for use in a public context. When the translation of the New Testament appeared in 1923, it was written in a smooth American English, showing (as might be expected) much knowledge of the Greek text. Goodspeed did the New Testament, and a colleague in Old Testament at the University of Chicago, Smith, translated the Old Testament, which appeared in 1927. The two were combined in one edition in 1931. The translation, especially of the New Testament, was highly criticized, much of it being unfair criticism, because of Goodspeed's teaching at the University of Chicago, considered by many to be too theologically liberal an institution to produce a responsible translation of the Bible, and because of wording that Goodspeed used that was different but in fact more accurate than the Authorized Version.

To this point, most of the new versions of the Bible in English had been done by Protestants, with the Catholics using the Douai-Rheims-Challoner version (New Testament in 1582, Old Testament in 1609–10, revised in the eighteenth century by Richard Challoner; and reprinted numerous times in the nineteenth century), a version that suffered from its being a translation of a translation, albeit an ancient one (it was a translation of the Vulgate), and done in conscious reaction to Protestantism. Because of its numerous archaisms, a revision of this translation was thought necessary, and the British Catholic scholar Ronald Knox was selected to do this. A man of literary accomplishment, besides theological knowledge, as well as being a convert from Anglicanism, he completed his translation of the New Testament in 1945 and the Old Testament in 1949. His attempt to render the language of the Vulgate into what a native English-speaker would say, and to overcome the limits of a translation, was clearly to his credit. Since 1943, however, Catholic scholars were allowed (and after Vatican II Catholic scholars were greatly encouraged) to utilize the original languages in their work. Thus, the fact that his version was based upon the Vulgate, which severely limits its effectiveness as a translation of the original Hebrew and Greek texts, rendered it somewhat anachronistic.

The last of the important personal translations takes this survey into the second half of the century, but its origins, purpose, and accomplishments merit its inclusion here. Out of work that he did with British youth during the Second World War, J. B. Phillips became aware of the need to communicate the Bible to those who had no background in biblical English. He decided to produce a translation that reflected spoken English, with the appropriate number of words to reflect the original in a smooth, flowing, and understandable language like that of a regular modern book. Beginning with his *Letters to Young Churches* (1947), which included Paul's epistles, Hebrews, and the catholic epistles (with a preface by C. S. Lewis, who had found much of merit in Phillips's translation), and following on with other parts (gospels in 1952, Acts in 1955, and Revelation in 1957), Phillips issued his entire New Testament in 1958. The popularity of this translation, as well as a desire not to have his version enshrined in the same way as some other translations had been, led Phillips to issue a revised edition in 1972, this time based upon the United Bible Societies' *Greek New Testament*, rather than that of Westcott and Hort, which he had originally used (see below on the texts used for translation). The translation is considered by many to be of high literary sensitivity, although others consider it too paraphrastic (see below on paraphrase vs. translation).

In the second half of the twentieth century there have been other personal translations produced as well, mostly of the New Testament, such as those by Gerrit Verkuyl known as the Berkeley Version (1959, though the New Testament appeared in 1945), by the Jewish scholar Hugh Schonfield, the first Jewish translator of the New Testament into English (1955), by the classical scholar E. V. Rieu as the Penguin Gospels (1952), and his son, C. H. Rieu, of the Acts of the Apostles (1957), by the classical scholar Richmond Lattimore (1962 for the Gospels and 1982 for Acts and the letters), by the Presbyterian minister Eugene Peterson (*The Message: The New Testament in Contemporary Language*, 1993), and the paraphrase of the American Standard Version by Kenneth Taylor into what he calls the Living Bible (1971). A revision of the last, purporting to make use of the Hebrew and Greek texts, has now been published (1996). The translation of the New Testament in 1966 of the Today's English Version, which became the New Testament portion of the Good News Bible (1976), was done by essentially one person, Robert Bratcher, but that is considered below, since it was a project sponsored by the American Bible Society and never promoted as a personal translation. Nevertheless, those above represent significant monuments in the history of Bible translation, for a number of reasons. Not least is the amount of effort devoted by a number of individuals to overcome the resistance to any other translation but the Authorized Version in English-speaking circles. There is on top of that the phenomenal amount of learning required to translate either or both Testaments, as well as the decisions that must be made regarding how to render words and phrases and pitch them appropriately for the use and audience of the particular version. Without these individual efforts, the history of Bible translation would certainly be much different. At the least, they paved the way for the major translation efforts of the second half of the century.

Whereas the first half of the century produced a number of personal translations of the Bible, the second half of the century has been dominated by group translational projects sponsored by Bible societies and other committees, such as had originally translated the Authorized Version and produced the Revised Version and American Standard Version. Having suffered setbacks with the

Revised Version, and recognizing continuing admiration, even veneration, for the Authorized Version, such translational projects undoubtedly had been slow in developing in the first half of the century. When such projects did get under way, they were dependent for their efforts upon the groundwork laid by the huge effort expended in personal translations, by people who had first taken up the task of developing readable modern English versions. A noteworthy exception to this is the Twentieth Century New Testament, a version by a small group of twenty men about the turn of the nineteenth century (1902). This group of ministers and laymen, none of them scholars, with common concern that the Bible be understood by readers in their own language as they use it, worked together over a number of years to produce this translation. The translation, which organized the New Testament in chronological rather than the usual order, is considered to be a pioneering effort in producing a modern English version, though it took a number of years before subsequent efforts by committees became widespread.

By far the most significant committee-made Bible in the English-speaking world of the twentieth century, in no small part because of the numerous imitative projects that it spawned, is the Revised Standard Version. The Revised Standard Version is itself a revision of the American Standard Version, the American version of the Revised Version. The International Council of Religious Education, which later became the National Council of the Churches of Christ in the USA, a group that had membership from a range of denominations, was given the copyright of the American Standard Version, and they took it upon themselves to set up a committee in 1937 to oversee its revision. The committee had a broad range of representation of American denominations. The translation was meant to preserve such language of the Authorized Version as could be preserved, but to take into account the findings of biblical scholarship, including that of textual criticism, and render this into a form of English that could be used for both public and private reading. Some of the more noteworthy changes were the use of the best Hebrew and Greek texts available. For the Old Testament, this included the Masoretic Hebrew text, supplemented by a few readings from some of the recently discovered Dead Sea Scrolls (especially Isaiah). For the New Testament, this meant an eclectic text based on the sixteenth (1936) and seventeenth (1941) editions of Nestle's Greek New Testament, with reference to other Greek texts (see further below). The Revised Standard Version went back to the practice of the Authorized Version in rendering the same word by differing English words, according to context and interpretation. There was also serious reconsideration of the use of pronouns, 'thee' and 'thou' being abandoned except when addressing God, with the odd result that 'you' was used when speaking to the pre-resurrected Jesus and 'thou' used when speaking to the resurrected Christ. The Revised Standard Version met with mixed reactions when the New Testament was published in 1946, and both Testaments in 1952. For over twenty-five years, until the New International Version was published, it was the predominant English version (over 12 million were reportedly sold in the first ten years alone), and continued to undergo a number of modifications and revisions under the auspices of its continuing Bible Committee. These included a revised edition in 1962, a Roman Catholic version with Apocrypha (translated in 1957) (New Testament in 1965; entire Bible in 1966), and a Revised Standard Version Common Bible with 3 and 4 Maccabees and Psalm 151, books accepted by Orthodox churches, in 1973. The negative reaction to the Revised Standard Version was at times vitriolic, but as is so often the case in instances such as this, much of it was misdirected and misguided. For example, there were accusations that theological truths had been lost in the translation. Some of these accusations overlooked the fact that in certain places many of these truths were still reflected, but they were often not to be found where the underlying original text did not include such theological wording. The consensus has been that the Revised Standard Version in most ways accomplished its purpose.

The committee was not content with its product, however, and the translation underwent a more thorough revision in what was published as the New Revised Standard Version in 1989. Beginning in 1974, the committee began work on this new edition, conscious of continuity with the Authorized Version through the Revised Standard Version and the American Standard Version, and wishing to make their new edition as cognizant of recent scholarly work, especially in Semitic languages. For the Old Testament, the standard critical scholarly text, based on the medieval Masoretic text, was still used, while being open to further correction from other ancient manuscripts. Texts for the apocryphal and deuterocanonical books were drawn from a range of manuscripts. The New Testament relied on the latest edition of the United Bible Societies' Greek text (third, with knowledge of the fourth), which is similar to the Nestle–Aland 26th edition (1979). Several other noteworthy departures from previous editions are the elimination of archaic second-person references even to God, and avoidance of what they call linguistic sexism, that is, any reflected bias of English towards the masculine gender, through the lack of an inclusive third-person singular pronoun. This has been the most controversial issue regarding this translation, since, as the editorial committee realized from the start, owing to the structure of the original languages and of English, it was impossible to be entirely consistent without being misleading. Thus, in some passages, masculine-oriented language was retained.

One of the major problems facing those producing personal translations was making sure that they were not falling into the trap of drawing upon their knowledge of previous translations. On the other hand, many translations produced by committees see themselves as following a tradition of constant revision, such as the Revised and New Revised Standard Versions. The New English Bible, however, attempted to be a completely new translation. In 1947 a committee was formed that brought together major church groups in Britain, as well as the British and Foreign Bible Society and the National Bible Society of Scotland, with the committee first headed by C. H. Dodd until 1965, when G. R. Driver became co-director with him. As might have been expected with scholars of this calibre, attention was paid to the Greek and Hebrew texts, the former being issued in a separate publication by R. V. G. Tasker (1964) to illustrate the decisions made in this eclectic text, and the latter reflecting a number of textual judgements based upon Driver's penchant for comparative philology, especially the use of Arabic. The translation, which was first issued for the New Testament in 1961 and the complete Bible with Apocrypha in 1970, followed a set of almost certainly unattainable goals. It was meant to have a timeless quality that avoided both archaisms and modernisms, not preserving the language of former versions, and written in such a way that it could be used for reading aloud. In its translation theory, the New English Bible was meant to be rendering by the sense or meaning of the passage and not literalistically or word by word. The result was to be expected. Although in places the New English Bible reads very well, it was criticized by many for its not finding the right level of style. Some thought that it had gone beyond what the average intelligent reader could understand, while others thought that it was rather more prosaic in its phrasing and expression. Designed for a British audience, it never found a place with American readers, for whom it

Members of the translation panel of the New English Bible New Testament, working under the chairmanship of C. H. Dodd.

Sir Godfrey Driver (1892–1975), co-director with C. H. Dodd of the New English Bible. Driver chaired the Old Testament panel.

usually sounded quite foreign. An attestation that this translation did not fully achieve its goal of timelessness is confirmed by the revision published in 1989 as the Revised English Bible. Committee representation had been expanded to include Roman Catholics. The desire to create a Bible for worship, as well as one intelligible to a range of users, is reiterated. To this effect, only 'you' pronouns are used, and inclusive-gender is used where reference is to both genders. Whether the goals of this version are any more attainable than the previous only time will tell.

At about the same time as British Protestant scholars were working on the New English Bible, there were several other translation projects worth noting. In Britain, there was a Catholic initiative to produce an English version directly from the original Hebrew and Greek, rather than from the Latin Vulgate. French scholars working in Jerusalem had produced a translation called La Bible de Jérusalem, which appeared in one volume in 1956. English-speaking Catholic scholars, including the well-known novelist and medievalist J. R. R. Tolkien, taking their model and inspiration (as well as the textual notes), from the French version, produced their own rendering of the Hebrew and Greek (checked against the French version), publishing the Jerusalem Bible in 1966. The Jerusalem Bible often has felicitous renderings, without the encumbrance of residual Authorized Version English still to be found in the Revised Standard Version, and was designed especially as a study Bible. The Jerusalem Bible has rightly established itself in Catholic circles, but it is not used as frequently in Protestant circles, where there is probably suspicion of the translation, perhaps perpetuated by some of the Catholic-oriented notes and interpretations. The Jerusalem Bible was revised and reissued as the New Jerusalem Bible in 1985, although some have thought that its revisions often take a more literalistic bent than the earlier version. In the United States, the equivalent Catholic translation was the New American Bible. Originally known as The Confraternity Bible, this version took a long time to appear in its final form, owing to changing policy on translation by the Roman Catholic church. The New Testament, first translated from the Vulgate, was issued in 1941, and the Old Testament from the Hebrew in 1969. Re-translation of the New Testament from Greek delayed issuing of the entire Bible until 1970. If nothing else, this version is a monument to perseverance, and is often used by Roman Catholics in the United States. The general flavour of the version has maintained some traditional Bible translation language, while utilizing some of the developments of the twentieth century, such as rendering the same word by different English words depending upon context.

Also in the United States, and at about the same time, there were three other major Bible translation projects under way. A conservative foundation undertook publication of a new version of the Bible, out of concern that the virtues of the American Standard Version were being lost in the spate of translations since 1901. Some might have thought this a good thing, but this foundation obviously did not, and appointed a committee to translate the Bible from the latest scholarly Hebrew and Greek texts, into a style of English that was contemporary but reflected its translational heritage. The New American Standard Bible was published with the New Testament in 1963 and the entire Bible in 1971 (and revised in 1995). The result was a version that has proved highly useful for students of the original languages, because of the literalness of the translation, but something that is far from readable as modern English. For example, returning to pre-twentieth-century translational practice, each verse is printed separately, rather than in paragraph form, and words not in the original but thought necessary by the translators are put in italics, a practice that cannot be maintained consistently, not least because it is difficult to define what constitutes literal translation. When rendering the Greek tense-forms, the New American Standard Bible utilizes an outmoded understanding, so that the English reads very unnaturally, perpetuating the idea that the Bible must sound difficult to be the Bible.

The second project was the translation of the Good News Bible or Today's English Version. The brain-child of the important linguist Eugene Nida (see below), this version attempts to enshrine the principles of translation that Nida developed in several important monographs. These principles are discussed below, but essentially involve rendering the Bible into the equivalent in modern English of how a contemporary reader would have understood and reacted to the living language of the text. As a result, all sorts of technical and biblical language are avoided, expressing the text in short sentences utilizing limited vocabulary. This programme is at the heart of what is called dynamic or functional equivalence translation theory, as opposed to formal equivalence translation. Sponsored by the American Bible Society, the New Testament was translated from the United Bible Societies' *Greek New Testament* (1st edn., 1966) by Robert Bratcher, which appeared in 1966 as Good News for Modern Man: The New Testament in Today's English Version, with subsequent editions. The Old Testament, done by a small group of translators from Kittel's Biblia Hebraica (3rd edn., 1937), appeared in 1976 with the New Testament in what was called the Good News Bible, with the Apocrypha following in 1979. To date, well over 70 million of these Bibles have been sold, and it has been widely used by those for whom English is not their first language and as an aid in the translation process of rendering the Bible into the languages of cultures for whom the Bible is their first written document. It is obvious that the Good News Bible has been a tremendous success, although there were many who cast aspersions on it because of what they perceived as theological deficiencies. Most of these theological accusations seem now to have been unfounded. There are many more issues raised by the translational method itself, discussed below. In many ways reflecting the same translational tradition, although with more attention to its place at the end of an entire history beginning with the Authorized Version, is the Contemporary English Version. Utilizing the latest Hebrew (Biblia Hebraica Stuttgartensia, 1977) and Greek texts (UBS Greek New Testament 3rd and 4th edns., 1975 and 1993), this translation employs the principles of dynamic or functional equivalence, while at the same time wishing to be seen as a translation that preserves the virtues of the Authorized Version in its literary style. The Contemporary English Version was published in 1995, and aroused the same kind of response as did the Good News Bible. It was falsely accused of a number of translational errors that reflected more on the traditional and conservative views of its reviewers. Nevertheless, the Contemporary English Version does seem to be trying to maintain a double standard in the claims that it makes regarding its innovative nature and its wanting to preserve certain traditional translational features. This perhaps reflects the realization that, for many Bible users, this is not a day and age that is theologically receptive to innovation; they want their Bible to sound like the Bible they are used to.

The third American translation to note here is the New International Version. The New International Version grew out of a concern of some American denominations for finding an existing translation that would provide a general-purpose Bible, as had been the Authorized Version, but would do so in contemporary English. When they were unable to find a suitable version (they rejected the Revised Standard Version), a committee was set up in 1965 to provide a new translation, enlisting the help of numerous other scholars. Since these scholars came from not only the United States but other English-speaking countries, such as Canada, Great Britain, Australia, and New Zealand, the version acquired its name. Despite the support of the New York Bible Society and the version's publisher, and no doubt because of the large numbers of people involved and the complex procedures used, entailing very slow results, the translational project was on the brink of failure a number of times. In many ways a conservative alternative to the Revised Standard Version, the New International Version used the standard Masoretic Hebrew text and a text very similar to that of the standard eclectic Greek New Testament. The New Testament was published in 1973, and the whole Bible in 1978. The result is a mixed product. At times the New International Version is colloquial and unstilted, while at other times it retains biblical language that is not transparent. Not as dependent upon the tradition of the Authorized Version as the Revised Standard Version, in some ways the New International Version is not as consistent in its style. The

Title page of The Contemporary English Version, 1995.

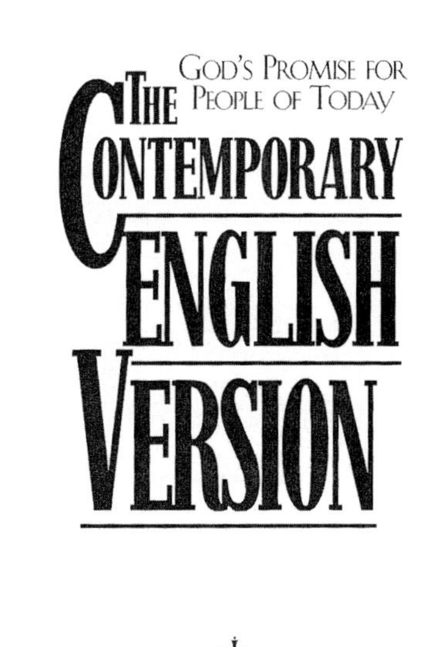

God's Promise for People of Today
The Contemporary English Version
Thomas Nelson Publishers
Nashville • Atlanta • London • Vancouver

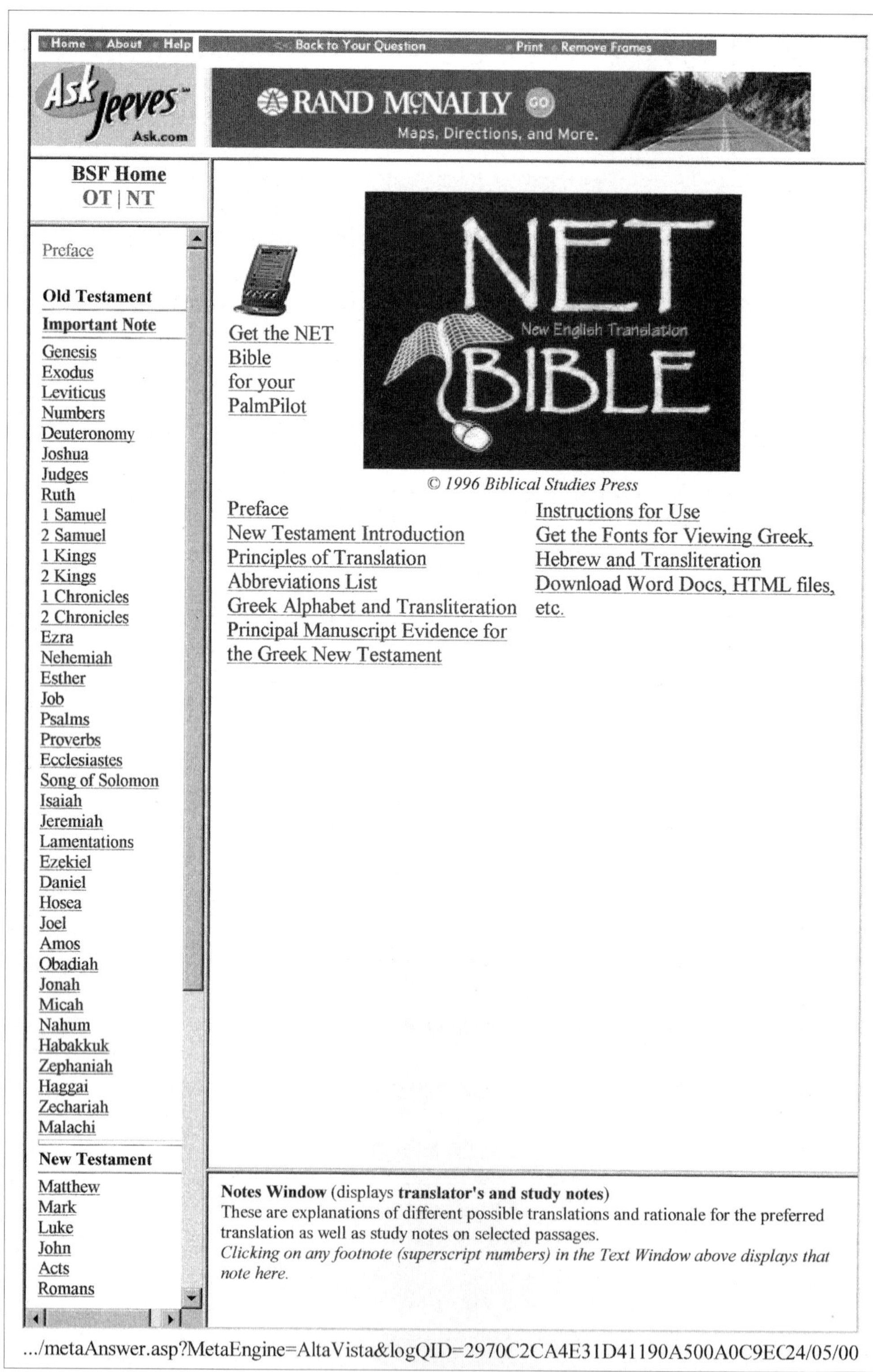
Home About Help
Back to Your Question
Print Remove Frames
Ask Jeeves
Ask.com
RAND McNALLY GO
Maps, Directions, and More.
BSF Home
OT | NT
Preface
Old Testament
Important Note
Genesis
Exodus
Leviticus
Numbers
Deuteronomy
Joshua
Judges
Ruth
1 Samuel
2 Samuel
1 Kings
2 Kings
1 Chronicles
2 Chronicles
Ezra
Nehemiah
Esther
Job
Psalms
Proverbs
Ecclesiastes
Song of Solomon
Isaiah
Jeremiah
Lamentations
Ezekiel
Daniel
Hosea
Joel
Amos
Obadiah
Jonah
Micah
Nahum
Habakkuk
Zephaniah
Haggai
Zechariah
Malachi
New Testament
Matthew
Mark
Luke
John
Acts
Romans
Get the NET Bible for your PalmPilot
NET
New English Translation
BIBLE
© 1996 Biblical Studies Press
Preface
New Testament Introduction
Principles of Translation
Abbreviations List
Greek Alphabet and Transliteration
Principal Manuscript Evidence for the Greek New Testament
Instructions for Use
Get the Fonts for Viewing Greek, Hebrew and Transliteration
Download Word Docs, HTML files, etc.
Notes Window (displays translator's and study notes)
These are explanations of different possible translations and rationale for the preferred translation as well as study notes on selected passages.
Clicking on any footnote (superscript numbers) in the Text Window above displays that note here.
.../metaAnswer.asp?MetaEngine=AltaVista&logQID=2970C2CA4E31D41190A500A0C9EC24/05/00

conservative nature of the translators can be seen, and is enshrined in the preface, which refers to the translators being 'united in their commitment to the authority and infallibility of the Bible as God's Word in written form'.

As might be expected in this computerized age, Bible translation has not escaped the desire to be technologically up-to-date. The result has been a number of translations that are now available in a variety of machine-readable forms, including availability on the internet and on CD-ROMs. Whereas most of these translations are electronic forms of previously made translations, one translation, the NET Bible (New English Translation), has been developed in both print and electronic form from the start. Distinctives of this translation are its availability for distribution through the net and its publication with extensive notes, which, commenting on a range of issues from language to theology, reveal a conservative orientation to understanding the Bible.

The NET Bible, which does not include the Apocrypha, is one of several electronic Bibles that are available on-line or on CD-ROM. In some cases they are multiple-version Study Bibles, including the original Hebrew and Greek.

This brief survey has only touched on a number of the more important or well-known translational projects—both personal and committee-based—that have taken place beginning with the Revised Version. There is no doubt that a huge amount of intellectual effort has gone into these projects, with at least something to commend almost every one of the versions, despite some of the caustic and ill-founded treatment that many of them have received, especially by those wishing to continue their veneration of the Authorized Version. Nevertheless, in the course of this discussion, a number of recurring issues have been raised that merit further examination.

THE TEXTUAL BASIS OF MODERN TRANSLATIONS

There has been a significant shift in the textual basis of the translations of the Bible, especially the New Testament. As mentioned above, the Catholic versions of the Bible had traditionally been based upon the Latin Vulgate, which meant that translations into English were translations of translations. As faithfully as these were made, they were bound to introduce wording and understandings that reflected the Latin rather than the original Hebrew and Greek. This was further complicated by the fact that various editions of the Vulgate underwent textual emendation and alteration, resulting, in the opinion of some, in an increasingly corrupt text, reflecting Byzantine and medieval readings. For those translations that returned to the original languages, however, there were still a number of issues to face.

In the study of the Hebrew Bible, the text has been relatively well established since the Reformation. Because Jewish scholars maintained the Masoretic text during the Middle Ages, this text was available for publication in the Renaissance, beginning in the early sixteenth century. In fact, the text by Daniel Bomberg in 1516–17, revised by Jacob ben Hayyim and published in 1524–5, provided the basis for the Hebrew text used by most scholars, up to publication of Kittel's Biblia Hebraica in its third edition in 1937 (followed by the Biblia Hebraica Stuttgartensia in 1977), when the St Petersburg manuscript (tenth century) became the basis of that and subsequent Hebrew texts. For the Apocrypha, most translations use a standard edition of the Septuagint, such as Rahlfs, and the Göttingen volumes where available, supplemented with Latin texts for certain books (e.g. 2 Esdras).

Debate over the Greek text to be used in translating the New Testament has had more widely diverging opinions, however. With the re-discovery of classical learning during the Renaissance, and the advent of movable type printing, there was impetus to publish the Greek text of the New Testament, despite the firm ecclesiastical hold of the Latin Vulgate. In a race to have his edition appear before that of Cardinal Ximenes and his Complutensian New Testament (printed in 1514 but not issued until about 1522), Erasmus published a text of the Greek New Testament in 1516, with a second edition in 1519, and a further three editions during his lifetime. This text was based on only a limited number of late Byzantine manuscripts (mainly two, supplemented by three or four others, dating to about the twelfth century), with some portions of Revelation a retroversion from Latin because none of his limited texts had all of the Greek text. In the preface to the second edition of their printing of a Greek New Testament in 1633 (this text resembled that of Erasmus but was based on one of Beza from 1565), the Elzevir printers referred to the text as the one that was 'received' by all. The *textus receptus*, or Received Text, as it became known, was used until the nineteenth century as the text for New Testament Greek scholarship. In the nineteenth century, owing to the discovery and publication of the major early codex manuscripts (fourth and fifth centuries), as well as the beginning of discovery of the Greek papyri (although these were not fully appreciated until the twentieth century), the textual basis of New Testament scholarship shifted. Constantin Tischendorf was one of the first, and arguably the most important, in establishing the importance of these recent textual findings, himself editing more Greek biblical manuscripts than any other person, before or after. He himself issued eight editions of the Greek New Testament, in the eighth edition especially utilizing Codex Sinaiticus, which he had discovered in St Catherine's Monastery in Sinai (1844, 1859). B. F. Westcott and F. J. A. Hort, however, were probably the most important systematizers of the principles of textual criticism. Their system of textual criticism is still widely used in creating what is called an eclectic text, that is, one that does not exclusively print one manuscript but collates a number of them. Their text relied heavily upon two major codices, Sinaiticus and Vaticanus, as the base against which other variant readings in other manuscripts were assessed. They published their text of the Greek New Testament, reflecting many of the recent manuscript finds, and their principles of textual criticism, in 1881. Since then, there have been other eclectic texts developed. In 1898, Eberhard Nestle created a hand-edition by collating the readings in Westcott and Hort's, Tischendorf's, and Bernhard Weiss's editions, with the result being a completely eclectic text. This edition has provided the basis of the Nestle–Aland New Testament (27th edn., 1993). In the early 1960s, in an effort to provide a Greek text with the interests of the Bible translator in mind, Eugene Nida instigated a project by the American Bible Society to publish an eclectic Greek New Testament, a project which soon had the support of many other Bible societies, and is published by the United Bible Societies (UBS). That edition, although originally independent, is now the same text as the Nestle–Aland text since its 26th edition (1979) and the third edition of the UBS text, which itself has reached four editions (1966, 1968, 1975 corr. 1983, 1993). This text now clearly dominates textual criticism of the Greek New Testament.

Brooke Foss Westcott (1825–1901), Regius Professor of Divinity at Cambridge (1870–90), Bishop of Durham (1890–1901). His edition of the Greek text of the New Testament (1881, with F. J. A. Hort) broke new ground and profoundly influenced subsequent research.

Despite the current pre-eminence of the Nestle–Aland/UBS editions, there are a number of texts that have formed the bases of the New Testament portions of versions of the Bible discussed above. The *textus receptus* formed the basis of the Authorized Version. We do not have the exact text that was used, but the reconstructed text was issued by F. H. A. Scrivener in 1881 as part of the revisions for the Revised Version, and is thought by him to reflect the fifth edition of Beza's text, published in 1598 (others have thought it reflects an edition published by Stephanus in 1550). Organizations such as the Trinitarian Bible Society have continued to keep editions of the *textus receptus* in print. Recently, an edition of the majority text, relying upon the Byzantine textual tradition and in many ways resembling the *textus receptus*, has been issued by Zane Hodges and A. L. Farstad (1982). There have been numerous revisions of the Authorized Version through the years, with at least two major revisions of this edition being made in the period with which we are concerned, both maintaining their reliance upon the *textus receptus*. The first of these is the King James II version, by Jay Green. An American project, the publication of the King James II in 1971 was a response to various modern translations, wishing to preserve the Bible that people were used to reading (undoubtedly meaning the Authorized Version, as if no others were being used). As a result, in places it attempts to make some of the archaisms of the Authorized Version more understandable to modern readers. The results are not convincing. A more serious effort is the New King James Bible. Rather than being the product of one person, which the King James II essentially was, the New King James Bible reflects the work of over 100 scholars from various denominations. They undertook to revise the Authorized Version in order to give access to the many 'spiritual treasures' of that version. It is unclear how creating a mongrel translation, combining modern and seventeenth-century English, can produce such a result. In any event, these two editions do not adequately address the crucial question of what text is being translated. They choose instead to stay with what is clearly an inferior text on the basis of modern text-critical principles, because of its limited basis and late manuscripts.

Among the other versions mentioned in the survey above, there are four texts, or kinds of Greek texts, that are used for translation of the New Testament. The first are those versions that use the Westcott and Hort edition. The Revised Version and American Standard Version in effect use Westcott and Hort, as originally did Phillips. The relationship between the text that Westcott and Hort were producing during the time that the Revised Version was being produced, and that version, has often been discussed and debated. The general thought is that they had a very strong influence, sharing their results with the translation committee and often voting in support of the Greek text based upon the two great Alexandrian codices, Sinaiticus and Vaticanus. This was much to the dismay of others, such as Scrivener, who apparently wished to retain more of the *textus receptus*. In 1881 Scrivener published the reconstructed text that the revisers thought lay behind the Authorized Version, with an appendix noting where the Revised Version had decided to follow a different reading. The second text to note is that of Hermann von Soden (1913), used by Moffatt for his translation. Von Soden performed a great feat in his compilation of his Greek text, but later scholarship has found fault with it at numerous points. Moffatt's is, to my knowledge, the only major version to follow this text for a modern English translation. The third Greek text to note is the one that follows the eclectic text of Nestle (beginning in 1898), first revised by Kurt Aland and now by Barbara Aland. Since the Nestle–Aland text has become the standard text for scholarly use, with the largest number of textual variants noted, it is not surprising that it has been used by a number of translations. The Revised Standard Version appears to have used the sixteenth and seventeenth editions (1936, 1941) of this Greek text, with consultation of a number of other editions then available. The New Revised Standard Version makes it clear that the Nestle–Aland/UBS text is used, which (as mentioned above) since the third edition of the UBS Greek New Testament (1975) is identical with the Nestle–Aland 26th edition (1979). The New American Standard Bible is based upon the 23rd edition of the Nestle–Aland edition of the Greek New Testament, and Phillips used the UBS text in his revision in the early 1970s. The fourth category is those versions that have created and used their own eclectic New Testament Greek text. Weymouth published the Greek text that he translated (*The Resultant Greek Testament*, 1886), which was based upon a collation of the major published editions available in the nineteenth century, including those that followed the *textus receptus* and the Alexandrian textual tradition. Besides Weymouth, however, since Scrivener in 1881, so far as I know only the New English Bible has issued the Greek text used. Tasker in 1964 published the Greek text followed by the New English Bible, with appended notes regarding variant readings. Other translations are usually content with notes that indicate where there are serious variations in the text and the reading they have accepted, although usually noted in English. Regardless of whether one can determine the exact text followed in every instance, it is clear that since the time of the Revised Version, there has been a definite rejection of the *textus receptus* as the basis of modern English translations, and the acceptance of the Alexandrian textual tradition in the form of various eclectic texts. This is a significant change in the basis of New Testament translation, and is bound to have implications, even if the translations themselves only reflect them in changes and deletions in certain passages (e.g. Mark 6: 9ff.).

The disjunction between the use of the (non-eclectic) Masoretic text in Hebrew Bible studies (essentially the St Petersburg manuscript) and the clear predominance of the eclectic text in New Testament Greek studies raises important questions, however. These questions cannot all be answered here, but some merit brief comment. One notes immediately that there are two apparently contradictory principles at work within biblical textual criticism. With the discovery of the Dead Sea Scrolls (1947), as well as knowledge of other Hebrew manuscripts and versions (e.g. Targumim), it would be possible for Hebrew Bible scholars to create an eclectic text of the Old Testament for study and use in translation. On the other hand, with the number of complete or nearly complete early codices, such as Sinaiticus and Vaticanus, it would be possible for New Testament scholars to use a single manuscript as the basis of their study and translation. In fact, early complete New Testament manuscripts are much closer to the time of writing than are any of the Hebrew manuscripts, making at least a prima-facie case for their use. In any event, it is an oddity that two different principles of textual criticism coexist in such a way. Some have recently suggested that an eclectic text should be used for Old Testament study, utilizing the recent Dead Sea Scrolls more heavily in reconstructing the original Hebrew text. Another way forward might be to utilize single manuscripts for both Old Testament and New Testament study and translation. An advantage of using a single manuscript is that it represents an actual text that was historically utilized and transmitted within a faith community, something that cannot be said about the modern eclectic text. This text is the product of nineteenth- and twentieth-century scholarship, and was never a text used by an ancient church or synagogue. Although textual eclecticism has the goal of reconstruction of the original text, this is a goal that can never be convincingly attained, short of discovering the original manuscripts themselves. In future translation work, attention perhaps should be paid to the issue of eclecticism versus single text traditions.

ISSUES IN MODERN TRANSLATION

As noted in the brief survey above, there have been a number of different trends in modern Bible translations. Without entering into the technical jargon involved when discussing these translations, I have tried to note that there have been several different streams of translations, with numerous tributaries. Several of these streams of translation are distinguished by how they approach the question of meaning in the original language, and how that meaning is conveyed in the language of translation. There are a number of issues facing any translator of the Bible. These include recent debate on the theory of translation, language change and the changing purpose of translations, and the issue of inclusive language.

Dynamic or formal equivalence translation theory

In 1964 Eugene Nida consolidated research that he had been doing for almost twenty years on the principles of translation, especially Bible translation, and published a new and almost unparalleled theoretical work on the principles of translation, entitled *Toward a Science of Translating*. This was followed by an application of his theories to Bible translation in *The Theory and Practice of Translation*, written with Charles Taber (1969), and took its most recent form in *From One Language to Another: Functional Equivalence in Bible Translating*, written with Jan De Waard (1986). For years Executive Secretary for Translations of the American Bible Society, Nida continues to do important linguistic research, besides the many biblical linguistic projects that he has initiated (e.g. the UBS Greek New Testament, Good News Bible, and Contemporary English Version, to mention only a few). I believe it is fair to say that he has had a far larger impact on translation theory, in particular the translation of the Bible into languages previously without a written language, than almost any other person, certainly than almost any other person in the twentieth century. The debt that biblical studies owes to him is tremendous, whether or not one accepts his theories. Many do not agree with his theories of translation, but one must understand them if one expects to know much about recent developments in Bible translation.

The major starting-point of Nida's work is rejection of the traditional means of translation, often referred to as formal equivalence. It is enshrined in the tradition of the Authorized Version, Revised and American Standard Versions, Revised Standard Version, and New American Standard Version, to name but a few. Formal equivalence attempts a word-oriented translation, with emphasis upon preserving the features of the original language, with respect to vocabulary, syntax, and tone, so far as this is possible in the translated language. By contrast, Nida advocates what is called dynamic or functional equivalence. Dynamic equivalence is defined by recognizing that each language has its own characteristics, many of which cannot be transferred to another language without loss of effective communication. Nevertheless, as translation between modern languages demonstrates, there is nothing in one language that cannot be said in another. Hence, emphasis is upon the message, rather than its form. The assumption is that writers of documents, including the writers of the biblical texts, expect to be understood by their readers. The reproduction of this meaning is what the translator attempts to do, by finding the closest natural equivalent expression in the new language, whether it is English or a language having the Bible translated for the first time. Dynamic equivalence involves appreciation of a number of factors in its implementation, including cognizance of the varied functions of language, and the needs of the audience using the translation. In many ways reflecting a similar orientation to language as is reflected in the linguist Noam Chomsky's early work on transformational grammar (e.g. *Syntactic Structures*, 1957), Nida developed his concept of kernel sentences as a means of handling grammatical problems within this theory. Rather than transfer items, such as individual words, from the surface structure of one language to another, Nida proposes a process by which one breaks down the source language into its underlying structure or kernel, and then transfers this meaningful unit across from one language to another, restructuring the kernel into the appropriate expression of the receptor language. Thus, the expression in Greek literally rendered 'love of God' can be analysed into the kernel 'God loves'.

The classic example that Nida has used through the years is Mark 1: 4, which is often rendered literalistically with something like 'John preached a baptism of repentance for the forgiveness of sins'. Nida contends that 'baptism of repentance' and 'forgiveness of sins' are phrases that reflect the literal expression in Greek but carry very little meaning for a contemporary reader. He believes that there are five kernel sentences in this verse: (1) John preached something (which the following phrase captures), (2) John baptizes people, (3) the people repent,

(4) God forgives something, and (5) the people sin. Nida believes that a sentence such as 'John preached, "Repent and be baptized, so that God will forgive the evil you have done"' captures the sense of the verse.

Nida's principles were largely behind the Good News Bible, as well as the more recent Contemporary English Version. About 30 years ago, he encouraged projects to provide translations that would in some way enshrine his principles in a translation that could be used by field translators, who either did not have adequate knowledge of the original language or who needed a check on their own understanding. In 1973 the Translator's New Testament was issued by the British and Foreign Bible Society, but the equivalent Old Testament project failed. The reasons for its failure are related to what some have seen as the major shortcomings of his theory of translation. The range of discussion of Nida's theories cannot be entered into here, apart from noting some of the major questions that have been raised. Many would disagree with the major presupposition that equivalent meaning in the receptor language is either possible or worthy of attempt. To be fair to Nida, he is certainly not the first to have had the transfer of meaning as a goal of translation. Benjamin Jowett, the great classical scholar and translator of Plato, among other ancient authors, worked from this perspective. This perspective was also consciously in the minds of E. V. Rieu and J. B. Phillips when they translated. Nevertheless, ancient languages are sufficiently removed in place and time that modern interpreters cannot hope always to be able to reproduce the same meaning, or to elicit the same effect as the biblical writers did, especially since one often has very little knowledge of what that effect might have been. If this is removed as a possible or achievable goal, then one is left with close analysis of the language or formal analysis. However, whereas it is easy to posit a distinction between meaning and form, virtually all translators must have some concept of meaning, the question being how closely they choose to stay to the original text. The attempt to determine this meaning, rather than leave the matter open, is not one that Nida devised, but was articulated in the previous century by Jowett, and has been articulated since by others. However, there are many instances where, even if one believes that the original audience understood the text (but is it certain that they always did?), modern interpreters are still not certain of that meaning. Any translation that forces one to decide the meaning of each passage, therefore, runs the risk of excluding viable options for meaning that may be better off left ambiguous and subject to further consideration.

The influence of Nida on Bible translation continues to be felt. As a result of his work, most modern translators are far more aware of a greater range of issues in Bible translation, even if they do not agree on the principles for all of these issues. There is, for example, a much greater respect for the larger context in which translation occurs, including not only the world and culture of the original authors and readers, and the current receptors, but also in terms of the entire text as a discourse. One is also much more conscious of the possibilities and limitations of translation, and how one can influence meaning through the process of translation. Many of the features of the grammar of language that were taken for granted in the past now are seen to have hidden complexities that must be addressed in understanding and translating. These issues will undoubtedly continue to be confronted and debated in future Bible translation projects—or at least they should be.

The question of the difference between translation and paraphrase is appropriately raised at this point. Often a distinction is drawn between these two types of Bible rendering, usually either with paraphrase being denigrated as something less than faithful to the original, or with translation being put down as wooden and impenetrable by the untrained. There is some truth, but much falsehood, on each side. In one sense, all translations are paraphrases, in that it is impossible to reproduce the original language word for word. Even selecting the translational equivalent for each word is an act of interpretation and requires paraphrase. If one ever reads an inter-linear Bible, where an English equivalent is placed under each Greek or Hebrew word, one gets a sense of how a strict literalism results in nonsense. Therefore, in offering a critique of a version, it is not a significant criticism to label something a paraphrase. Originally, Phillips's version was called a paraphrase, but now it is thought of as a progressive translation, one of the best personal versions of the century. Much of the difficulty with resolving this debate is what Nida has been concerned with, in terms of establishing criteria by which one more than simply examines the words of the original language but looks at the larger patterns of meaning, and renders the text into the corresponding forms of the receptor language.

Language change and the changing purpose of translations

The brief history above shows that two of the major issues that have prompted the increase in the number of translations are the changes that have occurred in English through the centuries, and the changing purposes for which translations are made. These are closely related to each other.

In the same way as Shakespeare reads as English of a previous period, so does the Authorized Version. In fact, the Authorized Version itself reflected language that was already in many ways dated by its large-scale adoption of the language of previous translations, such as that of Tyndale and the Geneva Bible (it has even been argued that the Authorized Version deliberately archaized its sources, such as Tyndale's English!). What many devotees believe is the spiritual quality of this Bible is nothing more than its archaic language by today's standards. Much has changed in English since 1611. This includes some fairly significant and radical changes in the meanings of words, as well as changes in syntax and grammatical features, such as the use of pronouns ('thee' and 'thou', for instance). One of the major problems with the Authorized Version was that the style in which it was written soon became revered as a literary masterpiece. These features were often equated with theological features, and, the more this became enshrined due to archaism, the more difficult it became to promote a revision of the text, even though this was more and more needed. The Revised Version attempted such a revision but failed, to a large extent because the revisers did not go far enough in revising the English to make it sound like late nineteenth-century English, instead attempting to preserve the earlier wording as much as possible. The need for constant vigilance with regard to the text is shown by the fact that the next revision, the Revised Standard Version, was undertaken so relatively soon afterwards, and succeeded more satisfactorily because it took a more aggressive stance towards the issue of preservation of the language of the Authorized and Revised Versions. Taking an aggressive stance towards the tradition of the Authorized Version does not guarantee success, however, especially since one of the major difficulties of a translation is still to fight against its being compared directly with the Authorized Version. Undoubtedly owing to the Authorized Version, several

The Jerusalem Chamber of Westminster Abbey, used by translators of the Bible from the 19th-century Revised Version to the 20th-century Revised English Bible.

translations have taken the view that they are trying to create an equivalent of or replacement for the Authorized Version, putting the English into a timeless form. Such a goal is almost certainly one that cannot be achieved. In fact, it is probably not a virtue for a translation to become timeless. One of the reasons for the success early in the twentieth century of a number of personal translations was no doubt because they were not trying to replace the Authorized Version, and certainly not trying to create timeless translations, but rather trying to render the Bible into the modern English of their times. The contexts out of which these translations developed were often the translator's work with people, including young people, who did not have great familiarity with the traditional language of the Bible, and for whom the translator was creating something for their particular situation. Thus, in the light of these findings, it is perhaps wise to consider the changing nature of the English language when translating, such that translations may well serve their audiences best by forecasting and building in revision and updating (and the expectation of such revision and updating) at regular, periodic intervals to take into account developments in the language.

Related to this issue is that of the intended purpose of a translation. There are a number of linguistic contexts today in which it is unreasonable for a people or group to have more than one translation. These contexts might include those of extreme poverty, where it is impracticable for people to own more than one Bible when they can barely find enough money to survive. Another context is one in which the Bible is the first written document for a language group, and where the size of the language group or other considerations make it unlikely that more than one Bible will be produced in the immediate future. Whether one agrees that more than one translation is necessary or even desirable, the reality of the English-speaking world is that there are numerous affordable translations available to almost anyone who desires one. One of the effects of the Authorized Version was that it effectively limited the English-speaking world to one Bible for use for all purposes. Before the Authorized Version had become the most popular English Bible, English Bible readers were accustomed to hearing the Great Bible read from the pulpit, and often to having the Geneva Bible for private study—both of which functions were subsequently taken over by the Authorized Version. One of the distinctive contributions of personal translations early in the twentieth century was that individuals took it upon themselves to translate the Bible for a particular purpose. Often it was related to the lack of understanding that they sensed when working with a particular group of people, or in a particular context where greater understanding was required than the traditional translations seemed to offer. The individuals were able to effect translations for these particular contexts and help to bring about a loosening of the stranglehold that traditional translation had on Bible versions. Much of this was because of their recognition of the changing use of language.

The two functions of liturgical use and private study still continue to be the two primary uses of a Bible today. One can see, however, that the two functions are quite different. Today, among other things, a Bible for public reading must be euphonious enough that it does not cause the reader or the hearer to stumble in the process of reading and hearing, since only the reader and not the hearers usually have the printed page before them. Today, the sentences should be short enough so that the sense can be retained over the course of the reading, and not lost in a maze of subordinate clauses. The vocabulary should be different enough and vivid enough to convey the sense of the passage, retain the interest of the readers, and yet maintain coherence. The Bible might also be well served to have division markers with brief descriptive headings to guide the reader, and possibly the congregation that hears it read (as many versions currently have). In some contexts, it might be appropriate for the Bible used for public worship to be compatible with singing and public recitation. A Bible for private study may have very different characteristics—for example, the aurality of the study Bible is probably less important. One has the printed text in front of oneself, and can consult it, if there is some item of meaning or sense that is missed, or if a sentence is too long. For those acquainted with the original languages, a study Bible has the advantage of being able to reflect the original text more closely, in terms of using similar words for the same vocabulary in the translation or having sentence structure and length that are imitative of the biblical writer's style. For those without the languages, a study Bible may still retain some features that are better represented for reading than for hearing, such as vocabulary choice and sentence structure. There is also the possibility and usefulness of having study notes included in the Bible itself, either at the beginnings of books, at the back, or even on the same page, as marginal material. From this description, one can appreciate that a single individual might find use for several quite different translations.

As a result, it may well be appropriate to commend the fact that there is a wide variety of Bibles currently on the market since they provide opportunities for use of different Bibles according to varying purposes. For example, one might highly recommend a Bible such as the New American Standard Bible as useful for those studying the original languages, while rejecting it strongly as a general study Bible or reading Bible. Instead, one may endorse the Revised Standard Version or New Revised Standard Version for private study, and the Revised English Bible as a fluid reading Bible. In any case, it is probably wise to be cautious of any Bible that claims that it can be equally effective for all purposes. The history of English Bible translations in the modern era suggests that few have been able to serve effectively in both public and private capacities, since the requirements of each are significantly different.

Gender-free language

One of the most highly contentious issues in recent discussion of Bible translation is that of gender-free language. Known by several different terms, such as gender-neutral or -inclusive language, the issue is how one renders what is sometimes seen as gender-biased language in the original languages of the Bible into gender-free English, despite the fact that English seems to have its own gender bias by failure to have a gender-inclusive third-person singular pronoun.

The implications of these grammatical issues reflect on larger issues related to the male orientation of the biblical world, and how one might address that through translation.

The New Revised Standard Version and the Revised English Bible were the first Bibles with an established and widespread potential clientele to be published as gender-sensitive Bibles (the New Jerusalem Bible made some attempt to address the issue). The appearance of the New Revised Standard Version, more so than the Revised English Bible, caused some eyebrows to be raised. The success of the Revised Standard Version, the reputations of those involved in the translation, and the widespread and relatively mainstream placement of many of the Bible's users, however, meant that the new Version was generally welcomed. Critical scrutiny of the translation has been in terms of correction, rather than rejection of the concept of gender-inclusive language. The same cannot be said for attempts to introduce in the United States a New International Version revised to reflect gender-free language. Whereas such a Bible was published with not much fanfare in the United Kingdom (1995), a concurrent attempt in the United States brought a reaction of hurricane proportions. Battle lines were drawn between groups, much name-calling ensued, books were written on this translation and the issue of gender-free translations, and conferences were the sites of often acrimonious debate. In the end, the publisher withdrew the revised New International Version as a result of widespread pressure being exerted, including large-scale media campaigns. The United Kingdom edition, as a result, often had to be brought into the United States if the Bible was to be sold.

This type of exaggerated conflict is not unusual in theological debate in the United States, but one might still ask why this issue caused such a furore. The immediate issue stems from the linguistic questions involved. Like many languages, Greek and Hebrew are gendered languages. In other words, they have grammatical gender, that is, certain kinds of words must appear with a designation of gender (e.g. nouns in Greek are masculine, feminine, or neuter). This gender often follows natural gender, but not always so (e.g. 'woman' is feminine, but 'child' is neuter, even though the ancient Greeks knew the difference between male and female children). The pronoun system is similar. Greek also used these gendered categories in such a way that, if there were to be a single male in an audience of women, reference to the group would require a masculine word-form. An example is the use of the Greek word 'brethren', which is masculine, when speaking to a group of Christians that might include numerous women. Further, there are certain words that are used to speak of representative individuals, and these words, such as 'man', are gendered also. The questions this grammatical system raises are compounded by a similar system in English, with reference to representative figures often using the third-person singular pronoun, 'he'. A further set of questions raised by gendered language involves how one speaks of God. In Greek, the word for 'God' that is used in the New Testament is grammatically masculine, so grammatical reference is made with masculine pronouns. Grammatically, concord of a masculine noun and masculine pronoun may be required, but recent theological discussion has raised the question of the 'sexuality' of God. Is it now advisable to speak of God being masculine or feminine, or masculine and feminine, or are these terms even relevant at all? In the Bible, especially the Old Testament, there are numerous depictions of God in terms of masculine imagery, but there are also depictions in terms of feminine images. This has further implications for a number of related issues, such as how to refer to Jesus Christ, since in traditional theology he is both 'man' and 'God', and the nature of the Trinity, which has at least two masculine members (and one grammatically neuter member!). In any case, there are questions raised by all of these issues.

The gender-free Bibles have attempted to overcome some of these difficulties by adopting a number of translational features. These are to be found in several different types of translational situations. For example, in some contexts it is easy to change a reference to a group that includes women to something that has the word 'they' in it. Or, when the word 'man' in Greek is used in a generic sense, one might well use the word 'humanity' or 'humankind'. In other contexts, where a word is used that refers to a group with women, use of a masculine *and* a feminine form might suffice, such as 'brothers and sisters', where earlier translations may have had only 'brothers'. However, beyond this point, there are a number of further difficulties raised by renderings. For example, there is the problem with God mentioned above, and there is the problem of Jesus Christ, who is clearly depicted in the New Testament as both a man, and as the saviour of humankind. For many, it is not an issue that Jesus is still referred to as a man, so long as his being the Christ is seen not to be gender-based. For some, however, this raises issues related to some of the earliest Christological controversies of the church, regarding the human and divine natures of Jesus Christ and their interrelationships. There is further difficulty with the title that Jesus often uses of himself, 'son of man', which raises questions by its twofold gendered reference. Although some have proposed alternatives (is 'offspring of humanity' quite what is meant?), the traditional language is usually retained. One soon realizes that tension can often be created between the gendered basis of the original language and attempts to eradicate such reference in modern English.

One of the common questions raised by gender-free translations is the relationship between the gendered nature of the original languages, which seems to be based both in the languages themselves and in distinctly patriarchal kinds of societies, and the desire to be gender-free in a modern English rendering. It is at this point, perhaps, that one should entertain the possibility of the use of several modern translations, depending upon their purpose. One of the purposes of the gender-free translation is to provide a Bible that does not exclude fully half of all Christians by sexually marginalizing women through language. It is difficult to deny that overly literal renderings of the biblical language strike the modern ear as often more exclusive than ever was intended in the original. This is particularly important in public contexts of worship and Bible reading. However, one cannot escape the reality that the Bible was originally written not in late twentieth-century English, whether that be British or American English, but in ancient languages with cultures that may have been restricted by grammar or insight, or both, into gender-related issues. For one who is attempting to come to terms with this world, through study of the Bible, perhaps a gendered version that reflects in many instances the gender-laden language of the original text is more useful, if for no other reason than it makes one aware of the issues involved.

CONCLUSION

The last hundred years have seen a number of significant changes in the English Bible. From essentially the use of one major translation, this century has witnessed a veritable explosion in the number of Bibles produced, for differing purposes and according to different principles. Some have seen this as a pernicious development, because either they are desirous of protecting a particular traditional Bible or they sense a breakdown of reverence and respect for the Bible, because each seems to be translating as is right in one's own eyes. With the proliferation of Bibles and the amounts of money that publishing companies make in selling them, one must raise the question of the ultimate purpose of many of these translations. Nevertheless, continuing attempts to make the Bible relevant in a world changing both linguistically and culturally, as well as developments in principles of translation theory, have encouraged the creation of new versions as well. We now stand at the end of a great tradition of Bible translation that is not as dependent upon the Authorized Version as in previous times. This is due in no small part to the individual work of many different people, some working on their own, and greater numbers working in committees. It is difficult to know the direction that future Bible translation will take, but it is clear that the last hundred years or so have completely transformed the translation of the Bible into English.

THE STUDY AND USE OF THE

BIBLE

Preface

JOHN ROGERSON

Until comparatively recently the history of biblical interpretation was something of a Cinderella subject in Britain. Dubbed 'the study of the study', it was regarded in some quarters as a diversion from the main business of biblical studies, which was to study the languages, textual transmission, historical background, and exegesis of the Bible. This attitude was understandable. Modern scholarship, assisted by such resources as archaeology, cognate Semitic languages like Akkadian and Ugaritic, or the recovery of Hellenistic Greek from papyri discovered in Egypt, was unlikely to learn very much from the scholarship of earlier ages that did not have the benefit of these discoveries.

However, it has been increasingly recognized that while many of the methods used in biblical studies are objective, the results that they yield can be affected by 'external' factors. The most obvious are chance discoveries, such as the Dead Sea Scrolls; but new techniques and conclusions from archaeology or new insights in the interpretation of cultures in social anthropology can all play a part, and there is also no doubt that theological considerations can affect the results of biblical studies. A second point is that it has become increasingly difficult to distinguish a pre-critical period of biblical scholarship from a modern critical period. Of course, there have been key points in the history of interpretation when new insights radically altered subsequent scholarship, but it is also the case that there is much less that is really new about modern critical scholarship than is often supposed. To take one example, the radical criticism of the psalms in the nineteenth and twentieth centuries proposed that many were to be dated to the Maccabean period, that is, the second century BCE. However, such possibilities were already noted, if not necessarily accepted, in both medieval Jewish scholarship and by Puritan commentators. Again, it has often been pointed out that the use of different divine names in the Pentateuch that led to the Pentateuch being divided into several literary sources in the eighteenth to twentieth centuries had already been noted and discussed by early Jewish exegetes, even if they had not resulted in documentary theories of composition.

The most important outcome of the renewed interest in the history of interpretation is that it has become clear that the study of the Bible has always been critical, in the sense that scholars have used a knowledge of languages other than Hebrew and Greek as well as philosophical and scientific knowledge about the world and human growth and development in their interpretation of biblical passages. Early Jewish interpreters used the Aramaic Targumim (expanded translations) as aids in interpretation and, with the rise of Islam and the spread of Arabic, Jewish scholars whose first language was Arabic used that language to lay the foundations for all subsequent study of Hebrew grammar and lexicography. Arabic culture also rediscovered the philosophy of Aristotle, and this came to influence biblical interpretation in the Middle Ages. For example, Maimonides' masterpiece *The Guide of the Perplexed* (1190 CE) played an important role in convincing Christian interpreters that they should take the ceremonial laws of the Old Testament more seriously. Questions were also raised by the scientific knowledge of succeeding generations. It was recognized that the creation of light on the first day of creation and that of the sun on the fourth day raised the question of the nature and source of the light created on the first day. This was only one of many problems that were addressed as early as the fourth century, and it gives the lie to the idea that it was only in the nineteenth century that there was a clash between the Bible and science.

Study of the Bible's interpretation can engender a new respect for earlier scholars and a certain amount of humility in present-day scholarship. The achievements of two thousand years of interpretation are outlined in the section that follows; but it is also important to take note of George Bebawi's contribution on the eastern churches. Here, there is a quite different tradition of interpretation compared with that in the west, and it provides much food for thought.

8 The Early Church

HENNING GRAF REVENTLOW

THE USE OF THE OLD IN THE NEW TESTAMENT

The study and use of the Bible in the church begins with the church itself. Jesus of Nazareth quoted the Bible and taught his disciples how to behave according to a radicalized Mosaic law (Matt. 5: 21–48). His proclamation of the kingdom of God actualizes a basic issue in the Old Testament: God as king of Israel his people, residing on Mt Zion. To begin with he seems to have identified his mission with the task of the messenger who has to bring good news to the oppressed (Isa. 61: 1f.; cf. Luke 4: 18f.; Matt. 11: 5), but more and more he might have regarded himself as the vicarious sufferer (cf. Mark 10: 45 with Dan. 7: 13; Isa. 43: 3f.; 53: 10–12) for the sins of the 'many'. During the last supper he speaks about his blood as the 'blood of the covenant' (Mark 14: 24; parallels) alluding to Exod. 24: 8, where the blood of the offerings is dashed by Moses on the people for atonement. His quotation of Psalm 22: 2 on the cross (Mark 15: 34/ Matt. 27: 46, still preserved in the original Aramaic) indicates the same self-understanding. After his death and resurrection he is said to have opened the minds of his disciples to comprehend the scriptures (Luke 24: 45): from now on the scriptures ('the law of Moses, the prophets and the psalms') are to be interpreted as 'written about me' (Luke 24: 44).

The bottom of a gold glass bowl found in a Roman catacomb and designed as a funeral gift (second half of 4th century). It depicts a young man surrounded by various scenes from the Bible.

The first Christians regarded the death and resurrection of Jesus as events that happened 'according to the Scriptures': a formulation occurring twice in what seems to be one of the earliest Christian confessions as quoted by Paul (1 Cor. 15: 3–5). The Jewish-Christian Bible (later called the Old Testament) was taken as a book of prophecy (Rom. 1: 2) pre-announcing the gospel of Jesus as the Christ. This Greek translation of the Hebrew title Messiah was soon used like a personal name. Paul in his letters quotes the Old Testament about 90 times using it as a basis for his theology in a rather peculiar way. In the Gospel of Matthew, the repeated catchword 'fulfil' (Matt. 1: 22f.; 2: 15,17f, 23; 4: 14–16; etc.) shows that the evangelist sees the whole story of Jesus the Christ as already implied in the words of Old Testament texts. Another model for the relationship between the two convenants is typology. It appears in the letter to the Hebrews, where the basic idea is the parallelism between the institutions of the time of the fathers and now in the 'last days' (Heb. 1, 2f.). The parallelism means increase. In all his offices Jesus is superior: As the son he is more than the angels (Heb. 1–2), he is more than Moses (3: 1–6), more than the Jewish high priest (4: 14–5: 10), in the order of Melchizedek (7; cf. Gen. 14: 7–20), but mediator in a heavenly sanctuary of a better covenant (8f.). His sacrifice is valid once for all (10: 1–18).

The revelation to John is the only apocalyptic book included in the New Testament. It consists of a wealth of pictures illustrating the expectation that the end is close, in which after a period of severe persecution of the believers (by the emperor Domitian) Jesus Christ will return to his everlasting rule. Nearly all of them are taken from the Old Testament, which is quite familiar to the visionary, who lives in the last decade of the first century.

THE APOSTOLIC FATHERS

The earliest documents in the post-canonical period are the 'Apostolic Fathers'. Two of them excel in their opposite evaluation of the Old Testament. The Epistle of Barnabas, actually a theological treatise, probably written in the first quarter of the second century in Egypt or Asia, is like Hebrews built up of Old Testament quotations as theological arguments. Barnabas does not start with the Christ-event as something superior to all that happened in Old Testament times, but for him the complete Old Testament is obligatory as a document of revelation; every theological argument has to be verified from its wording. On the other side the whole salvation history before Christ and every Old Testament institution lose their independent value, as the author denies rigidly any Jewish claim upon the Bible. The Jews have lost it forever (4: 7), when Moses broke the tablets of the law at Sinai (Exod. 32: 19). Therefore circumcision (9: 4), diet laws (10), and sabbath (15) are invalid. The interpretations Barnabas presents are traditional (cf. 1: 5; 9: 4). He understands the complete Old Testament as prophecy (1: 7). Abraham, Jacob, Moses, David (as psalmist), Isaiah, Jeremiah, Ezekiel, and Daniel are called prophets. Their prophecies exclusively point to Jesus Christ and his coming (5: 6). Fulfilments in the Old Testament itself are excluded. Especially the passion of Jesus is predicted (6: 7). Barnabas 7: 3–11 gives close parallels to every detail of the passion history; often a catchword (the red colour of the cloak, Mark 15: 17; the wood of the cross) is the connecting link. Cultic regulations in the Old Testament are explained spiritually (10: 2f.). The prophetic cult criticism is adopted and intensified. Instead, the author admonishes his readers to inquire as to the ethical demands of the Lord (2: 1). This intention stands in the background of the main part of the treatise (2–17), culminating in the motive of the two ways (18–20; cf. Didache 1–5). However, Barnabas also knows about the remission of sins by the passion of Christ (5: 1; 5: 5; 7: 2f., 5; 14: 4), which is received with baptism (11: 1).

Whereas Barnabas sees a break between the institutions of the Old Testament and the church of Christ, 1 Clement (an official letter of the congregation of Rome to the congregation of Corinth; 1: 1) stresses the continuation. The main intention of the missive, written about the end of the first century, when news about an insurrection in Corinth against the leaders of the congregation reached the capital (1: 1; 14: 2; 46: 9; 51: 1; 52: 2; 57: 1; 63: 1), is to admonish the insurgents to bow their necks under the rule of the legitimate presbyters (57: 1f.). But the author—as it seems, himself a presbyter and preacher—would also mix other topics into his lengthy tract. The Old Testament plays an important role in his arguments. Figures of the Old Testament are mentioned in chapter 4 as warning examples for the bad consequences of jealousy and envy: Cain and Abel, Jacob and Esau, Joseph and his brothers, Moses' flight from Egypt, Aaron and Miriam, Dathan and Abiram, Saul's persecution of David. Noah's and Jonah's penitential sermons (Jonah 3) show that the insurgents can save themselves by penance (7: 6–7). Chapters 9–12 contain a long chain of examples of pious believers, famous for their faith, their obedience and especially their hospitality. In chapter 16 Jesus Christ himself is introduced as prototype of humility, proved by a long quotation of Isaiah 53: 1–12, followed by Psalm 22: 7ff. Chapters 17–18 mention Elijah and Elisha, Abraham, Job, Moses, David (citing Ps. 51: 3–19) as righteous men who remained humble. For 1 Clement, the faithful of the Old Testament are witnesses of a belief to be imitated by the present Christian generation. There is no break in the history of salvation. In chapter 32 the priests and Levites, 'the lord Jesus according to the flesh', the kings and rulers of Judah, and all the tribes as descendants of Abraham are together the ones who came to honour by the will of God. Chapter 20 casts a look on the wonderful order of the universe and its creator; creation motifs also appear in the concluding prayer in chapters 59–61. Chapters 21–38 contain additional admonitions. Also in this passage many quotations from the Old Testament are interspersed. Chapters 40–44 explain (in contrast to Heb.) that the Old Testament orders and offices can be regarded as analogous to the orders and offices in the church. Thus, for instance, the distinction between bishops, presbyters (priests), and laymen is already prefigured in the Old Testament and the cult-orders in Jerusalem are a model for the Christian liturgy. Clement's first epistle mirrors a type of theology which probably was common in the communities of the period; the distance to Paul's thoughtful reflections is obvious.

EARLY APOLOGETICS: JUSTIN MARTYR

Justin (born about the turn of the second century; martyred 165), as a young Platonist was convinced by the Bible, understood as prophecy, of the superior truth of Christian faith compared with Gentile philosophy (cf. his *Dialogue with Tryphon the Jew*, 3–8). Later, in his own apologetics, he uses the same arguments for winning the unbelieving intellectuals. Of his two surviving treatises, written after 150, one is adressed to the emperor Antoninus Pius (138–61) and his sons (the 'First Apology'), the other (in form of a dialogue—a literary convention since Plato—with a Jew) to wavering Christians and educated Hellenistic proselytes acquainted with Jewish traditions and the Bible. Persecution of the Christians by the state on one side, because they refuse to take part in the official cult of the emperor, and growing anti-Christian propaganda by the Jews since the sharp separation between synagogue and church on the other side, are the background. Justin's arguments in his writings mostly belong to the traditional arsenal of early Christian apologetics. In 1 Apology 30–60 all the passages of the Old Testament are listed which already were regarded as messianic by the Jews and by the Christians as fulfilled in Jesus as the Christ. The following points are predicted by the prophets (1 Apol. 31: 7):

(1) That he has come,
(2) that he has been borne by a virgin,
(3) and grown up to a man,
(4) that he cured every illness and disease and raised the dead,
(5) that he has been hated and misjudged and crucified ...
(6) that he died and was raised from death and was carried up into heaven, being the son of God ...
(7) and that he sent out some [disciples] to every kind of people to proclaim this,
(8) and that people among the Gentiles would believe him more [than the Jews].

All these themes are discussed in detail. Answering the question whether the scriptures can be used at all as a prophetic testimony for Jesus as the Messiah (1 Apol. 36–49), Justin points to the Holy Spirit as the real author of the Bible. Its inspiration guarantees its hidden unity in spite of the diversity of the voices speaking in it. Tryphon (whether a historic person or a fictitious dialogue-partner) reliably represents the objections of contemporary Judaism against the Christians: They have deserted God by trusting a man; they are obliged to keep the law in all its details to obtain God's mercy; the messiah, if ever born, remains unknown, even to himself, until Elijah comes to make him known (Dial. 8, 3f.). In the discussion (Dial. 33–67) on the birth from the virgin (Isa. 7: 14) Tryphon goes back to the Hebrew text: The 'young woman' giving birth to a child is the mother of the future king Hezekiah, whereas Justin uses the Septuagint form 'virgin' to prove the spiritual conception of Jesus.

A GNOSTIC HERETIC: MARCION

A widespread movement in the second century and a strong rival of the church was the so-called Gnosis which combined a Platonic world-view with a spiritual form of Christian belief. Marcion, a wealthy shipowner, was a contemporary of Justin, whose teachings were already known throughout the whole Roman empire (cf. 1 Apol. 26: 1–5; 58: 1). According to Marcion, there are two gods: one,

The Eusebian canons produced by Eusebius, bishop of Caesarea from *c.*313 to 340, indicated parallel passages in the gospels at a time when the Bible had no verse or chapter divisions; here in a 7th-century parchment, probably made in Constantinople.

the minor, is the creator of the world (demiurge) and the god of Israel, the other is the redeemer who has revealed himself in Christ. This theory is part of Marcion's thoroughgoing gnostic dualism: he distinguishes strictly between law and gospel, between the material and the spiritual world. He seems to have regarded himself as a follower and pupil of Paul's: for his separate church, he selected a 'purified' canon of early Christian scriptures, in which the ten letters of Paul regarded as genuine received a central position. Paul's dialectic between law and gospel, to be restored from alleged falsifications, was the starting-point of his thought. But actually he separated the gospel from the law. In order to gain a scriptural basis, he introduced a special Marcionite gospel: a shortened Luke without chapters 1–3. The gospel means the liberation of man by the redemption effected on the cross by the redeemer, a heavenly being, coming down from heaven on a sudden without any previous announcement. Theories about messianic prophecy or typology in the Old Testament have to be abandoned. Whereas the demiurge is a judge, the 'strange' god does not judge or punish: he is nothing but love. 'I create darkness' a shortened version of Isaiah 45: 7, is the proof text for Marcion's speculation that the demiurge is, though righteous, not good. Other negative attributes of the Old Testament god (he becomes angry, he avenges himself, he is a warrior) show that he cannot be the father of Jesus Christ. Therefore the Old Testament cannot be regarded as holy scripture for Christians. Marcion was not against the Jews, but in his opinion their Bible was reserved exclusively for them. His dualism is seen in the undialectic separation between good and bad, while his belief that redemption only liberates the souls, shows the Gnostic origin of his ideas. The main church had to fight a hard struggle against Gnosticism, and its victory was never final, because similar world-views exist to the present day.

HARMONY OF THE TESTAMENTS: IRENAEUS OF LYONS

The most famous fighter against Gnosticism (especially the followers of Valentinus) in the second half of the second century was Irenaeus, bishop of Lugdunum (Lyons). His book against the Gnosis (preserved only in Latin translation: *Adversus haereses*, Against Heresies) combats the Gnostics on the battlefield of both testaments. In his time the four gospels, Acts, and the letters of Paul were already widely read and accepted as holy scriptures, though the official close of the canon in the western churches cannot be dated before the end of the fourth century. As the Gnostics founded their theories above all on New Testament texts, focusing on the letters of Paul, also the anti-Gnostic apologetics had to be based on their authority.

Though developing a theory of redemption was the first aim of the Gnostics, Irenaeus' central intention is to prove the unity of God against them. This he does on the basis of the scriptures, especially of the New Testament in the making. Two-thirds of his biblical quotations are taken from this part of the Bible. This proof is concentrated in book III of his work. Here he shows first that

there is only one God, the creator of all things (chs. 6–15), and secondly that there is just one Christ, son of God become man and word become flesh (chs. 16–23). He stresses the apostolic origin of the four gospels against the selection of one, shortened to fit the heretical opinions of the Gnostics, and stresses their harmony. He also proves the harmony between both testaments. Against the Gnostic division of the one Christ into two he stresses that the human Jesus and the 'Christ' belong to the divine pleroma. The proofs are taken from John 1: 14 and 18 and other texts showing that it was Jesus who became son of man as the Christ and son of God. In the passage about the first and second Adam (III, 21: 10–23: 8) the catchword 'recapitulation' marks Irenaeus' idea of a salvation history: the history of mankind, described in the Old Testament as a history of disaster, is started by Jesus anew with his coming, now as a history of salvation. The criticism of the Old Testament ethics by the Gnostics is answered by the thesis of the two 'economies': granted that people of Old Testament times were still imperfect—humans could just learn by experience, and this took time! (IV, 38: 1.; 39: 1). Therefore the word of God became a child with the childhood of humankind (IV, 38: 2). Accommodation and education (IV, 14: 2) characterize God's acts in history. The triune God (the 'word') was already present in paradise and appeared to the patriarchs and the prophets. The same God proclaimed the law; the gospel is its fulfilment. Irenaeus understands the commands in the Sermon on the Mount as the better law and can even speak of the 'law of the gospel' (IV, 16: 1–4). But he mentions also the temporal end of the law in the time of John the Baptist (IV, 4: 2). He accepts also the traditional view that the Holy Spirit acts in the scriptures (II, 28: 2). He uses allegorical forms of exegesis, detecting 'spiritual' meanings. All in all, his well-rounded theological system, based on the scriptures, being forced upon him by the struggle life or death against the Gnostics, characterizes Irenaeus as the first systematic but also biblical theologian.

THE DEEPER SENSE OF THE SCRIPTURES: ORIGEN

Origen, born of Christian parents *c.*185 in Alexandria, the centre of the Hellenistic world, opened in his city about 206 a Bible school, which he later transformed into a sort of academy for advanced studies. He regarded teaching, commenting, and preaching the Bible as his mission. For the emendation of the biblical text he produced a synopsis of the Hebrew Bible with the Septuagint and other Greek translations in four (later six) columns (the Hexapla). In Alexandria and even during several journeys which took him to Rome, Arabia, Antioch, and Athens, he dictated commentaries on different books of the Bible (Psalms, Lamentations, Genesis, later also on the Gospel of John, the letters of Paul and the prophets). Criticism of his approach forced him to write a defence: 'Peri Archôn' (*De principiis*—On the Beginnings). From 233 on he stayed (with some interruptions) in Caesarea. There he preached (as a presbyter) sometimes every morning on Old Testament texts, and in the evening services three times a week on New Testament passages. The sermon on the Old Testament was open also to the catechumens, on the New Testament only to the baptized members of the congregation. This shows his differing esteem for the testaments. He died after 251.

For understanding Origin's exegetical methods one must know about the intellectual background in Alexandria. There the Jewish philosopher Philo (first half of the first century CE) applied the Platonic/Stoic hermeneutics of the Hellenistic academy to the Bible. Also in Origen's opinion a Christian should not be content to understand only the literal sense like the simple-minded. Guided by an initiated teacher, he should progress to a deeper knowledge, detecting the spiritual sense of a passage. How this method functions can be seen above all in Origen's sermons. For instance, preaching on the stations of Israel's wandering through the desert in Numbers 33, he likens Israel's exodus from Egypt to the spiritual exodus of the Christian from a heathen lifestyle and/or the exodus of the soul from the body with death. The stations remind him of the stations a Christian has to pass on the way to the Father. To accept the divine law is the first station on this way, but the appeal to a moral outset is built upon the ground that God in Christ meets halfway with grace. The ascension of the soul to heaven is the core of Origen's theology; its traces are detected in a Bible explained by allegory. For his understanding of the Song of Songs, Genesis 1: 26f. and 2: 7 are decisive: God has created two men: one in his likeness, one out of dust from the ground. According to 2 Corinthians 4: 16 these are the 'outer' and the 'inner' man. The main catchwords of the Song of Songs are to be comprehended spiritually: the book as a whole traditionally means the love of the church for her bridegroom, Christ. For the single believer it shows the highest step in the three-stage ascent to God: the vision of the Divine. It is an intellectual rise: a progress mediated first by moral teachers, then by the word of God itself. The way Origen treats the New Testament, especially in his sermons, is more simple, but based on a similar dualistic world-view. Especially the gospels, as treated in his commentary on Matthew, have for him two levels: the literal/historical wording describes the human life of Christ, the spiritual aspect discloses his divinity.

THE LITERAL SENSE IS IMPORTANT: THEODORE OF MOPSUESTIA

Antioch (the modern Antakya) was in the fourth century one of the biggest cities in the Roman empire and most of its inhabitants since Constantine were Christians. But it was also a centre of Greek learning. There Theodore was born in 352. After a classical education he converted to Christianity in 368, and joined the loosely monastic community Asceterion, founded by Diodore of Tarsus for ascetic life and Bible study. Consecrated priest *c.*383, he became bishop of Mopsuestia in Cilicia in 392, remaining there until his death in 428. He dedicated most of his life to teaching and writing commentaries on nearly all books of the Bible, of which only a small part has survived, because Theodore posthumously (553) was condemned as a heretic. His exegetical method is similar to that of his teacher Diodore (of whom still less is preserved) and represents the so-called

Antiochene school. In his commentary on the Psalms he first tries to arrive at a correct text, comparing the Septuagint with other Greek translations and also amending Hebraisms in its style. For each psalm, he places a summary (Hypothesis) at the head of his comments; often he does not accept the superscription of the Septuagint. Embracing the tradition of David as the author of the psalms, he seeks an occasion for each psalm in David's life. Cases in which the background is later he explains by David's prophetic foreknowledge. He even classifies the psalms under categories as hymns of praise, doctrinal psalms, prayers of pentitence, etc. Theodore denies a direct prophecy of Christ in the psalms, except in the traditionally messianic Psalms 2, 8, and 45 (44). Similarly in his commentary on the Twelve Prophets he seeks to begin with fulfilments of the prophecies in the history of Israel. Every prophet acted in a special historical situation and did not care about the distant future. The prophets did not know of the Trinity. However, there is also a 'hyperbolic' element in their utterances, and therefore, in a few cases, one can detect a typological aspect pointing to Christ. Besides, the history in the Old Testament has its aim in Christ, in the frame of God's plan of salvation for all humankind. Later Theodore also wrote a commentary on John's Gospel, in which he detected a more exact chronological sequence of events than in the synoptic gospels. But in John he has dogmatic problems, especially in the prologue, which partly seems to contradict his adoptianist Christology. All in all, Theodore is a remarkably independent exegete, whose insights sometimes already anticipate the modern critical exegesis.

A BIBLE REVISED FROM THE 'HEBREW TRUTH': JEROME

Jerome (Hieronymus), probably born in 331 of wealthy Christian parents in Dalmatia, studied classical Latin culture and later rhetoric with a famous schoolmaster in Rome. During a stay in Trier he was touched by the monastic ideal. About 372, coming to Antioch, he learned Greek and attended Bible courses with Apollonius of Laodicea, who belonged to the Antiochene school. For a while he retreated to the hermits into the adjoining desert and lived in a cave. He also took Hebrew lessons with a Jew. After some years of travel, in 382 he arrived in Rome, where Pope Damasus I (366–84) made him his secretary and suggested he should produce a revision of the different Latin texts of the Bible used in the western congregations. Jerome completed a revision of the four gospels. He also gave biblical lessons. Followed by two noble Christian ladies: Paula and her daughter Eustochium, he left Rome in 385 for Palestine. In Bethlehem they founded a monastery for men and another for women. There he remained for the rest of his life. He wrote several (eclectic) Bible commentaries, but his most important work was the production of a complete new Latin Bible. He started with a revision of the Septuagint text of the Psalter, comparing it with the other Greek translations and the Hebrew text. Introduced as official text in Gallia (Gallican Psalter) it later supplanted Jerome's psalm translations from the Hebrew. After the revision of some other books Jerome abandoned this project. Having improved his Hebrew

Jerome and a lion, from a woodcut by Albrecht Dürer. The open books contain the beginning of Genesis in Hebrew, Greek, and Latin.

knowledge by learning from a Jew, he started anew, now translating from the Hebrew original, finishing the so-called Vulgate (common Bible) about 406. In his prologue to the books Samuel to Kings he also restricted the canon to the size of the Hebrew Bible and stated the sequence of the biblical books accordingly. Though this new version was much better than the existing ones, it took until the ninth century before it was officially received in the whole western church.

A BISHOP PREACHING ON THE BIBLE TO HIS FLOCK: AMBROSE OF MILAN

Ambrose, born in 339 as son of a high military commander, became a state official and about 370 governor of Liguria and Emilia, with his headquarters in Milan, in this period the main residence of the emperor and the most important

Portrait of Ambrose, from a triptych above the altar, *c.*1470.

city in Italy. When the Arian bishop died, a struggle about the succession between Arians and Catholics arose. Hurrying to the cathedral to intercede, the layman Ambrose spontaneously was elected bishop. This he remained until his death in 397. In spite of his successful political activities to restrain Arianism, most of his time Ambrose dedicated to his congregation in preaching and the care of souls. Based upon a comprehensive classical education and rhetorical training, he used his abilities for his famous sermons on biblical texts. Preaching belonged to his duties as bishop in the eucharistic services. He held the Bible in high esteem. His exegesis is moralistic, but also allegoric; he prefers texts from the Old Testament. But his theology is Christocentric: the gospel in Jesus Christ is the essence of his message. Dogmatics is influential with him. He tries to find reasons for the catholic (Nicene) position in the Bible. He combines classical and Christian traditions in his sermons. Old and New Testament he regards as a unity. He also wrote an apologetic work on Genesis against Appelles, a rationalistic pupil of Marcion. Against supporters of Gentile philosophy he stresses in his work 'Hexameron' that Moses lived much earlier than the Greek philosophers. In his catechetic addresses he speaks about word and sacrament as belonging together.

MONASTIC LIFE WITH THE BIBLE: JOHN CASSIAN

Characteristic of Christian monasticism is an intense life with the Bible. The cradle of monasticism is Egypt. John Cassian (*c.*360–432), later founder of his own monastery in Marseilles, about 392 visited the Egyptian monks in the desert and described their life and traditions. Each monk had a biblical codex in his cell during the day which was collected and locked away during the night. Many hours a day were dedicated to biblical 'meditations': reading aloud from the Bible and memorizing the texts. Handicraft and work on the fields were also accompanied by Bible recitations; psalm-singing attended the work. Several times during day and night the monks would gather for prayer, psalm-singing, and reading a text of the Old and the New Testament respectively. So they knew most of the Bible by heart. Bible-teaching mostly had a moral and spiritual purpose; the use of commentaries was suspect.

AUGUSTINE: A BIBLICAL HERMENEUTICS

Augustine, the most important theologian of late antiquity, born in 354 in North Africa, and educated in classical rhetorical studies, became a Christian in 387 and bishop of Hippo in 396, staying in this office until his death in 430, when the Vandals beleaguered his town. Commentaries are just a minor part of his works, but he wrote one of the first Christian hermeneutics: *De doctrina Christiana* (On Christian Doctrine). In the frame of a Neoplàtonic theology—God is the highest good one has to love intellectually, though combined with the commandment to love one's neighbour—the place of the Bible is not easy to determine. Augustine calls 'temporal dispensation' God's acting in history, including Israel, witnessed

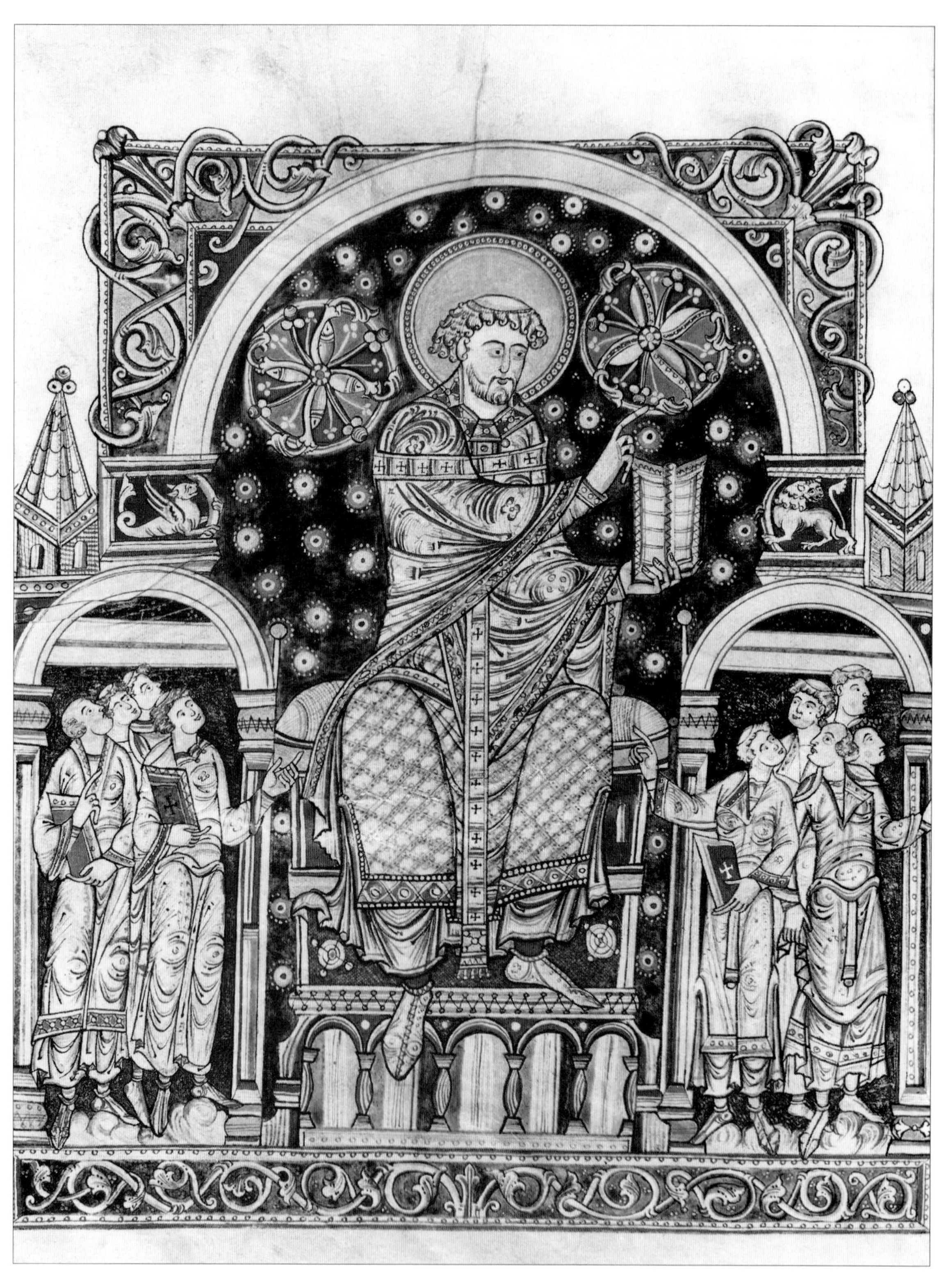

in the Old Testament and culminating in Jesus becoming a human being. It happens as a sign (*sacramentum*) adapted to the weakness of human understanding. The Bible mainly is a book of ethics, though also containing doctrines to believe. Because originally spoken words are the instruments by which humans communicate the movements of their minds to other people, writing is the way to fix the fleeting sounds. The scriptures are partly written in pictures and parables, some of them not easy to understand. But there are enough easier ones comprising all you need. In a scheme of seven steps for the ascension of the soul to God (VII. 9–11) the first three include the study of the Bible. One has to begin with reading the books which are acknowledged by all or most catholic churches, learning them by heart, understanding first the easier passages, then explaining from the easier the more obscure ones. For unknown signs (i.e. words) one should know Hebrew and Greek. Strange expressions in Latin may have their origin in a too literal translation. Augustine prefers the Old Latin version (Itala), in Greek the Septuagint, even where the Hebrew original varies. Here he differs from Jerome. He did not know Hebrew. For the choice between a literal and an allegorical understanding he gives the rule, that the literal is sufficient wherever it leads to love (XV.23). Morally offensive acts of biblical persons are to be explained allegorically, if other explanations fail.

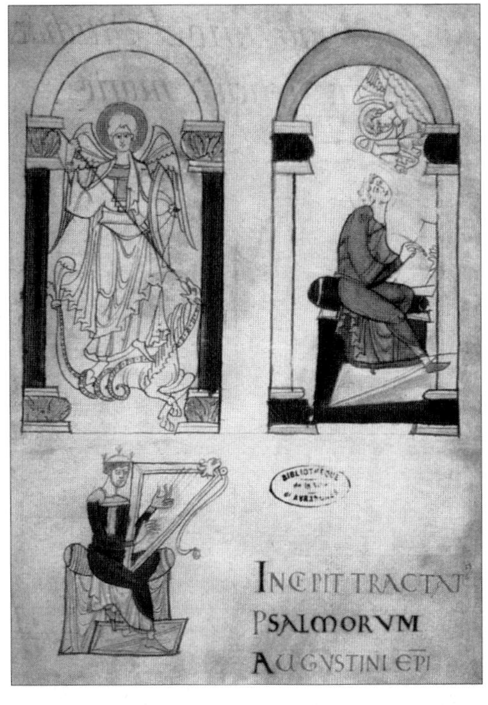

The initial and illuminated page of a commentary by Augustine on the Psalms (second half of 11th century) includes king David, and Michael defeating the dragon.

Augustine closes book III of his work by a look at the *Liber regularum* (Book of Rules) of the Donatist layman Tichonius, which mostly have a technical character. Rule 1 says that Christ and his body, the church, belong together; rule 2 that the church is divided in the true and the mixed church; rule 4 speaks about the kind and the individual; rule 6 about 'recapitulation' (in stories sometimes events that happened earlier are told later); rule 7 states that in speaking of the devil either his person or his body, the godless, can be meant.

Augustine's commentaries do not show that he put his theories into practice. His enormous impact later was in the field of theological thinking. But the Bible remained important for him, especially in his sermons.

(*Facing*) Augustine teaching in the midst of his students, from a manuscript of *The City of God*, Canterbury, 12th century.

9 The Middle Ages to the Reformation

G. R. EVANS

THE USES OF SCRIPTURE

From the patristic period to the Reformation scripture was the foundation text of all intellectual endeavour. All formal education was a preparation for reading it and its study the supreme task of the most advanced scholars of the medieval universities.

PREACHING THE WORD

Scripture was not always read as an academic exercise, and in the period after the end of the ancient world that was not the natural way to come to it. The purpose of the study of scripture was edification. It was the Word of God and it was 'given' to teach God's people about him and bring them to him. So it was first and most characteristically used in preaching.

Sermons of the patristic period could be very long. Augustine of Hippo (354–430) would preach for an hour or more, with his audience as involved as though they were at a theatre. He gave several long series (for example, on the Psalms, on St John's Gospel) in the course of which he expounded whole books of the Bible. The analysis was detailed and would have been testing for the listener, although the text is full of life and anecdote. Gregory the Great was still preaching in the same style at the end of the sixth century.

During the early Middle Ages the pattern of preaching changed for two main reasons. The number of individuals capable of preaching freshly composed sermons depended upon the number educated to a sufficient level, and those were for some centuries very few. It became usual for preaching to diminish to a mere reading of the surviving 'published' sermons of Augustine and Gregory and other 'Latin Fathers'.

The second reason was the loss of Latin as the language of normal exchange in the west. It gradually became the language of the 'learned' and so the text of scripture and these old sermons could not be understood by ordinary people in parishes. Largely uneducated clergy concentrated on the liturgy and left out sermons altogether.

In the late eleventh century Guibert of Nogent wrote a pioneering book on how to preach a sermon, which was the first of a series produced until the mid-thirteenth century. These revolutionized the practice of preaching and brought it to life again. By the end of the twelfth century (Alan of Lille) 'the art of preaching' had become a recognized branch of rhetoric. Formally taught in this way, the technique was to take a short passage of scripture as a 'text' (rather than to progress through a whole book of scripture). The theme was then developed by dividing the meanings of the key terms in the text and analysing each in turn.

The work of a scribe and his helper, illustrated in a manuscript of Augustine's *City of God*, c.1140.

During the same century a few preachers of exceptional talent arose who could speak without such props. Notable among these was Bernard of Clairvaux. His sermons read like Augustine's. They are shot through with biblical allusions and citations and direct quotations, to the point where half or more of each sentence is scriptural. Some are lengthy expositions of scripture, even a series on a single book, the Song of Songs, which he did not finish and which set a fashion among would-be imitators who aspired to complete it. Bernard's powers as a preacher were not merely verbal, although his skills with words were outstanding. He understood, as the ancient rhetoricians had done, that delivery is important. There is a story of his

The 14th-century Dominican priory in Dubrovnik, southern Croatia. The Dominican friars played a leading role in spreading knowledge of the Bible through their preaching.

preaching in Latin to a German-speaking audience and reducing it to tears. When the translator got up to explain to them what Bernard had said, the audience was far less moved by the sense than they had been by the delivery.

The orders of friars, which were founded first and foremost to preach, had different needs in their use of scripture. The Franciscans were wandering preachers, who sought to bring souls to Christ with their sermons. The Dominicans were founded to preach against heresy in the north of Spain and the south of France. Their task involved combating holders of unorthodox beliefs mainly of two types: the 'Waldensian' and the 'Albigensian'. The Waldensians were in some senses proto-Lollards, and they had among their number individuals well briefed in scripture and able to exchange quotations with any preacher who came against them. So the Dominicans needed at the outset a higher level of education and a clear understanding of the ways in which texts of scripture could best be set against one another to counter unorthodox positions.

During the thirteenth century, the two orders became rivals for the chairs in Europe's universities and both became highly focused on training the minds of their recruits. They produced a series of Bible-study aids and theological handbooks. The relationship between the two is important and intricate.

Preachers needed a variety of *practical* aids, all of which can be seen developing by the end of the twelfth century, but which were taken much further by the friars. They needed 'dictionaries' of biblical terms, so that they could look up a word which was to feature prominently in a sermon and see where else and in what other senses it occurred in scripture. They needed reference-books of illustrative stories and parallels and brief patterns of argumentation. They needed handbooks of 'authorities'. But, and this remained perhaps especially true for the Dominicans, they also needed arguments. An example of that type of aid is Peter the Chanter's *De tropis loquendi*, from the end of the twelfth century. This Parisian scholar is also the author of a *Verbum abbreviatum*, which is a digest and handbook to the Bible, but it is the *De tropis loquendi* which is most instructive in demonstrating the development of genres to meet specific needs. Peter the Chanter put two things together in this book. He confronted the problem Augustine had addressed in his 'Harmony of the Gospels', that scripture appears in places to disagree with itself. He used the teaching of logicians on methods of identifying and resolving sophistries. He thus provided the preacher with a means of tackling embarrassments in the exposition of any text he might be dealing with in which this problem arose. The requirements by way of preachers' aids were in fact identical with those recognized in the teaching of ancient rhetoric.

The various processes in the production of a book in the middle ages are indicated in the medallions in the margins of the 12th-century Ambrosius codex.

WRITTEN COMMENTARY AND THE DEVELOPMENT OF THE UNIVERSITY LECTURE

The theological reference-books developed by the friars were the culmination of a lengthy process. Scholars after the patristic period did not lose sight of the importance of study of the Bible and here a new pattern began to emerge, of 'written' commentary, which could be studied by monks together with the old sermons. Indeed, it consisted partly of extracts from such sermons, conveniently arranged alongside the text.

A leading exponent of this new trend was Bede. He was supplied with sources brought from the first Benedictine monastery at Monte Cassino in southern Italy by the travelling scholar Benedict Biscop. He seems to have had some perception of the need future generations would have for study-aids, and those he provided were strongly focused on scripture. He wrote commentaries of his own, beginning to fill some of the gaps in the authorities he had access to, and drawing upon extracts from those authorities so as to put together a tapestry of quotations.

Bede's commentary on the Gospel of Luke; a manuscript in the British Library.

This mode of Bible study persisted in monastic and later in cathedral schools. These differed in that the monastic schools of the west, all still Benedictine until the twelfth century, were normatively 'enclosed'. Exchange of books for copying and of letters went on between them, and the occasional scholarly traveller might bring new ideas. But in general such schools were only as good as the best teachers in the monastery at any given time. Bec in the time of Anselm (late eleventh century) was exceptional in that, it was said, Anselm could make 'seeming-philosophers' even out of 'rustics'.

The cathedral schools were much more open to scholarly exchange and could become centres of controversy, as did Laon at the end of the eleventh century. At Laon in particular—though other cathedral schools were actively involved—there were attempts to fill gaps in the existing coverage of commentaries available on the books of the Bible, so as to create a complete 'gloss' or 'commentary' on the whole of scripture. The Bible had always been studied—and indeed often thought of—as a series of books, rather than as the 'Bible'. Its sheer size meant that it was practical and convenient to bind it in individual books. Certain of these books were much more used than others. Accordingly, there had always been a certain patchiness in commentary. During the twelfth century almost every lecturer who commented on the Bible at all would do so on the Pauline epistles and the Wisdom literature of the Old Testament, and most especially the Psalms. Some of the prophets might remain untouched decade after decade in the schools, although some lecturers would take up themes within the Old Testament, as Hugh of St Victor did with Noah's Ark; Richard of St Victor with the vexed question how the Temple in Ezekiel could possibly stand up, with its given dimensions; Alan of Lille with the 'six wings of the cherubim' in Isaiah.

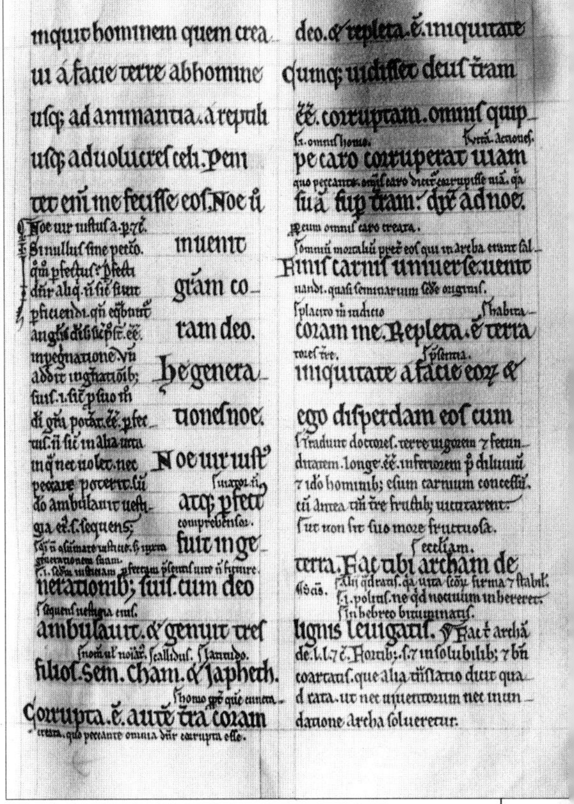

The *Glossa ordinaria* were important marginal and interlinear comments on the biblical text, here seen in a 13th-century manuscript of Genesis 6: 7–14 in the Latin Vulgate.

The unevenness of coverage now had to be repaired, because there was a new density of demand. The twelfth century saw the rise of schools which were to grow into the first universities, and pressure of student requirements for a syllabus and systematic instruction. A *Glossa ordinaria* or standard gloss came into being by the second half of the century, formed partly out of old work, partly out of new, so that a student could in principle obtain guidance on any portion of scripture he needed to study.

But students outside the continuing monastic tradition were not reading on their own. They 'read' a text with a master, who 'lectured' upon it to them. That meant taking a short portion of the text and expounding it. The lemmata were given complete by some masters (for example, Gilbert of Poitiers), so that it would be possible to reconstruct the text from them if it had been otherwise unavailable.

Anselm of Canterbury (1033–1109) was born in northern Italy and spent thirty years at the abbey of Bec, where he gained a profound knowledge of Scripture, before becoming Archbishop of Canterbury in 1093. This portrait by André Thevet dates from 1584.

This was a concession to the problem that students were unlikely to have the full text before them as they listened. (This practical difficulty of the expense and availability of books was addressed in the thirteenth-century universities by pragmatic booksellers, who would rent the relevant fascicules to students as the lecture-course proceeded.)

In the earliest commentaries we have, from the Carolingian period, the tendency is to concentrate at a fairly elementary level upon the difficult words. The trend thereafter was more and more to address the ideas in the text, and to try to deal with seeming contradictions piecemeal. Then came the need to tackle larger and larger theological problems to which portions of the text pointed. An example is a passage in Peter Abelard's commentary on Romans in the middle of the twelfth century. He found himself dealing with the question why God became man. He rehearsed all the arguments then currently fashionable, including that of Anselm's *Cur Deus Homo*, in order to reject them, then advanced his own, which was that Christ's primary purpose was to set an example of the way to live a perfect human life. But this excursus is extremely lengthy, and it was becoming a problem that the sequence of the lecture could be badly disrupted by such large pieces of 'commentary'.

It should be emphasized that it was not only scripture which was lectured on in this way. The method of instruction on any set text was exactly the same, and although the Bible was always far and away the most important, the method of approach to it was pedagogically standard for its time.

Because of the difficulty about the interruption of long asides, a new pattern of study was developing during the twelfth century out of this 'reading' (*lectio*) of a text of scripture with a commentary before an audience of students. These first 'lectures' led to the first 'disputations'. Some books of the Bible had more than one ancient commentary and the commentators did not always agree. So when he got to a given passage a lecturer might have to pause and give his view of the right answer. Thus 'topics' became isolated, and there survive from the school at Laon in this period a series of 'Sentences' on such themes. 'Sentences' are *sententiae* or 'opinions'.

In the course of the next century these 'topics' began to swell to a size which made them disruptive of the sequence of the lecture, and it is clear from surviving lectures that students would interrupt with questions. So the disputed passage or theme would be set aside for special consideration later in the day at a *disputatio*. These, too, grew, until it became an essential part of a scholar's training that he learn to handle disputed questions in a formal way, first posing the problem, then assembling all the arguments on one side and on the other, and finally deciding or 'determining' the matter. A higher degree in the later medieval universities (Master or Doctor) was a warrant that a scholar had reached a level where he could lead such *disputationes* and thus be a university teacher himself.

The most-used textbook of theology in the Middle Ages was a product of this development. Peter Lombard wrote his *Sentences* in the second half of the twelfth century to try to put the perplexing proliferation of topics into a logical order and thus provide a reference-book for students.

These sessions of pitting arguments against one another included the use not only of authorities from scripture itself and from the Fathers commenting upon it, but also from secular classical philosophical sources. Here, and in the increasing focus on disputed questions, was a trend which led students in medieval

Eadwine the scribe, from the Eadwine Psalter, *c.*1150–60.

universities away from the sequential study of the scriptures and made it appear perhaps less central, although there was never a time when scripture ceased to be the primary authority.

THE NATURE OF AUTHORITY

Fundamental to the approach of the late patristic and medieval period to the study of scripture was a respect for its authority. *Auctoritas* could be used in various ways, to refer to the individual author who was himself an 'authority', to refer to the text which was being cited as authoritative, or to the nature of the weight an opinion carried.

There were three 'levels' of authority in medieval thinking. Scripture came indisputably first and highest. Then came *auctores* who were Christians, and especially those now (though not in the earlier Middle Ages) referred to as the Fathers. Last came secular authorities, such as Cicero and Aristotle. Contradiction between authorities on different levels could normally simply be resolved in favour of the higher.

There was also a sense that the *antiqui* outweighed the *moderni*, being closer to the source. The high Middle Ages saw a debate on the question where the boundary lay between such ancient authorities and those who carried less weight because they were recent, and it was argued that merely being dead placed an authority in the first class. In twelfth-century compilations of authorities surviving in some of the English cathedral libraries and elsewhere, it is striking that Anselm of Canterbury, Bernard of Clairvaux, and Hugh of St Victor appear alongside Augustine and Gregory the Great as though they were of equal standing. But this pattern does not persist and the same 'latter-day Fathers' persisted without noticeable additions to their number in the later Middle Ages.

The key idea perhaps is that which later twelfth-century teachers ascribed to Bernard of Chartres. He is alleged to have described the scholars of his own day as dwarfs standing on the shoulders of the giants of old. It was possible for the dwarfs to see further than the giants. But there was no question whose was the greater stature.

This attitude of awed respect mutated by the end of the Middle Ages to the realization that an earlier author was 'only a man', and that a later scholar's opinion might be as good as his. But that in its turn depended upon the consideration that even the greatest Christian authors must differ from the author of scripture in that they were merely human. And here we come to the question of the divine inspiration of scripture.

It was taken for granted by all students of scripture in the Middle Ages that the text of the Bible was literally and directly inspired. The picture of an evangelist sitting writing with the Holy Spirit in the form of a dove with its beak in his ear is an iconographical commonplace.

Nevertheless, there was discussion in the later Middle Ages of the exact role of the human authors of scripture and some toying with the possibility that they had not always heard accurately what the Holy Spirit was saying to them. The puzzle of a prophet saying 'I am not a prophet' (*propheta non sum*) threw up sharply the question whether the human authors of scripture had not perhaps made at least some human, and therefore fallible, contribution.

Then there was the question of the status of the translation from which, in practice, all medieval commentators of the west were working. Jerome's Vulgate became the standard text from the fifth century until the sixteenth, when its accuracy was seriously questioned by textual critics working from the manuscripts for the first time. In fact not all their criticisms were well-founded because in some instances the Byzantine manuscripts they were using were less reliable than the sources Jerome had had before him.

Jerome himself was unequivocal that he was not inspired. The translation he provided was his own, not God's provision of a Latin text. Nevertheless the habit of close analysis and commentary led to the Vulgate text's being treated throughout the Middle Ages as though God himself were indeed the author of every word. Much ink was used, for example, in discussing the opening of the book of Job: *vir unus*, because the *unus* is a grammatical oddity; it was argued that God does nothing by chance, and if he says that there was 'one man' not 'a man' in the land of Uz he must do so for a reason.

Jerome uses the word *interpres* to describe himself as a translator, but that is of course the same word as one would have to use for an interpreter. That is a reminder that translation is also interpretation. The selection of one word rather than another can alter the reader's understanding significantly. That is very apparent in the early sixteenth-century English renderings which were sensitive to what then seemed undesirable connotations of such words as 'church' (for which 'congregation' might be substituted) and the mare's nest of difficulties which surrounded 'bishop', 'priest', 'minister'.

THE SENSES OF THE TEXT

The notion that a text might mean more than one thing was already securely established in the patristic period, and indeed it had early been found necessary to postulate that for some passages of scripture, which seemed on the face of it peculiarly unedifying, there might be no literal meaning at all, but only figurative ones. As late as Augustine's day, it was unclear what pattern the figurative senses might form, and several systems were in play. In the *De doctrina Christiana* Augustine himself favoured the method of Tichonius the Donatist, a striking testimony to the desperate need for help in this area, since Augustine campaigned remorselessly against the Donatists of North Africa as schismatics.

The system which came into established use in the west throughout the Middle Ages appears to have been worked out by Gregory the Great. He took the surface meaning of the text, its literal or 'historical' sense as the foundation, and built upon it three higher senses. (There was never any question throughout the patristic and medieval periods that the figurative senses were preferable, because

they were taken to be the 'spiritual' meanings, and therefore closer approximations to what God had meant to say.)

The first of these Gregorian higher senses was the allegorical. 'Allegory' could be used loosely to cover all the figurative senses, but in its strict sense it involved some transference of usage from the ordinary meanings of words to give them a spiritual application. For example, the 'lion of Judah' is Christ. This notion involved some conscious play with the term *proprietas* (propriety). On this analysis, the 'proper' sense became the allegorical one, so that *brachium* 'properly' meant 'Christ' rather than 'arm', which is its literal meaning.

The second higher sense was the tropological or moral. Thus when Gregory composed his *Moralia in Job*, in the company of his friends in the community, during his period in Constantinople, he concentrated especially on bringing out the moral lessons he found in the book of Job.

The third sense was the anagogical or prophetic. To draw that out was to show how the text pointed forward either to the future in this world, or, more usually, eschatologically, to the world to come. A habit of looking for 'types' in the Old Testament of figures or events in the New was universal, and it was then possible to move onwards into the future and suggest where the repeating pattern might lead next. A significant and controversial exponent of this method was Joachim of Fiore, who sought by this means to discover when the end of the world would come and to point to signs of the 'old age of the world' in present events. But before him the more respectable figures of Rupert of Deutz and Anselm of Havelberg in the first half of the twelfth century had been doing something very similar.

No meaning which could be got out of scripture which was in keeping with orthodoxy could be thought of as an invention, since God would necessarily have thought of it first and placed it in the text ready to be found by the spiritually minded reader.

Gregory the Great, who was Pope from 590 to 604 and a great biblical commentator, is here portrayed (*left*) with Augustine, in the central panel from the Fathers of the Church altarpiece, in the Alte Pinakothek, Munich.

DISSIDENCE AND LAY BIBLE STUDY

The capacity of heretics to use the Bible for their own ends, notable from the twelfth century, was linked to dissident moves to have scripture in the vernacular. This was a reflection in part of the rise of an urban middle class in the twelfth-century towns, who were articulate and entrepreneurial and did not take kindly to the notion that they must depend upon a priesthood they could see to be poorly educated for their salvation and for the instruction of their souls.

The Waldensians of the twelfth century became the Lollards of the fourteenth and fifteenth, not necessarily by direct inheritance, but certainly in the close similarity of many of their preoccupations. There is evidence that the Lollards formed Bible study-groups in private houses, and that on occasion they reached a remarkably high standard of criticism. They were looking to be pilots of their own souls, and to minister to themselves in matters of the Word.

There is an irony in this, in that one of the main objects of the hatred of Wyclif himself was the Friars, whom he described, with members of other religious orders, as *sectae*. Much of his ill will was generated by internal warfare in the University of Oxford, where there were academic parties representing the various orders. But in fact it was the friars perhaps above all who were actively providing a ministry of the Word in a period when that had become partly separated from the ministry of the Sacraments. The focus of the eucharist was the act of consecration, and Masses were commonly said without the inclusion of sermons.

10 The Reformation to 1700

DAVID WRIGHT

In the early modern period which is the subject of this chapter, a handful of developments combined to transform the use of the Bible. Together they promoted the transition from the pre-modern to the modern era of biblical study. These changes interacted with each other, and indeed some of them may not have taken place without the precipitating impact of one or more other advances. Among the most significant were the following:

- the invention and steady development of printing;

- within the context of Renaissance humanist studies, the recovery of scholarly attention to the text of the Bible in its original languages of Greek and to a lesser extent of Hebrew;

- the translation of the Bible in part or whole into the vernacular languages of sixteenth-century Europe;

- the movements of the Protestant Reformation which all in different ways were inspired by a rediscovery of central biblical teaching about God's provision for human salvation in Jesus Christ, and all with different emphases recognized God's Word in scripture as the supreme authority in the church in determining issues of Christian belief and practice;

- the emergence of more strictly historical methods of analysing the books of the Bible which in the later seventeenth century fostered the beginnings of what became known as biblical criticism.

Such a listing barely discloses the truly massive energies devoted to the Bible by expert and non-expert alike, not least because it was for much of this period a hotly contested book. The early phases of the Reformation effectively wrested it free of the restrictive control of the Roman Catholic Church, to the accompaniment of sharp and unresolved controversy. In some cases unauthorized translation or possession of a New Testament or Bible was punished by martyrdom. At the same time, disagreements among Protestants in interpreting some passages in scripture cut deep enough to preclude their sitting down together at the Lord's supper.

Larger differences, especially over the relationship between the Old Testament and the New, soon divided reforming radicals such as the Anabaptists from mainstream or magisterial Reformers—and no less from the Catholic Church also. The radicals in turn indicted the 'new papacy' of the Protestants, despite their biblical confession, as no less tradition-bound than the Roman papacy, while leading church Reformers tarred radicals and Catholics alike with the brush of sundering the Spirit, whether in the church or the believer, from the divine Word. Catholics concluded that evangelical defences of infant baptism against Anabaptist attack without clear biblical warrant looked little different from the reliance on unwritten tradition for which evangelicals so often condemned Catholics.

Through it all the religious face of Europe was being transfigured by the Bible—by lectures, disputations, and commentaries still in the Latin of the international academy and the religious professionals, by sermons and catechizing in the language of the populace, by public debates between opposing authorities in front of citizen assemblies called to vote for or against the new biblical gospel, by placards, posters, woodcuts, and cartoons, by vernacular service-books and liturgical lections and numerous other media of the open Bible. This chapter can trace only a highly selective path through a vast kaleidoscopic landscape whose making engaged prodigious endeavours and mighty passions.

THE PRINTED BIBLE

It is easy to exaggerate the advantages of the first printed Bibles over manuscript copies produced to the highest professional standards. In portability, selling price, accuracy (to start with, no better or worse than the manuscripts used by the typesetters), and even uniformity of text (given the practice of continuing correction in the midst of an edition), Johann Gutenberg's printings of the Latin Vulgate at Mainz in Germany in the mid-1450s marked no dramatic advance. Yet the potential of this new technology was in its day as world-changing as the IT revolution ushering in the third Christian millennium. 'He prints as much in a day as was formerly written in a year', spoken of another fifteenth-century printer, may have been a pardonable exaggeration. Of Gutenberg's famous 42-line Bible perhaps only a couple of hundred were produced, some on paper, the rest on vellum. Each vellum copy used the skins of 170 animals.

But by 1500 editions regularly ran to 1,000 or 1,500 copies, and 100,000 Bibles may well have been in print. William Tyndale's New Testament, the first printed in English, saw 3,000 copies off the press in Worms in 1525, and print-runs of this size must soon have been normal. Multiplied by the number of editions—by 1640 about 300 for the English Bible and about 150 for the New Testament—such figures roughly indicate the quantities involved. Bible publishing became big business.

The size of the Bible book had already come down considerably by the end of the fifteenth century. A Paris Bible of 1510 by Hopyl in five parts measured not much more than 3in. by 4in. (7.5 × 10 cm.). The first English New Testament to fit the pocket was William Whittingham's translation published at Geneva in 1557, whose text would soon form part of the Geneva Bible of 1560. This became the most widely used English version, only gradually displaced by the Authorized or King James Version of 1611.

This Geneva New Testament and Bible were the first in English to number verses throughout. Robert Estienne (Stephanus), member of a distinguished family of scholar-printers who worked first in Paris and then in Geneva, introduced his own system of verse division and numeration in his Greek New Testament of 1551 at Geneva. Somewhat earlier Santi Pagnini, an Italian Dominican who was one of the most important Catholic Bible scholars of the early sixteenth century, had numbered the verses throughout his Latin Bible of 1528 at Lyons, but his scheme failed to catch on. The Bible itself was noteworthy also as a fresh translation from the original Hebrew and Greek. The very first to provide both division and numbering of verses throughout was Robert Estienne's 1553 folio Bible in French.

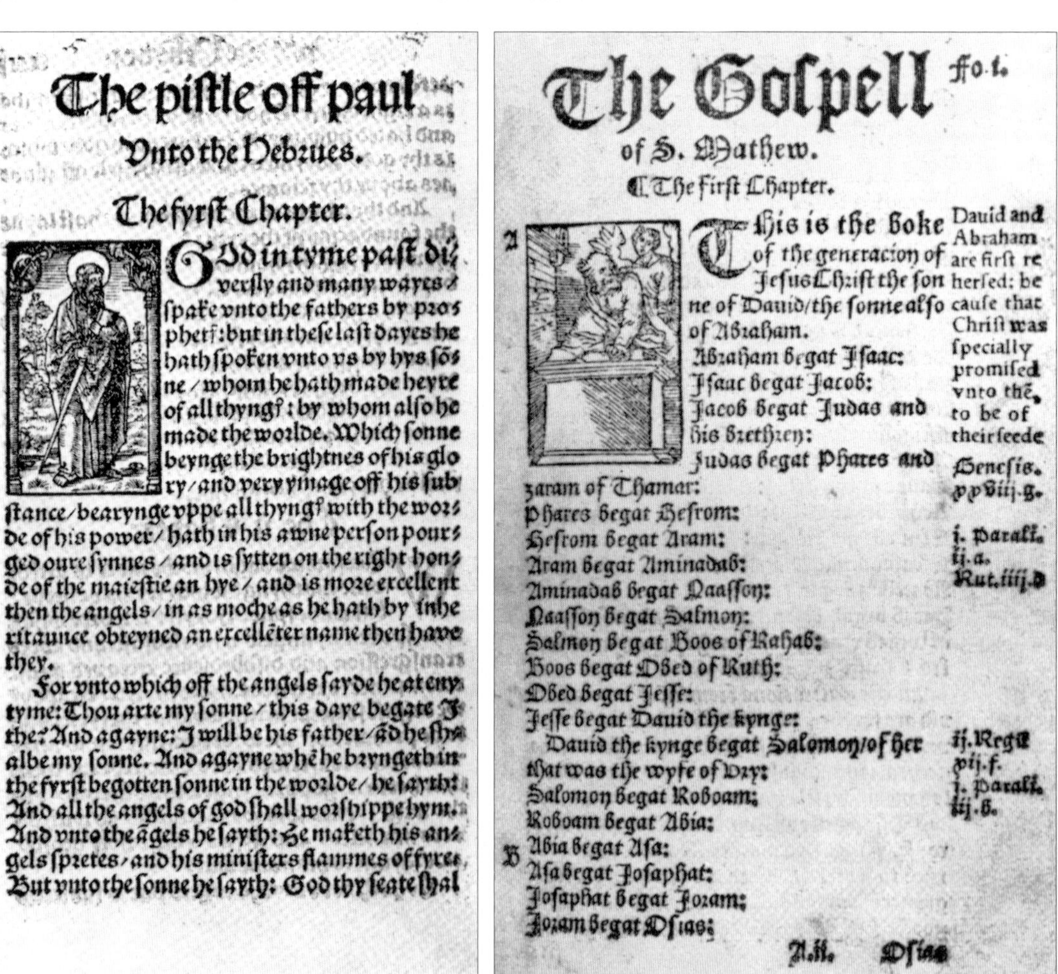

The pistle off paul
Vnto the Hebrues.
The fyrst Chapter.

GOd in tyme past diversly and many wayes / spake vnto the fathers by prophetes: but in these last dayes he hath spoken vnto vs by hys sonne / whom he hath made heyre of all thyngs: by whom also he made the worlde. Which sonne beynge the brightnes of his glory / and very ymage off his substance / bearynge vppe all thyngs with the worde of his power / hath in his awne person pourged oure synnes / and is sytten on the right honde of the maiestie an hye / and is more excellent then the angels / in as moche as he hath by inheritaunce obteyned an excellenter name then have they.

For vnto which off the angels sayde he at eny tyme: Thou arte my sonne / this daye begate I the? And agayne: I will be his father / and he shall be my sonne. And agayne whe he bryngeth in the fyrst begotten sonne in the worlde / he sayth: And all the angels of god shall worshippe hym. And vnto the angels he sayth: He maketh his angels spretes / and his ministers flammes of fyre. But vnto the sonne he sayth: God thy seate shal

The Gospell Fo. i.
of S. Mathew.
The first Chapter.

A This is the boke of the generacion of Jesus Christ the sonne of David / the sonne also of Abraham.
Abraham begat Isaac:
Isaac begat Jacob:
Jacob begat Judas and his brethren:
Judas begat Phares and zaram of Thamar:
Phares begat Hesrom:
Hesrom begat Aram:
Aram begat Aminadab:
Aminadab begat Naasson:
Naasson begat Salmon:
Salmon begat Boos of Rahab:
Boos begat Obed of Ruth:
Obed begat Jesse:
Jesse begat David the kynge:
David the kynge begat Salomon / of her that was the wyfe of Vry:
Salomon begat Roboam:
Roboam begat Abia:
B Abia begat Asa:
Asa begat Josaphat:
Josaphat begat Joram:
Joram begat Osias:
A.ii. Osias

David and Abraham are first rehersed: because that Christ was specially promised vnto them, to be of their seede. Genesis. xxviij.g. i. Parall. ij.a. Ruth. iiij.d. ij. Regum vij.f. i. Parall. iij.b.

Tyndale's New Testament of 1526 (*left*), printed in Worms, and the corrected edition produced in 1534 in Antwerp. In both cases, the use of illustrations and the general layout were influenced by Luther's New Testament.

Prior to the introduction of verse-numbering, location within a chapter was often assisted by marginal markers, A, B, C, etc., every fifteen lines or so. Chapter divisions and numbers had appeared in printed Latin Bibles from the outset, and summaries even prefaced chapters in a Latin Bible of 1480 from Ulm. But little or no gap was given between chapters or even books, in a black solidity of unbroken text running 'from Genesis to Revelation without stopping for breath'. Gradually

A printed black-letter Bible in Latin, produced in Basel in 1509. A space has been left for an illumination to be done, and the printed text resembles a hand-written copy.

The Complutensian Polyglot, published in Alcalá in 1522 and sponsored by Cardinal Ximenes. Here, the Hebrew text of Leviticus 1 includes the Latin and Greek versions as well as the Aramaic Targum of Onkelos.

the layout of the page became more and more reader-friendly, with page numbers in arabic figures first in Erasmus's New Testament of 1516 (see below), page-headings identifying the biblical book in question, and clear divisions first between the two Testaments (in a 1511 Venice Bible with a frontispiece to the New Testament for the first time), then between books and between chapters. More significant for easy legibility was the switch from heavy black letter type to roman (not far different from what you are reading on this page). This had been tried in the fifteenth century for Latin Bibles (and used for Italian ones from the earliest), but it became established only after Erasmus's pioneering New Testament of 1516.

Although several of these changes in printing practice facilitated the greater access to the Bible advocated by the Reformers, they often preceded Reformation pressures. Thus roman type was used in a series of small-size several-part Latin Bibles printed at Paris from 1523. Even standardized numbering of verses, which made possible greater speed and precision in appealing to the biblical text, especially in controversy, emerged more as a predictable development than a confessionally led innovation. In any case, facility in finding a crucial place in one of the gospels was of limited value without a uniform text. For that there was no alternative but resort to the original languages.

THE BIBLE IN HEBREW AND GREEK

Among the leading Reformers, especially of a more humanist stripe, some reserve is discernible towards the teaching of Hebrew. This is evident in Philipp Melanchthon, 'the tutor of Germany', nervous lest Hebrew studied too early corrupt the purity of the classical tongues of Latin and Greek. Nevertheless, Luther, Calvin, Martin Bucer, and Peter Martyr Vermigli were not the only Reformers to acquire a commendable expertise in Hebrew—Calvin to the extent of being able to preach in French and lecture in Latin on the Old Testament with nothing but a Hebrew Bible in front of him.

Hebrew Bibles had been printed since 1488, when the first complete edition was issued in Soncino, near Mantua in Italy. Three other editions, all likewise by Jewish scholars, appeared before 1500. The two-part Brescia printing of 1492–4 was used by Luther in translating the Old Testament into German. Christian interest in printing the Hebrew text first bore fruit in the six-volume Polyglot ('multi-lingual') Bible printed in Spain at Alcalá (and known as Complutensian from the place's Latin name) during 1514–17. Papal authorization delayed publication until 1522, depriving it of the distinction of being the first publicly available Greek New Testament. The Alcalá Polyglot deserves recognition as a high water mark of pre-Reformation scholarship on the text of scripture.

Daniel Bomberg at Venice was the first Christian printer to issue a Hebrew Old Testament (together with Targumim and rabbinical commentaries) in 1516–17. Far more mould-breaking for religious awakening was Erasmus' Latin–Greek *Novum Instrumentum* (Basel, 1516). As the first published Greek New Testament (even if provided chiefly to justify the fresh Latin translation), as well as

Primitiua heb. | Ter. Heb. | Leui. | Ca.i. | Träsla. B. Hiero. | Träsla. Gre. lxx. cü interp. latina

Träsla. B. Hiero.

tabernaculü deferebat pficiscebätur filii isrl p turmas suas. Si pëdebat desup: manebät i eo dë loco. Nubes qppe dñi incubebat per dië tabernaculo & ignis in nocte: videntibus cunctis populis israel per cunctas mäsiones suas.

Explicit liber Exodi.

Incipit vaiechra. i. liber Leuiticus. Cap. i.

Vocauit ät moysen & locutus ë ei dñs de tabernaculo testimonii: dicës. Loqre filiis israel: & dices ad eos. Hö qui obtulerit ex vobis hostiam domino de pecoribus idest, de bobus & ouibus offerens victimas: si holocaustum fuerit eius oblatio ac de armëto: masculü immaculatü offeret ad ostiü tabernaculi testimonii ad placandum sibi dominum. Ponetq; sup caput hostie manus & acceptabilis erit: atq; in expiatione eius pficiës. Immolabitq; vitulum coram domino: & offerent filii aaron sacerdotes sanguinem eius fundentes per altaris circuitum: quod est ante ostium tabernaculi. Detractaq; pelle hostie artus in frusta concident: & subiicient in altari ignem strue lignorum ante compo sita: & membra que sunt cesa desuper ordinätes:

Primitiua chal. | Interp. chal. | Transla. Chal.

Interp. chal.

tabernaculü proficiscebätur filii israel per oës mansiones suas. Et si nö eleuabat nubes: nö proficiscebätur vsq; in die qua eleuabatur. Nubes enim dñi erat sup tabernaculü per dië: & ignis erat in eo p noctë in oculis oïs domus israel in oïbus mäsionibus suis.

Explicit liber exodi.

Incipit liber leuiticus. Ca. i.

Vocauit aüt moysen & locutus est dñs cum eo de tabernaculo federis: dicens. Loquere cü filiis israel: & dices eis. Homo q obtulerit ex vobis oblationë corä dño: de pecoribus de bobus & de ouibus offeretis oblationes vras. Si holocaustü fuerit eius oblatio de bobus: masculü integrü offerat: ad ostiü tabernaculi federis offerat illü: vt sit ei placabile corä dño. Imponetq; manü suä sup caput holocausti: & acceptabile erit ei ad ppiciandü p eo. Imolabitq; vitulü corä dño: & offerët filii aaron sacerdotes sanguinë: & aspgent sanguinë sup altare p circuitü qd est in ostio tabernaculi federis. & detrahet pellë holocausti: & diuidet illud per membra eius: & ponët filii aaron sacerdotis ignë sup altare: & ordinabüt ligna super ignë. Ordinabuntq; filii aaron sacerdotes membra typographically avant-garde, it and subsequent editions (revised, but not always for the better) enlightened several early Reformers in the meaning of key words or statements in the New Testament. They thus became 'Erasmians' before coming out as 'Martinians', that is, Lutherans. When Jesus challenged hearers to 'Repent', he did not mean 'Do penance' (as the Latin of the Vulgate was taken to

This reproduction from Erasmus' *Novum Instrumentum* of 1516 shows the beginning of Paul's letter to the Romans in the Greek on the left, with a Latin translation on the right.

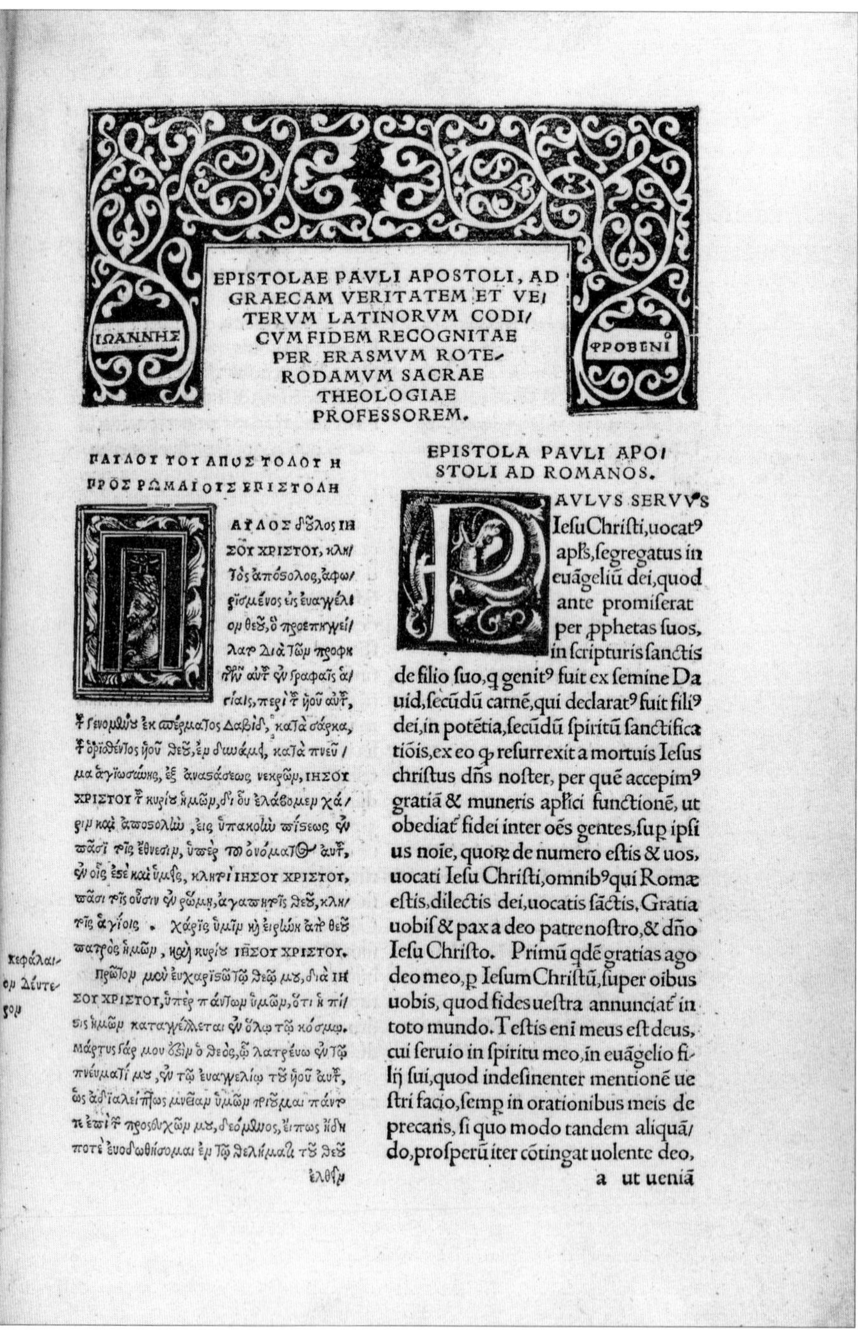

EPISTOLAE PAVLI APOSTOLI, AD GRAECAM VERITATEM ET VETERVM LATINORVM CODICVM FIDEM RECOGNITAE PER ERASMVM ROTERODAMVM SACRAE THEOLOGIAE PROFESSOREM.

ΠΑΥΛΟΥ ΤΟΥ ΑΠΟΣΤΟΛΟΥ Η ΠΡΟΣ ΡΩΜΑΙΟΥΣ ΕΠΙΣΤΟΛΗ

ΠΑΥΛΟΣ δοῦλος ΙΗ
ΣΟΥ ΧΡΙΣΤΟΥ, κλη/
τὸς ἀπόστολος, ἀφω/
ρισμένος εἰς εὐαγγέλι
ον θεοῦ, ὃ προεπηγγεί/
λατο διὰ τῶν προφη
τῶν αὐτοῦ ἐν γραφαῖς ἁ/
γίαις, περὶ τοῦ υἱοῦ αὐτοῦ,
τοῦ γενομένου ἐκ σπέρματος Δαβίδ, κατὰ σάρκα,
τοῦ ὁρισθέντος υἱοῦ θεοῦ, ἐν δυνάμει, κατὰ πνεῦ/
μα ἁγιωσύνης, ἐξ ἀναστάσεως νεκρῶν, ΙΗΣΟΥ
ΧΡΙΣΤΟΥ τοῦ κυρίου ἡμῶν, δι' οὗ ἐλάβομεν χά/
ριν καὶ ἀποστολὴν, εἰς ὑπακοὴν πίστεως ἐν
πᾶσι τοῖς ἔθνεσιν, ὑπὲρ τοῦ ὀνόματος αὐτοῦ,
ἐν οἷς ἐστὲ καὶ ὑμεῖς, κλητοὶ ΙΗΣΟΥ ΧΡΙΣΤΟΥ,
πᾶσι τοῖς οὖσιν ἐν ῥώμῃ, ἀγαπητοῖς θεοῦ, κλη/
τοῖς ἁγίοις. Χάρις ὑμῖν καὶ εἰρήνη ἀπὸ θεοῦ
πατρὸς ἡμῶν, καὶ κυρίου ΙΗΣΟΥ ΧΡΙΣΤΟΥ.
κεφάλαι- Πρῶτον μὲν εὐχαριστῶ τῷ θεῷ μου, διὰ ΙΗ
ον δεύτε- ΣΟΥ ΧΡΙΣΤΟΥ, ὑπὲρ πάντων ὑμῶν, ὅτι ἡ πί/
ρον στις ὑμῶν καταγγέλλεται ἐν ὅλῳ τῷ κόσμῳ.
μάρτυς γάρ μου ἐστὶν ὁ θεὸς, ᾧ λατρεύω ἐν τῷ
πνεύματί μου, ἐν τῷ εὐαγγελίῳ τοῦ υἱοῦ αὐτοῦ,
ὡς ἀδιαλείπτως μνείαν ὑμῶν ποιοῦμαι πάντο
τε ἐπὶ τῶν προσευχῶν μου, δεόμενος, εἴπως ἤδη
ποτὲ εὐοδωθήσομαι ἐν τῷ θελήματι τοῦ θεοῦ
ἐλθεῖν

EPISTOLA PAVLI APOSTOLI AD ROMANOS.

PAVLVS SERVVS
Ieſu Chriſti, uocatꝰ
apl̃s, ſegregatus in
euãgeliũ dei, quod
ante promiſerat
per pphetas ſuos,
in ſcripturis ſanctis
de filio ſuo, q genitꝰ fuit ex ſemine Da
uid, ſecũdũ carnẽ, qui declaratꝰ fuit filiꝰ
dei, in potẽtia, ſecũdũ ſpiritũ ſanctifica
tiõis, ex eo q reſurrexit a mortuis Ieſus
chriſtus dñs noſter, per quẽ accepimꝰ
gratiã & muneris apl̃ici functionẽ, ut
obediat fidei inter oẽs gentes, ſup ipſi
us noie, quorũ de numero eſtis & uos,
uocati Ieſu Chriſti, omnibꝰ qui Romæ
eſtis, dilectis dei, uocatis ſãctis. Gratia
uobiſ & pax a deo patre noſtro, & dño
Ieſu Chriſto. Primũ qdẽ gratias ago
deo meo, p Ieſum Chriſtũ, ſuper oibus
uobis, quod fides ueſtra annunciat in
toto mundo. Teſtis eni meus eſt deus,
cui ſeruio in ſpiritu meo, in euãgelio fi/
lij ſui, quod indeſinenter mentionẽ ue
ſtri facio, ſemp in orationibus meis de
precans, ſi quo modo tandem aliquã/
do, proſperũ iter cõtingat uolente deo,
a ut ueniã

mean). Paul's declaration about God's righteousness in Romans 1: 17ff. referred not to punitive or judicial *iustitia* (Latin could not distinguish between 'justice' and 'righteousness') but to God's gift of righteousness to penitent sinners.

Erasmus was the dominant figure among the 'biblical' humanists who directed the humanist drive back to the sources of classical Greek and Roman learning into Christian channels—the New Testament but also the church Fathers of the early centuries. The second part of his *Novum Instrumentum* of 1516 was a commentary in the form of *Annotations*, expanded in successive editions down to 1535, from which one can trace the developing learning and thought of this witty and provocative scholar. Numerous nuggets found their way into the margins of later New Testaments. Erasmus also wrote *Paraphrases* of the New Testament, similarly in Latin, the language which ensured his Europe-wide influence. Yet he expressed his strong support for vernacular renderings of sacred scripture so that (with reference to the *Paraphrases* in particular) it might reach 'the farmer, the tailor, the stonemason, prostitutes, pimps, and Turks'. Among the vernaculars which fulfilled this hope for the *Paraphrases* was English. King Edward VI ordered in 1547 that Erasmus' *Paraphrases* of the gospels be set up in all parish churches for everyone to read.

The Greek text of the New Testament provided by Erasmus was an imperfect instrument. His manuscript base was narrow, some verses he retroverted into Greek from the Vulgate on finding them missing from his manuscripts in Greek, and in his third edition (1522) he inserted 1 John 5: 7–8, the so-called Johannine comma, on learning of a single Greek manuscript that contained its undoubtedly inauthentic testimony to the Trinity. The 1534 Paris Greek Testament produced by Simon de Colines, stepfather of Robert Estienne, came nearer to a critical edition, using Erasmus, the Complutensian text, and unnamed manuscript sources which obviously furnished some good readings. But although used by Calvin, it seems, for a few years in the 1540s, the Colines edition was overshadowed by the Erasmian series.

It was again the achievement of the Estiennes to move the infant science of New Testament textual criticism a significant step forward. The edition Robert Estienne published at Paris in 1550 was the first to contain an *apparatus criticus*, that is, a record in the margins of variant readings of the Greek text collated from manuscripts by his son Henri. Theodore Beza built on Estienne's work in his Greek Testament of 1565, using more of Henri Estienne's collations and a wider range of manuscripts. But two weighty manuscripts at his disposal, including the one later known from his donation of it to Cambridge University in 1581 as Codex Bezae Cantabrigiensis, he used sparingly because of the divergence of their texts from the standard version.

There were in truth relatively insignificant differences between the Greek texts of Erasmus, the Complutensians, Estienne, and Beza. They each purveyed a text close to what underlay the King James translation of 1611, commonly referred to as the Byzantine Text, but also as the 'Received Text'. This Latin phrase, *textus receptus*, caught on from the preface to the neat and economic Greek Testament issued at Leiden in 1633 by the Elzevir press: 'You have then a text received by all.'

THE BIBLE IN THE LANGUAGE OF THE PEOPLE

Vernacular Bible translations did not begin with the Reformation. The first German Bible was published at Strasbourg in 1466. By 1522, when Luther's fresh New Testament appeared, almost twenty German editions had been issued. Unlike the Vulgate, from which they were all translated, these volumes were well illustrated, especially in the Old Testament. An Italian Bible was first

The so-called 'December Testament' of Martin Luther was the second impression of his German translation of the New Testament, published in 1522. The opening of John's Gospel is illustrated.

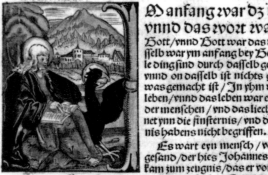

Sanct Johannes. LXI.

Das erste Capitel.

Gen.1. JM anfang war dz wort. vnnd das wort war bey Gott/vnnd Gott war das wort/das selb war ym anfang bey Gott/Alle ding sind durch dasselb gemacht/vnnd on dasselb ist nichts gemacht was gemacht ist/Jn yhm war das leben/vnnd das leben war eyn liecht der menschen/vnd das liecht scheynet ynn die finsternis/vnd die finsternis habens nicht begriffen.

Matth.3. Marci.1. Luce.3. Es wart eyn mensch/von Gott gesand/der hies Johannes/der selb kam zum zeugnis/das er von dem liecht zeugete/auff das sie alle durch yhn glewbten/Er war nicht das liecht sondern dz er zeugete von dem liecht/Das war eyn warhafftigs liecht/wilchs alle menschē erleucht/durch seyn zukunfft yñ disse welt/Es war ynn der wellt/vnd die welt ist durch dasselb gemacht/vñ die welt kandt es nicht.

Er kam ynn seyn eygenthum/vñ die seynen namen yhn nicht auff/Wie viel yhn aber auffnamen/den gab er macht/Gottis kinder zu werden/denen/die da an seynen namen glawben/wilche nicht von dem geblut/noch von dem willen des fleyschis/noch von dem willen eynes mannes/sondern von Gott geporen sindt.

Math.1. Luce.2. Vnd das wort wart fleysch/vnd wonete vnter vns/vnd wyr sahen seyne herlickeyt/eyn herlickeyt als des eyngepornen sons vom vatter/voller gnade vnd warheyt.

Johannes zeuget von yhm/schreybt vnd spricht/Diser war es/võ dem ich gesagt habt/Nach myr wirt komen/der fur myr gewesen ist/denn er war ehe denn ich/vñ von seyner fulle/haben wyr alle genommen/gnade vmb gnade/denn das gesetz ist durch Mosen geben/die gnade vnd warheyt ist durch Jhesum Christ worden/Niemant hatt Gott yhe gesehen/der eyngeporne son/der ynn des vatters schos ist/der hats vns verkundiget.

(gnad vmb gnad) Unser gnad ist vns geben/vmb Christus gnade/die ym geben ist/das wyr durch yhn/das gesetz erfullen vnnd den vatter erkennē/da mit heuchley auff hore vnd wyr ware rechtschaffne menschen werden.

Vnd dis ist das zeugnis Johannis/da die Juden sandten võ Jerusalem priester vnd Leuiten/das sie yhn fragten/wer bistu? Vnnd er bekandt vnd leugnet nicht/vnd er bekandt/ich byn nicht Christus/vnd sie fragten yhn/was denn? Bistu Elias? Er sprach/Jch byns nicht. Bistu eyn Prophet? vnd er antwort/Neyn/Da sprachen sie zu yhm/Was bistu denn/das wyr antwort geben denen/die vns gesand haben? Was sagistu võ dyr selbs? Er sprach/ich byn eyn ruffers stym ynn der wusten/Richtet den weg des hern/wie der Prophet Jsaias gesagt hat. [illegible]

Vnd die gesand waren/die waren/von den Phariseern/vnnd fragten yhn vnd sprachen zu yhm/warumb teuffestu denn/so du nit Christus

L stus

printed at Venice in 1471, while in France an extensive *Bible historiée*—a kind of thorough paraphrase with glosses—was delivered from presses in Lyons before and after 1500.

Martin Luther's *Das Neue Testament Deutzsch* (Wittenberg, 1522) was made, with some help from Melanchthon, direct from Erasmus's Greek (2nd edn., 1519) and in a German meant to be generally accessible. Although a folio in size, it cost only as much as a manual worker's weekly wage. Luther and colleagues pressed on with the Old Testament, and the whole Bible in High German was published at Wittenberg in 1534, and the same year in Low German at Lübeck, the work of unknown revisers of Luther's masterpiece. These Bibles included the apocryphal (deuterocanonical) books, translated largely from the Vulgate and Septuagint. Collaborative revision continued almost unbroken until Luther's death in 1546.

This German Bible not only blazed the trail for other vernacular translations made by Reformers from Hebrew and Greek, but won unchallenged acceptance in German-speaking territories. Frequent reprints, especially of sections or individual books; the thoroughly German character of the translation, making it a landmark in the development of literary German, not least in vocabulary ('I endeavoured', Luther said, 'to make Moses so German that no one would suspect he was a Jew'); the woodcuts domesticating biblical scenes and personages in modern Germany; and not least the growing demand for direct access to holy scripture nurtured by the ever-louder clamour for Reformation—all ensured the widest readership and audience. As Luther set out in his *Letter on Translation* of 1523, in defence of his addition of 'alone' to 'justified by faith', common-language Bibles responded to an evangelical and theological imperative. That famous Reformation slogan, 'Scripture alone', is not frequent in Reformation literature, but it voiced the conviction that the highest authority in faith and works resided in the Word of God written—'Scripture supreme', we might say. Luther, Zwingli, and many others had been preaching and lecturing from the Greek New Testament before the new vernacular versions entered into print. When Zwingli in 1519 in Zürich set out to preach right through Matthew's Gospel, not merely on the selected liturgical lections, he not only reintroduced a practice followed by distinguished expositors of the early centuries, like John Chrysostom and Augustine, but he also exemplified a new-found confidence in the clarity and certainty of the biblical Word of God.

Publication of the Bible in the language of the people without ecclesiastical authorization defied the Catholic Church's assumption that scripture was subject to its control. This claim was not yet as well defined as it would become in response to the Protestant challenge. The Council of Trent in 1546 declared the Vulgate the 'authentic' Latin version of the Bible, on the grounds of its centuries-long use and its approval by the church. In lectures, disputations, sermons, and expositions the Vulgate must be employed. Furthermore, it was not to be interpreted 'contrary to that sense which holy mother Church, to whom it belongs to judge of their true sense and interpretation, has held and holds'. No Bible or part thereof or commentary thereon was to be published without explicit church permission.

This decree left much unsaid or unsettled. It did not as such exclude vernacular translations made presumably from the Vulgate's Latin and certified by appropriate ecclesiastical officers. English-speaking Roman Catholics would for three centuries use the Douai–Rheims Bible (New Testament 1582, Old Testament

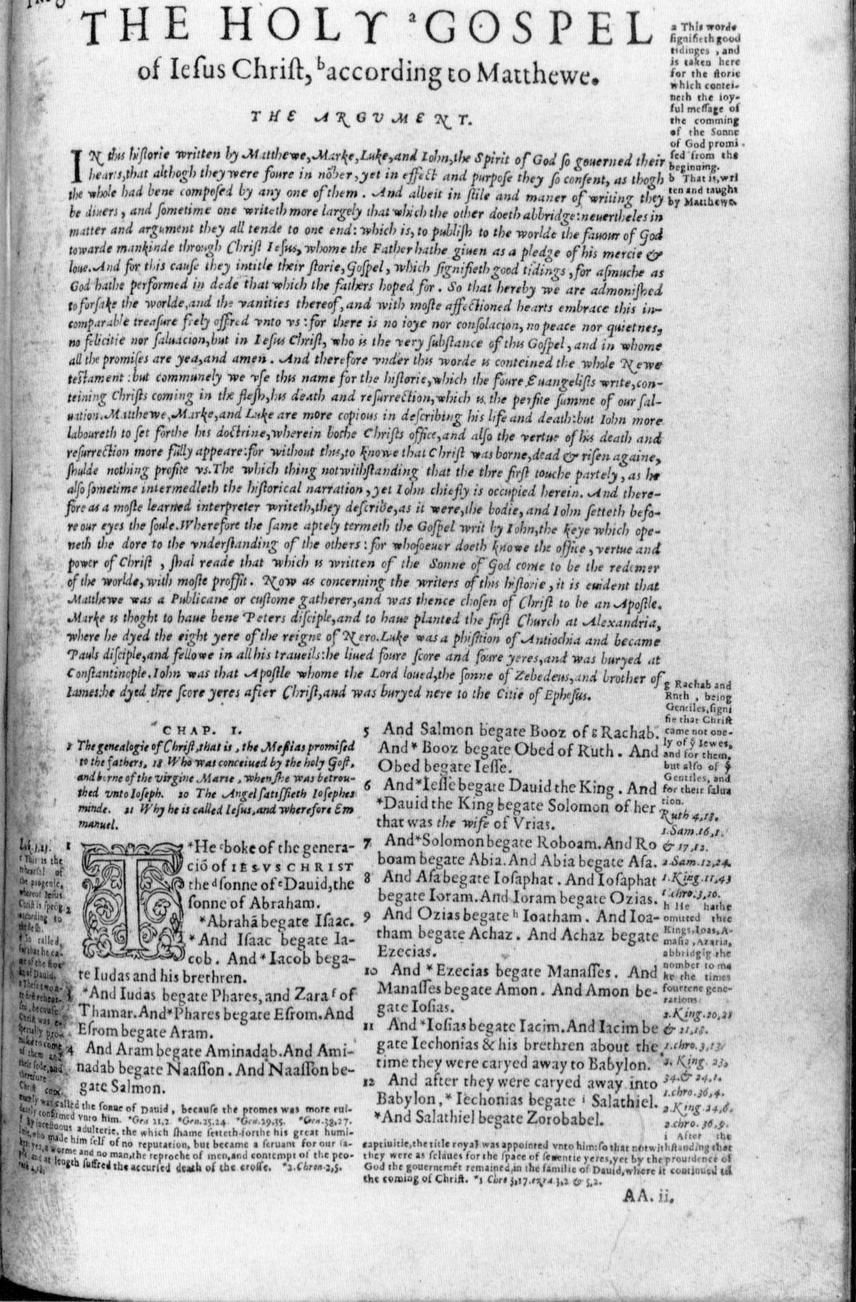

The generacion of Christ. 2

THE HOLY [a]GOSPEL

of Iesus Christ, [b]according to Matthewe.

a This worde signifieth good tidinges, and is taken here for the storie which conteineth the ioyful message of the comming of the Sonne of God promised from the beginning.

b That is, writen and taught by Matthewe.

THE ARGUMENT.

IN this historie written by Matthewe, Marke, Luke, and Iohn, the Spirit of God so gouerned their hearts, that althogh they were foure in nõber, yet in effect and purpose they so consent, as thogh the whole had bene composed by any one of them. And albeit in stile and maner of writing they be diuers, and sometime one writeth more largely that which the other doeth abbridge: neuertheles in matter and argument they all tende to one end: which is, to publish to the worlde the fauour of God towarde mankinde through Christ Iesus, whome the Father hathe giuen as a pledge of his mercie & loue. And for this cause they intitle their storie, Gospel, which signifieth good tidings, for asmuche as God hathe performed in dede that which the fathers hoped for. So that hereby we are admonished to forsake the worlde, and the vanities thereof, and with moste affectioned hearts embrace this incomparable treasure frely offred vnto vs: for there is no ioye nor consolacion, no peace nor quietnes, no felicitie nor saluacion, but in Iesus Christ, who is the very substance of this Gospel, and in whome all the promises are yea, and amen. And therefore vnder this worde is conteined the whole Newe testament: but communely we vse this name for the historie, which the foure Euangelists write, conteining Christs coming in the flesh, his death and resurrection, which is the perfite summe of our saluation. Matthewe, Marke, and Luke are more copious in describing his life and death: but Iohn more laboureth to set forthe his doctrine, wherein bothe Christs office, and also the vertue of his death and resurrection more fully appeare: for without this, to knowe that Christ was borne, dead & risen againe, shulde nothing profite vs. The which thing notwithstanding that the thre first touche partely, as he also sometime intermedleth the historical narration, yet Iohn chiefly is occupied herein. And therefore as a moste learned interpreter writeth, they describe, as it were, the bodie, and Iohn setteth before our eyes the soule. Wherefore the same aptely termeth the Gospel writ by Iohn, the keye which openeth the dore to the vnderstanding of the others: for whosoeuer doeth knowe the office, vertue and power of Christ, shal reade that which is written of the Sonne of God come to be the redemer of the worlde, with moste proffit. Now as concerning the writers of this historie, it is euident that Matthewe was a Publicane or custome gatherer, and was thence chosen of Christ to be an Apostle. Marke is thoght to haue bene Peters disciple, and to haue planted the first Church at Alexandria, where he dyed the eight yere of the reigne of Nero. Luke was a phisition of Antiochia and became Pauls disciple, and fellowe in all his traueils: he liued foure score and foure yeres, and was buryed at Constantinople. Iohn was that Apostle whome the Lord loued, the sonne of Zebedeus, and brother of Iames: he dyed thre score yeres after Christ, and was buryed nere to the Citie of Ephesus.

CHAP. I.

1 The genealogie of Christ, that is, the Messias promised to the fathers. 18 Who was conceiued by the holy Gost, and borne of the virgine Marie, when she was betrouthed vnto Ioseph. 20 The Angel satisfieth Iosephes minde. 21 Why he is called Iesus, and wherefore Emmanuel.

1 *He [c]boke of the genera-
ciõ of IESVS CHRIST
the [d]sonne of [e]Dauid, the
sonne of Abraham.
2 *Abrahã begate Isaac.
*And Isaac begate Ia-
cob. And *Iacob bega-
te Iudas and his brethren.
3 *And Iudas begate Phares, and Zara [f]of
Thamar. And *Phares begate Esrom. And
Esrom begate Aram.
4 And Aram begate Aminadab. And Aminadab begate Naasson. And Naasson begate Salmon.
5 And Salmon begate Booz of [g]Rachab.
And *Booz begate Obed of Ruth. And
Obed begate Iesse.
6 And *Iesse begate Dauid the King. And
*Dauid the King begate Solomon of her
that was *the wife* of Vrias.
7 And *Solomon begate Roboam. And Ro
boam begate Abia. And Abia begate Asa.
8 And Asa begate Iosaphat. And Iosaphat
begate Ioram. And Ioram begate Ozias.
9 And Ozias begate [h]Ioatham. And Ioa-
tham begate Achaz. And Achaz begate
Ezecias.
10 And *Ezecias begate Manasses. And
Manasses begate Amon. And Amon begate Iosias.
11 And *Iosias begate Iacim. And Iacim be
gate Iechonias & his brethren about the
time they were caryed away to Babylon.
12 And after they were caryed away into
Babylon, *Iechonias begate [i]Salathiel.
*And Salathiel begate Zorobabel.

Luk. 3, 23.
c This is the rehearsal of the progenie, whereof Iesus Christ is sprong according to the flesh.
d So called, for that he came of the stocke of Dauid.
e These two are first rehearsed, because Christ was especially promised to come of them and their sede, and therefore Christ continually was called the sonne of Dauid, because the promes was more euidently confirmed vnto him. *Gen 21, 2. *Gen. 25, 24. *Gen. 29, 35. *Gen. 38, 27.
f By incestuous adulterie, the which shame setteth forthe his great humilitie, who made him self of no reputation, but became a seruant for our sakes: yea, a worme and no man, the reproche of men, and contempt of the people, and at length suffred the accursed death of the crosse. *2. Chron. 2, 5. Ruth 4, 18.

g Rachab and Ruth, being Gentiles, signifie that Christ came not onely of ye Iewes, and for them, but also of ye Gentiles, and for their saluation.
Ruth 4, 18. 1. Sam. 16, 1. & 17, 12. 2. Sam. 12, 24. 1. King. 11, 43 1. chro. 3, 10.
h He hathe omitted thre Kings, Ioas, Amasia, Azaria, abbridgig the nomber to make the times fourtene generations.
2. King. 20, 21 & 21, 18. 1. chro. 3, 13. 2. King. 23, 34. & 24, 1. 1. chro. 36, 4. 2. King. 24, 6. 2. chro. 36, 9.
i After the captiuitie, the title royal was appointed vnto him: so that notwithstanding that they were as sclaues for the space of seuentie yeres, yet by the prouidence of God the gouernemẽt remained in the familie of Dauid, where it continued til the coming of Christ. *1 Chro 3, 17. ezra 3, 2 & 5, 2.

AA. ii.

The Geneva Bible of 1560, the version used by Shakespeare, was very popular on account of its forceful renderings, handy size, Roman type-face, layout, and accompanying notes and comments.

1609–10), so named from the two locations in France of the English Catholic college responsible for it. Translated from the Vulgate with a closeness that at times provided a highly Latinized English (e.g. 'supersubstantial bread' in the Lord's Prayer in Matthew 6: 11, but not in Luke—for the Vulgate strangely rendered the difficult Greek word 'daily' in the Lucan version; 'He exinanited Himself' in Philippians 2: 7), it was equipped with a prologue and notes that ensured dogmatic correctness of interpretation. It was surely intended to counter the marginal

216

THE HOLY GOSPEL OF IESVS CHRIST ACCORDING TO IOHN.

CHAP. I.

The 1. parte: THE ACTES of Christ before his manifestation, whiles Iohn Baptist was yet baptizing.

The preface of the Euangelist, commending Christ (as being God the Sonne incarnate) to the Gentils, and setting out the blindnes of the Ievves in not receiuing him. 19 Then, the testimonies of Iohn Baptist, first to the solemne legacie of the Ievves: 29 secondly, vvhen he savv IESVS come to him: 35 thirdly, to his ovvne Disciples also, putting them ouer from him self to IESVS. Vvho made it plainer to them that he is Christ, 40 and so began he also to haue Disciples.

The Gospel at the third Masse vpō Christmas day. And euery day at the end of Masse.

N THE beginning "vvas the WORD, 1
and the WORD vvas "vvith God, and
"God vvas the WORD. † This vvas in 2
the beginning vvith God. † Al things 3
vvere made "by him: and vvithout him
vvas made \`nothing. That vvhich vvas
made', † in him vvas life, and the life vvas 4
the light of men: † and the light shineth in darkenesse, and 5
the darkenesse did not comprehend it. † There vvas a man 6
sent from God, vvhose name vvas Iohn. † This man came 7
for testimonie: to giue testimonie of the light, that al might
beleeue through him. † He vvas not the light, but to giue 8
testimonie of the light. † It vvas the true light, vvhich ligh- 9
teneth euery man that commeth into this vvorld. † He vvas 10
in the vvorld, and the vvorld vvas made by him, and the
vvorld knevv him not. † He came into his ovvne, and his 11
ovvne receiued him not. † But as many as receiued him, "he 12
gaue them povver to be made the sonnes of God, to those
that beleeue in his name. † Vvho, not of bloud, nor of the 13
vvil of flesh, nor of the vvil of man, but of God are borne.
† AND "THE VVORD VVAS MADE FLESH, 14
and dvvelt in vs (and vve savv the glorie of him, glorie as it
vvere of the only-begotten of the Father) ful of grace and
veritie.

\`*nothing that vvas made.*

ET VERBVM CARO FACTVM EST.

The Douai New Testament, published in 1609 in Douai in northern France, was prepared by Roman Catholic scholars, and translated from the Latin Vulgate. Its clear type-face and layout should be noted.

William Tyndale translating the Bible, from the painting by W. Johnstone.

notes of the 1560 Geneva Bible. The latter, often unfairly stigmatized as extremist, were generally Protestant rather than markedly Calvinist; so they emphasize justification by faith and frequently target the papacy. Sometimes Douai–Rheims and Geneva were closer than either expected, for the latter deliberately allowed for the perpetual virginity of Mary in its notes on the apparent brothers of Jesus and related texts.

The Council of Trent also instructed that in future 'the Holy Scriptures, especially the old Vulgate edition, be printed in the most correct manner possible'. The Council could not specify which printing of the Vulgate was *authenticum*. The lack was supplied by an edition produced under the authority of Pope Sixtus V in 1590 and issued in a revised text under his successor Clement VIII in 1592. This 'Clementine' Vulgate has never been formally superseded, although Trent's silence has allowed the Roman Church in the modern era to function with the Hebrew and Greek scriptures no less than other scholastic and ecclesial communities. The Clementine Bible had two further editions, in 1593 and 1598. The practice of continuing correction while printing was in process meant that copies of the same edition do not agree in all respects. Such a risky procedure resulted in the third edition being the least correct.

THE ENGLISH BIBLE

English Bible translation began in earnest with the Wycliffite versions in the fourteenth century. Although made from the Vulgate (but not by John Wyclif himself), they were inevitably controversial because unauthorized, and made more so by the teachings of Wyclif and his followers. They were banned and fresh English translation forbidden (1407). Nevertheless, manuscripts of the Wycliffite translations continued to circulate, and the possession and public reading and preaching of English scriptures became a trademark of Lollardy and sufficient to ensure condemnation as heretical.

Thus the fresh translations of the Bible into English initiated by William Tyndale began life under a menacing cloud. By common consent Tyndale was a genius of a translator whose work had immense influence on the Authorized Version. His New Testament, made on the basis of the Greek but aided by Luther's German, Erasmus's Latin, and other resources, had to be printed on the Continent (Cologne and Worms, 1525) but copies were soon smuggled into England and Scotland. Tyndale went on to translate parts of the Old Testament but only the Pentateuch and Jonah were published. He kitted out his New Testament with prefaces, prologues, and marginalia often of Lutheran origin or inspiration.

Another English Bible translator of genius was Miles Coverdale, later bishop of Exeter. He dedicated his 1535 Bible, the first complete one in English, to Henry VIII. He used Tyndale wherever it was available. Coverdale's translation of the Psalms went on to exercise a profound influence on English religious consciousness through its inclusion in the Book of Common Prayer.

(*Right*) Miles Coverdale's Bible of 1535, produced in Cologne. The general layout owed much to German Lutheran printed Bibles.

(*Above*) Portrait of Miles Coverdale (*c.*1488–1568), who was Bishop of Exeter (1551–3), and a former assistant of Tyndale. He prepared the Great Bible of 1539, whose revised Psalter (1540) was retained in the Book of Common Prayer of 1662.

The gospel of S. Mathew.

The first Chapter.

A Luc.3.d This is the boke of the
generacion of Jesus
Christ ỹ sonne of Da-
uid, the sonne of Abra-
Gen.21.a ham. Abrahã begat
Gen.25.c Isaac: Isaac begat
Gen.29.f Jacob: Jacob begat
Judas ⁊ his brethrẽ:
Gen.38.e Judas begat Phares ⁊ Zarã of Thamar:
Gen.46.b Phares begat Hesrom:
Ruth.4.d Hesrom begat Aram:
1.Par.2.a Aram begat Amminadab:
Num.1.a Aminadab begat Naasson:
Naasson begat Salmon:
Salmon begat Boos of Rahab:
Boos begat Obed of Ruth:
Obed begat Jesse:
1.Reg.16.a Jesse begat Dauid the kynge:
2.Re.12.c Dauid the kynge begat Salomon, of her
1.Par.3.b 3.Re.11.g that was the wyfe of Vry:
Salomon begat Roboam:
Roboam begat Abia:
Abia begat Asa:
Asa begat Josaphat:
B Josaphat begat Joram:
Joram begat Osias:
2.Par.26.d Osias begat Joatham:
2.Par.27.b Joatham begat Achas:
2.Par.28.d Achas begat Ezechias:
4.Re.20.c Ezechias begat Manasses:
4.Re.21.d Manasses begat Amon:
4.Re.21.e Amon begat Josias:
4.Re.23.f 24.25 Josias begat Jechonias and his brethren
aboute the tyme of the captiuyte of Ba-
bylon.
1.Par.3.c And after the captiuyte of Babylon, Je-
Agg.1.a chonias begat Salathiel:
1.Esd.3.a Salathiel begat Zorobabel:

Zorobabel begat Abiud:
Abiud begat Eliachim:
Eliachim begat Azor:
Azor begat Sadoc:
Sadoc begat Achin:
Achin begat Eliud:
Eliud begat Eleasar:
Eleasar begat Matthan:
Matthan begat Jacob:
Jacob begat Joseph the hußbande of Ma-
ry, of whõ was borne that Jesus, which is
called Christ.
All the generacions from Abrahã to Dauid are fourtene generacions: From Dauid
vnto the captiuite of Babylon, are fourtene generacions. From the captiuite of Babylon vnto Christ, are also fourtene generacions.
The byrth of Christ was on thys wyse: C
When his mother Mary was maried to Jo- Luc.1.b
seph * before they came together, she was
foũde with chylde by ỹ holy goost. But Joseph her hußbande was a perfect man, and
wolde not bringe her to shame, but was myn
ded to put her awaie secretely. Neuertheles
whyle he thus thought, beholde, the angell
of the LORDE appered vnto him in a dreame, sayinge: Joseph thou sonne of Dauid, feare not to take vnto the Mary thy wyfe. For
that which is cõceaued in her, is of ỹ holy
goost. She shall brynge forth a sonne, and
thou shalt call his name Jesus. For he shall Phi.2.a Act.4.a
saue his people from their synnes.
All this was done, ỹ the thinge might
be fulfilled, which was spoken of the LORDE
by the prophet, sayinge: Beholde, a mayde Esa.7.c
shall be with chylde, and shall brynge forth
a sonne, and they shall call his name Ema-
nuel, which is by interpretacion, God wt vs.
Now whan Joseph awoke out of slepe
he did as the angell of ỹ LORDE bade hym,
and toke his wyfe vnto hym, and knewe her
not, tyll she had brought forth hir fyrst bor- Luc.2.a
ne sonne, and called his name Jesus.

* Some reade: before they sat at home together.

The II. Chapter.

When Jesus was borne at Bethleẽ A
in Jury, in the tyme of Herode the
kynge, Beholde, there came wyse
men from the east to Jerusalẽ, sayinge: Where is the new borne kynge of the Jues? We
haue sene his starre in the east, and are come
to worship him.
When Herode ỹ kynge had herde thys,
he was troubled, ⁊ all Jerusalẽ with hym,
and he gathered all the hye Prestes and
Scribes of ỹ people, ⁊ ared of them, where Christ shulde be borne. And they sayde vn-

AA ij

Revisions and editions based chiefly on Tyndale and Coverdale continued steadily for a decade. Sorting out the different printings of Coverdale is still an unfinished task. In 1537 a revision known as 'Matthew's' Bible, in reality the work of John Rogers, was the first to carry royal authorization, but the Great Bible which Thomas Cromwell in 1538 ordered to be set up in every parish church in England was another Coverdale version (1539).

Scotland produced no vernacular Bible of its own. A manuscript Scots recension of a Wycliffite New Testament made by Murdoch Nisbet, an Ayrshire Lollard, incorporated a Lutheran preface and marginal notes based largely on a Coverdale printing, but the manuscript remained unpublished until the twentieth century. It was, therefore, English Testaments and Bibles that early Scottish evangelicals were condemned for possessing and teaching. One such was Thomas Forret, vicar of Dollar, who was burned before the castle in Edinburgh in 1539.

Reading from a chained Bible in the crypt of Old St Paul's, a painting by Sir George Harvey. The onlookers include the bearded Bishop of Winchester, Stephen Gardiner in conversation with the Vicar General, Lord Cromwell.

His biblical preaching had provoked George Crichton, bishop of Dunkeld, to declare 'I thanke God, that I never knew quhat the Old and New Testament was!'—an utterance that for a time set a proverbial standard for ignorance. The cause of vernacular scripture for Scotland was eloquently championed from the Continent by Alexander Alesius, an Edinburgh native won to Lutheranism in St Andrews, in an appeal to James V.

In England, policies concerning the free availability of English Bibles varied with the ups and downs of the Reformation movement. During the Catholic reaction under Queen Mary, translation went abroad with the Protestant exiles, to Geneva in particular. Here in 1560 the Geneva Bible of which mention has already been made was published—not to be confused with the French Genevan Bible, which Calvin and his fellow pastors steadily improved over a number of years. The English was the work of William Whittingham and colleagues. It became the most widely used English Bible for a century or more, but, although dedicated to Elizabeth I, it never possessed authorization from crown, parliament, or church. Archbishop Matthew Parker initiated a revision of the Great Bible, which on publication in 1568 became known as the Bishops' Bible but, despite being required usage for every church in England, it never challenged the Genevan version in popularity. The latter was of course the Bible of Shakespeare. It was also the first Bible to be published in Scotland—the Bassendyne Bible issued in 1579 in Edinburgh. The appearance of the Geneva Bible in 1560 coincided with the Reformation settlement in Scotland. John Knox's close ties with Geneva helped ensure a speedy and long-lasting acceptance of this translation in Scotland. That he had any part in its translation in Geneva can almost certainly be discounted, but he cited verses from its Old Testament in his major defence of predestination a year of two before 1560.

In 1611 was launched the Authorized or King James Version (AV), which within a generation or so—longer in Scotland—overtook the Geneva Bible in common use. The first suggestion for a new translation came from the General Assembly of the Church of Scotland meeting in 1601 in the small Fife burgh of Burntisland. (In 1946 it was again the General Assembly which set in train the production of the New English Bible.) An expert team of translators set to work at James I/VI's direction, but royal patronage and the words on the title-page 'Appointed to be read in Churches' are all the 'authorization' it received. It was not a wholly fresh translation but more a revision, taking the Bishops' Bible as a basis but consulting other versions, especially Douai–Rheims and Geneva, as far back as Tyndale, as well as the Hebrew and Greek. It achieved a literary felicitousness that still today makes it the favourite English Bible in surprising quarters, among the traditionally pious and the cultured irreligious. Its influence on the English language both written and spoken has been immeasurable. Its prose rhythms, in metres that often reflect the translators' mental formation in classical Greek and Latin verse, have made it a high preference for public reading, in settings where its use for private devotion and study has long been abandoned. The translators' preface (which takes its own biblical quotations from the Geneva

In these scenes from the Nuremberg Bible (1483), depicting one of the plagues in Egypt and the Song of Moses, Moses has horns thanks to a Latin mistranslation of a Hebrew word meaning both 'ray' and 'horn' at Exodus 34: 29.

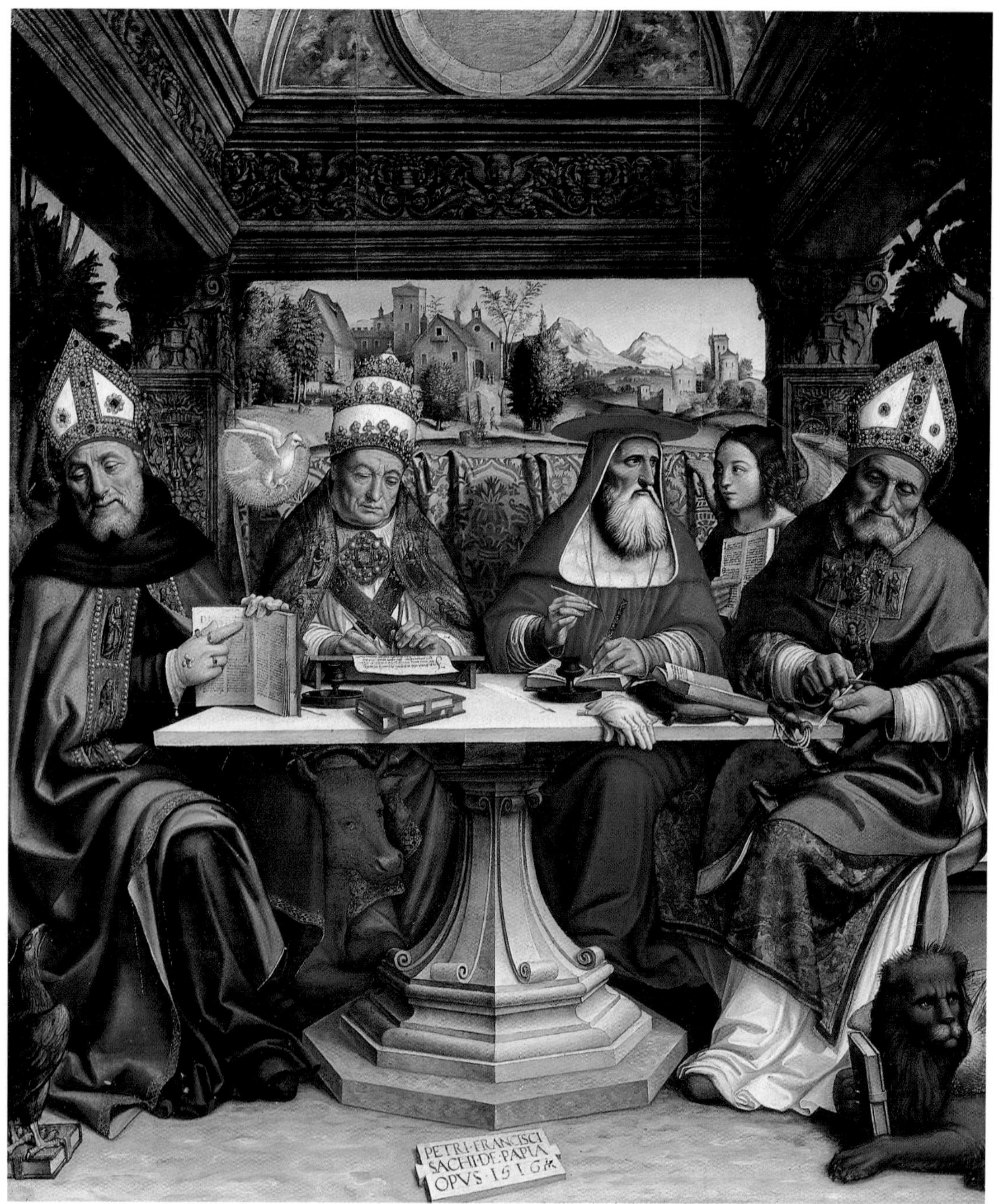

The Four Doctors of the church, Augustine, Gregory the Great, Jerome, and Ambrose by Pier Francesco Sacchi, 1516.

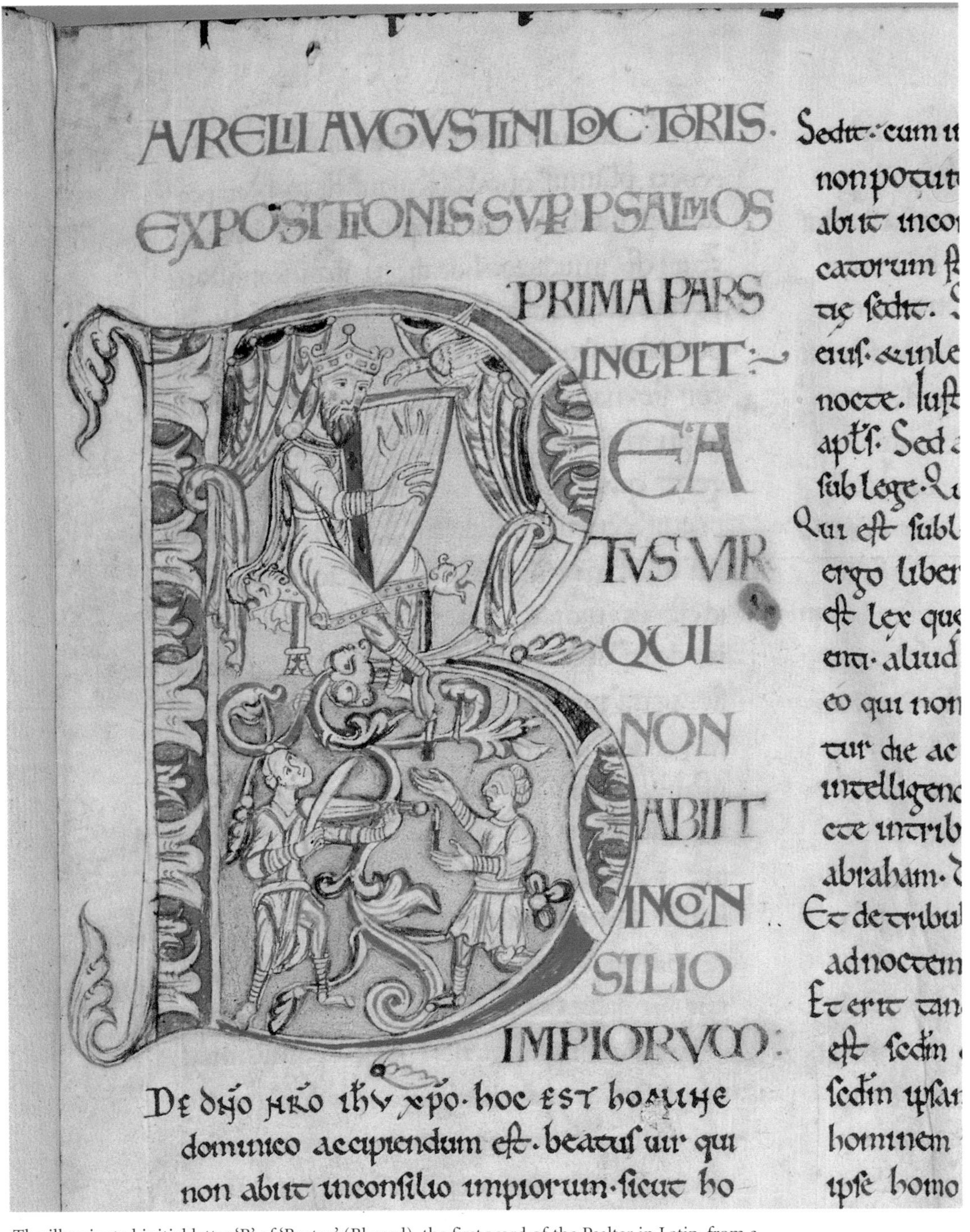

AVRELII AVGVSTINI DOCTORIS.
EXPOSITIONIS SVP PSALMOS
PRIMA PARS
INCIPIT:
BEATVS VIR QVI NON ABIIT IN CONSILIO IMPIORVM:
De dño nr̃o ihũ xp̃o. hoc est hominе
dominico accipiendum est. beatus uir qui
non abiit in consilio impiorum. sicut ho

The illuminated initial letter 'B' of 'Beatus' (Blessed), the first word of the Psalter in Latin, from a late-11th-century manuscript of the commentary by Augustine, portrays David playing the harp and being inspired by the dove-like Holy Spirit.

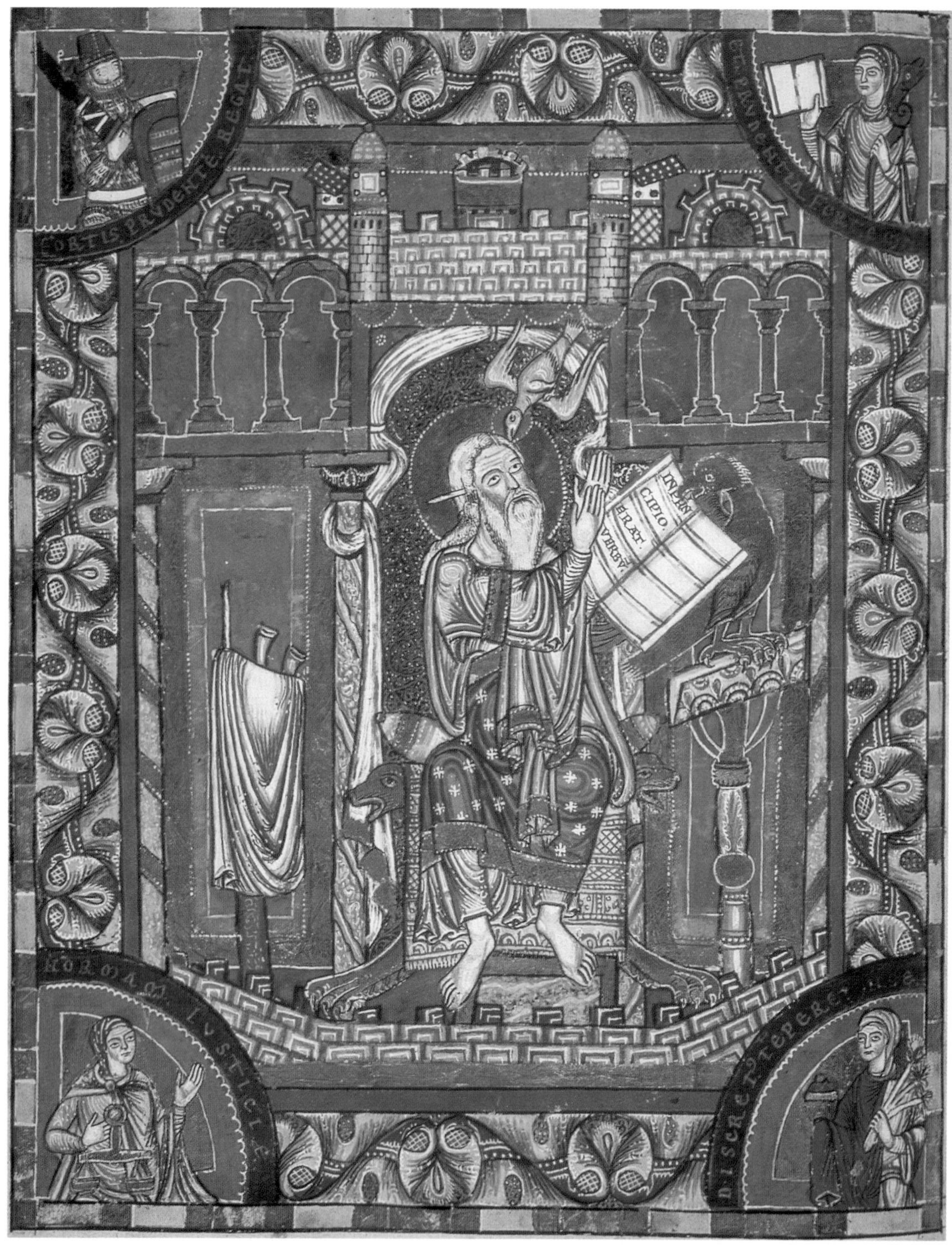

St John the Evangelist, from an illuminated page of the 10th–11th-century Gospels of Henry the Lion. The dove-like Holy Spirit is speaking into the evangelist's ear.

The Sermon of John the Baptist (1604). John the Baptist preaching is placed by Pieter Bruegel the Younger in the Flemish countryside, reflecting the local field-preaching which encouraged a movement of revolutionary reform in 1566.

Christ appearing to St Mary Magdalene at the Tomb, by Rembrandt, 1638.

The Shadow of Death by Holman Hunt, 1870–3.

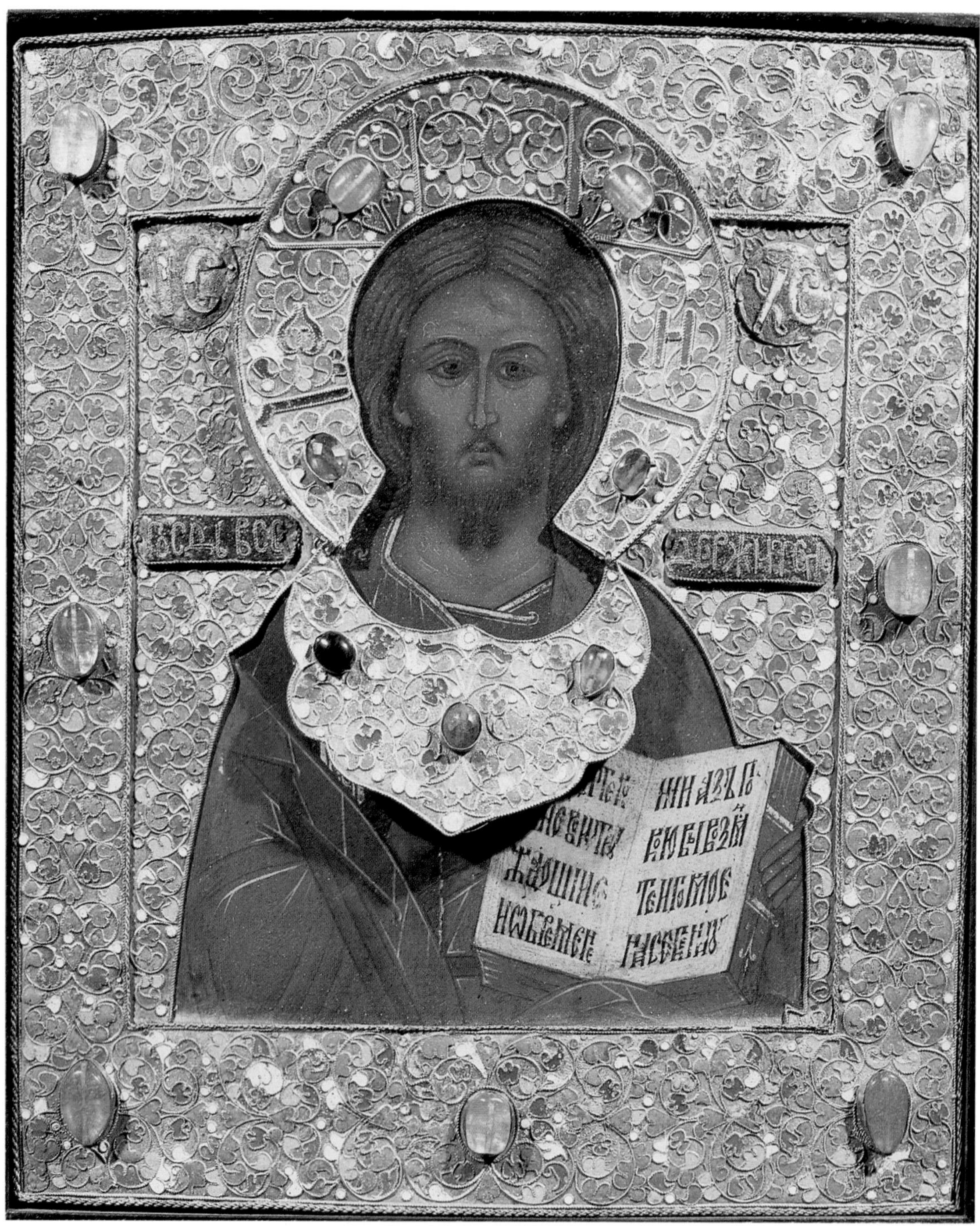

Icon of Christ Pantocrator, from the Russian School, 19th century.

The generation Chap.j. of Chriſt.

THE GOSPEL ACCORDING to S. Matthew.

CHAP. I.

1 The genealogie of Chriſt from Abraham to Ioſeph. 18 Hee was conceiued by the holy Ghoſt, and borne of the Virgin Mary when ſhe was eſpouſed to Ioſeph. 19 The Angel ſatiſfieth the miſdeeming thoughts of Ioſeph, and interpreteth the names of Chriſt.

HE booke of
Luke 3. 23. the *genera-
tion of Jeſus
Chriſt, the
ſonne of Da-
uid, the ſonne
of Abraham.
*Gen.21.3. 2 *Abra-
*Gene.25. 26. ham begate
*Gen.29. 35. Iſaac, and
*Gen.38. 27. *Iſaac begate Jacob, and * Jacob be-
*1.Chro.2. 5. ruth.4. 18. gate Judas and his brethren.
3 And * Judas begate Phares and
Zara of Thamar, and *Phares begate
Eſrom, and Eſrom begate Aram.
4 And Aram begate Aminadab,
and Aminadab begate Naaſſon, and
Naaſſon begate Salmon.
5 And Salmon begat Boos of Rachab, and Boos begate Obed of Ruth,
and Obed begate Jeſſe.
*1.Sam.16. 1. and 17. 12. 6 And * Jeſſe begate Dauid the
King, & * Dauid the King begat Solo-
*2.Sam.12. 24. mon of her that had bin the wife of Urias.
*1.Chro. 3. 10. 7 And * Solomon begat Roboam,
and Roboam begate Abia, and Abia
begate Aſa.
8 And Aſa begate Joſaphat, and
Joſaphat begate Joram, and Joram
begate Ozias.
9 And Ozias begat Joatham, and
*2.King. 20.21. 1. chro.3.13. Joatham begate Achas, and Achas be-
gate Ezekias.
10 And * Ezekias begate Manaſſes,
and Manaſſes begate Amon, and A-
mon begate Joſias.
11 And || Joſias begate Jechonias || Some read, Ioſias begate Iakim, and Iakim begat Iechonias.
and his brethren, about the time they
were caried away to Babylon.
12 And after they were brought to
Babylon, *Jechonias begat Salathiel, * 1.Chro.3. 16,17.
and Salathiel begate Zorobabel.
13 And Zorobabel begat Abiud, and
Abiud begat Eliakim, and Eliakim begate Azor.
14 And Azor begat Sadoc, & Sadoc
begat Achim, and Achim begat Eliud.
15 And Eliud begate Eleazar, and E-
leazar begate Matthan, and Matthan
begate Jacob.
16 And Jacob begate Joſeph the
husband of Mary, of whom was borne
Jeſus, who is called Chriſt.
17 So all the generations from A-
braham to Dauid, are fourteene generations: and from Dauid vntill the ca-
rying away into Babylon, are foure-
teene generations: and from the cary-
ing away into Babylon vnto Chriſt, are
fourteene generations.
18 ¶ Now the *birth of Jeſus Chriſt *Luke 1. 27.
was on this wiſe: When as his mother
Mary was eſpouſed to Joſeph (before
they came together) ſhee was found
with childe of the holy Ghoſt.
19 Then Joſeph her husband being
a iuſt man, and not willing to make her
a publique example, was minded to put
her away priuily.
20 But while hee thought on theſe
things, behold, the Angel of the Lord
appeared vnto him in a dreame, ſaying,
Joſeph thou ſonne of Dauid, feare not
to take vnto thee Mary thy wife: for
that which is conceiued in her, is of the
holy Ghoſt.

A 2 21 And

The Barker, London edition of the Authorized or King James Version of 1611. As against the Geneva Bible, it employed Gothic type-face and was much more sparing in its comments.

Bible) justifies their decision not to adopt the same English word for every occurrence of a Hebrew or Greek term—partly on the quaintly modern grounds that to do so would by omission discriminate against 'a great number of good English words'. Later the Revised Version (1881–95) would reverse this policy, and perhaps the AV went too far in favour of variation, for example in Romans 5: 2, 3, 11, where the same Greek verb is rendered 'rejoice … glory … joy'. It was from the AV that generations of English speakers learned to celebrate the Nativity as simply a season of 'good will towards men' (Luke 2: 14), and became preoccupied with their 'soul'. Coverdale's psalms remained in the Book of Common Prayer, but the other lections were now taken from the AV of 1611.

The AV omitted marginal notes (but not cross-references) except where required on a particular point of translation. The Genevan notes have been over-criticized for their doctrinal tendentiousness, as has its actual translation. The AV deliberately opted for more ecclesiastical terms like 'church' instead of Geneva's 'congregation' and 'baptism' instead of 'washing'. On the other hand it deliberately rejected 'the obscurity of the Papists' in using original Hebrew or Greek merely transliterated like 'azymes, prepuce, pasche', as Douai–Rheims preferred.

AIDS TO RIGHT UNDERSTANDING

Marginal notes also served to explain historical, geographical, or other details not part of general knowledge. As such they belonged to the variety of aids for the student of the Bible that multiplied alongside, and often inside, the early printed editions. A concordance of the Vulgate—that is, an alphabetical list of all its Latin words with location-references (still imprecise, before verse-numbering)—was printed in 1479. A Jewish scholar's concordance of the Hebrew Bible published by Daniel Bomberg at Venice in 1523 became the basis for later versions, and was itself used by Martin Bucer of Strasbourg for his Psalms commentary of 1529. At Frankfurt in 1607 Conrad Kircher brought out a three-volume concordance of the Greek of the Septuagint together with Hebrew equivalents. The earliest concordance of the Greek New Testament was the work of Sixtus Betuleius (Birck), issued at Basel in 1546, while another by Henri Estienne at Geneva in 1594 marked another of this printing family's services to sixteenth-century Bible learning. Luther's New Testament and whole Bible were soon followed by German concordances, in 1524 and 1546 respectively. Thomas Gybson in 1535 published a concordance to Coverdale's English New Testament. John Merbecke (Marbeck), better known for his musical contributions to worship, got his concordance to the whole English Bible printed in 1550—but only winning a pardon after being sentenced to death in 1543 for daring to produce it. Later printings of the Geneva Bible included a concordance by Robert Herry.

The first printed grammars of the Hebrew language built on the foundation laid by Rabbi David Kimchi (d. 1235) and a commentary on it by another Jewish grammarian, Elias Levita (1468–1549). Christian pioneers of Hebrew language study included Johannes Reuchlin (especially *De Rudimentis Hebraicis*, 1506),

Conrad Pellikan (a brief introduction, 1503/4), Wolfgang Capito of Strasbourg (1525), and Santi Pagnini (Hebrew grammar printed by Robert Estienne of Paris in 1546). The most important was Sebastian Münster of Basel (d. 1552). Taught by Levita and Pellikan, he produced several Hebrew grammars and the first of Aramaic (1527), and was without rival in transmitting the best of Jewish expertise, represented above all by Levita, to Christian scholastic circles. The study of Hebrew in Basel was later revitalized by Johann Buxtorf (d. 1629), who was succeeded in the chair of Hebrew by his son, grandson, and great-grandson, all named alike.

The study of the Greek of the New Testament took time to shake itself free of the dominance of classical Greek, of which there was no lack of grammars in print. Forty appeared in as many years, including an elementary one by Melanchthon in 1518. Erasmus himself was followed by others such as Beza in reflecting on the differences between the two, but grammars of New Testament Greek alone were not produced until the mid-seventeenth century (Caspar Wyss, 1650; Georg Pasor, 1655), but still classical parallels proved impossible to ignore. Earlier discussions attributed the distinctiveness of New Testament Greek to Hebraisms or to the purity inspired by the Holy Spirit. Its recognition as the koine (common) Greek of the Hellenistic world was slow in emerging.

Hebrew lexicons looked back to the early work of Kimchi (published before 1480). Significant productions by Christians included those by Reuchlin (1506, in his *De Rudimentis*), Münster (1523), Pagnini (1529), and Buxtorf the Elder (1607). The sixth volume of the Complutensian Polyglot was a vocabulary of Hebrew and Aramaic (printed 1515), and the fourth contained a Greek–Latin glossary of the New Testament, Ecclesiasticus, and Wisdom. When printed in 1514 this was the earliest of its kind, but publication was held up until 1522. Georg Pasor's *Lexicon Graeco-Latinum* (1619) was an altogether more scholarly effort. The Estiennes produced outstanding Latin and Greek dictionaries, Robert's *Thesaurus Linguae Latinae* (from 1532) and Henri's *Thesaurus Linguae Graecae* (1572). Both were immense advances on anything then available, especially the Greek *Thesaurus*, which continued to be republished into the nineteenth century. But these were general humanist productions with no special interest in the biblical languages.

Modern students of the Bible have at their disposal a rich variety of introductions, handbooks, dictionaries, and encyclopedias. The sixteenth century witnessed the publication of a number of individual works which from one angle or another in varying measure essayed the task of inducting readers into sound knowledge of the Bible. Several of Erasmus's writings furnished introductions to New Testament books, Santi Pagnini issued an introduction (*Isagogae*) 'to the mystical senses of Holy Scripture' (1536), and the English Puritan divine, William Whitaker (d. 1595), regius professor at Cambridge, compiled a *Disputatio* on scripture against Roman Catholic positions on such issues as the distinction between canonical and non-canonical books, vernacular translations and scripture's authority, perspicuity and interpretation (1600). Several writings

(*Both pages*) The beginning of the book of Psalms in the Antwerp Polyglot, 1569–72

א

1 אשרי האיש אשר לא הלך בעצת
רשעים ובדרך חטאים לא עמד
ובמושב לצים לא ישב :
2 כי אם בתורת יהוה חפצו
ובתורתו יהגה יומם ולילה :
3 והיה כעץ שתול על פלגי מים אשר פריו יתן
בעתו ועלהו לא יבול וכל אשר יעשה יצליח :
4 לא כן הרשעים כי אם כמץ אשר תדפנו רוח :
5 על כן לא יקמו רשעים במשפט וחטאים
בעדת צדיקים :
6 כי יודע יהוה דרך צדיקים ודרך רשעים תאבד :

ב

1 למה רגשו גוים ולאמים יהגו ריק :
2 יתיצבו מלכי ארץ ורוזנים נוסדו יחד על
יהוה ועל משיחו :
3 ננתקה את מוסרותימו ונשליכה ממנו
עבתימו :
4 יושב בשמים ישחק אדני ילעג למו :
5 אז ידבר אלימו באפו ובחרונו יבהלמו :
6 ואני נסכתי מלכי על ציון הר קדשי :
7 אספרה אל חק יהוה אמר אלי בני אתה אני
היום ילדתיך :
8 שאל ממני ואתנה גוים נחלתך ואחזתך
אפסי ארץ :
9 תרעם בשבט ברזל ככלי יוצר תנפצם :
10 ועתה מלכים השכילו הוסרו שפטי ארץ :
11 עבדו את יהוה ביראה וגילו ברעדה :
12 נשקו בר פן יאנף ותאבדו דרך כי יבער כמעט
אפו אשרי כל חוסי בו :

LIBER PSALMORUM.

PSALMUS I.

1 EATUS *vir qui non abijt
in consilio impioru, & in via
peccatorum non stetit, & in
cathedra derisorum non sedit.*
2 *Sed in lege Domini voluntas eius, & in lege eius medi-*
3 *tabitur die ac nocte. Et erit tanquam lignum
transplantatum iuxta riuos aquarum, quod fru-
ctū suum dabit in tempore suo, & folium eius
nō defluet, & omne quod fecerit prosperabitur.*
4 *Non sic impij, sed tanquam puluis quem*
5 *proiicit ventus. Propterea non resurgent
impij in iudicio, neque peccatores in congrega-*
6 *tione iustorum. Quoniam noscit Dominus
viam iustorum, & iter impiorum peribit.*

PSAL. II.

1 Q*Vare congregauerunt gentes, et tribus me-
ditabuntur inania?*
2 *Consurgent reges terræ, & principes tra-
ctabunt pariter aduersus Dominum & aduer-*
3 *sus Christum eius. Dirumpamus vincula eorum, & proijciamus à nobis laqueos eorum.*
4 *Habitans in cælis irridebit, Dominus subsannabit eos.*
5 *Tunc loquetur ad eos in ira sua, & in furore suo conturbabit eos.*
6 *Ego autem ordinaui regem meum, super
Sion montem sanctum meum.*
7 *Annunciabo Dei præceptum: Dominus
dixit ad me: Filius meus es tu, ego hodie genui*
8 *te. Postula à me, & dabo gentes hæreditatem tuam, & possessionem tuam terminos
terræ.*
9 *Franges eos in virga ferrea, ut vas figuli
conteres eos.*
10 *Et nunc reges intelligite, erudimini iudi-
ces terræ.*
11 *Seruite Domino in timore, & exultate in
tremore.*
12 *Adorate purè, ne fortè irascatur, & pereatis de via, cùm exarserit post paululum furor
eius: beati omnes qui sperant in eum.*

תרגום

א

טובוהי דגברא דלא הליך במלכת רשיעין ובארח חייבין לא קם ובסיעת ממיקני לא אסתחר : 2 אלהן בנימוסא
דייי רעותה ובאורייתה מרנן יימם ולילי : 3 ויהא כאילן דנציב על סיפי מוי דאנבה מבשל בעדניה ואטרפוי לא נתרין
וכל דלבלבוי דסלקלב מגרגר ומצלח : 4 לא היכנא רשיעי אלהן כמוצא דתשקפנה זעפא :
5 מטול כן לא יקומון רשיעי ביום דינא רבא וחטאי בסיעתהון דצדיקי : 6 מטול דגלי קדם ייי ארחתהון דצדיקי וארחתהון
דרשיעי תהובד :

ב

1 למה מתרגשין עממיא ואמיא מרננין סריקותא : 2 קיימין מלכי ארעא ושלטוניא יתחברין כחדא למרדא קדם ייי ולסנאי עם
משיחה : 3 אסרין נתרע ית אסרתיהון ונטליק מנן ית שושלותהון : 4 דיתב בשמיא ידחך מימרא דייי ידחך להון :
5 בכן ימלל להון בתקפה וברגזה יבהלנון : 6 ואנא רביתי מלכי ומניתה על ציון טור קדשי : 7 אשתעי דאלהא קימא ייי אמר
[illegible] חביב כבר לאבא את לי זכאה כאילו יומא דין בריתך : 8 בעי מני ואתן נכסי עממיא אחסנתך ואחודתך סיפי ארעא : 9 תתברנון
[illegible] בחוטרא דפרזלא היך מאן דפחר תתרעינון : 10 וכען מלכיא אשכלו קבלו מרדותא נגידי ארעא : 11 פלחו קדם ייי ברחלתא
[illegible] ברתיתא : 12 קבלו אולפנא דילמא ירגז ותהובדון ארחא מטול דייתור כזעיר תקפה טב לכל דסברין במימרה :

PSALTERIVM.

Psalmus Dauid, sine titulo apud Hebræos.

PSALMVS I.

BEATVS vir qui non abiit 1
in cõsilio impiorum, & in
via peccatorum non ste-
tit, & in cathedra pestilen
tiæ non sedit.
*Sed in lege Domini vo- 2
luntas eius, & in lege eius meditabitur die
ac nocte. *Et erit tanquam lignum quod 3
plantatum est secus decursus aquarum,
quod fructum suum dabit in tẽpore suo:
& folium eius non defluet; & omnia quę-
cunque faciet, prosperabuntur. *Non sic 4
impij, non sic; sed tanquam puluis quem
proiicit ventus à facie terræ. *Ideò non 5
resurgent impij in iudicio, neque peccatores in consilio iustorum. *Quoniam nouit 6
Dominus viam iustorum, & iter impiorum peribit. Psalmus Dauid. II. 1
QVare fremuerunt gẽtes, & populi me-
ditati sunt inania? *Astiterunt reges 2
terræ, & principes conuenerunt in vnum,
aduersus Dominum & aduersus Christum
eius. *Dirumpam' vincula eorum, & pro- 3
iiciam' à nobis iugũ ipsorum. *Qui habi- 4
tat in cælis, irridebit eos, & Dominus subsannabit eos. *Tunc loquetur ad eos in ira 5
sua, & in furore suo conturbabit eos. *Ego 6
autem constitutus sum rex ab eo sup Sion
montem sanctum eius, *Prædicans præce- 7
ptum Domini. Dominus dixit ad me: Filius me' es tu, ego hodie genui te. *Postu- 8
la à me, & dabo tibi gentes hæreditatem
tuam, & possesionem tuam terminos ter-
rę. *Reges eos in virga ferrea, *tãquã vasa fi 9
guli cõfringes eos. *Et nunc reges intelli- 10
gite, erudimini omnes qui iudicatis ter-
ram. *Seruite Domino in timore, & ex- 11
ultate ei in tremore. *Apprehendite disci- 12
plinam, nequando irascatur Dominus, &
pereatis de via iusta. Cùm exarserit in bre-
ui ira eius, beati omnes qui cõfidũt in eo.

ΨΑΛΤΗΡΙΟΝ.

Ψαλμὸς τῷ δαυίδ, ἀνεπίγραφος παρ' ἑβραίοις.

α'.

1 Μακάριος ἀνὴρ ὃς οὐκ ἐπορεύθη ἐν βουλῇ ἀσεβῶν, καὶ ἐν ὁδῷ ἁμαρτωλῶν οὐκ
ἔστη, καὶ ἐπὶ καθέδρᾳ λοιμῶν οὐκ ἐκάθι-
2 σεν. *ἀλλ' ἢ ἐν τῷ νόμῳ κυρίου τὸ θέ-
λημα αὐτοῦ, καὶ ἐν τῷ νόμῳ αὐτοῦ μελε-
3 τήσει ἡμέρας καὶ νυκτός. *καὶ ἔσται ὡς τὸ ξύλον τὸ πε-
φυτευμένον παρὰ τὰς διεξόδους τῶν ὑδάτων, ὃ τὸν καρπὸν
αὐτοῦ δώσει ἐν καιρῷ αὐτοῦ, καὶ τὸ φύλλον αὐτοῦ οὐκ ἀποῤ-
ῥυήσεται, καὶ πάντα ὅσα ἂν ποιῇ, κατευοδωθήσεται.
4 *οὐχ οὕτως οἱ ἀσεβεῖς, οὐχ οὕτως, ἀλλ' ἢ ὡσεὶ χνοῦς
ὃν ἐκρίπτει ὁ ἄνεμος ἀπὸ προσώπου τῆς γῆς.
5 *διὰ τοῦτο οὐκ ἀναστήσονται ἀσεβεῖς ἐν κρίσει, οὐδὲ ἁ-
μαρτωλοὶ ἐν βουλῇ δικαίων.
6 *ὅτι γινώσκει κύριος ὁδὸν δικαίων, καὶ ὁδὸς ἀσεβῶν
ἀπολεῖται.
1 Ψαλμὸς τῷ δαυίδ. β'.
Ἱνατί ἐφρύαξαν ἔθνη καὶ λαοί, ἐμελέτησαν κενά;
2 *παρέστησαν οἱ βασιλεῖς τῆς γῆς, καὶ οἱ ἄρχοντες συ-
νήχθησαν ἐπὶ τὸ αὐτό, κατὰ τοῦ κυρίου καὶ κατὰ τοῦ χριστοῦ
3 αὐτοῦ· *διαρρήξωμεν τοὺς δεσμοὺς αὐτῶν, καὶ ἀποῤ-
ῥίψωμεν ἀφ' ἡμῶν τὸν ζυγὸν αὐτῶν.
4 *ὁ κατοικῶν ἐν οὐρανοῖς ἐκγελάσεται αὐτούς, καὶ ὁ κύριος ἐκμυκτηριεῖ αὐτούς.
5 *τότε λαλήσει πρὸς αὐτοὺς ἐν ὀργῇ αὐτοῦ, καὶ ἐν τῷ
6 θυμῷ αὐτοῦ ταράξει αὐτούς. *ἐγὼ δὲ κατεστάθην βα-
7 σιλεὺς ὑπ' αὐτοῦ ἐπὶ σιὼν ὄρος τὸ ἅγιον αὐτοῦ, *διαγγέλ-
λων τὸ πρόσταγμα κυρίου. κύριος εἶπε πρός με, υἱός μου εἶ
8 σύ, ἐγὼ σήμερον γεγέννηκά σε. *αἴτησαι παρ' ἐμοῦ, καὶ
δώσω σοι ἔθνη τὴν κληρονομίαν σου, καὶ τὴν κατάσχεσίν
9 σου τὰ πέρατα τῆς γῆς. *ποιμανεῖς αὐτοὺς ἐν ῥάβδῳ
10 σιδηρᾷ, ὡς σκεῦος κεραμέως συντρίψεις αὐτούς. *καὶ νῦν
βασιλεῖς συνέτε, παιδεύθητε πάντες οἱ κρίνοντες τὴν γῆν.
11 *δουλεύσατε τῷ κυρίῳ ἐν φόβῳ, καὶ ἀγαλλιᾶσθε αὐτῷ
12 ἐν τρόμῳ. *δράξασθε παιδείας, μή ποτε ὀργισθῇ κύριος,
καὶ ἀπολεῖσθε ἐξ ὁδοῦ δικαίας. ὅταν ἐκκαυθῇ ἐν τάχει ὁ
θυμὸς αὐτοῦ, μακάριοι πάντες οἱ πεποιθότες ἐπ' αὐτῷ.

CHALDAICAE PARAPHRASIS TRANSLATIO,

IN LIBRVM PSALMORVM. B. ARIA MONTANO INTERPRETE.

BEatitudo viro qui non iuit in consilium impiorum, & in via peccatorum non stetit, & cum societate derisorum non sedit.
2 Sed in institutione Domini voluntas eius, & in Lege eius meditatur die ac nocte.
3 Et erit tanquam arbor quæ plantata est super riuos aquarum, cuius fructus maturescit in tempore suo, & folia eius non
defluunt, & omne germen eius quod germinat, granescit & proficit. 4 Non sic impij, sed sicut stipula quam
proiicit ventus. 5 Propterea non consistent impij in die iudicij magni, neque peccatores in societate iustorum.
6 Quoniam manifesta est ante Dominum via iustorum, & via impiorum perdetur.

PSAL. II.

QVare fremunt populi, & nationes meditantur vanitatem? 2 Consurgunt reges terræ, & potentes conuenerunt in vnum, vt
deficiant à Domino, & certent cum Messia eius. 3 Dicunt, Dissoluamus vincula eorum, & proiiciamus à nobis funes eorum.
4 Qui sedet in cælis, ridebit: Verbum Domini subsannabit eos. 5 Tunc loquetur ad eos in fortitudine sua, & in ira sua interturba-
bit eos. 6 Et ego vnxi regem meum, & constitui ipsum super Sion montem sanctum meum. 7 Recitabo Dei pactum: Dominus
dixit mihi: Dilecte sicut filius est patri, tu mihi purus es, ac si die ista creauissem te. 8 Postula à me, & dabo diuitias populorum hæreditatem tuam, & possessionem tuam fines terræ. 9 Confringes ipsos velut in virga ferrea, tanquam vas fictile conteres eos.
10 Et nunc reges intelligite, recipite eruditionem duces terræ. 11 Seruite coram Domino in timore, & orate in tremore. 12 Recipite
doctrinam, ne fortè irascatur, & amittatis viam. Cùm exarserit paululum furor eius: bonum omnibus qui sperant in verbo eius.

Bb 2

catalogued the books of the Bible, sometimes as the first section of a larger listing of Christian writers. But in this period no genre established itself comparable to later works of reference or introduction.

Deserving of special mention is the *Bibliotheca Sancta* (Holy Library) of Sixtus of Siena (d. 1569), a convert from Judaism, whose colourful career as a Catholic friar and teacher was crowned by the production (1566) of this remarkably comprehensive encyclopaedia of biblical scholarship. It merited numerous subsequent editions, including a revision by the Scots Jesuit John Hay, and was still being published in the mid-eighteenth century. Lutherans, Calvinists, Anglicans, and Catholics all spoke well of it. In 1678 in his *Histoire critique* (Critical History) of the Old Testament, Richard Simon, one of the forerunners of later biblical criticism, declared that there were few works with as much sense and learning on the Bible as that of Sixtus. Its eight books cover the distinction between canonical, 'deuterocanonical' (a term he introduced), and apocryphal books, and provide a basic introduction to each book. The third book, often printed separately, deals with biblical interpretation, and is followed by a dictionary of writers on scripture, two books on numerous contested passages in each testament in turn, citing extensive patristic material, and finally books on heresies and heretics motivated by rejection or criticism of parts of the Bible. Particular interest has attached to his extraordinarily schematic and detailed analysis of the different ways of tackling the interpretation of scripture. His sources included the rhetorical and scholastic traditions, but his work reflects also the fresh learning and resources of Renaissance biblical study. Sixtus thus has been credited with creating the science of biblical introduction. Nothing comparable was forthcoming from Protestant authorship for some time. When it came, from Johann Heinrich Alstedt (d. 1638), a German Calvinist from Herborn, his *Triumphus* of the Sacred Writings, subtitled 'Biblical Encyclopaedia' (1625), was a more advanced compilation, harvesting much humanist learning on the biblical books in their historical setting.

The modern study Bible had its closest sixteenth-century counterpart in the French Genevan Bible of 1559 (with many features carried over into the English Genevan version the next year). Each book is prefaced by an introduction ('Argument') running across both columns, and each chapter by a summary of the content. Heavy textual or doctrinal annotations fill the margins, even attaching to the title of, say, Matthew's Gospel. The Bible itself is preceded by Robert Estienne's summary of Christian doctrine and John Calvin's 'That Christ is the end of the law' (which first appeared as the foreword to the New Testament in Olivétan's French Bible of 1535). Diagrams and folding maps are incorporated, an index or two at the end, and many copies had bound in a collection of metrical psalms, a form of common prayer, and Calvin's Genevan Catechism of 1542.

Thus scripture was not 'alone', even in a context such as Calvin's Geneva where it was accorded the highest authority. Both authority and interpretation were contested issues, which could not be left to unaided apprehension direct from the scriptural text.

Portrait of Martin Luther by an unknown artist.

EXPOUNDING THE BIBLE

Sixtus's *Bibliotheca* covered both methods for discovering the sense of scripture and forms of presentation of its meaning once found. Among them was *enarratio*, the public exposition of scripture, the designation Martin Bucer gave to his Latin translation for the benefit of brethren in France of Luther's German homilies (postils) on the lections from the gospels and epistles (1525–6). As professor of the Bible in Wittenberg Luther had lectured in Latin on the Psalms, Romans, and Galatians before he challenged fellow scholars to debate over 95 propositions in 1517. In virtually every local situation where the Reformation put down roots, vernacular preaching went hand in hand with learned instruction more akin to lecturing. The whole Reformation movement was almost an orgy of preaching, from the masterly gospel expositions Luther delivered on returning to Wittenberg in May 1522 to retrieve the cause of moderate reform after Carlstadt's disruptive radicalism in his absence, to the remarkable sermon 'on the plough' (and ploughers) preached by Hugh Latimer, bishop of Worcester, at St Paul's Cross, London, early in January 1548, and John Knox's first public preachment, on Daniel 7 and the coming of Antichrist, at St Andrews in 1547.

The simple plaque in St Peter's Cathedral in Geneva that honours Calvin describes him only as 'servant of the Word of God'. One of his earliest biographies records what are in effect four forms that that service took in Geneva. Calvin was first a lecturer before he was made a pastor, and from his lectures came many of his published commentaries in Latin. Preaching in French consumed enormous energies, with an average ten sermons a fortnight, each an hour long, at the height of his Genevan ministry. Then every Friday at the pastors' open Bible study, called in French the Congrégation, whether at the outset or in rounding off Calvin frequently gave a short exposition. Finally, in the meetings of the consistory, the organ of pastoral discipline in Reformed communities like Geneva, Calvin regularly addressed a biblically grounded remonstrance to the person found wanting in some aspect of behaviour.

Calvin was to be sure exceptional, but not in the prominence and focused effort devoted to letting the biblical message have free course among the people. As Luther once memorably put it:

> All I have done is to put forth, preach and write the Word of God, and apart from this I have done nothing. While I have been sleeping, or drinking Wittenberg beer ... it is the Word that has done great things ... I have done nothing; the Word has done and achieved everything.

INTERPRETATIONS OF THE BIBLE

Luther and Calvin, then, were two of the sixteenth century's most enthusiastic and outstanding teachers and preachers of the Bible. Yet the existence in most parts of the world in the 21st century of separate Lutheran and Reformed/ Presbyterian churches recalls the fact of Protestant disagreements on the right interpretation of scripture in the era of the Reformation. The beginning of discord is normally located at Marburg in 1529 when Luther and Zwingli could not reach a common mind on the meaning of 'This is my body' in the Lord's supper. Luther insisted on an objective, literal sense, while Zwingli preferred a symbolic one, 'This bread represents my body.' The dispute had wide ramifications. It provided ready-made ammunition for Catholic critics who made polemical play of the disunity that inevitably followed the abandonment of the *magisterium*, the teaching authority, of Rome. It also gave the lie to the evangelical conviction of the clarity or perspicuity of scripture, which Zwingli had set forth in *The Clarity and Certainty of the Word of God*. More worryingly, this particular falling out raised—or confirmed—suspicions of erroneous beliefs about Christology, the church's doctrine of the person of Christ, at once both human and divine. Surely his glorified humanity was in heaven, at God's right hand, rather than present on myriad communion tables? Did this then mean that his human and divine natures were now divided from each other, if he was present in the eucharist only in his divinity?

In reality, serious and far-reaching though this 'supper-strife' proved to be, a deeper fissure had already opened up over the relationship between Old and New Testaments. It is not too unfair to characterize the Anabaptists as New Testament Christians. The analogy of infant circumcision was irrelevant to Christian baptism, which in the New Testament was given only to professing believers. The precedent of Israel's waging of wars and infliction of capital punishment taught nothing to the followers of Jesus, called to renounce the sword. Before the Marburg colloquy in 1529, Swiss Anabaptists had been executed in Zwingli's Zürich for acting on these beliefs. It is arguable that the question how the Old Testament relates to the New is among the biggest issues facing world Christianity today, given that by far the fastest growing sector, of Pentecostals and their kin, stands in an Anabaptist lineage.

To a subtler degree, this issue also left mainstream Reformers in disarray. Luther much more readily found Christ and the Trinity and the gospel in the Old Testament than Calvin did. The latter was accused of being a 'Judaizer' for his inadequately Christianized reading of the Hebrew scriptures. He could preach on Job 19: 25 with no apparent awareness of a possible Christological reference in 'redeemer'. Yet paradoxically Calvin and other founding fathers of the Reformed tradition of Protestantism gave a more prominent place to the Old Testament and especially its God-given law than Lutheran or Anglican Protestants did. Whereas for Luther the chief function of law—which was not the whole truth about the Old Testament or to be found only there in the Bible—was to convict of sin and lead to the grace of the gospel, Calvin and others viewed the Mosaic law more prominently as itself God's gracious guidance for the life of the Christian and the community.

In part this difference had roots in the contrasting personal histories of Luther, the religiously conscience-racked monk, and Calvin, the legally trained humanist whose 'conversion' to evangelical faith was, it seems, an altogether smoother taming to teachableness. More significantly it reflected the greater rigour with which Calvin applied perhaps the Reformation's greatest contribution to biblical study—the recovery of the straightforward, literal (not literalistic—poetry was still poetry) sense as determined by appropriate linguistic, grammatical, and historical enquiry. As Calvin wrote in his first commentary, on Paul's Romans (1540), 'Almost the only duty [of the commentator] is to lay open the mind of the writer whom he has undertaken to explain.' If he kept this objective in view, his writing would be marked by lucid succinctness (*perspicua brevitas*). Calvin's *Romans* is a great deal slimmer than most recent commentaries on the epistle. His measure of success can be gauged from the fact that his volumes on most books of the Bible are today consulted by students and expositors far more than those of any of his contemporaries.

It has recently become commoner for scholars writing on sixteenth-century biblical exegesis to emphasize its continuities, and not only its discontinuities, with medieval patterns. Yet it remains broadly true that allegory and multi-level interpretation fell very largely out of favour in short order. Allegory is by no means absent from Erasmus or Luther, nor wholly lacking in Calvin, yet the massiveness of the transition to a preoccupation with the single literal sense, which was the spiritual sense, that is, intended by the Spirit's inspiration for the spiritual instruction of the faithful, is incontrovertible. And so John Chrysostom was, as an exegete, the Reformers' favourite among the early Fathers, even though as a theologian Augustine was unrivalled.

Historically driven scrutiny of the scriptures inevitably raised critical questions, about authorship, for example. Sixtus of Siena recognized the multi-author origins of the psalms, and Calvin was not greatly bothered by uncertainty about the authorship of one or two minor epistles. Towards the end of our period, the French biblical scholar Richard Simon (d. 1712), in his 'Critical History of the Old Testament' (1678), by internal analysis concluded that Moses was not the author of the Pentateuch, although much of Simon's work was more conservative, countering the more radical critical opinion of Spinoza (d. 1677). But the extent to which Reformation impulses in biblical study anticipated later biblical criticism has often been overestimated. What is undeniable is that, in devoting to the translation, elucidation, and proclamation of the teaching of the Bible the boundless energy and impressive expertise at their command, the Reformers and their followers were motivated by the conviction that they were entrusted with the very oracles of God.

11 1700 to the Present

RONALD CLEMENTS

The beginning of the eighteenth century witnessed a significant turning-point in the interpretation of the Bible, initially largely determined by the controversies and conflicts which had dominated the previous century. From the perspective of the English church, set against the background of the wider European scene, the concern to secure the position of a truly national church was of paramount importance. This entailed a clear and firm rebuttal of Catholic claims and the strong assertion of truly Protestant principles of biblical interpretation. Europe was itself now divided between Catholic and Protestant, with correspondingly distinct traditions on the subject. In Great Britain the differences between Lutheran and Calvinist approaches were further challenged by the concerns of the philosophical Deists to render the biblical revelation conformable to straightforward rational principles of universal religious truth. Yet it was just such a reasoned and reasonable defence of religious truth which held out promise of bypassing the extremes which had generated past conflicts.

What was needed was a balanced acknowledgement of the authority of the Bible, a reasoned methodology in its interpretation, and a politically stabilizing endorsement of the claims of the English crown against Catholic pretensions. Consequently, to show how the biblical revelation was in accord with the dictates of reason was clearly a primary task for biblical interpretation.

Within such a concern a number of major themes dominated discussion, each of which gradually blossomed into an independent subject of theological research by the middle of the nineteenth century. Each developed appropriate goals and methods of enquiry which, to an increasing extent, began to stand apart from the others. Foremost was a concern with the relationship between the Bible and the ever-enlarging body of scientific knowledge. The need to harmonize the biblical world-view with the new scientific understanding which was giving rise to an entirely new cosmology set the primary task. Alongside this historical, rather than cosmological, issues began progressively to become the centre of biblical research. Theology itself became historically oriented to such an extent that historical reconstructions shaped the form of theological enquiry. Central among such questions were those relating to the life and person of Jesus of Nazareth. In line with this the preparation in the Old Testament for the advent of the Messiah became increasingly focused on its historical, rather than its theological, character. Instead of messianic prophecies the idea of a historical preparation—a 'salvation history'—became the central theme.

THE BIBLE AND THE NATURAL WORLD

During the seventeenth century the understanding of the universe, of the nature of matter, and consequently of the manner in which the creative power of God had originated and continued to sustain the world had all been subjected to major reappraisal. The work of Isaac Newton had transformed the understanding of the physical universe in a fundamental way. This necessarily called for a serious rethinking of the way in which the teaching of the Bible could be harmonized with this new knowledge, if its position as the primary foundation document for intelligent religious discussion were to be maintained. Newtonian physics was establishing a coherent picture of an ordered universe in which reasoned observation could trace the interconnections and interactions of its varied parts. Heaven and earth formed one world in which a harmonious order prevailed. The 'hand of God' which maintained a providential control over all things visible and invisible was seen to be a 'hand' that conformed to recognizable laws. Human beings could observe, quantify, and define what these laws were.

As an expression of this belief in 'the laws of nature', the experimental methods of Robert Boyle (1627–91) had demonstrated ways in which the operation and effects of such laws could be examined. Such experiments in physics and chemistry were bringing about a transformation of human understanding of the natural world. Arguments for the existence of God, and evidence of the divine control over human life and destiny, could themselves now be constructed on the basis of recognition of this orderliness. Order, with its openness to scientific demonstration in natural laws, pointed to the controlling hand of a Divine Designer. It was arguable that the very foundations of science took their origin in the religious belief in this supreme Divine Architect.

In this context the traditional religious reports of miracles became puzzling witnesses to aberrations from the given order which demanded explanation. They represented a break in the coherence of all things which God had established at creation. So the concept of nature, and of a world order governed by natural laws, began to form the primary testimony to the divine origin and purpose of all things. Natural revelation appeared a surer guide to the reality of God than the special revelation contained in the Bible. What was needed was an interpretation of the latter which showed it to be in harmony with the former.

A series of lectures founded by Robert Boyle and delivered between 1692 and 1732 addressed these issues: *A Defence of Natural and Revealed Religion.* Their overall aim was symptomatic of the desire for a new path of biblical interpretation. William Whiston's eight sermons of 1707, *The Accomplishment of Scripture Prophecies*, and Thomas Burnett's sixteen sermons of 1724–5 reflected the new

scientific cosmology that was emerging. Burnett's title was *The Demonstration of True Religion in a Chain of Consequences from Certain and Undeniable Principles.*

(*Facing*) Moses and Aaron before Pharaoh, portrayed by Gustave Doré from *Bible Illustrations*, 1866. The rod cast down before Pharoah becomes a serpent. Miracle stories such as this were problematic in the new age of historical realism.

There was clearly need to show how the reported miracles of the Bible could be shown to be compatible with the laws of nature, or at least be regarded as necessary departures from them. Had there been an age when the natural order had not conformed to its present orderly patterns, or were the biblical accounts of miracles merely literary perceptions and enlargements of natural events, the reporting of which required to be understood differently in the modern era? The stories of miracles, instead of forming incontrovertible evidence of the special providential interventions of God, became problematic. Their presence in the Bible relegated them to the margins of historical truth, at the same time making the real history of the Bible a more prominent focus of research.

In no small measure the understanding of biblical prophecy also demanded a comparable change. If the physical universe is an objective reality which is subject to certain observable laws, is not the course of events which occur within it subject to comparable laws? So the causes and consequences of historical events required to be researched and interpreted in a more scientific way. The matter was of importance to the popular understanding of the Bible, since the foretellings and fulfilments of prophecy provided the primary point of connection between the Old and New Testaments. The issues here also soon became adapted to a study of the historical events which provided a background to the biblical literature.

It is not surprising therefore to find that Thomas Sherlock's lectures, *The Use and Intent of Prophecy in the Several Ages of the Church* (1724), introduced a significant measure of openness between prophecy and its later fulfilment. Prophecy was seen to have two meanings—a literal one confined to the prophet's own understanding of the original prophecy and a fuller, spiritual one belonging to its God-intentioned fulfilment. Thereby a deterministic view of history was avoided and space was provided for an enlargement of prophetic hope in line with the traditional interpretation of a divine plan of redemption, progressively disclosed through a chain of prophets. The issue was of considerable importance, since, besides seeking to resolve the questions raised concerning the application of Old Testament prophecies to Jesus, it also challenged the Puritan tendency to regard the course of church history as secretly foretold, in coded fashion, in the books of Daniel and Revelation.

Thomas Young (1773–1829), physicist and Egyptologist who played a key role in deciphering the demotic text of the Rosetta Stone.

More immediately pressing for biblical interpretation was the emerging awareness that the biblical evidence regarding the chronology of the prehistoric period of earth's existence posed difficulties. Isaac Newton had wrestled with the mathematical data, and Archbishop Ussher's contention that the original date of earth's creation was 4004 BCE, with Jesus himself having been born in 4 BCE, was increasingly cast into a realm of uncertainty. The issue was important, for it reflected directly on the status of the biblical evidence for the prehistory of the earth, and had wide-ranging implications for the compatibility of the data of biblical texts with scientific learning. Although the books of Genesis and Revelation were most directly affected, the very status of revealed knowledge, embodied in biblical data, was at issue, and with it the whole question of the Bible's authority as a source of truth. With it, too, went a far-reaching shift in the understanding of time, since belief in a predetermined pattern of millenia, before and after the birth of the Messiah, provided a popular portrayal of the expected age of the universe.

The publication in 1830 of Sir Charles Lyell's *The Principles of Geology* marked a watershed in the attempts to maintain a reasoned compatibility between biblical interpretation and the natural

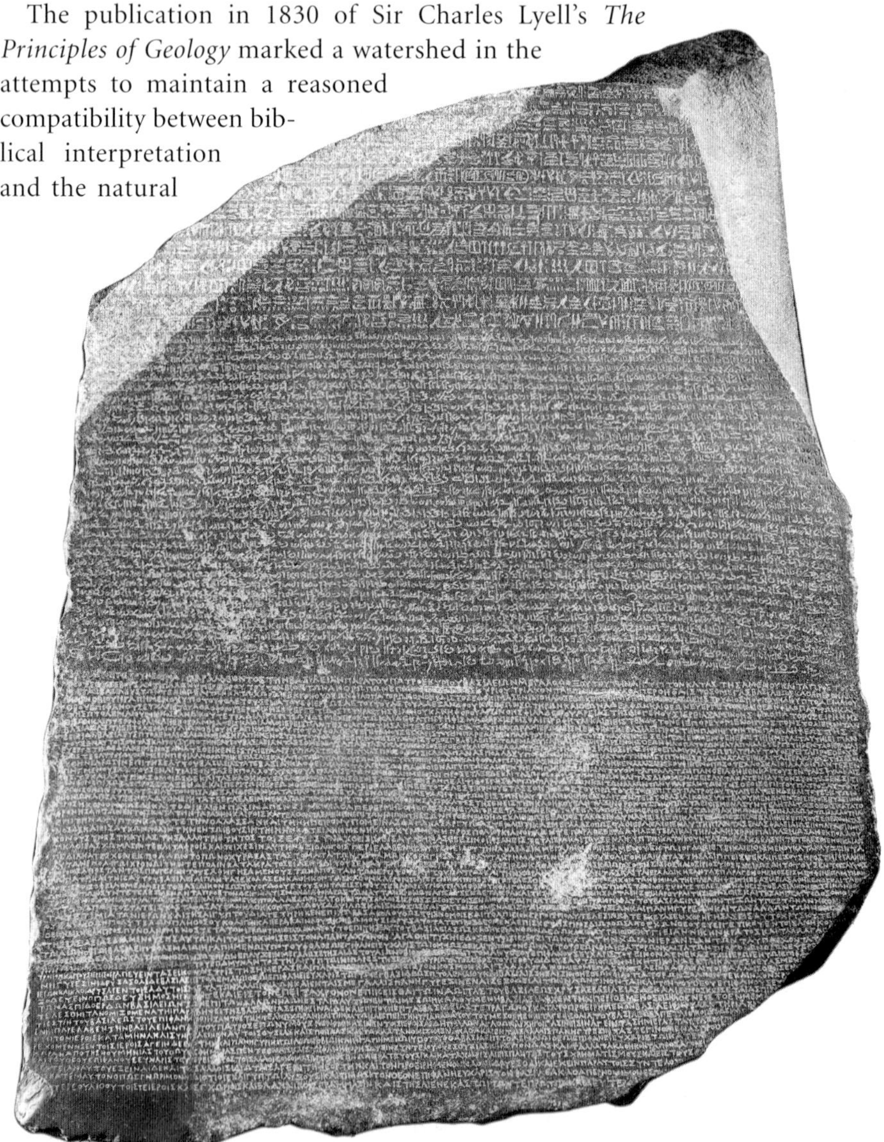

The Rosetta Stone, dated to 196 BCE and discovered at the end of the 18th century in Egypt, contained a royal decree written in Egyptian hieroglyphic and demotic scripts, and Greek. It made the decipherment of hieroglyphic possible.

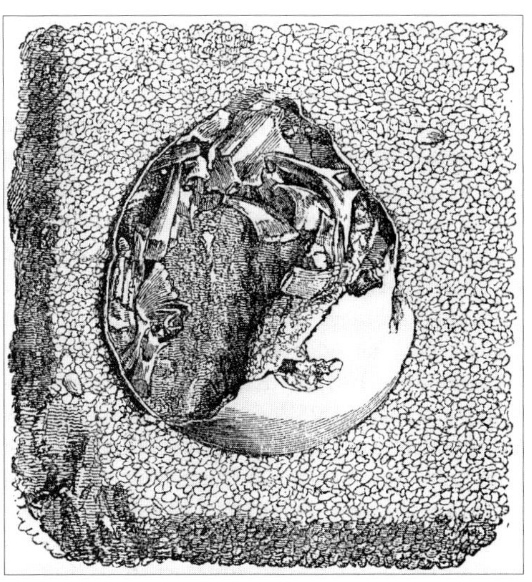

Plate from *The Principles of Geology* by Charles Lyell (1853), showing the fossilized egg of a turtle from Ascension Island. Lyell's researches cast doubt upon the apparent biblical view that the world was created in 4004 BCE.

sciences. In spite of his retention of belief in specific acts of divine creation for every species of animal life, Lyell's researches showed that the earth was, on geological evidence, of immensely greater antiquity than had previously been accepted. Even the most strained interpretative constructions placed upon the assertions of the book of Genesis, such as the claim that the biblical 'days' of creation could be understood as longer periods, could scarcely be adapted to the new perspective.

Accordingly, even before Charles Darwin's publication of *The Origin of Species* (1859), the presence of fossil remains in rock formations had shown that the age of the universe was greater than a simple biblical chronology could sustain. The order of the natural world which had appeared to William Paley (1743–1805) to speak so eloquently of their Great Designer, was now seen as an order that had undergone immense changes. The geology of the earth, including its puzzling evidence of the fossil remains of long-extinct species, revealed that the earth and its inhabitants do not form a static and uniform reality. Belief in the simultaneous creation of all species, and their providentially arranged interdependence, was increasingly seen as requiring substantial modification. Order and design, which held distinct forms of life in a measure of equilibrium, could now be seen as the result of a long process of interaction, accomplished through an extended period of time. Darwin's thesis regarding the evolutionary origin of species through a prolonged series of separations was the final bombshell that altered forever the traditional assumption that science and biblical testimony could sit comfortably side by side.

Yet much of the difficulty lay with the very confidence that had previously insisted that the perceptions of the natural world contained in the Bible, regarding its history and workings, were to be accorded the same status as were now given to the conclusions of scientific observation and experiment. Since it was already a commonplace recognition of theology that the biblical writers had conveyed their messages and ideas through senses like our own, based on modes of understanding current at the time, the sharpness of the conflict that arose over Charles Darwin's thesis might have been ameliorated.

Already by the middle of the eighteenth century the classical scholar C. G. Heyne (1729–1812) had introduced the term 'myth', drawn from its ancient Greek context, to describe the many Greek and Roman tales of visitations of gods among humankind and of fabulous beasts and journeyings. By the end of the century the German theologian J. S. Semler (1725–91) had applied the concept to some of the biblical material, and this was carried further by J. G. Eichhorn (1752–1827) in an effort to classify the categories and nature of the biblical writings. Eichhorn's major work on the subject consisted of three volumes entitled *Die Urgeschichte*, published in 1790–3.

The Battle Field of Science and the Churches. This cartoon of the 1870s ranges the miraculous improbabilities of the Bible, taken literally, against the advances of science. On the science side are two biblical scholars, M. M. Kalisch and Bishop J. W. Colenso.

During the following century the term gained wide currency as a description of certain biblical stories, and Eichhorn's work was popularized and developed in England by S. T. Coleridge (1772–1834). In the theological writings of G. L. Baur (1755–1806) and J. S. Vater (1771–1826) it was employed as a classification for the entire world-view reflected in the earliest biblical books. For them the Bible's own central story bore an essentially mythological character. By the end of the century the mythological aspect of features in Genesis, Daniel, and Revelation was widely accepted.

Yet, in spite of its usefulness in classifying certain types of biblical story, the term 'myth' remained clouded and problematic for biblical interpretation throughout the nineteenth century. Most of the reason for this lies in the central attention during this period to issues of formal history and historical factuality. In such a perspective myth became widely and popularly used to refer to the unhistorical, or marginally historical, elements of the biblical literature. Therefore it was reflected in stories and narratives which were less amenable to the historian and, as such, was regarded with suspicion.

Consequently it was left to the twentieth century to attempt a less harsh, and less negatively conceived, contrast between myth and history, but by this time much confusion had arisen and it proved difficult to restore to the term any significant degree of clarity or usefulness. Nevertheless, it was in a desire to return to the claim that the entire world-view of the Bible must be regarded as pre-scientific, and incompatible with a modern understanding cognizant of contemporary scientific cosmology, that the term was revitalized, most notably by Rudolf Bultmann (1884–1976). His programme of 'demythologizing' the New Testament narratives, publicized in the war-torn 1940s, represented a *tour de force* in attempting to discount the conflict between scientific knowledge and biblical perceptions of the natural world.

THE HISTORY OF JESUS THE MESSIAH

The end of the seventeenth century had witnessed the publication by the celebrated philosopher John Locke (1632–1704) of a study entitled *The Reasonableness of Christianity*. First published anonymously in 1695, it sought to place the Christian faith, and its affirmation concerning the person and status of Jesus, on the most basic level conformable to human reason. It regarded the oldest and most fundamental Christian confession to be that Jesus is the Messiah (= the Christ, from the Latin term for 'Anointed One'). In spite of Locke's own denials that he was advocating a unitarian (Socinian) doctrine which denied the divinity of Jesus, the tendency was strongly in this direction. Yet if this was indeed the earliest Christian confession then the early Christian church had, during the first three centuries of its history, transformed its simplicity and recognizable Jewish origin into a far more complex metaphysical one.

The immediate consequence of Locke's claim, aimed at setting a non-controversial foundation of faith for the national church, was to engender a series of debates over the nature of prophecy and the accuracy with which the Old Testament foretellings of the coming of the Messiah could be directly matched to their New Testament fulfilments. The 'argument from prophecy' was clearly the primary evidence which could be used to defend the New Testament claim that Jesus was the promised Messiah. Yet Jewish scholars had long questioned the impartiality of the textual citations from the Old Testament psalms and prophets which pointed to a fulfilment in the life and ministry of Jesus of Nazareth.

The mathematician William Whiston (1667–1752) and the philosopher-disciple of John Locke, Anthony Collins (1676–1729), had sought to deal with the issue. Where Whiston had questioned the trustworthiness of the Jewish preservation of the Hebrew text when disagreements over the interpretation of several Old Testament passages were evident, Collins had strongly favoured this Jewish tradition over the conventional Christian one. The refutation of Collins's claims was left to Richard Bentley (1662–1742), but their widely reported nature is reflected in G. F. Handel's composition of *The Messiah* (first performed in 1741) as a national confession of faith.

G. F. Handel (1685–1759) from an engraving around 1780 by Francesco Bartolozzi (1727–1815) based on the drawing by Giovanni Battista Cipriani (1727–1785). His most famous work *The Messiah* reflects contemporary debate about argument from prophecy.

Locke's contention that Jesus had not originally been designated Son of God, and that this marked a later Hellenized interpretation, pointed strongly to the more human aspects of the figure of the Redeemer. The issue was of considerable historical importance because it drew attention to the keenly felt gap between the simple humanity and compassion of the stories of Jesus in the gospels and the elevated status of the Second Person of the Holy Trinity worshipped in the Christian creeds. The entire seventeenth-century desire to promote a reasonable interpretatation of Christian faith had naturally looked to recover the oldest, and therefore assumed purest, form of Christian confession, as a primary goal.

Moreover, the Protestant tradition of the church had never lacked for radical thinkers and reformers, many of whom regarded the Reformation of the church as an unfulfilled goal. The monolithic development of Christian doctrine during the earliest Christian centuries, and the biblical interpretations on which it rested, were viewed with suspicion as precursors of the errors of the medieval church. The desire to return to the simplicities of the earliest Christian expressions of faith remained attractive. Accordingly, rescuing Jesus from the overweight of doctrine with which the church Fathers of the second and third centuries had burdened him appeared as reasonable a quest in eighteenth-century Europe as it had been two centuries earlier. To many the Christian church still presented itself as a powerful, enigmatic, and frequently oppressive authority.

Key figures in the first stages of this eighteenth-century search to recover the true history of Jesus were the German dramatist G. E. Lessing (1729–81) and H. S. Reimarus (1694–1768), a professor of oriental languages in a Hamburg *Gymnasium.* At his death Reimarus had left an unpublished work, entitled *Apology for Rational Worshippers of God.* This drew heavily upon the arguments of Matthew Tindal and other English Deists of the preceding century. As librarian to the Duke of Brunswick in Wolfenbüttel, Lessing published a number of fragments of Reimarus's work which raised serious questions as to how much of the gospel record offered a true and reliable account of Jesus. Could knowledge of the original Jesus be recovered at all? Lessing's piecemeal, and somewhat disingenuous, publication of these challenges under a thin veil of anonymity was in line with his own sympathies and questions about Christian claims. What was important about Reimarus's work had been the claim that it was not only the early church which had added to the portrait given in the four gospels of the New Testament, but these gospels were themselves heavily overladen with speculative and mythological features. The real historical Jesus had to be uncovered beneath the biblical tales of the oriental wonder-worker.

So by the beginning of the nineteenth century a number of different impulses combined to intensify the quest to establish a reliable and convincing portrait of the real historical Jesus. This became the *cause célèbre* of biblical interpretation during the following century. Historical scholarship had been given a major new task, and was rapidly sharpening new tools with which to perform it.

During the Enlightenment in France such men as Voltaire (François-Marie Arouet, 1694–1778) and Denis Diderot (1713–84) had recognized that biblical history needed to be understood by the same canons of criticism as other history. Edward Gibbon (1737–94) had followed the French lead in subjecting the decline of the Roman empire and the rise of the Christian church to a fresh, essentially critical and non-theological, scrutiny. Similarly the Scottish Jesuit Alexander Geddes (1737–1802) had sought to apply to the Bible the critical evaluation of sources that were to become hallmarks of this fresh approach to history-writing. In England the distinguished scientist and dissenting churchman Joseph Priestley (1733–1804) took up afresh the task which had remained the

Edward Gibbon (1737–94) whose history of the fall of the Roman empire became a model for writing critical, non-theological accounts of biblical history.

The frontispiece to the *Encyclopédie* of D. Diderot (1713–84).

ENCYCLOPÉDIE,

OU

DICTIONNAIRE RAISONNÉ

DES SCIENCES,

DES ARTS ET DES MÉTIERS,

PAR UNE SOCIÉTÉ DE GENS DE LETTRES.

Mis en ordre & publié par M. *DIDEROT*, de l'Académie Royale des Sciences & des Belles-Lettres de Pruſſe; & quant à la PARTIE MATHEMATIQUE, par M. *D'ALEMBERT*, de l'Académie Royale des Sciences de Paris, de celle de Pruſſe, & de la Société Royale de Londres.

Tantùm ſeries juncturaque pollet,
Tantùm de medio ſumptis accedit honoris! HORAT.

TOME PREMIER.

A GENEVE,

CHEZ CRAMER L'AINÉ & Compagnie.

M. DCC. LXXII.

goal of two centuries of English dissenting scholarship. His *History of Early Opinions concerning Jesus Christ* (1786) had proved something of a rallying-cry for the revival of unitarian views of the person of Jesus, and a strong insistence on his human, compassionate, and socially revolutionary mission.

D. F. Strauss (1808–74), the German theologian whose radical *Life of Jesus* (1835) produced major shock waves in the theological and ecclesiastical world. It was translated into English by George Eliot (Mary Ann Evans).

The portrait of the 'historical' Jesus that was drawn was still largely an impressionistic reconstruction based on the stories of the gospels and focused on the ancient titles accorded to their central figure. Yet, already by the year 1800, questions were being raised in Britain and Germany concerning the time of origin of the four surviving gospels and the possible sources upon which they had drawn. A major turning-point in the quest to recover a critical historical portrait of the figure of Jesus came through the publication by the German scholar D. F. Strauss (1808–74), of a work entitled *Das Leben Jesu, kritisch bearbeitet*, 2 vols., 1835 (ET *The Life of Jesus Critically Examined*). Its early publication in English translation by the novelist George Eliot (Mary Ann Evans) in 1846 made awareness of the issues a prominent focus of international attention. Strauss had studied in Tübingen and was an eager follower of the philosopher G. W. F. Hegel, his primary concern being to reinterpret the central features of Christian doctrine in terms of the interactions of the divine and human Spirit which lay at the heart of Hegel's thinking. *The Life of Jesus* was a preparation for this larger doctrinal undertaking and Strauss's main contention was to insist on the mythological nature of the gospel testimony to Jesus. What are presented as a series of marvellous events in the Redeemer's life, fulfilling ancient prophecies, can be seen to have been shaped by the need to reveal the meeting of the divine and human Spirit in the person of Jesus. The very formulation of the gospel stories showed the artificiality of their construction. To what extent they were historically true remained clouded in doubt and uncertainty.

D. F. Strauss had raised a major issue in a fresh way, but had done little to establish any clear agenda of research into primary historical questions which could be further investigated. Too many questions were left unanswered concerning the origin of the gospels, the order of their composition, and the possible sources on which they had drawn. Had there been an earlier Aramaic gospel which they had used, as the English scholar Herbert Marsh (1757–1839) had speculated? Was St Matthew really the earliest of them? In spite of the wide publicity given to his critical views about the historical Jesus, Strauss was too committed to philosophical speculation and doctrinal reformulation to pursue such issues.

A

DICTIONARY OF THE BIBLE

COMPRISING ITS

ANTIQUITIES, BIOGRAPHY, GEOGRAPHY, AND NATURAL HISTORY.

EDITED

BY WILLIAM SMITH, D.C.L., LL.D.,

IN THREE VOLUMES.—VOL. I.

AARON—JUTTAH.

LONDON:

JOHN MURRAY, ALBEMARLE STREET.

1863.

The title page of William Smith's *Dictionary of the Bible* (1863), an important landmark in British biblical scholarship.

More central to biblical scholarship, and more lasting in its consequences, was the work of Strauss's contemporary, the Tübingen scholar F. C. Baur (1792–1860), who sought to reconstruct a more comprehensive picture of the historical development of early Christian doctrine. Central to this was a revised estimate of the creative role of the apostle Paul, whom Baur saw as the primary architect of Christianity as a religion of Gentiles. This entailed reconstructing a picture of a major clash between early Jewish and Gentile elements within the nascent church. He viewed the actual course of the birth of Christianity as very different from that portrayed in the book of Acts. This was essentially a work of apologetic for the Gentile church which prevailed over the Jewish sectarian group from which it had sprung.

For Baur the apostle Paul had been altogether a more controversial figure than hitherto supposed, and the major New Testament writings had been composed in circumstances of conflict and bitter argument. Only by studying the ideas and forces which shaped this formative development of the church could the groundwork be established for understanding the language and titles which had been heaped by the earliest gospel writers upon the person of the Redeemer.

These developments in Germany caused alarm and anxiety in Britain but for long gained little strong following there. However, in parallel with the German scholarship of the period there emerged a critical and strongly influential development in France. This was primarily focused on the University of Strasbourg with its strong Protestant affiliations. This combined the insights and critical methods of French historians which had begun half a century earlier and did much to focus the issues for the twentieth century. Central figures were Timothée Colani (1824–88), Eduard Reuss (1804–91), and, after 1875, H. J. Holtzmann (1832–1910). Reuss was undoubtedly one of the formative figures in introducing new methods and perspectives of biblical interpretation to both Old and New Testaments. Only the late publication of his researches into the origins of the Old Testament led to the relative neglect of recognition for their originality.

The most celebrated and widely read author of a reconstruction of the historical life of Jesus was Ernest Renan (1823–92). Briefly associated with a professorship of Hebrew in Paris, Renan attempted an imaginative work entitled *La vie de Jésus*, published in 1863, which proved immensely popular. It was soon translated into English and a host of other languages. Although it followed a popular critical line of argument that, behind the four written gospels there lay two main sources—an early Aramaic one which underlay the teaching of Jesus in

St Matthew's Gospel and a Greek reminiscence of the deeds of Jesus recorded by St Mark, its main appeal lay in its broad philosophical attempt to modernize the biblical narrative into a more straightforward, and less theological, human story.

It was the line of research of the earliest gospel tradition by H. J. Holtzmann which marked a fresh step forward. This gave new impetus to a carefully planned enquiry into the interrelationships of the first three gospels, the order of their composition, and the possible sources which underlie them. It was the most celebrated of Holtzmann's pupils, Albert Schweitzer (1875–1965), who subsequently became the best-known reviewer and judge of the course of the nineteenth-century 'Jesus of History' quest. This was in his study *Von Reimarus zu Wrede*, published in 1906 (ET *The Quest of the Historical Jesus*, 1910).

Central to Schweitzer's conclusions, and developing claims that had been initiated earlier by Colani, was the contention that the real historical Jesus had been a fiery apocalyptic preacher, proclaiming the imminent breaking-in of the kingdom of God, who would overthrow tyrannical human powers. Only when this hope had failed to find fulfilment had Jesus tried forcibly to initiate a challenge to Judaea's ruling powers, which had ended in his death and left his followers with the necessity for rethinking and reformulating an understanding of who he really was.

Scripture reading in a night refuge, by Gustave Doré, from *London*, 1872. In the 19th century an emphasis on Jesus' socially revolutionary mission made the Bible a powerful force for social reform.

The shrine containing what is traditionally regarded as the tomb of Christ, in the church of the Holy Sepulchre, Jerusalem. A litho by David Roberts, 1849.

By the time of the First World War the thesis of Schweitzer stood as both a milestone of past researches and a starting-point for fresh enquiry. Increasingly this focused on the quest to find the sources which the authors of the surviving gospels must have used. Three paths were followed up. The first of them, exemplified in the writings of Rudolf Bultmann and Martin Dibelius, enquired after the oral traditions of preaching, echoes of which are still recognizable in the form of the gospel narratives. The second path followed up suggestions set out a century earlier, arguing that many of the sayings of Jesus, especially in the presumed 'teaching source' that lies behind the gospels of St Matthew and St Luke, showed evidence of their translation from an Aramaic, or Hebrew, original. The third path was directed towards a revised study of the overlaps and interrelationships of the narrative contents of the first three gospels, thereby carrying into new areas problems noted, and assumed to have been resolved, in the late nineteenth century. The conviction that an early written document containing much of the teaching of Jesus, which two of the gospel-writers drew upon, has remained a widely held conclusion of such research. Overall, however, the gap between a reconstruction of the actual course of the life and death of Jesus of Nazareth and the presentation of the Messianic Redeemer portrayed in the gospels has proved a difficult one for biblical interpretation to cross.

The annals of the Assyrian king Sennacherib (705–681 BCE), the so-called Taylor Prism, which gives an Assyrian version of Sennacherib's campaign against Judah and king Hezekiah in 701 BCE.

THE HISTORY OF ANCIENT ISRAEL

Closely matching the nineteenth-century quest for the historical Jesus there emerged a similarly focused concern to reconstruct the actual course of the rise and historical development of ancient Israel. Once again it was the impact of the French Enlightenment, with its prominent concern with historical research as a means of understanding the nature of human existence and civilization, which served to initiate fresh questions. Paris at the end of the eighteenth century had provided a haven for several British scholars in which they had found encouragement to examine afresh the nature of the Bible.

At first the interest was primarily into their literary forms and poetic nature. This was a field of enquiry which had been begun by the French priest Richard Simon (1638–1712), and which had been carried further by the Englishman Robert Lowth (1710–87), by J. G. Herder (1744–1803) and J. G. Eichhorn in Germany. Few scholars had more energetically pursued the task of classifying the various types of literature to be found in the Bible, and commenting on their religious worth, than W. M. L. de Wette (1780–1849). Yet the goal of such enquiries had not been historical, even though a new impetus towards historical questions had already begun to transform studies of the classical civilizations of ancient Greece and Rome.

Hammurabi receiving the law from the sun god. The top of the stele containing the laws of Hammurabi, king of Babylon (1792–1750 BCE).

It was primarily this concern which now turned attention to the historical books of the Old Testament. How much real history did they report? By the early 1820s scholars were beginning to subject the lengthy histories of Herodotus, Thucidydes, and Tacitus to fresh critical examination. Should not the narratives attributed by tradition to Moses be subjected to a similar critical scrutiny? In Britain it was Henry Hart Milman (1791–1868), an eager disciple of Edward Gibbon, who initiated the task, at first almost by accident. His *The History of the Jews*, published in 1829 as the first of a three-volume popular history of the

Jewish people, dealt with the biblical story as far as the late Old Testament period. It had been sponsored on account of the revived interest in Jews and Judaism that had arisen in the wake of the Napoleonic Wars and the extent to which the Napoleonic constitution had made possible the ending of a ghetto-bound existence for many of them.

Milman's little book was no monument of scholarship, but it highlighted the possibility of recasting the historical narratives of the Old Testament into the form of a real history, explaining away the miraculous element and regarding the biblical assertions of a divine plan as the cover for belief in a providential destiny. What was now called for was a more wide-ranging critical re-examination of the nature and time of origin of the historical narratives of the Old Testament. The scholar who took up this challenge was the German H. G. A. Ewald (1803–75), who laid out the mammoth task of reconstructing Israel's story in a five-volume work (1843–55), carrying it through from its beginnings until the birth of the early Christian church (two volumes on the Apostolic Age were added in 1858–9). In spite of Ewald's grand design and energetic fulfilment, the work sufficed largely to highlight yet again the problems relating to a critical evaluation of the sources. It was of significance that Ewald, whose political views made him a controversial figure in Germany, received a wide following in Great Britain, appearing as the scholar most likely to succeed in combining faith and piety with scholarly integrity. Yet his achievements were only partially successful and too many questions were left unanswered for the *History* to be more than an interim work of scholarship.

GEORGE SMITH 1840-1876
and the Babylonian Flood story:
a centenary exhibition

George Smith (1840–76), the Assyriologist who first identified the Babylonian story of the Flood among tablets in the British Museum.

It was Ewald's pupil and follower Julius Wellhausen (1844–1918) who was destined to pursue more rigorously the task addressed by Ewald. He recognized the primacy of the need to reasses the historical worth, and time of origin, of the historical books of the Old Testament. Thus his major publication devoted to the subject in 1878 was entitled in its second edition of 1883 *Prolegomena to the History of Israel.* In spite of Wellhausen's ambition to write the story of the rise of a great nation, in the manner that B. G. Niebuhr and T. Mommsen had attempted for ancient Rome, the central feature of this work was a critical evaluation of the course of Israel's religious development. It was this which held the key to an understanding of the various documents which had been woven into the construction of the two largest Old Testament compositions—the Pentateuch and the Former Prophets. Although now existing as two single wholes, these are, in reality, built up from a number of separate source documents. To identify and define these was a necessary prerequisite to recovering the basic course of ancient Israel's history.

An early display of Egyptian antiquities by G. Belzoni in the British Museum, *c.*1847. The Museum played a major role in promoting a changed attitude to biblical history.

Wellhausen had endeavoured to carry through a historian's task, although it was his literary achievement of identification and reconstruction of the four primary documents from which the Pentateuch had been composed that became most directly associated with his name. This documentary reconstruction has passed into history as the Graf–Wellhausen hypothesis, bringing into the story reference to Karl-Heinrich Graf (1815–69), a German schoolmaster who had studied in Strasbourg under Eduard Reuss. Graf had anticipated Wellhausen in reconstructing a picture in which the course of Israel's cultic institutions and rules had passed from simple forms into elaborate realities. It was the key by which the major literary components of the Pentateuch could be identified and dated. Graf had himself clearly learned the necessity of this critical historical perspective from his Strasbourg teacher Eduard Reuss, with whom he maintained an important correspondence.

The initial response to Wellhausen's proposals in church circles was strongly negative, and took time to be assimilated. Strong refutations were published, among the most widely read and influential of them being *The Problem of the Old*

Testament (1906) by the Scottish scholar James Orr (1844–1913). In Germany, Great Britain, and America, however, by the beginning of the twentieth century, Wellhausen's literary reconstructions of the sources of the Pentateuch had come to be regarded by most critical scholars as the best solution to an admittedly difficult problem.

By 1900 these literary problems no longer appeared in need of major review and to complement them there was now emerging a new area of research of great promise. This lay in the archaeology of the Holy Land itself and of the neighbouring lands which had been the cradles for the civilizations of ancient Egypt and Mesopotamia. Although its beginnings are to be found in a survey of the historical geography of the region, which had begun in 1838–9 with the explorations of the American Edward Robinson, it soon grew into extended excavation of the most prominent sites. These led to the establishing of major institutes and organizations for the systematic prosecution of archaeological research in the region.

Initially the meagre results in the Holy Land itself were largely compensated for by the immense achievements of similar archaeological research in the neighbouring territories. Egypt, Assyria, and Babylon all had immense importance for the Bible, not least in rendering possible a means of establishing a credible chronology of events. In many respects it was the rediscovery of the achievements of the civilizations of ancient Egypt, Babylon, and Assyria which was to have the most profound effect upon the interpretation of the Bible. The closeness of the links between the biblical world and that of the ancient Near East could now be examined more closely and at first hand. Much of the defensive apologetic of the biblical writings, which had led to grotesque and negative estimates

Cherubim figures from the temple of 'Ain Dara' 67 km (42 miles) north-west of Aleppo, Syria.

The frontispiece of Handel's oratorio *Jephtha* (1751). Handel's setting of the story gave it a happier ending than appears in the biblical account.

of the quality of life in antiquity, could now be set in a clearer light. Even the skills and techniques of writing and the production of literary works, such as those preserved in the Bible, could be given a cultural context which they had not previously possessed.

THE DEVOTIONAL INTERPRETATION AND USE OF THE BIBLE

Scientific study of the Bible has frequently appeared to have as its primary duty the task of formulating biblical teaching, whether of ideas or events, in such a manner that their importance and meaning is made plain, and their congruity with other branches of knowledge is not imperilled. Yet this has frequently carried it into areas of deep controversy and has brought into the forefront technicalities and problems in which the private Bible-reader, or even the preaching minister of the church, has little interest. Great Britain in the seventeenth century had suffered nation-wide conflicts in which the interpretation of the Bible had played a significant role. Puritans against Royalists, Catholics against Protestants, and Rationalists against Literalists had all served to make the Bible a subject bringing dissension. Across Europe since the Reformation many comparable conflicts had been evident. It is not surprising therefore that many serious Christian readers of the Bible felt that the very purposes for which it existed were being betrayed.

It is in reaction to this that we should give attention to the emerging influence and attraction of what can best be described as a renewed focus on the devotional use and meaning of the Bible. Clearly such an interest had always existed in the church, and the great devotional writings of the Middle Ages had included handbooks of Psalms, readings for Books of Hours, and imaginative, if sometimes fanciful, homilies on biblical stories. It appeared that the central importance of the Bible to the Reformation had served to lend fresh intensity to controversies regarding its meaning and especially its political import. What was the nature of the Christian society which the Bible heralded? Clearly what had actually been achieved in forming a European Christian civilization had frequently been far from spiritually uplifting. Yet small printing houses and the eagerness of devout readers to enrich their spiritual understanding had between them continued to generate a large number of popular tracts, homilies, and devotional aids which remained aloof from the centres of academic and ecclesiastical control.

The renewal of concern with the personal and spiritual meaning of the Bible found a powerful advocate in German Pietism in the eighteenth century with the commentaries of J. A. Bengel (1687–1752). The legacy of Bengel's approach, with the intensity of its heart-searching inwardness, was to receive lasting influence through its embodiment in the works of Johann Sebastian Bach, supremely in the *St Matthew Passion* and *St John Passion.*

In England it was the dissenting commentator Matthew Henry (1662–1714) who produced in 1708–12 commentaries on the Old Testament, the gospels, and Acts which provided a largely uncontroversial, and personally meaningful,

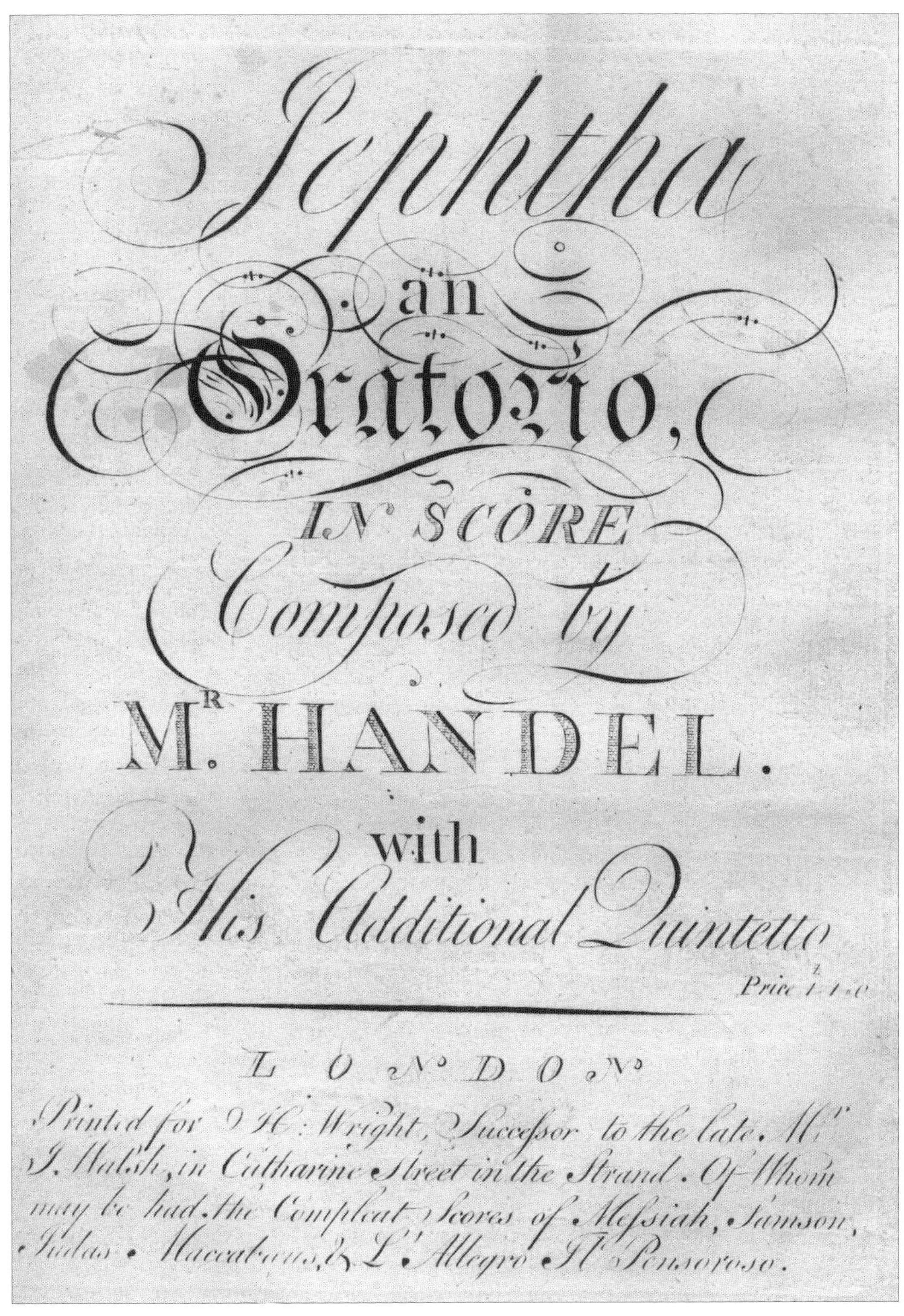
Jephtha
an
Oratorio,
IN SCORE
Composed by
M.R HANDEL.
with
His Additional Quintetto
Price 1.1.0
LONDON
Printed for I. H. Wright, Successor to the late Mr. J. Walsh, in Catharine Street in the Strand. Of Whom may be had the Compleat Scores of Messiah, Samson, Judas Maccabaeus, & L'Allegro Il Pensoroso.

approach to the Bible. Writing from a Puritan standpoint, but setting aside the issues which had been the subject of political controversy during the preceding century, Henry sought to provide the general reader with ideas and images, culled from the Bible, which were morally edifying and capable of providing spiritual direction and meaning to the individual life. John Wesley's *Notes on the New Testament* (1754, 1765) drew heavily upon the approach and ideas adopted by Henry. The work set a precedent followed by others such as Thomas Scott (1747–1821), who adapted the rather heavyweight style of Puritan commentating to a more popular level. The approach adopted showed that the Bible need not be read solely as a political tract, nor as an affront to science or reason, but could retain a strongly personal and religious meaning.

If J. S. Bach's music gave a new range and depth to the German Pietistic approach to the Bible, an even more wide-ranging popularizing and spiritualizing of its message was achieved in the oratorios of G. F. Handel (1685–1759). Besides the composition of *The Messiah*, Handel's treatment of a wide selection of historical narratives concerning Joshua, Solomon, and other biblical heroes and heroines drew popular interest to these narratives. Even such unlikely subjects as the tragedy of Jephthah's daughter could be infused with sensitivity to the tragedies and disappointments which becloud human existence.

The conventicles and private meetings for prayer and Bible study which had given strength and confidence to the religious and political tensions of the seventeenth century in England provided a context for the nurture of private biblical interpretation and exposition. In no small measure such meetings took place outside the jurisdiction of episcopal church oversight, and often with little guidance from university-trained scholars. A comparable style of Bible study and personal reflection received fresh encouragement through the Class-meetings of early Methodism. After the Napoleonic conflicts at the beginning of the nineteenth century a new wave of popular lay interest in the Bible emerged, partly fuelled by disenchantment with the established churches throughout Europe and partly in reaction against the radicalism of academic approaches to the Bible. Accordingly the older Puritanism gave way to a new Evangelicalism which fostered a strongly conservative approach to the interpretation of the Bible.

During the latter half of the nineteenth century, there emerged both in Britain and America the holding of annual conferences for the study of the Bible, marked by the active promotion of such conservative viewpoints. In turn these conferences led to the setting up of private academies and Bible schools which have upheld an active and influential role in the teaching, interpretation and public promotion of Bible-reading.

Such revitalizing of concern to place the Bible at the centre of ecclesiastical and personal life, with a tightly drawn profile of a biblical lifestyle, has served to keep the Bible prominent in public affairs, often outside the defined borders of the church. Such groups have consistently favoured traditional views regarding the authorship of the biblical writings and a very positive stance over matters concerning its historical veracity and reliability. More extreme forms of this conservatism in the early twentieth century have given rise to the concept of fundamentalism, but overall they have served to encourage and promote a strong interest in the Bible and its central role in the history of humankind's religious quest.

It is largely in recognition of this popularity of private Bible study that a major feature of twentieth-century biblical scholarship has lain in the desire to provide fresh, clearly intelligible translations of the ancient Hebrew and Greek texts. The formal requirements of worship, which strongly characterized the older translations into the major languages of Europe, have often appeared too stilted and artificial for the needs and abilities of such modern readers. Accordingly broad paraphrases of ancient idioms and concepts, aimed at providing clarity of meaning, have been encouraged as a means towards aiding the private reader. The need for simplicity and immediacy of impact have served as guidelines for promoting an extraordinary number of modern versions of the biblical text. These have largely been directed towards the needs of the private reader rather than the formalities of church use and in this they have largely succeeded. The consequence has been that, even though the traditional role of the Bible in church life and intellectual circles has appeared much weakened by the cultural and religious pluralism of modern Western-style societies, the private study of the Bible has flourished and continued to enjoy great popularity and vitality.

12 The Bible in the Eastern Churches

GEORGE BEBAWI

The Transfiguration of Christ, Russian icon, Novgorod School, 15th century, from the Holy Theotokos Dormition Church on the Volotovo Field near Novgorod.

It is important to remember the two communities of eastern Christianity, the Chalcedonian and the non-Chalcedonian Orthodox churches. Greek, Russian, Romanian, Coptic, Syrian, Indian, Armenian, and Ethiopian churches form the bulk of eastern Christians. This is not the place to discuss the old Christological debate, which destroyed the Eastern Communion and has remained a living problem since the fifth century. Christology is the main dividing line between the two bodies.

Biblical studies and commentaries in Greek, Syriac, Arabic, Armenian, and Slavonic have existed from the days of the great Fathers of the church through the Middle Ages and up to the present day. The Fathers, since Origen of Alexandria wrote his commentaries, drew on the techniques of the Greek 'Grammaticus', which was employed in Alexandria to establish and explain classical works of the great writers. Thus the aim to establish a good reading of the text by comparing textual variations was introduced as early as the beginning of the third century. The geography of Palestine and the etymology of words were used to give a more accurate meaning of words and names. This has continued throughout the history of both eastern churches.

It is beyond the scope of this chapter to provide the reader with a summary of a heritage which stretches over 1,400 years or even to summarize the various schools of theology which presuppose the various ways of understanding the Bible in the eastern context. What concerns us here are the basic features, which may be regarded as common among the biblical scholars of the eastern churches.

THE BIBLE AND WORSHIP

Christian history and theology did not start with theological controversies but with worship. The separation between church and synagogue came as a result of the new forms of worship, namely baptism and the Lord's supper; both sacraments contained the seeds of future creeds. Whatever was the complicated history of the development of either sacrament, what is clear from the outline of both in the New Testament and later on is enough to point to the cause of the

separation. With the coming of Gentiles to join the new movement, confession of faith became a necessity. The confession that Jesus is Lord was the major element, which brought a new attitude to the Old Testament and a different way of understanding it by the new members. This is reflected in the book of Acts, the Gospel of John, Romans, Galatians, and later on in Justin Martyr's Dialogue with Trypho and other related documents of the second and the third centuries. The divinity of Jesus, his resurrection, and the acceptance of Gentiles in the new faith remained, throughout the period of the formation of the great doctrines of the churches (325–415), the key issues which changed the understanding of the Old Testament and contributed to the formation of the New Testament canon.

Whatever we can say about the origin and the influence of Jewish prayers on the prayers of the new movement, it is apparent from the oldest collection of the prayers of the Didache and later liturgical collections such as the Apostolic Tradition that Christian teaching is centred on the person of Jesus. This shaped the new prayers and reflected the awareness of the new communities that they were related to God the Father of Jesus Christ in a new way that demanded a different mode of understanding the Old Testament. This made all the difference between those who recognized Jesus as the Messiah, and saw in him the fulfilment of the Old Testament's divine promises and prophecies, like Justin Martyr, and others who refused to accept Jesus' messiahship.

The debate is centred on the significance of having mere events or the life of Jesus as the key, which unlocks the meaning of the words of Old Testament. This was expressed in worship, which made all the difference and inspired ancient Christians to read the Old Testament differently and even to decide later on what should be included in the New Testament canon. The debate between Justin and the Jew Trypho is not centred on the meaning of words in a text, but on the meanings of words and texts in the light of the events of the life, the teaching, and the death and resurrection of Jesus Christ. This basic idea must be realized as we read the old documents of the first centuries, especially those which are related to the Christian–Jewish dialogue. In other words we do not encounter a collection of texts which prove this or that of the Christian teaching, but we read a Christian reflection on the Old Testament which is guided and seen in the light of the life of Jesus as the Messiah. This does not weaken or undermine the New Testament, but rather points to more than the basic and primary question among them: how did ancient Christians read and understand the Bible?

Truth for the early Christians was not an idea, but the Son of God Incarnate, that is, the person of Jesus Christ. Thus in relation to the personal understanding and to the personal relationship with the person of Jesus, words and texts must be understood. The reinterpretation of the Old Oracles is desirable and becomes a necessity which is determined by the New Revelation: one whose truth is not the law nor prophetic words but the person of Jesus Christ. In other words it is not by comparing one text with another that truth is revealed, but rather by reading the text in the light of the life of Jesus that the words are understood differently. The dialogue between Christ and the two disciples on the road to

Emmaus in Luke 24, which is given in a summary, betrays the liturgical origin of the whole passage. Those who have faith and can discern the new reality in the shadows of the old Oracles can see Jesus in Moses and the prophetic books. The new reality is the person of Jesus himself. Thus we can see in baptism in the early practice and in the Lord's supper the centrality of the person over the words and oracles. The meanings of any text can be determined by the events. The best example of this is in the writings of Origen of Alexandria. In his commentary on the Gospel of John, book x, he calls our attention to the discrepancy between John and the synoptic gospels:

> If the discrepancy between the Gospels is not solved, many dismiss credence in the Gospels as not true, or written by a divine spirit, or not successfully recorded. The composition of these Gospels in fact, is said to have involved both. Let those who accept the four Gospels, and who do not think the apparent discrepancy is to be solved, tell us when the Lord came to Capharnaum in relation to the difficulty we mentioned earlier concerning the forty days of the temptation which can have no place at all in John. For if it occurred six days after the time when he was baptised, since his ministry at the marriage at Cana of Galilee took place on the sixth day, it is then clear he has not been tempted, nor was he in Nazareth, nor had John yet been delivered up. (*Commentary on John*, x. 10, Eng. trans. The Fathers of the Church, 80, 256)

The words of Origen are clear. Origen does not dismiss the problem and the reliability of the four gospels. His solution will linger throughout centuries of eastern Christianity. He says later on that the 'spiritual meaning of the events supersedes what is recorded'. He says, 'On the basis of numerous passages also, if someone should examine the Gospels carefully to check the disagreement so far as the historical sense is concerned—we shall attempt to show this disagreement ... as we are able' (ibid. 257). The solution does not dismiss the problem. Origen says that if God appeared to four different men, each will record the manifestation differently. The analogy is used to explain that, 'in the case of the four evangelists who made full use of many things done and said in accordance with the prodigious and incredible power of Jesus, in some place they have interwoven in Scripture something made clear to them in purely intellectual manner, with language as though it were something perceptible to the senses' (ibid. 258). Origen saw the problem and his faith prompted him to say, 'I do not condemn, I suppose the fact that they have also made some minor changes in what happened so far as history is concerned, with a view to the usefulness of the mystical object of [those matters]' (ibid.).

The truth is what Origen called 'spiritual' which is the faith of the church as embodied in what was called at that time the Rule of Faith and later the creed. The Rule of Faith, which was the oldest form of confession adopted and adapted in most of the ancient Christian communities, preceded the canon of the New Testament. In fact a close examination of the debate with Gnosticism may reveal to us that the Rule of Faith itself was responsible for two things:

1. The exclusion of certain books and defining the understanding of the canon. It is faith in the Creator God, the God of the Old Testament, who is also the Redeemer and the Father of Jesus Christ as was declared in the Rule of Faith that retained the Old Testament books, which confirmed the reading of the selected New Testament and excluded a number of other books such as the Nag Hammadi collection.

2. Even later on, the whole debate with Arianism was about the confession of faith not about particulars of the Old Testament or the New Testament texts. Modern studies on Arianism have been able, after a long period of fascination with the biblical arguments exchanged between the two sides, to discover that soteriology was the guiding hermeneutical principle which divided Orthodoxy from Arianism. In other words the meaning of biblical texts is defined by the practice of the church which in turn is defined by the confession of faith. This remained the same during the debate with Nestorianism. If we exclude all the personal elements and hatred of Cyril and Nestorius, the words of the Creed of Nicea (325) expressed the hermeneutical principle, the understanding and the approach to the biblical texts and to the Christological questions which were raised at that time.

The Bible did not give rise to the church or to Israel, because both had a similar starting-point, the events of their relationship with God. The Bible is certainly what gave birth to the Reformation, but not to the ancient church in both east and west. In other words the Bible was read in the light of the relationship between God and the people of God.

Faith preceded the formation of the canon. This was altered during and after the Reformation because the Reformation had its birth within the church as a movement aiming at renewal and guided by reading the Bible differently from the church of the Middle Ages. Thus the various disciplines of biblical studies which came into existence in the west are in harmony with the origin and the development of Reformed Christianity. The coming of the Catholic Church to this arena and in response to the challenge of the Reformation is also an integral part of common European culture and the historical relationship of both Catholic and Reformed churches.

The eastern churches seem not to be affected by the late western tools and schools of the interpretation of the words and the texts of the Bible. Even in Greece, Russia, and the established Orthodox Theological Institutes in France and the USA, Orthodox theologians remain committed to the above guiding principles, the Creed and the practice of the church. Worship remains the essential school of biblical interpretation. The Bible must be explained according to the Creed, the liturgical life of the church, and the monastic ideal of Christian holiness.

In the works of Orthodox theologians, the Bible is understood as part of the life and history of the church. Holiness and Christian life in its Orthodox monastic forms are the goal of all interpretation and speculation. St Athanasius of Alexandria gives a fairly defined name to this approach to the Bible, the 'Ecclesiastical Meaning', of the Word of God must be according to the 'Scope of Salvation'. These two terms must not be confused with the anti-Arian apologetic

The Holy Trinity, by Andrei Rublev (*c*.1370–1430), Russia.

arguments. Arianism has put on the language of the scripture as a garment to deceive the foolish, but the Arian interpretation is 'foreign' because it is misinterpretation according to the 'private sense'. The ecclesiastical sense of the words of the Bible is in the 'Scope of Salvation', which is the unity of the Godhead, the divinity of the Son, his death, and resurrection. This is what Athanasius called the biblical 'double account of the Saviour' the first of which speaks of his divinity and the second of which speaks of his humanity, 'This is the Scope of Salvation which is to be found throughout inspired Scripture'. In other words the Bible must be understood according to the confession of faith and the message of salvation.

Modern scholars very often express their surprise that all the Fathers quote John and Paul in the same line. The New Testament like the Old Testament is one book, which must be read according to the faith of the church, not according to the writer. Although some of the Fathers like Origen were aware that some writers have particular words and style, nevertheless they all are witnesses to the faith. Patristic writings contain the seeds of biblical criticism, but they lie there undeveloped because the goal of Christian life is 'Deification' or 'Participation in the divine Nature'.

In this sense it is accurate to say that the special place of the Bible in ancient Christianity was and is in eastern Christianity a witness to the faith of the church as declared and experienced in worship. This experience is what gave the books their name: the New Testament. The eastern Fathers never used the expression 'Authority of the Scriptures'. St Augustine and the Latin Fathers used it in a limited way and it became a common expression with the arrival of St Thomas Aquinas. The differences between 'Authority' and 'Witness' are important to notice. The witness of the Bible to the faith of the church does not come from the words or the texts but from the events and their interpretation. This interpretation is to be discovered in worship and specially in the experience of salvation. It is

Byzantine icon of the Virgin and Child Enthroned, between St Gregory Nazianzus and St John Chrysostom, 12th century.

also important to remember that the eastern churches, through the writings of the Fathers, never regarded the Old Testament as equal to the New Testament. The earliest reference to this approach is to be found in the Didascalia, the Apostolic Constitutions, and the Homilies of the Fathers especially John Chrysostom. Also two books of the New Testament, Revelation and the letter to Philemon, are not included in the lectionaries of the Coptic and the Byzantine churches.

It was baptism, the eucharist, and other forms of worship that shaped the attitude to the Bible in early Christian worship. The Word of God was read in the gatherings of the church especially on the Lord's day and this remained the obvious attitude to the word of God till the fourth century when the Homilies of the Fathers were written and Commentaries were composed very often to explain the community's participation in the life of Christ. The discourses of the Fathers to the catechumens on baptism such as those of Cyril of Jerusalem or John Chrysostom are full of biblical images that may shock the readers. Most of the biblical texts were selected for instruction and for preparing the candidates for baptism. The Fathers do not apologize for the way they explain the biblical texts because the Bible is the main book for instruction. It has the seeds of all the teaching of the church. It is the church's first book and its proper use was never questioned.

THE TRANSFORMATION OF THE HISTORICAL MEANING OF THE TEXT

It seems obvious that if worship is the reason for reading the Bible, the historical meaning will become secondary for any worshipping community, even in the twenty-first century. One good example among many others is in the words of St Cyril of Alexandria, after commenting on the first miracle of Jesus at Cana of Galilee. Cyril of Alexandria says: 'The historical account then will stop here, but I think we ought to consider the other view of what has been said, and to say what is signified'. What is signified is not the changing of the water to wine, but the marriage of humanity to the divinity of the Son who is the Bridegroom. The marriage is consummated on the third day, the day on which humanity was raised from the dead. (*Commentary on John*, II.1.11; Eng. trans. The Fathers of the Church, 1, 157). This is further given a better illustration by Maximos the Confessor who says:

> the sacred Scripture, taken as a whole, is like a human being. The Old Testament is the body and the New is the soul, the meaning it contains, the spirit. From another viewpoint we can say that the entire sacred Scripture, the Old and the New, has two aspects: the historical content which corresponds to the body, the deep meaning the goal at which the mind should aim, which corresponds to the soul. If we think of human beings, we see they are mortal in their visible properties but immortal in their invisible qualities. So it is with Scripture. It contains the letter, the visible text, which is transitory. But it also contains the spirit hidden beneath the letter, and this is never extinguished and this ought to be the object of our contemplation. Think of human beings again. If they want to be perfect, they master passions and mortify the flesh. So it is with Scripture. If it is heard in a spiritual way, it trims the text, like cir-

> cumcision. Paul says: 'Though our nature is wasting away, our inner nature is being renewed every day' (2 Cor. 4: 16). We can say that also of the Scripture. The further the letter is divorced from it, the more relevance the spirit acquires. The more the shadows of literal sense retreat, the more the shining truth of the faith advances. And this is exactly why Scripture was composed. (Mystagogia, 6 PG 91'684)

The historical meaning was never ignored but the Bible, as the book of the living word of God cannot be taken as a collection of only historical events. The language of the Bible is part of the variety of sacred symbols. If we look from outside, the language of the Bible seems to be 'filled with incredible and contrived fantasy'. God has a womb (Ps. 2: 7 and Ps. 110: 3, Septuagint). He speaks like someone who is using his breath (Ps. 45: 1). Even the Father has a bosom which embraces the Son (John 1: 18) and others which are listed in the ninth letter of Pseudo-Dionysius. According to Pseudo-Dionysius they are written in this way because the 'theological tradition has dual aspect', to reveal the mystery which is understood by the initiated and thus it has to use symbols; and the second is to put the initiate in the presence of God. Pseudo-Dionysius speaks in the same way as Origen of Alexandria; no one can understand the Bible without the inspiration of the Holy Spirit. The work of the Spirit is not only in inspiration but also in the interpretation. Pseudo-Dionysius supports his teaching by referring to the parables of Jesus, which do not give an open teaching but the hide the mystery of the divine activities under symbolism.

Modern theologians such as Dumitru Staniloae develop the patristic approach to the Bible by contrasting the Orthodox understanding with the Protestant method of 'demythologization' with its link via existentialism to the 'inner meaning of the text' which can be distinguished from the form of Revelation. According to Staniloae the word of God is not an outer shell or a form peculiar to the time of its composition. What we read in the New Testament forms 'Typologies'. The biblical language has to be adapted to modern language by taking into consideration the core of Revelation. This core of Revelation is the 'spiritual understanding' of divine revelation.

It must be made clear that Revelation is the Son Incarnate, not the Bible itself. Thus the faith of the church is the guide to the meaning of the text as expressed throughout its history. New meanings do not come from the text but from the faith, which expresses itself using modern words but is guided by the Acts of Revelation and the Images of Revelation.

The teaching of Christian faith and understanding of the gospel must be related first to the acts of God in Christ. Staniloae finds a confirmation of his approach in the teaching of the Second Vatican Council and in Protestant theologians such as Oscar Cullmann and others who belong to the *Heilsgeschichtliche Schule.* The ancient Christian teaching, universal up till now, is that God is not an 'objective entity' but is a person who enters into dialogues through acts. Creation is the first act of God. By creation God revealed his will and continued to do so in the acts of salvation of Israel. The One God in the Decalogue is the one God who 'gets Israel out of Egypt'. His worship is due to this great act of salvation. It is the event which defines the meaning of the words. Events and words are not two separate entities. Staniloae, like other Orthodox theologians, sees in the Bible multiple images, which form the icon of salvation. These images can change according to the needs of our time and according to the kind of preaching but the icon must remain as an icon of salvation. The best illustration of this is in the famous icon of Christ the Pantokrator. He is painted carrying the New Testament gospels. The message is that no one can understand one without the other.

THE BIBLE AND MONASTICISM

From the monastic traditions we learn three basic facts that have survived up till now:

1. The memorization of the scriptures according to the rules of Pachomius: novices must learn by heart the Psalter and the New Testament. It is in this context that the memorization or learning by heart became the most obvious mark

Abbot Mena with Christ. Coptic painting on wood, 6th–7th century.

of early monasticism. The scriptures are called the 'breath of God', and monks were encouraged to sing the psalms, recite them, and meditate on them in order to gain inward purification and holiness.

The prophet Elijah, Pskov School (panel) by Russian School, 13th century.

2. Reading the scriptures does not necessarily mean reading all of them. Certain texts assumed a prominent place in the life of some of the Desert Fathers. Particular words remained a goal to be achieved in the inner life. More specifically, at least in the Coptic tradition, a monk is called the 'bearer of the cross', and for someone like John the Dwarf the cross is a law of life. 'Live by the Cross, in warfare, in poverty of spirit, in purity of soul' (Saying 34). Meditation on the scriptures is described as follows by Leclercq: 'For the ancients, to meditate is to read a text and to learn it "by heart" in the fullest sense of this expression, that is, with one's whole being: with the body, since the mouth pronounced it; with the memory which fixes it; with the intelligence which understands its meaning and with the will which longs to put it into practice' (*The Love of Learning*, 26). Or, to use the words of another scholar, the Desert Fathers lived in the Bible, in other words, they used it, not just to read it and meditate on it, but applied it to the environment itself. St Seraphim gave names to certain parts of the forest such as Gethsemane, Calvary, and so forth. It was not just reading the scriptures and applying them to the environment but also taking statements which were uttered by the great heroes of faith, as a law for their personal life. The words of the prophet Elijah ('As the Lord lives, in whose presence I stand today') meant, for St Antony of Egypt, to regard every day as a fresh beginning.

3. Monasticism reshaped eastern Christian life as a whole. The Bible is read for edification and truth is examined in order to be applied to the personal life of every individual. The Bible was not criticized, because it is the breath of God, which has brought the message of salvation. Thus Antony of Egypt heard the words of our Lord to the rich young man and went and sold everything and followed the commandment. Thus we reach the famous saying 'you cannot become a disciple and a judge at the same time'. Eastern Christianity, which regards the life of holiness as a mark of true faith, does not favour biblical criticism, because the Bible was read to judge us rather than to be judged by us.

THE BIBLE IN CONTEMPORARY EASTERN CHRISTIANITY

Since Origen of Alexandria bequeathed to us the use of philology, logic, art, grammar, geography, history, and textual variations, commentators on the scriptures have never abandoned this approach. Tracing back words in their Hebrew origin or in the Septuagint remained an essential element in understanding the biblical text, in order to establish the best and the clearest reading of the Bible. But two important remarks must be noted. In the late work of the very learned Bishop Theophylact of Bulgaria, his commentaries on the four gospels reveal an adherence to the patristic method.

Icon of St John of Patmos, traditionally believed to be the author of the Fourth Gospel, the Johannine letters, and the book of Revelation, from the Trinity-Sergiev Monastery, late 15th century.

1. Defining the goal of the text by reading it as part of a theme rather than an isolated two or three lines.

2. The variations between the Gospel of John and the synoptics were treated according to the Rule of Faith; that is to say the problem is noted and discussed according to the articles of the creed. In other words, the historicity of the sayings of Jesus in the Gospel of John was not raised, despite their different context and style and in spite of the fact that they are not reported in the other three gospels because

(*a*) they do not contradict the confession of the church;

(*b*) they confirm the teaching of the church especially regarding the eucharist and the doctrine of the Trinity. Thus the historicity of the Gospel of John is not a question that can be raised as a subject because the Gospel of John is part of the Christian life which is deeply rooted in the doctrine of the Trinity, the divinity of Jesus, and the celebration of the eucharist. The dichotomy between the Bible and theology has never succeeded in splitting theology, faith, and worship. In many Orthodox schools of theology of higher theological education, very able scholars teach new methods, which were developed in Europe in the last hundred years. These new methods confirm the old approach; tradition comes before the formation of the canon and the reliability of the confession of faith.

It is essential to note that the doctrine of biblical revelation as was developed in western Christian theology since Thomas Aquinas is not known in eastern Christian theology. God revealed himself in Christ and he is the only divine revelation.

13 The Bible in Judaism

PHILIP ALEXANDER

THE CENTRALITY OF THE BIBLE IN JUDAISM

Judaism is now so Bible-centred, so obviously a 'religion of the Book', that it takes an effort to remember that this was not always the case. But if we go back far enough into Jewish history, to pre-exilic times (before 586 BCE), there is little evidence that the written word played anything like the central role then that it was later to play. Important religious texts did exist—collections of laws, histories, wisdom literature, prophecies, and oracles—but their relationship to the Bible we now have in our hands is far from clear, they were accessible only to a small literate élite, and their impact on religious life was at best indirect. Religious life for most ancient Israelites would have focused on the crises of the life-cycle (birth, marriage, death) and on the rhythms of the agricultural year, with occasional visits to the local shrine, the 'high places' (while these still stood), or to the Temple in Jerusalem. Priests would have verbally dispensed Torah (teaching) in response to specific personal or communal problems, and occasionally prophets or other holy men would have appeared to deliver 'the word the Lord'.

In the Second Temple period (538 BCE–70 CE), however, sacred scripture became central to Judaism and Judaism acquired its enduring character as a 'religion of the Book'. The reasons for this development are complex and not yet fully understood. Four interconnected factors played a part. The first was the rise of the scribes to a position of religious authority. There had been a scribal class in Israel going back possibly at least to the time of King David. Scribes worked in the administration of the state, keeping records and archives and dealing with diplomatic correspondence. Increasingly in the Second Temple period, however, they claimed that their competence extended beyond bureaucracy into the religious sphere, and they began to challenge the religious authority of the priests. Secondly, a canon of sacred literature emerged which was regarded by all sections of the community as authoritative for religious belief and practice. The core of this canon, comprising the Pentateuch, the Prophets (including the historical books), and some of the Writings (notably the Psalms), was well established by the end of the Second Temple period, though it remained 'fuzzy' at the edges and the texts of the individual books were far from fixed. Thirdly, going hand in hand with the emergence of a canon of authoritative scripture, was a widespread belief that prophecy had come to an end. God no longer spoke directly to his people. He had already said all that Israel needed to know to live life in accordance with his will, which could be discerned by studying the words of the ancient prophets. Finally, these developments on their own would hardly have been decisive in making scripture central to Judaism without a significant increase in literacy. There is evidence to suggest that an elementary school system, based on the study of the Torah, was established in the Palestinian Jewish communities in late Second Temple times. It was probably this, more than anything else, that made possible the application of the Written Torah to the everyday life of the ordinary Jew.

These profound changes, which had begun much earlier, were probably consolidated by the Hasmonaeans (165 BCE onwards), who in forging a new national identity for Jews did much to redefine Judaism and to establish its place in the Hellenistic world of its day. Certainly by late Second Temple times the centrality of the Written Torah is evident in Judaism and all the competing sects and parties that arose in the wake of the Hasmonaean Revolution felt that they had to justify their positions from scripture and to claim to be its correct interpreters. An abundance of Jewish literature survives from Second Temple times, thanks in part to the discovery of the Dead Sea Scrolls. Most of that literature circles round scripture and can be seen as, in some shape or form, commentary upon it. Scripture played a central role in all areas of Jewish life. The Torah of Moses was regarded as the national constitution of the Jews, the basis of their religious polity and identity. In some sense, though much extended and interpreted, it was applied in the Jewish lawcourts. Torah was publicly read in synagogues and at the great religious festivals in the Jerusalem temple. It was taught and studied in the schools from primary up to tertiary level. It was the ultimate court of appeal for the numerous sects and parties which jostled and debated with each other as they strove to win the hearts and minds of ordinary Jews. The Written Torah was probably even more central to everyday life for the Jews of the far-flung Jewish diaspora than it was for their Palestinian co-religionists who lived nearer the Jerusalem temple. The most important of these diaspora centres was at Alexandria in Egypt, where there was a large, prosperous, and well-educated Jewish community. A number of Alexandrian Jews acquired a good Greek education and produced syntheses of Jewish and Greek ideas which were to be of incalculable importance for the subsequent development of European thought.

A portrait of Moses reading from the Torah, from the West Wall of the ancient synagogue at Dura Europos (*c.*250 CE). The synagogue's paintings have been reassembled in the National Museum in Damascus, their original location being on the Euphrates in northern Syria.

Commentary on scripture took a variety of literary forms:

1. First there were lemmatic commentaries, that is, commentaries in the normally accepted sense of the term: the commentator quotes a verse of scripture, comments upon it, quotes the next verse of scripture and comments upon it, and so on till he comes to the end of the passage or text with which he is concerned. A good example of this type of commentary are the Dead Sea Pesharim such as Pesher Habakkuk, commentaries on the prophetic books which see them as foreshadowing the history of the Dead Sea Community at the end of days. The Alexandrian Jewish philosopher Philo (*c.*20 BCE–50 CE) also produced a series of lemmatic commentaries on the Pentateuch in which he attempted to create a fusion of Torah and the philosophy of Plato (see e.g. his *On the Giants* dealing with Gen. 6: 1–4, and *On the Unchangeableness of God* dealing with Gen. 6: 4–12).

2. Secondly, there was the lecture type of commentary in which the expositor explains a section of scripture in an integrated way, drawing out what he sees to be its leading ideas without systematically going through it verse by verse. Philo also uses this type of commentary on Torah in his voluminous writings (note e.g. his *On the Creation of the World* [Gen. 1–3] or his *On Joseph* [Gen. 37–50]). The origins of this style may lie in the synagogue sermon, but it is more likely that it derives from lectures delivered in the schools.

Columns VII (*right*) and VIII from the Pesher (commentary on the book of Habakkuk, from Qumran (Dead Sea Scrolls)).

3. A third type of commentary, the 'problematic', works systematically through a text posing and answering questions (see e.g. Philo's *Questions on Genesis:* 'Why did the serpent accost the woman and not the man?' [Gen. 3: 2]; 'Why does God ask, "Where are you?" [Gen. 3: 10], when he knows everything?'). Again Philo is the classic exponent of this catechetical style of commentary which, like the lecture style, probably originated in the schools.

4. A fourth type of commentary is often referred to as Rewritten Bible. This retells a part of the biblical story with omissions and expansions, integrating into it later legends and traditions to form a seamless new narrative. Examples of Rewritten Bible can be found in the Book of Jubilees (originally written in Hebrew), in the Genesis Apocryphon (in Aramaic), and in the biblical sections of Josephus' *Antiquities of the Jews* (in Greek).

5. A fifth type of commentary is codification. This applies only to the legal sections of the Torah. The classic Second Temple period example of this genre is the great Temple Scroll from Qumran. Based on the book of Deuteronomy, this rearranges the biblical material into a more coherent topical order, integrating into it the other relevant biblical data, together with explanatory expansions and non-biblical laws.

6. A sixth type of biblical commentary is anthology. Scrolls were clumsy and expensive and scholars resorted to the practical expedient of excerpting from the longer texts the verses which particularly interested them. These might be verses linked by a single theme, or proof-texts to support a particular doctrine. The process of extracting and juxtaposing verses from different parts of the Bible (with or without explanation) constitutes a kind of rudimentary commentary. Examples of such anthologies are attested among the Dead Sea Scrolls (e.g. 4QFlorilegium). There is also good reason to believe that collections of biblical testimonies and proof-texts circulated among the early Christians.

7. Finally there is proof-text. This is where a verse of scripture is quoted, introduced by a citation-formula such as 'as it is written', or 'as it is said', or 'as scripture says', in order to clinch an argument. The use of proof-text is particularly common in the Dead Sea Scrolls (note e.g. the Damascus Document) and in the early Christian writings. Its origins lie in the inter-sectarian debates which raged in Judaism in the late Second Temple period.

CLASSIC RABBINIC MIDRASH

The Second Temple period was one of the most religiously dynamic and creative in the history of Judaism. It came dramatically to an end when the Romans destroyed the Jerusalem temple in 70 CE. The most significant post-destruction development was the emergence of rabbinic Judaism—the form of Judaism which has dominated Judaism down to modern times. There was no sudden triumph of rabbinism after 70. Initially the rabbis, like their spiritual forebears the Pharisees at the end of the Second Temple period, were a sect within Judaism, whose power-base within the community was in the rabbinic schools (the *Batei Midrash*). They were opposed initially by the land-owning class, whom they refer to as 'peoples of the land' (*'ammei ha-'aretz*) and by other groups competing for the hearts and minds of Israel, including the Jewish Christians, whom they call 'heretics' (*minim*). However, by the third century CE the rabbis seem to have been accepted as the reli-

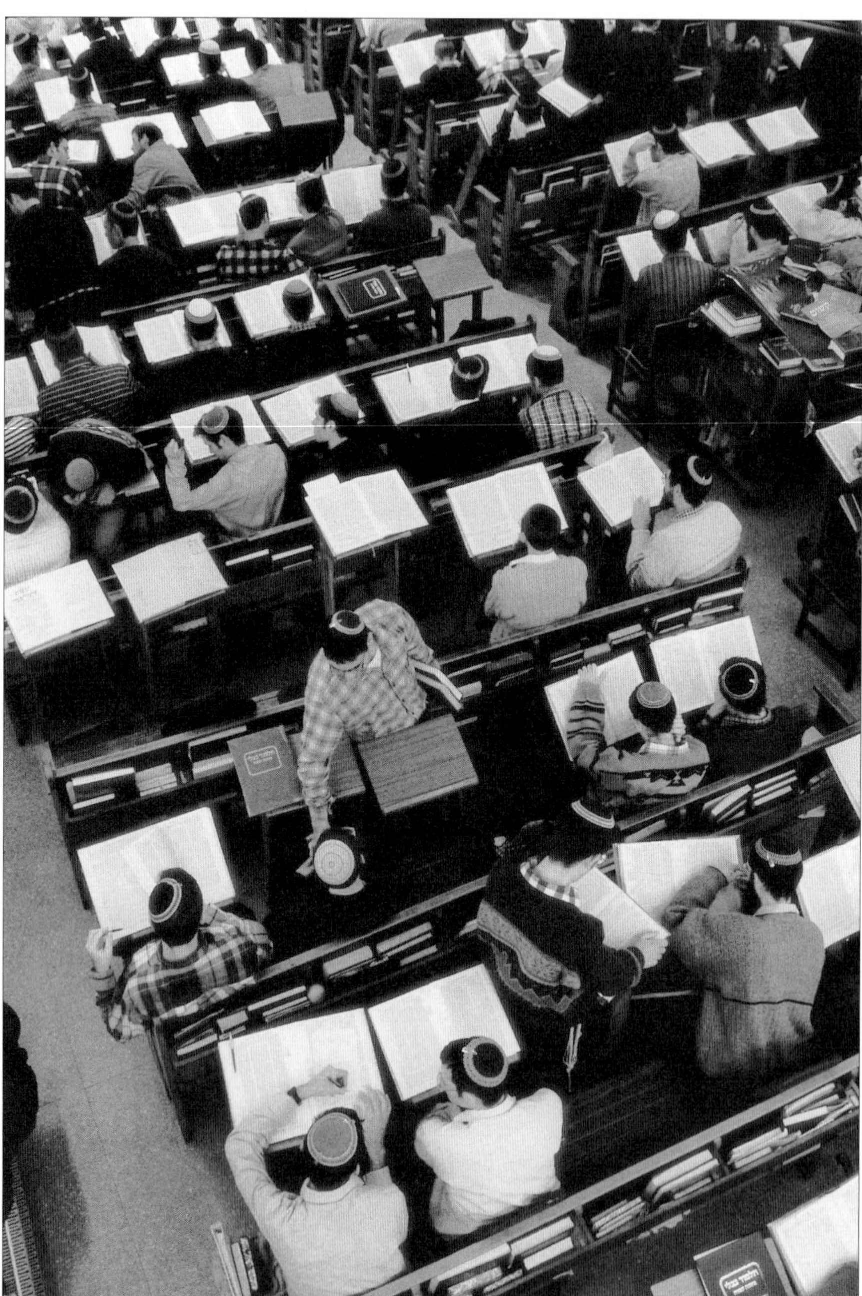

A modern Jewish rabbinical seminary (Yeshivah). The students study in pairs, perpetuating a practice that goes back to antiquity.

gious authorities by the majority of Palestinian Jews. The turning-point probably occurred about 200 CE during the lifetime of Judah ha-Nasi. Judah, a wealthy landowner, was recognized by the Romans as the political leader (the Patriarch) of the Jewish community. He was, at the same time, leader of the rabbinic party.

The rabbis were a scholarly group whose religious activities centred on the study and exposition of Torah. They accepted as inspired scripture the present-day synagogue canon (though some doubts, finally quashed, were expressed about the inspiration of the Song of Songs and about Ecclesiastes). Within scripture pride of place was given to the first five books—the Torah of Moses. These were regarded as containing within them, whether implicitly or explicitly, all that Israel needed to know in order to live its life in conformity to the will of God. As one rabbinic maxim put it: 'Turn Torah over and over again, for everything is in it. Reflect upon it. Grow old and worn in it, and do not stir from it, for you have no better rule than it' (Mishnah, *Pirqei 'Avot* 5: 22). In addition to the Written Torah, the rabbis held in high esteem certain traditions passed down, they believed, ultimately from Moses himself, which supplemented and clarified the Written Torah. These traditions were subsequently designated Oral Torah, and came in the end to carry the same authority as the written text itself. In effect this Oral Torah defined the parameters of the correct interpretation of the Written Torah. Interpretations of the Written Torah (such as those advanced by Jewish Christians to justify their teachings) which did not accord with the tradition of the rabbinic schools were *ipso facto* deemed illegitimate. However, within the framework of the Oral Torah considerable diversity of opinion was allowed. The Oral Torah was by no means rigid and monolithic. The text of the Written Torah was polysemic and even contradictory conclusions, if drawn correctly from it by competent authority, could be seen as equally 'words of the living God'. This introduced a flexibility into the system, which was vital in adapting Torah to ever-changing historical circumstances. In a sense the rabbis embraced a kind of doctrine of continuous revelation. All necessary truth was encoded in the Written Torah given to Moses on Sinai, but the meaning of the Torah only unfolds through the activity of the scholars who expound it generation after generation and apply it to changing historical circumstances. And only at the end of history will all the latent meaning of Torah be fully realized.

The rabbis' programme of study in the post-70 period concentrated initially on the codification of law. This programme eventually reached its culmination in the law-code known as the Mishnah, which tradition holds was promulgated about 200 CE under the auspices of Judah the Patriarch. The Mishnah is not a 'cut-and-dried' code, like the Code Napoléon. It contains within it considerable differences of opinion. Nor is it a straightforward commentary on the Torah, though it presupposes the Torah throughout and frequently cites it directly to support a particular position. Rather, in a manner reminiscent of the Temple Scroll, it offers a systematic and thematic statement of the law which harmoniously combines the data of the Torah with clarificatory expansions and with well-established custom and tradition.

Despite its systematic incorporation of so much of the Torah, it is the Mishnah's independence of Torah that first strikes the reader. It is a self-contained, essentially free-standing document, which raises acutely the problem of its relationship to the Torah of Moses. This problem was addressed by the rabbis over the next 300 years in broadly two ways. First, the Mishnah itself was carefully studied and expounded in the rabbinic schools, and in the process biblical bases for its views from time to time were proposed. This process of direct commentary on the Mishnah resulted in the two Talmuds—the Palestinian or Jerusalem Talmud, which was finally edited about 400 CE in the school of Tiberias, and the Babylonian Talmud, which was finally edited about a century later in Babylonia, where rabbinic schools had also become well established. Secondly, a programme was initiated of reading and commenting upon the Torah in the light of the Mishnah. This produced the classic Rabbinic Bible commentaries known as the Midrashim. There was, doubtless, a tradition of Bible-exegesis within the rabbinic schools prior to the editing of the Mishnah, and some of these traditions have been incorporated into the Midrashim, but it was probably the publication of the Mishnah, and the need to link the Oral Torah to the Written Torah, that generated the compilation of all the major Rabbinic Bible commentaries that have survived from the Talmudic period. The creation of Midrash continued unabated down to roughly the ninth century, by which time the whole of the Pentateuch, the Five Scrolls (Ruth, Esther, Song of Songs, Lamentations, and Ecclesiastes), and much of the rest of the Hebrew Bible had been provided with detailed commentary. The Pentateuch, not surprisingly, attracted the lion's share of the attention, and in the case of some of its books several different commentaries survive. These commentaries fall into three main groups. First, the Tannaitic or Halakhic Midrashim comprising the Mekhilta of Rabbi Ishmael on Exodus, Sifra on Leviticus, and Sifrei on Numbers and Deuteronomy. Secondly, Midrash Rabbah comprising commentaries on Genesis, Exodus, Leviticus, Numbers, and Deuteronomy, and on each of the Five Scrolls. And thirdly, the Homiletic Midrashim, the Pesiqta of Rav Kahana and Pesiqta Rabbati, which are based on the cycle of special biblical readings used in the synagogue during the festivals.

The exposition of scripture offered in these works is highly distinctive. For possibly the first time in Jewish Bible commentary the principle of polysemy is explicitly embraced, that is to say, the Bible is held to possess different simultaneously valid levels of meaning. The text tends to be treated atomistically, verse by verse, or phrase by phrase, with little attempt to discover the ongoing 'argument' of a passage or book. The potential of scripture is maximized: there is a tendency to deny that scripture is ever redundant or simply repeats itself. Repetitions are systematically nuanced to provide slightly different meanings. Scripture is treated as an interlocking whole and harmonized to remove contradictions. There is virtually no sense of historical development, 'no before and no after in Torah': it is saying the same things throughout. In some forms of Midrash the text of scripture can be reduced effectively to a set of symbols to be manipulated by the commentator apparently at will, as when the numerical value of the words is computed for exegetical purposes (a device known as *gematria*). However, an important distinction is observed between the exposition of the legal parts of scripture (the Halakhah) and the exposition of the non-legal, narrative portions (the Aggadah). The former were treated much more conservatively, well within the range of techniques which one would expect sober jurisprudents to employ. The latter, however, can be subjected to extreme forms of manipulation to make them yield the homiletic, theological, or moral points which the commentator desires to make.

As their highly learned character shows, these commentaries were all compiled within the rabbinic schools. However, one of the sources on which they drew was the long and rich tradition of Bible exposition within the synagogue. Scripture played a central role in the synagogue service. The Pentateuch was systematically read in Hebrew on sabbaths over a three-year or a one-year cycle. A second reading, known as the Haftarah and drawn from the second division of the synagogue canon, the Prophets, was added to the Torah reading, and the Psalms and other parts of the third division of the canon, the Writings, were also extensively used in the liturgy. Exposition of scripture was presented in synagogue in two main forms, first through the Targum, a rendering of the Hebrew Bible lections into Aramaic, and secondly, through the sermon.

Rabbinic tradition claims that Ezra instituted the Targum. Whether or not this is correct, the practice of translating the Hebrew Bible into Aramaic certainly goes back to Second Temple times. As the numerous surviving medieval copies suggest, the old oral Targum delivered in synagogue was often much more than a literal translation of the Hebrew. It could involve extensive paraphrase of the biblical text. The relationship of the synagogue Targum to the classic rabbinic Midrashim has long been a matter of dispute. It used to be assumed that the exegesis of the Targumim was heavily derivative from the Midrashim (there was a reluctance to grant the Targumists any originality), but it is more likely that influence operated in both directions, and that the Targum provided a rich source of commentary for the Midrashists when they were first developing the systematic exposition of scripture. The influence of the Targum on early classic Midrashim such as Genesis Rabbah is very clear. The Targumim were certainly valued highly by the medieval Jewish commentators, and are printed alongside the biblical text in the great modern Rabbinic Bibles. The Targum, as befits its life-setting, offers on the whole a popular, homiletic exposition of scripture. It became the model for a whole series of later Bible paraphrases into Judaeo-Arabic, Ladino (Judaeo-Spanish), and Yiddish (Judaeo-German), which powerfully shaped the Jewish popular religious imagination.

The sermon also as an institution seems to have predated the emergence of the classic Midrashim and to have contributed substantially to their content. One form which it took was a short homily preceding the reading of the Torah and based on the first verse of the Torah lection. It was regarded as 'opening' the scripture reading and was known in Hebrew as a *Petihah.* The preacher began by quoting a verse, usually from the third division of the canon, which on the face of it had nothing whatsoever to do with the Torah reading. He then ingeniously demonstrated that there was, in fact, a link. The *Petihah* was used to engage the audience's interest in the Torah reading, to demonstrate the unity of scripture, and to make various theological and moral points. There are remnants of many hundreds of these *Petihot* scattered all over the classic Midrashim. They are testimony not only to the eloquence and ingenuity of the preachers but to the Midrashists' reliance on their expositions of scripture. Though it has never carried the same prestige as the more formal, systematic Bible commentaries, the sermon has remained an important genre of Jewish Bible commentary down to the present day, and sermon collections form an extensive if somewhat neglected body of exegetical literature.

THE MIDDLE AGES

The classic Midrashim form the bedrock of all subsequent Jewish Bible interpretation. There was a late flowering of Midrash in the seventh and eighth centuries, in part inspired by the rediscovery by Jewish scholars of Second Temple-period traditions. (In many ways the quintessential work of this later Midrash is the innovative work known as *Pirqei de Rabbi Eliezer* [The Chapters of Rabbi Eliezer]). The Midrashim continued to be studied and great Midrashic compilations (such as the *Yalqut Shim'oni* and *Midrash ha-Gadol*) were being produced as late as the thirteenth century, but Midrash as a creative mode of Bible exegesis effectively came to an end in the ninth century CE, and new styles of exegesis took its place.

The reasons for this change of direction are complex, but they can all be traced back in one way or another to the new intellectual and religious climate inaugurated by the rise of Islam. In the early Middle Ages Jewish scholars for the first time began to show an interest in the grammar of biblical Hebrew and in philological solutions to biblical problems. The Midrashists of the Talmudic period were, in their way, fine Hebraists with great sensitivity for the nuances of biblical Hebrew, but they had little scientific understanding of the workings of Hebrew grammar. The inspiration for this new interest in grammar was the work of the great Islamic grammarians who were, with astonishing sophistication, laying the foundations for the scientific description of Arabic. Arabic and Hebrew are closely cognate languages and it became clear to Jewish scholars that much of what was being said about the former was equally applicable to the latter.

This new interest in philology went hand in hand with a concerted attempt to fix in all its aspects the text of the Hebrew Bible. The Torah scroll as used in synagogue contains basically only the consonantal text. It does not mark vowels nor does it indicate the punctuation of the verse. The reader is supposed to supply these from memory in accordance with oral tradition. A group of Jewish scholars, known collectively as the Masoretes, began to devise ways of marking the vowels and the punctuation by using tiny symbols that were written in around the consonantal text. The Torah scroll as used in synagogue was left in its traditional form, but great master-codices were produced (such as the St Petersburg and Aleppo codices) which gave the text fully vocalized and accented (to show its sense-units), together with an elaborate series of marginal notes highlighting unusual words and grammatical forms. These master-codices form the basis of all modern printed editions of the Hebrew Bible. The work of the Masoretes went well beyond merely recording how the Hebrew was pronounced in synagogue. Their system of vowel notation is actually much more refined than any cantor could ever reproduce, at least consistently. Behind it lies a profound attempt to systematize the phonetics of Hebrew and to regularize its grammar.

A page from Codex Reuchlin 1 showing the fully vocalized and accented Hebrew text along with marginal Masoretic notes.

The Jewish religious movement known as Karaism played an important role in mediating Islamic philology to the Jewish world and in forcing orthodox Rabbanite scholars to take an interest in Hebrew grammar. Karaism, supposedly founded by Anan ben David in the eighth century, rejected the authority of the Talmud and advocated a return to the Bible as the sole arbiter of faith and practice. The Karaites seem to have been particularly open to the Islamic science of their day and used it effectively to attack what they saw as the naïveté and illogicality of rabbinic literature. Karaism made significant inroads into rabbinic Judaism in the ninth and tenth centuries and forced a response from the Orthodox establishment. Orthodoxy found a doughty champion in Saadia Gaon (882–942). Born in the Fayyum in Egypt, Saadia, after a period of study in Galilee, ended his life as the head of the great rabbinic academy of Sura in Baghdad. Though a defender of rabbinic orthodoxy, Saadia was no mere traditionalist. He was a master of Arabic and participated fully in the great cultural renaissance which was going on in Baghdad in his day under the patronage of the Abbasid caliphs. He decided to fight the Karaites with their own weapons by showing that Rabbanism was fully compatible with the best contemporary philosophic and scientific thought. He advocated a more philological approach to the Hebrew Bible and reflected this interest in a series of biblical commentaries which can be taken as marking the beginning of medieval Jewish Bible exegesis.

Saadia's advocacy ensured that the philological approach to the Bible was acceptable to rabbinic scholars. This approach, which naturally led to a greater stress on the literal (*peshat*) sense of scripture, was pervasive in early medieval Jewish Bible commentary and was one of the hallmarks of medieval exegesis as distinct from Midrash. It is widely regarded as reaching its peak in the work of Abraham ibn Ezra and David Qimhi.

Abraham ibn Ezra (1089–1146) was born and reared in Spain, but from 1140 onwards he lived a wandering life which took him to Italy, Provence, northern France, and even England. Despite his travels his literary output was prodigious. It probably originally included commentaries on the whole of the Hebrew Bible, though some of these are now no longer extant: Ibn Ezra stressed the role of human intellect in understanding prophetic revelation, and his commentaries show a notable independence of mind, which led later Jewish thinkers such as Nahman Krochmal to claim him as a forerunner of the modern critical approach to the Bible. He usually begins his discussion of a verse with a close analysis of its grammar and language and then proceeds to relate the verse to its context and to the overall argument of the passage. His style, though sharp and often witty, is notoriously obscure, and in places his comments read like preliminary notes (which, given his peripatetic lifestyle, might well be the case). Sometimes he tantalizes the reader by stating 'There is a mystery here', without saying what it is. Later scholars provided his work with super-commentaries which attempted to make it accessible to a wider public.

David Qimhi (*c.*1160–*c.*1235), whose family hailed from Spain but who lived in Narbonne in Provence, took essentially the same line as Ibn Ezra. However, his style is much more lucid and readable, and this was to make him by far the most accessible proponent of the philological approach. He was highly valued by Christian Hebraists at the time of the Reformation (when his *Compendium* (the *Mikhlol*) was the standard Hebrew grammar), and the influence of his ideas on the Protestant Bible translations, such as the Authorized Version of 1611, has been well documented.

A slightly earlier scholar, Rabbi Solomon Yitzhaqi (1040–1105), or Rashi as he is better known, completes, along with Abraham ibn Ezra and David Qimhi, the great triumvirate of medieval Jewish Bible commentators whose work is always included in Rabbinic Bibles. In fact Rashi is universally acknowledged to be the single most influential Jewish exegete of all time. His work was, and largely still is, the first resort for any educated Jew who wants to know what a verse of the Bible means. Whereas Abraham ibn Ezra and David Qimhi represent the Spanish school of commentary, which was shaped essentially in an Islamic milieu, Rashi is the supreme representative of the northern French school, which functioned in a Christian environment less intellectually advanced than the Islamic world, and much more hostile to Judaism. The result of this was that the northern French Jews tended to be more conservative and inward-looking than their co-religionists

The Rashi Study House attached to the Old Synagogue of Worms, where Rashi (Rabbi Solomon Yitzhaqi, 1040–1105) studied as a young man.

This traditional likeness of the great Jewish philosopher Maimonides (1135–1204) was used on a postage stamp issued in Israel in 1953 to mark the International Congress of the History of Science.

in Spain, Provence, and North Africa. Rashi was born in Troyes and studied in the rabbinical seminaries of the Rhineland, before returning to his native town and setting up his own school. He taught scripture diligently all his life, and commentaries by him, or attributed to him, are extant for all the books of the Hebrew Bible with the exception of Chronicles. Rather different versions of his commentaries survive in the manuscripts, suggesting that he regularly revised his views. In some cases the texts may have been edited by his pupils. Rashi, like Ibn Ezra and Qimhi, stresses the plain sense (*peshat*) of scripture, but his grasp of philology is less advanced than theirs, and he cites a great deal more Midrash. However, his choice of *derash* (the search for deeper and symbolic senses) is noticeably careful: he avoids the more fanciful ideas and selects traditions that are reasonably compatible with the plain sense. His penchant for *derash* was criticized by his grandson and pupil, Samuel ben Meir, himself a significant commentator, but it gives his work a homiletic edge, and is a major reason for its popularity and influence.

Philology pushed medieval Jewish Bible commentary in the direction of the plain sense of scripture. An upsurge of philosophy and mysticism, however, was to push it more in the direction of allegory. Philosophy, which had been introduced into rabbinic Judaism by Saadia in the ninth century, received a major boost with the publication in the late twelfth century of Maimonides' *Guide of the Perplexed*. The fact that Maimonides (1135–1204) was acknowledged to be the greatest Jewish legalist of his day gave his philosophical *magnum opus* an authority that could not be ignored. The purpose of the *Guide* was to show that the teachings of the Torah and the teachings of philosophy were compatible. To do so Maimonides had to interpret the Torah at times in a non-literal way, particularly when it spoke of God in anthropomorphic terms. Though Maimonides himself did not write any commentaries on the Bible, his influence in fostering a philosophical approach to biblical exegesis was profound. It is clear, for example, in the writings of Qimhi.

So long as the philosophical approach meant, as in Qimhi or Ibn Ezra, a reliance on reason and intellect to discover the meaning of scripture, it was not necessarily in conflict with the plain sense, even when it insisted on treating scriptural language as metaphorical, or in finding in scripture the ethics of the philosophers. However, when commentators began to find allusions to the metaphysics of the philosophers in the Bible they often resorted to allegory. In a sense, though they were unaware of it, they were returning to a very much older style of philosophical commentary which had been perfected in the first century by Philo of Alexandria. The Provençal scholar Levi ben Gershon (1288–1344) was the most distinguished advocate of this style of philosophical Bible commentary. Though he retained a strong interest in the *peshat*, from time to time he falls into outright allegory as, for example, when he takes the two Cherubim that faced each other across the Ark of the Covenant (Exod. 25: 20) as symbolizing the Active and the Passive Intellect.

Allegory was even more widely and, indeed, indiscriminately used by the mystics. There had been a mystical tradition in Judaism at least from the second century CE which had been anchored in certain key texts in scripture, Ezekiel 1 (Ezekiel's vision of the Chariot of God), Genesis 1 (the Account of Creation), and the Song of Songs. Judaism, however, experienced a powerful upsurge of mysticism in the thirteenth century partly as a reaction to the rationalism of the philosophical movement. There were important schools of Jewish mystics in the Rhineland (the Hasidei Ashkenaz), in Spain and Provence (the Cabbalists), and in Egypt (the Jewish Sufis of the circle of Moses Maimonides' son Abraham). Like the philosophers these mystics used allegory to prove that their ideas were contained in Torah. The most important of the mystical commentaries is the Book of Splendour (the Zohar), which claims to be the discourses of the great second-century Palestinian rabbi Simeon bar Yohai, but is generally believed to have been composed at the end of the thirteenth century by the Spanish Cabbalist Moses de León. The Zohar, which systematically reads the mystical ideas of the Spanish Cabbala into the Pentateuch and the Five Scrolls, is an extreme example of mystical allegorizing. Cabbalistic interpretation also features, in a more sober and veiled fashion, in the important commentaries on the Pentateuch by the Spanish scholar Moses Nahmanides (1194–1270), together with much discussion of the plain and the homiletic senses. Nahmanides' standing as one of the great Jewish legalists of his day did much to make the Cabbala and mystical exegesis of Torah respectable.

By the thirteenth century it had become abundantly clear that a number of very different approaches to Torah had emerged. The need to classify these and to clarify their relationship to each other had become urgent. This was done most systematically by the Spanish commentator Bahya ben Asher (d. 1320). He distinguished four styles of exegesis: the way of *peshat* (the plain sense), the 'Way of Midrash', the 'Way of Intellect' (philosophy), and the 'Way of Cabbala' (mysticism). Bahya was, in effect, picking up on a fourfold classification of the senses of scripture earlier propounded in the Zohar under the mnemonic PARDES ('paradise'), in which p stands for *peshat*, d for *derash*, r for *remez* (allegory), and s for *sod* (mysticism). In keeping with the well-established rabbinic doctrine of the polysemy of the Torah, all the approaches were treated as valid: scripture has many senses and levels of meaning. However, as Bahya and the Zohar make clear, there is a hierarchical relationship between the senses, the mystical being the most profound and significant. The Pardes-schema was intended primarily to privilege mystical interpretation, but at the same time it could exercise restraint upon it. It was always possible to argue that the higher levels of meaning should be approached only through the lower, and, by invoking an ancient rabbinic dictum, that in the last analysis scripture can never depart from its plain sense, the wilder fantasies of mystical interpretation could, in principle, be curbed.

THE RENAISSANCE AND EARLY MODERN PERIOD

Two commentators, Isaac Abravanel (1437–1508) and Obadiah Sforno (1475–1550), can be taken as marking the transition to the post-medieval phase of Jewish Bible commentary. Though both at many points are indistinguishable from their medieval predecessors, both also manifest some rather new features. Abravanel, besides being a scholar, was a statesman and man of the world who successively held positions at the courts of Portugal, Castile, and Venice. His breadth of experience is everywhere evident in his commentaries, and is shown in his knowledge of Christian exegesis and in his willingness to accept Christian interpretations when they do not conflict with tradition. Instead of treating the text atomistically he tried to divide it into thematic sections and to expound the argument as a whole. And he revived the 'problematic' style of commentary, which, as we have seen, was first extensively employed by Philo. Sforno was something of a Renaissance man, with an excellent secular education which he drew on to good effect in his commentaries on the Torah. A physician by training and profession, he attempts from time to time to use contemporary science to throw light on scripture.

Abravanel and Sforno promised much, but they proved to be heralds of a false dawn, for their successors, for complex reasons, did little to develop their insights. Instead, the sixteenth to eighteenth centuries were dominated by a deadening spirit of conservatism in Jewish Bible exegesis. They saw the appearance of two large popular works, which deeply influenced the ordinary Jews' understanding of the Bible, but which are largely homiletic compilations of traditional materials. The first of these was the *Tze'enah u-Re'enah*, a Yiddish paraphrase, with numerous explanatory additions, of the weekly Torah readings and of the Five Scrolls. Compiled in the 1590s by the Polish scholar Jacob ben Isaac Ashkenazi, the work was supposedly intended for women (its title is derived from the exhortation to the 'daughters of Jerusalem' in Song of Songs 3: 11 to 'go forth and behold'), who did not have the benefit of a Hebrew education. It is likely, however, that it was widely read by men as well. Where the Yiddish-speaking Ashkenazi Jews of Germany and eastern Europe had the *Tze'enah u-Re'enah*, the Sefardis, descendants of the Jews expelled from Spain in 1492, had the *Me'am Lo'ez*. This great encyclopaedic Bible commentary in Ladino (Judaeo-Spanish), begun by Jacob Culi (*c.*1685–1732), is a miscellany of edifying texts drawn from the Mishnah, the Midrashim, the Talmud, the Zohar, and the medieval commentators, interlaced with anecdotes, legends, and folklore, all arranged so as to illuminate the biblical text. The first volume on Genesis was published in 1730, but the work took over 150 years to complete. Pitched at a higher educational level than the *Tze'enah u-Re'enah*, the *Me'am Lo'ez* is commonly regarded as a masterpiece of Ladino literature.

Also typical of the generally conservative, traditionalist attitude towards Bible commentary characteristic of the period were the voluminous biblical commentaries of the Sefardi Moses Alshekh (*c.*1507–1600), and of the Ashkenazis David Altschuler and his son Hillel—*the Fortress of Zion* (*Metzudat Tziyyon*) and the *Fortress of David* (*Metzudat David*) (both eighteenth century). There were, however, signs of that a radically new approach was emerging. The first glimmerings of this are to be found in the *Me'or 'Einayim* of the Italian scholar Azariah de Rossi (*c.*1511–1577). De Rossi, who had an excellent secular education and was something of a polymath, introduced for the first time a genuinely historical and critical spirit to the study of early Jewish literature. He made use of classical Greek and Latin writers, as well as of the Jewish literature of the Second Temple period, the Apocrypha, the pseudepigrapha, and the writings of Philo. He read widely in Christian patristic and medieval texts. He proved that the *Book of Josippon*, which Jewish scholars relied heavily upon for their knowledge of the Second Temple period, was a medieval composition, only loosely related to Josephus, and was far from historically reliable. He challenged the traditional Jewish chronology of the Persian period, and showed a pioneering interest in archaeology and numismatics. De Rossi was very circumspect in applying his new critical and historical method to the Bible, but it was only a matter of time before it would be extended to Holy Writ as well. The radical spirit of the *Me'or 'Einayim* was immediately recognized by the Jewish

The Portuguese Synagogue in Amsterdam, dedicated in 1675, two years before the death of Benedict Spinoza (1632–77).

religious authorities, who put it under a ban as soon as it was published. Over 200 years later, however, it was to have a considerable impact on the scholars of the Jewish Enlightenment.

The other harbinger of a new critical approach to the Bible was Baruch Spinoza (1632–77). Spinoza was brought up in the prosperous and, in some ways, intellectually radical, Sefardi Jewish community of Amsterdam, and may have studied with the most famous Amsterdam Jewish scholar of the day, Menasseh Ben Israel. One of the most uncompromisingly independent thinkers of western philosophy, Spinoza applied his general philosophical principles specifically to the study of the Bible in his *Tractatus Theologico-Politicus* (1670). He laid great stress on free and fearless enquiry, on recovering the historical origins of the biblical books, on determining when they were written, for whom and in what language, and on tracing how they were subsequently received and transmitted. He argued that Moses was responsible for only parts of the Pentateuch, but that most of this work was composed very much later, probably by Ezra. He suggested that the book of Psalms was compiled only in Second Temple times, and that the book of Daniel was not as early as it purports to be. Though Spinoza claimed, with some justification, that he was developing insights already adumbrated by medieval Jewish commentators such as Ibn Ezra (Ibn Ezra had suggested that Moses could not have written the whole of the Pentateuch, and detected the hands of two authors in the book of Isaiah), his rationalist approach to scripture alarmed both the Jewish and the Christian religious authorities. The Jewish community expelled him in 1656, and his works have remained under ban within Judaism ever since. Yet he was read by Jewish intellectuals and exerted considerable influence on some of the thinkers of the nineteenth-century Jewish Enlightenment.

FROM THE JEWISH ENLIGHTENMENT TO THE PRESENT DAY

The Jewish Enlightenment (the Haskalah), an offshoot of the eighteenth-century European Enlightenment, marks the next turning-point in the development of Jewish Bible exegesis, and, indeed, has effectively determined its course down to the present day. The Haskalah proclaimed the primacy of reason and opposed the restriction of traditional Jewish education to the Talmud, advocating instead that Jews should study secular subjects and generally integrate into the surrounding non-Jewish culture. Initially the movement was centred on the circle of Moses Mendelssohn (1729–86) in Berlin. Mendelssohn, himself one of the leading philosophers of the German Enlightenment, was a doughty defender of Judaism to the non-Jewish world of his day and argued tirelessly for the amelioration of the Jews' lot in society. At the same time he inaugurated an educational programme directed towards his co-religionists, the aim of which was to prepare them to take their place in non-Jewish society. The main instrument of this programme was a translation of the Hebrew Bible into German, accompanied by an extensive commentary known as the *Biur*. The *Biur*, a collaborative effort with Solomon Dubno, Naphtali Hirz Wessely, and many others, offered an interesting

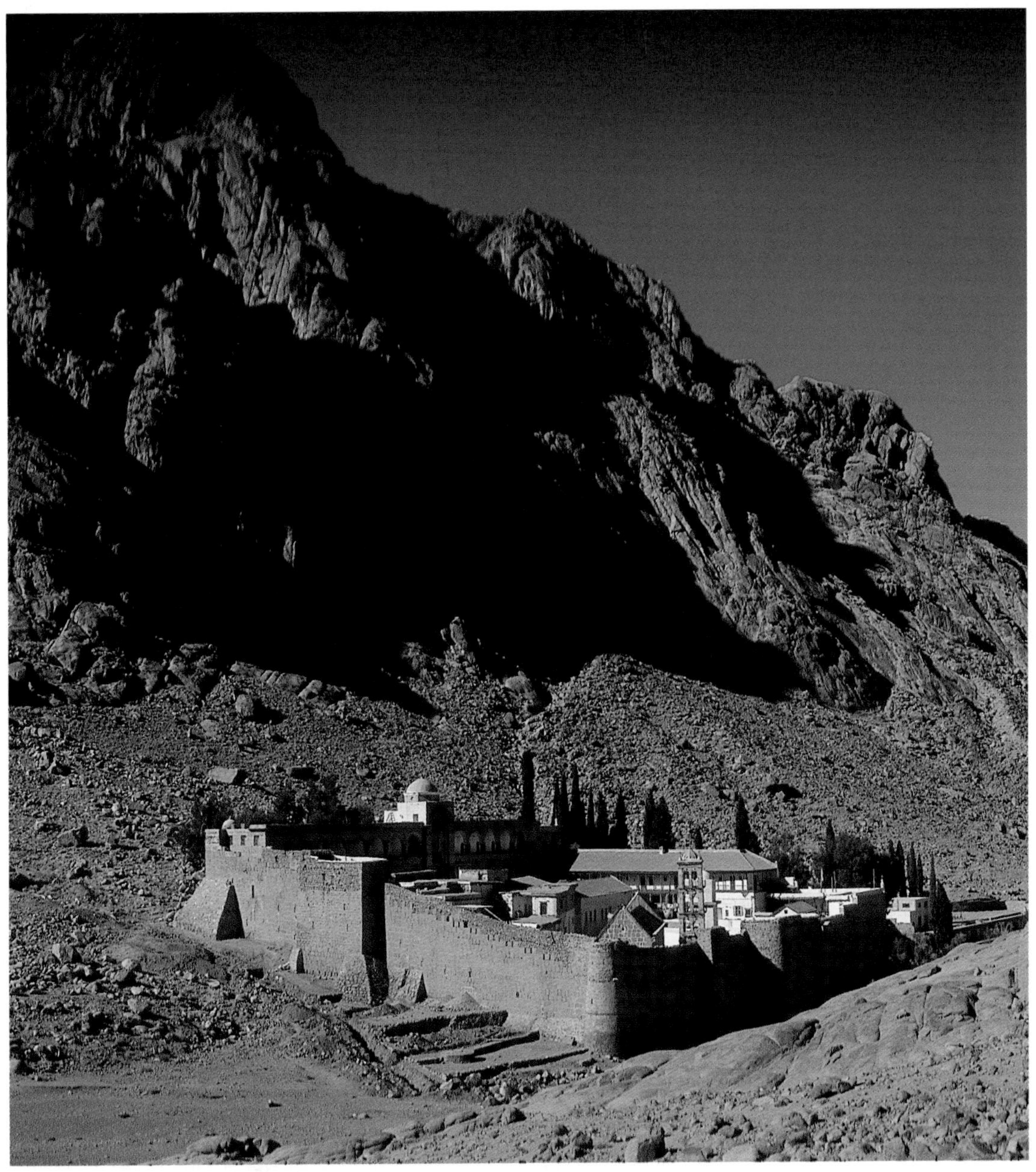

St Catherine's monastery on Mt Sinai. It was here that Constantin Tischendorf discovered the famous and important Greek Codex Sinaiticus in 1844.

The Resurrection of Christ, with the angels rolling away the stone from the sepulchre, by William Blake (1757–1827).

A close-up of a synagogue scroll of the Torah (Numbers 28: 15–22) with a silver pointer, known as a *yad* or hand, to avoid touching the scroll. The Hebrew is unpointed and the letters are embellished with small strokes (*taggin*).

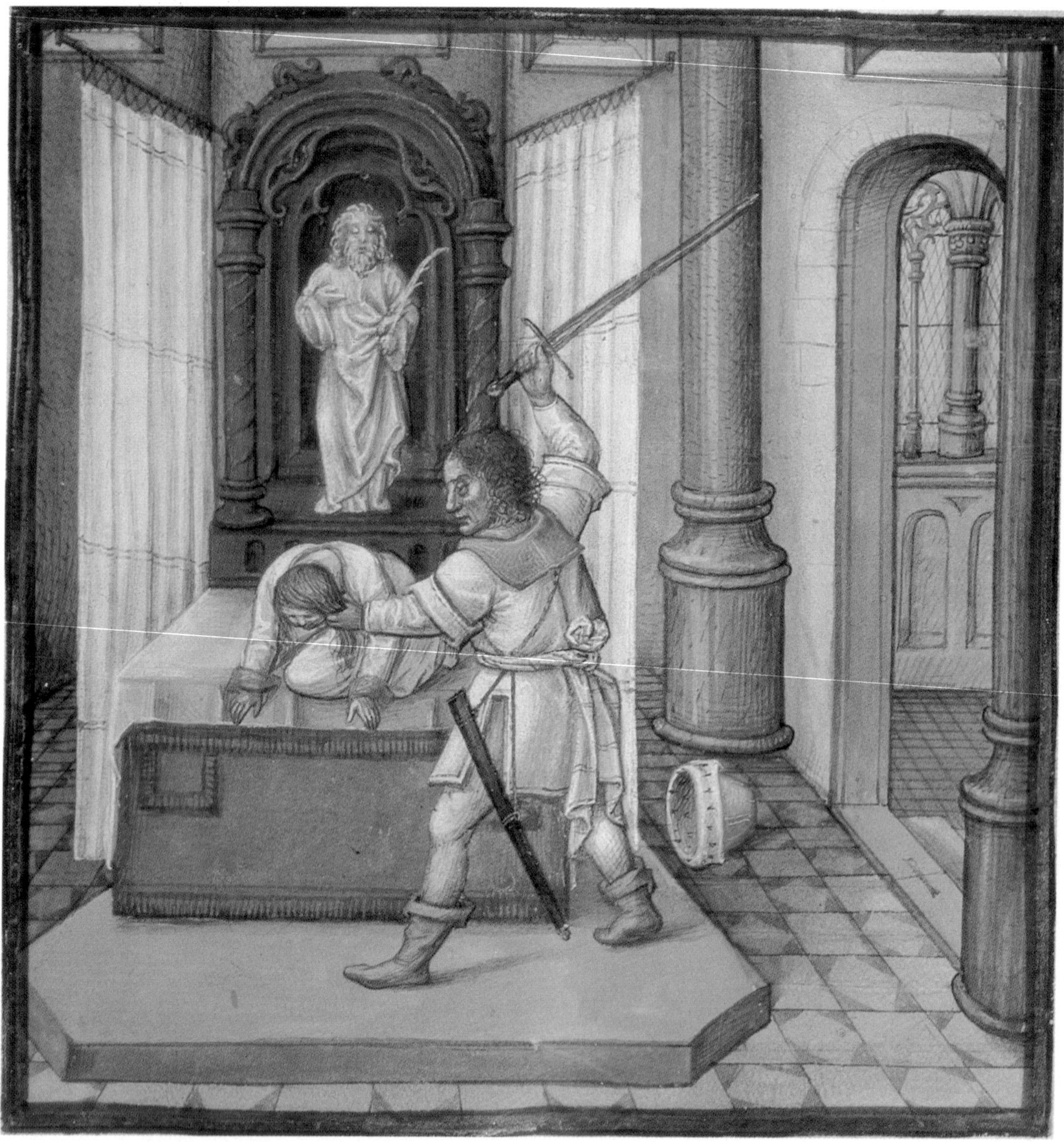

The Sacrifice of the Daughter of Jephthah (Flemish School, 15th century). Jephthah had vowed to sacrifice the first person he met on his return from battle if he was victorious (Judges 11). Later interpreters, including in Handel's oratorio *Jephtha*, gave the story a happier ending.

Virgin and Child, after Martin Schongauer (*c.*1430–91).

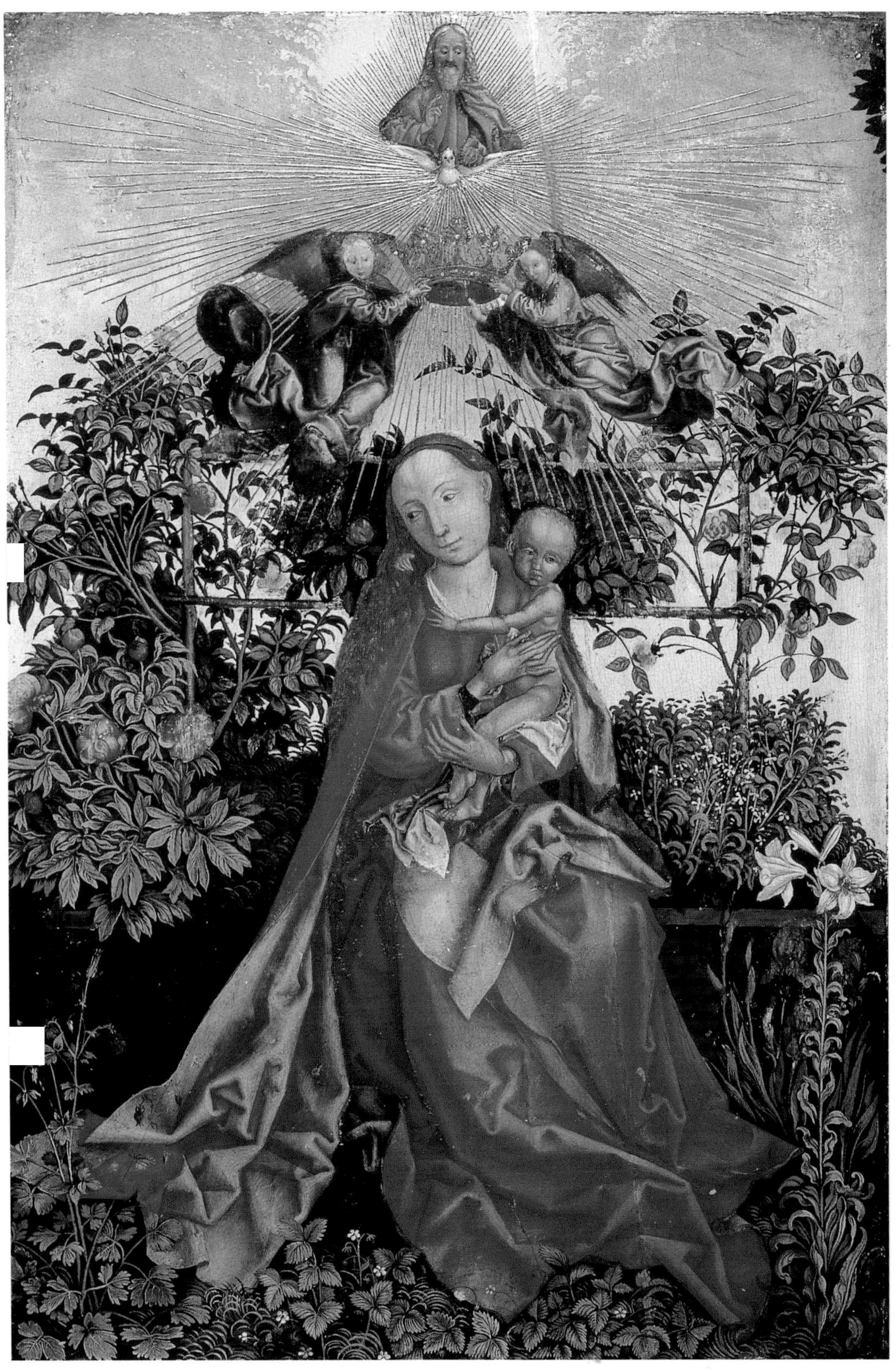

The Baptism of Christ. The anonymous mural in Santa Trinidad Cathedral, Haiti, reproduces not only local colour, but the traditional artistic view that Christ was baptised by the pouring of water on his head and not by total immersion.

Jesus walks on Water. A contemporary painting by Laura James.

The front cover of the 10th/11th-century Lindau Gospels, embellished with gold, jewels, enamel, and ivory.

blend of traditional Jewish Bible interpretation and the new biblical researches of Lowth, Herder, and Eichhorn. It stressed the aesthetic aspects of the Bible and constantly tried to show that the Bible's moral teachings conformed to the deepest insights of the Enlightenment. In retrospect the *Biur* now strikes the reader as relatively tame, but in its historical context it was truly revolutionary and aroused strong opposition from the rabbinic authorities of its day.

Encouraged by the teachings of Mendelssohn, a number of young German Jews began to attend the University of Berlin and to absorb the radical historical-critical methods of the classicist F. A. Wolff and others. A number of these young

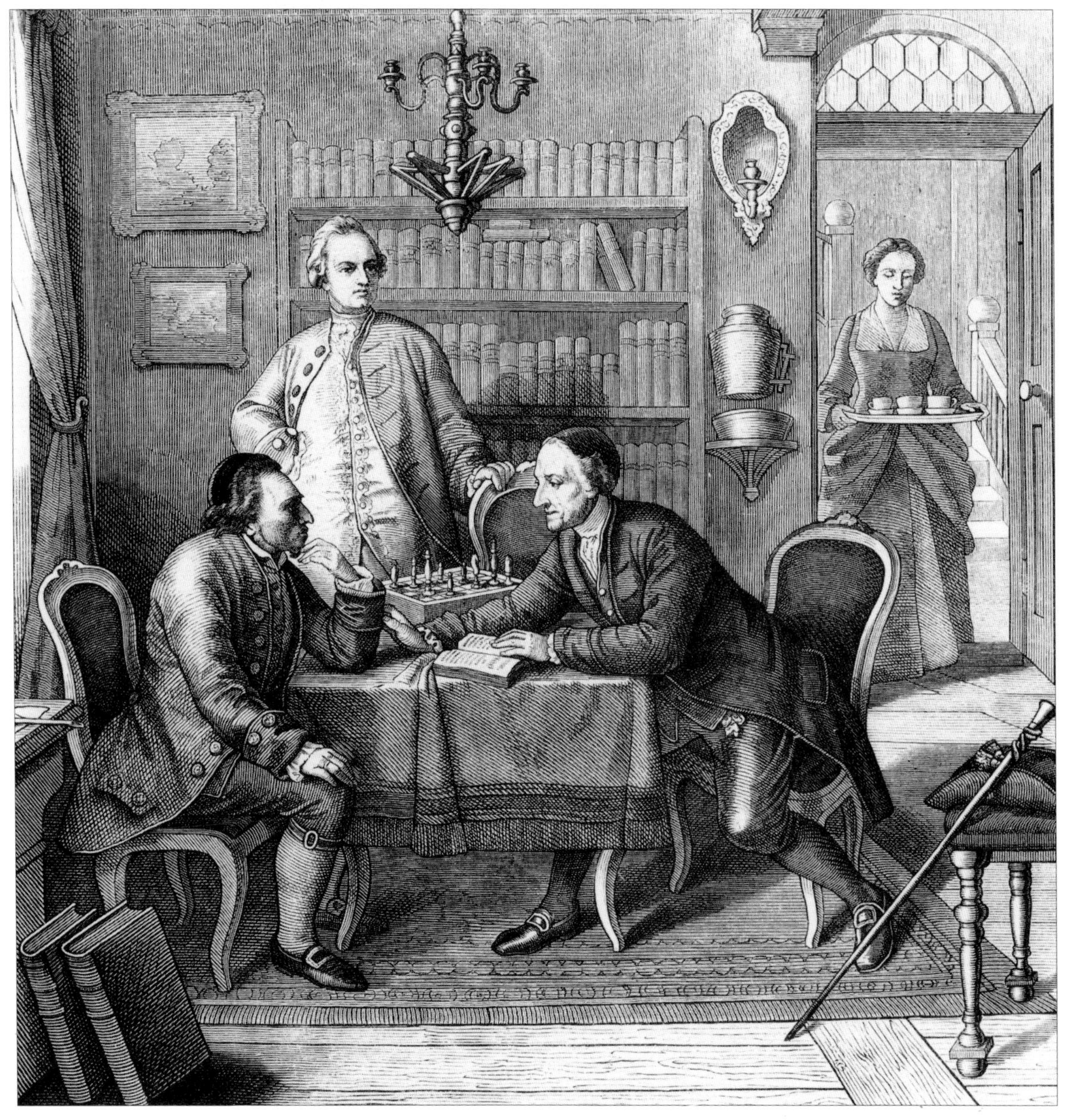

Moses Mendelssohn (1729–86), a leader of Jewish thought of the Enlightenment, in discussion with Gotthold Ephraim Lessing and Caspar Lavater.

Leopold Zunz (1794–1886), aged 70. Zunz was one of the founders, in 1819, of the movement known as the Science of Judaism.

scholars (prominent among whom were Leopold Zunz and Isaak Markus Jost) came together in Berlin in 1819 to found the Society for the Culture and Science of Judaism (*Verein fuer die Cultur und Wissenschaft der Juden*). The movement thus begun (often referred to as the Science of Judaism) for the first time applied a consistent critical and historical approach to ancient Jewish sources. Much of its effort was directed towards post-biblical Jewish literature, but it also made some notable contributions to the scientific study of the Hebrew Bible. Its leading biblical scholar was the Italian Samuel David Luzzatto (1800–65). Luzzatto in his Bible commentaries, like the *Biur*, offers a blend of traditional Jewish exegesis and modern scholarship. However, his modernism is much more thoroughgoing. He appeals to Semitic philology, uses the ancient versions, and is even prepared (cautiously) to emend the biblical text. Like the *Biur* he also shows sensitivity towards the literary and poetic aspects of the Bible.

The earlier Science of Judaism scholars, when they engaged with the Bible, tended to concentrate on text and philology, disciplines known at the time as 'lower criticism'. Significantly they showed little interest in the more religiously sensitive issues of 'higher criticism', such as the source analysis of the biblical documents, and when they did were inclined to take a conservative line (Luzzatto accepted the Mosaic authorship of the Pentateuch and the unity of the book of Isaiah). Higher criticism, however, in the end made its mark on Jewish biblical scholarship. This came about largely because of the increasing integration of the Jews into the modern intellectual world. But, curiously, the rise of Zionism also seems to have played a part. Higher criticism arose because scholars began to take history seriously: they did not simply accept the ancient accounts at face value but wanted to get behind them and find out what had really happened. Zionism involved a return of the Jews to history. It stimulated a strong interest in the biblical period, when Jews had enjoyed political and cultural independence in their ancient homeland. Zionism played down, and even denigrated, the achievements of rabbinic Judaism over the past 2,000 years, because they were seen as dominated essentially by an exilic mentality. The influence of higher criticism and of the new biblical research can be seen in the essays of the Zionist thinker Ahad ha-Am (Asher Ginzburg, 1856–1927), who called for the creation of a Jewish culture that was fully in keeping with the advances of modern scholarship and science. Abraham Kahana (1874–1946), was one of the first to work this programme out in terms of Bible commentary and to make the fruits of modern research accessible to Jewish readers. He inaugurated an extensive Hebrew-language commentary on the Bible written by himself and by scholars of the calibre of H. P. Chajes. S. Krauss, A. Kaminka, F. Perles, and M. L. Margolis. The commentary appeared between 1903 and 1930, and, though never completed, had covered much of the Hebrew Bible by the time it was discontinued.

From the 1930s onwards there has been a growing stream of Jewish commentaries on the Bible fully within the historical-critical tradition, and, although these may be distinguishable by their language (Hebrew), or their style (from time to time they may quote classic Jewish commentators and sources), in terms of their substance and general approach they are basically indistinguishable from the academic commentaries produced by non-Jewish scholars. Jewish academic study of the Bible seems at present to be following faithfully the twists and turns of biblical scholarship, on which it is exercising an increasing influence. It flourishes in two main centres: in Israel, where, hardly surprisingly, it tends to stress the archaeological and ancient Near Eastern context of the Hebrew Bible, and in the United States, where it tends to be more open to interdisciplinary cross-currents and to the changing fashions of scholarship within the academy.

Apart from liberal, highly academic institutions such as Hebrew Union College, Cincinnati and the Jewish Theological Seminary, New York, the critical and historical study of the Bible among Jews has effectively moved out of the religious sphere into academia. Perhaps even more than in the Christian world a gap has opened up between the religious and the academic study of the sacred texts. Scripture, however, continues to play its traditional central role in the religious life of the individual Jew and of the synagogue, but in these spheres a conservative and increasingly fundamentalist approach prevails. The emergence of the critical school in the nineteenth century did not go unchallenged. There were significant Orthodox commentators who argued fiercely against it. Two of these were Samson Raphael Hirsch (1808–88), the leading exponent of Neo-Orthodoxy, and Meir Leibush Malbim (1809–79), both of whom produced substantial and significant commentaries on parts of the Bible from a traditional perspective. Hirsch and the Malbim were men of great intellectual ability and independence, and their influence continues to be felt within Orthodoxy down to the present day, but within Orthodoxy the tide now seems inexorably to be running in the direction of fundamentalism.

This can be illustrated from the development of religious Bible commentary in the English-speaking world. Before the Second World War a typical (and influential) Bible commentary among English-speaking Orthodox Jews would have been *The Pentateuch and Haftorahs* (1929–36) edited by J. H. Hertz, then Chief Rabbi of the United Hebrew Congregations of the British Empire, in collaboration with a number of Anglo-Jewish scholars. Writing broadly within the tradition of Hirsch, Hertz proclaimed in his introduction to the work: 'Jewish and non-Jewish commentators—ancient, mediaeval and modern—have been freely drawn upon. "Accept the truth from whatever source it comes", is sound Rabbinic doctrine—even if it be from the pages of a devout Christian expositor or of an iconoclastic Bible scholar, Jewish or non-Jewish.' He accepted some of

זה השער ליי
צדיקים יבאו בו
מה טבו אהליך יעקב משכנותיך ישראל
נדבת
שמעון ומרים קוהנה
ה״ו

the findings of modern biblical scholarship and science, and although he rejected many others (including the documentary theory of the origins of the Pentateuch), he at least gave these views something of an airing and attempted to refute them by argument. After the Second World War the leading Jewish religious publisher in England, the Soncino Press, produced a new commentary on the Bible for Jewish readers. In the historical books, the Prophets, and the Writings this took modest account of biblical scholarship, though to nowhere near the same extent as Hertz had done in the Pentateuch, but in the Pentateuch it adopted the ultra-safe expedient of simply producing an anthology of the medieval commentators. This anthological approach seems to have become the norm in Orthodox Bible commentary. It is standard in the most popular of present-day religious commentaries, the Art Scroll Tanach Series of Mesorah Publications, New York. These commentaries, which are attractively produced, take absolutely no account of modern philological, historical, or critical study of the Bible, nor even of the more radical options of the great classic Jewish commentators, but offer the reader simply an extremely pious anthology of pre-modern and highly traditional exegesis.

Interior of a modern synagogue showing an open scroll of the Torah (Pentateuch) together with the pointer or *yad* (hand). In the background a second scroll of the Torah dressed in its mantle standing in the Holy Ark.

14 The Bible in Literature

DAVID JASPER

The books of the Bible, from Genesis to Revelation, are undoubtedly the single greatest influence on the development of English literature, and the reasons are twofold. First, the traditions and stories of the Bible are constituted within a body of narratives and images that have a unique authority within both the Jewish and the Christian traditions, sustained in doctrine and culture. Secondly, translations of the Bible into English from the sixteenth century with the work of scholars like William Tyndale and Miles Coverdale and culminating in the great King James Version of 1611 bequeathed to literature a wealth of phrase and image which persists in our common culture to this day. Phrases like 'the root of the matter' (Job 19: 28), 'lick the dust' (Ps. 72: 9) are now so much part of everyday language that their biblical origins are all but forgotten.

Although it is always dangerous to refer to the Bible *as* literature, much of both the Old and New Testaments is, in both Hebrew and Greek originals, literature of the highest quality, and quite self-consciously so. Genesis contains stories and narratives which have inspired in their turn some of the greatest works in Western literature, notably in modern times Søren Kierkegaard's *Fear and Trembling* (1843), from Genesis 22, and Thomas Mann's tetralogy *Joseph and his Brothers* (1933–43). Job ranks with the works of Aeschylus and Shakespeare as a foundational example of tragic literature; the Song of Songs has had some influence on almost all of the great love poetry of the West after the classical period. In the four gospels, the great parables of St Luke and the accounts of the Passion alone are literary masterpieces apart from their importance within a sacred tradition. Yet the distinction should be borne in mind as the place of the Bible *in* literature is both a literary and a religious phenomenon, one Christian critic, T. S. Eliot, going so far as to suggest that 'the Bible has had a *literary* influence upon English literature *not* because it has been considered as literature, but because it has been considered as the report of the Word of God'. Considered as, in the words of the translators of the Authorized Version, 'a fountain of most pure water springing up into everlasting life', the resonances of its narratives and poetics adorn a dramatic shape and struggle between God and his people which lie at the very heart of our greatest literature, so that William Blake (1757–1827) can affirm, categorically, that 'the Old and New Testaments are the Great Code of Art'. In the Middle Ages a poet was called a 'Maker', from the Greek word *poiesis* ('a making'), such that Samuel Taylor Coleridge (1772–1834) famously described the 'primary imagination' as 'a repetition in the finite mind of the eternal act of creation in the infinite I AM', referring back directly to the voice of God from the burning bush in Exodus 3, and Jesus' claim in John 8: 58, 'Before Abraham was, I am'. The poet, then, is most profoundly 'godlike', and at the same time the most heinous of blasphemers—a paradox which characterizes the inextricable relationship between the Bible and literature, seen

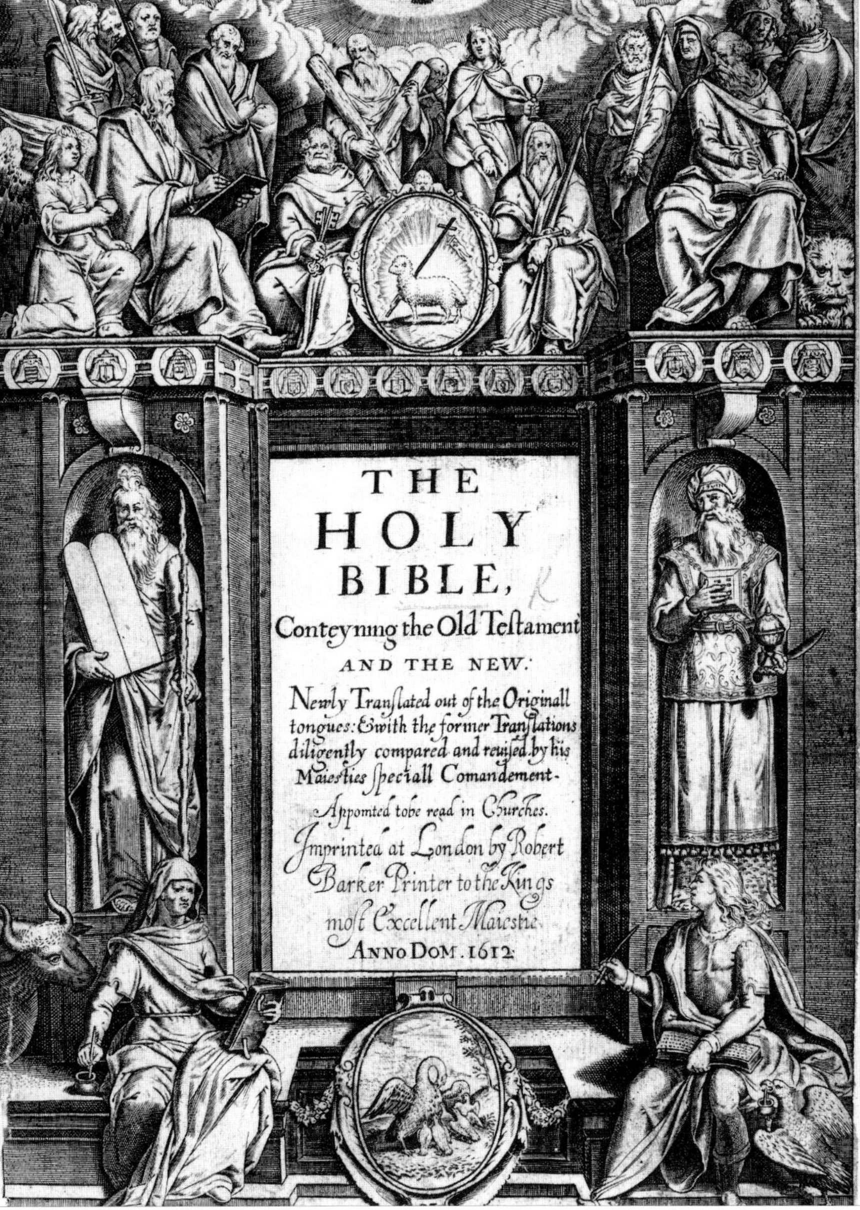

THE HOLY BIBLE,
Conteyning the Old Teſtament
AND THE NEW:
Newly Tranſlated out of the Originall tongues: & with the former Tranſlations diligently compared and reuiſed, by his Maieſties ſpeciall Comandement.
Appointed to be read in Churches.
Imprinted at London by Robert Barker, Printer to the Kings moſt Excellent Maieſtie.
ANNO DOM. 1612.

The title page of Robert Barker's edition of the King James or Authorized Version of the Bible of 1611, bearing the date 1612. This version was never, apparently, actually 'authorized' and had to compete with the Geneva Bible until 1660.

variously as the Bible *as* literature, the Bible *in* literature, and, most disturbing of all, literature *as* 'Bible'. It explains also the profound insight of Blake in *The Marriage of Heaven and Hell* (*c.*1790): 'The reason Milton wrote in fetters when he wrote of Angels & God, and at liberty when of Devils & Hell, is because he was a true Poet and of the Devil's party without knowing it.' Since Milton's fellow poet Andrew Marvell (1621–78) expressed his fear of the 'ruin of sacred truths' in *Paradise Lost* (1667), critics from Dr Samuel Johnson in the eighteenth century to David Daiches in our own time have edgily acknowledged the dangerous creativity of Milton's 'rewriting' of the Genesis story. The Christian tradition has always needed, and, like Plato in his *Republic*, always feared the poets and artists.

The earliest great 'Christian' poem in English, the eighth-century *Dream of the Rood*, has a remarkable history, its earliest evidences being divided between fragments engraved on a stone cross in Ruthwell in Dumfriesshire and a complete version in the *Codice Vercellae* of the ninth century now in Vercelli in Italy on the pilgrim route to Rome. Deeply rooted in the liturgical rehearsals of the Passion narratives, the poem's literary form draws upon pagan poetic traditions of the riddle and late Latin examples of prosopopeia (the endowment of inanimate objects with speech). In the *Dream of the Rood* the cross itself speaks of its experience of Christ's sufferings and death, drawing widely upon the biblical references within the liturgy of Holy Week, from Psalm 35: 1–2 ('Plead my cause, O Lord, with them that strive with me') to Galatians 6: 14 ('But God forbid that I should glory, save in the cross of our Lord Jesus Christ') and Philippians 2: 8 ('and became obedient unto death, even the death of the cross').

Medieval English literature is saturated with biblical allusions, from extended meditations like *Patience* (*c.*1360), which draws particularly on the Beatitudes (Matthew 5: 3–11) and the story of Jonah, to religious lyrics and 'macaronic' verse (poems in two or more languages, usually Latin and English, as in the great 'In the vale of restless mind', with its Latin refrain from the Song of Songs), and William Langland's dream poem *Piers Plowman* (*c.*1380). But it is Geoffrey Chaucer, especially in *The Canterbury Tales* (*c.*1387) who engages with scripture most imaginatively. Thus, for example, 'The Parson's Tale' is a learned instance of a medieval sermon drawn from biblical texts, while the Prologue to 'The Wife of Bath's Tale' begins with a lengthy reflection on John 4, Jesus' meeting with the Samaritan woman at the well, turning it to the advantage of the Wife of Bath, herself often married, as she questions the words of Jesus:

> 'Thou hast yhad five housbondes,' quod he,
> 'And that ilke man that now hath thee
> Is noght thyn housbonde,' thus seyde he certeyn.
> What that he mente therby, I kan nat seyn.

But perhaps the most significant and sustained example of literary intertextuality with the Bible in medieval English literature is to be found in the great cycles of the mystery plays which, quite literally, enacted the whole drama of the biblical narrative from the creation in Genesis to the end of all things in the Apocalypse.

The only surviving illustration from Tyndale's first, fragmentary, New Testament of 1525. An angel provides the evangelist (probably Matthew) with a bottle of ink.

Like the *Dream of the Rood*, these plays are rooted in the church's liturgy, beginning probably as far back as the tenth century with the so-called *Quem quaeritis* within the Easter liturgy as a dramatization of the moment in Luke 24: 5, when the two men in shining garments ask the women at the tomb, 'Why seek ye the living among the dead?' From these simple beginnings, drama moved from the church building into the market place and developed into the great 'cycles' which began with the story of Adam and Eve and focused particularly on the events of the gospels. The most developed of all these plays are the pageants of the so-called Wakefield Group in the Towneley Cycle, probably dating from the first half of the fifteenth century, and the most famous of them is the *Secunda Pastorum* (*The Second Shepherds' Play*), in which the nativity story is brilliantly counterpointed with the pantomime of Mak the sheep stealer and his wife Gyll in a parody of the Bethlehem stable, as Gyll hides the stolen lamb in a cradle and pretends to have just given birth.

These biblical dramas died out, for various reasons, by the later sixteenth century, and though essentially folk drama, they have certain literary affinities with the great early translations of the Bible into English, above all by William Tyndale (*c.*1494–1536), who rendered the New Testament into English in 1534 directly from the Greek, to release the common reader from 'the popish doctors of dunce's dark learning, which with their sophistry, served us, as the Pharisees did the Jews'. Tyndale combined learning with an earthy command of English and is by far the single greatest source for the great King James Version of the Bible of 1611 which, despite its inital lack of popularity, is probably the one most influential piece of *literature* in the English language. In the words of Robert Carroll and Stephen Prickett, its most recent editors:

> The translators' willingness to allow ambiguity of meaning and, at the verbal level, their minute attention to the music of its words, phrases, and even cadences, meant not merely that the biblical texts were given a new (and arguably quite spurious) unity, but also that the English language received a new stylistic model.

Yet it must be borne in mind that the King James Version was not the Bible of Spenser, Shakespeare, or John Donne, and that the sixteenth century saw an energetic battle between different English versions of the Bible. By far the most popular version was the Geneva Bible of 1560, often known as the 'Breeches Bible' (from its rendering of Genesis 3: 7, 'they [Adam and Eve] ... made themselves *breeches*'). This version was the work of English Protestant exiles in Geneva and drew heavily on Tyndale, as well as Calvin himself and various French Bibles. Although never formally authorized, its popularity was largely due to its publication in a cheap edition rather than as an expensive folio, and it was the first English Bible to be divided into chapters and verses. But its literary importance was ensured because it was clearly the Bible of Shakespeare. Later, many of its particular renderings were incorporated into the King James Version.

Against this popular tradition set by Tyndale and the Puritan Miles Coverdale (chiefly remembered for his translation of the Psalms) were opposed those like

Bishop Stephen Gardner of Winchester (*c.*1490–1555), who insisted on a more Latinate English closer to the form of the Vulgate Bible. The debate was both theological and literary, for the failure of the attempt to make the English Bible Latinate and ecclesiastical profoundly affected the course of English literature and even language, and it was Shakespeare, above all, who turned the vitality of 'biblical' English into the greatest of literature. Pre-eminently, perhaps, the figure of Falstaff emerges from and dies into the language of the Bible; for his defence of being a highwayman—'Why, Hal, 'tis no sin for a man to labour in his vocation'—draws with splendid irony upon St Paul's exhortation to the Christian community in 1 Corinthians, while in his death in *Henry V*, Falstaff is eulogized by Mistress Quickly as the figure of Lazarus reclining in 'Abraham's' bosom (Luke 16; 23; though she changes this to 'Arthur's' bosom), and dying he repeats snatches from Miles Coverdale's version of Psalm 23.

Throughout his work, Shakespeare echoes the phrases and rhythms of the English Bible, often in counterpoint, particularly in the tragedies. So, for example, we find in *Antony and Cleopatra* repeated use of Revelation, from the description of Cleopatra as the great harlot of Revelation 17, to Antony as a 'fallen star', after the star named Wormwood in Revelation 8: 10–11. But, above all, throughout the play there is a counterpointing with Revelation 21–2, as Antony begins by styling his obsession with Cleopatra as a 'new heaven' (Rev. 21: 1), and Cleopatra herself dies with the words, 'Husband, I come' (Rev. 22: 20).

On more than one occasion, Samuel Taylor Coleridge, one of the greatest Shakespearian critics as well as himself a poet, compares Shakespeare's language with that of the Bible, and specifically its capacity to entertain ambiguity and sustain mystery with such precision. 'In the Scriptures themselves', Coleridge remarks, 'these plays upon words are to be found as well as in the best works of the ancients and in the most delightful parts of Shakespeare.' No less significant, but of quite a different character, Coleridge maintains, is John Milton's relationship with the Bible:

> Many Scriptural poems [suggests Coleridge] have been written with so much of Scripture in them that what is not Scripture appears to be not true, and like mingling lies with the most sacred revelations. Now Milton, on the other hand, has taken for his subject that one point of Scripture of which we have the mere fact recorded, and upon this he has most judiciously constructed his whole fable.

In other words, *Paradise Lost* stands as an epic poem independently of Genesis 3, the poet legitimately building upon one brief but theologically crucial episode in the Bible to fulfil a particular purpose, that is, in Milton's own words, 'to justify the ways of God to men' (*Paradise Lost*, book I, line 26). The poem, therefore, is a theodicy designed, as Dr Samuel Johnson in the eighteenth century put it, 'to shew the reasonableness of religion, and the necessity of obedience to the Divine Law'. Unlike Shakespeare, Milton is self-consciously scholarly and theological in his use of the Bible, his English style elaborately Latinate. Thus, the first 25 lines of *Paradise Lost* are a patchwork of biblical allusion and theological reflection, mixed also with classical and Renaissance learning from Hesiod and Ariosto, in the epic style. Herein lies the continuity between Milton and the earliest days of English religious poetry based on the Bible and biblical themes, a continuity grounded in the intermingling of Christian, biblical, classical, and pagan reference and literary form, and nowhere is this more acutely and creatively evident than in the writing and art of the most 'biblical' of all English poets, William Blake.

Blake saw himself as nothing less than a reincarnation of Milton, and his poetic inclination was similarly towards the epic. In his manuscript epic 'Vala' or 'The Four Zoas' (*c.*1795–1808), Blake mingles a 'pagan' mythical language with a deeply Christian and biblical poetics in which the Crucifixion lies at the heart of history as both cosmic and apocalyptic. Blake is perhaps the most 'scriptural' of all English poets, even more than Milton writing poetry which is deeply continuous with the Bible yet profoundly contrary to traditions of biblical interpretation in an agreement of opposites that proposes a dialectical identity of heaven and

'Pandemonium' from the illustrations by John Martin (1789–1854) to Milton's *Paradise Lost*.

hell and 'a vision of a kenotic movement in the Godhead leading to the redemption of a cosmic humanity'. In his late poem 'The Everlasting Gospel' (*c*.1818), Blake identifies the High Priest Caiaphas with the bishops and hierarchy of the Church, suggesting that

> ... Caiaphas was in his own Mind
> A benefactor to Mankind:
> Both read the Bible day & night,
> But thou read'st black where I read white.

The most important books of the Bible for Blake are Ezekiel and Revelation, both apocalyptic texts, and his epic vision celebrates a kenosis, or self-emptying of the Divine (see Phil. 2: 8), and the cross as a manifestation of an utterly alienated God.

> For the Divine Lamb, Even Jesus who is the Divine Vision,
> Permitted all, lest Man should fall into Eternal Death;
> For when Luvah sunk down, himself put on the robes of blood
> Lest the state call'd Luvah should cease; & the Divine Vision
> Walked in robes of blood till he who slept should awake.
> ('Vala', or 'The Four Zoas', 2nd Night, lines 261–5)

Though formally uneducated, Blake was clearly well aware of some of the most significant movements in biblical criticism in the eighteenth century, not least the revolutionary 'discovery' of biblical poetics by Bishop Robert Lowth (1710–87), so that, in John Drury's words, 'biblical criticism here enables biblical creativity, and in the mind of a poet who understands ... the structure of the canonical books and will not "resist his genius", the bounds of the canon are splendidly broken.'

Strangely, perhaps, the closest to Blake of eighteenth-century poets is the nonconformist hymn-writer Isaac Watts (1674–1748), in his sense of biblical dialectic, supremely in his poem 'Crucifixion to the World by the Cross of Christ', a meditation on Galatians 6: 14, still sung in churches today as the Passiontide hymn 'When I survey the wondrous cross', although the crucial verse (which Blake would have loved) is invariably omitted from hymn books:

> His dying crimson like a robe
> Spreads o'er his body on the Tree,
> Then am I dead to all the globe,
> And all the globe is dead to me.

Here Christ's blood becomes his regal garment, his death becomes our death to wordly things, and his death (as in John 19: 30) becomes his moment of victory.

In Blake, as throughout Romanticism in both England and Germany, a new mythological approach to the Bible combined with a new understanding of history to promote a sense of the need for a modern mythology and an appropriation of the Bible into literature even as biblical criticism, as an academic pursuit, was isolating the biblical texts from the rest of 'secular' literature. Not only were biblical narratives and the 'design of biblical history' finding their way into the developing genre of the novel, but the ancient interpretative practice, present in the Bible itself, of typology was reinstated in nineteenth-century literature, thereby profoundly affecting the secular culture of the Victorian age. Thus, Charlotte Brontë's *Jane Eyre* (1847) is a pre-eminent example of what Thomas Carlyle (1795–1881) called 'natural supernaturalism', an appropriation of the biblical drama of fall and redemption ending in a rediscovered 'Eden', and the work of one who, as a daughter of the vicarage, was constantly exposed to the reading of

William Blake's *The Book of Urizen* (1794). Blake's illustrations drew biblical imagery into his own poetry.

the Bible through the liturgical year. In addition Brontë was powerfully influenced by the biblicism of John Bunyan's great allegory *The Pilgrim's Progress* (1678, 1684), whose status in the nineteenth century was almost that of the Bible itself.

For the Victorians, one biblical passage stands out as a typological image ubiquitously present in literature. It is Deuteronomy 34: 1–4, the brief account of Moses' view of the Promised Land from the summit of Mount Pisgah as he dies seeing the goal of his journeying but finally denied access into Canaan: 'And the Lord said unto him, This is the land which I sware unto Abraham, unto Isaac, and unto Jacob, saying, I will give it unto thy seed: I have caused thee to see it with thine eyes, but thou shalt not go over thither' (Deuteronomy 34: 4). In Charles Kingsley's novel of the working classes, *Alton Locke* (1850), the Promised Land becomes America as the hero emigrates from the miseries of Europe, only to die of consumption on the voyage across the Atlantic:

> Yes! I have seen the land! Like a purple fringe upon the golden sea, 'while parting day dies like the dolphin', there it lay upon the far horizon—the great young free new world! and every tree, and flower, and insect on it new!—a wonder and a joy—which I shall never see ... No,—I shall never reach the land.

Elsewhere in prose, in a passage which he planned to use in the second volume of *Modern Painters* (1846), John Ruskin contemplates the beauty of the Alps between Chamouni and Les Tines as a kind of metaphorical Pisgah granting a glimpse of eternity: 'And then I learned—what till then I had not known—the real meaning of the word Beautiful.' Ruskin here draws upon not only the Bible, but after it, Milton's use of the Pisgah experience in the last two books of *Paradise Lost*, innumerable nonconformist and evangelical hymns such as Isaac Watts's 'A Prospect of Heaven makes Death easy' ('There is a land of pure delight'), and finally the poetry of Wordsworth and Coleridge.

Among Victorian poets, Tennyson uses the Pisgah sight to describe the death of King Arthur at the end of *The Idylls of the King* (1842), Swinburne returns to it in his poem 'Evening on the Broads' (1880), but perhaps most interesting is Matthew Arnold's use of it in *Empedocles on Etna* (1852). For Arnold's Empedocles is a latter-day Moses, or rather his Victorian antithesis, for he receives no vision of the future and for him there is no Promised Land but only death without consolation. The ironic echoes of Deuteronomy 34 in *Empedocles* flow from the pen of the Arnold of 'Dover Beach' (1867) for whom the 'sea of faith' has finally withdrawn. But there is another side to Arnold, evidenced in his later studies of biblical interpretation, *St. Paul and Protestantism* (1870), *Literature and Dogma* (1873), and *God and the Bible* (1875). In *Literature and Dogma* Arnold attempts to recover the Bible as work of literature, its terms to be understood as poetry and as a magnificent achievement within the corpus of 'World literature' (a phrase taken from Goethe's term *Weltliteratur*) alongside Aeschylus, Sophocles, Dante, and Shakespeare. In chapter 1, Arnold suggests that theologians have claimed a *scientific* precision for words like 'grace', 'new birth', and 'justification' which, to St Paul, were *literary* terms, and he insists that in the Bible there is 'a sense of the

James Joyce (1935) by Jacques-Emile Blanche. Joyce's *Finnegans Wake* (1939) was described by Thomas Altizer as 'the culmination of our Western literature ... a culmination that is ending or apocalypse itself'.

inadequacy of language in conveying man's ideas of God, which contrasts strongly with the licence of affirmation in Western theology'. Arnold, then, returns to the Bible and to poetry as an escape from the hard-edged 'science' of the nineteenth century, a soft-focus Bible with its tentative 'language *thrown out* at an object of consciousness not fully grasped, which inspired emotion'. Here, clearly, a particular understanding of the nature of poetic language has a profound effect upon Arnold's understanding of the nature of theology itself.

In stark contrast to Arnold, the language and poetics of early twentieth-century modernism are sharp and precise in their interactions with the Bible. If the novelist D. H. Lawrence (1885–1930) continues the traditions of Victorian fiction in, for example, the Edenic themes and imagery of *Lady Chatterley's Lover* (1928), a year earlier a poem by T. S. Eliot (1888–1965), 'Journey of the Magi', is a crisp intertext with Matthew 2, its images as hard and penetrating as the coldness which they describe. But by the far the greatest 'biblical' epic in the first half of the twentieth century, greater even than Thomas Mann's Joseph tetralogy, is James Joyce's *Finnegans Wake* (1939), described by Thomas Altizer as 'the culmination of our Western literature ... a culmination that is ending or apocalypse itself.' The *Wake* embodies a liturgical action which is centred on the Eucharist, in writing and text, re-enacting the biblical narrative from Genesis to Revelation in a manner not achieved even by Blake, Joyce's poetic predecessor. It opens in Dublin, which is Eden, 'riverrun, past Eve and Adam's, from swerve of shore to bend of bay', in a final triumph of Romanticism's mythological aspirations. On the first page, in which 'bland old isaac' rubs shoulders with Sir Tristram, is suffered a fall 'of a once wallstrait oldparr is retaled early in bed and later on life down through all christian minstrelsy'.

Though deeply Catholic, even as the Geneva Bible and the King James Version are deeply Protestant, Joyce's remarkable, intricate and punning language is actually within the tradition of English of Chaucer, the English Bibles of the sixteenth century, and Shakespeare, with its ease of punning, its entertaining of ambiguity, and its sharp refusal of definition. Its last lines, with their themes of adoration and 'coming' relate to the visionary last two chapters of Revelation.

> Yes. Carry me along, taddy, like you done through the toy fair. If I seen him bearing down on me now under whitespread wings like he'd come from Arkangels, I sink I'd die down over his feet, humbly dumbly, only to washup. Yes, tid. There's where. First. We pass through grass behush the bush to. Whish! A gull. Gulls. Far calls. Coming, far! End here. Us then. Finn again! Take. Bussoftlhee, mememoree! Till thousendsthee. Lps. The keys to. Given! A way a lone a last a loved a long the

In this end there is a beginning, for the end of this last sentence is the first sentence of the whole book, but as in Revelation 21, it is a creation made anew.

Twentieth-century fiction has remained fascinated with the Bible, though usually far more pedantically than in Joyce's work. In the second half of the twentieth century, encouraged no doubt by cinema's fascination with the stories of the Bible, there has been a flourishing sub-genre in fiction which retells biblical narrative. One of the more successful books by English novelists in recent years is Howard Jacobson's *The Very Model of a Man* (1992), a complex, post-modern revisiting of the story of Cain with satirical leanings which are not always under control. Feminist writers have repeatedly taken up the legends of Mary Magdalene, a figure compiled from a variety of gospel references to different women, though of these only Carolyn Slaughter's *Magdalene* (1978) and Michèle Roberts's *The Wild Girl* (1984) can claim to be serious literature. In a note at the beginning of her novel, Roberts reflects:

> Medieval and later tradition in art, hagiography, legends, poems and plays collapses the figure of Mary Magdalene, briefly mentioned in the Gospels, into that of Mary of Bethany, the sister of Martha and Lazarus, and also into that of the sinful woman who anoints Christ. Although many modern scholars distinguish separate figures in the gospel accounts, I have chosen to follow the tradition of centuries, the spinning of stories around a composite character.

The Nuptials of God (1922) by Eric Gill (1882–1940). Mary Magdalene is the curving female form pressing against Christ, who is covered by the waves of her hair flowing to the ground.

Although her claims are, to an extent, scholarly—she refers, for example, to her use of the Nag Hammadi gospels—Roberts is following an ancient synchretistic tradition in literature which is present even in the Bible itself. Thus she claims in *The Wild Girl* 'to imagine another long-lost gospel retrieved from its burial place'. Biblical scholarship, on the other hand, has tended, at least in more recent centuries, to be dissective, separating out different strands entangled in the biblical texts and their traditions in the interests of historical precision and careful thought. Nowhere has this literary/theological tension been more acutely felt then in the long list of novels, dating well back into the nineteenth century, which explore, in one way or another, the 'life of Christ'. These may refer to the gospel narratives directly or indirectly, and critical reaction to the best of them has tended to be a confused mixture of literary appreciation and religious confusion or outright disapproval. Critics, even in the twentieth century, have, it seems, never quite overcome Marvell's fear of the 'ruin of sacred truths', or else feel uncomfortable at the intrusion of the gospel story into fictional narrative. Thus, for example, criticism has remained divided over William Faulkner's Pulitzer Prize-winning *A Fable*

(1954), an extended parable of Christ's Passion set within the First World War, while the recent film by Martin Scorsese has ensured both the notoriety as well as the place within literature of Nikos Kazantzakis's *The Last Temptation* (*O Teleftaios Peirasmos*, 1959), described by Peter Bien, its translator, as 'the summation of the thought and experience of a man whose entire life was spent in the battle between spirit and flesh'.

Still from Scorsese's film *The Last Temptation of Christ*, with Willem Dafoe as Jesus.

In this brief chapter it has not been possible to be inclusive, but only to refer briefly to some of the major instances in English literature of the Bible *in* literature. Almost no mention has been made of literature outside the English tradition. Little has been said of modern poetry. Perhaps here mention should be made of Geoffrey Hill and particularly his collection *For the Unfallen: Poems 1952–1958* (1959) in which 'Canticle for Good Friday' stands out as a remarkable meditiation on the cross from the perspective of Doubting Thomas. Neither has anything been said, except fleetingly, of the Bible in postmodern fiction, plays, and poetry.

The intention has rather been to provide a generous overview of the subject from the earliest times in English literature. For more detail, by far the best (and essentially the *only*) reference book is David Lyle Jeffrey's *A Dictionary of Biblical Tradition in English Literature* (1992). Useful also is the two-volume anthology of poetry based upon specific passages of the Bible from Genesis to Revelation, *Chapters into Verse* (1993), edited by Robert Atwan and Laurance Wieder. Finally, *The Bible and Literature* by David Jasper and Stephen Prickett (1999) is an annotated collection of literary passages based on selected biblical readings, with detailed introductory essays and bibliographies.

CONTEMPORARY INTERPRETATION

Preface

JOHN ROGERSON

An Oxford don once related the advice that he had been given in the late 1930s when he was looking for a research topic in Old Testament studies. The advice was to learn Hittite. The potential for research in the Old Testament had been exhausted, it was thought, and new discoveries were only likely to come from the study of surrounding cultures.

It is easy to be critical of such an attitude, and to forget that academic disciplines go through periods of both apparent stagnation, when prospects of progress seem slight, and of vibrant creativity when scholars almost fall over themselves to get onto a bandwagon that seems to offer unlimited possibilities. The late 1930s stood unknowingly on the threshold of the discovery of the Dead Sea Scrolls. Similarly, the early 1960s stood unknowingly on the threshold of the advent of methodologies such as structuralism, deconstruction, feminist criticism, and liberation theology.

There is no doubt that the past 30 years have witnessed one of the most exciting and creative periods in the whole history of biblical interpretation. One of the features of this period has been that biblical interpretation has become less dominated by the interests of 'professionals'. All of the scholars whose work is described in the chapters on the study and use of the Bible were professionals in the sense that they were experts in one or more of the many fields that are associated with the study of the Bible: scribes, copyists, linguists, textual critics, exegetes, translators, historians, printers. This ought to be reassuring. The study of the Bible, if it is to be done with the utmost seriousness, requires training in a number of disciplines whose mastery can take many years. However, the need for expertise also created a situation in which biblical interpretation became the province of a guild whose legitimate concerns were understandably narrowly conceived. The needs and interests of 'ordinary people' were neither disdained nor overlooked by professional biblical scholars, as many popular commentaries and other works on the Bible by them indicate; but the 'ordinary people' had to be content with receiving what the professionals considered they needed.

The advent of liberation theology in particular has shifted this balance, because it had its origin not in the lecture room or the private studies of scholars, but in the struggles of oppressed people in the 'two-thirds' world, oppressed people who dared to believe that the Bible had a message directed to their material as well as their spiritual well-being. The story of the Exodus has been important here, for it has been observed that salvation for the Israelites was a material matter, in that it involved liberation from physical slavery and the granting of freedom. Liberation theology has similarly produced an understanding of Jesus, which has emphasized his political involvement on behalf of the poor and oppressed of his day.

Partly influenced by liberation theology, but also arising spontaneously, have been the feminist movements and the European liberation theology movement in biblical interpretation. These have been much more the concerns of professional scholars, but in the case of the movements described by Luise Schottroff in Chapter 16(*c*) they have included the attempts of ordinary churchgoers to relate the Bible to contemporary issues such as apartheid, nuclear disarmament, and the disparities in wealth between the first and the 'two-thirds' worlds.

Some of the results of broadening the scope of those whose interests affect biblical interpretation have been disturbing, but the newer methods of interpretation and the pluralism that they have brought with them look set to become a permanent feature of biblical studies. This makes it imperative that professional scholars collaborate with those who are helping 'ordinary people' to see how the Bible addresses their situations, not so that professional scholars can reclaim a right to be the sole arbiters in matters of biblical interpretation, but so that exegesis is safeguarded from arbitrary and fanciful interpretations that rob the Bible of its power to challenge people and to give them high aspirations.

15 Feminist Scholarship

YVONNE SHERWOOD

The Bible is strangely full—and empty—of women. There is Eve, whose name means Life but who is 'born' of a man, and who, at least according to the 1 Timothy 2: 13–14 reading of Genesis, is a Pandora-creature, guilty of the first transgression. There are women who ensure that the plot continues to the next chapter: Esther and Deborah who fight for or deliver their people; the midwives in Exodus who save male Israelite babies, and Moses' mother, who saves one baby in particular; the women in Matthew who carry the news of the resurrection, as well as women such as Sarah, Rachel, Rebekah, Hannah, Manoah's wife, Ruth, Elizabeth, and Mary the mother of Jesus, who give birth to heroes and provide crucial links in the genealogical chain. There are women who are the victims of violence (Dinah, the Levite's concubine in Judges 19); exemplary women (the widow and her offering, the haemorrhaging woman who touches Jesus' garments); women in positions of authority (Hulda, Deborah, Prisca); dangerous women (Jael, Delilah, Herodias, and her daughter); women with strange peripheral roles (Lot's wife who turns into a pillar of salt, Abishag who acts as a human blanket in 1 Kings 1: 1–4). And there are metaphorical women, female symbols of the awful and the ideal: Woman Wisdom; the restored Jerusalem as city jewel and suckling mother (Isaiah 66); the church as bride of Christ; the whore-nation in the prophets; the 'strange woman' of Proverbs, whose lips drip with honey and whose speech oozes with oil ...

Even if feminist biblical criticism confined itself to texts about women (which it does not), evidently there would be plenty of material—and silences—to go on. And, as might be expected of a book written by many authors over several centuries and appropriately named 'the library' (*ta biblia*), the Bible by no means offers a homogeneous view of woman.

Over the last two centuries, and particularly over the last few decades, a whole new range of female 'characters' have emerged—Sojourner Truth, Anna Julia Cooper, Elizabeth Cady Stanton, Mary Wollstonecraft, Emmeline Pankhurst, Simone de Beauvoir, Betty Friedan, Germaine Greer, to name just a few. And these figures, who have arguably had more opportunity to speak for themselves than their biblical counterparts, have posed considerable challenges to our perceptions of society and justice. Some of the early views and demands of these women are now enshrined in Western law: few would deny a woman's right to vote, for example, or contest Emmeline Pankhurst's claim that 'a husband should not imprison his wife to enforce conjugal rights'. And because of the feminist movement and campaigns for human rights, there is increasing awareness of issues such as sex discrimination in the workplace, unequal pay, and unequal access to positions of power, or, more starkly, issues of wife-battering, or the lower social valuation of female children (resulting in less access to education, abortion, even child-death). The global women's movement has not only offered a different (and disturbing) perception of the world by compiling

The Rescue of Lot (Genesis 19: 23) by Gustave Doré, 1865. In the background the calcified figure of Lot's wife is to the right of the burning cities of Sodom and Gomorrah.

(Above) Mary Wollstonecraft (1759–97) portrayed by John Opie *c.*1790. She was author of *A Vindication of the Rights of Women* and an anti-slavery activist in mid-19th-century America.

(Above middle) The former slave and abolitionist Sojourner Truth (1777–1883), originally Isabella Van Wagener, around 1860.

(Above right) Emmeline Pankhurst (1858–1928) around 1910. She was a prominent campaigner for women's suffrage in Britain.

evidence about women's lives, but has also questioned the very structures of epistemology—our ways of knowing and of seeing. Although there is no official feminist 'creed', the following two claims can be seen as foundational to the modern feminist movement:

1. Knowledge, religion, society, and human institutions are androcentric (male-centred). That which is considered to be normative, standard, or neutral is in fact skewed towards the interests of men. When feminists change words like 'mankind' to 'humankind', they are doing more than tweaking language. They are making the point that the interests, ideas, and beliefs of this alleged universal—man—do not represent their own interests, ideas, or beliefs, and that reading themselves into 'mankind' involves a dangerous kind of self-forgetfulness (or self-abnegation).

2. *Sex* is a biological given at birth, but *gender* (the templates we have in our minds of what it means to be 'masculine' and 'feminine') is something we learn from culture. The roles are not equally distributed: as Simone de Beauvoir famously put it in *The Second Sex*,

> Woman is defined and differentiated with reference to man and not he with reference to her; she is the incidental, the inessential as opposed to the essential. He is the Subject, he is the Absolute—she is the Other.

Western thought tends to be constructed around hierarchies in which one term is elevated and one demoted: pairs such as day–night, objective–subjective, active–passive, self–other, mind–body, and masculine–feminine. 'Woman' as a category often acts as a negative mirror for positive male attributes: thus the characteristically emotional and passive female acts as a foil for the rational and active male.

Since these rather stark claims can make the issues seem more simple than they are, it needs to be stressed that feminism is not about the *absolute* and *conscious* victimization of women by men. Even in the most patriarchal societies, as Gerda Lerner notes, 'women are not totally powerless, or deprived of rights, influences and resources', and because men and women are born into a world and a way of seeing which habitually privileges the male over the female, the denigration of women is often unconscious, and complied with by women. Like all creeds and foundational statements, these are being constantly interrogated and reworked (the ideas of sex and gender in particular are currently very controversial). And of course no one is claiming that male and female genders are always everywhere the same: learning to be a woman in twentieth-century London is something very different to learning to be a woman in twentieth-century China or Iran, or, indeed, in ancient Israel.

As feminism exerts an increasing (and contested) influence on society, the difficult question asked by feminist biblical critics is how to work between these two bodies of knowledge—feminism on the one hand and the Bible on the other. The fact that traditional biblical scholarship tends to regard feminist questions as peripheral, and that mainstream feminist scholars studiously avoid the Bible (even as they engage with other patriarchal edifices, such as Freudianism) suggests a common perception that there is something absolutely incompatible about the Bible and feminism, and that both might be compromised and demeaned by even speaking to the other. As early as 1895, Elizabeth Cady Stanton, the compiler of *The Woman's Bible*, speaks on the one hand of educated women who dismiss the Bible as having 'lost its hold on the human mind', and on the other of male biblical scholars who refuse to 'wipe the dew from their spectacles' and 'see that the world is moving'. Because many feminists and mainstream biblical critics regard feminist biblical scholarship as something of an oxymoron, feminist biblical critics are doing something doubly transgressive, doubly perverse. And it is a credit to their ingenuity that the conversations that they create between feminism and the Bible are more subtle than slanging matches and more interesting than sweet-talking mediation sessions.

There are almost as many ways of engaging the Bible and feminism in conversation as there are feminist critics. Though 'feminist biblical criticism' may suggest something homogeneous, monolithic, even a kind of bland sisterhood, the voices it encompasses are extremely diverse, as are the feminisms. For some, feminism is a position intricately theorized through the work of French psychoanalytic critics such as Hélène Cixous or Luce Irigaray; for others it is a label aquired simply through arguing for equality ('I myself have never been able to find out precisely what feminism is,' wrote Rebecca West, famously. 'I only know that people call me a feminist whenever I express sentiments that differentiate me from a doormat or a prostitute.') For some, feminist biblical criticism is about reclaiming the Bible for women in Jewish or Christian communities; for others, it is about exploring the influence of the Bible on contemporary society. A good example of the 'dissonant buzz' in contemporary scholarship can be found in Ilana Pardes's study 'Creation According to Eve', where she analyses how Elizabeth Cady Stanton, Simone de Beauvoir, Kate Millett, Phyllis Trible, and Esther Fuchs read Genesis 1–3, and sets up a round-table discussion between the critics.

The diversity of feminist biblical scholarship makes it clear that there is no universal category 'woman' with which to replace the abstract 'man'. Feminism has learned this in painful ways, as, attacked by African-American, 'two-thirds' world, and working-class women for its parochialism, it was forced to examine its own middle-class, white, myopic constructions of 'what women want' and 'who women are'. As early as 1892, the African-American activist Anna Julia Cooper protested that 'the coloured woman of today' occupies a 'unique position' in that she is confronted by both a 'woman question' and a 'race problem' and is an 'unacknowledged factor in both'. Elizabeth Cady Stanton demonstrated the problem in rather a different way when, even as she set about the radical work of compiling *The Woman's Bible*, she addressed herself to 'American women of wealth and refinement'—emphatically *not* the Chinese, Africans, Germans, and Irish, and lower-class women. Gradually critics are realizing that colour and working-classness and Jewishness (for example) cannot be added on to feminism as sub-categories ('I am a feminist, comma, black, comma, and working-class') but that 'feminism' is fundamentally shaken up, and changed, by each 'qualifying' identity statement. To demonstrate the difference of view, some African-American critics call themselves 'womanists', to distinguish themselves from a feminism that does not speak for them (this move mirrors the way in which feminists refused to see themselves properly represented in the so-called universal—man). In biblical scholarship, the work of womanist, Latin-American and Asian feminist biblical critics such as Renita Weems, Teresa Okure, Ada Maria Isasi-Diaz, and Kwok Piu-Lan, and Jewish feminists, such as Amy-Jill Levine and Judith Plaskow, has exposed the white Euro-American Christian focus, even the anti-Judaism of early feminist work. A sense of the growing diversity and self-awareness of contemporary feminist criticism can be found in volume one of *Searching the Scriptures*, where critics from Latin America and Africa offer perspectives on the 'Bible' and 'feminism' in ways that problematize white Christian perceptions of both. Provocatively, the differences in power that can be seen among women working on the Bible can also be found among women in the Bible: Sarah (the wife, the free woman) obviously has power over the Egyptian slave-woman, Hagar, which she wields quite freely in Genesis 16 and 21. Paul demonstrates the problem for Jewish women when, in Galatians 4: 21–31, he uses the inequality between slave and free woman, Sarah and Hagar, to describe the inequality between Christians and Jews, children of the promise and children of the flesh.

Hagar, portrayed by the black 19th-century American artist Edmonia Lewis, is presented in noble and dramatic posture, as opposed to the biblical account of her as a servant driven out by Abraham and Sarah.

Given the plurality of voices in feminist biblical criticism, many attempts have been made to sift and categorize critics and plot them on some kind of spectrum. Since feminism is not a method but an *ideology* (within which there is considerable room for manœuvre) attempts have been made to categorize critics ideologically. In feminist studies generally distinctions have been made between liberal feminists (who espouse a universalist view of human nature, a sense of the general sameness of human beings), radical feminists (who emphasize difference), and Marxist and socialist feminists (who focus on the social production of gender categories). In feminist biblical studies, ideological distinctions have been made using the Bible and theological tradition as a starting-point: Carolyn Osiek is interested in whether critics *collude* or *collide* with the biblical text and tradition, in whether they are 'loyalist' like Phyllis Trible or 'rejectionist' like Mary Daly (Daly achieved notoriety by, among other things, claiming that, were the positive material in the Bible to be collected together, there would be just about enough for a 'salvageable pamphlet'). But not only do such categorizations fail to do justice to the complexity of a single critic, and indeed the biblical canon, but they also tend to prioritize the Bible and the Christian tradition over feminism as the basis of judgement. Not only are such approaches reductive but they completely bypass the interests of a critic like Mieke Bal, who emphatically maintains that she does not treat the biblical text as a 'feminist manifesto', or a uniformly patriarchal document, and considers this a misleading question to ask of her own—or indeed anyone else's—work. Classification by methodology can be more helpful: since feminist biblical criticism uses as wide a range of methodologies as 'mainstream' scholarship, it is useful to know, for example, that Carol Meyers draws on anthropology and sociology, or that Elizabeth Castelli is influenced by post-structuralist literary theory. But since feminists often weave different approaches together, this kind of classification is in danger of producing Polonius-like descriptions of a critic as anthropological-sociological-historical-critical (Mieke Bal, for example, reads Judges through historical, anthropological, theological, and literary lenses). It also ignores the way in which feminism often transforms the methodologies that it uses, and how, as one feminist literary critic aptly put it, it is ideally 'responsive to all the critical schools and methods but captive of none'.

This introduction is more concerned with outlining a feminist critique of the Bible, and then describing how scholars work in the space opened up by that critique, than with classifying feminists ideologically or methodologically. That is, it concentrates on what is distinctive about a feminist approach—the difference of view. It begins by outlining the basis of the critique—the problems that the Bible and the interpretative tradition raise for feminist readers—and then it looks at ways feminist critics have found to engage with these texts. But these two sections are not about simply denigrating the tradition and then rehabilitating it: I hope to show that feminist critiques and responses are more diverse in their aims and their approaches than that.

CRITIQUE: SPEAKING AGAINST THE BIBLICAL TEXTS

Feminist criticism by definition begins with the critique. When the object of critique is the Bible it can be tempting to rush to apologetic before the problems are fully articulated. But to do this is to run the risk of not making it absolutely clear why a modern feminist reader often feels like an alien and stranger on the Bible's pages.

Adam and Eve, a fresco from the Stanza della Segnatura by Raphael, *c.*1508–11, presents the biblical story in Genesis 3 in a traditional manner.

The first phase of feminist critique, in biblical studies and theology as in other branches of the humanities, concentrates on exposing negative images of women, and in picking out texts that, to use Marie-Theres Wacker's wonderful play on Luther's phrase, would make 'right strawy epistles for the Women's Bible'. This process—known as *Images of Women* criticism—began when Elizabeth Cady Stanton and her team first began literally cutting out biblical passages about women and then exposing why the representations were problematic, and it is still a dominant feature of feminist biblical critique today. Outside the guild of biblical scholarship, the figure of Eve—spare rib, helper, derivative, bringer-of-sin-and-death-into-the-world—became iconic for the feminist movement (famously *Spare Rib* became the title of a 'Women's lib' magazine). Within the field, the critique went beyond Genesis 1–3, and engaged precisely with those less well-known texts, the ones barely preached on or discussed, the ones tucked away in dark corners of the canon. In Old Testament/Hebrew Bible studies, Phyllis Trible famously and painfully exposed four 'texts of terror'—the stories of Hagar, Tamar (daughter of David), Jephthah's daughter, and the Levite's concubine—women who are rejected, raped, murdered, cut up into pieces, and sacrificed in the fulfilment of a paternal vow. These texts so graphically militate against women's interests and women's bodies that they could be said to act as a rallying cry for women engaging with the Hebrew Bible (rather as the dismembered concubine's body in Judges 19 is meant to act as a rallying cry for the tribes of Israel to go to war).

As well as treating the lives of real women, the feminist critique has looked at the ways in which, to use Karen King's apposite phrase, biblical authors 'use women to think with'. One of the most notorious uses of woman-as-metaphor is the harlot-nation in the prophets: a metaphor applied to Israel, Judah, Samaria, and Nineveh, graphically detailed in Ezekiel 16 and 23, Hosea 1–3, Jeremiah 22: 20–3, and Nahum 3: 5–6, and critiqued by a whole host of feminist commentators including Mary Shields, Cheryl Exum, Athalya Brenner, Tikva Frymer-Kensky, Renita Weems, and Fokkelein van Dijk-Hemmes. The marriage metaphor, in which God is male and the nation, or sin, is female, expresses a damaging inequality between genders; it also legitimates male violence against women as the relationship becomes 'pathological' (Frymer-Kensky) and the imagery turns (to use Athalya Brenner's provocative phrase) 'pornoprophetic'. The idea that God has the right to punish his sinful people may, as Renita Weems suggests, be a 'congenial theological point', but what about when that punishment gets entangled with highly disturbing language about lifted skirts, exposed genitalia, bared breasts, and the story of a woman who is stripped, beaten, starved, and paraded naked in the sight of her lovers (Hosea 2)? For some the language is innocuous because it is 'only a metaphor', but metaphors have a dangerous tendency to leak into reality, and 'some metaphors create more problems than they solve' (Weems). The Hebrew Bible itself demonstrates this when it shows how the metaphorical language of the rape of a city too often collides with the 'real' rape of the female inhabitants (see Judges 5: 30; cf. Deuteronomy 21: 10–14).

A feminist critique of the Bible cannot progress very far focusing only on concrete images of women; it needs to articulate the absence of women, the silence about women's lives. Phyllis Trible focuses on texts where women are graphically, violently fragmented; Cheryl Exum articulates how women's *stories* are fragmented, and how they often have walk-on bit parts in the stories of men. Women are often peripheral, named only by possessive patrynomic, or as a man's possession—Jephthah's daughter, the Levite's concubine, Lot's wife. And not only is Yhwh a male God who deals primarily with males (he is the God of Abraham,

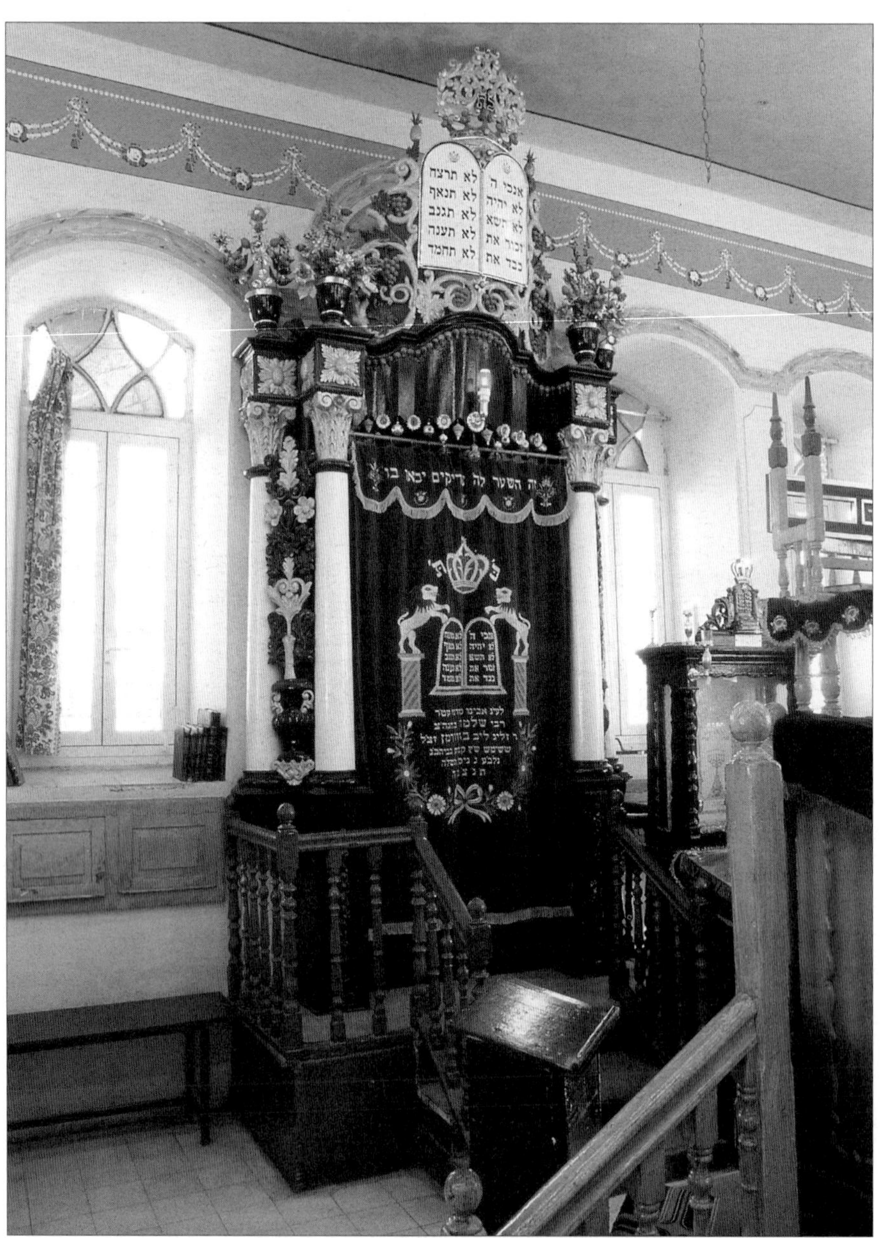

The Ten Commandments in their conventional abbreviated form appear beneath the crowns at the top and on the black curtain of the 'Ark' containing the scroll of the Torah in a synagogue.

Isaac, and Jacob rather than Sarah, Rebekah, and Rachel) but the textual perspective is one of a male author addressing an audience of males. Sarah is painfully invisible from the narrative of the Akedah (Genesis 22) and the Ten Commandments, with their instruction 'not to covet your neighbour's ox, ass, or wife' obviously assume a male addressee who owns an ox, ass, and wife. (As well as uncovering texts that have always made readers uncomfortable, and articulating why they make them uncomfortable, feminist criticism is also about reading more familiar texts in unfamiliar ways.)

A portrayal of Sarah and her son Isaac from *Testament: The Animated Bible*. While Sarah is absent from the biblical account of the 'sacrifice' of Isaac (Genesis 22), the *Animated Bible* inserts her into the story.

In this illustration from a 1260 Psalter, one woman anoints the head of Jesus (Mark 14: 3–9) while another anoints his feet (Luke 7: 36–8). Feminists point out that both women are nameless in the narratives, even though their behaviour is praised as exemplary.

There are some passages in the Old Testament/Hebrew Bible that, like Eve, seem to be absolutely iconic of the injustices challenged by the feminist movement. Leviticus prescribes forty days of uncleanness after the birth of a boy child and eighty after the birth of a girl, and values women at 30 shekels, men at 50—you can read these texts as starkly mathematical illustrations of gender inequality, even as an ancient example of differential wages (but for a different reading see Meyers, Discovering Eve). The Law of the Sotah in Numbers 5 painfully exposes double sexual standards with all the vividness and horror of medieval witch-hunts, and there is no clearer illustration of patriarchy than the Genesis genealogies in which fathers beget sons who beget more sons (as if women were somehow removed from the biological process, and daughters were never born). Texts like these are not only on a direct collision course with values that we think of as distinctively feminist, but they sometimes assault those basic understandings of equality and human rights that have been enshrined and normalized in law.

Lest a sense of discomfort with the Hebrew Bible propel us into a kind of feminist neo-Marcionism, scholars have also challenged the idea that the New Testament can be seen as a kind of proto-feminist refuge for women battered by their reading of the 'Old'. The New Testament does indeed reflect a different view of gender: it reflects the androcentric social structures of the Graeco-Roman world. Elizabeth Schüssler Fiorenza warns the woman reader to proceed with 'caution' since the New Testament 'could be dangerous to [her] health and survival'; while Daphne Hampson warns that, though not a misognynist, the Jesus of the gospels is certainly not a feminist, even by the most minimalist definition. The story of the New Testament orbits around men—a male Christ, male disciples, male church elders, male authors or pseudonyms (Matthew, Mark, Luke, John, Paul, Peter) and male addressees (Timothy, Philemon), and passages like 1 Thessalonians 4: 4 assume a male audience just as naturally as the Ten Commandments when it talks of 'taking a wife for yourself'. Women looking for traces of women's roles in the early church are often employed in a process of *cherchez la femme*, picking at tantalizingly brief allusions, for example to the *diakonos* Phoebe in Romans 16: 1–2. Like their Old Testament/Hebrew Bible counterparts, female characters often hover in the background, in the sub-plot, and can also suffer from namelessness and anonymity: Matthew's Gospel may praise the woman who anoints Jesus, and may condemn Judas and Peter for their betrayal and denial, but, as Schüssler Fiorenza points out, the name of the betrayer is remembered, but the name of the faithful (female) disciple is forgotten. Moreover, in Luke's version the woman is described as a prostitute, an example of the sinners with whom Jesus interacts, rather than a prophetic figure annointing Jesus before his death. The New Testament, like the Old, has its more notorious 'strawy' texts, texts such as the pastoral epistles, which seem so keen to repress women's active roles. And occasionally these texts can themselves become 'texts of terror': Tina Pippin, for example, sees the Whore of Babylon (Revelation 17–18) as the bloody culmination of the woman-as-whore metaphor in the prophets, and is profoundly disturbed by the depiction of Rome as female, at the moment when

hate is most powerfully unleashed against her. Ephesians uses the conventional patriarchal household structures of the *paterfamilias* as a reflection of unity and harmony; Romans 7: 1–6 uses a wife's obligations to her husband as a metaphor for the obligation of Christians to the law, and so on. The examples may be less stark than in the Old Testament/Hebrew Bible but, as Susan Durber points out, sexism may be most dangerous when it is at its least violent and obvious—when it simply seduces the reader into accepting a normal, male point of view.

If the Bible, as Phylis Bird puts it, is largely a 'collection of writing by males from a society dominated by males', then so too is commentary. Feminist meta-commentary (or commentary on commentary) shows how the scholarly tradition has often unthinkingly reinscribed biblical prejudices against women, and in some cases written gender inequalities larger than in the original text. The garden of Eden has, as Trevor Dennis puts it, been crammed full of theological 'litter' that has made Eve into the 'devil's gateway', 'the unsealer of the tree', and 'the one who crushed the image of God' (as Tertullian sweetly put it). But other biblical characters have also been distorted: Sarah's laughter has been amplified and castigated; the Samaritan woman at the well has been described by commentators as a 'five-times-loser' or a 'tramp'; the woman who anoints Jesus' feet has been condemned for her 'hysteria'; while popular cultural interpretation has made Mary Magdalene into a prostitute, established Delilah and Bathsheba as culpable *femmes fatales*, and totally created the eroticized figure of 'Salome'. Sometimes male commentators have underplayed the roles of women: Phoebe, the *prostatis* (the feminine form of *prostates*, generally translated leader, chief, patron, guardian, protector), is usually denied the strong role that the text seems to give her; Junia (fem.) the *apostolos* in Romans 16: 7 undergoes a sex-change in modern translations to become Junias (masc.); while commentators explain the role of Prisca (co-worker with Paul, together with her husband Aquila) on the basis that perhaps she had special access to 'women's areas' (maybe she was the ancient equivalent of the Sunday school teacher). As well as exposing the andro-centricism of scholarship, feminist metacommentary may also expose how male commentators are caught out by their own criticisms of the woman-in-the-text (Moore), or how, even as they condemn feminist criticism for its unscholarly subjectivity, they sometimes stray into subjectivity themselves (Sherwood).

'Reading as a woman' is not something that comes naturally, instinctively, just by being a woman, because women are socialized to identify themselves with a male point of view. But critical reflection on the text can be a necessary act of self-protection from biblical ideology, a way of preventing oneself reading with, and so complying with, the scapegoating, denigration, and silencing of women. By training themselves to become resisting readers of the Bible, feminists have become among the first ideological critics, the first to articulate their difference from the biblical texts. The effect on 'the Bible' is disorientating: the book that is usually associated with liberation is shown to be, in some ways, unliberating; the book that has habitually been invoked to comment on society is critiqued from the standpoint of twentieth-century social values; and the visionary book is

The tattooed Salome, by Gustav Moreau (1826–98). Salome has become the embodiment of men's desires, and fears, about women.

J'ai baisé ta bouche, Jokanaan, an illustration by Aubrey Beardsley in Oscar Wilde's *Salome* (1894) shows Salome holding the dripping head of John the Baptist, and representing herself as a gorgon.

shown to be myopic about women's rights and women's questions. Having articulated the tensions between the Bible and feminism, the critic can no longer assume that the voice of the biblical texts and tradition will merge with her own. But this is not the end of the conversation, but the beginning, as the feminist responses below show.

CONVERSATION: SPEAKING WITH THE BIBLICAL TEXTS

No feminist is prepared bleakly to catalogue women's oppression: all critics want to combat that oppression with strong, confident, women-affirming voices. For some critics, such as Mary Daly, or Daphne Hampson, these voices emphatically cannot be found in the text and the tradition, and the only strong female voice is the voice of the critic, breaking free and defining herself against an irredeemable legacy. Other feminist critics tease out positive voices from the text/tradition that they can relate to and magnify (although they would disagree as to the extent to which those voices were intended by the authors). For some this is a political and religious act, a way of staking a place in the Bible and tradition. For others it is a reflection of a different kind of belief—a belief that even a system like patriarchy has gaps and holes in it, and that traces of women's voices, and women's power, will inevitably leak through, even in the most androcentric of texts.

One of the most obvious ways of finding footholds in the biblical tradition is by identifying women-friendly role models and women-friendly texts. As a feminist critique has developed naming texts of terror, so an informal, positive canon-within-the-canon has also separated out. Many critics talk self-consciously of doing something magpie-like, of gathering up the most sparkling, attractive texts, like lost coins (Loades), or finding texts that are more 'bread' than 'stone'-like (Schüssler Fiorenza). The Song of Songs is for many a 'non-sexist' text, even an 'antidote to patriarchy': Trible sees it as a kind of feminist paradise to compensate for an Eden that has gone sour for womankind. The book of Ruth can offer a similarly idyllic space: reversing the usual pattern, the husbands and fathers sink into the sub-plot (they die in the first few verses) and Boaz sits in the wings as Ruth, Naomi, and a female chorus take centre stage. The book of Luke is a book which foregrounds women; it praises them and offers a kind of equality of symbolism whereby for every male parable and male example there is an equal and opposite parable centred on a female character.

In addition to these book-length islands in a biblical sea of androcentricism, feminist analysis has also pointed to a whole group of exemplary, even powerful, female characters (Esther, Ruth, Abigail, the 'woman of worth' in Proverbs 31, the faithful women in the gospel parables, Lydia, Prisca, Phoebe) and has teased out other promising textual strands. Galatians 3: 28 offers 'the clearest statement of women's equality to be found in the Christian scriptures' (Briggs), while Hosea 4: 14 can be read as a timely antidote to Hosea 1–3, and the unequal metaphor whereby sin is female harlotry, but righteousness and constancy is male (Marie-Theres Wacker). Male leaders, in moments of compassion, mourning, or care are

Naomi entreating Ruth and Orpah to return to the land of Moab, by William Blake (1757–1827), is a reminder that the book of Ruth is a women-centred story.

described in maternal terms: Jesus is like a mother-hen (Matthew 23: 37–9; Luke 13: 34), Paul, in Galatians 4: 19, describes himself as a woman labouring for his children, and in 1 Thessalonians 2: 7 and 1 Corinthians 3: 12 casts himself as nurturing mother/wet nurse of the church. Promisingly for feminist theology, there even seem to be moments where female metaphors meet the image of God: the God of Hosea 11 is a maternal figure, teaching Ephraim to walk (Schüngel-Straumann), and Deutero- and Trito-Isaiah not only restore Jerusalem as radiant bride and suckling mother, but offer the radical images of God as midwife and woman giving birth (Isaiah 42: 14; 66.9). However, by far the most promising figure for feminist theology is Woman Wisdom, Hebrew *Hokhmah*, Greek *Sophia*, who appears in the book of Proverbs and ben Sira (Ecclesiasticus) as the female love-object of the male seeker after wisdom *and* as one who sits beside the divine throne, as co-creator and beloved of God. These images of Wisdom, influenced by ancient oriental and Egyptian goddess cults, have become increasingly important in feminist scholarship, theology and liturgy (to appreciate the extent of the impact of Sophia, see the collection of essays in the section 'Revelatory Discourses: Manifestations of Sophia' in *Searching the Scriptures*, ii).

As this positive counter-canon has multiplied so have the voices of caution. Positive images of women do not always represent women's interests, warns Esther Fuchs, since female characters in male-authored texts 'reveal more about the wishful thinking, fears, aspirations, and prejudices of their male creators than about women's authentic lives'. Women in Luke may be numerous and exemplary, observes Jane Schaberg, but they are exemplary for their aptitude for 'following' and 'subordinate service' (roles which hardly challenge the roles of women under patriarchy); moreover, since women are often socialized to be unassertive and socially deferential, might it not be dangerous for them to read a gospel extolling humility, and directed at a male will-to-power? Pure proto-feminist utopias such as the Song of Songs may be dangerously over-romanticized: at the end of Ruth our heroine disappears, once she has given birth to Obed father of Jesse father of David. With the possible exception of Wisdom, female metaphors for God, Jesus, and the apostles tend to reinscribe those traditionally 'feminine' attributes of compassion, kindness, caring, and motherliness, and so by celebrating them we may be unwittingly deifying woman's role as nurturer and carer.

In other disciplines in the humanities, such as English literature, feminist analysis has moved from critiquing representations of women in male-authored texts (Images of Women criticism) to a new emphasis on women's writing. The idea of canon has been challenged, and rediscovered authors, such as Charlotte Perkins Gilman and Radclyffe Hall, have been put on the curriculum. In biblical studies and theology the decentring of the canon and an interest in writing by women has been expressed in different, less straightforward ways. The canon of study has been expanded (*Searching the Scriptures* is interested in potentially radical theological ideas in extra-canonical texts, as well as the New Testament canon, though obviously not on the assumption that these texts were written by women) and figures such as Hildegard of Bingen and the fabulously named Gertrud the Great have become rehabilitated in the history of interpretation. Within the canon, however, rediscovering women's voices is a far more tenuous business, since it is difficult to ascertain where (or even if) women's texts and traditions survive. Mary-Ann Tolbert tentatively makes the point that, given the spread of female literacy, 'it is not impossible that the author of Mark was female', while Athlaya Brenner and Fokkelein van Dijk-Hemmes propose that books like the Song of Songs show the influence of F (or female) sources.

Brenner and van Dijk-Hemmes's suggestion that there are some F sources behind a dominant M (male) tradition is reminiscent of conventional 'source' studies—of Pentateuchal criticism's J, E, D, and P, or gospel-study's Q. They seem to be echoing source criticism, even as they do something radically new (they never argue that women wrote these texts down, only that these texts seem to be strongly influenced by a woman's perspective). This kind of echoing and ingenuous reuse or redirection of mainstream critical methods is characteristic of much feminist biblical scholarship. Phyllis Trible reflects the etymological remanœuvres that you find in many commentaries when, in a famous reading of Genesis 2–3 (in *God and the Rhetoric of Sexuality*) she stresses the link between *ha-adam* (usually translated 'the man') and *ha-adamah* ('the earth') and suggests that the 'man' is actually an androgynous 'earth creature', who splits to become male and female. Trible reads Genesis 2–3 as a mirror of the more egalitarian creation account of Genesis 1: 28, where male and female are created simultaneously and equally. And as Trible mirrors the linguistic ingenuity of male commentators, and squeezes an egalitarian reading out of the word *adamah*, so critics like Carol Meyers, Phyllis Bird, and Elizabeth Schüssler Fiorenza draw on historical-contextual approaches to uncover a less one-sided view of history. In *Discovering Eve*, Carol Meyers uses anthropological models to look at the influence of factors such as high female mortality rate, disease, economic and household structure on the lives of real-life 'Eves'; Phyllis Bird examines institutions of cultic prostitution and the religious activity of women; and Elizabeth Schüssler Fiorenza, in *In Memory of Her*, attempts to reconstruct the obscured role of women in the early church. These critics, and many others, attempt to create a space for women in history, a historical room of their own (which is often lacking in the text).

For many feminist critics it is important to argue using objective, mainstream methodologies, or versions of them, lest feminist critics be simply dismissed to a zone of 'creativity' and 'subjectivity'. Other critics, such as Alice Bach, are influenced by post-structuralist critiques of objectivity, and are involved in self-consciously re-imagining the texts from a woman's perspective (on the grounds that all scholarship, ultimately, is subjective). This kind of criticism can be rebellious and enthralling: what would Vashti's story sound like, or Gomer's or Potiphar's wife's? The stories may be playful, but the issues raised are serious: for example Balz-Cochois's Gomer 'talks' powerfully of her alienation from a male-oriented cult.

Though feminist conversations with the Bible have been productive in many ways, perhaps the most powerful theme to emerge is the idea that *the Bible begins its own critique*. Rosemary Radford Ruether, who describes her approach as a *feminist theology of liberation*, understands the prophetic tradition as a 'golden thread' running through scripture, and pulls at this thread to unravel the one-sidedness of biblical tradition. For many critics, the Magnificat and its Old Testament/Hebrew Bible prototype the Song of Hannah offer an important model for inversion and subversion, for lifting up the low and excluded, and questioning the authority of the mighty. Other critics fasten on to moments where women within the Bible arguably speak out against their own marginalization: moments such as the daughters of Zelophehad's interrogation of the inheritance law (Numbers 27: 1–11), or the questions of the Syro-Phoenician woman who argues her right for inclusion and, uniquely, bests Jesus in an argument (Mark 7: 24–30). As Mary Ann Tolbert points out, Jesus has already taught others that religious customs should not stand in the way of doing good for those in need (Mark 2: 23–8; 3: 1–6); now the Gentile-woman-outsider pushes the principle and argues that social conventions should not do so either. Following her cue feminist critics outside the text also push biblical principles, by relentlessly pursing the logic of the texts until they expose their own blind spots. For example, scrupulously following the logic of Luke, Jane Schaberg reasons that if the 'greatest' are those who serve, and if the models of service throughout the book are female, then surely women should be promoted to leadership. This process of following the logic of the text, and its liberating implications, beyond the text's own limits is increasingly becoming known as 'feminist deconstruction'.

THE FUTURE OF FEMINIST SCHOLARSHIP

Feminist biblical scholarship, like feminist study in general, is constantly becoming more sophisticated, more expansive, as it builds on the work of previous generations. New fields of enquiry are opening up: critics are becoming increasingly interested in the afterlives of biblical women, in art, film, and popular culture, and the consideration of gender has inevitably led to questions about masculinity, homosexuality, and issues of power and inequality, as well as questions specifically limited to the 'female'. Yet even as the field is expanding, it also goes on, quite simply, articulating *why* the Bible is problematic for so many contemporary readers, and why feminist critics must ultimately be something more than a sort of special-interest group on the margins of the academy. After all, women are quite a distinctive 'minority'—the only 'minority' that makes up 52 per cent of the world.

16(a) Liberation Theology: Latin America

M. DANIEL CARROLL R.

FUNDAMENTAL COMMITMENTS

Latin American liberation theology conceives of its primary responsibility as doing theology from a lived experience with the poor in solidarity with their struggle for a life free from oppression. This starting point reorients the whole nature of the theological enterprise, which then is defined as the effort to reflect critically on harsh contextual realities in the light of Christian faith. Theology is a 'second act' that reshapes that faith, once the nature of social, economic, and political injustice is understood.

People scavenging at a landfill site in Honduras illustrate the harsh realities of poverty, hunger, and violence in Latin America, the context in which Christians must incarnate their faith.

(*Above left*) Children in front of their home in La Paz, Bolivia, are a reminder that over half of their population is under the age of 15. It is the young who suffer most and who face an uncertain future.

(*Above right*) Undated picture of Archbishop Oscar Romero, who was assassinated while celebrating Mass in a church in San Salvador on 24 March 1980. Romero was regarded as a martyr, especially by the poor.

Theology, therefore, cannot be an abstract science. It must be engaged in praxis—that is, in concrete actions guided by a perspective designed to bring social transformation within history and in the here and now. It cannot be individualistic, but rather must be elaborated in collaboration with the marginalized. Liberation theology has coined a number of expressions that capture well its intent: 'doing theology from the underside of history' means that the focus is on 'orthopraxis' (efficacious deeds for change congruent with Christian ethical mandates rather than simply assent to correct doctrines) from a 'preferential option for the poor' (the conscious choice to prioritize the poor in theological and ecclesiastical matters), often in conjunction with the 'base ecclesial communities' (groups which try to read scripture in and for the context in contrast to the approaches of traditional hierarchical structures).

The majority of liberation theologians are Roman Catholic, and they have had to go to great lengths to defend their adherence to that church's teachings and to the Magisterium before a papacy that is viewed as quite conservative. John Paul II,

Bartolomé de Las Casas (1474–1566), called the 'Apostle of the Indians' for trying to humanize the colonization of Southern America by the Spanish. The portrait dates from the end of the 17th century.

although apparently sensitive to the needs of the poor, has replaced several radical bishops, criticized those clergy holding public office (especially in Sandinista Nicaragua, 1979–90), and on occasion silenced individual theologians. The most famous case of censure was that of the Brazilian Leonardo Boff in 1985; he subsequently resigned from the priesthood. There has been support as well for movements considered more loyal to the Vatican, such as the Opus Dei and the charismatic renewal. Sometimes liberation theologians have held their views at great personal cost over and beyond the pressure from church authorities. Some were forced into exile by the governments of their countries. Others, both a number of pastoral workers and also a few internationally recognized figures (in particular, Bishop Oscar Romero and the Jesuit Ignacio Ellacuría of El Salvador), were assassinated and are claimed as martyrs for liberation theology.

The liberationist framework requires that theologians consider themselves 'organic intellectuals', a concept borrowed from A. Gramsci. They are not to be an élite separated from the life of those who suffer. Speaking for the oppressed is impossible—even immoral—unless theologians are connected with the poor and grasp their plight. To accomplish these ends theology must be properly informed of the mechanisms of oppression that it desires to see changed. Hence the need for the social sciences.

Various streams of Marxism have long held sway in institutions of higher learning in Latin America. It is, then, no surprise that liberation theology would turn to Marxism in order to comprehend social issues. A number of liberationists studied in Europe and there also became acquainted with Marxist thought. Marxist theories are viewed as the most appropriate method to analyse Latin America's woes. It has offered some important categories of liberationist thought, such as dependency theory, praxis, capital as a fetish, the organic intellectual, and the hope of a socialist state. These theologians, however, have never adopted Marxism wholesale. The appropriation of Marxism has varied from theologian to theologian, and use has been selective and critical. For example, they have rejected the atheism of some official Marxist thought, while appreciating Marxist explanations for their nations' poverty. They also consider certain aspects to be compatible with the critiques of wealth and power found in the Bible and Christian tradition.

This manner of doing theology in the Latin American context has profound implications for the study of scripture. To begin with, this perspective claims to be an epistemological break from other Western theologizing, which has ignored oppression in the text and in life itself. The decision to read from the perspective of the poor encompasses more than an ethical stance *vis-à-vis* social injustice; it requires an entire reformulation of theological method and content. In addition, the goals of biblical study now are redefined as fostering 'conscientization' (that is, sensitizing the social consciousness of the people of God), exposing hegemonic readings of the Bible that might perpetuate present injustice, and promoting more liberating interpretations of scripture. As precedents for its biblical work in the service of the lowly, liberation theology points to the multiple passages in the Bible concerning poverty and political abuse, to the impassioned treatises of the seventeenth-century Dominican friar Bartolomé de las Casas which were designed to protect the indigenous from the horrors of Spanish colonization, and to Christian social teachings over the centuries.

SPECIFIC HERMENEUTICAL PROPOSALS

Several theologians have made particular contributions to this general orientation to the study of the Bible, which further clarify the process or add new theoretical dimensions and insights.

Liberation theology must be done *en el camino*, on the way and in interaction with everyday life in all its dimensions. These boys 'on the way' in the Chimaltenango Province of Guatemala are carrying corn (maize) crops.

One of the earliest and best-known discussions on Latin American hermeneutics came from Segundo, who elaborated the now celebrated liberationist version of the 'hermeneutical circle'. This circle contains four elements. First, a new way of experiencing one's context from the perspective of the oppressed leads to an ideological suspicion of what has been accepted as the normal state of affairs in society. Secondly, this ideological suspicion is then applied to theology, and thus its content and history are questioned. Thirdly, from this challenging horizon there follows another way of experiencing theology in everyday life as well as a hermeneutical suspicion of the manner in which the biblical text has been interpreted. The fourth and final step is the development of a different hermeneutic, one which will be more cognizant of what is at stake in theological method and of the relationship between the Bible and social reality. This circle is to be dynamic, constantly seeking more insights for liberating praxis.

Segundo has also suggested a pedagogical approach that he calls 'deutero-learning', which is based on a particular kind of distinction between faith and ideology. The former, he says, are the values grounded in a transcendent worldview. For the believer, these are determined by Christian faith. By ideology he means a specific system of means and analysis for any given context. This differentiation is then applied to the interpretation of scripture, where he would encourage readers not to try necessarily to imitate the choices and actions of biblical characters (which would reflect an ideology of the past), but rather to perceive the values that are being communicated through the text (faith) and which now must be incarnated in our time in a fashion more appropriate to the modern context (an ideology for the present). For instance, that Jesus did not more actively confront the political leaders of his day should be viewed as his option for his own time and place, first-century Palestine. What continues to matter is his commitment to the poor. This faith obligation would need to be worked out in another manner within the different world that is Latin America today. In this way, Segundo attempts to move beyond debates on historicity and the possible ethical limitations of certain texts.

Croatto appeals to modern literary theory and acknowledges his debt to the philosopher P. Ricoeur. His approach stresses the autonomy and potential of the biblical text: rereadings (*relecturas*) and appropriations of the Bible, specifically of its foundational events (such as the Exodus), generate fresh meanings in new contexts. This series of successive rereadings for liberation constitute for Croatto part of the text's reservoir of meaning and its openness towards the future. In other words, the biblical text is not a dead letter whose significance must remain fixed by the original writer and audience. The text lives and becomes alive as it is read by people in similar circumstances of oppression. The ability to discover these new meanings, however, would especially 'pertain to' and 'be pertinent for' the oppressed and those in solidarity with them.

Clodovis Boff helpfully differentiates between three levels of theological and hermeneutical work. There is first the popular level, which would refer to those who work directly with and live among the oppressed. Here, any sort of biblical reflection must be concrete, directly relevant, and intelligible to the masses, who often have little or no formal education. Next, there is the pastoral level that involves those at a higher level of church care and governance, such as the bishops (Boff speaks as a Roman Catholic). Finally, there are the professional theologians, who have the vocation and training to be able to spend time and effort on the actual articulation of this new way of doing theology. Even though this last group at times might write for and speak to audiences other than the poor of their local communities (such as international forums, or European and North American academic institutions), they should not lose their links with the socio-economic and political reality of Latin America. All three levels share a common vision and the same commitments. Ideally, there should be a constant, mutual cross-fertilization between them through visits, publications, consultations, and congresses.

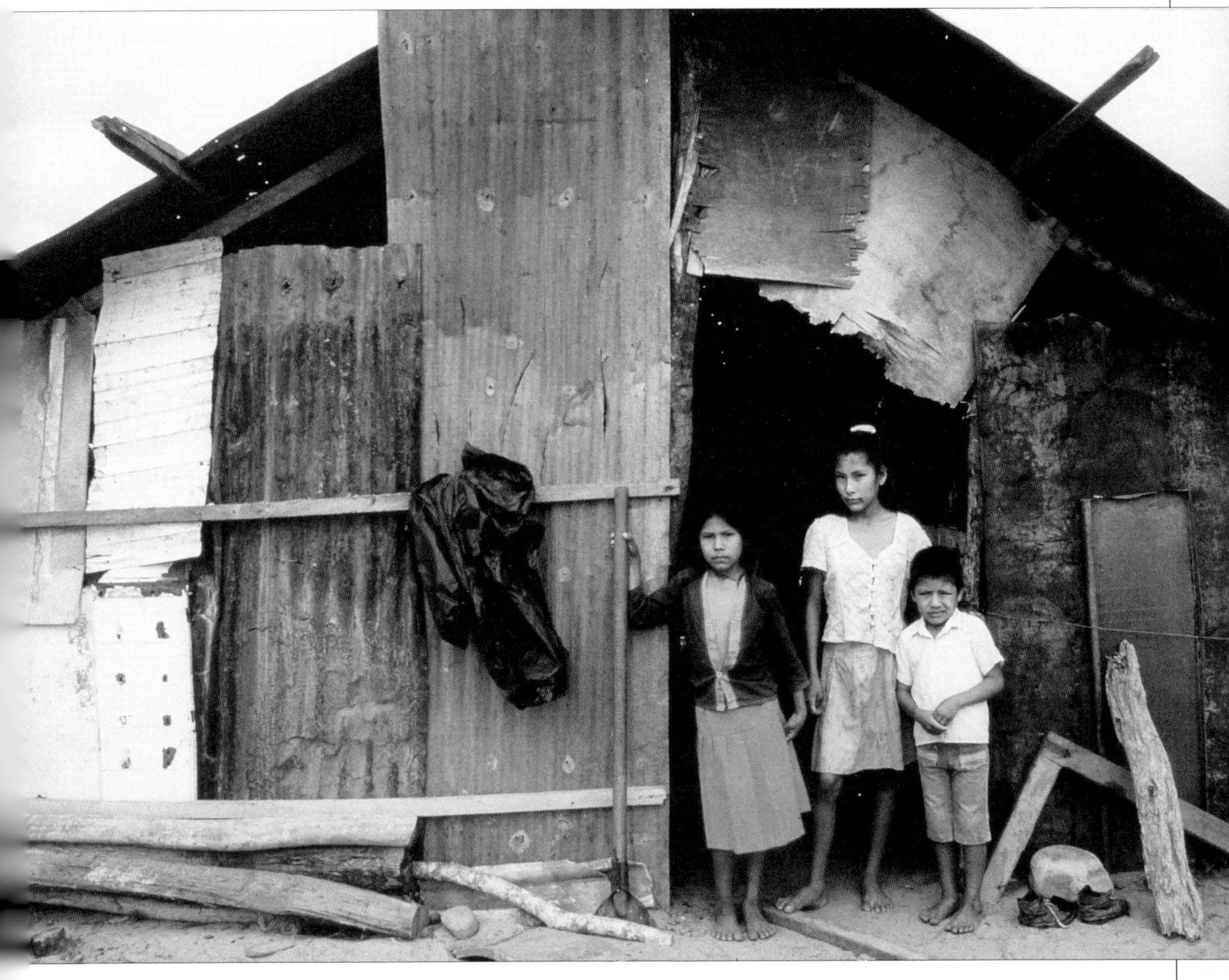

Young land squatters in Santa Cruz, Bolivia, are examples of the poor whom, liberationists hope, God will lead out of oppression to new life, as he delivered the Israelites from slavery at the Exodus—a key narrative in this context.

This concern for the broad spectrum of liberationist theology is evident as well in Boff's discussion of the three mediations necessary for theological and biblical studies from a liberationist perspective. This approach has many affinities with Segundo's hermeneutical circle. The fundamental mediation must be socio-analytic. This aspect strives to achieve some sort of solid illumination concerning the underlying historical and structural causes of the continent's injustice. Since the ultimate goal is social transformation, any such investigation must move beyond reformist or palliative solutions. At this point, Boff indicates the insights available from a discriminating utilization of Marxist thought. The second mediation is hermeneutical. The interpreter moves to the biblical text with a certain lens illumined by the first step. The Bible now can be read alongside and for the poor. The interpreter and the community will seek out those biblical themes and passages which seem to speak most directly to their situation. Some of these would include the kingdom of God, the Exodus (the suffering of the masses under an oppressive system and the response of God to their cries), prophetic denunciations of economic injustice and religious hypocrisy, various elements of the life of Jesus in the gospels (such as his care for the disenfranchised, the confrontations with religious leaders, and his trial and death at the hands of the political authorities), and important declarations by Jesus that define the nature of his ministry and the exigencies for his followers (especially Luke 4: 16–30 and Matt. 25: 31–46). Boff closes with the practical mediation, as all reflection should be geared to positive action. He expands the purview of this mediation to embrace also contemplation and worship.

LIBERATION THEOLOGY AND THE BIBLICAL TEXT

A full presentation of liberationist hermeneutics must move beyond a discussion of its basic hermeneutical commitments to an analysis of the actual study of the biblical text itself and its appropriation (if at all) of scholarly methods. On the one hand, a reading of liberation theology biblical work makes it clear that a variety of textual methods are utilized. At the same time, critical methodology is not eschewed, but rather is re-evaluated and then applied with a set of criteria not normally considered within traditional Western academic circles.

In an echo of Boff's first level of reflection, Mesters describes the nature of popular readings of the Bible among the base ecclesial communities. He posits three features of the interaction of the Bible which characterize the reading by the poor. Mesters holds that they sense a 'freedom with the biblical text'—it truly becomes alive and accessible—once it is seen to engage with the difficult realities of social life. Accordingly, the poor can enjoy a 'familiarity' with its stories and poems, because in its pages they perceive many parallels with today's world. The Bible is a mirror of their experiences, a source of analogies which enriches faith. It becomes truly theirs. Thirdly, this appropriation of the Bible generates a 'fidelity' in its application, as they attempt to live in a manner consistent with the meaning they glean for their own lives.

The Good Samaritan pictured within a tropical setting by Rodolfo Arellano.

Mesters also distinguishes between the pre-text, the context, and text. The first term refers to the situation of the people that will affect the handling of the Bible. A full awareness of their circumstances, however, cannot be limited to just the immediate personal emotional and physical needs of the poor but also must extend to include the social and systemic dimensions. Only then can scripture be read for all its worth and power. For Mesters the proper context for this sort of study and incarnation of the Bible is the church community. These believers must exemplify the quality of life and relationships that they hope to see someday when society itself is transformed. A realistic pre-text without this context can lead to a strident ideological stance with an inadequate orientation from the Christian faith; on the other hand, to remain solely within a limited contextual reading without the insights of the pre-text can result in an apologetic perspective. Ideally, a reading by the oppressed moves from the pre-text to the text and into the context.

What might be the role of the professional exegete in this process? Mesters in no way wants to discount the importance of scholarship, but he does point out that the particular logic and argumentation of the academy are far removed from the interest that the poor have in the Bible. They are not concerned with the details of hypothetical textual reconstructions and philological and historical debates. Exegetes who truly desire to be a part of this way of reading scripture must now learn to listen to the concerns of the people and endeavour to put their expertise at their service. This commitment might entail redirecting energies and research, but Mesters would insist that scholarly input, correctly utilized, can help popular readings from becoming overly subjective and arbitrary.

While Mesters and others have dedicated themselves to working with the base communities and developing an appropriate approach to the Bible for that setting, for the last three decades other liberationists have written an impressive array of scholarly works for a wider audience. These can be considered of at least two types. To begin with, there are the professional theologians, who appeal to biblical research as they elaborate their themes. In addition, there are also a number of prolific exegetes trained in both Old and New Testament scholarship.

Gutiérrez is arguably the best-known liberation theologian from Latin America. His works are replete with references to particular texts and biblical motifs. Though he tends to cite the Bible in a precritical manner, Gutiérrez on occasion does refer to certain critical positions in his argumentation and in footnotes. He has written on Job, but his is not a commentary in the classical sense. As his subtitle, *God-talk and the Suffering of the Innocent*, indicates, this work is more of an extended reflection on the difficult task of discerning how one might speak about God and reality from within a context of oppression and extreme poverty. In his exposition he contrasts a prophetic posture from the contemplative mode of doing theology and living out a

Cena Campesina (Peasant Meal) recalling the Last Supper, painted by the Nicaraguan artist Manuel García in 1978.

life of faith. The former identifies with God's solidarity with the poor; the latter is grounded in the mystical discovery of the grace of God within adverse circumstances. Both kinds of God-talk were necessary for Job's struggles. They also prefigure the ministry of Jesus and what is found among the poor today.

Several prominent theologians, such as Leonardo Boff, Sobrino, and Segundo, have produced impressive Christological studies. For centuries in Latin American Roman Catholicism the two most powerful images of Jesus have been 'el niño Jesús' (the Baby Jesus) of Christmas and the bloodied crucified Jesus of Good Friday. In contrast to these traditional figures, which engender sympathy and compassion but who are defenceless and powerless, liberation scholars claim the historical Jesus as foundational for any effective Christology for their context. They tend to interact, however, with studies done years ago and not the most recent research on Jesus that is subsumed under what is now called the 'Third Quest'. This is explainable, in part, because several of the liberation works appeared before these newer trends. Nevertheless, it could be said that what is actually offered in some of these Christologies as the 'historical Jesus' is a certain portrait constructed from the gospel narratives that highlights the practices and experiences of Jesus which seem to cohere with the social realities of today's poor. 'Historical' in this sense would mean realistic and plausible from the perspective of the oppressed.

Among liberationist technical biblical scholars several deserve special mention. In an early exegetical study spanning both testaments, Miranda sought to identify the basic message of the Bible. This, he proposed, is the constant divine demand for interhuman social justice, a stance with much in common with Marxism. Miranda makes extensive use of classical source and tradition criticism, yet he is critical of how such approaches have willingly ignored or misrepresented the pertinent biblical data.

Pixley has also based much of his work on critical theory, but he has appealed to sociological approaches. In both his commentary on Exodus and his history of Israel he has utilized Gottwald's explanation of the emergence of Israel as a peasant rebellion against Canaanite overlords. The proper theological framework for this Old Testament scholar is the Exodus, which defines the God of Israel as a deity of liberation and establishes that the ideal for this people was an egalitarian society.

Taking a very different methodological tack, the Old Testament scholar J. S. Croatto traces the reappropriation of the 'foundational event' of the Exodus throughout the biblical material in order to demonstrate its ongoing relevance for the diverse communities that produced the Bible and for today. He also has suggested that it is necessary to consider how this reappropriation can be ascertained not only by a careful reading of the received text of the Bible, but also from a certain notion of canon formation through redactional stages. For instance, in consonance with many critical scholars, Croatto separates Amos 9: 11–15 from the rest of that prophetic book as a post-exilic addition. The subsequent attachment of this new ending, he asserts, would show that the later community reinterpreted the earlier message in the light of its new circumstances. This redactional process would illustrate how a text can take on new meaning. Of course, today one works with the completed canon, but the dynamic of an ever-living word from God would still apply.

Not all liberationist exegetes, of course, focus on the Old Testament. Even though in 1981 Tamez did publish a piece which was composed of word studies of Old Testament terms for oppression, more recently she has produced two significant New Testament works. A commentary on James highlights the letter's condemnation of the oppression of peasants by the rich and attempts to read it from the perspective of the poor. In the published version of her doctoral work at the University of Lausanne she attempts to reformulate the doctrine of justification in terms of the theology of liberation. From her point of view, this

Modern Migration of the Spirit, from the *Epic of American Civilization* (1932–4), mural by the Mexican artist José Clemente Orozco (1833–1949).

classic belief, as reread today from a continent lacking in socio-economic justice, should now be understood as offering good news to the poor and all those who suffer discrimination. Tamez criticizes how the doctrine has been disconnected from the social realities of Latin America to the detriment of the masses of its violated poor. Justification should affirm the dignity of those exploited by the systemic sins of modern society and empower all excluded persons to transform their context for the possibility of enjoying the gift of life in all of its dimensions. This orientation suggests new ways of appreciating the significance of the life, death, and resurrection of Jesus.

Technical biblical studies of these and other scholars continue to appear. One valuable source for a wide variety of authors is the journal *RIBLA* (*Revista de interpretación bíblica latinoamericana*). All of these diverse manners of studying the Bible, whether from precritical or more scholarly perspectives, however, are expressions of a militant mode of reading within the struggle for liberation. For liberation theology no reading should be simply for intellectual stimulation or personal edification.

RESPONSES AND ALTERNATIVES

The reaction to this way of looking at and living out scripture has been varied. As was pointed out earlier, the Vatican under John Paul II has tried to counteract some of the influence of Latin American liberation theology. Over the years the Roman Catholic Church has taken official steps in relation specifically to those hermeneutical postures and biblical interpretations. For example, in August 1984 the Congregation for the Doctrine of the Faith, which is headed by Cardinal Ratzinger, issued the 'Instruction on Certain Aspects of the "Theology of Liberation"'. This document accused liberation theology of being overly materialistic, naïve in its utilization of Marxism, and manipulative of the biblical text. It is also possible to trace a shift in the stances taken at the Bishops' Conference in Medellín (1968) from those postures that prevailed at the Conferences of Puebla (1979) and Santo Domingo (1992). The latter two were convened by Pope John Paul II. In both cases, there was much pre-conference debate and manœuvring concerning liberationist perspectives, and the results of these proceedings included, for instance, the softening of some of the strong language against the hegemonic economic systems (even though a pastoral commitment to the poor was maintained). The hierarchy was able to ensure, too, that the activities of the base communities be brought under the authority of the local bishops. In other words, the Vatican has moved in several ways to curtail the hermeneutical and theological space of liberation theology.

Another developing, but very heterogeneous, mass religious movement among the marginalized over the last few decades has been the explosion of evangelical churches of a wide spectrum of theological traditions, especially of the pentecostal variety. It has been said that liberation theology opted for the poor, but that the poor opted for the pentecostal churches. This interesting demographic phenomenon continues to be the target of sociological and anthropological research. The surprising lack of actual participation in the base communities by the poor and the broad impact of these evangelical churches is now admitted by certain liberationists. While this reality has been the source of consternation or even has been deliberately downplayed by some, others would say that liberation theology and evangelicalism share certain common ethical concerns and also have much to learn from one another about ministering among the poor.

There has been an effort by not a few evangelicals to propose more contextualized readings of the Bible. This perspective is best represented by the Latin American Theological Fraternity, which has sponsored consultations and congresses to probe the significance and responsibilities of evangelicalism within Latin America. Members have published exegetical and theological works, which interact with liberation theology and try to respond constructively to the many challenges of the continent. Differences with liberationists centre primarily on convictions concerning the Bible as divine revelation, the prominence given to some Marxist analysis, and the utilization of certain critical textual methodologies.

PROSPECTS FOR THE FUTURE

Changes in the world situation over the last decade have had a profound effect on the fortunes of liberation theology. For example, the collapse of the former Soviet Union and Eastern Europe and the electoral defeats of the Sandinistas in

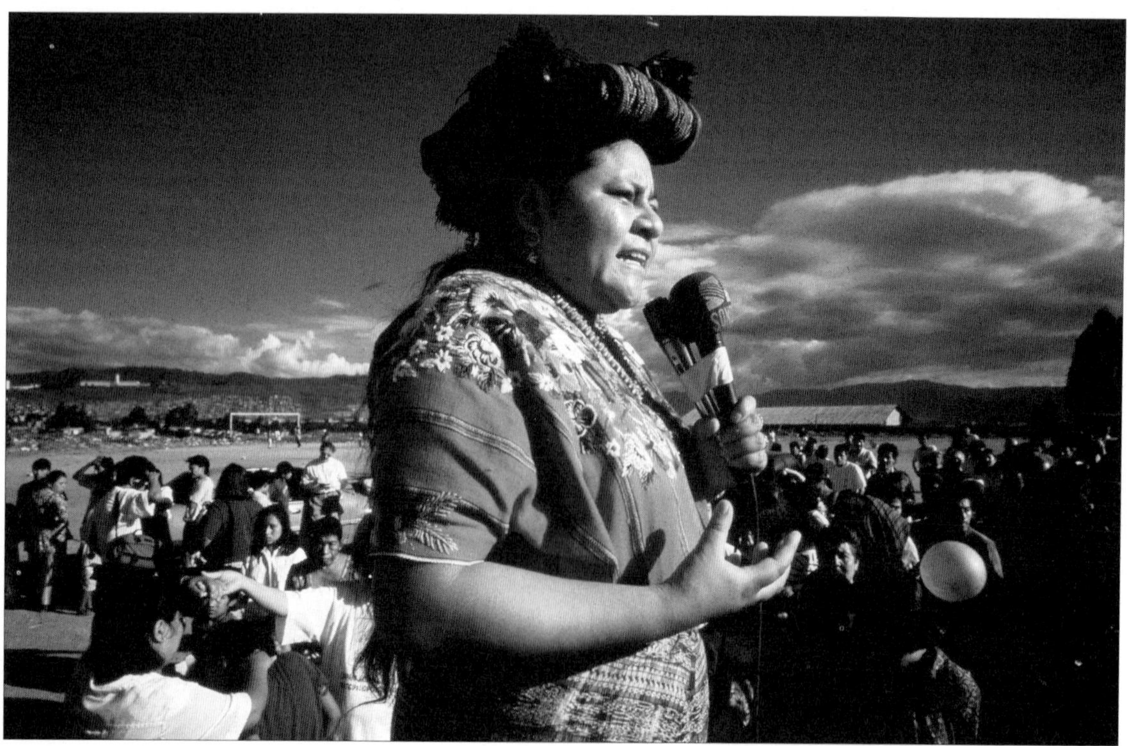

Rigoberta Menchú, Nobel Peace Prize winner and Guatemalan poetess, speaking at a rally in the urban shanty town of Mesquital. A Mayan woman, she is probably the most well-known symbol of the indigenous rights movement in Latin America.

Nicaragua (1990, 1996) have created a crisis in the Latin American left and influenced liberationists as well. The hope of a more equitable socio-economic system, embodied for some in the socialist hope, appears to have disappeared before the pressures of a global capitalistic economy. From a very different angle, among those who champion postmodernity, there is a question about whether it is still possible at this juncture in world history to elevate one particular perspective (in this case, the 'preferential option for the poor') above all others.

The reaction of liberation theologians to these new political and cultural realities has implications for their use of the Bible. At one level, all feel that the conditions of Latin America require the continued commitment of their theological and biblical work to the cause of the oppressed. The material life of the poor has not improved, perhaps even has worsened in the last few years, and scripture still must speak to that context. Yet, for some there has been a change in tone. Though there are those who still feel somewhat sanguine about the possibility of having a significant impact on the Latin American continent, others are more circumspect and feel that the task ahead must be more limited to small, local pastoral projects.

There are also liberationists who seek to pursue with renewed energy themes that now are emerging with increasing relevancy in the nascent fragile democracies of Latin America—particularly the status and options of women (not totally ignored in the past, but now receiving greater attention), ecology, and the indigenous. Richard, for instance, believes that liberation hermeneutics has much to offer the elaboration of a theology for the indigenous and their struggle for civil and religious rights. Liberationists who desire to explore this area are also considering the appropriateness and the role of the pre-Columbian scriptures and indigenous traditions in these efforts. Nevertheless, the response from the indigenous themselves has not been entirely positive. There is the perception that liberation theology has been most interested in systemic problems of a particular sort and that it has not been sensitive enough to deep cultural and ethnic issues, which can cross class lines and national boundaries in complex ways. Any contribution from liberation theology, though appreciated, can be viewed too as a word brought by those from outside the indigenous communities.

Whatever the precise future of liberation theology and its study of the Bible, it surely will continue to influence how the Bible is read and incarnated beyond its own circles. On the one hand, much of its hermeneutical and biblical work has helped to reshape how some First World biblical scholars now approach the text. Translations from the Spanish and Portuguese, even of journal articles, continue to appear.

On the other hand, liberation theology has forced all of the Christian traditions in Latin America to wrestle theologically and pastorally with the social, political, and economic problems of the context. It has demonstrated the importance and cost of reflecting upon the inescapability of doing theology from a particular point of view and within a defined set of commitments. In sum, liberation theology's way of doing theology and using scripture is an enduring legacy for Latin America and the rest of the world.

16(b) Liberation Theology: Africa and the Bible

GERALD WEST

INTRODUCTION

'Further developments in African Christianity will test the depth of the impact that the Bible has made upon Africa', says Kwame Bediako in the final sentence of his 'Epilogue' to Ype Schaaf's book *On their Way Rejoicing: The History and Role of the Bible in Africa.* Bediako's statement points to the significant role the Bible has played in the formation of African Christianity. Unfortunately, however, this formulation perhaps gives the impression that the encounter between the Bible and Africa is in one direction: from the Bible to Africa. The Bible, in this formulation, is the subject and Africa is the object. The Bible as subject, it would seem, is static and has an essential and self-evident message which has had a series of effects upon Africa.

What if we make Africa the subject and the Bible the object? We would then have the following formulation: *further developments in African Christianity will test the depth of the impact that Africa has made upon the Bible.* This statement points to the role that Africa has played in the interpretation, and construction, of the Bible. Africa is no longer acted upon, but is itself an actor. The Bible is no longer the agent, but is the object of the actions of others (African others).

By placing these two sentences alongside each other we can speak of the encounter between Africa and the Bible as 'a transaction'. The word 'transaction', with its economic and legal connotations, is used here to signify that this process is not innocent. When, for example, the Bible was brought to Africa by the missionaries and colonialists, it was part of a 'package deal'. However, the missionaries and colonialists did not always have their own way. As Tinyiko Maluleke reminds us, 'While oppression and imperialism have been real and ruthless, Africans have at a deeper level negotiated and survived the scourge—by relativising it, resisting it, and modifying it with uncanny creativity.' We could make the same point concerning the Bible. While the Bible has been used for purposes of oppression and imperialism, both because of the ideologies of those who have used it and because of the ideologies intrinsic to it, ordinary Africans have at a deeper level negotiated and transacted with the Bible and partially appropriated the Bible—by relativizing it, resisting it, and modifying it with uncanny creativity.

AN INTERPRETATIVE HISTORY OF THE BIBLE IN AFRICA

An important aspect of the Bible in Africa, then, is an account of the transactions that constitute the history of the encounters between Africa and the Bible. Historical accounts of the encounters between Judaism and/or Christianity and Africa are rich and detailed in their analysis of most aspects of these transactions, but consistently exclude the Bible. This is the case in the otherwise excellent recent work by Elizabeth Isichei, *A History of Christianity in Africa: From Antiquity to the Present*, where the historical, sociological, geographical, cultural, economic, and religious dimensions of, for example, the emergence of North African Judaism centuries before Christ and then Christianity in the beginning of the first century, the initial interface between Judaism/Christianity and Islam, the impact of Portuguese (Catholic and Protestant) evangelization and exploitation between 1500 and 1800, the nineteenth-century missionaries and colonialists, and the expansion of Christianity through African evangelists in the twentieth century are all described and analysed in detail, but the biblical and hermeneutical are hardly mentioned.

Even Ype Schaaf's book, *On their Way Rejoicing: The History and Role of the Bible in Africa*, belying its title, provides little analysis of the Bible's interpretative history in Africa. Much is implicit, as with the work of Isichei, but explicit analysis is absent. Though Schaaf deals with the topic of translation of the Bible in great detail, this discussion does not lead into any inventory of its interpretative history.

So while the accounts we have of the encounters between Africa and Judaism and/or Christianity are well documented, the encounters between Africa and *the Bible* are partial and fragmentary. That the Bible is seldom treated separately from the arrival and reception of Judaism and/or Christianity is not surprising, particularly as it can be argued that the Bible is analytically bound up with being a Jew and/or a Christian. However, without disputing the interconnectedness of the Bible and Judaism and/or Christianity, the nature of the interconnectedness ought to be examined more carefully. We should not assume, for example, that the reception of Christianity and the reception of the Bible always amount to the same thing. Vincent Wimbush's interpretative history of the Bible among African Americans provides compelling reasons for analysing the reception of the Bible as distinct from but related to the reception of Christianity.

Furthermore, if Wimbush is right in asserting that the array of possible modes of interpretation or interpretative strategies forged in the earliest encounters of African Americans with the Bible are foundational in that all other African-American readings are in some sense built upon and judged by them, then such analysis has tremendous hermeneutical significance (relevance in theorizing about methods of interpretation) for our current context. The early African-American encounters with the Bible have functioned, according to Wimbush, 'as phenomenological, socio-political and cultural foundation' for subsequent periods. While there are many significant differences between African-American transactions with the Bible and indigenous African transactions with the Bible, there are also many striking similarities which make Wimbush's analysis heuristically valuable.

Writing from the Kenyan context, Nahashon Ndungu would seem to support elements of Wimbush's analysis. He notes that when the Akurinu Church emerged among the Gikuyu in Kenya there was a deliberate rejection of the beliefs and practices of the mission churches and a turn to the Bible, from which they identified their own teachings and practices. A more comprehensive account of such transactions is necessary if we are construct a picture of early African encounters with the Bible and if we are to understand the interpretative resources of ordinary Africans today.

(SCHOLARLY) AFRICAN RESOURCES FOR READING

The discussion so far makes it clear that Africans do not transact with the Bible 'empty-handed'. Beside their distinctive experiences of reality, both religio-culturally and socio-politically, and the particular questions that such experiences generate, Africans have a range of hermeneutic strategies for transacting with the Bible. Knut Holter has characterized the interpretative strategies of African Old Testament biblical scholarship as consisting predominantly of comparative studies between the African experience and the Old Testament. At a more general level, there is the assumption that there is some common ground between the world-views of traditional Africa and Old Testament Israel, and at a more practical level there are detailed expositions of the religio-cultural affinities between the two. This predilection for comparative studies allows African experience and the Old Testament to 'encounter and mutually illuminate each other'. By allowing the religio-cultural heritage ('the myths') and the socio-political situation ('the meanings') of Africa to interface with the Old Testament, Holter argues, African biblical scholars have much to offer their colleagues in the North.

However, and this is an important aside, when Holter examines Northern/First World/Western biblical scholarship he finds that African biblical scholars are marginalized, both in terms of their personal presence at international—that is Western—meetings and in terms of their scholarly production. Holter sees two factors as contributing to this marginalization. First, Northern scholarship has a very narrow conception of what constitutes biblical scholarship, and secondly, African scholars do not have the financial resources to enter the academic biblical studies market place of current literature, data bases, and conferences.

Within the predominantly comparative approach of African biblical scholarship, and Holter's comments concerning African Old Testament scholarship would cover African New Testament scholarship as well, African scholars make use of the full array of critical methods that constitute the tools of the trade of biblical scholarship: historical-critical, sociological, literary, and reader-response methods. But, because most African biblical scholars have been trained in the North in contexts where the historical-critical methods still hold sway and because resources, like books, reflecting more recent developments in biblical scholarship are expensive and therefore inaccessible to Africans, historical-critical tools tend to be the most prevalent.

(ORDINARY) AFRICAN RESOURCES FOR READING

But when it comes to ordinary African interpreters of the Bible, they are not as constrained as their scholarly compatriots in the strategies they use to appropriate the Bible. Their strategies, in Wimbush's words, 'reflect a hermeneutic characterized by a looseness, even playfulness, vis-à-vis the biblical texts themselves'. While much more work needs to be done on how ordinary Africans interpret the Bible, how they 'read', whether literate or illiterate, matters in Africa because African biblical scholarship is inclusive of scholars and nonscholars, the rich and the poor.

Noah, his family, the Ark and its animals. A linocut by John Muafangejo, 1979.

This is not merely a nostalgic or romantic yearning for a lost naïveté; there are a number of sound reasons for this. First, because African biblical scholarship concentrates on the correspondence between African experience and the Bible, it locates itself within the social, political, and ecclesiastical context of Africa. Biblical scholarship belongs in the church and the community, not only in the academy. Secondly, recent trends in biblical scholarship—such as postmodernism, reader-response criticism, and liberation hermeneutics—push biblical scholarship in Africa in the direction of the ordinary 'reader'. Thirdly, most African biblical scholars recognize that there are elements of ordinary readings in their own 'scholarly' reading processes. Fourthly, remaining connected to the various forms of contextual theology in Africa (including the theology of African women, Black Theology, African theology, etc.) requires that socially engaged African biblical scholars recognize the foundational (in Wimbush's sense) resources that ordinary 'readers' of the Bible bring with them to this task.

Africa also has a wealth of other African resources for reading the Bible. The extensive examples of African art that exegete and comment on the Bible are an amazing resource. From the narrative art interpretations of Azariah Mbatha to the three dimensional sculptures of Bonnie Ntshalintshali (see p. 337), to the eloquent linocuts of John Muafangejo (see pp. 333, 340), and the work of many others, we have a wealth of local indigenous interpretative resources. Mbatha's woodcuts, for example, both in their form and in their images, are excellent examples of resisting conversation—of African transactions with the missionaries, colonialism, and the Bible. The woodcut, an African form, seizes and remakes the left to right and top to bottom conventions of colonial text to tell an African story of struggle from a European-brought book (the Bible).

TEXTUALITY AND ORALITY

In the African context ordinary African interpreters work with a remembered as well as a read Bible. As Itumeleng Mosala reminds us, ordinary Africans, particularly in the African Independent churches, 'have an oral knowlege of the Bible'. 'Most of their information about the Bible comes from socialization in the churches themselves as they listen to prayers and sermons.' This reality, however, does not imply the absence of the Bible as text, for although the Bible as text is not central to the 'reading' practices of most ordinary Africans, it does have a presence. Even those who are illiterate have considerable exposure to biblical texts being read. Reflecting on the Kenyan context Ndungu notes that 'even the illiterate members [of the Akurinu African Independent Church] take pains to master some verses which they readily quote when they give their testimonies'. These same members often carry copies of the Bible so that 'if need arises they can always request a literate member to read for them'. The remembered Bible and the read Bible reside side by side.

In a recent article, 'Confessional Western Text-Centred Biblical Interpretation and an Oral or Residual-Oral Context', Jonathan Draper cautions us not to minimize the complexity of the relationships between literacy and orality. That literacy and the Bible often went hand in hand in the missionary/colonial encounter is common knowledge, and is a much emphasized point in all accounts of transactions between the Africa and the Bible. Draper's research, however, probes more deeply and raises difficult questions. How do textually oriented readers and orally oriented 'readers' work together with the Bible? When we 'read' the Bible are we dealing with the same thing? What are the prevailing interpretative practices in these respective communities? What implications does textual biblical and theological training have pedagogically for preparing people to minister in predominantly oral communities? Is the path away from orality towards textuality inevitable, and how should we implicate ourselves in this process?

TRANSACTING THROUGH TRANSLATION

When the Bible itself as text becomes the focus of the encounter between Africa and Judaism and/or Christianity, the emphasis is almost always on translation. For example, Schaaf's *The History and Role of the Bible in Africa* is primarily about the history and role of *translation* of the Bible in Africa. From the translation of the Hebrew Bible into Greek (the Septuagint) in Alexandria about 260 BCE, to the first translations of the Bible into African languages in the early 1500s (Coptic, Arabic, Ge'ez), to the present where parts of the Bible have been translated into more than 230 African languages, translation has been a central aspect of Africa's transactions with the Bible.

Bediako goes as far as to say that 'to the credit of the modern missionary enterprise, the more recent missionary history of Africa ... can justly be regarded as the history of Bible translation'. Drawing on and developing the work of David B. Barrett, Kenneth Cragg, Philip Stine, Ype Schaaf, and especially Lamin Sanneh, Bediako argues that when missionaries or mission societies made the Bible available to an African people in that people's own language, their grip on the gospel was loosened and so too their proprietary claim on Christianity. Translation enabled the Bible to become 'an independent yardstick by which to test, and sometimes to reject, what Western missionaries taught and practised' and in so doing 'provided the basis for developing new, indigenous forms of Christianity'.

The full weight of Bediako's argument, and here he leans heavily on Sanneh's work, is found in the final phase of the argument where it is claimed that in the vernacular Bible Africans were able to discover 'that the God of the Bible had preceded the missionary into the receptor-culture' and that 'Christianity had, in fact, been adequately anticipated'. Translation in this sense is much more than a technical discipline, it is a metaphor for forms of inculturation.

While most translation in Africa to date has focused on particular translation problems in particular languages, Bediako's elaboration of translation as a metaphor for inculuration opens up other, less explored, areas. For example, what forms of Christianity emerge in a context where the first texts translated into the local languages are Genesis and then Luke? Such was the case in the coastal villages of East Africa among the freed slaves during the period 1840–70. This question is given additional force because, as Schaaf notes, these Christians 'became the African pioneers of the missions who early in the twentieth century would spread the gospel among the peoples of East Africa'. If both Bediako and Wimbush are right in their respective arguments—that translation into the vernacular loosens the control of the missionary on the message and that the hermeneutic strategies that local communities adopt in order to appropriate the message for themselves are foundational—then more careful analysis of such transactions would be extremely valuable.

THE AMBIGUITY OF THE BIBLE

The encounter between indigenous South Africans and the Bible is usually recounted in broad strokes: 'When the white man came to our country he had the Bible and we had the land. The white man said to us "let us pray". After the prayer, the white man had the land and we had the Bible'. This anecdote, Takatso Mofokeng argues, expresses more precisely than any statement in the history of political science or Christian missions 'the dilemma that confronts black South Africans in their relationships with the Bible'.

> With this statement, which is known by young and old in South Africa, black people of South Africa point to three dialectically related realities. They show the central position which the Bible occupies in the ongoing process of colonization, national oppression and exploitation. They also confess the incomprehensible paradox of being colonized by a Christian people and yet being converted to their religion and accepting the Bible, their ideological instrument of colonization, oppression and exploitation. Thirdly, they express a historic commitment that is accepted solemnly by one generation and passed on to another—a commitment to terminate exploitation of humans by other humans. ('Black Christians', 34)

The dilemma of the Bible has been at the centre too of Itumeleng Mosala's work. In an early essay, 'The Use of the Bible in Black Theology', he publically questions the status of the Bible in Black Theology. Mosala's basic critique is directed at Black Theology's exegetical starting-point which 'expresses itself in the notion that the Bible is the revealed "Word of God"'. He traces this view of the Bible as 'an absolute, non-ideological "Word of God"' back to the work of James Cone. He finds it even in the work of the 'most theoretically astute of black theologians', Cornel West. More importantly, according to Mosala, 'South African black theologians are not free from enslavement to this neo-orthodox theological problematic that regards the notion of the "Word of God" as a hermeneutical starting point.' Mosala underlines the pervasiveness of this view of the Bible by subjecting Sigqibo Dwane, Simon Gqubule, Khoza Mgojo, Manas Buthelezi, Desmond Tutu, and Allan Boesak to a similar critique. More recently, Tinyiko Maluleke has extended this critique to African theologians north of the Limpopo river, including Lamin Sanneh, Kwame Bediako, John Mbiti, Byang Kato, and Jesse Mugambi.

Mosala's contention is that most of the Bible 'offers no certain starting point for a theology of liberation within itself'. For example, he argues that the book of Micah 'is eloquent in its silence about the ideological struggle waged by the oppressed and exploited class of monarchic Israel'. In other words, 'it is a ruling class document and represents the ideological and political interests of the ruling class'. As such there 'is simply too much de-ideologization to be made before it can be hermeneutically straightforward in terms of the struggle for liberation'. The Bible, therefore, cannot be the hermeneutical starting-point of Black Theology. Rather, those committed to the struggles of the black oppressed and exploited people 'cannot ignore the history, culture, and ideologies of the dominated black people as their primary hermeneutical starting point'.

However, this does not mean that Mosala totally rejects the Bible. While the Bible cannot be the primary starting-point for Black Theology, 'there are enough contradictions within the book [of Micah, for example] to enable eyes that are hermeneutically trained in the struggle for liberation today to observe the kin struggles of the oppressed and exploited of the biblical communities in the very absences of those struggles in the text'. Because the Bible is 'a product and a record of class struggles', black theologians are able to detect 'glimpses of liberation and of a determinate social movement galvanized by a powerful religious ideology in the biblical text'. But, he continues, it 'is not the existence of this which is in question. Rather, the problem being addressed here is one of developing an adequate hermeneutical framework which can rescue those liberative themes from the biblical text'.

In a later essay Mosala gives some indication of how black theologians ought to appropriate the Bible. He identifies two sources of Black Theology: the Bible and African history and culture. 'Black Theology has roots in the Bible insofar as it is capable of linking the struggles of oppressed people in South Africa today with the struggles of oppressed people in the communities of the Bible', but because the oppressed people in the Bible 'did not write the Bible', and because their struggles 'come to us *via* the struggles of their oppressors', 'Black Theology needs to be firmly and critically rooted in black history and black culture in order for it to possess apposite weapons of struggle that can enable black people to get underneath the biblical text to the struggles of oppressed classes'. Furthermore, Black Theology also needs to be 'firmly and critically rooted in the Bible in order to elicit from it cultural-hermeneutical tools of combat' with which black people can penetrate beneath both the underside of black history and culture

Pharaoh's Dream of the lean and fat cows, by the South African sculptor Bonnie Ntshalintshali. In Genesis 41 Joseph interprets the dream as foretelling seven years of plenty followed by seven years of famine.

and contemporary capitalist settler colonial domination to the experiences of oppressed and exploited working class black people.

Similarly, for Mofokeng the Bible is both a problem and a solution. The 'external' problem of the Bible is the oppressive and reactionary use of the Bible by white Christians. The internal problem is the Bible itself. Like Mosala, Mofokeng is critical of those who concentrate on only the external problem, those who 'accuse oppressor-preachers of *misusing* the Bible for their oppressive purposes and objectives', or who accuse 'preachers and racist whites of not practising what they preach'. It is clear, Mofokeng continues, that these responses are 'based on the assumption that the Bible is essentially a book of liberation'. While Mofokeng concedes that these responses have a certain amount of truth to them, the crucial point he wants to make is that there are numerous 'texts, stories and traditions in the Bible which lend themselves to only oppressive interpretations and oppressive uses because of their inherent oppressive nature'. What is more, any attempt 'to "save" or "co-opt" these oppressive texts for the oppressed only serve the interests of the oppressors'.

Young blacks in particular, Mofokeng states, 'have categorically identified the Bible as an oppressive document by its very nature and to its very core' and suggest that the best option 'is to disavow the Christian faith and consequently be rid of the obnoxious Bible'. Indeed, some 'have zealously campaigned for its expulsion from the oppressed Black community', but, he notes, with little success. The reason for this lack of success, Mofokeng argues, is

> largely due to the fact that no easily accessible ideological silo or storeroom is being offered to the social classes of our people that are desperately in need of liberation. African traditional religions are too far behind most blacks while Marxism is, to my mind, far ahead of many blacks, especially adult people. In the absence of a better storeroom of ideological and spiritual food, the Christian religion and the Bible will continue for an undeterminable period of time to be the haven of the Black masses par excellence.

Given this situation of very limited ideological options, Mofokeng continues, 'Black theologians who are committed to the struggle for liberation and are organically connected to the struggling Christian people, have chosen to honestly do their best to shape the Bible into a formidable weapon in the hands of the oppressed instead of leaving it to confuse, frustrate or even destroy our people.' ('Black Christians', 40).

The Bible will probably continue to be a site of struggle, although the shape of the struggle will change as South Africa begins to conduct a deeper dialogue with the rest of Africa and particularly as African women give voice to their experiences and readings of the Bible.

LIBERATION AND INCULTURATION BIBLICAL HERMENEUTICS

The liberation of South Africa has accelerated academic exchanges between South (and southern) Africa and Africa north of the Limpopo river and brought the liberation hermeneutical perspective of the South African (and to some extent southern African) experience of the Bible into sustained dialogue with the inculturation hermeneutical perspective of West, East, North, and Central Africa.

The foregrounding of culture, ethnicity, and Africanness in South Africa in the post-apartheid context has opened biblical scholarship to the rich resources further north where culture has always been the predominant domain of transactions with the Bible. But just as South African biblical scholarship has much to learn, so too it has much to contribute. Issues of Africanness, ethnicity, and culture cannot be separated from the complex matrix they share with issues of race, class, and gender. African biblical scholarship north of the Limpopo has been strangely silent on these matters, but that silence is being broken, particularly by African women, who are tired of being asked to wait while more important (male) matters are dealt with. They wait no longer.

African women, then, are providing a way for dialogue and collaboration between the liberation hermeneutical perspective of South Africa (where the predominant hermeneutic disposition is one of suspicion towards the Bible) and the inculturation hermeneutical perspective of West, East, North, and Central Africa (where the predominant hermeneutic disposition is one of trust towards the Bible). For African women, theologies of bread (with an emphasis on liberation) and theologies of being (with an emphasis on inculturation) are inextricably intertwined.

As a further example of the need for dialogue between liberation and inculturation hermeneutics, the role of the Bible in the 'ethnic' conflict in Rwanda remains to be examined, but when it is the relationship between culture and class will have to be carefully examined, given a social history in which social class divisions within a single cultural group were manipulated by colonial powers to produce ethnic forms of identity.

THE BIBLE AND OTHER AFRICAN INTERTEXTS

The Bible is only one of the sacred or classic texts that Africa has or has encountered. Besides the many sacred oral 'texts' of indigenous African religions, Africa has received the Koran and, to a lesser extent, the sacred texts of Hinduism. The encounter between Africa and each of these sacred texts has always been an encounter with the oral 'texts' of African traditional religions, and while African biblical scholarship has been slow to explore these transactions explicitly, African theological scholarship has not.

Besides an examination of the transactions between the Bible and sacred indigenous oral 'texts', the transactions between the more recently arrived sacred texts themselves is beginning to be investigated. In those parts of Africa where Christianity and Islam substantially encounter each other this task cannot be ignored, and some analysis and reflection is being done. However, the challenge remains in those areas (like South Africa) where Christianity is overwhelmingly dominant. How we should go about this task is an important question, and while we will have to find our own ways of proceeding, the rich experience of Asian biblical scholarship in this regard may be of use.

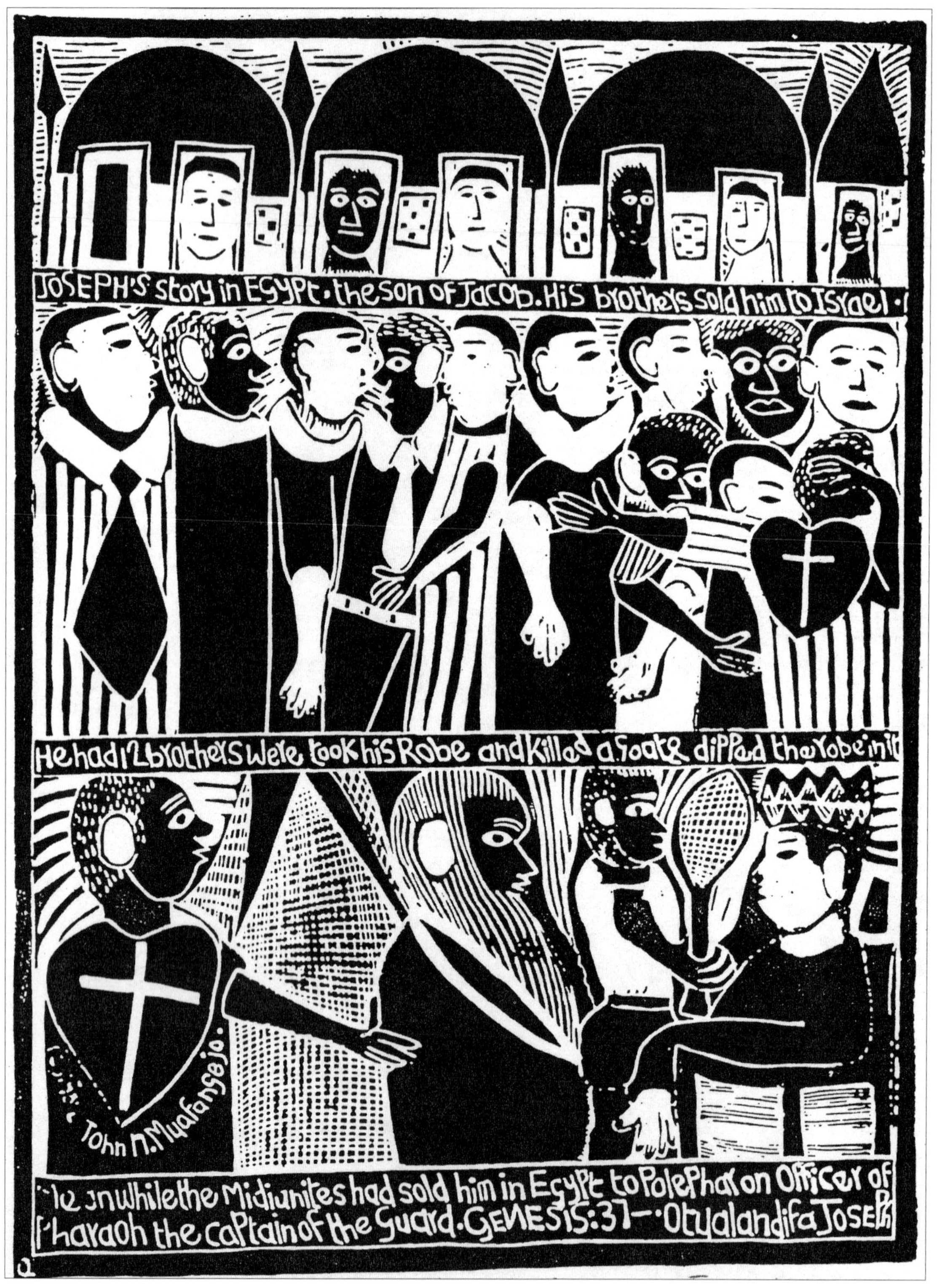
JOSEPH'S story in EGYPt · the son of Jacob. His brothers sold him to Israel ·
He had 12 brothers were took his Robe and Killed a Goat & dipped the robe in it
John M. Muafangejo
while the Midiunites had sold him in Egypt to Polephar on Officer of
Pharaoh the captain of the Guard. GENESIS 15:37 -- · Otualandifa JOSEPH

THE BIBLE AS 'THE WORD OF GOD'

Joseph's Story in Egypt, a linocut by John Muafengejo, portrays the events of Genesis 37. The subject of slavery has a particular resonance in Africa.

The encounter between Africa and the Bible has always been more than an encounter with a book. Wimbush's description of the earliest encounters between the Bible and African Americans as characterized by a combination of rejection, suspicion, and awe of 'Book Religion' has strong echoes in the encounters on the African continent. While the Bible did play a role in the missionizing of Africa, initially its role was not primary and so its impact was indirect. 'It was often imbedded within catechetical materials or within elaborate doctrinal statements and formal preaching styles.' When Africans did encounter the Bible it was from the perspective of cultures steeped in oral tradition. From this perspective the concept of religion and religious power circumscribed by a book was 'at first frightful and absurd, thereafter ... awesome and fascinating'. As illiterate peoples with rich, well-established, and elaborate oral traditions, the majority of the first African slaves were suspicious of and usually rejected 'Book Religion'. However, as Wimbush notes, 'it did not take them long to associate the Book of "Book religion" with power'.

The power that the Bible is, for most Africans, is 'the Word of God', but quite what is meant by this phrase is not clear. The analyses of Mosala, Mofokeng, and, more recently, Maluleke in this respect offer useful insights, but more careful analysis is required of exactly what particular black and African theologians mean by their various uses of the phrase 'the Word of God', particularly when we take into account that ordinary African interpreters of the Bible are not as transfixed and fixated by the text as their textually trained pastors and theologians; as Wimbush has indicated, their hermeneutics is characterized by 'a looseness' towards the biblical text. If they do speak of the Bible as the 'Word of God', they do so in senses that are more metaphorical than literal; 'the Book' is as much a symbol as a text. Maluleke is right when he says that, while many African Christians 'may mouth the Bible-is-equal-to-the-Word-of-God formula, they are actually creatively pragmatic and selective in their use of the Bible so that the Bible may enhance rather than frustrate their life struggles'.

AFRICA IN THE BIBLE

Until recently not much attention has been given *in Africa* to the presence and place of Africa in the Bible. Such interest has usually been the preserve of African-American biblical scholars. But increasingly African biblical scholars are showing interest in biblical references or allusions to the people and places of Africa and the role of Africa in the formation of the Bible. As Africa recovers its dignity and its 'Africanness', so too it is recognizing, recovering, and reviving its presence in the past—including the Bible.

A WORD ON 'AFRICA' BY WAY OF CONCLUSION

Throughout this chapter the proper name 'Africa' has been used in an unproblematized manner. Postmodern studies remind us, however, to be cautious about inherited constructs, particularly when they are the constructs of the dominant and dominating discourse. Such is certainly the case with 'Africa'. Why, for example, do introductions to the Bible, histories of Israel, maps of the Bible lands, dictionaries of the Bible, and the work of church historians and theologians minimize the role of Africa? Might we, for example, consider Mesopotamia as a part of north-east Africa? 'Africa' is one of the constructs of Western colonialism, imperialism, and capitalism. Africans themselves have had little say in the way 'Africa' has been constituted by the dominant discourse of discovery, civilization, colonialization, industrialization, and capitalization.

Problematizing and destablizing the proper name 'Africa' is a painful and potentially dangerous thing to do, just as we are recovering and revelling in our 'Africanness'. But we will have to deconstruct the dominant discourse's constructions *as* we construct our own understanding of 'Africa' and 'African'. African biblical studies clearly have a contribution to make, connecting as they do with every aspect of Africanness.

16(c) Liberation Theology: Europe

LUISE SCHOTTROFF
TRANSLATED BY JOHN ROGERSON

By 'liberation theology' I understand theology that arises from the processes of liberation in social communities. The interpretation of the Bible from the perspective of liberation theology can be found in many countries of Europe. However, this article can only deal with the subject from a particular perspective: that of a West German feminist liberation theologian. A survey of European liberation theology has not yet been undertaken; neither is there any systematic account of liberation theology in the German context. Because there are no institutions through which liberation theology is organized there are scarcely any conferences dedicated to it, and the material is often 'grey' literature. Research into the history of liberation theology in Europe is badly needed.

Viele kleine Leute
an vielen
kleinen Orten,
die viele
kleine
Schritte tun,
können
das Gesicht
der Welt verändern

A postcard widely used by the European base communities movement reads 'many lowly people in many unimportant places who take many small steps can change the face of the world'.

The term 'liberation theology' has its origins in the work of the liberation theologians of Latin America after which it came to be applied to the contextual theologies of other parts of the 'two-thirds' world. From here it can be connected with contextual theologies of the First World whether or not they actually regard themselves as liberation theologies. For a long time there was reluctance in the European context to use the term liberation theology for theologies of the First World, in order not to provoke the misunderstanding that it was possible in Europe to copy or to take over the liberation theology of Latin America and in this way to perpetuate European colonialism. For this reason many European theologians, such as Metz and Greinacher, prefer to use the terms 'political' theology or 'prophetic' theology for their work, or 'theology of life'. On the other hand there are male and female theologians who deliberately use the term liberation theology in order to express their respect for and solidarity with the liberation theologians of the 'two-thirds' world, and to make clear that liberation theology is a world-wide religious movement. This is done, however, without relinquishing the connection to specific regional contexts. It is often argued that there can be no liberation theology in Europe because there are no base communities as in Latin America, and that it is necessary for such base communities to come into existence in Europe first. In what follows I shall none the less designate as liberation theology the work of those groups that have read the Bible in connection with specific movements of liberation and have worked for the liberation of people regardless of whether they have adopted the term liberation theology or not. The 'Christian renewal movement' (Tamayo), for example, can be regarded as an instance of European liberation theology and base communities. Basic

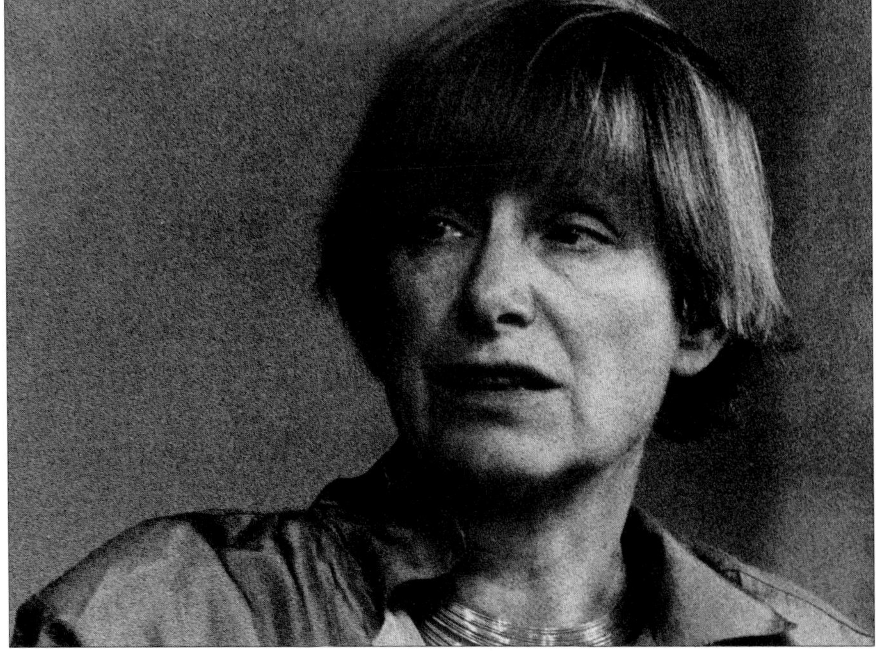

The German feminist Dorothee Sölle, whose statement of Christian belief (Credo) was used at the 'Political Night Prayer' in Cologne (1968–72).

structures similar to those of the liberation theology of the 'two-thirds' world can be recognized in European theologies and readings of the Bible that have arisen from praxis, whether they have been adopted from the 'two-thirds' world or not.

Instances of liberation theology readings of the Bible in West Germany since about 1965 can be mentioned here as examples. Of particular historical significance for liberation theology reading of the Bible in the European context is the 'Political Night Prayer' in Cologne (1968–72; the group began in 1966). An ecumenical group of about 40 people addressed contemporary political questions in the course of worship services of a hitherto unknown form. This group understood itself as a 'new congregation' which was separate from the local parish congregation. The services were based upon three steps: analysis, meditation, and orientation to praxis (information, meditation, action). Prayers and readings of the Bible therefore grew from the analysis of contemporary political injustice. Two examples can be given: the Soviet invasion of Czechoslovakia on 20 August 1968 was, together with the United States war in Vietnam, analysed as genocide at a service on 1 October 1968 and at the same time was enlisted for the continuation of the western policy of détente. The first step of the analysis ended in the quotation of Matthew 5: 21: 'You have heard that it was said to those of ancient times, "You shall not murder"; and "whoever murders shall be liable to judgement."' With the heading 'today these words mean' they were interpreted as 'those who think that it is only the communists who have let their masks drop and that the politics of détente is therefore false, make themselves guilty.' The saying of Jesus was interpreted in terms of the political controversy so that the actor and the victim within the meaning of the biblical text received a name and address according to the situation of the community reading the Bible. The second example comes from the Credo of Dorothee Sölle that was recited at the same act of worship and which brought the charge of heresy against the night prayer in general and Dorothee Sölle in particular, from both the Catholic Vicar-General and the Bishop (*Präses*) of the Protestant church in Rhineland:

> I believe in Jesus Christ who was right when he, an individual who like us could do nothing, worked for the transformation of all conditions and perished as a result. … I believe in Jesus Christ who is resurrected in our life in order that we should become free from prejudice and presumption, from anxiety and hate and that we should further his revolution. (D. Sölle and F. Steffensky, *Politisches Nachtgebet*, 27)

The Christology of this Credo understands the relationship to Christ not as a relationship from above to beneath, but sees Christ by and in those who pray. No distinction is made between the historical Jesus and the Christ of faith although this distinction currently affects academic and popular theological discussions. Also, the relationship to the Jesus of history is understood as faith. The historical experiences of the life of Jesus are seen as analogous to the social experiences of the community of the present world. It is taken as given that it is possible to compare power, injustice, and work for justice in one's own situation with that of the epoch of Jesus and other epochs of history. The 'political night prayers' that were held in Cologne have enjoyed widespread influence, both in their forms of worship which combined political analysis with meditation and liberating praxis, and particularly in the use of the prayer texts of the night prayer.

Two books were particularly important for the liberation theology Bible readings in the middle 1970s: *The Gospel in Solentiname* (first volume translated into German in 1976) and Fernando Belo's *Lecture matérialiste de l' Évangile de Marc* which appeared in French in 1976 and in German in 1980. Both books were read in Christian political groups and the impulse that they gave was developed by these groups for their own work. In *The Gospel in Solentiname* Ernesto Cardenal recorded the conversations of the male and female peasants in Solentiname concerning the Bible during and after Holy Mass. In these conversations, centred on biblical texts, a connection was made between the social analysis of the experiences of the population of Nicaragua of poverty and oppression under the Somoza regime and the reading of biblical texts in their social-historical context. Teresita says in connection with Luke 1: 48: 'he has looked with favour on the lowliness of his servant',

> one must recognize that at the time when Mary called herself a servant or slave, slavery was the accepted state of affairs ... Slavery still exists today but under another name. Today the slaves are the proletariat or the peasants. I believe that Mary therefore called herself a slave so as to show solidarity with the oppressed. Today she would perhaps have called herself a member of the proletariat or a peasant woman of Solentiname. (p. 30)

From the point of view of European Christian biblical scholarship *The Gospel in Solentiname* was naïve. However, it opened up a new way into the Bible for theologically educated people who were working together in such groups as Third World solidarity groups. They discovered the vitality of the Bible read in a social-historical way, and they discovered that biblical hermeneutics can involve theoretical and practical reflections upon the social situation of the reader as a member of an affluent society. The poverty and oppression of the male and female peasants of Solentiname became a political and spiritual challenge to wealthy Christians in western Europe.

The rediscovery of the power of the Bible in concrete political confrontations was also strongly affected by the 'materialist reading' deriving from French priests. Fernando Belo wrote a scholarly commentary on the Gospel of Mark in which social history at the time of the gospel and in the present was read with the help of a Marxist concept, and the actions of Jesus were described as actions with hands (the economy), feet (the path to the Kingdom of God), and eyes (opposing the ruling ideology). The concept of messianic praxis that was developed from this became the core of a 'materialist ecclesiology'. The writings of Michel Clévenot popularized materialist readings of the Bible in wider circles: *Approches matérialistes de la Bible* (1976) and *The Counter-Gospel of Anatole* (1975, 1979). The materialist readings of the Bible were carried on above all by the new groups that came into existence under the title 'Christians for Socialism'. This movement was

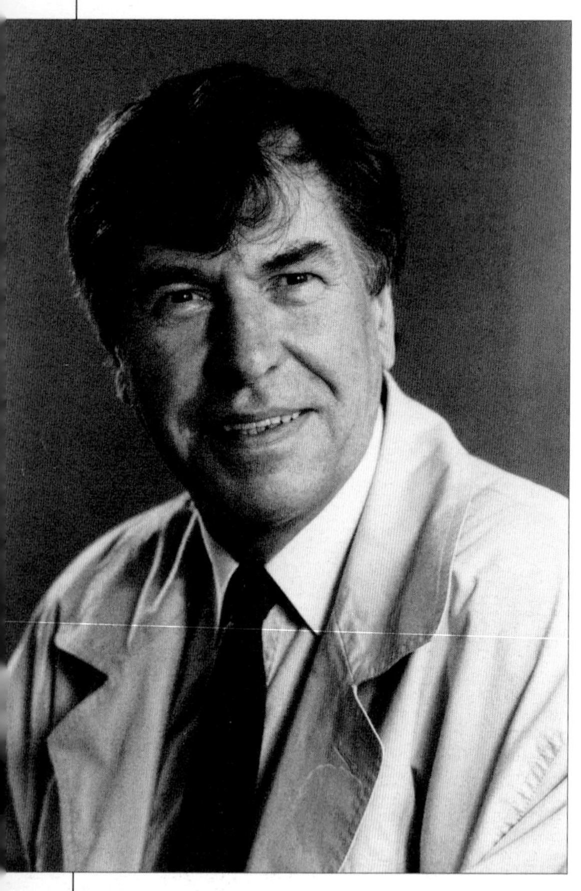

Professor Willy Schottroff (1931–97), a pioneer of European social-historical interpretation of the Bible.

founded, so far as Europe was concerned, in Bologna, Lyons, and Arnhem in Holland in 1973 in deliberate imitation of the 'Christians for Socialism' movement which was formed in 1970 during the elections in Chile and which soon had groups in the whole of Latin America. Books and lectures by the French Protestant Georges Casalis and the German Catholic Kuno Füssel enabled materialist reading of the Bible to be consolidated and extended.

In 1977 the 'Heidelberg Working Group for Social-Historical Interpretation of the Bible' was formed, a group in which biblical scholars, church workers, and members of the laity worked together on the social questions of their time. The biblical scholarship which several of the members carried out in the universities was no longer to be oriented to academic consensus and thus to an academic career, but was to be oriented towards the work of groups that were engaged for world-wide justice as in the 1980 World Council of Churches document *Towards a Church in Solidarity with the Poor*. The group did not call its work 'materialist'. This was not in order to distance its work politically from the 'lecture matérialiste' but because the social-historical reading of the Bible was carried on from the scholarly point of view in the tradition of academic exegesis of the Bible in Germany (that of H. Gunkel's 'Form Criticism', the history of life and customs, and archaeology) and did not belong to the philosophical tradition of French structuralism from which the 'lecture matérialiste' derived. Instead, the social analysis was undertaken by this group in a pragmatic and biblically oriented way. Questions were posed which came from the tradition of Marxist analysis of class: questions concerning power, authority, and money, and freedom from this unjust system. The Bible was discovered as a social-historical source in its own right. The group was also involved from the outset in Jewish–Christian dialogue: it engaged critically with the stereotypes of Christian anti-Judaism, and was from the beginning involved with the feminist theological movement that arose at about the same time. The biblical interpretations of this group were taken up in many church groups that were working for justice and peace.

Through work on the Bible which several of its members presented at German Protestant Church conferences (*Kirchentage*) from 1981 onwards, this way of reading the Bible became more widely known in church circles. The group still exists and it is concerned, for example, with questions of financial markets and globalization.

The peace movement against the stationing of new American middle-range atomic weapons reached its high point in 1981–6, NATO having decided on 12 December 1979 to re-equip western Europe with US middle-range rockets. The movement initiated a sharp political debate which was taken seriously in many circles. This debate was at the same time a debate about the Bible and particularly the Sermon on the Mount and Christian identity. Dutch and German responses from the Reformed Church gave an uncompromising 'no' to atomic weapons as a command of Christian faith, which became a paradigm for more than just the Reformed Churches. The debate about the Sermon on the Mount touched on fundamental questions: should Christians base their actions on the Sermon on the Mount when social or national decisions are concerned, or is the Sermon on the Mount valid only for the private lives of individuals who accept that powerlessness is the right way for them personally? The spiritual strength of the peace movement expressed itself in services of worship often immediately outside the camps where the atomic rockets were stored, in isolated forests. Here, affected by the place where the service was being held and the efforts of those taking part in many forms of work for peace often without any explicit analysis of the political situation in the worship, the prayers and the psalms became the language of hope

Over 20,000 people demonstrated in Brussels on 25 October 1981 against the deployment of American Pershing and Cruise missiles in Western Europe and the presence of Soviet SS-20 missiles in Eastern Europe. Such issues were at the heart of European liberation theology.

in a situation that suggested resignation. Those who took part in the services saw themselves as a congregation. The spiritual strength of these elements of worship also characterized the resistance of the citizens of the German Democratic Republic which contributed to the destruction of the wall between eastern Europe and the capitalist countries in 1989. There were hymns which used the same language in both the West German Peace Movement and the services of resistance in the GDR: 'May God keep us, May God protect us and be with us on our ways. Be a fountain and bread in the desert, Be with us with your blessing' (text, Eugen Eckert, 1985; melody Anders Ruuth, *c.*1968, 'La Paz del Señor'). The peace movement was the point of departure for the 'conciliar process' in the context of Europe, which additionally brought about a broad anchoring of impulses from liberation theology in the churches.

Important places for liberation theology readings of the Bible were and are projects carried out by women who did not see themselves as feminist in the narrow sense, but who were often bound up in a personal way with the feminist-theological movement. Two such projects can be mentioned here; first, the women's boycott campaign 'Do Not Buy Any Fruits of Apartheid 1977–1992'. The anti-racist decision of the World Council of Churches in 1969 had provoked a bitter controversy in the churches about the theological evaluation of racism as a sin, and the willingness for church finances to be used for the liberation struggle of non-whites. The women's boycott took up the cause of the movement for solidarity with the black population of South Africa in the context of the ecumenical programme against racism, and developed the politics of the shopping basket into an instrument of resistance from below, with implications for future forms of resistance. This movement also had its spiritual origins in joint services of supporter groups and their Bible readings.

The second project was, the Women's World Day of Prayer, whose history goes back to the nineteenth century. It is a movement of lay women from about 170 countries which spans confessional and national barriers. It sharpens awareness of the world-wide political situation and the particular context of those who pray, through the detailed information provided by those who have written the liturgy for that particular year concerning their regional situation. It is exemplary in its contextualization of faith and Bible reading, and as a spiritual workshop of women.

In the feminist-theological movement only some of the women explicitly regard themselves as feminist liberation theologians; nevertheless their actual interpretation of the Bible is strongly indebted to liberation theology. This expresses itself in the aim of the liberation of women, who must not be seen as isolated but as part of the overall liberation of men, women, and children from the structures of sexism but also of racism and economic and ecological exploitation. The connection with liberation theology expresses itself further in the methodological requirement of contextualization, and sometimes also in the requirement of a paradigm change in scholarship. The reception of feminist liberation theology from Latin America as well as other lands of the 'two-thirds world' increases with the awareness for the necessity of inter-cultural dialogues.

For the further development of European liberation theology and Bible reading, notice must be taken of Kairos Europa, which has developed 'an alliance for the freedom from the dictatorship of the de-regulated global economy and its culture of competition' (see the European Kairos document, 1998). Also, feminist liberation theology reading of the Bible will have an effect in the future in the work of the women of the European Society of Women in Theological Research.

The hermeneutical basis of liberation theology readings of the Bible in the context of Europe can be described as a structure which, in spite of the varying contexts and presuppositions of those who take part, is relatively homogeneous. In the first political night prayer in Cologne of 1 October 1968 it was affirmed that

> in prayer, humans express themselves in the presence of God. They express themselves in their pain over the not-yet-present kingdom of God and they express their hope for the coming of this kingdom. … Christ took sides because he put himself on the side of truth and justice, and we will be recognized as his followers by taking the same stand.

Hope and taking a particular stand are regarded as vital steps in this reading of the Bible and they can be supported biblically from the gospels of the New Testament in particular. In the same way the orientation towards praxis of faith can be defended against the Lutheran charge of legalism. 'When Jesus says "Go and do likewise" should that be regarded as being under the law? Are we not rather being given an example … in a demand that presupposes the ability to be free to live differently?' (Sölle and Steffensky, *Politisches Nachtgebet*, 136). With this is bound the implication of a critical and new Christian anthropology as opposed to that of traditional Christian, and above all Lutheran, dogmatic theology. Sin is confused in Protestantism with weakness. 'In fact by sin we understand neither individual personal matters that mostly have to do with the area of sexuality, nor that Protestant global feeling of powerlessness according to which we can do nothing in our own strength. … We are the collaborators of sin simply by the fact that we belong to the Northern rich world' (ibid. 236). Also the challenge of the dualism of this world and of the world to come, in the hope in resurrection, is clearly formulated here (as in the Credo from Dorothee Sölle on 1 October 1968). The recognition that this hermeneutic is in contradiction to the predominant theology of the churches and universities becomes particularly clear. Dorothee Sölle has always worked out the hermeneutical structures of a European liberation theology in opposition to those of the predominant Christian theology and in connection with this has spoken of two 'theologies'.

No dialogue between the two different theologies has taken place because the representatives of the predominant theology almost entirely ignore the new liberation theology in their own context and have not found it necessary to engage in dialogue with it because the impulses of liberation theology have no institutional anchoring. The unequal division of power relationships is expressed in this act of ignoring, and becomes obvious in the few written observations of those who represent the traditional theology. Eduard Lohse, for example, in an article published in 1981 has answered the ecumenical challenge of the poor churches to the rich churches with the observation that this challenge must be taken seriously and that the Western churches should be guided by the New Testament. The relevant New Testament passages, for example Matthew 5: 3 and Mark 10: 25, are interpreted by him to mean that the rich should not set their hearts on riches but should give gladly and support the churches of the poor. He interprets Mark 10: 42 as follows: here one is reminded 'in all sobriety that there exist in this world and will continue to exist power and authority, distress and need, wealth and poverty' (p. 63). The social-historical book by Luise Schottroff and W. Stegemann, *Jesus of Nazareth: Hope of the Poor* (1978) and the *Lecture matérialiste* (he names Belo and Casalis) are dismissed by him as Marxist ideology and countered with the argument that these expositions of the New Testament do not really match the sense of the biblical words (p. 53). The defective hermeneutical awareness of this position expresses itself in the fact that historical-critical interpretation of the Bible as practised by the author and his colleagues is regarded as the only correct method. No attempt is made to question the presuppositions of his own interpretation. The certainty with which the almsgiving practice of the rich is insisted on as the only true interpretation of the Bible is at the same time an expression of the political power relationships between the First and the 'two-thirds world'. The critical challenges from the 'two-thirds world' are handled with goodwill while at the same time it is asserted that their voices utter confused sounds (p. 52). The challenges to the exegesis and political praxis of wealthy theologians from the same context are dismissed with the anti-Communist argument (they are 'ideology') and the academic argument (they are not satisfactory scientifically). This article makes clear what is otherwise almost never openly documented in printed texts. Similar arguments have been used against all the groups and persons described so far in this essay, not in dialogues but in conversations with like-minded people between institutions ('such people cannot expect to get a post in a university or a relevant invitation to academic conferences, etc.'). A limitation of academic awareness and a distancing from liberation theology praxis in one's own context is also a feature of the 1994 book by Thomas Schmeller. It shows that in the very place where at least Latin American liberation theology has made a breakthrough into the Western academic context it is not able to penetrate the barriers of the Western academic and political consensus. Schmeller simply denies that the 'lecture matérialiste' is liberation theology (p. 279). Here the strategy of established academic institutions becomes implicitly visible; it aims to make liberation theology invisible in one's own context in order to avoid raising social questions.

In the following outline of a liberation theology reading of the Bible two steps will be taken: taking key passages from the New Testament I shall place in juxtaposition the outlines of traditional interpretation which I must always call the predominant one, and a liberation theology exposition from my perspective. I shall simply sketch the liberation theology interpretation without referring to particular references in order to make clear that this interpretation is anchored in the community of groups oriented to liberation theology and is not only the work of a particular person.

Matthew 5: 3, 'Blessed are the poor in spirit, for theirs is the kingdom of heaven'/Luke 6: 20, 'Blessed are you who are poor, for yours is the kingdom of God'. The blessing of the poor and the criticism of the divine incompatibility of wealth (compare Mark 10: 25) are understood in the traditional Western exegesis, as has already been made clear, in the sense of the benevolence of the wealthy. Alternatively they are interpreted moralistically: only those who make wealth their sole aim distance themselves from God; wealth as such is not the problem. In the liberation theology interpretation God's bias for the poor is emphasized. God's action for justice begins with the 'last' (Matthew 20: 16). Justice is a process in which the poor of the world are placed in the centre. The 'teaching office of the poor' means, 'that the poor pose the questions, for example about water' (D. Sölle, *Mystik und Widerstand*, 353). The belief in God of the rich begins with listening to this question of the poor. The history of liberation theology interpretation of the Bible in Western contexts shows that the demand of the gospel of the poor is a stumbling-block in a particular way. The peace movement is concerned with issues that immediately affect the interests of the people of Western Europe. The liberation theology interpretation of the biblical message of peace has found a much broader basis than the gospel of the poor. It touches the political and economic identity of the Western world and causes anxiety about the (further) loss of prosperity. The gospel of the poor makes visible that injustice upon which the prosperity and might of the Western world is based.

The story of the disciples plucking ears of corn on the sabbath (Mark 2: 23–8 and parallels) is interpreted in the traditional exegesis in an anti-Jewish manner. Jesus brings freedom from the Sabbath and from the Jewish law that enslaves humankind. The freedom from law in the gospel confronts petty Pharisaic observance of the Sabbath and legalism: 'the Sabbath was made for humankind', while in Judaism 'humankind was made for the Sabbath'. The hunger of the disciples of Jesus, which is the reason for plucking the ears of corn, appears simply as a convenient means of confrontation with Pharisaic or Jewish legalism. A liberation theology interpretation of the incident starts from the hunger of the disciples and with it that of the Jewish people at the time of Jesus. According to Mark 2: 23–8 and its parallels the Sabbath presumes that people will have had enough to eat when they praise God. The bodies of humans are a part of their relationship to God. Thus the violation of the Sabbath commandment is the expression of a need that is so great that it displaces the Sabbath. The Jewish interpretation of the law is positively utilized and it is assumed, in agreement with the Pharisees, that God in creation made the Sabbath for human beings. The liberation theology interpretation of the Bible in the German context has devoted considerable energy since its beginning in the 1970s to the critical revision of traditional Christian anti-Judaism and in co-operation with Jewish–Christian dialogue has also made it possible for wider church circles to become aware of this problem. I refer for this discussion here simply to an important and much read book by F. Crüsemann. Particularly influential was the vigorous debate among feminists over the anti-Judaism of the initial feminist biblical interpretation movement. In liberation theology interpretation of the Bible hope is understood as part of belief, and resignation as distancing from God. The hope of believers centres on the parables and pictures of the kingdom of God in the New Testament. The traditional Western idea of the kingdom of God, which comes from academic exegesis but has affected circles beyond that, spoke of a 'delay in the parousia' and the 'mistake' of the expectation of the imminent arrival of the kingdom of God on the part of Jesus and Paul. The kingdom of God became a subject for the study of religions and was no more a vital dimension of faith. In addition it was interpreted dualistically: we live in this world, the kingdom of God is a hope beyond this earth and death. For the political night prayers in Cologne a central part of faith was hope for the kingdom of God and joy that it was possible to work together in order to establish the kingdom of God on earth. The prayers and the hymns that arose in liberation theology working groups deal again and again with the nearness of God and the kingdom of God. 'Nearness' is not understood in the sense of a linear chronology, as in the concept of the delay of the parousia. 'The kingdom of God is at hand' (Mark 1: 15 and parallels) is a promise of the nearness of God that encourages and strengthens those who believe. 'Nearness' is a relational term and cannot be pressed into a time scheme. Naturally the eschatology of the New Testament contains elements of an apocalyptic myth which, as myth, has not become untrue but is true in the sense that poetry expresses truth. Jürgen Ebach has developed an important social historical account of Jewish and Christian apocalyptic in the context of liberation theology work.

The critical questions concerning Paul which have been widely discussed in the feminist theological movement have a pre-history in liberation theology and philosophy (Ernst Bloch). Paul has been criticized because of his texts that are oppressive to women. In 1 Corinthians 11: 2–16 the woman is not, like the man, called the image of God; there is a theologically based hierarchy of Christ–man–woman. He is also criticized because of his theology of the cross. According to this criticism his theology of the cross is an instrument that prevents the human race from taking responsibility for itself (thus Ernst Bloch) and which also prescribes for women the role of sacrifice. Here the deepest divisions between the insights of (feminist) liberation theology in the European/Western context and in Latin American liberation theology become apparent. In contemporary Latin America the experience of martyrdom and its Catholic piety, for example, in the stations of the cross, have made possible a positive view of the theology of the cross. In many circles of the feminist movement the theology of the cross has been particularly criticized. Meanwhile feminist and liberation theology discussion in the Western context has become more cautious and more often includes historical reflection on the social-historical context of the crucifixion of Jesus by representatives of the oppressive *Pax Romana*, as well as on the theology of the cross in early Christianity.

However, the criticism of Paul is only one side of the liberation theology dispute with Paul. Liberation theology anthropology with its criticism of the traditional Christian view of sin (see above), its concept of 'structural sin', and the social-historical research which has arisen in connection with liberation theology have led to a new engagement with Paul and a new theological evaluation of him. I can illustrate this new reading on the basis of Galatians 2: 16:

> we know that a person is justified not by the works of the law but through faith in Jesus Christ. And we have come to believe in Christ Jesus so that we might be justified by faith in Christ, and not by doing the works of the law, because no one will be justified by the works of the law.

The traditional interpretation is as follows: on the basis of the works of the law 'the Jew' seeks justification before God. For this reason the law leads people into sin, namely to pious achievement which desires to gain salvation by human efforts and to break free from God or even reject him. Through the death and resurrection of Christ, God has acted on behalf of those who are caught up in this sin and has made the godless righteous. The law is now abrogated as a way of salvation. It now has significance for Christian belief only as an ethical tradition. The 'ritual law', above all circumcision, is no longer binding on Christians. The circumcision of non-Jewish Christian males brings them under the law and not to righteousness before God. The key for a new reading of the theology of Paul is the understanding of sin. Paul says nowhere that the desire of people to fulfil the law is sin. He says that all sin because all have broken the law, that is, they do not live according to the will of God (compare Romans 2: 17–24; 3: 9ff; 7: 14–25). It is the false way of living which destroys the life that God wills. The false way of life comes from structural sin whose power is omnipresent and which turns people into murderers. The death and resurrection of the Messiah Jesus indicate God's intervention on behalf of the life of an alienated humanity. Now we are free from the domination of false praxis. We are able 'to walk in new life' (Romans 6: 4), that is, to live according to the Torah. Paul represented rigorously the following standpoint: without belief in Christ, life according to the will of God, the Torah, is not possible. Most of the Jews of his time, assuming that they knew it, did not accept this standpoint, to Paul's sorrow. His standpoint, however, did not mean that he no longer regarded himself as a Jew. Here both the traditional anti-Jewish reading of Paul's view of the 'the law' and his anthropology and idea of sin can be seen in a completely new light. Paul thus becomes the advocate of a clear analysis of the death-dealing social structures of that time, and as a teacher of loyalty to the law.

Liberation theology reading of the Bible in the West European context arose from the work of the political night prayer, Third World solidarity groups, the peace movement, and the women's movement. It already has a long history. It has its roots in the life-and-death questions of Western society, in which Christians have worked together for the alteration of death-dealing structures. Their identification as liberation theology, which is not always made, corresponds, however, to their dialogue and solidarity with the 'two-thirds world', and their analysis which identifies Western power and Western prosperity as the cause of the poverty of the poor: world-wide and in their own country.

17 Epilogue

JOHN ROGERSON

Several of the preceding chapters have dealt with contemporary interpretations of the Bible, in particular those dealing with feminism, European liberation theology, and interpretation in Latin America and Africa. The aim of the present chapter is to return to the academic scene and to outline the changes that have taken place in the past thirty years in biblical scholarship. These changes have brought much vitality to the discipline; but they have also introduced a good deal of confusion, which this chapter will attempt to sort out. It will end by discussing the phenomenon of so-called postmodernism.

THE PLURALISM OF METHODS IN RECENT SCHOLARSHIP

There is no doubt that the diversity and pluralism that have become part of the everyday scene in biblical studies have brought great benefits to students and scholars alike. When I began my teaching in Durham in 1964, we were still fighting some of the battles of the nineteenth century. Students were sharply divided into two camps, liberals and conservatives, and the major issue that divided them was that of authenticity. To take one example, were the closing verses of the book of Amos, those that speak of raising up 'the booth of David that is fallen' (Amos 9: 11) the words of the eighth-century prophet Amos, or the work of later editors dating from the time when the temple (the booth of David) was in ruins between 587 and 515 BCE? Conservative students wanted to maintain the authenticity of the words, that is, that they indeed derived from the eighth-century prophet. Most, if not all, of their teachers were liberals, who regarded the words as later additions. The whole discussion was controlled, however, by the fact that there was only one method that the conservatives and liberals could use in their approach to the text. This was the method that tied biblical interpretation to the search for the intended meaning of the biblical writers and which, in the case of prophetic books, tried to discover the authentic words of the prophets as opposed to material that scholars classified as later editorial additions. In New Testament studies the gospels were treated as repositories of the words of Jesus, which, once the authentic words had been separated from later additions made by the early church, could be used to reconstruct the mission and intentions of Jesus.

There were laudable theological impulses behind this method. If the prophets were men of God speaking the word of God to their contemporaries in concrete historical circumstances, one wanted to hear these inspired utterances and was less interested in the work of later editors. If Christianity was primarily concerned with the mission and message of Jesus, one wanted to know what he actually said. There was also the hidden assumption that editors were less 'inspired' than prophets who proclaimed 'thus saith the Lord', and that additions to the words of Jesus by the early church were less 'inspired' than his genuine utterances. It is true that even in 1964 there were scholars in Scandinavia and Britain who were trying to introduce a more flexible approach to prophetic books into Old Testament scholarship, via the idea that prophetic books were produced by prophetic schools, or by disciples of prophets. But these trends had only a small measure of success compared with the impact made by literary, structuralist, and final-form methods in interpretation.

Suddenly, we were being warned again the 'intentionalist fallacy', that is, the fallacy that we could discover the intentions of writers or that these intentions were necessarily the most important factor in interpreting a text. We were made aware of latent meanings; we were shown how texts could be interpreted in terms of their binary oppositions, how plot and character contrast functioned in the final form of a text. To scholars who had been trained to interpret texts diachronically, that is, to peel off their literary layers like layers of an onion so as to penetrate back to the earliest units of which they were composed and then to work out how all the layers had been added to make up the whole onion, structuralist or final-form criticism came as a blinding revelation.

Ferdinand de Saussure's example of the chess match can convey something of what the new approaches offered. If we see a chess match adjourned at, say, move nineteen, we do not need to know what moves one to eighteen were in order to appreciate the state of the game and whether one player has an advantage. That will be clear from the relation of the pieces to each other. Moves one to eighteen will, of course, be important to experts, who may discern in them a strategy by one player that will become important. The value of the chess match example for our purposes is that, crudely generalizing, we can say that prior to the advent of literary and structuralist methods in biblical studies it seemed as though we spent much of our time trying to guess, on the basis of the state of the game at move nineteen, what the earlier moves had been, so that we could properly understand the state of play at move nineteen! The discovery that the final form of the text, that is, the game as adjourned at move nineteen, contained its own resources for interpretation, brought a new dimension to biblical studies.

If we go back to the example of Amos 9: 11–15, the new dimension did not settle the question whether or not these were the words of the eighth-century prophet. But they did make it legitimate to study the book of Amos in its final form as opposed to scholarly attempts to discover the authentic utterances of

Amos. The text now assumed a new importance in its own right. Previously, it had been more of a means to an end, that end being the recovery of the historical Amos. Conservative students, at least, could now study Amos in a manner that could be defended intellectually, and scholarship had moved on from the battles of the nineteenth century. In the case of the gospels, these could be studied as compositions in their own right, and not simply as repositories for possible authentic sayings of Jesus.

But biblical studies is a fast-moving field. No sooner had structuralism and final-form criticism been assimilated than other new approaches arrived, including deconstruction, feminism, liberation theology, and, later, ideological criticism. Each of these approaches had, and has, a positive contribution to make to interpreting the Bible. Deconstruction looks for features in a text that appear to undermine it. At the end of Psalm 23, for example, the psalmist affirms that he will dwell in the house of the Lord for ever. This is an odd place for a shepherd to want to be, and the statement at once puts into question the pastoral images that the psalm contains about lying down in green pastures, passing through deathly valleys, and enjoying banquets in the presence of enemies. Of course, it has long been known that shepherd imagery in the ancient Near East was used of kings, and Psalm 23 is possibly a royal psalm. However, by 'deconstructing' the imagery of the psalm, the concluding statement about dwelling in the Lord's house invites and initiates a deeper examination of the psalm than does the observation that it may be a royal psalm.

Feminist criticism has made biblical studies aware of issues that were previously overlooked, not least, the whole question of sexuality. Phyllis Trible's pioneering *God and the Rhetoric of Sexuality*, parts of which appeared as separate articles in 1973, showed how an approach to the Bible that was driven by the modern concern to redress historic discrimination against women could open up familiar texts to all sorts of new insights. Once the approach was established, men as well as women were able to contribute to feminist criticism, a good example being an essay by John Sawyer pointing out that the second half of Isaiah, as well as containing material on the male servant of God, also has a good deal to say about the female daughter of Zion. Feminist criticism also made the discipline aware of gender-derived translation distortions, as in Psalm 22: 9. English translation, from Coverdale (1540) to the Revised English Bible of 1989 translated this verse as

> thou (you) art (are) he that took me from my mother's womb,

thus obscuring the fact that in this verse God is implicitly likened to a female midwife. The New Revised Standard Version

> yet it was you who took me from the womb

is both closer to the Hebrew, and makes possible the connection with the feminine imagery.

Liberation theology had a similarly illuminating contribution to make. It emphasized that, for ancient Israel, salvation was something material and social; and it challenged biblical scholars to examine their own political attitudes and to place their extremely privileged positions alongside the marginalized and persecuted positions of prophets such as Amos and Jeremiah. Liberation approaches rediscovered texts that were generally overlooked. For example, everyone knows that the sin of Sodom was an attempted public homosexual orgy. But liberation theology emphasizes another view of the sin of Sodom, that in Ezekiel 16: 49:

> This was the guilt of your sister Sodom: she and her daughters had pride, excess of food, and prosperous ease, but did not aid the poor and needy.

Again, liberation theologians brought to light and emphasized the pathos of Lamentations 5:

> We have become orphans, fatherless; our mothers are like widows. We must pay for the water we drink; the wood we get must be bought. With a yoke on our necks we are hard driven: we are weary, we are given no rest. We get our bread at the peril of our lives, because of the sword in the wilderness ... Our skin is black as an oven from the scorching heat of famine. Young men are compelled to grind, and boys stagger under loads of wood. The old men have left the city gate, the young men their music. The joy of our hearts has ceased; our dancing has been turned to mourning.

Who can fail to be moved, not only by these verses, but by the knowledge that they have brought hope to the poor and distressed in Latin America? The simple discovery that their plight is described in the Bible has been the beginning of hope for some.

Finally, and briefly, a word about ideological criticism. This is an approach that asks questions about the interests of those who produced the various texts of the Bible. Whom did they represent, and what were their aims in writing as they did?

I have tried to outline, then, the impact made on biblical studies by the methods that established themselves in the 1970s and 1980s, and I have noted that they had positive things to offer. But they also brought negative possibilities. Along with feminists whose aim was to redeem the biblical text for those concerned with women's issues were feminists who believed that the Old Testament was irredeemable. It was so much the product of a patriarchal society in which women were oppressed that it could serve as no more than evidence for an oppression that needed to be redressed. Women's voices in ancient Israel had been silenced and were hardly heard, if at all, in the Old and New Testaments. Their story needed to be recovered, with the help of archaeology and by reading behind the Old Testament text.

The same ambiguity could be found with liberation theologians. Whereas the first wave of them used the Old Testament, and especially the story of the Exodus, positively to advocate social and material liberation in Latin America and Southern Africa, voices were later to be heard questioning whether texts produced by ruling and oppressing classes could, in fact, be liberating for oppressed people today.

The approach most likely to bring negative considerations to bear on the Bible was ideological criticism, especially in a Marxist-derived form which regarded ideology as a false consciousness that blinded people to the truth and which needed to be unmasked. While it was, and is, perfectly legitimate to enquire, for example, into the interests of those who produced the Ten Commandments—they were evidently property- and slave-owning circles—such questioning can be unsettling to anyone who regards the Decalogue as an expression of God's will for ancient Israel and a key element in traditional Christian ethics. To be told that the Ten Commandments originated in class supremacy, rather than a theological attempt to define human responsibility, can be disturbing.

I have kept until last the question of deconstruction, because it raises fundamental questions about biblical interpretation, and because dealing with these questions will lead to the main aim of this chapter, which is to outline a theory of scholarship which will accommodate the best insights of recent approaches while marginalizing their negative aspects.

Earlier, I presented deconstruction in a favourable light as a reading device. It is now necessary to indicate its negative sides and the long-term effects that they have had upon biblical studies. Inevitably, this outline can only touch on a complex subject.

I began by going back to structuralism and the new possibilities that it offered to biblical interpretation. I described it as a move that brought the text back into the centre of attention in contrast to methods that I caricatured as resembling the peeling of an onion. But structuralist approaches were also approaches which removed the text from any social and historical context. If the stress was upon how the plot was constructed, and how the characters related to each other, it was not necessary to ask questions about the social and historical contexts in which a text was produced. Thus, decontextualizing the text was the literary equivalent of Saussure's distinction between language system (*langue*) and language use (*parole*) and his concentration upon language system, which was investigated in terms of its own organization and structures, unrelated to social context. This in turn was connected with the theory of the arbitrariness of the linguistic sign—a grey area, but one which was taken to mean that meaning within the language system was determined by the internal relationships between signs rather than by a connection between a sign and external reality.

Before I elaborate this further, I want to stress that there were gains in decontextualizing certain biblical books and in paying attention to their final form and their internal structures. When I was a student, we were required to study the book of Ruth in the following way. We were expected to accept that it was written in the fifth century BCE as a protest against the narrow, nationalistic policies of Ezra and Nehemiah, and we were expected to be able to discuss the problems of relating the practice of levirate marriage in the book (the marriage between Ruth and Naomi's kinsman Boaz) to the law of levirate marriage as stated in Deuteronomy 25: 5–10. We were also expected to discuss whether the book's concluding genealogy, which makes the Moabitess Ruth the grandmother of King David, was a later addition, or was the datum that the book of Ruth had been written to explain. What was never explained to us was that the book had a narrative arch, from the hopelessness of Naomi in a foreign land and with no male dependants at 1: 5, to the concluding verse of the story (prior to the genealogy) at 4: 17 with the exclamation 'a son has been born to Naomi'; nor was it pointed out that the narrative developed via the contrasts between Naomi and Ruth on the one hand and Boaz and the nearer kinsman, who refused to marry Ruth, on the other. These, and many others gains brought by literary structuralism masked the negative aspects of such approaches.

COMMUNICATIVE INTENTIONS AND TEXTUAL INTERPRETATION

Deconstruction developed from that part of Saussure's theory that was taken to assert that meaning was internal to linguistic systems and not dependent on objects in the external world. It was a small step to the view that texts, whatever their nature, should be regarded as pieces of literature to be closely read, and not as works that in any way related to an external world. In the words of Anthony Giddens, 'The thesis of the arbitrary character of the sign, as Saussure developed it, tends to elide the difference between texts which claim to deliver some veridical description of the world and those that are fictional' (*Social Theory Today*, 210). In *The Truth about Postmodernism*, Christopher Norris discusses deconstructionist writers such as J. Hillis Miller, who believe that 'philosophical texts are in no way different from novels or poems, and should therefore be read chiefly with an eye to their covert metaphors, fictive strategies and structures of rhetorical implication' (p. 183). On this view, Kant's *Critique of Pure Reason* ceases to be an attempt to explore the possibilities and limits of empirical knowledge and becomes a text no different from a poem or novel, to be studied for its rhetorical and other techniques.

The view that texts do not relate to an external world has serious implications for a collection such as the Bible that claims to record the dealings of God with a historical people in a specific cultural setting and which claims that 'God was in Christ reconciling the world to himself' (2 Cor. 5: 19). Some of these implications have found expression in recent work. Thus, it is common to regard God in Old Testament texts not as an external reality in whom the Old Testament writers believed, but simply as a character in a story. Jesus, in the gospels, can be regarded in the same way. Equally serious is the assumption that because all texts are literary texts in spite of what they claim to be, literary methods have priority over historical or philosophical attempts to interpret texts. This has led to the assertion that the historical books of the Old Testament, such as Samuel and Kings, should be read primarily as literary narrative, and should not be used to reconstruct the history of ancient Israel.

One further outcome of the negative side of newer, literary-based approaches to the Bible needs to be introduced before the attempt is made to move in a positive direction. Reader-response criticism has rightly drawn attention to the need for reflection upon reading and readers when interpretation is being considered. It is obvious that readers come to texts from vastly differing backgrounds, and that what they make of texts depends upon their interests and where they are coming from. The correspondence page of the *Times Literary Supplement* provides weekly evidence that reading is not an innocent activity! But does it follow from the fact that readers have different interests that affect their reading, or that authors can be so easily misunderstood (as they constantly point out on the correspondence page of the *TLS*) that texts only have the meanings assigned to them by interpretative communities? That this latter possibility is the case has been strikingly urged by my colleague David Clines in a recent essay. Commenting on the practice of reading against the grain of a text Clines writes:

> Strictly speaking, texts do not have grains any more than they 'have' meanings. Authors would like to put grains in their texts, of course, and readers are forever finding grains in texts, even though they are not there. But since authors do not own their own texts, not forever, authors' intentions do not constitute the reality of the texts they compose or determine their meaning. And from the readers' side, what counts as the grain of the text for them is no more than what some interpretative community or other decides to call the grain. So when I am reading against the grain, I am really reading against the practice of an interpretative community, sometimes even against myself and my own first reading. Strictly speaking, the text is not to blame for the thoughts that come into my head when I am reading it, but I am not always speaking strictly; like most people, in everyday speaking and writing I go on ascribing meaning and grain to texts. (*Interested Parties*, 207 n. 38)

There are many points in this statement with which I can agree, but I content myself with the observation that it privileges for itself what it denies to other texts. It clearly has a communicative intention, not to mention a grain, and these are the work of the author and certainly not dependent on the practice of an interpretative community. At the same time, it is difficult to disagree with the view expressed in the quotation that a person's second reading of a text might vary radically from that same person's first reading. What is needed is a theoretical framework that can accommodate the main important insights brought to biblical studies by literary structuralism, deconstructive techniques, and interest approaches such as feminism and liberation theology, without reaching the conclusion that all texts must be treated as literary texts and that meanings are only the practice of interpretative communities. Such a theoretical framework is found, in my view, in Anthony Giddens's theory of 'talk'.

In his essay 'Structuralism, Post-structuralism and the Production of Culture' Giddens criticizes the work of Saussure and those who have followed him, for separating language and language structure from the social environments of language use. 'Linguistic competence', he writes, using Noam Chomsky's adaptation of Saussure's language system, 'involves not only the syntactical mastery of sentences, but mastery of the circumstances in which particular types of sentence are appropriate ... mastery of the language is inseparable from mastery of the variety of contexts in which language is used' (*Social Theory Today*, 199–200).

Giddens's next step is to note that in day-to-day communication it is possible for speakers to interrogate each other to ensure that what they intended to say has been properly understood. (The *TLS* correspondence page serves the same function!) Giddens defines as 'talk' the activity that links culture and communication via agents and their social setting, and then makes the important observation that 'talk' is situated in space but not in time. A conversation, for example, takes place in a particular social space occupied by two or more people, and depends upon a whole range of non-linguistic factors. To give an example of my own, the word 'round' spoken in a pub has different implications from when it is used at a choir practice. Once the conversation is ended it no longer exists. If it is written down, however, it occupies time in the sense that other people can have access to the conversation even centuries after it has taken place. But the transfer of the conversation from social space to time means that it is removed from the social context in which it was generated, including the non-linguistic factors and shared conventions which were a vital part of it. As a piece of writing, the recorded conversation becomes a cultural object capable of being interpreted in varying ways, and thus having meaning potential beyond the original communicative aims of the conversation.

Several things are implied in this analysis. First, in talk, closure and fixity of meaning are aimed at and achieved by the fact that parties to it can check to see that they have been properly understood. It is only when something is written down that language is turned away from fixity of meaning and becomes open to multiple interpretation. But, secondly, even in writing something down an author has a communicative intention (compare once more the *TLS* correspondence page) and it ought to be possible to interrogate a text in order to discover its communicative intention. Giddens writes:

> we can ask what was the communicative intent involved in a given section of a text. Where the author is unavailable, we can seek to answer such a question by investigating the forms of mutual knowledge implied in what the author wrote. This entails in turn that there are criteria for the accuracy of interpretations. But these criteria, and the types of material that must be known to confirm them, are complicated. They essentially involve enquiring into the settings of production of the text as a work. They mean knowing a good deal about the way in which the author set out to produce the text and the intellectual resources drawn upon in its production ... they also involve knowing about the audience to whom the text was primarily addressed ... Texts are written within various conventions of form, style and readership. (ibid. 220)

Translated into the specifics of biblical studies we have here, it seems to me, a powerful justification for the classical methods of source criticism and form- and redaction criticism; a justification for the need for a knowledge of the social and intellectual milieu of ancient Israel within the larger ancient Near East and of the early church in its Judaeo-Hellenistic-Roman context. We have a defence of scholarly attempts to establish the communicative intentions of the biblical writers.

But we also have a justification for refusing to be satisfied simply with trying to establish the communicative intentions of the writers. As written texts become separated in time and social setting from the conditions in which they were produced, they become capable of bearing multiple meanings. As Giddens says, writing of artefacts, with which texts have much in common,

> All artifacts which have a durable character can become more or less completely separated both from the contexts of their initial production and from the projects of those who created them. All artifacts similarly may be put to purposes, or even 'interpreted', in ways of which their producers may never have dreamed. (ibid. 221)

Giddens's approach, with its firm rejection of divorcing language and the production of texts from their social context, coupled with the recognition that texts as artefacts can be open to multiple interpretation and use, enables us to put the methods that can currently be found in biblical studies study into a credible framework.

The biblical writers had a communicative intention within their historical and social world, and the discovery of that communicative intention is a primary task in biblical studies, and one that calls for a great deal of specialist knowledge. The biblical writers did not produce their texts with the intention of allowing scholars in the twentieth century to address feminist and social and political issues, nor to deconstruct their texts or to apply to them close reading and literary structuralist techniques developed in the twentieth century. Yet all of these latter strategies are legitimate activities, and they have enriched biblical studies. It is important, however, that we do not allow the tail to wag the dog, which is what happens when it is claimed that there is no difference between a philosophical text and a poem, that literary methods are prior to historical-critical methods, and that texts do not have meanings or grains intended by authors.

We have come round, then, to reaffirming the importance of historical criticism as a means of discovering the intentions of the biblical writers. Does this mean that we are only back to where we were in 1964, with our arguments about the authenticity of the closing verses of Amos 9? Certainly not. If the historical-critical method is reinstated as having a prime position in biblical studies, it is a historical-critical method chastened and, in my opinion, improved by the attacks that it has suffered at the hands of advocates of the other methods discussed in this chapter and illustrated elsewhere in this volume.

HISTORICAL CRITICISM REASSESSED

If I compare myself now with what I can remember about the beginning of my teaching in 1964, I can say that in 1964 I was not aware of women's issues, nor of the way in which my political attitudes might affect my scholarship. I did not think of books such as Ruth and Jonah or the gospels as literary works to which purely literary techniques could be applied. None of this change of perspective affects, of course, the communicative intention of the biblical writers in producing their texts; but it has affected how I understand my task as a practitioner of historical criticism, and to that extent I hope that it has enabled me to do the work better.

Historical criticism has benefited, then, from its encounter with newer methods. But these newer methods need to benefit from historical criticism, especially a historical criticism informed by sociology and anthropology. I have argued that Giddens's sociological approach to texts makes it possible to challenge certain deconstructionist strategies. But challenges also need to be made to feminist and liberation approaches to the Bible.

A commonplace of feminist criticism is that women were oppressed and marginalized in the patriarchal society of ancient Israel, a charge that has brought the accusation from some feminists that such scholarship is anti-Jewish, and which has caused scholars such as Luise Schottroff (see her essay above) to seek for a feminism that is not anti-Jewish. Liberationists point similarly to oppression of peasants by the ruling classes. Now these assertions may be correct; but they do not become correct simply by being asserted. Such claims have to be established, if that is possible, by reference to evidence about the nature of ancient Israelite society, by the roles of women within that society, by how power was actually exercised. Feminist anthropologists such as Henrietta Moore have pointed out that it is difficult to generalize about gender roles, and that such roles are determined by the cultural contexts in which people live. Gerald West has drawn attention to what have been called 'hidden transcripts', that is, rumours, gossip, folk-tales, gestures, jokes, which are the strategies of resistance among so-called powerless groups and which need to be taken into account in analysis of how power is actually exercised. It may be, of course, that we lack the means of discovering the answer to some of these questions; in which case, we should say that we do not know what the position of women and peasants was in ancient Israel. That would not alter the fact that, in the history of interpretation of the Bible, certain texts have been used to advocate male headship over women; but that is another matter.

In a way, the Bible is like people whose faults are the most obvious thing about them but who turn out to have many sterling qualities on deeper acquaintance. If, to use George Steiner's analogy in *Real Presences* about respecting a text as one would respect a stranger, we concentrate not on the obvious faults of the Bible but its virtues, it presents many striking features. The feature that constantly impresses me is the degree of criticism that is brought to bear upon the chosen people of Israel and its leaders, and upon the failure of the disciples of Jesus to understand him or be loyal to him. Confining ourselves to the Old Testament, it is possible to find self-satisfied and nationalistic sentiments in the Old Testament portrayal of Israel, but these are far outweighed by unfavourable comments on Israel's radical failure to fulfil its vocation. These unfavourable comments stem from a deeply realistic understanding of human nature in general, and its propensity for inhumanity, insincerity and violence. The Old Testament at its best longs for a transformed world, a world of nature that is at peace with itself (this is the implication of the vegetarian world of the envisaged new creation of Isaiah 11: 1–9 and 65: 17–25) inhabited by humans who are not deprived by human or natural evil of life, or food, or habitation. It witnesses to people trying to live out this hope in the context of a cruel and ambiguous world that is none the less, and against much evidence, believed ultimately to be in the hands of a God whose mercy and justice will have the last word. The witness to such a hope, in both Old and New Testaments, is what gives the Bible its abiding value even in a so-called postmodern world, if that is a correct designation of the world today.

POSTMODERNISM AND BIBLICAL STUDIES

It is a commonplace of academic discourse that we are living in a postmodern era, although there is little agreement about whether 'post' is to be understood in a temporal or a structural sense. Understood as a temporal term, 'postmodern' denotes a period of time that has succeeded the 'modern' period. Understood structurally, 'postmodern' denotes features of thought that are not necessarily new, such as a distrust of grand narratives, but which are in conflict with what are often, perhaps unfairly, regarded as legacies of the Enlightenment. My own view is that it is more accurate to say with Anthony Giddens, in his *Modernity and Self-Identity*, that we are living in late modernity, and that the phenomena that are pointed to as indicators of postmodernity are developments from within modernity itself. I can also agree with Zygmunt Bauman's definition of post-modernity as 'modernity without illusions'.

In his *Postmodernism: A Reader* Thomas Docherty reminds us that the whole topic, this amorphous thing, as he calls it,

> remains ghostly—and for some, ghastly—for the simple reason that the debate around the postmodern has never been properly engaged. The term itself hovers uncertainly in most current writings between—on the one hand—extremely complex and difficult philosophical senses and—on the other hand—an extremely simplistic mediation as a nihilistic, cynical tendency in contemporary culture.

Something of the confusion that arises from the lack of clarity about the meaning of 'postmodern' can easily be illustrated. Jean François Lyotard, one of the most important theorists of postmodernism, wrote in a letter to Jessamyn Blau in 1985,

> There is a sort of grief in the Zeitgeist. It can find expression in reactive, even reactionary, attitudes or utopias—but not in a positive orientation that would open up a new perspective ... Technoscientific development has become a means of deepening the malaise rather than allaying it. It is no longer possible to call development progress. It seems to proceed of its own accord, with a force, an autonomous motoricity that is independent of us. It does not answer to demands issuing from human needs. On the contrary, human entities—whether social or individual—always seem destabilized by the results and implications of developments ... We could say that humanity's condition has become one of chasing after the process of the accumulation of new objects (both of practice and of thought). (Docherty, *Postmodernism*, 49)

There is much in this statement with which I can agree, but which is also reminiscent of the book of Ecclesiastes in the Old Testament, with its insistence that much of life at the time of the writer (probably the late fourth century BCE) was vanity and a chasing after wind. From this perspective, there is nothing new about 'postmodernism', a point made trenchantly by Terry Eagleton in a review in the *TLS* on 2 January 1998 of a book by M. J. Devany, *Since at Least Plato … and Other Postmodernist Myths*:

> M. J. Devany … brings to aspects of postmodern thought the grossly unfair advantage of a knowledge of the history of philosophy. One thing in which that knowledge instructs her is just how old-hat most postmodernism is. Moral relativism, the arbitrary sign, the world as 'constructed' rather than as given, the mediated nature of knowledge, the self as processual rather than stable: all of these doctrines of course are at least as old as Plato, and no doubt as Adam. 'Antirealism', as Devaney caustically puts it, 'is as much of a foundational principle in western philosophy as realism is'. This is bad news for those credulous souls who believe that all this avant-garde speculation started with Saussure, or Jacques Derrida, before whom all philosophy was a dreary mixture of native realism and autocratic rationalism.

Eagleton's broadside, however, indicates that for some advocates of postmodernism what is being claimed in its name *is* a feature of a new age, a new age in which relativism in ethics and 'deregulation' in the interpretation of texts have produced a situation in which almost anything goes. Christopher Norris, in an attack upon Lyotard, accuses him of deliberately skewing Kant's philosophy in order to achieve 'a wholesale aestheticisation of ethical discourse which redefines "autonomy" in private-individualistic terms, and which blocks the appeal to any wider community of intersubjective understanding' (*Reclaiming Truth*, 41). From some feminist quarters comes the accusation that postmodernism is a male phenomenon that has succeeded in 'reconstituting an overwhelmingly male pantheon of proper names to function as ritual objects of academic exegesis and commentary'. It is necessary to reclaim 'women's work and women's names, as a context in which debates about postmodernism might further be considered, developed, transformed (or abandoned)' (M. Morris in Docherty, *Postmodernism*, 378, 381).

Within the context of biblical studies some, but by no means all, of the advocates of deconstructionist, ideological, and feminist critiques of biblical texts regard themselves unashamedly as postmodernists and as subscribing to some of the positions that are anathema to critics such as Eagleton and Norris. My own view is much closer to that of Eagleton and Norris than to that of those whom they attack. At the same time, I am strongly drawn to what are often regarded as the typical features of postmodernism, if only because they express standpoints that I find represented in the Bible, and which seem to me to be realistic assessments of the human predicament. The first is a distrust of grand narratives, that is, explanatory theories designed to make sense of the whole of reality. Such theories can also be found in the Bible, as in the view of the 'wisdom' literature of the Old Testament that virtue will always be rewarded and evil will always be punished; but at its most profound, in books such as Job and Ecclesiastes and in Psalms of Lament, the Old Testament challenges such simplistic outlooks. Secondly, there is a distrust in postmodernism of the Enlightenment belief that human reason has the capacity to emancipate humanity from dogma and superstition so that the human race can make its own history and destiny. The Bible, of course, knows nothing of the Enlightenment; but it has a good deal to say about what happens when the human race believes that its destiny is best left to humanity. The opening chapters of Genesis are powerful commentaries on this viewpoint. Thirdly, there is an awareness that things that seem to be innocent in themselves, such as knowledge and education, can and do conceal powerful ways in which some groups of people can exercise power over other people and thus control them. The Bible is well aware of the problems of the exercise and abuse of power.

My own position, then, is that I share the distrust of grand narratives, accept that aspects of the Enlightenment project led to German fascism and Stalinist totalitarianism, and am very conscious of the autonomy of other people and the need to respect them. I prefer, however, the term late modern to postmodern because I believe in the Enlightenment project, and because radical criticism of that project from within is not essentially new. I also view with alarm some of the implications of postmodern theories, such as that texts only have the meanings that can be accepted by interpretative communities. Some of the versions of ethics that have come to the fore under the aegis of postmodernism also seem to me to be capable of justifying practices such as apartheid, although I would never want to imply that such an outcome would be intended or welcomed by those who are ethical relativists.

However, the actual definition of our present intellectual condition, whether we call it postmodern or late modern, is less important than the fact that, in the humanities at least, we are operating in a different world compared with that of forty years ago. If, as has been argued above, Giddens's theory of 'talk' makes possible a sensible reconciliation between the need to search for the communicative intentions of biblical texts and to allow that, separated from their original contexts of production, such texts can be interpreted in new and creative ways, the opportunities presented by the current pluralism in biblical studies will yield positive results without leading to absurdities that contradict common sense and the realities of human lives.

Further Reading

General Reference

D. N. Freedman (ed.), *The Anchor Bible Dictionary*, 6 vols. (New York, 1992).

P. R. Ackroyd and C. F. Evans (eds.), *The Cambridge History of the Bible*, i. *From the Beginnings to Jerome* (Cambridge, 1970).

G. W. H. Lampe (ed.), *The Cambridge History of the Bible*, ii. *The West from the Fathers to the Reformation* (Cambridge 1969).

S. L. Greenslade (ed.), *The Cambridge History of the Bible*, iii. *The West from the Reformation to the Present Day* (Cambridge 1963).

J. B. Pritchard, *Ancient Near Eastern Texts Relating to the Old Testament*, 3rd edn. (Princeton, 1969).

B. M. Metzger and M. D. Coogan (eds.), *The Oxford Companion to the Bible* (New York, 1993).

H. C. Kee, E. M. Myers, J. Rogerson, and A. J. Saldarini, *The Cambridge Companion to the Bible* (Cambridge, 1997).

D. L. Jeffrey, *A Dictionary of Biblical Tradition in English Literature* (Grand Rapids, Mich., 1992).

R. J. Coggins and J. L. Houlden, *A Dictionary of Biblical Interpretation* (London, 1990).

THE MAKING OF THE BIBLE: I. THE HISTORICAL BACKGROUND

1. Old Testament Background

G. I. Davies, *Ancient Hebrew Inscriptions: Corpus and Concordance* (Cambridge, 1991).

N. Gottwald, *The Tribes of Yahweh: A Sociology of Liberated Israel, 1250–1050 B.C.E.* (London, 1979).

D. W. Jamieson-Drake, *Scribes and Schools in Monarchic Judah: A Socio-Historical Approach* (Sheffield, 1991).

J. W. Rogerson (ed.), *Beginning Old Testament Study* (London, 1998).

——and P. Davies, *The Old Testament World* (Cambridge, 1989).

G. Vermes, *The Complete Dead Sea Scrolls in English* (London, 1998).

2. The Apocrypha

J. H. Charlesworth (ed.), 'Apocrypha' in *Anchor Bible Dictionary* (New York, 1983), i. 292–4.

J. C. Dancy, *The Shorter Books of the Apocrypha* (Cambridge, 1972).

D. Ewert, *From Ancient Tablets to Modern Translations: A General Introduction to the Bible* (Grand Rapids, Mich., 1983).

B. M. Metzger, *An Introduction to the Apocrypha* (New York, 1957).

3. The New Testament

J. K. Elliott, 'Manuscript, the Codex and the Canon', *Journal for the Study of the New Testament*, 63 (1996), 105–23.

H. Y. Gamble, *Books and Readers in the Early Church: A History of Early Christian Texts* (London, 1995).

E. Hennecke, *The New Testament Apocrypha* (ed. W. Schneemelcher and J. Clark) 2 vols. (Louisville, Ky, 1991, 1993).

B. M. Metzger *The Canon of the New Testament: Its Origin, Development, and Significance* (Oxford, 1987).

THE MAKING OF THE BIBLE: II. TEXT AND TRANSLATION

4. The Hebrew Bible

P. S. Alexander, 'Jewish Aramaic translations of Hebrew scriptures', in M. J. Mulder (ed.), *Mikra: Text, Translation, Reading and Interpretation of the Hebrew Bible in Ancient Judaism and Early Christianity* (Assen/Maastricht/Philadelphia, 1988), 217–53.

F. I. Andersen and A. D. Forbes, *Spelling in the Hebrew Bible* (Rome, 1986).

J. Barr, *Comparative Philology and the Text of the Old Testament* (Oxford, 1968), 194–222.

B. Chiesa, *The Emergence of Hebrew Biblical Pointing: The Indirect Sources* (Frankfurt am Main/Cirencester, 1978).

M. B. Cohen, *The System of Accentuation in the Hebrew Bible* (Minneapolis, 1969).

F. M. Cross and S. Talmon (eds.), *Qumran and the History of the Biblical Text* (Cambridge, Mass., 1975).

M. Fishbane, *Biblical Interpretation in Ancient Israel* (Oxford, 1985).

C. D. Ginsburg, *Introduction to the Massoretico-Critical Edition of the Hebrew Bible*, proleg. H. M. Orlinsky (New York, 1966).

L. L. Grabbe, 'Survey of literature on the authenticity of Masoretic vocalization', in *Comparative Philology and the Text of Job: A Study in Methodology* (Missoula, Mont., 1977), 179–97.

P. Kahle, *The Cairo Genizah*, 2nd edn. (Oxford 1959).

G. Khan, 'Tiberian Hebrew Phonology', in A. S. Kaye (ed.), *Phonologies of Asia and Africa* (Winona Lake, Minn., 1977), 85–102.

——'The Syllabic Nature of Tiberian Hebrew Vocalization', in A. S. Kaye (ed.), *Semitic Studies in Honor of Wolf Leslau* (Wiesbaden, 1991).

——'The Medieval Karaite Transcriptions of Hebrew in Arabic Script', *Israel Oriental Studies*, 12 (1992), 157–76.

——'The Tiberian Pronunciation Tradition of Biblical Hebrew', *Zeitschrift für Althebraistik*, 9 (1996), 1–23.

S. Kogut, *Correlations between Biblical Accentuation and Traditional Jewish Exegesis: Linguistic and Contextual Studies* (Jerusalem, 1994).

S. Leiman, *The Canonization of Hebrew Scripture: The Talmudic and Midrashic Evidence* (Flamden, 1976).

C. McCarthy, *The Tiqqune Sopherim and Other Theological Corrections in the Masoretic Text of the Old Testament* (Freiburg/Göttingen, 1981).

E. J. Revell, *Biblical Texts with Palestinian Pointing and their Accents* (Missoula, Mont., 1977).

——*Hebrew Texts with Palestinian Vocalization* (Toronto, 1970).

S. Talmon, 'The Three Scrolls of the Law that were Found in the Temple Court', *Textus*, 2 (1962), 14–27.

——'The Old Testament Text', in P. R. Ackroyd and C. F. Evans (eds.), *The Cambridge History of the Bible*, i. (Cambridge, 1970), 159–99.

E. Tov, *Textual Criticism of the Hebrew Bible* (Minneapolis/Assen/Maastricht, 1992).

——*The Text-Critical Use of the Septuagint in Biblical Research*, 2nd edn., rev. and enlarged (Jerusalem, 1997).

E. Würthwein, *The Text of the Old Testament: An Introduction to the Biblia Hebraica*, tr. E. F. Rhodes from *Der Text des Alten Testaments—Eine Einführung in die Biblia Hebraica von Rudolf Kittel*, 4th edn. (Stuttgart, 1973; London, 1980).

I. Yeivin, *Introduction to the Tiberian Masorah*, tr. and ed. E. J. Revell (Missoula, Mont., 1980).

5. The Apocrypha

Articles on the books dealt with in this chapter in the *Anchor Bible Dictionary* and J. H. Charlesworth (ed.), *Old Testament Pseudepigrapha* (New York, 1983).

6. The New Testament

There are two excellent introductions to the text of the New Testament:

K. and B. Aland, *The Text of the New Testament*, 2nd edn. (Grand Rapids, Mich., and Leiden, 1989). Containing much up-to-date information generated by the Münster Institute, this study is especially strong in describing the materials and in its study of various textual problems according to the editorial principles behind the Nestle–Aland text.

B. M. Metzger, *The Text of the New Testament*, 2nd edn. (Oxford, 1968; or 3rd edn., Oxford, 1992). This gives a description of the manuscripts and other materials, a history of the discipline, and a discussion of textual methods and problems. It is the best traditional introduction.

See also:

B. D. Ehrman and M. W. Holmes, *The Text of the New Testament in Contemporary Research: Essays on the Status Quaestionis. A Volume in Honor of Bruce M. Metzger* (Grand Rapids, Mich., 1995). A collection of 'state of the art' studies by experts in the various fields of study.

D. C. Parker, *The Living Text of the Gospels* (Cambridge, 1997). An introduction along new lines, which studies the materials and a number of passages in the light of the question whether there is an 'original' text. No knowledge of Greek is required to understand it.

More generally, the whole history of the text and versions is covered in various sections of *The Cambridge History of the Bible*, 3 vols. (Cambridge, 1963–70).

There are a number of general introductions to Greek and Latin palaeography. For a book more precisely on the former as it applies to the New Testament, see:

B. M. Metzger, *Manuscripts of the Greek Bible: An Introduction to Greek Palaeography* (New York/Oxford, 1981).

For Latin manuscripts:

M. T. Gibson, *The Bible in the Latin West* (The Medieval Book 1; Notre Dame, Ind./London, 1993).

Other books on subjects discussed above:

H. Y. Gamble, *Books and Readers in the Early Church: A History of Early Christian Texts* (New Haven, 1995). An excellent study of the use and context of early Christian manuscripts.

B. M. Metzger, *A Textual Commentary on the Greek NT*, 2nd edn. (Stuttgart, 1994).

W. L. Petersen, *Tatian's Diatessaron: Its Creation, Dissemination, Significance, and History in Scholarship*, Supplements to *Vigiliae Christianae*, 25 (Leiden, 1994).

F. H. A. Scrivener, *A Plain Introduction to the Criticism of the New Testament for the Use of Biblical Students*, 2 vols.; 4th edn., rev. E. Miller (London/New York/Cambridge, 1894). Outdated both in theory and in its list of materials, it still provides the fullest history of scholarship.

Among other kinds of material, there is the video *The Desert Speaks: The World of Papyrus*, produced by the Institut für Neutestamentliche Bibelwissenschaft, Salzburg, which tells the story of the great papyrus finds and illustrates the process of conservation.

There are outstanding permanent exhibitions of biblical manuscripts and incunabula in various libraries, including the British Library (where Codex Sinaiticus, Codex Alexandrinus, the Lindisfarne Gospels, and other treasures may be seen), Trinity College, Dublin (The Book of Kells), and the Chester Beatty Collection, Dublin (a great variety of books and manuscripts).

7. Modern Translations

F. F. Bruce, *History of the Bible in English: From the Earliest Versions* (New York, 1978).

D. Ewert, *From Ancient Tablets to Modern Translations* (Grand Rapids, Mich., 1983).

F. C. Grant, *Translating the Bible* (Edinburgh, 1961).

E. A. Nida, *Toward a Science of Translating, with Special Reference to Principles and Procedures involved in Bible Translating* (Leiden, 1964).

——and C. R. Taber, *The Theory and Practice of Translation* (Leiden, 1969).

H. Pope, *English Versions of the Bible* (St Louis, 1952).

S. E. Porter and R. H. Hess (eds.), *Translating the Bible: Problems and Prospects* (Sheffield, 1999).

E. H. Robertson, *The New Translations of the Bible* (London, 1959).

S. M. Sheeley and R. N. Nash, Jr., *The Bible in English Translation: An Essential Guide* (Nashville, 1997).

L. A. Weigle with C. F. D. Moule, 'English Versions since 1611, with a Note on the New English Bible', in *The Cambridge History of the Bible*, ii. *The West from the Reformation to the Present Day* (Cambridge, 1963), 361–82.

The Prefaces to the various translations often provide much useful information. Several committee-based translations have also published explanations of their work. These have been prepared for the Revised Version by several of those who participated, the Revised Standard Version, the New English Bible, and the New International Version, among others.

THE STUDY AND USE OF THE BIBLE

8. The Early Church

P. R. Ackroyd and C. F. Evans (eds.), *The Cambridge History of the Bible*, i. *From the Beginnings to Jerome* (Cambridge, 1970).

P. R. L. Brown, *Augustine of Hippo* (London, 1967).

R. M. Grant and D. Tracy, *A Short History of the Interpretation of the Bible*, 2nd edn. (Minneapolis, 1989.).

J. N. D. Kelly, *Jerome: His Life, Writings and Controversies* (London, 1975).

M. Sæbø (ed.), *Hebrew Bible/Old Testament: The History of its Interpretation*, i. *1. Antiquity* (Göttingen, 1996).

M. Simonetti, *Biblical Interpretation in the Early Church: An Historical Introduction to Patristic Exegesis* (Edinburgh, 1994).

9. The Middle Ages to the Reformation

G. R. Evans, *The Logic and Language of the Bible*, i. *The Earlier Middle Ages* (Cambridge, 1984); ii. *The Road to Reformation* (Cambridge, 1985).

G. W. H. Lampe (ed.), *The Cambridge History of the Bible*, ii. *The West from the Fathers to the Reformation* (Cambridge, 1969).

J. Leclercq, *The Love of Learning and the Desire for God: A Study of Monastic Culture* (New York, 1962).

B. Smalley, *The Study of the Bible in the Middle Ages* (Oxford, 1952; 3rd edn., 1983).

10. The Reformation to 1700

M. W. Anderson, *The Battle for the Gospel: The Bible and the Reformation, 1444–1589* (Grand Rapids, Mich., 1978).

G. Bedouelle and B. Roussel (eds.), *Le Temps des Réformes et la Bible* (Bible de tous les temps, 5; Paris, 1989).

F. F. Bruce, *The English Bible* (London, 1961).

S. L. Greenslade (ed.), *The Cambridge History of the Bible*, iii. *The West from the Reformation to the Present Day* (Cambridge, 1963).

D. K. McKim (ed.), *Handbook of Major Historical Interpreters of the Bible* (Downers Grove, Ill, 1998).
T. H. L. Parker, *Calvin's Preaching* (Edinburgh, 1992).
——*Calvin's Old Testament Commentaries* (Edinburgh, 1986).
——*Calvin's New Testament Commentaries*, 2nd edn. (Edinburgh, 1993).
J. Pelikan, *Luther the Expositor: Introduction to his Exegetical Writings* (St Louis, 1959).
A. Rabil, Jr., *Erasmus and the New Testament: The Mind of a Christian Humanist* (San Antonio, Tex., 1972)
D. Wilson, *The People and the Book: The Revolutionary Impact of the English Bible, 1380–1611* (London, 1976).
D. F. Wright (ed.), *The Bible in Scottish Life and Literature* (Edinburgh, 1988).

11. 1700 to the Present

General Studies of the Period

W. Baird, *The Interpretation of the New Testament, i. From Deism to Tübingen* (Minneapolis, 1992).
J. Barton and R. Morgan, *The Interpretation of the Bible* (Oxford, 1988).
J. Drury (ed.), *Critics of the Bible, 1724–1873*, Cambridge English Prose Texts (Cambridge, 1989).
W. G. Kümmel, *The New Testament: The History of the Investigation of its Problems* (London, 1973).
N. Smart and J. P. Clayton (eds.), *Nineteenth-Century Religious Thought in the West*, 3 vols. (Cambridge, 1985), esp. vol. iii. *Biblical Interpretation and Modern Science.*
B. Willey, *The Eighteenth-Century Background: Studies in the Idea of Nature in the Thought of the Period* (London, 1940).

Biblical and Historical Criticism

S. Neill and T. Wright, *The Interpretation of the New Testament, 1861–1986* (Oxford, 1988).
J. W. Rogerson, *Old Testament Criticism in the Nineteenth Century: England and Germany* (London, 1984).
E. S. Schaffer, *'Kubla Khan' and the Fall of Jerusalem: The Mythological School in Biblical Criticism and Secular Literature, 1770–1880* (Cambridge, 1975).
B. Willey, *Nineteenth-Century Studies: Coleridge to Matthew Arnold* (London, 1949).

Popular Interpretation and Use of the Bible

G. M. Marsden, *Fundamentalism: The Shaping of Twentieth-Century Evangelicalism, 1870–1925* (New York, 1980).
B. Thwaite and T. Thornton, *Prophecy*, Themes in History (Stroud, 1997).
T. P. Weber, *Living in the Shadow of the Second Coming: American Premillenialism, 1875–1982*, rev. edn. (Chicago, 1983).
D. F. Wright (ed.), *The Bible in Scottish Life and Literature* (Edinburgh, 1988).

12. The Eastern Churches

Apostolos Athanssakis, *The Life of Pachomius*, Early Christian Literature Series, 2 (Missoula, Mont., 1975).

P. M. Blowers (ed.), *The Bible in Greek Christian Antiquity* (Notre Dame, Ind., 1997).
J. Chrysostom, *Discourse against Judaizing Christians*, tr. Paul W. Harkins, The Fathers of the Church, 68 (Washington, DC, 1977).
Pseudo-Dionysius, *The Complete Works: The Classics of Western Spirituality* (London, 1987).
J. Leclerq, *The Love of Learning and the Desire for God: A Study of Monastic Culture* (New York, 1962).
Origen of Alexandria, *Commentary on the Gospel According to John Books 1–10*, tr. R. E. Heine, The Fathers of the Church, 80 (Washington, DC; 1989).
——*Commentary on the Gospel According to John Books 13–23*, tr. R. E. Heine, The Fathers of the Church, 89 (Washington, DC, 1993).
Theophylact Bishop of the Ochrid and Bulgaria, *The Explanation of the Holy Gospels*, 4 vols. (House Springs, Miss., 1997).
Pachomian Koinonia, *The Lives, Rules and other Writings of Saint Pachomius and his Disciples*, 3 vols. Cistercian Studies Series, 45, 46, 47 (Kalamazoo, Mich., 1980–2).
E. Werner, *The Sacred Bridge: Liturgical Parallels in Synagogue and Early Church* (New York, 1970).
F. Yates, *The Art of Memory* (Chicago, 1966).

13. The Bible in Judaism

E. R. Bevan and C. Singer (eds.), *The Legacy of Israel* (Oxford, 1927).
C. Pearl, *Rashi* (London, 1988).
M. Sæbø (ed.), *Hebrew Bible/Old Testament: The History of its Interpretation*, i. *1. Antiquity* (Göttingen, 1996).
E. Silberschlag, *From Renaissance to Renaissance: Hebrew Literature from 1492–1970* (New York, 1973).
C. Sirat, *A History of Jewish Philosophy in the Middle Ages* (Cambridge/Paris, 1985).
M. Steinschneider, *Jewish Literature from the Eighth to the Eighteenth Century* (New York, 1965)
F. E. Talmage, *David Kimhi: The Man and his Commentaries* (Cambridge, Mass., 1975).

14. The Bible in Literature

T. S. Eliot, 'Religion and Literature', *Selected Essays*, 3rd edn. (London, 1951).
O. B. Hardison, Jr., *Christian Rite and Christian Drama in the Middle Ages* (Baltimore, 1965).
D. Jasper, *The Sacred and Secular Canon in Romanticism: Preserving the Sacred Truths* (London, 1998).
D. Norton, *A History of the Bible as Literature*, i (Cambridge, 1993).
S. Prickett, *Origins of Narrative: The Romantic Appropriation of the Bible* (Cambridge, 1996).
B. Qualls, *The Secular Pilgrims of Victorian Fiction* (Cambridge, 1982).
W. Tyndale, 'W. T. unto the Reader', in D. Daniell (ed.), *Tyndale's New Testament: Modern-Spelling Edition* (New Haven, 1995).
T. Ziolkowski, *Fictional Transfigurations of Jesus* (Princeton 1972).

CONTEMPORARY INTERPRETATION

15. Feminist Scholarship

Collections

E. Schüssler Fiorenza (ed.), *Searching the Scriptures*, i. *A Feminist Introduction* (London, 1994).

——(ed.), *Searching the Scriptures*, ii. *A Feminist Commentary* (London, 1995). This includes E. Castelli on Romans and S. Briggs on Galatians.

C. A. Newsom and S. H. Ringe (eds.), *The Women's Bible Commentary* (London, 1992). This includes J. Romney Wegner on Leviticus and J. Schaberg on Luke.

E. Cady Stanton (ed.), *The Woman's Bible: The Original Feminist Attack on the Bible* (first published 1895; Edinburgh, 1985).

Work by individual authors

A. Bach, *Women, Seduction, and Betrayal in Biblical Narrative* (Cambridge, 1997).

A. Y. Collins (ed.), *Feminist Perspectives on Biblical Scholarship* (Chicago, 1985).

T. Dennis, *Sarah Laughed: Women's Voices in the Old Testament* (London, 1994).

E. Schüssler Fiorenza, *In Memory of Her: A Feminist Theological Reconstruction of Christian Origins* (London, 1983).

A. Loades, *Searching for Lost Coins* (London, 1987).

C. Meyers, *Discovering Eve: Ancient Israelite Women in Context* (Oxford, 1988).

Y. M. Sherwood, *The Prostitute and the Prophet: Hosea's Marriage in Literary-Theoretical Perspective* (Sheffield, 1996).

P. Trible, *God and the Rhetoric of Sexuality* (London, 1978).

——*Texts of Terror: Literary-Feminist Readings of Biblical Narratives* (Philadelphia, 1984).

R. J. Weems, *Battered Love: Marriage, Sex, and Violence in the Hebrew Prophets* (Minneapolis, 1995).

16. Liberation Theology

(*a*) Latin America

P. Berryman, *Stubborn Hope: Religion, Politics, and Revolution in Central America* (New York, 1994).

M. D. Carroll R., *Contexts for Amos: Prophetic Poetics in Latin American Perspective* (Sheffield, 1992).

——'God and his People within History and among the Nations: Considerations for a Contextualized Reading of Amos 1 & 2 from Latin America', *Tyndale Bulletin*, 47/1 (1996), 49–70.

G. Cook, *Crosscurrents in Indigenous Spirituality: Interface of Maya, Catholic and Protestant Worldviews*, Studies in Christian Mission, 18 (Leiden, 1997).

J. S. Croatto, *Exodus: A Hermeneutics of Freedom* (Maryknoll, NY, 1981).

——*Biblical Hermeneutics: Toward a Theory of Reading as the Production of Meaning* (Maryknoll, NY, 1987).

G. Gutiérrez, *On Job: God-Talk and the Suffering of the Innocent* (Maryknoll, NY, 1987).

C. Mesters, *Defenseless Flower: A New Reading of the Bible* (Maryknoll, NY, 1989).

J. Míguez Bonino, *Christians and Marxists: The Mutual Challenge to Revolution* (Grand Rapids, Mich., 1976).

J. P. Miranda, *Marx and the Bible: A Critique of the Philosophy of Oppression* (Maryknoll, NY, 1974).

J. Pixley, *On Exodus: A Liberation Perspective* (Maryknoll, NY, 1987).

——*Biblical History: A People's History* (Minneapolis, 1992).

C. Rowland and M. Corner, *Liberating Exegesis: The Challenge of Liberation Theology to Biblical Studies*, Biblical Foundations in Theology (London, 1990).

J. L. Segundo, *The Liberation of Theology* (Maryknoll, NY, 1976).

——*Faith and Ideologies: Jesus of Nazareth Yesterday and Today*, i (Maryknoll, NY, 1984).

J. Sobrino, *Jesus the Liberator: A Historical-Theological Reading of Jesus of Nazareth* (Maryknoll, NY, 1993)

E. Tamez, *Bible of the Oppressed* (Maryknoll, NY, 1981).

——*The Scandalous Message of James: Faith without Works is Dead* (New York, 1990).

——*The Amnesty of Grace: Justification by Faith from a Latin American Perspective* (Nashville, 1993).

L. E. Vaage, *Subversive Scriptures: Revolutionary Readings of the Christian Bible in Latin America* (Valley Forge, Pa., 1997).

(*b*) Africa

D. T. Adamo, *Africa and the Africans in the Old Testament* (San Francisco, 1998).

K. Appiah-Kubi and S. Torres (eds.), *African Theology en route: Papers from the Pan-African Conference of Third World Theologians, Accra, December 17–23, 1977* (Maryknoll, NY, 1977).

K. Bediako, 'Epilogue', in Y. Schaaf, *On their Way Rejoicing: The History and Role of the Bible in Africa* (Carlisle, 1994), 243–54.

P. Frostin, *Liberation Theology in Tanzania and South Africa: A First World Interpretation* (Lund, 1988).

E. Isichei, *A History of Christianity in Africa: From Antiquity to the Present* (Grand Rapids, Mich., 1995)

T. S. Maluleke, 'Black and African Theologies in the New World Order', *Journal of Theology for South Africa*, 96 (1996), 3–19.

T. A. Mofokeng, 'Black Christians, the Bible and Liberation', *Journal of Black Theology* 2 (1988), 34–42.

I. J. Mosala, 'Race, Class, and Gender as Hermeneutical Factors in the African Independent Churches' Appropriation of the Bible', *Semeia*, 73 (1996), 43–57.

——and B. Tlhagale (eds.), *The Unquestionable Right to be Free* (Johannesburg, 1986).

N. Ndungu, 'The Bible in an African Independent Church', in H. W. Kinoti and J. M. Waliggo (eds.), *The Bible in African Christianity* (Nairobi, 1997), 58–67.

Y. Schaaf, *On their Way Rejoicing: The History and Role of the Bible in Africa* (Carlisle, 1994).

R. S. Sugirtharajah (ed.), *Voices from the Margin: Interpreting the Bible in the Third World* (Maryknoll, NY, 1991).

G. O. West, *Biblical Hermeneutics of Liberation: Modes of Reading the Bible in the South African Context*, rev. edn. (Pietermaritzburg/Maryknoll, NY, 1995).

——*The Academy of the Poor: Towards a Dialogical Reading of the Bible* (Sheffield, 1999).
V. L. Wimbush, 'The Bible and African Americans: An Outline of an Interpretative History', in C. H. Felder (ed.), *Stony the Road We Trod: African American Biblical Interpretation* (Minneapolis, 1991), 81–97.

(*c*) Europe

E. Cardenal, *The Gospel in Solentiname*, 4 vols. (Maryknoll, NY, 1977–84).
M. Clévenot, *Materialist Approaches to the Bible* (Maryknoll, NY, 1985).
F. Crüsemann, *The Torah: Theology and Social History of Old Testament Law* (Edinburgh, 1996).
E. Lohse, 'Das Evangelium für die Armen', *Zeischrift für die neutestamentliche Wissenschaft*, 72 (1981) 51–64.
C. Rowland and M. Corner, *Liberating Exegesis: The Challenge of Liberation Theology to Biblical Studies*, 2nd edn. (London, 1991).
T. Schmeller, *Das Recht des Anderen. Befreiungstheologische Lektüre des Neuen Testaments in Lateinamerika* (Münster, 1994).
L. Schottroff, *Lydia's Impatient Sisters: A Feminist Social History of Early Christianity* (Louisville, Ky, 1995).
——'Spirituality in a Household of Deprivation and Affluence: The Perspective of a Western German Feminist Theologian 1995', *Feminist Theology. The Journal of the Britain and Ireland School of Feminist Theology*, 13 (1996), 31–46.
——'Through German and Feminist Eyes: A Liberationist Reading of Luke 7: 36–50', in A. Brenner (ed.), *The Feminist Companion to the Hebrew Bible and the New Testament* (Sheffield, 1996), 332–41.
——'Working for Liberation: A Change of Perspective in New Testament Scholarship', in F. F. Segovia and M. A. Tolbert (eds.), *Reading from this Place*, ii. *Social Location and Biblical Interpretation in Global Perspective* (Minneapolis, 1995), 183–98.
W. Schottroff and W. Stegemann (eds.), *God of the Lowly: Socio-Historical Interpretations of the Bible* (Maryknoll, NY, 1984).
D. Sölle, *Political Theology* (Philadelphia, 1974).
——*Mystik und Widerstand* (Hamburg, 1997).
World Council of Churches, *Towards a Church in Solidarity with the Poor: Commission on the Churches' Participation in Development* (Geneva, 1980).

17. Epilogue

Z. Bauman, *Postmodern Ethics* (Oxford, 1993).
D. J. A. Clines, *Interested Parties: The Ideology of Writers and Readers of the Hebrew Bible* (Sheffield, 1995).
M. J. Devaney, *'Since at least Plato ...' and Other Postmodern Myths* (Basingstoke, 1997).
T. Docherty (ed.), *Postmodernism: A Reader* (New York, 1993).
A. Giddens, 'Structuralism, Post-Structuralism and the Production of Culture', in A. Giddens and J. Turner (eds.), *Social Theory Today* (Cambridge, 1987).
——*Modernity and Self-Identity: Self and Society in the Late Modern Age* (Cambridge, 1991).

H. L. Moore, *Feminism and Anthropology* (Minneapolis, 1988).
M. Morris, 'Feminism, Reading, Postmodernism', in Docherty, *Postmodernism: A Reader*, 368–89
C. Norris, *The Truth about Postmodernism* (Oxford, 1993).
——*Reclaiming Truth: Contribution to a Critique of Cultural Relativism* (London, 1996).
J. F. A. Sawyer, 'Daughter of Zion and Servant of the Lord in Isaiah: A Comparison', *Journal for the Study of the Old Testament*, 44 (1989), 89–107.
G. Steiner, *Real Presences: Is There Anything in What We Say?* (London, 1989).
P. Trible, *God and the Rhetoric of Sexuality* (Philadelphia, 1978).
G. West, 'And the Dumb do Speak: Articulating Incipient Readings of the Bible in Marginalized Communities', in J. W. Rogerson *et al.* (eds.), *The Bible in Ethics: The Second Sheffield Colloquium* (Sheffield, 1995), 174–92.

Acknowledgement of Sources

The publishers wish to thank the following who have kindly given permission to reproduce illustrations on the pages indicated. In a few instances we have been unable to trace the copyright holder prior to publication. If notified, the publishers will be pleased to amend the acknowledgements in any future edition.

ABBREVIATIONS
T = Top B = Bottom L = Left C = Centre R = Right

Colour plates All pictures are between the pages quoted

(112–3) 1: Private Collection/Bridgeman Art Library. 2: Prado, Madrid/Bridgeman Art Library. 3: Sonia Halliday Photographs. 4: Staats-und Universitatsbibliothek, Hamburg. 5: Palazzo Pitti, Florence/Bridgeman Art Library. 6: Jane Taylor/Sonia Halliday Photographs. 7: Fitzwilliam Museum, University of Cambridge Ms 3-1954 f. 13r/ Bridgeman Art Library. 8: Sonia Halliday Photographs.
(208-9) 1a: Private Collection/Bridgeman Art Library. 1b: Private Collection/Bridgeman Art Library. 2: Louvre, © RMN-Arnaudet. 3: The Master & Fellows of Trinity College Cambridge. 4: Private Collection/Bridgeman Art Library. 5: Hermitage, St Petersburg/Bridgeman Art Library. 6: The Royal Collection © 2000 Her Majesty Queen Elizabeth II. 7: Manchester City Art Galleries/Bridgeman Art Library. 8: Richardson & Kailas Icons, London/Bridgeman Art Library.
(272-3)1: Ancient Art & Architecture Collection. 2: Editions Assouline, photo Laziz Hamani. 3: Victoria & Albert Museum, London/Bridgeman Art Library. 4: Musée Condé, Chantilly Ms 139/1363 f. 7r/Bridgeman Art Library. 5: Isabella Stewart Gardner Museum, Boston, Mass./Bridgeman Art Library. 6: Santa Trinidad Cathedral, Haiti/Bridgeman Art Library. 7: Private Collection/Bridgeman Art Library. 8: The Pierpoint Morgan Library/Art Resource, NY.

Black and white illustrations All pictures are on the pages quoted

3: Courtesy Professor J. W. Rogerson. 4: Courtesy Professor R. Smend. 6: © The Israel Museum, Jerusalem, Collection Israel Antiquities Authority. 7: Cairo Museum. 8: Z Radovan, Jerusalem. 10: photo AKG, London. 12: City of David Archaeological

Project. 14: Trustees of the British Museum. 15: Louvre, © RMN-Franck Raux. 16-17: Trustees of the British Museum. 19: University of Pennsylvania Museum (neg. #S8-56181). 20: Louvre, © RMN. 21: John Rylands University Library of Manchester. 22-23: Israel Museum, Jerusalem, photo David Harris. 24: Leipzig University Library. 32: © National Gallery, London. 35: The Dean and Chapter of Winchester. 38: © RMN-Hervé Lewandowski. 39: By permission of the British Library. 42: Deutsches Archaologisches Institut, Rome. 49: Cambridge University Library. 55: By permission of the British Library. 64: Institute of Microfilmed Hebrew Manuscripts, Jewish National & University Library, Jerusalem. 65: Beth Hatefutsoth, The Nahum Goldmann Museum of the Jewish Diaspora, Tel Aviv. 67: Cambridge University Library. 68–69: Israel Museum, Jerusalem, photo David Harris. 71: Hulton Getty. 73: Israel Museum, Jerusalem, photo David Harris. 75: © Biblioteca Ambrosiana. All rights reserved. 76: Cambridge University Library. 81: Cambridge University Library. 87: Cambridge University Library. 90: By permission of the British Library. 93: Ben-Zvi Institute, Jerusalem. 95: Cambridge University Library. 99: The Schøyen Collection Ms 46. Location: Oslo & London/Courtesy Sotheby's. 103: By permission of the British Library. 107: Alte Pinakothek, Munich/Bridgeman Art Library. 110: Photographie Giraudon. 111: By permission of the British Library. 114: By permission of the British Library. 119: Courtesy The Queen's College, Oxford. 123: Mary Evans Picture Library. 124: Alpine Club Library. 125: By permission of the British Library. 127: John Rylands University Library of Manchester. 130: Bibliotheca Bodmeriana. 135L: Oxford University Press. 135R: The Governing Body of Christ Church, Oxford. 137: Courtesy of Mansfield College, Oxford. 142: Oxford University Press. 143: © The Times. 145: © The American Bible Society. 146: © NETBible.com. 149: The Dean & Chapter of Durham. 156: © Dean & Chapter of Westminster. 166: The Metropolitan Museum of Art, Rogers Fund, 1916. (16.174.2) All rights reserved. 171: By permission of the British Library. 176: photo AKG, London. 178: Florence, Biblioteca Medicea Laurenziana, Ms laur. Plut. 12.17, c. 3v. With the authorization of the Ministero per i Beni e le Attivita' Culturali. Further reproduction without permission is forbidden. 179: Bibliothèque Municipal, Avranches. 181: National Library, Prague. A XXI/I, Collection Prague Metropolitan Chapter of St Vitus Cathedral. 182: Ancient Art & Architecture Collection. 183: Staatsbibliothek, Bamberg, Msc. Patr. 5, fol. 1v. 184: By permission of the British Library. 185: The Dean & Chapter of Worcester. 186: Mary Evans Picture Library. 187: The Master & Fellows of Trinity College Cambridge. 190: Alte Pinakothek, Munich/Bridgeman Art Library. 198: By permission of the British Library. 202: By permission of the British Library. 203: By permission of the British Library. 205: Hulton Getty. 206L: Oxford University Press. 206R: By permission of the British Library. 207: Hulton Getty. 209: By permission of the British Library. 215: Germanisches Nationalmuseum, Nuremberg. 221: Hulton Getty. 222: Trustees of the British Museum. 223: By permission of the British Library. 224: By permission of the archives of Imperial College of Science, Technology & Medicine, London. 226: photo AKG, London. 227: photo AKG, London. 228: By permission of the British Library. 229: photo AKG, London. 232: By permission of the British Library. 233: Trustees of the British Museum. 234: Louvre, © RMN-Hervé Lewandowski. 235: Trustees of the British Museum. 236: Illustrated London News. 237: Courtesy Professor R. E. Clements. 239: Henry

Watson Music Library, Manchester. 243: Museum of Art, Novgorod/Bridgeman Art Library. 247: Tretyakov Gallery, Moscow/Bridgeman Art Library. 248: Victoria & Albert Museum, London/Bridgeman Art Library. 251: Louvre, Paris/Bridgeman Art Library. 252: Tretyakov Gallery, Moscow/Bridgeman Art Library. 254: Private Collection/ Bridgeman Art Library. 257: Z Radovan, Jerusalem. 258: Israel Museum, Jerusalem, photo David Harris. 260: Editions Assouline, photo Laziz Hamani. 265: Badische Landesbibliothek, Karlsruhe. 267: Courtesy of the Jewish Museum, London. 268: Courtesy Clive Rosen, Israel-Judaica Stamp Club. 271: Courtesy Portuguese-Israeli Synagogue, Amsterdam. 273: Staatsbibliothek Berlin-©Preussischer Kulturbesitz, Musicabteilung mit Mendelssohn-Archiv, MA BA 140. 276: Editions Assouline, photo Laziz Hamani. 279: By permission of the British Library. 281: By permission of the British Library. 284: The Royal Collection © 2000 Her Majesty Queen Elizabeth II. 286: Trustees of the British Museum. 288: By courtesy of the National Portrait Gallery, London. 289: V & A Picture Library. 290: Universal (Courtesy Kobal). 297: photo AKG, London. 298 L & R: photo AKG London. 298C: Hulton Getty. 300: National Museum of American Art, Washington DC/Art Resource, NY. 302: Vatican Museums & Galleries, Vatican City/Bridgeman Art Library. 304: Z Radovan, Jerusalem. 305: Courtesy S4C. 307: Bibliothèque Municipal, Besançon. 309: Paris, Musée Gustave Moreau © photo RMN-RG Ojeda. 310: Private Collection/The Stapleton Collection/Bridgeman Art Library. 312: V & A Picture Library. 316: Nigel Dickinson/Still Pictures. 317L: Mark Edwards/Still Pictures. 317R: Associated Press. 318: photo AKG, London. 319: Jorgen Schytte/Still Pictures. 321: Ron Giling/Still Pictures. 326: Baker Library, Dartmouth College, Hanover, NH/Instituto Nacional de Bellas Artes y Literatura/© Orozco Valladares Family/Bridgeman Art Library. 328: Nigel Dickinson/Still Pictures. 333: © John Muafangejo Trust. 337: Johannesburg Art Gallery, South Africa. 340: © John Muafangejo Trust. 344: Courtesy Martin-Luther-Kirche, Rottenburg am der Fulder. 345: Courtesy Continuum International Publishing Group, photo Hans Lachmann. 348: Courtesy Prof. Dr. Luise Schottrof. 349: Gamma/Frank Spooner Pictures.

Picture research by Celia Dearing

Index

Bold numbers denote reference to illustrations